Land Law

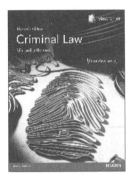
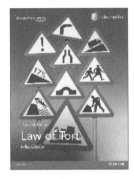
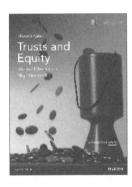
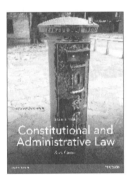

Land Law

PAUL RICHARDS

PEARSON

Harlow, England • London • New York • Boston • San Francisco • Toronto • Sydney • Auckland • Singapore • Hong Kong
Tokyo • Seoul • Taipei • New Delhi • Cape Town • São Paulo • Mexico City • Madrid • Amsterdam • Munich • Paris • Milan

Pearson Education Limited
Edinburgh Gate
Harlow CM20 2JE
United Kingdom
Tel: +44 (0)1279 623623
Web: www.pearson.com/uk

First Published 2014 (print and electronic)

ISBN: 978-1-4082-8738-5 (print)
     978-1-4082-8740-8 (PDF)
     978-1-292-01626-9 (CSeTxt)

British Library Cataloguing-in-Publication Data
A catalogue record for the print edition is available from the British Library

Library of Congress Cataloging-in-Publication Data
A catalog record for the print edition is available from the Library of Congress

10 9 8 7 6 5 4 3 2 1
18 17 16 15 14

Print edition typeset in 9/12 pt StoneSerITCStd by 35
Print edition printed by Ashford Colour Press Ltd, Gosport

NOTE THAT ANY PAGE CROSS REFERENCES REFER TO THE PRINT EDITION

Brief contents

Contents

Part 1 Introduction and the acquisition of land

Part 2 The estates in land

Part 3 The ownership of land

Preface

There is no question that Land Law is not easy. Ask any lawyer who has studied the subject and most will say the same thing. But difficulty should not be an excuse to avoid the subject and, anyway, a student aspiring to complete a law degree, with aspirations of qualifying as a solicitor or barrister, has no choice in the matter. Equally, difficulty should not be a reason for not finding the subject fascinating, despite its challenges. Some might say that it is a dry subject – but out of all the legal subjects this is the one which we all recognise, lawyer or not. We all live on the land and thus we interact with it every day. We travel on lanes, roads and motorways, passing rivers, streams, fields, gardens, homes (stately and more modest), offices and factories and all these are governed by the principles which are to be found within this book. To a greater extent than any other legal subject, we have the evidence of it before us. More often than not, the very landscape that is in front of us is carved out of the legal regime that is land law. So what better way to envisage the subject than to close the book, walk around your neighbourhood and visualise the legal principles that lie before you? But land law is about much more than this since it is about relationships: husbands, wives, cohabitees, lenders and borrowers, landlords and tenants, trustees and beneficiaries. The subject is therefore dynamic and, if it is approached in this light, you will become engrossed in its twists and turns and the puzzles that it presents. The language of land law is very different as well and at times you can be forgiven for thinking that you have entered into some sort of Tolkienesque world.

To understand the subject you have to know the language and the only way to do this is to read . . . and then read again until you become conversant with this fascinating world. A word of warning here – I have made no attempt to avoid the use of legal terminology as part of a trendy way of presenting the material. This only presents the material in an artificial manner that is not based in reality and does a disservice to those seeking to gain a full picture of the subject. And land law is indeed a picture, though not one you will recognise at first, since it is conjured up in the form of a jigsaw. The chapters appear as standalone units but to treat them as such will provide you with a shallow understanding of the subject. All the chapters form part of the jigsaw and, as you study each one, so a picture will slowly emerge. Some of you, as with a jigsaw, will see the picture emerge very early on, others may not – but persist and the veil will be raised from your eyes.

This book is not intended to be a 'crammer'; it is far too long to pretend to be such anyway, but is intended to provide you with an understandable and readable insight into the complexities of the subject in a structured, logical manner so that your knowledge and understanding are cumulative. Reading around the subject will also help you to immerse yourself in it and each chapter provides you with some guidance here.

This text is not written as some definitive statement of land law and for this you should refer to texts such as *Elements of Land Law* by Gray and Gray or *The Law of Real Property* by Megarry and Wade. The intention is to provide a halfway house between the student's own lecture notes and these more substantive and authoritative texts.

In time-honoured tradition, all errors and omissions are entirely my responsibility and I welcome any suggestions that readers might think will improve the text.

It would be remiss of me not to thank those who have provided assistance and encouragement in the writing of this book. Thanks therefore go to Donna Goddard and latterly Christine Statham, and to the rest of the team at Pearson Education, for their support in the writing of this book and for the Foundations Studies in Law Series generally. Their ideas, efforts and enthusiasm have contributed greatly to both and I am grateful for their patience when the production of the manuscript appeared to be slow at times. I would also like to express my thanks to the staff of the Law School and my other former colleagues at the University of Huddersfield for their support and advice over the years I spent there. Special thanks are due to Emma Hatfield, Rebecca Kelly and Catherine Stanbury for providing me with advice and acting as a sounding board for parts of the text. In particular I would like to express my profound gratitude to my former secretary, Joanne Battye, who took on the enormous task of typing the manuscript and without whom I doubt this book would have been completed. I am pleased she can now have a 'normal' weekend!

I thank my sons, Phillip and William, for their continued support and companionship and hope that they fulfil their ambitions in life. I also thank my partner, Maggie, for her patience and encouragement – particularly on those 'lost' weekends when I was tied to my desk, working on the manuscript – and for reminding me that I needed to be writing as I reached for a fly fishing rod! I would also like to thank my brother Tony for providing intervals of sanity when we could chat over a meal, usually as a precursor to seeing some atrocious movie.

Following my retirement from being Head of the School of Law at the University of Huddersfield in 2012, it has been a great pleasure to write this book as it has enabled me to return to the sustained academic writing that managing a law school often rendered impossible. It has been a particular joy to write a book on Land Law since this was my first love in entering academic life 35 years ago. I should perhaps add that retired I have not! My involvement in academic life since retirement has proved to have been busier than ever and those visions of practising the gentle art of fly fishing or meandering through my beloved mountains of the Lake District and the Himalaya have so far proved elusive but now this book has been completed . . . ?

Paul Richards
November 2013

Guided tour

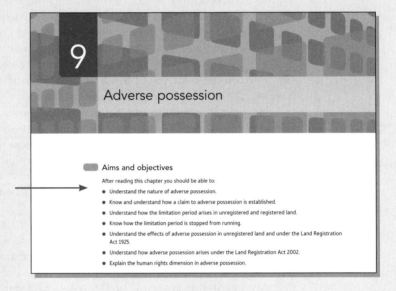

9

Adverse possession

Aims and objectives

After reading this chapter you should be able to:

- Understand the nature of adverse possession.
- Know and understand how a claim to adverse possession is established.
- Understand how the limitation period arises in unregistered and registered land.
- Know how the limitation period is stopped from running.
- Understand the effects of adverse possession in unregistered land and under the Land Registration Act 1925.
- Understand how adverse possession arises under the Land Registration Act 2002.
- Explain the human rights dimension in adverse possession.

Aims and objectives at the start of each chapter help focus your learning before you begin.

Case summaries highlight the facts and key legal principles of essential cases that you need to be aware of in your study of land law.

Baxter v Mannion [2011] 1 WLR 1594

In this case, Baxter ('B') applied to the Land Registry to be entered as the registered proprietor of a field by way of adverse possession. The registrar gave notice of the application to Mannion ('M'), who failed to respond to the notice within the prescribed period of 65 days (Schedule 6 para 3(2) and the Land Registration Rules 2003 r.189). B was therefore entered as the registered proprietor of the field. M then applied for rectification of the register on the basis that B had not been in adverse possession of the land and therefore the registration of B as the registered proprietor was a mistake under Schedule 4 para 5. M's application was upheld by the adjudicator and the High Court on the basis that B had not satisfied the substantive requirements of proving adverse possession.

B argued that Schedule 4 para 5 only allowed for a challenge on procedural grounds. This was rejected by the Court of Appeal since there was no indication that 'mistake' was confined in this way. Further, the Court of Appeal considered that Schedule 4 para 6(1) would not apply to prevent rectification in that there was no evidence of fraud. It was, however, considered that under Schedule 4 para 6(2) it would be unjust not to order for rectification since otherwise M would lose his land for the sake of a bureaucratic process, whilst B would gain land when he had never been in adverse possession.

Figures and diagrams are used to strengthen your understanding of complex legal processes in land law.

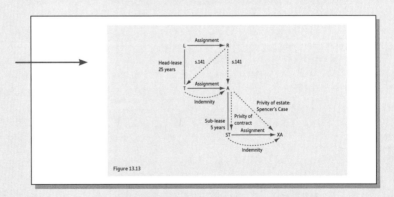

Figure 13.13

Summary

Licences

- A licence confers no interest in land; essentially it is a personal right given by a licensor to a licensee that prevents what would otherwise be regarded as a trespass.

- The concept of a licence covers a myriad of different situations, ranging from parking a car through to a long-term permit to occupy land.

- One vital distinction between a lease and a licence is that the former gives a tenant exclusive possession of the land, even as regards landlords. A licence confers no such right and a landowner is free to enter the land at will.

- There are no formal requirements for the creation of a lease, though sometimes they may be conferred in a deed, particularly if the licence is attached or incidental to creation of an estate or interest in land.

- The relationship between the licensor and the licensee is essentially a contractual one.

Chapter summaries located at the end of each chapter draw together the key points that you should be aware of following your reading, and provide a useful check for revision.

Further reading

Brown, 'E-conveyancing: Nothing to Fear' (2005) 155 *New Law Journal* 1389

Dixon, 'Registration, Rectification and Property Rights', 46 *Student Law Review*, Autumn

Dixon, 'The Reform of Property Law and the Land Registration Act 2002: A Risk Assessment' [2003] 67 *The Conveyancer and Property Lawyer* 136

Law Commission (2001) *Land Registration for the Twenty-First Century: A Conveyancing Revolution*, Law Com No. 271

Law Commission/HM Land Registry (1998) *Land Registration for the Twenty-First Century: A Consultative Document*, Law Com No. 254

Tee, 'The Rights of Every Person in Actual Occupation: An Enquiry into Section 70(1)g of the Land Registration Act 1925' (1998) *Cambridge Law Journal* 328

Suggestions for **Further reading** at the end of each chapter encourage you to delve deeper into the topic and read those articles which help you to gain higher marks in both exams and assessments.

3 Notice attributed to a person by virtue of the registration of a land charge in accordance with the Land Charges Act 1972.

All three forms of notice need to be distinguished.

notice to quit Method by which a landlord or tenant may terminate a periodic tenancy.

option to purchase A right whereby the holder can require an estate owner to convey that estate to the option holder. A form of estate contract.

overreaching Method by which interests in land are shifted from the land into the proceeds of sale, thereby enabling a purchaser to take the legal estate free of any equitable interests existing behind a trust of land or strict settlement, provided they pay the capital (purchase) monies to at least two trustees or a trust corporation.

perpetually renewable lease A lease which contains a covenant by the landlord that they will from time to time renew the lease (i.e. grant a new one to the tenant) at the termination of the current lease. Such leases are automatically converted into a term of 2000 years – see LPA 1922 s.145.

personal property Property other than freehold land.

personal representatives Persons authorised to administer the estate of a dead person:

(a) executors – appointed by will;
(b) administrators – appointed by the court where the deceased died intestate (or where an executor is unwilling or unable to act).

personal rights Rights which attach only to

Reference sections have a stepped coloured tab to allow you to navigate quickly to key information within the text.

Glossary

A full **Glossary** located at the back of the book can be used throughout your reading to clarify unfamiliar terms.

As we have seen throughout this book, land law has a language very much of its own, based on Latin, Norman-French, Anglo-Saxon and English. This terminology frequently creates difficulty for students since many of the expressions have a technical meaning and even apparently familiar words are given a different meaning. To understand the subject of land law you need to be familiar with the language and the best way to do this is to read the material as often as you can.

This glossary aims to explain the meanings of words and phrases which commonly arise in the subject. The glossary does not provide an exhaustive list, though the most frequently used expressions are explained here. If you do come across a term you do not understand immediately, take steps to ascertain its meaning in the context in which it is used, and add it to the glossary.

abatement The removal of an obstruction to the exercise of an easement by the dominant tenement owner.

absolute (of an interest) neither conditional nor determinable by some specified event.

abstract of title A summary of all matters which affect the title offered by the vendor, including the various dispositions; it is the narrative summary of title, consisting of documents or events affecting the title, that must be supplied by a landowner to a purchaser under a contract of sale. See LPA 1925 s.10. See also **epitome of title**.

acquiescence Failure to take steps to prevent

alienation The transfer of interests in property from one owner to another. This can be by way of sale, gift or some other transaction.

animus possidendi The intention to (adversely) possess the land of another.

annexation The attaching of the benefit of a restrictive covenant to the dominant tenement so that it will run with the land.

ante-nuptial Prior to marriage.

appurtenant
1 A right which is attached to the land by agreement between the parties.
2 A profit à prendre which benefits a piece of land, and not merely the owner of it.

Table of cases

Table of Statutes

Table of Statutory Instruments

Acknowledgements

We are grateful to the following for permission to reproduce copyright material:

Figures

Figure 5.1 reproduced with kind permission of Land Registry. The Official Copy of Register of Title is Crown copyright and is reproduced with the permission of Land Registry under delegated authority from the Controller of HMSO; Figure 11.10 reproduced with kind permission of Land Registry – Transfer of whole of registered title(s). **http://www.landregistry.gov.uk/ _media/downloads/forms/TR1.pdf**. The Form TR1 is Crown copyright and is reproduced with the permission of Land Registry under delegated authority from the Controller of HMSO.

Text

Extracts on page 42, 77 from Midland Bank Trust Co Ltd v Green [1981] 1 AC 513; Extracts on pages 52, 239 from Errington v Errington and Woods [1952] 1 KB 290; Extract on page 59 from National Provincial Bank Ltd v Hasting Car Mart Ltd [1965] AC 1175; Extract on page 71 from Pritchard v Briggs [1980] Ch 338; Extract on page 75 from Lazarus Estates Ltd v Beasley [1956] 1 QB 702; Extract on page 76 from Re Monolithic Building Co [1915] 1 Ch 643; Extract on page 76 from Miles v Bull [1969] 1 QB 258; Extract on page 95 from Yandle & Sons v Sutton [1922] 2 Ch 199; Extracts on pages 105–6, 243 from Yaxley v Gotts [2000] Ch 162; Extracts on pages 108, 246 from Ramsden v Dyson (1866) LR 1 HL 129; Extract on page 142 from National Provincial Bank Ltd v Hastings Car Mart Ltd [1964] Ch 9; Extract on page 142 from Land Registration for the Twenty-First Century: A Conveyancing Revolution, **http://lawcommission.justice.gov.uk/docs/lc271_land_registration_for_the_twenty-first_century.pdf**; Extracts on pages 146–7 from National Provincial Bank Ltd v Hastings Car Mart Ltd [1964] Ch 665; Extracts on pages 148, 150 from Williams & Glyn's Bank plc v Boland [1981] AC 487; Extract on page 160 from Baxter v Mannion [2011] 1 WLR 1594; Extracts on pages 173, 175, 178, 180, 234 from Street v Mountford [1985] AC 809 (HL); Extracts on page 175 from Prudential Assurance Co Ltd v London Residuary Body [1992] AC 386; Extract on page 177 from AG Securities v Vaughan [1990] AC 417; Extract on page 180 from Marcroft Wagons Ltd v Smith [1951] 2 KB 497; Extracts on pages 181, 191 from Bruton v London and Quadrant Housing Trusts [2000] 1 AC 406; Extract on page 191 from Industrial Properties (Barton Hill) Ltd v AEI Ltd [1977] QB 850; Extract on page 196 from National Carriers Ltd v Panalpina (Northern) Ltd [1981] AC 675; Extract on page 200 from Attorney General of Belize v Belize Telecom Ltd [2009] 1 WLR 1988; Extract on page 207 from Billson v Residential Apartments Ltd [1992] 1 AC 494; Extract on page 211 from Akici v LR Butlin Ltd [2006] 1 WLR 201; Extract on page 218 from Lee-Parker v Izzet [1971] 1 WLR 1688; Extract on pages 176–7 from Aslan v Murphy [1990] 1 WLR 766; Extract on page 237 from Hurst v Picture Theatres Ltd [1915] 1 KB 1; Extracts on pages 243, 248 from Cobbe v Yeoman's Row Management Ltd [2008] 1 WLR 1752; Extract on page 243 from Crabb v Arun District Council [1976] 1 Ch 179; Extracts on pages 246, 252 from Gillett v Holt [2001] Ch 210; Extracts on pages 247, 248 from Thorner v Major [2009] 1 WLR 776; Extract on page 249 from Amalgamated Investment and Property Co Ltd v Texas Commerce International

Bank Ltd [1982] QB 84; Extract on page 251 from Pascoe v Turner [1979] 1 WLR 431; Extract on page 255 from Stack v Dowden [2007] AC 432; Extract on pages 237–8 from Tanner v Tanner [1975] 1 WLR 1347; Extract on pages 244–5 from Taylor Fashions Ltd v Liverpool Victoria Trustees Co Ltd [1982] QB 133; Extracts on pages 274, 276 from J A Pye (Oxford) Ltd v Graham [2003] 1 AC 419; Extract on page 290 from Re Buchanan-Wollaston's Conveyance [1929] Ch 738; Extracts on pages 301, 304, 366 from Mortgage Corporation v Shaire [2001] Ch 743; Extract on page 307 from Re Citro (A Bankrupt) [1991] Ch 142; Extract on pages 300–1 from Transfer of Land: Trusts of Land (Law Com. No. 181), **https://www.gov.uk/government/uploads/system/uploads/attachment_data/file/ 228750/0391.pdf**; Extract on page 333 from WestdeutscheLandesbankGirozentrale v Islington Borough Council [1996] AC 669; Extract on page 335 from Oxley v Hiscock [2005] Fam 211; Extract on page 343 from Burgess v Rawnsley [1975] Ch 222; Extracts on pages 358, 359, 360, 366 from Gissing v Gissing [1971] AC 886; Extracts on pages 358, 362, 363–4 from Lloyds Bank plc v Rosset [1991] 1 AC 107; Extract on page 359 from Pettitt v Pettitt [1970] AC 777; Extract on page 366 from Sharing Homes, **http://lawcommission. justice.gov.uk/publications/sharing-homes.htm**; Extract on page 371 from Cohabitation: The Financial Consequences of Relationship Breakdown – Executive Summary, **http:// lawcommission.justice.gov.uk/docs/lc307_Cohabitation_summary.pdf**; Extract on page 385 from Dunlop Pneumatic Tyre Co Ltd v Selfridge & Co Ltd [1915] AC 847; Extract on page 393 from Boyer v Warbey [1953] 1 QB 234; Extract on page 394 from Landlord and Tenant: Privity of Contract and Estate (Law Com. No. 174, 1988), **https://www.gov.uk/ government/uploads/system/uploads/attachment_data/file/229015/0008.pdf**; Extract on page 409 from Crest Nicholson Residential (South) Ltd v McAllister [2004] 1 WLR 2409; Extract on page 411 from Rogers v Hosegood [1900] 2 Ch 388; Extract on page 414 from Elliston v Reacher [1908] 2 Ch 374; Extract on page 414 from Re Dolphin's Conveyance [1970] Ch 654; Extracts on pages 416, 421, 422 from Rhone v Stephens [1994] 2 AC 310; Extract on page 422 from Re Gadd's Land Transfer [1966] Ch 56; Extract on page 437 from Crow v Wood [1971] 1 QB 77; Extract on page 438 from Copeland v Greenhalf [1952] Ch 488; Extract on page 438 from Reilly v Booth (1890) 44 Ch D 12; Extract on page 441 from London and Blenheim Ltd v Ladbrooke Parks Ltd [1992] 1 WLR 1278; Extract on page 447 from Nickerson v Barraclough [1981] Ch 426; Extract on page 448 from Pwllbach Colliery Co Ltd v Woodman [1915] AC 634; Extracts on pages 449, 451 from Wheeldon v Burrows (1879) 12 Ch D 31; Extract on page 451 from Sovmots Investment Ltd v The Secretary of State for the Environment [1979] AC 144; Extract on page 451 from Wheeler v JJ Saunders Ltd [1996] Ch 19; Extract on page 452 from R v Oxfordshire County Council Ex parte Sunningwell Parish Council [2000] 1 AC 335; Extract on page 463 from Tehidy Minerals Ltd v Norman [1971] 2 QB 528; Extract on page 463 from Swan v Sinclair [1924] 1 Ch 254; Extract on page 464 from James v Stevenson [1893] AC 162; Extract on page 479 from Samuel v Jarrah Timber and Wood Paving Co Ltd [1904] AC 323; Extract on page 481 from Knightsbridge Estates Trust Ltd v Byrne [1939] Ch 441; Extract on page 482 from Rigby LJ in Noakes v Rice [1900] 2 Ch 445; Extracts on pages 482, 483 from G & C Kreglinger v New Patagonia Meat and Cold Storage Ltd [1914] AC 25; Extract on page 486 from Multiservice Bookbinding Ltd v Marden [1979] Ch 84; Extract on page 490 from Cuckmere Brick Co Ltd v Mutual Finance Ltd [1971] Ch 949; Extract on page 492 from Four Maids Ltd v Dudley Marshall (Properties) Ltd [1957] Ch 317; Extract on page 492 from Quennell v Maltby [1979] 1 WLR 318; Extracts on page 495 from China and South Sea Bank Ltd v Tan Soon Gin [1990] 1 AC 536; Extract on page 496 from Cheltenham and Gloucester Building Society plc v Krausz [1997] 1 WLR 1558; Extract on page 520 from Newbiggin v Adam (1886) 34 ChD 582.

In some instances we have been unable to trace the owners of copyright material, and we would appreciate any information that would enable us to do so.

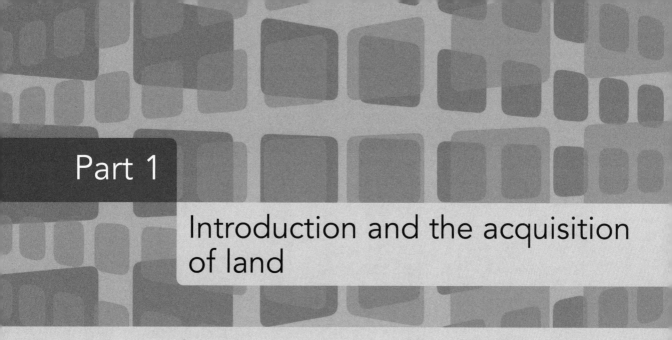

Part 1

Introduction and the acquisition of land

1

Land law – some basic concepts

Aims and objectives

At the end of this chapter you should be able to:

- Understand what is meant by land.
- Distinguish between real and personal property.
- Recognise the objectives in studying land law.
- Gain an understanding of land as a three-dimensional concept.
- Distinguish between fixtures and fittings.
- Classify the different types of property.

Land as legal construct

As a species, we are tied to land, and since mankind ceased to be hunter gatherers and began to settle on a given piece of land, rules emerged as to land ownership and use. It is difficult to imagine any society that does not measure the relationship of its members to each other and the environment in which they live and work. Today the concept of property is central to the social and economic life of our society.

The law of property provides rules that confer the notion of ownership on land and goods. The law is also concerned with our relationship with that property, including the de facto possession of it. To ignore this perspective creates a misconception on the part of the student embarking on the study of the law of property that one is simply looking at a body of rules and principles that regulates one's rights and obligations in relation to that part of the general law relating to property. It is important to establish that, whilst the layperson might talk in terms of owning a 'thing', lawyers do not perceive property in this way but in terms of a multiplicity of interests that might exist within property and which may, in turn, give rise to a variety of different actions. This concept may seem obscure but it can be illustrated by considering that in relation to a piece of land there may be rights pertaining to the land in respect of the owner, a tenant, a building society or bank, the owner of a right of way, a neighbour who has a restrictive covenant over the property, or, indeed, the spouse of the owner.

Another aspect that arises in relation to property, as opposed to one's rights in the property, is the right to exclude others from it. Thus an owner can exclude a trespasser from entering the property. This right to exclude can apply to persons who have competing rights in the property.

Example

A could mortgage his house to Bank B and then take out another mortgage with Bank C. If A becomes insolvent then both B and C may each claim a proprietary interest in the house and will attempt to exert their priority to each other in order to recover the money they have lent to A.

So far we have talked of 'land law' and 'property law' but the two are not necessarily the same thing. By 'land law' we mean that we are studying what is generally referred to as the law of 'real property'. This has a technical meaning but here we are distinguishing land from other forms of property, such as tables, chairs, cars, copyrights, etc. This work is primarily concerned with land law or real property, which to a degree can be used interchangeably, though there are nuances attached to the expression 'real' which we will define and clarify later on.

Undoubtedly, the study of land law is not easy – speak with any lawyer and they will confirm this. Indeed, it was described by Oliver Cromwell as an 'ungodly jumble'! Many students therefore approach this subject with a significant amount of trepidation and the subject has a reputation for being difficult and, for some, uninteresting. It is, however, a dynamic subject and not necessarily academic – after all, we live on and amongst land or real property every day of our lives. The very landscape of the towns, cities and countryside that we live in is a construct that is often derived from legal rules and principles. Sometimes it is easy to think of land law being contained within a text such as this one, but one only has to open one's eyes and look around to see many of the concepts appearing in the world about us as we travel through our towns, cities and countryside.

Land law is different from other areas of law in that it has a terminology and vocabulary all of its own. Many of the terms are derived from Latin, Norman French and the feudal system that underpins the subject. This adds another level of confusion and the student must become conversant with this terminology and vocabulary in order to understand the subject. Essentially, it is like learning a new language and, as with learning a language, the best way of dealing with this is to read and use it as much as possible. Perhaps an example here will give you some idea of the difficulty. When you look in the estate agent's window, you will notice that the properties being sold are often termed 'leasehold' or 'freehold'. The former is fairly self-explanatory at this point, but the expression 'freehold' is known to the lawyer as a 'fee simple absolute in possession'. The expression 'fee' indicates that the estate is one that is capable of being inherited, the expression 'simple' indicates that the estate can pass down through both lineal (father to son to grandson) as well as collateral (father to uncle to a company) descendants – that is, unrestricted rights. The expression 'simple' indicates that there are no conditions attached to the land and 'possession' indicates that there is a present entitlement to the estate/land. This is clearly a bit of a mouthful and largely meaningless to the layperson, so for short we use the expression 'freehold' to describe what it is one is buying.

Unlike many subjects that the student may have studied so far, which can be divided up into distinct topics that can be studied in isolation from each other, land law cannot be studied in a piecemeal fashion. Each topic forms a component of the whole. The subject is therefore a bit like a jigsaw. The picture comprises many pieces and to view the picture properly one needs to put them all together in the correct place. The same is true of land law, and the more one reads and progresses in one's study of the subject, the clearer the picture becomes.

There are some advantages with land law in that it is a fairly structured subject and because we are dealing with 'property' or 'proprietary' rights in land (a freehold, for example) as opposed to personal rights (a licence), the structure is fairly rigid since proprietary rights can exist for many years – or even centuries – as they attach to the land itself, whilst personal rights are fairly transient and exist between individuals, much like a contract. The subject is also very much statute-based – largely because, in 1925, a whole raft of inter-connecting pieces of legislation was created by Parliament and much of the modern law is derived from this body of legislation, though there have been some amendments, such as the Trusts of Land and Appointment of Trustees Act 1996. The subject has nevertheless grown organically from case law and statute law and there is no top-down consolidating legislation that pulls it all into a coherent body of law. Whilst it is imperative to know the modern land law, one also has to know something of its origins since otherwise it is impossible to understand the modern context.

What are the objectives in studying land law?

The objectives are twofold:

(i)   to know and understand the rights and liabilities attached to the land; and

(ii) to provide a foundation for the study of conveyancing practice.

What is the distinction between land law and conveyancing? Land law involves the rights and liabilities pertaining to the land in a passive sense, whilst conveyancing is the activity that creates and transfers rights in a piece of land. The two of course overlap and cannot exist in isolation from each other. The result is that, whilst this book is primarily about land law, by its very nature it must include elements of conveyancing, though the finer intricacies of that subject have to be left for further study at a later stage. That is not to say that conveyancing is not important since it is the conveyancing of land from one person to another that defines ownership or 'title' to the property, what piece of land is actually being transferred, how long the transferee may hold the land for, what interests that person may have in relation to adjoining property, what interests others may have over the transferee's property and what restrictions may be placed on the land by public authorities.

The last point is interesting since, whilst we will be mostly dealing with the operation of private law, it is as well to be aware that the public law, such as the requirement for planning permission to develop the land, also has an influence here. This aspect is a relatively modern development and very much a late-nineteenth- and twentieth-century concept. It dictates much of the way our towns and cities are laid out and constructed. Nevertheless, one should not underestimate the influence that private land law has had on our environment by way of restrictive covenants. Victorians, if they could be transported via a time machine to the present, would be astonished at the design of our modern buildings and the materials used in their construction – however, they would also be able to recognise that the way our streets, towns and cities are formed still complies with restrictions developed in their own era. It is therefore important that to understand English land law one must of necessity understand the historical context that lies behind the subject as it is this that underpins the present-day law.

Little of this book will be concerned with planning law as a body of public law – this is a separate subject in its own right. That is not to say that we are inured from its influence and we refer to it when, and if, it is relevant to our study of land law. Our study of land will therefore fall into two broad areas:

(i)   rights over one's own land; and

(ii) rights over land owned by another person.

So . . . what is land?

A good starting point here is the definition stated in the Law of Property Act 1925 ('LPA') s.205 (1)(ix):

> 'Land' includes land of any tenure, and mines and minerals, whether or not held apart from the surface, buildings or parts of buildings (whether the division is horizontal, vertical or made in any other way) and other corporeal hereditament; also a manor, an advowson, and a rent and other incorporeal hereditament, and an easement, right, privilege, or benefit in, over, or derived from land; . . . and 'mines and minerals' include any strata or seam of minerals or substances in or under any land, and powers of working and getting the same . . . ; and 'manor' includes a lordship, and reputed manor or lordship; and hereditament 'means any real property which on an intestacy occurring before the commencement of this Act might have devolved upon an heir'.

What emerges from this definition is that it is not really a definition as such, that defines exactly what land is, but it rather informs us in what things land may consist, hence it talks in terms of the fact that 'Land includes . . .'. The other thing we can see from this 'definition' is that it uses some fairly unusual words that are somewhat arcane and not easily understood. It is, however, useful to dissect this provision and look at each element in turn.

'. . . land of any tenure . . .'

Broadly speaking, this takes us back to the estate agent's and how property is described there. You will recall that properties are often described as 'leasehold' and 'freehold'. More will be said about these later on, but basically when we see the expression 'leasehold' we think in terms of land being held for definite periods of time, such as a 999-year lease, a yearly lease or a weekly lease. Freehold land means that the owner can own the land forever and, as such, it is for an indefinite period of time. The land can be sold or passed on through inheritance. A lease can be created out of a freehold estate but not the other way around, since a freehold, by definition, is longer than a lease, so it is not possible to carve something greater out of a limited interest, which is something smaller.

If one looks at a house from a road, it is not possible to tell if it is a freehold or a leasehold estate – one would have to see the title deeds to discern this distinction. Both therefore appear to be land but historically land comprises 'real' property (sometimes referred to as 'realty' – *not* 'reality', which is something entirely different!). We need to distinguish real property from 'personal' property (sometimes referred to as 'personalty' – *not* 'personality', which, again, is something entirely different!). Personal property comprises things such as chairs, tables, etc., which are referred to as 'chattels' in property law. The expression 'chattel' is derived from the Anglo-Saxon word for cattle.

Freehold property is 'real' property whilst leasehold property is 'personal' property. This seems strange since, as stated earlier, if one looks at a house one cannot see if it is freehold or leasehold, though they are, in fact, very different types of land. The reason that freehold land is real property derives from what could be recovered if one was dispossessed of the land. The expression 'real' is derived from the Latin word 'res' which means 'thing'. Thus, if one were dispossessed of one's land, one could recover the land itself, the 'thing', as opposed to merely receiving damages. The expression 'personal' property is derived from the Latin 'in personam' and here, if there is a dispute about ownership of the property, the courts would either order the return of the item or award damages instead.

One would have thought that the classification of property would have been based on whether it is immoveable or moveable, i.e. land and chattels, Whilst this distinction was, in fact, recognised, leasehold land was regarded as existing outside of the feudal system of landholding and was therefore designated as personal property. Thus, if one was dispossessed of leasehold property, the only redress was damages, as one did not have the right to bring a 'real' action to recover the property itself. In fact, this rule changed in 1499, when it was decided that leaseholders were entitled to recover their land, but by that time leaseholds were firmly established as personal property and there they remain. So the classification of leaseholds as personal property arises from a law that was changed over 500 years ago! To show the connection with land and the personal nature of leaseholds they are designated as 'chattels real'.

'. . . and mines and minerals, whether or not held apart from the surface, buildings or parts of buildings (whether the division is horizontal, vertical or made in any other way)'

This part of the definition indicates that land includes mines and minerals, which may be owned in their own right, for instance by a mining company, or by the owner of the land itself that sits above the mineral – ('whether or not held apart from the surface'). This requires some qualification since some minerals are excluded from this arrangement; thus gold and silver belong to the Crown as of right – *Case of Mines* (1568) 1 Plowd 310. The Crown is also entitled to other minerals by virtue of statutory authority, as in the case of coal (Coal Industry Act 1995) and oil (Petroleum Act 1998).

What the definition also tells us is that land ownership is a three-dimensional concept and it applies not just along a flat horizontal plane but also into the ground and into the airspace above it. Thus we can look at a block of flats and we can see the notion of land not only belongs to those at ground level but also to those in the flats above the land. Similarly, in a street of terraced houses each person will enjoy owning their own part of the street. The principles also apply to underground ownership – you only have to walk along a street and you will very often notice grills at payment level which provide light or access into the underground cellar – indeed, sometimes cellars are converted into flats in their own right.

So if a person owns a house with a piece of garden, what exactly does that person own? The principle is summed in the common law maxim 'cuius est solum eius est usque ad caelum et ad inferos' – 'he who owns the surface owns everything up to the heavens and down to the depths of the earth'.

To the depths of the earth

We have already looked at some aspects of subsoil ownership in terms of minerals but the principle goes further than this since there is a presumption at law that one owns the land and subsoil to the middle of the highway ('ad medium filum') and, of course, some cellars extend beyond the surface boundary of the property owned.

One interesting area to do with the subsoil concerns the issues arising from items found in or on the land and issues involving buried treasure.

As far as items found in the ground are concerned, these belong to the occupier of the land. In the case of ***Attorney General of the Duchy of Lancaster v Overton (Farms) Ltd*** [1981] Ch 33 it was held that a hoard of Roman coins was not treasure trove as the coins did not have sufficient gold or silver content and therefore they belonged to the owner of the land and not the Crown.

Objects found on the land will belong to either the finder or the occupier of the land; however, for the latter to claim the property he must demonstrate that he has a 'manifest intention to exercise control over the land'.

This issue arose in the case of ***Parker v British Airways Board*** [1982] 1 All ER 834 where a bracelet was found on the floor of an airport terminal. The claimant handed the bracelet to an employee of British Airways, stating that if the owner could not be found then it should be given to him, the claimant. In fact, British Airways could not find the true owner and therefore sold the bracelet. The claimant sued for damages, alleging that he had a better title to the bracelet than the airline. The Court of Appeal held that, since the bracelet was not attached to the land, British Airways did not have automatic priority to the bracelet over the finder who was in the lounge lawfully and not a trespasser. Lord Donaldson stated:

> An occupier of a building has rights superior to those of a finder over chattels on or in, but not attached to, that building if, but only if, before the chattel is found, he has manifested an intention to exercise control over the building and the things which may be on or in it.

The court stated that the test to be used to determine ownership was whether British Airways exercised a 'manifest intention to exercise control over the lounge and all things which might be in it'. The court found that, since British Airways did not regularly search the lounge for any lost objects and, indeed, did not do so at all, it clearly did not have the manifest intention to exercise control over the building and thus the claimant was entitled to the proceeds of the sale.

'Manifest intention' can derive from the nature of the premises themselves and Lord Donaldson considered that a bank vault would be such a place. On the other hand, a waiting room or a car park would not raise a presumption of manifest intention.

It is important that any finder of property is present on the land lawfully in order to claim any objects that he or she finds and, of course, the actual position of the object is important in deciding ownership. Both these aspects can be seen in the case of ***Waverley Borough Council v Fletcher*** [1995] 4 All ER 756 where a brooch was found buried in a park by the defendant, using a metal detector. Auld LJ stated that 'The distinction is now long and well established' in regards to items found in or attached to land and items found on land. He stated that an owner or lawful possessor of the land has a superior right to items buried in the ground, whilst in the case of items found on the land the finder has a superior right, provided the owner has not manifested an intention to control the land and things upon it. He stated that such intention will normally be lacking in a shop or other such places, but there would be a high degree of control in a house, or a bank vault. In particular, an owner of an estate who had not occupied it for a considerable period could not claim a better right than a finder, since he or she clearly has no control over the property or anything upon it. In this case, therefore, the defendant could not claim the brooch or the proceeds of sale. One other factor that was taken into account was that the local authority did not permit the use of metal detectors or digging in its parks and therefore the defendant had no licence to be carrying out that type of activity and, in essence, was a trespasser.

Treasure is treated rather differently from the principles we have just been looking at. The principle at common law used to be that gold and silver found hidden in the land belonged to the Crown. There has to be a significant quantity of gold and silver in the contents – hence the fact that in **Attorney General of the Duchy of Lancaster v Overton (Farms) Ltd** above, the Roman coins were not regarded as treasure since the silver content only represented 10% of the weight. Originally, when treasure was found, the finders of the treasure trove were paid compensation for the find by the Crown. The problem with this approach to treasure trove is that it largely ignored some quite important archaeological finds which did not amount to treasure trove because they were not gold or silver and such items were essentially being lost to the nation. The Treasure Act 1996 abolished the common law principles and provided a more far-reaching definition of what treasure comprises. Under the Treasure Act 1996 s.1:

(1) Treasure is—
    (a) any object at least 300 years old when found which—
        (i) is not a coin but has metallic content of which at least 10 per cent by weight is precious metal;
        (ii) when found, is one of at least two coins in the same find which are at least 300 years old at that time and have that percentage of precious metal; or
        (iii) when found, is one of at least ten coins in the same find which are at least 300 years old at that time;
    (b) any object at least 200 years old when found which belongs to a class designated under section 2(1);
    (c) any object which would have been treasure trove if found before the commencement of section 4;
    (d) any object which, when found, is part of the same find as—
        (i) an object within paragraph (a), (b) or (c) found at the same time or earlier; or
        (ii) an object found earlier which would be within paragraph (a) or (b) if it had been found at the same time.
(2) Treasure does not include objects which are—
    (a) unworked natural objects, or
    (b) minerals as extracted from a natural deposit,
    or which belong to a class designated under section 2(2).

Other categories were added to the definition by virtue of the Treasure Designation Order (2002) SI 2002/2666:

(3) Designation of classes of objects of outstanding historical, archaeological or cultural importance
    The following classes of objects are designated pursuant to section 2(1) of the Act.
    (a) any object (other than a coin), any part of which is base metal, which, when found is one of at least two base metal objects in the same find which are of prehistoric date;
    (b) any object (other than a coin), which is of prehistoric date, and any part of which is gold or silver.

The effect of the above provisions is that any items within the definition which are found in or attached to land or on the surface must be reported to the coroner within 14 days of the find. An inquest is then held to determine the status of the items, whether treasure or not. There is a code of practice to determine if the items will be offered to museums and the rewards that will be paid to finders and landowners. Usually, there is a presumption that a reward will be split 50:50 between the landowner and the finder, unless they have already come to an agreement which the court may have regard to. A finder who is a trespasser or who has delayed or not reported their find may have their reward reduced or even forfeited.

Up to the heavens

The owner of the land owns the airspace above their property. The expression 'usque ad caelum' is based on Roman law principles which hardly stand up in today's age of airliners and satellites and it is clear that a landowner cannot literally own land to the heavens – even nations in public international law cannot decide where airspace and outer space ends and begins, despite the presence of the Outer Space Treaty 1967.

So how far above one's land does one actually own? The question arose in the case of **Bernstein v Skyviews** [1978] QB 479 where the owner of a large estate brought an action for trespass against Skyviews for overflying the estate and taking aerial photographs of it. The claimant considered that Skyviews had infringed the airspace above his property. It was held that the owner of land owned such of the airspace as was necessary for the ordinary use and enjoyment of his property and the structures upon it. Above that height the owner of land had no more rights than anyone else and thus aircraft flying at a normal height would not be trespassing in the claimant's airspace. Consequently, he lost his case.

It should also be noted that the Civil Aviation Act 1982 s. 76 provides that no action for trespass lies in respect of an aircraft over property at a height above the ground which, having regard to wind, weather and all the circumstances of the case, is reasonable.

Outside of aircraft, occupation of a person's airspace without their consent constitutes a trespass. Thus in the case of **Woolerton and Wilson Ltd v Richard Costain Ltd** [1970] 1 WLR 411 in September 1969 the defendants erected a tower crane on a building site which was so confined that the crane could only be positioned in one place, which resulted in the crane's jib overhanging into the plaintiffs' airspace and 50 feet above the ground. The defendants admitted that that they had committed a trespass and offered substantial amounts of money for permission to continue the trespass while the building was being constructed. The plaintiffs nevertheless refused permission, even though there was no risk to their premises, and claimed for an injunction to restrain the trespass. The court held that, whilst it was no excuse that the trespass did not commit any harm and that the proper remedy was to award an injunction, in this case the granting of the injunction would be suspended until November 1970, when the building would be completed.

There are many other cases involving similar sorts of trespass, such as the case of **Kelsen v Imperial Tobacco Co.** [1957] 2 QB 334 which involved an advertising hoarding encroaching on the airspace of a neighbour's land. It must be stressed that it does not matter if the trespass does not cause any damage or does not interfere with the ordinary use of the land; the fact is that if anything encroaches on to a neighbour's airspace this becomes a trespass.

'. . . and other corporeal hereditament . . .'

The expression 'hereditament' is now quite an old-fashioned one and somewhat obscure. It is the subject of further definition within s.205, where it states:

> . . . and hereditament 'means any real property which on an intestacy occurring before the commencement of this Act might have devolved upon an heir'.

The expression 'hereditament' refers to real property which passed to an heir on intestacy prior to 1926. The expression 'corporeal' (from the Latin *corpus* meaning 'body') tells us that it refers to physical property over which ownership is exercised; thus the expression 'corporeal hereditament' refers to land, building, trees, minerals, etc. which are part of or fixed to the land that an heir would inherit. The expression therefore describes all the property an heir entitled to real property would inherit. Prior to 1926, there were a number of cases that considered what property formed part of the inheritance and this provision is really there to confirm the decisions in these old cases. It has little relevance in the modern world of property law, though the expression is still useful in describing what land comprises.

Defining what is meant by a corporeal hereditament, however, raises the important question as to what we actually own when we have ownership of a piece of land. Indeed, one of the important questions that arises when purchasing land is what exactly we are buying – not just in terms of the land but the fixtures and fittings that may or may not form part of the purchase.

The issue of fixtures and fittings reveals the issue as to what the land comprises. Land is, of course, an immoveable form of property and chattels are moveables, but when does a chattel become fixed to the land so as to form part of it? The position is summed up in the maxim 'quicquid plantatur solo, solo cedit' meaning 'whatever is fixed to the land becomes part of the land'. To take the example of a tap – clearly this is a moveable object, a chattel, when one picks it up in the shop; however, once it is fitted to the sink it becomes part of it and part of the house itself and therefore part of the land. The tap now changes in characteristic since it changes from being a chattel to being a 'fixture'.

Example

One of the great points of contention that often arises when one is purchasing a house is what items actually come with the house. Let us take another example, a garden urn, which the owner of Blackacre, A, has put on her patio. A now sells the house to B and, prior to B taking possession, A takes the garden urn with her to her new house. Now B quite liked the garden urn when he inspected the property so he is quite upset to find that it has now gone. B considers that the garden urn is part of the deal. If the garden urn is a fixture, then he is indeed entitled to it and can demand that A returns it. On the other hand, if the garden urn is a fitting, then A is entitled to keep the urn and take it with her. The question as to whether an item is a fixture or a fitting is answered by determining the degree to which the chattel is attached or annexed to the land or not.

In the latter part of the nineteenth century it came to be recognised that what was a fixture depended on the purpose for which the chattel was brought on to the land. Thus if the garden urn in our example was brought on the land with the intention that it was to be enjoyed in its own right, then it remains a chattel. It does not matter whether the chattel was attached or secured to the land in any way – for example, the garden urn could have been secured to the land by cement. On the other hand, if the chattel was placed on the land so that it became part of the landscaping of the garden, then it may become a fixture notwithstanding that the chattel, or garden urn, is freestanding and capable of being moved. Thus it is the intention or purpose of the person bringing the chattel on to the land that may provide the answer as to whether a chattel is a fixture or fitting.

The case of **Holland v Hodgson** (1872) LR 7 CP 328 provides us with two tests to help determine whether a chattel has been annexed to the land. The case concerned whether looms in a factory formed part of the factory or not. Blackburn J stated that whether or not an object is a fixture or fitting depended on two tests:

1 the degree of annexation;
2 the purpose of the annexation.

Blackburn J considered that objects that only rested on the land by virtue of their weight were not usually considered as part of the land; nevertheless, if the intention was that they were part of the land then they would become fixtures. Blackburn J used a pile of stones as an example in his judgment. He stated that a random pile of stones in a field was not part of the land, but if the stones were built into a dry stone wall then clearly the intention is that they would form part of the land. It is for the person claiming that a chattel is part of the land to prove it. An object that is fixed to the land is presumed to be part of the land unless the circumstances indicate that it was intended that the object is to remain a chattel. Here the burden of proof is reversed and it is for the person claiming that the object is a chattel to prove it.

Berkely v *Poulet* [1976] 242 EG 39

This case concerned a dispute as to what items formed part of a piece of land that was sold at an auction. The dispute was concerned with a heavy marble statue weighing nearly half a ton that rested on a plinth, a sundial and some pictures that were set into panelling in a wall of the house.

The Court of Appeal considered the test set out in **Holland v Hodgson** and concluded that the pictures were placed on the walls to be enjoyed in their own right, as opposed to the intention to make them part of the house. The court considered that the sundial, which had been detached from its own plinth previously, was a chattel rather than a fixture. The statue, despite its weight, was also found to be a chattel since it did not form part of the 'architectural scheme' of the garden – unlike the plinth on which it rested, which the court concluded did form part of the land.

The case of **Berkely v Poulet** demonstrated that objects may remain as objects despite the fact that they are attached to the land. Thus the purpose of the annexation seems to be more relevant today than simply the degree of annexation. This can be seen by looking at the pictures in the case. Whilst they were clearly fixed within the panelling, it was proven that the intention was that they were not put there to form a permanent part of the property and therefore they remained as chattels and could be removed.

The decision in **Holland v Hodgson** was also considered later in the case of **Elitestone v Morris** [1997] 2 All ER 513.

Elitestone v *Morris* [1997] 2 All ER 513

The case concerned a chalet bungalow that rested on concrete blocks but was not attached to them in any way. The blocks were attached to the land. The chalet had been brought on to the land many years earlier and had been occupied by the defendants since 1971. The defendants occupied the land by way of a licence agreement on the basis that the occupier owned the chalet but paid rent to the landowner for the use of the land on which the chalet stood. There was then a change of owner, who increased the rent and served notice on the defendants to remove the chalet. In order to remain on the land, the defendants had to prove that they were Rent Act protected tenants but to do that they had to show that the chalet formed part of the land.

The Court of Appeal held that the chalet did not form part of the land since it was not attached to it and merely rested on it. The defendants appealed to the House of Lords, which reversed the decision of the Court of Appeal.

Their Lordships found that the chalet was not designed to be removed from the land without essentially destroying the chalet. The chalet was not like a mobile home or some other portable building and was not capable of being dismantled and re-erected elsewhere. Their Lordships decided that, whatever the original parties had previously agreed, the chalet had become part and parcel of the land.

Lord Lloyd of Berwick considered the terms 'fixture' and 'chattel' to be confusing in the context of a house or building and proposed a threefold method of classifying an object:

> An object which is brought onto land may be classified under one of three heads. It may be (a) a chattel; (b) a fixture; or (c) part and parcel of the land itself. Objects in categories (b) and (c) are treated as being part of the land.

Lord Lloyd stated that a house that cannot be removed at all except by destruction cannot have been intended to remain as a chattel. It must have been intended to form part of the land. The case therefore gives more weight to the degree of annexation test – i.e. the intention of the parties. Having said this, Lord Clyde considered 'intention' to be misleading and considered that it is the purpose the object is serving that is important, not the intention or purpose of the person who put the building there. The relevant issue is whether the object is 'designed for the use and enjoyment of the land or for the more complete and convenient use of enjoyment of the thing itself', thus applying an objective test as opposed to a subjective one.

The principles set out in **Elitestone v Morris** were applied in **Chelsea Yacht and Boat Club v Pope** [2001] 2 All ER 409 where a houseboat was attached to pontoons and was also attached to the river bed by an anchor and lines. The court held that the boat did not form part of the land, despite the fact it was connected to the various service mains. The degree of annexation was insufficient to fix it to the land.

Apart from chalets and temporary buildings, etc. what about ordinary household items? The case of **Botham v TSB plc** (1997) 73 P & CR D1 provides a good insight into the approaches of the court when considering the status of such items.

Botham v TSB plc (1997) 73 P & CR D1

In this case, the bank was entitled to take possession of the appellant's house as the appellant had fallen into arrears with his mortgage repayments. The appellant claimed that he had transferred the contents of the flat to his parents and as such the bank was not entitled to those items. A dispute arose as to which items were fixtures (and therefore the property of the bank) and which were classified as chattels and belonged to the appellant's parents. There were approximately nine different categories of items, most of which were considered to be fixtures and belonged to the bank.

The Court of Appeal came to a different conclusion, however, and looked at the degree to which the chattels could easily be removed from the property. The court considered that bathroom fittings, including mirrors, towel rails, soap dishes, taps and shower heads, and kitchen units were fixtures, given that they were necessary for the use of the rooms concerned, based on the degree of annexation and permanence involved. On the other hand, the white goods which formed part of the kitchen, along with the units, had only a slight degree of annexation, which was not sufficient for them to become fixtures, given their intended purpose and relatively short working life. In any event, if these had been on hire purchase, ownership would not have passed immediately to the householder until he had paid for them. The carpets and curtains were not capable of becoming fixtures, due to their temporary attachment and lack of permanent improvement to the building. Gas fires, although having both functional and decorative effects, were not capable of being fixtures, having a low degree of annexation. Light fittings attached to walls or ceilings, some of them on tracks, were held to be chattels, though light fittings that were fixed into recesses were regarded as having sufficient degree of annexation or permanence to be regarded as fixtures.

The case is useful in that it gives some idea of how the courts approach the issue of fixtures in property law. Suffice it to say that the cases in this area turn very much on their facts. The application of the traditional rules in **Botham** provides a practical solution to the problem – however, the law is very much a rough and ready set of guidelines built around the somewhat anachronistic principle of 'quicquid plantatur solo, solo cedit'. This in itself was a Roman law principle that does not sit well in a common law system but was nevertheless adopted by the medieval courts. The development of the law in terms of its degree and purpose rules is not a very satisfactory way of dealing with the matter, although in **Botham** at least the Court of Appeal applied the principles in a pragmatic manner. The issue of whether an item was intended to form a permanent improvement so that its removal would substantially damage the building or remove the usefulness of the item seems as good a way as any of deciding the matter.

'. . . and other incorporeal hereditament, and an easement, right, privilege, or benefit in, over, or derived from land . . .'

Just as 'corporeal hereditament' refers to physical property, so the expression 'incorporeal hereditament' refers to property that has no physical form and is intangible. The expression describes all sorts of rights that exist over the land. It can, as the definition indicates, mean rights such as easements, which may be such things such as private rights of way (not public rights of way, which are part of the law of highways). It may also refer to such things as riparian rights – for instance, the right to fish on someone's property. Incorporeal hereditaments may also take the form of restrictive covenants in which a landowner is limited in the way they may use their property. Many of these rights or interests will be discussed in much greater detail later on but it is important to understand that, as far as land law is concerned, we are concerned with proprietary rights. Proprietary rights are those which attach to the land and therefore they affect a landowner and his or her successors in title to the property. They are not therefore personal rights, as one finds between parties to a contract, which only affect those parties. To be a proprietary right, the right must be capable of being defined – what it is or is not; it must be capable of being transferred to a new owner; and, finally, it must exist for a reasonable period of time – in other words, it is not something that exists for a fleeting period of time: **National Provincial Bank Ltd** v **Ainsworth** [1965] AC 1175.

These rights can be expressly agreed between the parties – for instance, when a landowner is selling a part of their land to another. An example in the circumstances is where the landowner wishes to restrict what the purchaser can do with the land. For instance, the landowner may sell the property for residential purposes only since they do not want to be affected by any industrial activities taking place on the land or suddenly wake up one morning to find a pig farm next to their back garden. Sometimes the law implies these rights – for example, if a person purchases a piece of land that is surrounded by land belonging to someone else then they would not be able to gain access to their land without committing a trespass over the other's land. Here the law will imply a right of way since otherwise the surrounded piece of land would be moribund and useless. Such a scenario involves what the law refers to as a 'landlocked close', which it will not allow. Thus these rights can be vital in order to be able to enjoy or make use of one's own property.

Rivers, lakes and the sea

So far, we have talked a great deal about the meaning of land and how it is defined by reference to the LPA 1925 s.205 (1)(ix). However, this provision makes no mention of rivers, lakes and the sea. In order to find any reference to water in defining land we have to look at the Land Registration Act ('LRA') 2002 s.132(1) which states:

. . . 'land' includes –

(a) buildings and other structures,
(b) land covered with water, and
(c) mines and minerals, whether or not held with the surface;

On the face of things, this seems very straightforward and land covered with water – whether by a pond, lake, stream, river or the sea – is included in our definition of land. But all is not quite so simple since, with flowing water, it depends whether it is flowing through a defined channel or whether it seeps or percolates through the ground. It also depends on whether the flowing water is tidal or not. Thus rights in relation to water are not quite so straightforward and it is all a bit of a tangle.

Let us take a relatively simple part first: the sea and tidal waters. The presumption at law is that the Crown owns the foreshore. Although the Crown is the only true absolute owner of land, it may have granted ownership to another body for the exploration or extraction of minerals from the sea bed, for instance. Apart from the issue of ownership, non-owners also have navigation rights in certain channels. Similarly, the public have fishing rights in tidal waters though certain activities such as salmon netting in estuaries are specifically licensed by the government. However, it is true that some have distinct rights in law to do this that are analogous to a riparian right. Some of these rights go back many centuries. The public have a right to take bait from the foreshore in order to fish and have the right to collect shellfish from the foreshore whilst the tide is out.

In relation to the ownership of ponds and lakes, ownership of land continues beneath the water – as the definition above indicates, 'land' includes 'land covered with water'.

With regards to other matters relating to water, an owner of land has no property rights in water as regards water that percolates through their land or flows through it in a defined channel. Thus in **Home Brewery Co. Ltd v William Davis & Co. (Leicester) Ltd** [1987] QB 339 it was held that, where water percolates from higher ground, the owner of the lower property has no obligation to receive that water and may, if they so wish, dam or hold the water back, provided they do not act unreasonably in doing so. By the same token, at common law, a landowner may draw off any amount of water with no regard to their neighbours. Having said this, the Water Resources Act 1991, as amended by the Water Act 2003, now restricts such use without a licence unless the water is being used for the landowner's domestic needs.

Where water runs through a defined channel, the owner of land again has no property rights in the water, though they do have certain rights. Perhaps the most common of these is in relation to fishing, where the landowner has sole rights to fish. Sometimes there is a public right of navigation down a river but this right is for that alone and there is no right to fish. Here the right of navigation is similar to a right of way over land. Where an owner owns the land on one bank of a non-tidal river then their riparian rights only extend to the middle of the river, the presumption at law being that one owns the land and subsoil to the middle of the river ('ad medium filum'). Similar principles apply to highways.

Landowners also have rights with regard to the flow of a watercourse in that the landowner is entitled to an unaltered flow of water in terms of volume. This is subject to the upper landowners making ordinary and reasonable use of the water. There is no right of action if the level of the water decreases unless this causes damages or amounts to the tort of nuisance. A landowner has reciprocal duties with regards to landowners downstream of their property.

As stated at common law, a landowner may make ordinary and reasonable use of water within a water course. This includes the right to abstract water for domestic purposes, or farming or, in some areas, industrial processes, even if this means exhausting the water flow. In addition, the landowner can make extraordinary use of the flow, provided the water is restored to the river in the same quantity as it was originally abstracted. These common law rights are subject to very severe regulation by way of statute and no doubt in an age of global warming and water shortages such legislation will become more stringent in the future. Broadly speaking, it is an offence for a landowner to abstract water without a licence from a water authority, unless it is used for domestic purposes or agricultural purposes other than irrigation by way of spraying.

The classification of property

In looking back through the above chapter we can see that property is divided into two types: real property and personal property. Real property has a very specific meaning and in fact refers to freehold property which will be discussed in detail later on. It will be recalled that the expression 'real' relates to the ability to recover property in medieval times if one was dispossessed of it. All other property is personal property, which originally only gave a right to damages.

Personal property, in turn, is divided into chattels real and chattels personal. Chattels real refers to leasehold land. It will be recalled that whilst this is of course land, it owes its classification to a rule that ceased to exist 500 years ago; however, to show its links with land we have the reference to 'real' in its description.

Chattels personal are also subdivided into choses in action and choses in possession. The expression 'choses' originates from the French, meaning 'thing'. Choses in possession are physical property such as a chair, table or pen. They gain this classification since, if one is dispossessed of this property, it can be recovered by re-taking the item itself – taking physical charge of it. Choses in action are items that may have a physical form – however, the value in the item does not rely on that physical form but lies in the inherent value 'within' the item. For instance, a cheque is simply a piece of paper with no or little inherent value. It gains its value by what is written on the cheque – i.e. 'I promise to pay X £5000 signed Z'. Other examples of a chose in action are share certificates, copyrights and patents. The expression 'chose in action' derives from the fact that the property is personal property which can only be claimed or enforced by action and not by taking physical possession, as with choses in possession.

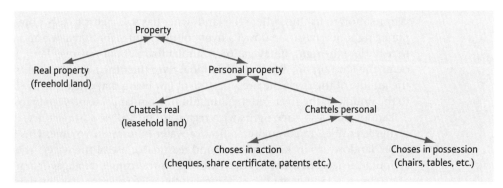

Figure 1.1

Summary

Land as legal construct

- Whilst property law provides rules relating to land and goods, it is also concerned with one's relationship with that property and other interested parties.
- Property law is concerned with one's rights in the property and the right to exclude others from it.
- There is a distinction between 'land law' and 'property law' – i.e. there is a distinction between 'real' property and 'personal' property.

The objectives in studying land law

- To know and understand the rights and liabilities attached to a piece of land.
- To provide a foundation for the study of conveyancing.

So . . . what is land?

Law of Property Act 1925 s.205(1)(ix)

'Land' includes land of any tenure, and mines and minerals, whether or not held apart from the surface, buildings or parts of buildings (whether the division is horizontal, vertical or made in any other way) and other corporeal hereditament; also a manor, an advowson, and a rent and other incorporeal hereditament, and an easement, right, privilege, or benefit in, over, or derived from land; . . . and 'mines and minerals' include 'any strata or seam of minerals or substances in or under any land, and powers of working and getting the same . . .'; and 'manor' 'includes a lordship, and reputed manor or lordship; and 'hereditament' means 'any real property which on an intestacy occurring before the commencement of this Act might have devolved upon an heir'.

'. . . land of any tenure . . .'

- Freehold land is held for an indefinite period of time, whilst leasehold land is held for a defined period of time.
- There is a distinction between 'real' property ('land') and 'personal' property ('chattels').
- Freehold land is classified as 'realty' based upon an action to recover the 'res' ("thing"); hence the expression a 'real' action that allows the 'thing' itself to be recovered, as opposed to simply an award in damages.
- Leasehold land is classified as 'personal' property based upon an action 'in personam'; hence the expression a 'personal' action. Such actions formerly only allowed damages to be awarded but later allowed the property itself to be recovered.

'. . . and mines and minerals . . .'

The principle of 'cuius est solum eius est usque ad caelum et ad inferos' – 'he who owns the surface owns everything up to the heavens and down to the depths of the earth'.

1. To the depths of the earth:

- Objects found in the ground belong to the occupier of the land
- ***Attorney General of the Duchy of Lancaster* v *Overton (Farms) Ltd*** [1981] Ch 33.

- Objects found on the land will either belong to the finder or the occupier of the land; however, for the latter to claim the property they must demonstrate that they have a 'manifest intention to exercise control over the land'.
- (*Parker* v *British Airways Board* [1982] 1 All ER 834).
- Treasure – at common law, gold and silver found hidden on the land belonged to the Crown; however, now see the Treasure Act 2006.

2. Up to the heavens:

The owner of the land owns the airspace above their property:

Bernstein v *Skyways* [1978] QB 479

Woolerton and Wilson Ltd v *Richard Costain Ltd* [1970] 1 WLR 411

Kelsen v *Imperial Tobacco Co.* [1957] 2 QB 334

'. . . and other corporeal hereditament . . .'

The expression 'hereditament' refers to real property which passed to an heir on intestacy prior to 1926. The expression 'corporeal' (from the Latin *'corpus'* meaning 'body') tells us that it refers to physical property over which ownership is exercised; thus the expression 'corporeal hereditament' refers to land, building, trees, minerals, etc. which are part of or fixed to the land that an heir would inherit. The expression therefore describes all the property an heir entitled to real property would inherit.

Fixtures and fittings

Whatever becomes fixed to the land becomes part of it and in this respect it is important to distinguish between fixtures and fittings. In doing this, one must recognise the difference between moveables and immoveables, as in the case of taps. Once the tap becomes fitted to a sink in the house it becomes immoveable, a fixture, and becomes part and parcel of the land.

In determining whether an item is a fixture or a fitting in *Holland* v *Hodgeson* (1872) LR 7 CP328 it was stated that two tests are used:

(i) the degree of annexation;

(ii) the purpose of the annexation.

Berkely v *Poulet* [1976] 242 EG 39

Elitestone v *Morris* [1997] 2 All ER 513

Chelsea Yacht and Boat Club v *Pope* [2007] 2 All ER 409

Botham v *TSB plc* (1997) 73 P & CR D1

'. . . incorporeal hereditament . . .'

This describes property that has no tangible form: for instance, easements and restrictive covenants. To be a proprietary interest the right must be capable of being definable; must be capable of being transferred to a new owner; and must exist for a reasonable period of time:

National Provincial Bank Ltd v *Ainsworth* [1965] AC 1175

Rivers, lakes and the sea

This is referred to in the Land Registration Act 2002 s.132(1). Land covered by water falls within the definition of land; however there are exceptions:

- Sea and tidal waters: The presumption at law is that the Crown owns the foreshore, though it may grant ownership to other bodies – for example, for the exploration of minerals. The public have fishing rights in tidal waters but note that specific licences may be required for certain activities, such as salmon netting.

- Flowing waters: An owner of land has no property rights in water as regards water that percolates through their land or flows through it in a defined channel: ***Home Brewery Co. Ltd* v *William Davis & Co. (Leicester) Ltd*** [1987] QB 339. See also: Water Resources Act 1991, as amended by the Water Act 2003.

- Where water runs through a defined channel the owner of land has no property rights in the water, though they do have certain rights – for example, fishing rights.

- Note: Public rights of navigation down a river. Owners of one bank of a non-tidal river have riparian rights to the middle of the river.

- See also rights of abstraction.

The classification of property

Real property = Freehold land

Personal property: Chattels real and chattels personal: choses in action and choses in possession.

Further reading

Baker, *An Introduction to English Legal History*, Oxford University Press (2007)

2

Estates and interests in land – an historical perspective

Aims and objectives

After reading this chapter you should be able to:

- Understand the nature of the feudal system.

- Understand the doctrine of tenures.

- Understand the doctrine of estates.

- Understand the nature of words of limitation.

- Know the origins of the common law and equity.

- Understand the nature of legal and equitable rights, with particular reference to the notion of the trust.

- Understand the impact of the bona fide purchaser of the legal estate for value without notice with particular reference to the doctrine of notice.

- Recognise the development of other equitable interests.

- Understand how equitable rights are created.

Introduction

Having seen what is meant by property in Chapter 1, we now need to see what rights and interests one can acquire in real property. For our purposes here we include leaseholds, even though these are, strictly speaking, personal property. In order to examine and understand what rights and interests one can acquire in real property we have to look back into history to the Norman Conquest in 1066.

When William invaded England, he brought a large army and rapidly established a strong central administration. This administration was based around the Curia Regis, or King's Court. The Curia Regis exercised judicial, administrative and political functions and comprised the King and his barons. William regarded England as his own personal property but he set about rewarding the barons, bishops and his other followers for the help they gave him in recovering England from Harold and the Anglo-Saxons. The barons wanted land as their reward and therefore William set about dividing his new kingdom into large estates and gave these to his chief supporters. William retained ownership of the land and indeed this principle remains the same today. It is important to remember that there is only one absolute owner of property – the Crown. The principle can be seen in modern times – i.e. the law relating to inheritance. Thus if a person dies without making a will, intestate, with no close relatives then his property reverts to the Crown as bona vacantia.

In return for the King's giving his barons and important followers large tracts of land, these 'tenants' not only had to swear fealty to the him but also had to provide him with services. Thus if a large piece of land was granted to A in Yorkshire he not only had to pay homage and swear fealty to the King, he might also have to provide his King with 100 armed horsemen for 40 days each year. This was the condition on which the land was held and, of course, it enabled the King to maintain an army. On the other hand, if B was given a large piece of land in Cheshire, as well as paying homage and swearing fealty, he might have to provide the King with 50 baskets of wheat or 10 cows.

The barons, as well as providing the King with certain services, would, in turn, divide their land up into smaller pieces or parcels of land for their principal followers, who would, in turn, have to provide services to them. This process of subinfeudation, or dividing the land up, continued down to the smallest piece of land, known as the manor. Pieces of land within the manor would also be given to the lord of the manor's immediate servants and agricultural labourers in return for the services he required. In this way, the whole of England was divided and sub-divided so that the social and economic organisation was based on landholding in return for services or 'tenure' and formed the basis of the feudal system.

The large landowners were known as 'tenants in capite' as they held their land directly from the King. The persons who actually occupied the land were known as 'tenants in demesne' wherever they appeared on the feudal ladder. Whether as tenants in capite or agricultural tenants, those persons that occupied land within the feudal system were known as 'mesne lords'. The process ensured that there is no land in England and Wales without an owner: 'nulle terre sans seigneur' (no land without a lord) since, even if no owner could be found, the land always belonged to the Crown. The feudal lords, whether the King or lords of the manor, were obliged to hold a court for their tenants in order to decide local disputes as to landholding. The Curia Regis was the King's Court and it was from this that a centralised system of justice developed into the common law courts. It was from this system of courts that the common law emerged.

The feudal system therefore looked like this:

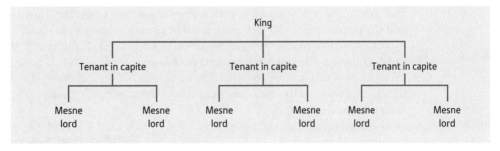

Figure 2.1

In addition to the King requiring services from his tenants in capite, he also controlled land by way of time. Generally speaking, William only made grants of land to a tenant for that tenant's lifetime, although it became common for the King to renew the grant in favour of the tenant's heir when the tenant died. Eventually, the life tenancy evolved into a 'fee tail', whereby the land would pass from the tenant to his descendants – i.e. from father to son, to grandson, to great grandson, etc. Still later, a 'fee simple' also evolved, where the land could pass to the tenant's heirs, whether descendants or not – i.e. from father, to son, to nephew, to the Church, etc. Both life and fee simple tenancies continue to exist today; however, fee tails were abolished by the Trusts of Land and Appointment of Trustees Act 1996.

The different tenancies were known as 'estates' and each estate designated how long a tenant held the land for. It is very important in this context not to mix up the notion of an estate being a tract of land with that of a concept of time. It is common in everyday language to talk of 'my landed estate' referring to a 1000-acre estate, but in the law when one refers to an estate one is referring to how long a person is to hold the land for. This difference is summed in the quotation from **Walsingham's Case (1579) 2 Plowd 547** which stated:

> . . . the land itself is one thing and the estate in the land is another, for an estate in land is a time in land, or land for a time.

The effect of this is that, whilst tenants in capite and tenants in demesne held estates in land, neither owned the land itself and each held it from the Crown. Indeed, as stated earlier, to this day all land is held from the Crown and the fee simple is the closest one comes to outright ownership of the land.

Two basic doctrines therefore emerge from the feudal system:

- the doctrine of tenures; and
- the doctrine of estates.

The doctrine of tenure

Generally

Under the feudal system, several different forms of land tenure existed. Essentially, the relationship between each lord and his tenant was a form of contract. The tenant performed his service in return for a landholding and was liable to forfeit his holding if he failed to perform his service or committed a crime or was found to be disloyal to his lord. In turn, the lord would protect his tenant and guaranteed his tenant's title against all comers. The lord also held a court for himself and his tenants. In fact, the relationship was something more than a contract since there was a bond of trust between the lord and the tenant that was sealed by the tenant paying homage to his lord.

The system of tenures progressed through each layer of the feudal system until one came to the very lowest, and poorest, in the order. These villeins, or serfs, simply had a small piece of land to work for their own purposes. Of course, being at the very bottom of the system, those in this category were always tenants, never mesne lords, since there was no one beneath them.

The lowest tenants, as opposed to villeins, usually held a 'manor' or 'vill'. Manors were usually quite small communities that were often gathered in a village around a fortified house. The village would often have a church and though this was based on ecclesiastical landholding that was centred around a parish, sometimes the local lord of the manor would have the right to appoint the priest by way of a right of patronage or 'advowson'. Essentially, the manor was a feudal state in its own right since all the tenants within it swore allegiance to their local lord, who held his own court. This local court controlled many of the activities within the manor, whether agrarian activities or controlling the conduct of the population within the manor. It might also control the production of flour and ale. The manors also had their own customs that were enforced through the local or seignorial courts until such time as the royal courts took over their jurisdiction by way of justices 'on circuit'. It was this and the enforcement of local customs with regard to landholding that gave rise to the development of the common law of England and, in particular, the evolution of the law of real property. These developments eventually weakened the jurisdiction of the local courts, leading to their demise, though the last were only abolished by the Courts Act 1971.

The services provided by tenants fell into three broad categories: military, civil and spiritual.

Military tenure

Knight service was the principal military tenure whereby a tenant was obliged to provide a number of armed horsemen, usually for 40 days. Military service imposed on a tenant in capite could be passed on to his tenants in turn by subinfeudation so that tenant in capite could meet his obligations to the King through his own tenants.

Another form of military service was 'castleguard' which, as the term suggests, required castle guarding duty. Yet another type of military service was 'cornage', which required a tenant to patrol borders.

Over a period of time, many of the traditional military services were commuted to a money payment known as 'scutage' and, whilst this was similar to the modern-day concept of rent, the jurist Henry de Bracton still considered it to be a form of military tenure.

Civil service

These types of service were usually provided by the tenants in capite for the monarch. The services were generically referred to as 'grand serjeanty' and were really personal services. These services were many and various and included putting food on the monarch's plate, looking after his wine, holding his head if he was seasick, counting his chessmen on Christmas Day and tending his garden. By the time Edward I (1272–1307) came to the throne, many of these types of tenure were in retreat – some became obsolete, others were changed to knight's service or commuted to payments of money. Some of the ceremonial favours were retained, with some even existing well into modern times: for instance, the duty to support the monarch's right arm holding the sceptre during the coronation can still be seen today.

'Petty serjeanty' referred to types of tenure which required the tenant to provide, not services, but small items such as horses, arrows, armour, wine or food.

Spiritual tenures

The two main types of tenure found here were 'divine service' and 'frankalmoign'. Divine service arose where land was granted to an ecclesiastical body or church in return for specific spiritual services, such as saying prayers for the lord on his birthday or Christmas Day. The service could include other favours, such as giving alms to the poor at Easter.

Frankalmoign arose where land was granted to an ecclesiastical body where no services were required to be performed and no 'fealty' or oath of allegiance was required. Thus, if land was granted to the local abbey but no specific services were required of the abbey, it was said to hold by way of frankalmoign.

Other types of tenure

Lower down the social order of the feudal system, the types of tenure were less defined. Peasants generally provided agricultural duties; these were either fixed or unfixed. If a peasant was required to help his lord by sowing his fields or helping with the harvest at certain times of the year, this type of tenure was called 'common socage', which was a free tenure and is the origin of the expression 'freehold' which we are all familiar with today. The expression 'socage' eventually became a generic term that referred to all forms of free tenure, other than knight service, serjeanty or spiritual service. On the other hand, if the peasant was required to provide services as and when his lord required him to do so, this type of tenure was called 'villeinage', which was an unfree tenure.

The majority of the land after the Norman Conquest was held in unfree tenure and here the tenant held the land at the will of the lord and could be evicted at any time. The tenant had no right of redress in the local seignorial court; nor would the royal courts protect him. Over a period of time, customs emerged that gave the tenant protection from his lord unless he had committed some act that merited the forfeiture of his land by the lord. These customary rules became more important since the common law itself would not recognise the rights of the tenant.

By the fifteenth century, the royal courts began to give protection to tenants of villein land against their lord and therefore the tenant was now protected not only by custom but by the common law itself. In practice, what was occurring here was that the common law would recognise the local custom and then enforce it. Where the tenure was recognised by the common law, it became known as 'copyhold'.

The expression 'copyhold' derived its name from the way the tenure could be transferred or conveyed to another. Copyholds could only be transferred by a process of surrender and admittance within the lord's court, where the tenant surrendered his land to the lord, who then admitted another to it. The process was recorded in the records of the court and the person to whom the land was transferred would be given a copy of the record to prove his title, hence the expression 'copyhold'. In time, these became valuable forms of tenure for the tenant and his heirs since the rent payable to the lord could not be increased and thus the value to the lord depreciated.

The 'incidents' of tenure

The services that a tenant rendered to his lord were not the only rights that the lord was entitled to. These 'incidents' of tenure imposed certain obligations on the tenant or certain rights in the landlord. So if A failed to perform certain services to his lord, B, then B's remedy was to seize A's chattels, such as cattle, and keep them until A performed his service to B. Thus B could levy 'distress' against A's goods: he 'distrained' them, and if A continued not to perform his service B could 'forfeit' (take) A's land and keep it.

Another significant incident was 'escheat'. In granting a tenure to a tenant, the lord might specify that the tenant would only have the land for his lifetime. On the tenant's death, escheat gave the lord the right to re-take the land to retain it or give it to another tenant. Often the landlord would find it convenient to give the land to the tenant's son since he might know the land and the other tenants and so there was some continuity in the management of the land.

The lord could grant the land to a tenant and his heirs, in which case the land would pass to the tenant, then his son, then his grandson, etc. It should be noted, however, that the expression 'heirs' did not necessarily mean direct heirs, such as sons, but also any blood relatives. These could be issue or collateral relatives such as brothers, sisters or nephews and nieces.

Escheat therefore is the right of a superior lord to re-take land on termination of a tenancy (that is, a feudal tenancy *not* a lease). If there was no mesne lord to whom the land could escheat, the land would be held directly from the King. The rule still applies today since, as we have seen, if a person dies without leaving close relatives, within the terms of the Administration of Estates Act 1925 s.46, the deceased person's estate devolves to the Crown as bona vacantia in lieu of any right of escheat (s.47(3)).

The demise of tenure

In truth, the doctrine of tenure as a means of giving land in return for services did not last very long, probably only around 200 years. Two pressures brought about the demise of tenure.

Firstly, in the feudal system there was theoretically no limit to the number of levels that could be created within the feudal pyramid or ladder. In their work *The History of Law* Vol. I at p.233 Pollock and Maitland stated:

> . . . theoretically there is no limit to the possible number of rungs, and . . . men have enjoyed a large power, not merely of adding new rungs to the bottom of the ladder, but also inserting new rungs in the middle of it.

This process of adding new rungs, known as 'subinfeudation', could arise by a tenant attempting to raise money by giving a purchaser a sub-tenancy – i.e. the purchaser becomes a tenant of the vendor himself. This process tended to extend the feudal ladder. For a while, subinfeudation was preferable to the vendor since it did not require the lord's consent and also because it could give the vendor an 'incident' or 'seignory' that might provide a benefit in the future – for instance, the possibility of an escheat from the purchaser.

The real loser here was the lord – mainly because of the potential loss of incidents of tenure. One of these was the incident of wardship, whereby, if a tenant died, leaving an heir who was an infant, the lord had the right to manage the land and take any profits until the heir came of age, subject to the lord having to pay for the heir's education and upbringing. In the context of subinfeudation, if the tenant subinfeudated (i.e. created another rung) during his lifetime he could, as part of the transaction, take a largely nominal service that was essentially worthless in favour of a large cash price. In this situation, when the lord took the seignory or wardship on the tenant's death, he would only have the benefit of a nominal seignory/service and the cash value would be in the tenant's wallet as cash, following the subinfeudation process.

Another effect of subinfeudation was that, as more rungs were added to the feudal ladder, there was less likelihood that an escheat would arise.

The second aspect that contributed to the demise of tenure was 'substitution'. A tenant, rather than subinfeudate, could convey his land to a new owner by way of substitution. This meant that the new owner took over the tenant's position on the feudal ladder. Originally, a tenant required the lord's consent to substitute – however, at some point in the thirteenth century it seems that the general rule developed that a tenant could transfer or 'alienate' his land by substitution without the lord's consent. This created two problems for the lord: firstly, the lord had no discretion over who was now to become his tenant: it could, for instance, be someone who proved to be a very poor tenant in terms of his husbandry of the land. Secondly, an old tenant could substitute in favour of a young tenant and therefore deprive the lord of his seignory of escheat and the possibility of obtaining valuable fees.

Undoubtedly, the greater evil as far as the lords were concerned was subinfeudation – not just for the reasons set out above, but also because the continued process extended the feudal ladder and made it unwieldy. This process was brought to a halt by the statute Quia Emptores in 1290. This enactment prevented tenants from alienating their land to others by way of subinfeudation and required transfer or alienation to take place by substitution. The enactment represented a shift of public policy in favour of the free transfer of land, but it had another profound consequence in that it heralded the end of the feudal system as no new mesne tenures could be created except by the monarch. The effect of this was that the feudal pyramid became flattened so that now fee simple owners of land held it directly from the Crown as tenants in chief. Quia Emptores is still operational today and continues to regulate the archaic doctrine of tenure. It ensures that any conveyances of fee simple estates must be out-and-out transfers, with no feudal or seignory services being capable of being reserved. The effect therefore was to make transfers commercial transactions and not ones of feudalism.

The statute did not apply to the Crown and thus all land is held by a subject in tenure from the Crown. This was an important exception since it meant that the Crown would have to transfer the land to a tenant with no possibility of an escheat. Consequently, if no mesne lord emerged, the land reverted to the Crown.

The doctrine of tenure was further eroded by subsequent legislative enactments, particularly the Tenures Abolition Act 1690, which converted all tenures into 'free and common socage' (or 'freehold tenure') and copyhold. Subsequently, the Law of Property Act 1922 converted all copyhold into freehold tenure: that is, socage. Thus all tenures were reduced to a common freehold tenure held directly from the Crown so that, technically, only the Crown holds the ultimate title to land and the closest an individual comes to holding absolute ownership is by way of freehold tenure. One word of warning needs to be given, however – freehold tenure has nothing whatsoever to do with the expression 'freehold' which we see in estate agents' windows. Although the expressions are the same, it is important to recognise that freehold tenure refers to the *quality* of the tenure whilst, as we shall see next, 'freehold' refers to the duration (or quantity) of the estate.

The doctrine of estates

Generally

As already mentioned, an 'estate' refers not to an area of land but to a period of time. It can be seen therefore that the ownership of land is a very different concept from that of ownership of chattels. In the case of chattels ownership is an absolute concept – there is either ownership by one or more persons or nothing at all. In the case of land, ownership is not absolute since it is held in tenure from the Crown. Furthermore, in relation to land there can be a multiplicity of estates and interests arising concurrently in the same piece of land and these are each related to a period of time, a 'temporal slice' or, more simply: 'For how long is the land to be held by a tenant?'

The doctrine of estates is of vital importance to the understanding of land law. It is useful to see this in an historical context first of all, but it is important to bear in mind that the Law of Property Act 1925 brought about radical changes to the doctrine of estates.

Prior to 1925, the common law divided estates into two classes: estates of freehold and estates of less than freehold (better known today as leases). Do not confuse freehold estates with freehold tenure or socage – the two are not the same, though the expression 'freehold' is often used to describe both.

Estates of freehold

At common law there were three freehold estates:

(a) the fee simple estate;

(b) the fee tail estate; and

(c) the life estate.

Fee simple

Generally

This type of estate is the primary one in land law as it is the one that comes closest to absolute ownership and is the largest estate a tenant can have in terms of time since potentially it can exist for an unlimited duration. The point is illustrated by referring back to Walsingham's case which was referred to on page 22. Here it was further stated that 'he who has the fee simple in land has a time in the land without end, or land for a time without end'.

The concept of the fee simple estate was that it existed as long as the original tenant or any of his heirs survived. The word 'fee' denotes that the estate is one of inheritance. The word 'simple' indicates that the estate will pass to any heirs, whether they be blood relatives or otherwise. Further, if the original tenant sold or transferred his fee simple to another person, that person would also be able to pass his estate to his own general heirs. The estate thus became virtually perpetual and would only end if a tenant died without leaving any heirs, at which point it would escheat to his lord, nowadays the Crown.

Types of fee simple

There are various forms of fee simple that require consideration.

Fee simple absolute The expression 'fee simple' has already been explained above but the word 'absolute' merely means that it stands to be potentially perpetual in that the fee simple itself is not subject to an event which might bring it to a premature end.

Determinable fee simple This type of fee simple will automatically cease on the occurrence of an event, which may never occur. Here the occurrence of the event will bring the fee simple to its natural end and the estate will then revert to the person who originally granted it.

Example

If a grantor (X) grants a fee simple to a grantee (Y) until she becomes a solicitor, when Y becomes a solicitor her fee simple estate comes to an end and the estate then reverts to X. The estate therefore comes to the end of its natural existence.

It is important that a determinable fee simple is distinguished from a conditional fee simple, which we will discuss next. Essentially, the difference lies in the words of the grant; thus words such as 'until', 'so long as' or 'whilst' tend to create a determinable fee since these set out the natural boundary or 'end point' of the estate.

Conditional fee simple This may take two forms: a condition precedent or a condition subsequent. With a *condition precedent*, the grantor sets a condition that marks the commencement of the fee simple. Thus the existence of the fee simple depends on the condition being met.

Example

X grants a fee simple estate to Y if he marries Z. When Y marries Z, he will take the fee simple absolute, which may then carry on indefinitely. Another example might be if A grants a fee simple to B if she qualifies as a solicitor. Again, once B qualifies as a solicitor, she takes a fee simple absolute.

In a fee simple subject to a condition subsequent, the occurrence of the condition brings the premature end to the fee simple absolute.

Example

X grants a fee simple to Y provided he does NOT marry Z. Here Y takes the fee simple absolute but this is brought to an end if he enters the forbidden marriage. Another example might be if X grants a fee simple to Y provided that she continues to practise as a solicitor. If Y decides to leave her profession, she will forfeit her fee simple.

A conditional fee subject to a condition subsequent is very different from a determinable fee simple and great care must be taken to distinguish between the two. In the former there is a clause added that defeats the existence of the fee simple, whilst in the latter the determining event sets out the duration or limits of the estate. Just as in a determinable fee simple, in a condition subsequent the words can provide a guide as to what is taking place: words such as 'provided that', 'but if', 'on condition that' or 'if it should happen' often point to a fee simple subject to a condition subsequent.

Fee tail

The expression 'fee' here again demonstrates that this is an estate of inheritance, whilst the word 'tail' indicates that the estate will continue whilst the grantee and his linear descendants continue to exist. Thus the estate will pass from father to son, to grandson, to great grandson, and so on. This is an example of 'male tail' but more rarely there can exist a 'female tail' whereby the estate passes from mother to daughter, to granddaughter, etc. Where the fee tail can pass through either sex, it is known as a 'general tail'.

It is worth noting that the 'fee tail' estate is sometimes referred to as an 'entail' or an 'entailed interest' or an 'estate tail'. The terms are all synonymous, though an 'entailed interest' generally refers to an equitable fee tail.

Fee tails are largely of historic interest since they were abolished by the Trusts of Land and Appointment of Trustee Act 1996 so that, since 1 January 1997, no new fee tails can be created. Any attempt to create such an estate will result in a fee simple absolute being created. Fee tails that existed before the above date can continue to exist, but on the death of the heir, the estate will be converted to a fee simple absolute for his or her descendant.

It should be noted that after the Law of Property Act 1925 fee tails could only exist as equitable interests, but more about this later on page 66.

Life interests

This type of estate exists for the lifetime of the grantee only, after which it terminates and reverts back to the grantor. Very often, the extent of the estate is measured by the life span of the tenant – however, it is possible for the extent of the estate to be measured by some other person's life: for example, 'a grant to A for as long as B lives'. This type of life estate is known as a life estate 'pur autre vie'.

What happens if the life estate owner predeceases the person on whom the extent of the estate depends – for example, if land is granted by X to A on the life of B but A predeceases B? Here A's estate passes to his own heirs until such time as B actually dies, when it will pass to X's heirs.

It is also possible to have life interests that are determinable or subject to a condition subsequent, just as we have seen in fee simple estates.

After the Law of Property Act 1925, life estates can only exist as an equitable interest in land.

Estates of less than freehold

Leases for a definite period of time

Originally at common law, only the three freehold estates above were recognised. Estates of less than freehold – or leaseholds, as we will now call them – were regarded as inferior and developed completely separately from the common law system of estates. Leaseholds developed as contracts that bound only the parties to the contract and, as such, were not regarded as property in terms of land ownership. Hence, as we have already seen in Chapter 1, leaseholds were regarded as personal property and holders were not fully protected against the claims of interlopers. Thus, where a leaseholder was deprived of his land, his only remedy lay in damages – a personal action – as opposed to a right in rem giving him a right to recover the land itself, a real action. It is for this reason that leasehold property remains a personal property classified as a 'chattel real'. However, the law eventually gave leaseholds full protection as a proprietary interest in the land and they became part of the law of estates.

In contrast with the estates of freehold, whose duration is of an indefinite period of time, leaseholds are characterised by durations either of a definite or certain period of time or capable of being made definite or certain. A tenant may therefore hold the land for a fixed term of certain duration – for example, a lease to X for 999 years, or a lease to Y for 99 years, or a lease to Z for 1 year. A word of warning needs to be given here. Occasionally, the grant of a lease may look very similar to a freehold estate – for example, a grant to 'A for 50 years if A so long lives'. On the face of things it appears that this is a life interest since, if A is already 50 years old, the probability is that she will die before her lease expires as she would then be 100 years old. The grant therefore appears to be the same as a grant 'to A for life'. Notwithstanding, it is important to remember that the maximum duration of the lease is set by the definitive time period of 50 years and therefore the estate remains a leasehold, not a freehold estate.

Another aspect of a lease being granted for a definite period of time is that it is impossible for the holder of a lease to create a freehold estate out of it. The reason for this is that a freehold estate being for an indefinite period of time could outstrip the period of the tenancy. Thus a leaseholder with a 999-year lease could not grant a fee simple absolute since this could exist almost in perpetuity and outlast the lease. In such a case the lease-holder is attempting to grant something greater than they themselves have, which is, of course, not possible. Effectively, in attempting to make such a grant, the leaseholder would merely be assigning his 999-year lease (or what remains of it) to the grantee.

Leases for a period of time capable of being made certain

Whilst we tend to think of leases for 999 years, 99 years or 1 year, etc. leases from month to month or year to year are also properly regarded as leases, even if it may look as though they may carry on indefinitely. The reason for this is that such tenancies are capable of being made definite by either party giving notice to the other. Thus at common law in a monthly tenancy either the landlord or the tenant could terminate the lease by giving the other one month's notice. From this moment the length of the lease (or tenancy – the terms are synonymous, though we tend to call leases for one year or more 'leases' and leases for shorter periods 'tenancies') becomes certain and becomes a lease for a 'fixed term of certain duration'. This position is now defined in the Law of Property Act 1925 s.205 (xxviii) which states:

> Term of years absolute means a term of years . . . but does not include any term of years determinable by life or lives . . . and in this definition 'term of years' includes a term for less than a year, or for year or years and a fraction of a year or from year to year.

Whilst leases and tenancies exist for a definite period of time, or for periods capable of being made certain, there are two particular types of tenancy that do appear to be for an indefinite period; these are tenancies at sufferance and tenancies by will. A tenancy at sufferance arises where a lease or tenancy has been terminated but the tenant remains in possession or 'holds over' without the landlord's permission. In such a situation, the tenant cannot be considered a trespasser since their original entry on to the property is lawful, but once the landlord enters the property, the tenant does indeed become a trespasser and they can be ejected from the premises. The expression 'tenancy at will', however, belies the fact that the tenant does not have an interest in land as such. It is considered that such tenancies arose in order to prevent a tenant acquiring an estate by way of adverse possession by virtue of their occupation of the land and thus preventing the landlord from establishing their title to the land.

A tenancy at will is a type of tenancy that continues indefinitely, although it can be brought to an end by either party giving notice to the other. Clearly, until this is done, there is a relationship of landlord and tenant between the parties; however, because there is no defined duration within the tenancy, no estate arises in relation to the land. This type of tenancy is therefore precarious and since the tenant has no estate as such he cannot transfer anything to a third party.

Words of limitation

Words of limitation define the estate to be taken by a transferee either in an inter vivos conveyance or in a will. The words mark out the extent or length of time for which the estate to be transferred. It is important to bear in mind that, technically, the words do not themselves convey the estate to a transferee. Originally, the correct word or phrase was required to limit the estate, thus to convey an estate of inheritance such as a fee simple, the word 'heirs' was required to be contained in the conveyance. To create a fee tail, the conveyor would have to ensure that the conveyance indicated that it was to an individual and then to their linear descendants. Thus it was usual to convey land to 'A and the heirs of his body'.

In modern times, the process has been simplified by the Law of Property Act 1925 s.60(1) which provides:

> A conveyance of freehold land to any person without words of limitation, or any equivalent expression, shall pass to the grantee the fee simple or other the whole interest which the power to convey in such land, unless a contrary intention appears in the conveyance.

The effect of this is that a grantor is assumed to transfer to the grantee the maximum estate that the grantor holds in the land, unless the grantor expressly states that the transfer will be for a lesser interest.

In relation to fee tails, it has already been established that these cannot be created following the Trusts of Land and Appointment of Trustees Act 1996. The question then arises as to what occurs if a person attempts to create such an estate today. If A conveys land to B with an entailed interest, the effect of this will be that B, rather than taking an entail, will take a fee simple.

With regard to life estates, the grantor will create a fee simple unless they show an intention to create a life estate, for instance by using the expression 'to A for life'.

Common law and equity

Generally

As we have seen already, William, after his victory at the Battle of Hastings, brought with him the Curia Regis or King's Court. This was not, however, a law court per se but a body of advisers who supervised the administration of the kingdom. A great deal of the administration of the law was based upon the seignorial courts that local lords held for their tenants. There were also courts for the shires, boroughs and hundreds – indeed, some of these survived into the twentieth century until the Courts Act 1971. The Salford Hundred Court of Record was such an example. Much of the law that was administered in these courts was based on local custom and sometimes the outcome depended very much on the status of the parties involved. Trial by battle or ordeal and trial by oath were common methods for determining success or failure in litigation. The King's Court did, of course, handle some cases since, just as mesne lords had seignorial courts for their tenants, so the King held court for his tenants in capite. The King's Court was not accessible by ordinary people at the time and was not considered a court of the people.

Despite the myriad courts that existed, the prominent position of the King placed him above all the courts. The royal court stood over everything. The administration of justice was nevertheless very uncertain. The position began to change in the reign of Henry II, who, following the disastrous reign of Stephen, restored a firm system of government and produced a coherent system of justice which formed the foundation of the common law that we know today. The three pillars on which this system was based were the role of the itinerant justices, the development of the royal courts and the writ system.

The itinerant justices

In order to enforce royal justice, Henry II appointed itinerant justices to tour the country, which was divided into six circuits which still exist today. The justices would move around their circuit and administered both civil and criminal justice. On the civil side, the justices administered the 'petty assizes', which required them to enquire into disputes brought before them. Originally, the justices would come to their decision based on local custom but after a while they would come together at Westminster and look at the various customs they had come across, choose the best and then apply these over the whole country, irrespective of the local customs. Thus the notion of the common law – i.e. a law applied 'commonly' over the whole country – began to evolve.

The development of the royal courts

The early kings were very much peripatetic rulers and moved around the country. This was clearly not a sound way of ruling a kingdom, since the whole entourage associated with the King's Court would move too. Eventually, bodies of administrators were based at a location, usually the Palace of Westminster, to carry out functions whilst the King was away. The first department to be based in this way was the Exchequer and eventually this developed into a formal court, the Court of Exchequer which dealt with taxation and a variety of fiscal matters.

The fact that the King's Court was not static and that the justices were itinerant posed a problem for some suitors since their access to justice was limited by the peripatetic nature of the judicial structure. These suitors needed a court that remained in one place and was accessible to them wherever they came from in the country. To address this problem, a static royal court, the Court of Common Pleas, was founded that functioned independently of the presence of the King at Westminster and was staffed by permanent justices. The Court of Common Pleas dealt with cases in which the King had no interest. In addition, a third court developed, the Court of the King's Bench, which was peripatetic in nature and accompanied the King.

It can be seen, therefore, that three principal royal courts emerged: the Court of Exchequer, the Court of Common Pleas and the Court of the King's Bench. Much of the jurisdiction of the courts overlapped but it is beyond the remit of this work to look at all these aspects in detail. Suffice it to say that the royal courts existed alongside the seignorial courts, though these declined over many years as suitors gradually moved over to the royal courts on the basis that they could get better, cheaper and more consistent justice from them.

The writ system

Usually, no action could be commenced in any of the common law courts until a writ had been issued to a suitor by the chancellor, who originally was an ecclesiastic. Each type of action had its own particular type of writ, known as a 'form of action'. Different writs had their own procedures and remedies. It was of fundamental importance for a suitor to obtain the correct writ since no action could succeed unless the correct writ was obtained. If there was no writ for a suitor's particular problem, then a new writ could be invented. Initially, this was quite easy to do (though even then there could be problems since sometimes a court would refuse to recognise a writ) and the number of new writs increased rapidly. This power to issue new writs was challenged by the barons – no doubt because they were losing business from their seignorial court to the royal courts. In the Provisions of Oxford 1528 it was agreed that the chancellor would issue no new writs except for those already recognised. The effect of this provision was that the common law became frozen within the bounds of the existing writs. The Statute of Westminster II 1285 chapter 24 In Consimili Casu provided that the clerks of Chancery should have limited powers to create new writs. Thus if there was an existing writ for an action and there was a similar case (in consimili casu)' which required a remedy for which none existed, then the clerks could create a new writ or refer the matter to Parliament. It remained the case, however, that if there was no original writ, nor one created in consimili casu, a suitor would have no right of action and therefore no remedy, unless he could persuade Parliament to create a new writ.

The role of the chancellor and the Court of Chancery

From what we have seen above, the writ system had two principal defects: firstly, there might be no writ for a suitor's particular cause of action, and, secondly, if a suitor chose the wrong writ then he lost his action in limine (at the outset). A further difficulty was that, even if a suitor obtained the correct writ, the remedies available were very limited, being largely the recovery of land and damages, which remain the common law remedies today. Additionally, in the seignorial local courts and the early common law courts there was every chance that a local mesne lord could influence the outcome of the case by bribing or intimidating court officials or juries, which were also introduced more widely in Henry II's reign.

The effect of these problems would be to leave a suitor without a remedy, or with a remedy that was inappropriate to his needs. A suitor did, however, have an action of last resort and that was to petition the King's Council directly. The right of the King's Council to dispense justice existed prior to the Norman Conquest and was a residuary right prior to the development of the common law courts. This right to petition the King's Council also has its origins within the political hierarchy of the feudal system. The monarch was clearly the head of the feudal system but he ruled by way of the 'divine right of kings', a political philosophy that would prove particularly problematical for Charles I much later on. The philosophy of the divine right of kings was that the King was appointed by God and therefore laws passed by the King were tantamount to being those of God himself. As part of this philosophy, the King was regarded as the 'fountain of justice' to which everyone should have access.

Petitions to the King's Council were addressed to the Council, which included the King, and were heard by the Council itself. Another important member of the Council was the chancellor. The chancellor was usually a bishop since, as chancellor, he was regarded as 'the keeper of the King's conscience'. As the number of petitions to the King's Council increased, it clearly became impossible for this council to hear these as well as dealing with major issues relating to the governance of the realm, foreign policy, etc. As a result, responsibility for hearing the petitions became delegated to the chancellor. Whilst he originally took the advice of judges, by the fifteenth century he would make decisions on his own authority. As the petitions to the chancellor became more and more frequent, there gradually came into existence a Court of Chancery in which the chancellor acted independently of the King's Council and administered a new system of justice called 'equity'.

The approach of equity to justice was entirely different from that applied by the common law courts, which applied the law according to strict principles hidebound by formality. Equity based its decisions on the simple application of what was just and fair – what was 'equitable'. The Court of Chancery was therefore a court of conscience that did not see itself bound by the rigour of the common law, which was concerned with simply administering the strict legal rights of the parties, irrespective of any moral or ethical consideration. In applying the simple notion of conscience, the Court of Chancery evolved new remedies that often met the needs of a suitor better. The idea was that a remedy would cleanse the conscience of a party by requiring him to act according to good conscience and, if he refused to do so, compelling him to act by the threat of imprisonment.

Example

A enters into a contract to purchase Blackacre from B for £10,000. B then refuses to proceed with the contract. At common law, A would be able to recover damages from B for breach of contract, but this does not really produce the remedy A needs. What A requires is for the contract to be fulfilled so that he obtains Blackacre. In equity, the Court of Chancery might consider that B has acted against his conscience and would grant an order of specific performance that required him to hand Blackacre over. If B refused, he would be put in prison until he agreed to hand the property over and thereby act according to his conscience.

The remedies of equity, such as specific performance and injunctions which could be used to compel someone to do or not to do something, acted against the person himself.

Equity is therefore said to act in personam, whilst the common law acts in rem. This nature of equity can still be seen today; thus if a person refuses to abide by the terms of an injunction they stand to be in contempt of court and may be imprisoned.

As a court of conscience, the Court of Chancery developed rules of equity that varied with the different views an individual chancellor proposed. This led to the maxim that 'equity varies with the length of the Lord Chancellor's foot'! In the late sixteenth and early seventeenth centuries, a code of principles for the administration of equity began to emerge under Lord Ellesmere, and by the end of the seventeenth century, under Lord Nottingham, the administration of equity had become a great deal more systematic. By the early nineteenth century, the rules of equity were almost as rigid as the common law. This evolution was, of course, necessary in order to have a system of principles that were certain and predictable rather than based on some nebulous concept such as conscience. Equity is generally a more flexible system than the common law and is important in that it mitigates the strict rules of the common law and adds a dimension of fairness to the law.

Conflict between common law and equity

Inevitably, over a period of time there came to be conflict between the common law courts and the Court of Chancery. This conflict often arose where a party had lost his case in a common law court which had applied strict principles but where the successful party had nevertheless acted unconscionably. In such a case, the losing party could take his case to the Court of Chancery, which would decide the case on very different principles. The Court of Chancery might order the successful party not to enforce his common law judgement on pain of imprisonment if he attempted to do so. This process disrupted the administration of the common law and this inevitably led to conflict. It is commonly assumed that this conflict was resolved in the Earl of Oxford's case (1615) 1 Ch Rep 1 where a dispute arose between Lord Chief Justice Coke, who was head of the common law courts, and Lord Ellesmere, who was Chancellor of the Court of Chancery. The conflict was resolved by Sir Francis Bacon at the behest of James I. The principle that emerged from this resolution is that where there is a conflict between the rule of common law and the rules of equity, the rules of equity will prevail over the common law. This is still a fundamental and important principle when studying land law.

Until 1875, the common law courts and the Court of Chancery operated completely separately; however, this was highly inefficient. In addition, over a period of time, the Court of Chancery, whose foundations rested on the principles of fairness and good conscience, became synonymous with corruption, expense and delay. Dickens' *Bleak House* and the case of *Jarndyce* v *Jarndyce* publicised the terrible impact the Court of Chancery had on the future of many families at this time. Simple cases could take five years or more before determination and a commission of enquiry in 1824 found huge sums of money, £39 million, held in the court as a result of undecided cases. The nineteenth century therefore saw a gradual reformation of the Court of Chancery. Ultimately, the reforms led to the Judicature Act 1873 whereby the superior common law courts and the Court of Chancery were fused into a single Supreme Court of Judicature comprising the High Court and the Court of Appeal, with the House of Lords, now the Supreme Court, as the final court of appeal outside of the Supreme Court of Judicature. The High Court was originally divided into five divisions, though there are now three: the Chancery Division, dealing with cases involving equity; the Queen's Bench Division that administers common law cases; and the Family Division, dealing mainly with matrimonial matters. Common law and equity are in fact dealt with across all three divisions since all three are merely divisions of one court, the High Court.

It is important to bear in mind that, whilst common law and equity are administered by the same courts, the systems are not themselves fused. It was stated earlier that, where the rules of common law and equity conflict, the rules of equity prevail over the common law. This principle is maintained in the Judicature Act 1873 s.25(ii). The effect is that equitable rights are still only enforceable by equitable remedies, though it should be noted that the Chancery Amendment Act 1858 s.2, now replaced by the Supreme Court Act 1981 s.49(1), allows damages to be awarded instead. Occasionally, conflicts between the two sets of rules still occurred, as can be seen in the case of *Walsh v Lonsdale* (1882) 21 Ch D 9.

Walsh v Lonsdale (1882) 21 Ch D 9

In this case there was an agreement for the lease of a mill for seven years at a rent payable quarterly in arrears, with a provision that entitled the landlord to demand a year's rent in advance. No formal lease was executed and therefore the lease was void – that is, it had no legal effect at common law. The tenant entered possession and paid the rent quarterly in arrears for 18 months. The landlord then demanded one year's rent in advance. The tenant failed to pay and the landlord sought to distrain, i.e. seize personal property to enforce the obligation. The tenant sued for damages for wrongful distress, arguing that, since no formal lease was executed, the lease was ineffective. The tenant argued that, since he had taken possession of the premises and paid by reference to a year, which the landlord accepted, he had a yearly periodic tenancy, not a seven-year legal lease, and that one of the terms of such a yearly tenancy was that rent was payable in arrears. The action of the landlord in distraining for the rent was therefore unlawful.

The Court of Appeal held that, since the lease was not executed, an *equitable* lease for seven years had arisen. The court referred to a maxim of equity that 'equity treats that as done which ought to be done' and there existed a *contract* for a lease for seven years which equity would recognise and, if necessary, enforce by an order for specific performance. The effect of such an order would be that equity would enforce the contract against both the parties. Equity would therefore treat this lease as though it had been properly executed by deed. The effect of this is that an equitable lease had been created on the same terms as the legal lease, had this been properly entered into by the signing of a deed. The tenant would therefore have to pay his rent in advance.

The case of *Walsh v Lonsdale* provides a good illustration of how the different rules of common law (or 'law') and equity interact in their separate ways. It would be a mistake, though, to think that where equity comes to a similar conclusion to the law the effects are the same. In *Walsh v Lonsdale*, equity considered that a seven-year lease had arisen; however, an equitable lease is *not* the same as a legal lease. The effect may be the same as between the landlord and tenant but not where third parties are involved. Legal rights are enforceable against the whole world, whilst equitable rights are good against all persons except a bona fide purchaser or a legal estate for value without notice – but more about that later.

The nature of legal and equitable rights

Whilst we have talked of two separate systems of law when discussing common law and equity, we have to be a little guarded. The common law is a complete system of law, whilst equity is not a complete system of law and exists to mitigate the harsh rigour of the common law and to meet any defects within it. Equity is, therefore, a gloss on the common law. Maitland in *Equity* (1909) p.19 goes further that this and notes that, 'At every point equity pre-supported the existence of common law.' Thus equity lays an additional body of rules over the common law, which normally provides an appropriate remedy. The point was referred to in **Lord Dudley and Ward v Lady Dudley** (1705) Pr Ch 241 by Sir Nathan Wright LJ who stated, 'Equity therefore, does not destroy the law, nor create it, but assists it.'

The result of this position is that, generally speaking, equity did not develop its own range of estates and interests in land but adopted those that already existed. Thus if we talk about the legal estates of fee simple, fee tail, life interests and leases, these could also exist as equitable fees simple, etc. The maxim is therefore that 'equity follows the law'.

Apart from the development of the differing estates, there also developed a whole range of interests whereby third parties had rights in another's land. We will deal with some of these later on in this book but, for example, a person might have a right of way over a neighbour's land – a right of easement; a person might have a right to enter another's land and take fish or wood – rights of profit of piscary and profit of estover respectively; a mortgagee will have certain rights to re-possess and sell the property to recover his security if the mortgagor defaults. All these different interests existed at common law but they also had their counterparts in equity. One exception to this is the restrictive covenant, which is a creature of equity and does not exist in a 'legal' form at common law.

Whilst equity followed the law, the fundamental difference between legal and equitable rights is that a legal right is a right in rem: that is, a right in the land itself. A legal right therefore is enforceable against the whole world. Thus if a person buys a piece of property that is subject to a legal right, they will be bound by it, whether they knew of the right or not. The legal right is 'attached' to the land itself. Equitable rights, on the other hand, are rights in personam and therefore only bound certain individuals, though eventually equitable rights bound everyone *except* a bona fide purchaser of a legal estate for value without notice of the equitable right. Equitable rights therefore over a period of time began to look more like rights in rem; however, strictly speaking, they are rights in personam.

It would be wrong to assume from the above that equity lived in the shadows of common law since it made a significant and fundamental contribution to the operation of land law. The two foremost contributions that equity made were the development of the trust and mortgages.

The notion of the trust

In order to understand land law it is essential that one understands the notion of the trust since it underpins much of what will be discussed in the rest of this book. It is perhaps best to begin by looking at an example of the circumstances in which an early trust might have arisen.

Example

A is going on a Crusade and he owns a piece of land, Blackacre. He has a particular problem – who is going to look after Blackacre whilst he is away? He could appoint an employee to look after the running of the farm on his estate, but who is going to make important decisions about Blackacre, such as buying and selling parcels (or pieces) of land? Whilst A has an infant son, the son cannot own property until he comes of age – just as today, in fact. A therefore asks a close friend, B, to look after Blackacre for him on behalf of himself, A, or, if he fails to return, for his wife and son until the son comes of age. A therefore transfers the legal fee simple estate into the name of B. The result of this is that B's name appears on the title deeds so that, for all intents and purposes, B now appears to be the legal owner of Blackacre.

In legal terms what we have here is that A is the 'grantor' in that he has transferred Blackacre to B, who is the 'grantee' to hold for the benefit of A, his wife and his son, who are all beneficiaries, subject to any conditions which he has stipulated.

What, in fact, A has created here is a trust, in which, as the creator, he is known as the 'settlor' ('S'). The person whom the settlor appoints to look after the property, B, is known as the 'trustee' ('T'). It should be noted that, for reasons we will examine later, it is usual to appoint two trustees. The persons for whom the property is to be held are known as the 'beneficiaries' ('B'). In dealing with trusts throughout this book we will use diagrams like Figure 2.2.

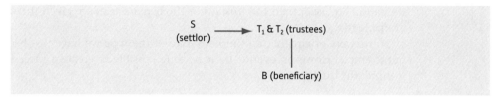

Figure 2.2

Let us go back to our example above. If A, the settlor, returns from the Crusades and B, the trustee, transfers Blackacre back to him then all is well and life carries on. But supposing A dies on the Crusades, then B will hold the land until A's son comes of age. Two years later, the son, the beneficiary, comes of age and claims the title to Blackacre. B refuses to transfer it and tells the son he is keeping the land, irrespective of the promises he made to A. The son now contests the title and goes to the common law courts to recover the title to Blackacre. He will not like the result since we must remember that the common law is very strict about issues of formality. The judge would simply ask, 'Whose name is on the title deeds?' 'Mine' retorts B and the judge would proclaim that B is the owner of Blackacre. B's right of ownership is therefore recognised by the common law and therefore he is said to be the *legal* owner of the estate Blackacre.

The son would obviously feel aggrieved by this decision and therefore he would then take his case to the Court of Chancery. As we have seen, the Court of Chancery would examine the case and consider that B had acted against his conscience and order him to transfer Blackacre to the son on pain of imprisonment if he refused to do so – remember: equity acts in personam. The Court of Chancery dispensing equitable jurisdiction would consider that B had acted in breach of trust. In recognising the son's right to Blackacre, we can now say that the son has an *equitable* estate in land, which is also sometimes referred to as the *beneficial* title. Our diagram now looks like Figure 2.3.

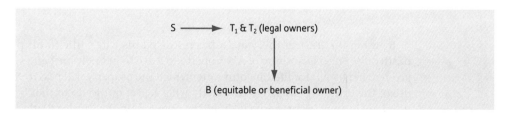

Figure 2.3

Equity imposed on trustees strict rules of good faith in carrying out their duties and failure to do so on their part meant that they could be liable for breach of trust. Equity did not deny that the trustees were the legal owners but compelled them to carry out the terms of the trust and, indeed, required them to control and manage the land in accordance with the trust.

The type of legal estate the trustees 'own' is determined by what the settlor has conveyed to them. It could be a fee simple or a life estate. As we have seen already, the words of limitation contained in the transfer or conveyance will determine this. Similarly, the words of limitation contained in the trust will determine the nature of the beneficiary's equitable estate, so the beneficiary could have an equitable fee simple or an equitable life interest. Equity follows the law in terms of limitation but, as we have seen, if no words of limitation are used, then the trustees or the beneficiaries are given the maximum estate available to the settlor.

Trusts were originally of a simple nature of the type we have just been looking at in our example. However, eventually it became possible to create a succession of interests 'behind' the trust.

Example

A is making a will, which is also a form of trust, in which he appoints two executors, or trustees, B and C. A has a wife, W, and a son, X. A would like to leave his property to his wife but he is concerned that, if he simply gifts all his property to W, this could adversely affect his son, X. For instance, W could remarry and, in turn, leave all her property to her new husband. Essentially, therefore, X would receive no inheritance from his father, A. In order to avoid this situation, A leaves his property to W for her lifetime only and then to his son X 'absolutely'.

In this scenario, the trustees B and C will hold the legal title to A's property when A dies, but B and C will hold the property on trust for W for her lifetime only and then, on her death, pass the property to X.

They will, in fact, transfer the legal title to X when he is of age or meets any condition that A chooses to place on his gift to X. Our diagram now looks like Figure 2.4.

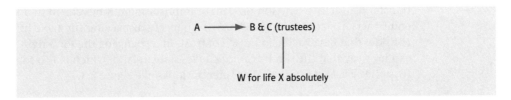

Figure 2.4

By using the trust in this way, A has restricted his wife's title to his property. On the death of W, she has nothing of A's property to leave to her new husband since any interest given to her by A is for lifetime only, after which the property will pass to X, his son. By the use of the trust, [A] has achieved exactly what he set out to do in that both beneficiaries now benefit from his property. It should be noted again that the legal title remains with the trustees, B and C; W will have an equitable life interest and X will have an equitable fee simple until W dies and then B and C will pass the legal title to him. The process therefore looks like Figure 2.5.

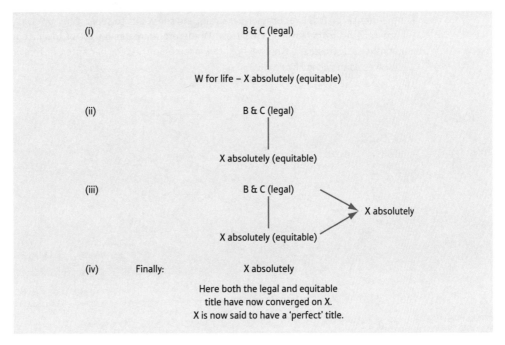

Figure 2.5

Just because B and C hold the legal title on trust for X alone does not mean the trust necessarily comes to an end. It might be the case that A, when he created the trust, imposed some conditions on it: for instance, X will not be entitled to the property until he becomes 25 years of age. Here B and C will continue to hold the legal title until X achieves this condition. At this point in time, another fundamental principle of the law of trusts emerges. Once the beneficiary meets the condition and is therefore absolutely entitled to the property, he or she can require, and indeed compel, the trustees to convey the legal estate to him or her. This rule is known as the rule in *Saunders v Vautier* (1841) 4 Beav 115. It is important since where a beneficiary is of full age and absolutely entitled to the property, in that there are no conditions that have to be met, there is no point in having the title split into a legal and equitable title. This just makes matters more complicated and is unnecessary. Once both the legal and equitable titles converge on the beneficiary, he or she is said to have a 'perfect' title. The position applies equally if there is more than one beneficiary. Provided all the beneficiaries are of full age and absolutely entitled, they can all compel the trustees to hand the property over so that they all take their share or entitlement to the property, though where there is co-ownership of land another trust comes into existence since the co-owners will hold the legal title on trust for themselves.

The process of simplification of the trust structure that we have examined in the rule in *Saunders v Vautier* can be seen also in relation to *sub-trusts*. What is a sub-trust?

Example

A grants Blackacre to two trustees, T_1 and T_2, to hold it on trust for W. The trustees rent Blackacre out so as to provide an income for W – say, £5000. In fact W, who is A's widow, decides that she does not need this money as she is already well provided for. On the other hand, W is concerned that her sister, R, is in poor financial straits and she wants to support her by giving her the income she receives from her husband's trust. W therefore creates a trust of this income by appointing another sub-trustee, t, who will hold the income on trust for her sister, R. The whole transaction evolves as shown in Figure 2.6.

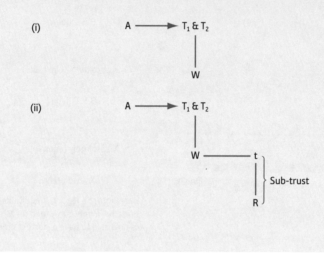

Figure 2.6

This picture is now quite complex but why have T_1 and T_2 paying this income to W, who then passes it to t, who then holds it on trust for R? In this situation it is possible to simplify the structure by W dropping out of the picture – there is no need for her to be there – unless, of course, she has some sort of obligations to perform (none in this situation). The picture now is as shown in Figure 2.7.

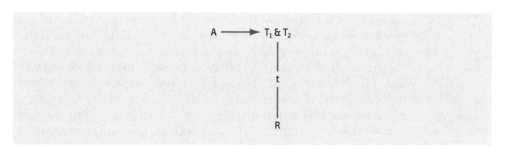

Figure 2.7

We have talked of equitable interest and beneficial interests and normally the person who has the former also has the latter. In the situation above, whilst W has an equitable interest, she does not technically have the beneficial interest. R has an equitable interest but she is the one gaining the benefit from the trust and therefore here it is R who is the beneficial owner.

The bona fide purchaser for value of the legal estate without notice

This fundamental concept in land law has been referred to in passing and it is now time to look at this doctrine in more detail. The doctrine of notice, as it is sometimes referred to, has been described as the 'polar star of equity' by Lord Henley LC in ***Stanhope v Earl Verney*** (1761) 2 Eden 81. It is still an important and significant doctrine that very much underpins land law.

If we refer back to Figure 2.1, we can see that S has given his property to the two trustees T_1 and T_2 to hold it on trust for B. If the trustees acted in breach of trust then originally B could enforce the terms of the trust against T_1 and T_2. Thus, if the terms of the trust forbade T_1 and T_2 from selling the land but they nevertheless did so, they would be held in breach of trust and B could take action against them as equity recognised the rights of B, the beneficiary.

B's rights against T_1 and T_2 would be limited to an action in damages. The property itself – for instance, Blackacre – would not be recoverable since T_1 and T_2 would have sold the legal title to Blackacre to a purchaser ('P'). The position therefore now looks like Figure 2.8.

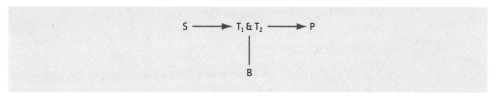

Figure 2.8

B's rights against T_1 and T_2 being limited to damages meant that, if T_1 and T_2 were insolvent or had disappeared, B's rights could not be enforced. It should also be borne in mind that, even if he could enforce his rights, the remedy of damages might not be an adequate remedy since he might actually want Blackacre, not damages. In such circumstances, B could be forgiven for thinking, 'Hold on a minute, I have lost the property that had been left to me and furthermore I cannot even get damages. Who else can I take action against? Can I sue P? Surely P should now hold Blackacre on trust for me and I should be able to enforce it against him?'

In order to get an answer to these questions, B, having an equitable interest, would take his case to the Court of Chancery. Originally, the Court of Chancery would in this situation 'follow the law' and would not enforce the trust against P, who would be said to have taken Blackacre 'free' from B's equitable interest.

Over a period of time, the Court of Chancery began to move from its original stance in certain circumstances. If the Court of Chancery discovered that P knew about B's equitable interest at the time he bought the property, then to deny B's rights could be to act against his, P's, conscience, so the court would allow B to enforce his rights under the trust against P. P therefore took Blackacre 'subject' to the rights of B. As the law evolved, the Court of Chancery began to enforce the equitable rights of B against all comers, thereby more closely resembling the common law principle that 'legal rights bind the world'. There was one exception to this principle in that equitable rights bound everyone *except* the bona fide purchaser for value of the legal estate without notice of B's equitable interest.

This individual was the epitome of what equity stood for – a person who had acted in good faith and not against their conscience. So high was the standing of the bona fide purchaser in the eyes of equity that they are often referred to euphemistically as 'equity's darling'.

We now need to examine each component of what makes up this individual.

Bona fide

The purchaser must have acted in good faith; however, this concept is clearly associated with the requirement that there must be an absence of notice of the equitable interest and indeed emphasises this requirement. In **Midland Bank Trust Co. Ltd v Green** [1981] AC 513, Lord Wilberforce stated at 528:

> The character in the law known as the bona fide (good faith) purchaser for value without notice was the creation of equity. In order to affect a purchaser for value of a legal estate with some equity or equitable interest, equity fastened upon his conscience and the composite expression was used to epitomise the circumstances in which equity would, or rather would not, do so. I think that it would generally be true to say that the words 'in good faith' related to the existence of notice. Equity, in other words, required not only absence of notice, but genuine and honest absence of notice . . . But it would be a mistake to suppose that the requirements of good faith extended only to the matter of notice, or that when notice came to be requested by statute, the requirement of good faith became obsolete. Equity still retained its interest and power over the purchaser's conscience . . .

Purchase for value

This composite expression emphasises the fact that the person who acquires the property must be a purchaser in the sense that they acquire the property other than 'by operation of law' – for instance, under the rules of intestacy. He must acquire the property either by way of a sale or by way of gift, either inter vivos or under a will.

'Value' means that the purchaser must have provided consideration that would be recognised as consideration in the law of contract. 'Value' includes money, money's worth (for example, stocks and shares, copyrights or indeed other land) and marriage, i.e. 'I give you my estate, Blackacre, if you marry my daughter' – it must be a future marriage or an ante-nuptial agreement. The value does not have to be the full value, provided it is paid before the purchaser has notice of the equitable interest. The courts will not make any inquiry as to whether the consideration or value is adequate and will not make a comparative evaluation. Basically, the courts merely establish that there is an economic value, not a relative value, and are not interested, in the absence of fraud, as to whether there is a bad bargain.

The application of this principle can again be seen in the case of **Midland Bank Trust Co. Ltd v Green** [1981] AC 513 where a father, to avoid an option granted to his son, sold a farm to his wife for £500 even though it was valued at £40,000. The Court of Appeal held that the sale at such an undervalued price could not amount to 'money or money's worth'. The House of Lords reversed the decision, stating that the court would not inquire into adequacy as long as the consideration was real. Thus simple love and affection have no economic value and would not be regarded as 'value' for this purpose.

The expression 'purchaser' has a wider meaning than someone who is simply purchasing property. The expression also includes a mortgagee, a bank for instance, which is lending money for the purchase of property. It should be remembered that, if the mortgagor/borrower fails to keep up the mortgage instalments, the mortgagee could re-possess and sell the property to recover its money. The expression also includes lessees since these are also purchasers, like a mortgagee, to the extent of their interests or pro tanto.

Of the legal estate

The purchaser must purchase a legal estate, a fee simple or a lease. Thus, in the example in Figure 2.8, if P purchases the legal fee simple from T_1 and T_2 then he satisfies this requirement.

This matter could be of importance in relation to the sub-trust which we examined on page 40 and displayed in Figure 2.9 as follows:

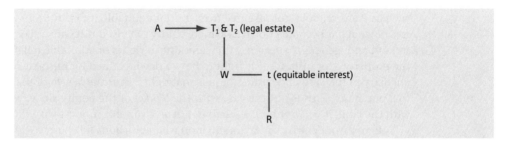

Figure 2.9

If t now sells his interest to P, will P take his interest subject to R's interest? The position now is as indicated in Figure 2.10.

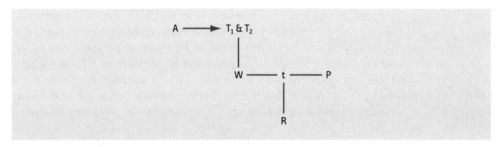

Figure 2.10

In such a situation, whilst P may be a bona fide purchaser for value, he is not a purchaser of a legal estate since t only has an equitable interest and one cannot create a legal right out of an equitable right. The legal estate remains in the hands of T_1 and T_2. Since P is not the purchaser of a legal estate, he takes his equitable interest from t subject to R's beneficial interest. The position is now as shown in Figure 2.11.

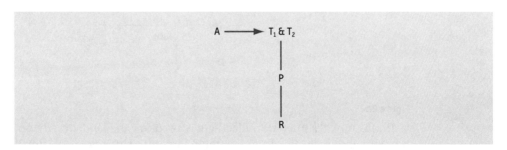

Figure 2.11

In practical terms, therefore, any benefits – such as rent – acquired by T_1 and T_2, are held in trust for P, who in turn holds it on trust for R.

When we look at the interests of P and R, we can see that they both have equitable interests and so this begs the question as to which interest takes priority over the other. The principle used to decide this matter is found in the maxim 'Where the equities are equal, the first in time prevails'. It is not therefore possible for P to say to R that he takes his interest free from R's interest since R's interest was in existence before P's interest and therefore R takes priority. This position can be more simply expressed by saying that since P is not a bona fide purchaser of the legal estate he takes subject to R's interest.

Where a purchaser of an equitable interest, without notice of a prior equitable interest, such as P above, does not take free from a prior equitable interest (R), he or she does take free of what has become known as a 'mere equity'. Mere equities are not equitable interests in land and, generally speaking, they amount to rights of equitable relief with respect to the property – for instance, the right to have a deed rectified for mistake. Mere equities are ancillary to the land and so are not personal rights; thus the *benefit* of the equity will pass to a purchaser. This is not the case with the *burden* of the equity since, whilst this passes with the land, it will not bind a purchaser of an equitable interest without notice.

You may wonder why we have a situation whereby a bona fide purchaser is allowed to take free of an equitable interest. Looking at Figure 2.8, why should P take free of B's equitable interest? The answer to this question lies in the pragmatism of the courts. It is easy to see that if purchasers, such as P, were always going to take subject to the beneficial interest (B) then purchasers were unlikely to want to buy land. Equity therefore recognised that, to prevent land from being inalienable, a person who fulfilled the requirements of the bona fide purchase rule should be able to take free of any equitable interest.

Basically, equity had to make a choice between two innocent parties, B and P. In such a situation, the Court of Chancery might compensate B by way of damages; however, one must also bear in mind that the purchaser would have paid for the legal estate. The Court of Chancery would therefore see to it that, whilst B has lost his equitable interest *in the land*, he has gained an equitable interest in the proceeds of the sale of the land and his interest is severed from the land. The transaction therefore evolves as shown in Figure 2.12:

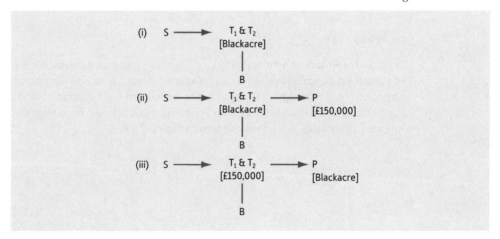

Figure 2.12

In this way, B's interest in Blackacre is swept off the land entirely, so that P takes the property absolutely free from equitable interests. This may seem unfair to B until one remembers that the proceeds of the sale are now held for him on trust by T_1 and T_2.

Without notice

The last requirement of the bona fide purchaser rule is that the purchaser must have taken the legal estate for value without notice of the equitable interest. There are three types of notice.

Actual notice

A person is deemed to have actual notice of all facts of which they have actual knowledge. It does not matter how they acquired that knowledge, provided it does not come by way of rumour or gossip.

By statute, a number of rights are registrable in the Register of Land Charges and such registration is deemed to be actual knowledge of those rights, even if the purchaser does not search the register – Law of Property Act 1925 s.198(1):

> The registration of any instrument or matter [in any register kept under the Land Charges Act 1925 or any local land charges register], shall be deemed to constitute actual notice of such instrument or matter, and the fact of such registration, to all persons for all purposes connected with the land affected, as from the date of registration or other prescribed date and so long as this registration continues in force.

Constructive notice

A person has constructive notice of any interest of which they would have acquired actual notice if they had made those inquiries or inspections that a prudent purchaser would reasonably have made. In *Jones v Smith* (1841) 1 Hare 43 two categories of constructive notice were indentified by Lord Wigram:

(a) cases of where there was actual notice on the part of the purchaser of some defects or incumbrances and a proper inquiry would have revealed the nature of the defects and incumbrances; or

(b) cases where the purchaser has deliberately or carelessly abstained from making those inquiries that a prudent purchaser would have made in purchasing the property.

The purchaser therefore can only plead the absence of notice if they had made proper inquiries but had not discovered the presence of the equitable interest. If they did not apply this due diligence standard to their inquires then they would be deemed to have constructive notice of the equitable interests. These rules are set out in the Law of Property Act 1925 s.199(i)(ii)(a).

(i) A purchaser shall not be prejudicially affected by notice of –
. . .

(ii) any other instrument or matter or any fact or thing unless – (a) it is within his own knowledge, or would have come to this knowledge if such inquiries or inspections had been made as ought reasonably to have been made by him;

The due diligence test involves two matters; firstly, inspection of the land; and, secondly investigation of the vendor's title.

Inspection of the land

The purchaser is expected to inspect the land with a view to seeing if some sort of adverse interest affects the land – for instance, the presence of a footpath may point to the existence of a private or public right of way over the property. Inspection of the premises may also point out the fact that the land is being occupied by some person other than the vendor. Thus, if the purchaser finds there is some person other than the legal owner occupying the premises, they must attempt to discover what interest that person holds in relation to the land, if any. A purchaser who fails to make such inquiries will be deemed to have constructive notice of the interest of the occupier. It could be that the occupier is a tenant under a lease as in *Hunt* v *Luck* [1902] 1 Ch 428.

If the legal owner is in occupation but there are others living there as well, the question arises as to whether a purchaser also has constructive notice of the rights of the other occupiers. A typical and not uncommon situation is if a husband has legal title to the property conveyed into his name alone but in fact holds the equitable interest on trust for himself and his wife. The issue that now arises is if the vendor attempts to sell the property to the purchaser without revealing the equitable interest of his wife. The purchaser when they inspect the property will no doubt see signs of the presence of the vendor's wife on the premises – for instance, women's clothes hanging on a clothes line. At this point, they should be making inquiry as to who else lives in the premises and what interest they have, otherwise they will be deemed to have constructive notice of the wife's interest; as held in *Kingsnorth Finance Co. Ltd* v *Tizard* [1986] 1 WLR 783.

Originally, in *Caunce* v *Caunce* [1969] 1 All ER 722 it was held that a wife's presence was not inconsistent with a husband claiming the legal title free from the wife's equitable interest under a trust and therefore a purchaser was not bound to enquire what interest the wife took in the property. In other words, the purchaser did not have constructive notice of the wife's equitable interest. This is somewhat arcane law and was based on a now discredited reasoning that the presence of the wife arose because she was the husband's wife; she was a mere shadow of her husband. The purchaser therefore did not have constructive notice of her interest. Their position as expressed in *Caunce* v *Caunce* changed following the case of *William and Glyn's Bank Ltd* v *Boland* [1981] AC 487 where it was held that the purchaser did have constructive notice of the wife's equitable interest and took subject to it.

Clearly, the lesson to be learned here is that if there are others living in the property with the vendor then inquiry must be made of these individuals as to what equitable interests, if any, they might claim. The principle is well stated by Lord Vaughan Williams in *Hunt* v *Luck*:

> . . . If a purchaser or mortgagee has notice that the vendor or mortgagor is not in possession of the property, he must make inquiries of the person in possession . . . and find out from him what his rights are, and if he does not choose to do that, then whatever title he acquires as a purchaser or mortgagee will be subject to the title or right of the [person] in possession.

Investigation of title

Apart from physically inspecting the land, a vendor must also investigate the title deeds relating to the land as they are deemed to have constructive notice of all rights that they would have discovered by such an investigation. Investigation of the title requires the vendor to examine all documents pertaining to the land for the period immediately prior to the purchase. In the absence of a special length of time set out in the contract, the Law of Property Act 1969 s.23 stipulates the period of time within which the vendor must investigate the title is at least 15 years. The vendor must search for a 'good root of title' at least 15 years old and search all documents from this good root of title to the time immediately prior to the vendor's purchase so that there is a continuous, unbroken chain of documents tracing dealings with the property. A good root of title is a document that deals with the whole of the legal and equitable interest in the land, provides a clear description of the property, and contains nothing that calls into question the title of the land. The good root of title therefore provides a 'base' on which to investigate the title. The assumption that is made is that the person purchasing the property at the time of the good root of title would also have investigated the title thoroughly at that time since they are expending money. A good root of title may be a conveyance or a mortgage, provided it meets the criteria. Essentially, it must be a document that involves a transaction in which value has been provided.

Example

A is purchasing Blackacre from B and in order to prove his title B produces a bundle of documents. These consist of:

(i) a conveyance to B when he bought the property from C 5 years ago;
(ii) a conveyance to C when he bought the property from D 11 years ago;
(iii) an assent transferring the property to D when she inherited Blackacre from her father, E, 20 years ago;
(iv) an assent transferring the property to E when he inherited Blackacre from his uncle, F, 25 years ago;
(v) a conveyance transferring Blackacre to F when he purchased it from G 40 years ago.

A, in investigating the title, has to find a good root of title at least 15 years old. Clearly, the conveyance in (i) is not adequate as it does not meet the time requirement. Similarly, the conveyance in (ii) is not more than 15 years old. The two assents in (iii) and (iv), whilst more than 15 years old, are not regarded as evidencing a purchase for value since they are documents that merely transfer the title to a beneficiary on the death of an owner. The result of this is that A must go back to the conveyance from G to F since this is a purchase for value which is *at least* 15 years old. In investigating the title, A will need to examine all documents evidencing the title from the conveyance in (v) in order to 'deduce' the title. Once A has all the documents, she is deemed to have constructive notice of all interests that she would have discovered had she investigated the title.

The purchaser is not concerned with any transactions that arose before the good root of title, though if they do investigate them or make inquiries about them then they may be affected by notice of any interests.

Imputed notice

If a purchaser employs an agent, such as a solicitor or licensed conveyancer, then any actual or constructive notice which that agent receives is imputed to the purchaser. This is set out in the Law of Property Act 1925 s.199(i)(ii)(b):

> in the same transaction with respect to which a question of notice to the purchaser arises, it has come to the knowledge of his counsel, as such, or of his solicitor or other agent, as such, or would have come to the knowledge of his solicitor or other agent, as such, if such inquiries and inspections had been made as ought reasonably to have been made by the solicitor or other agent.

Thus a purchaser is deemed to know what their solicitor or agent would have known, or should have known, if that solicitor or agent had investigated the title correctly. The effect therefore is that a purchaser cannot plead ignorance of the activities of their own solicitor or agent, which, of course, makes sense since otherwise it is highly unlikely that any purchaser would have notice of any equitable interest.

The doctrine of notice and successors in title

The protection given to a bona fide purchaser for value of a legal estate without notice also applies to a successor in title of that purchaser, even if that successor in title takes with notice of the interest. For instance, if P, who is a bona fide purchaser of the legal estate for value without notice, in turn sells the land to V, then V will also take free of the equitable interests. In this way, a sale of land to a purchaser without notice has a curative effect on the title so that successive acquirers of the title do not have to worry about the equitable interest.

The development of other equitable interests

The influence of equity went a great deal further than the development of trusts, though this is by far the most important development. The influence of equity can be seen inter alia in mortgages, informal leases, estate contracts and restrictive covenants.

Mortgages

A mortgage is essentially a means by which an owner of land could transfer their property to another, usually a bank or building society, in return for a loan. At common law, the loan had to be paid back on a specific date and failure to do so meant that the lender could not only take ownership of the property but also still recover the loan. Equity acted to prevent this draconian situation from occurring and developed what is now known as the 'equity of redemption'. Basically, equity regarded the conveyance of land to the lender as a mere security for the loan and therefore provided that the borrower could redeem – i.e. pay off the loan – at any time and not necessarily on the date fixed by law. Furthermore, if the legal date for redemption passed, equity would not allow the lender to take the property absolutely and would allow the borrower to continue to make payments on the mortgage.

The modern mortgage that we see today is largely a creature of equity that protects borrowers from the harsh common law principles. We will look at mortgages in more detail in Chapter 16.

Informal leases

The principles relating to informal leases also apply to informal mortgages and easements but for illustrative purposes we will confine ourselves to informal leases.

At common law, to create a legal estate the correct formalities have to be used: that is, a deed must be used. This requirement is now set out in the Law of Property Act 1925 s.52(1) which states:

> (1) All conveyances of land or any interest therein are void for the purpose of conveying or creating a legal estate unless made by deed.

Thus, if one tried to create a legal lease for seven years but no deed was executed, then no such lease was created. Equity, however, would recognise the lease as a contract for a lease, provided the contract was in writing to comply with the Law of Property (Miscellaneous Provisions) Act 1989 s.2(1) in accordance with the maxim 'equity treats that as done which ought to be done' – i.e. equity treated the position as if a deed had actually been executed. Equity would then enforce the contract by way of an order for specific performance and compel the landlord to give the tenant a deed. The requirement for a deed would have been completed and the lease would be converted into a seven-year *legal* lease. Until the deed had been executed, however, equity would recognise the lease and the tenant would have a seven-year *equitable* lease. We will look at leases and informal leases in Chapter 6.

Estate contracts

As we have seen with regard to informal leases, when there is a contract to purchase an estate in land then the purchaser immediately has an equitable interest in that land once the contract is executed properly. This equitable interest arises since the purchaser can enforce the contract by obtaining an order of specific performance from the Court of Chancery. Thus equity recognises and will enforce the contract.

This effect is particularly important in the case of options to purchase land. If a property developer wishes to purchase a piece of land, they may enter into an option with the landowner to purchase the land at some point in the future. This would be advantageous to the developer since they would not wish to build their stock of land for development by paying the full price every time. In this way, they can have the right to buy land by paying out a relatively modest amount to a landowner that gives them the right to buy it from the landowner at some time in the future, when they feel the time is right. This option gives the developer an equitable interest in the land which they can enforce, by specific performance if necessary, if the landowner refuses to comply with the contract.

It is important to distinguish an option from a right of pre-emption, which is only a right of first refusal that gives the developer a right to be first offered the land if and when the landowner decides to sell the land in the future. The developer cannot compel the landowner to sell here, unlike in an option, and thus a right of pre-emption does not give the developer an equitable interest in the land.

Restrictive covenants

The rule in the law of contract is that only the parties to a contract are bound and can enforce a contract, subject to certain modifications under the Contract (Rights of Third Parties) Act 1999. This basic rule of contract was modified by equity in the nineteenth century where a landowner (the 'covenantor') promised a neighbour (the 'covenantee') not to use their land for certain purposes to the benefit of the covenantee. Clearly, the covenant, or promise, could be enforced by and against the two parties as they were parties to the contract. The question then arose as to whether a successor in title to the covenantee could enforce the covenant against the covenantor or their successor in title. Equity decided that, if the covenant was negative in nature and the successor in title to the covenantor bought the land with notice of the restriction, then the covenantee or their successor in title could enforce the covenant against that person.

It is important that the covenant in question is negative or restrictive in nature. It should also be noted that restrictive covenants are wholly creatures of equity and have no counterpart at common law. This aspect will be discussed in a great deal more detail in Chapter 14.

How are equitable rights created?

So far, we have seen that equity played a highly significant role in the development of property law. It did this by way of enforcing obligations that arise out of the conscience of a defendant and intervening where it considered the common law acted unconscionably so as to modify the common law rules, or to impose obligations on a defendant. We now need to see how equitable rights came to be created. Broadly speaking, equitable rights are created in five separate ways.

Intention

An equitable right might arise where a grantor intended that only an equitable interest be created or transferred. A typical example here would be where a trust is created. Thus, for example, in creating his will a testator might wish to ensure that his son should not be allowed to have free discretion over his, the testator's property, until his son was considered responsible enough to be entrusted with such powers over the property. The testator would then arrange for his property to be passed to trustees on his death and for them to hold the property in their discretion until such time as the son was 25 years of age. Here, on the death of the testator, the legal estate would pass to the trustees who would hold the property on behalf of the son who held the equitable interest until such time as the son became 25 years of age.

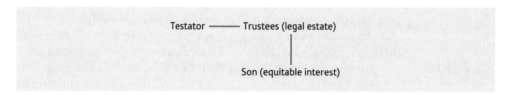

Testator ——— Trustees (legal estate)

Son (equitable interest)

Figure 2.13

A similar arrangement could be put in place if the testator had a child who was both mentally and physically disabled. Here the trustees would hold the testator's estate on a protective trust for the child, who would otherwise be unable to manage the estate because of his or her disability.

Similarly, it might also be the case that a testator might wish to transfer his fee simple estate to his wife for life and then to his children absolutely. In such a situation, this arrangement must exist behind a trust and therefore the wife would only receive an equitable interest during her lifetime and on her death the property would go to the children, just as we saw earlier in this chapter.

Operation of law

In certain circumstances the law itself imposes an equitable interest on a party – thus, a minor, i.e. someone under the age of 18 (Family Law Reform Act 1969 s.9), by virtue of the Law of Property Act 1925 s.1(6) cannot hold a legal estate in land, though the minor may still hold an equitable interest. So if the testator on their death leaves their property to a child then that property must be held on trust for the child by trustees until the child comes of age.

If a person attempts to convey land to a minor, that conveyance will not pass the legal estate to the minor. Here the conveyance operates as a declaration that the transferor holds the property on trust for the minor by virtue of the Trusts of Land and Appointment of Trustees Act 1996 s.2(6).

Capacity

As alluded to earlier, one cannot 'carve' a legal interest out of an equitable interest. However, a person who has an equitable interest can create another equitable interest by transferring their equitable interest to another, or creating an equitable mortgage of their interest, or, indeed, creating a sub-trust. Thus in the case of the trust created to a wife for life and then to the children above, the wife could sell her life interest or mortgage it a bank. In both cases the recipient could only have an equitable interest; the bank could only ever have an equitable mortgage.

Formality

The common law operated strict rules regarding formalities and eventually these were translated, following several enactments such as the Statute of Frauds 1677 and the Real Property Act 1845, into the Law of Property Act 1925 s.52(1) which provides that 'all conveyances of land or of any interest therein are void for the purpose of conveying or creating a legal estate unless made by deed'. In the absence of a deed, as we have already seen in the informal leases, an equitable interest will arise.

Whilst a deed must be used to create or convey a legal estate in land, it is not uncommon to find judges and others talking of 'grants', as in 'A grants a lease to B'. The expression 'grant' means that a deed is being used. It is vital to remember that, just because a deed is used, a legal estate or interest is not invariably being conveyed or created – all the Law of Property Act 1925 s.52(1) is saying is that a deed must be used, NOT that the estate or interest is invariably a legal one. Conversely, the Law of Property Act 1925 s.51(2) provides that 'the use of the word grant is not necessary to convey land or create any interest therein'.

Whilst a deed must be used to convey or create a legal estate or interest in land, the deed may not always actually refer to the interest. Thus it is possible to create a legal easement by virtue of the fact that this is *implied* into a deed. This is very much the exception to the rule which we will deal with later in Chapter 15.

Proprietary estoppel

This doctrine arises where a person, A, makes a promise to or otherwise encourages or acquiesces in a belief or expectation in another person, B, that B will become the owner of or obtain an interest in A's land and B has relied on that promise, encouragement or acquiescence to his or her detriment if A then denies B his or her expectation. In such a situation, equity will consider that A has acted against his or her conscience and will then use its discretion as to how B's belief or expectation can be satisfied, since B has acquired an 'equity' in the property. Equity is extraordinarily flexible in the application of the doctrine, as it can apply where there is a mistaken belief on the part of B or if there is a lack of formality. The doctrine, however, can be extremely powerful and can elevate what appears to be a simple personal right into something resembling a proprietary right – or, indeed, a proprietary right itself. An example of its operation can be seen in the cases of *Errington v Errington and Woods* [1952] 1 KB 290 and *Dillwyn v Llewelyn* (1862) 4 De GF & J 517.

Errington v *Errington and Woods* [1952] 1 KB 290

A father purchased a house in his own name and then allowed his son and daughter-in-law to live in the house, provided they paid the mortgage instalments. He told them that the house would be theirs when the mortgage was paid off. The couple lived in the house and paid the instalments. They were not contractually obliged to do this, though if they did, the house would be theirs. The father eventually died and his widow claimed possession of the house.

The Court of Appeal held that the agreement amounted to a contractual licence which could not be revoked and gave the couple equity to remain in occupation, provided the couple continued to pay the instalments, and that when these were paid the couple would be entitled to have the legal title conveyed to them.

Lord Denning summed up the situation at 295 as follows:

The father's promise was a unilateral contract – a promise of a house in return for their act of paying the instalments. It could not be revoked by him once the couple entered a performance of the act, but it would cease to bind him if they left it incomplete and unperformed, which they did not do . . . They acted on the promise and neither the father nor his widow, his successor in title, could eject them in disregard of it.

Dillwyn v *Llewelyn* (1862) 4 De GF & J 517

A father allowed his son to build a house on land that the father owned. There was an understanding that the father would convey the land to the son and, to confirm this, the father signed a memorandum, stating: 'H, together with my other freehold estate, are left in my will to my dearly beloved wife, but it is her wish, and I hereby join in presenting the same to my son for the purpose of furnishing him with a dwelling house.' No conveyance was entered into, however. On the father's death, the land was left to his widow for life, with remainder to the son for life, with remainders over to others. The son claimed to be entitled to have the fee simple conveyed to him.

The Court of Appeal held that the actions of the son subsequent to the signing of the memorandum gave rise to valuable consideration by the son and thus the imperfect gift was converted into a binding contract so that the son was entitled to have the legal fee simple conveyed to him. It was clear in this case that the father had actively encouraged his son to believe that he would convey the land to him and that the son had relied on this to his detriment so that it would be unconscionable for the father to deny his son the title.

Conclusion

So far, we have seen the historic context of how land law developed and the development of equity, which is of fundamental importance in the study of the subject. In the next chapter, we will turn our attention to how the structures we have been looking at are dealt with in the modern law.

Summary

Introduction

The doctrine of tenure

Generally

Note the contractual relationship between lords and their tenants.

Military tenure

- The nature of military tenure.
- Socage – the commutation of military service to the payment of money.

Civil service

- The nature of civil service: grand serjeanty; petty serjeanty.

(c) Spiritual service

- Divine service and frankalmoign.

(d) Other types of tenure

- Agricultural tenures – common socage.
- The nature of free and unfree tenures.
- The nature of copyhold.

The incidents of tenure

- Levying distress.
- Escheat – the right of the lord to take the land on the termination of the tenancy. See the modern application contained in the Administration of Estates Act 1925 s.46 and s.47(3) – bona vacantia.

The demise of tenure

- Creation of new tenures – wardship.
- The insertion of new 'rungs' into the feudal system and the reduction of escheat.
- Substitution and the problems for the lord.
- Statute of Quia Emptores 1290.
- Tenures Abolition Act 1690.

The doctrine of estates

Estates of freehold

Fee simple estates

Types of fee simple

- Fee simple absolute.
- Determinable fee simple.
- Conditional fee simple.
  - Condition precedent.
  - Condition subsequent.

Fee tail

- Nature of fee tails.
- Abolition: Trusts of Land and Appointment of Trustees Act 1996.

Life interests

- Nature of life interests and life interests pur autre vie.
- Life interests are now equitable interests following the LPA 1925.

Estates of less than freehold

Leases for a definite period of time

- This type of lease is granted for a definite period of time, e.g. 5 years or 999 years, unlike freehold estates which are created for an indefinite period of time.

Leases for a period of time capable of being made certain

Such leases are defined with the LPA 1925 s.205 (xxviii).

- Tenancies at sufferance.
- Tenancies at will.

Words of limitation

See LPA 1925 s.60(1).

Common law and lquity

Generally; the royal courts and the seigniorial courts

The role of the itinerant justices

The development of the royal courts

The writ system

- The 'forms of action'.
- Provisions of Oxford 1258.
- Statute of Westminster II (in consimili casu) 1285.

The role of the Chancellor and the revelopment of the Court of Chancery

The defects in the common law system

(a) No writ, no right.

(b) If the wrong writ was obtained then the action was lost in limine.

(c) The common law remedy of damages did not provide an appropriate remedy in certain cases.

(d) There was widespread corruption in the early seigniorial courts and early common law courts.

Correcting the defects

(a) The right to petition the King as the 'fountain of justice'.

(b) Petitions were originally heard by the Council, but eventually hearings were delegated to the Chancellor who, as a cleric, was regarded as the 'keeper of the King's conscience'. Justice was delivered on the basis of good conscience.

(c) Eventually, a Court of Chancery developed, which administered good conscience or 'equity'.

(d) The evolution of new remedies aimed to 'cleanse' the conscience of a suitor: injunctions and specific performance etc.

(e) Equity acts in personam, against the person, as opposed to the common law, which acts in rem by way of awards of damages.

Conflict between the common law and equity

In time, conflict arose between the common law courts and the Court of Chancery. This was eventually resolved in the Earl of Oxford's Case (1615) 1 Ch Rep 1 where it was stated that where there is a conflict between the rules of common law and the rules of equity, the rule of equity shall prevail.

Eventually, the common law courts and the Court of Chancery were merged into a single Supreme Court of Judicature by way of the Judicature Act 1873. The effect of s.25(ii) was that the rules of equity still prevailed over the common law and they exist as separate systems of law, albeit administered in the same system of courts – for example, see *Walsh v Lonsdale* (1882) 21 ChD 9.

The nature of legal and equitable rights

'Equity is a gloss on the common law.'

'Equity follows the law.'

The notion of a trust

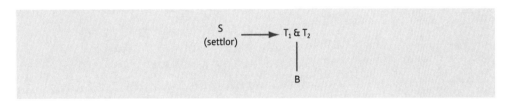

Figure 2.14

The bona fide purchaser for value of the legal estate without notice

The development of other equitable interests

The influence of equity went a great deal further than the development of trusts, though this is by far the most important development. The influence of equity can be seen inter alia in mortgages, informal leases, estate contracts and restrictive covenants.

How are equitable interests created?

Broadly speaking, equitable rights are created in five separate ways:

- intention;
- operation of law;
- capacity;
- formality;
- proprietary estoppel.

  Errington* v *Errington and Woods [1952] 1 KB 290

  Dillwyn* v *Llewelyn (1862) 4 De GF & J 517.

Further reading

Baker, *Introduction to English Legal History*, Oxford University Press (2007)

Hanbury and Martin, *Modern Equity*, Sweet and Maxwell (2012)

3

Estates and interests in land – a modern perspective

Aims and objectives

After reading this chapter you should be able to:

- Understand the structure of land law after 1925.
- Identify the different types of legal estates and interests that existed following the Law of Property Act 1925.
- Understand how equitable interests of a commercial nature were protected and the processes by which such interests could be identified.
- Understand the circumstances in which registered land charges bound third parties.
- Understand how equitable interests of a family nature were protected.
- Identify those interests that were of neither a commercial nor a family nature.

Introduction

In Chapter 2, we saw that there were several different types of estate – fee simple, fee tail life estates and terms of years (leases). The fee simple estates could also exist in a modified form as absolute, conditional or determinable estates. These estates could also exist in 'reversion'; thus, if A grants a life interest to B, then on the death of B the land reverts to A or his successors in title – for example, his heir. The estates could also exist in remainder, so A could grant a life interest to B and then to C in fee simple. Here C has a remainder and indeed the gift by A could be expressed as to 'B for life, remainder to C'. Here C will take the estate that formerly belonged to A, which may be a fee simple.

Prior to 1926 all the above estates and their modified forms could exist in either a legal form – that is, not under a trust – or an equitable form, existing behind a trust. For example, if A held the legal fee simple, he could grant B a legal life estate and then to C he could grant a legal fee simple until she ceased to be a solicitor, i.e. a determinable fee simple in remainder.

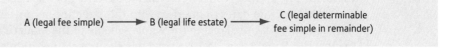

Figure 3.1

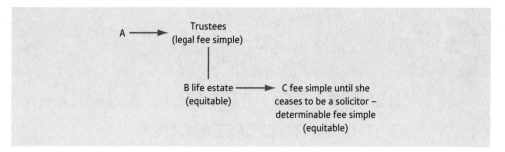

Figure 3.2

On the other hand, A could transfer the legal fee simple to trustees who would hold it on trust for B for life and then a fee simple to C provided she ceased to be a solicitor. Since the interest of B and C now exist behind a trust, these must now exist in an equitable form.

This somewhat confusing web of legal and equitable estates is also replicated when we consider what interests a person may have in the land of another, such as easements, mortgages and rent charges, for example. All these could exist in a legal or equitable form – remember, though, that restrictive covenants can *only* exist in an equitable form and have no counterpart at law. Of these, easements require further consideration, since they could be created for various durations – for example, an easement for life, or a fee simple or a fee simple for a term of years, say, 14 years. Whilst we consider easements in more detail later on, a legal easement generally had to be created in a deed and if this did not occur then the easement had to exist as an equitable easement. This distinction could have a profound effect for a purchase of the land and indeed for the owner of the easement.

The structure of land after 1925

As can be seen from the above, the state of land law prior to 1925 was hopelessly complex – the 'ungodly jumble' described by Oliver Cromwell. In 1925, though, a whole raft of legislation was passed to reform land law. There had been some attempts at reform prior to this date; however, the 1925 legislation provided a watershed and, indeed, still provides the foundation on which land law is based today.

When we discuss the 1925 legislation, we are essentially looking at six Acts of Parliament:

- Law of Property Act 1925
- Land Charges Act 1925
- Land Registration Act 1925
- Administration of Estates Act 1925
- Settled Land Act 1925
- Trustee Act 1925.

The Law of Property Act 1925 forms the central plank of this legislative regime, but all these Acts interconnect with one another to a greater or lesser degree. It is a brave legislative drafter indeed who dares to interfere with this structure, as any change could potentially have the effect of unbalancing the whole scheme of the modern land law. That is not to say that the draughtsmen in 1925 got it wholly correct; they didn't – and no wonder, given the complexity of the law prior to 1925. On the other hand, there have been changes to the

1925 legislation since it was passed, so that the law has moved with the modern perspective of property holding.

The legislators had two objectives in developing a modern land law structure. Firstly, they had to ensure that land would be freely alienable so that estates or interests could be transferred easily and securely, since no purchaser would want to risk their money if their investment would be subject to some sort of encumbrance that would render their investment worthless or less valuable. The position is summed up by Lord Upjohn in *National Provincial Bank Ltd* v *Hasting Car Mart Ltd* [1965] AC 1175 at 1233:

> It has been the policy of the law for over one hundred years to simplify and facilitate transactions in real property. It is of great importance that persons should be able freely and easily to raise money on the security of their property.

It is thus extremely important that third party purchasers (including mortgagees) are able to easily discover the extent to which proprietary rights, whether legal or equitable, affect their title. It has been seen that, prior to 1925, there were a myriad of legal rights that could arise in the land. The fundamental rule is that 'legal rights bind the world' and third party purchasers always take subject to these rights. Prior to 1925, therefore, third party purchasers were particularly vulnerable to such rights because of the number of legal and equitable interests that existed. Similarly, in the case of equitable rights, such rights bound everyone except a bona fide purchaser of the legal estate for value without notice of those equitable rights. Thus, if a purchaser bought a piece of land but had actual, constructive or imputed notice of an equitable interest, they were also bound by that interest. However, if the purchaser was a bona fide purchaser of the legal estate for value without notice of an equitable right, then they took free from it and the owner of the equitable interest had that interest 'swept' off the land and lost it. Both situations were unsatisfactory and a solution had to be created to deal with them.

Secondly, the legislators had to ensure that any regime had to cope with a title that was fragmented in that it had to be possible to create different interests in the land so that the legal regime supported interests of a family or a commercial nature.

These two objectives operated in tension with one another. To accommodate a fragmented title made the land less freely transferable. On the other hand, to accommodate a position that land was freely alienable invariably meant that the fragmentation aspect would be limited.

The legislation addressed the two objectives by radically overhauling the system of legal and equitable interests:

(a) The number of legal estates that could exist in the land was reduced to two and the number of legal interests that could exist in the land was reduced to five. Adopting such a structure meant that there were far fewer legal estates and interests that a purchaser was susceptible to being bound by and made the land more freely alienable.

(b) The effect of the reduction of the number of legal estates and interests was to dramatically increase the number of equitable interests that now existed. The legislators dealt with this increase in two ways:

    (i) Interests of a commercial nature became registrable so that they could more easily be discovered on investigation of the title. Registration was deemed to be actual notice of the interests. The effect of this was to reduce the impact of the doctrine of notice.

    (ii) Interests of a family nature were swept off the land and into the proceeds of the sale of the legal estate. This process is known as 'overreaching' and we will look at it more closely later. This change allowed for the second objective to be achieved – i.e. it allowed for the fragmentation of title to co-exist with the need for alienability.

A further development to aid the transfer of title to land was the introduction of a system of land registration by the Land Registration Act 1925. The idea behind this was that all aspects relating to a piece of land would be contained in a register administered by the Land Registry. In this way, a purchaser would not have to wade through bundles of title deeds to discover the estates and interests in relation to a piece of land, but could simply consult the register. This development gave rise to a further distinction in land law: unregistered and registered land.

The Law of Property Act 1925

The two legal estates

Having looked at the historical basis for land law, you should now be familiar with the expression 'estate' – remember we are looking at the notion of time, not area.

The Law of Property Act 1925 s.1(1) provides:

> The only estates in land which are capable of subsisting or of being conveyed or created at law are –
>
> (a)   an estate of fee simple absolute in possession;
> (b)   a term of years absolute.

With this simple section all the other estates now became equitable *interests* and could no longer exist in a legal form. Such equitable interests now had to exist behind a trust and were considered to be equitable interests of a family nature.

It is very important to remember that not all estates of fee simple absolute in possession or terms of years absolute are *necessarily* legal as it is possible for them to exist in equity. What the legislation is stating is that these estates are the only two *capable* of existing at law.

It is necessary to look at the two legal estates in more detail.

Fee simple absolute in possession

For an explanation of the expressions 'fee' and 'simple' see p. 4.

Absolute

This expression means that the estate is held without condition and distinguishes the estate from 'determinable' and 'conditional' fees which we examined on p. 27, where we saw that a grant by X to Y until she became a solicitor created a determinable fee. Such a grant would now be ineffective to create a *legal* estate to Y; it can now only exist as an *equitable* interest.

With regards to conditional fees – originally, these were also converted to equitable interests. Thus, in the example on p. 28, a grant by X of a fee simple to Y if he married Z also created an equitable interest. It will be recalled that a determinable fee sets out the natural boundaries of the estate. In a conditional fee, however, there is a grant of a fee simple absolute but this commences on the occurrence of the condition being met (a condition precedent) or being brought to a premature end by the condition occurring (a condition subsequent). So in a conditional fee there is a granting of a fee simple absolute. A conditional fee therefore should have fallen within s.1(1)a and be capable of existing as a legal estate. In order to correct this error the Law of Property Act 1925 s.7(1) was amended by the Law of Property (Amendment) Act 1926 so that a conditional fee simple is now 'for the purposes of this Act a fee simple absolute'.

'In possession'

This expression indicates that the interest confers an immediate right to occupy and enjoy the land from the date of the grant.

The expression must be distinguished from an interest 'in remainder' and an interest 'in reversion'. An 'interest in remainder' is an interest that 'falls into possession' at some date in the future when prior interests expire. Thus whilst the holder of the interest, the grantee, does, in fact, obtain a proprietary interest 'at the date of the grant', they only receive a present right to *future* enjoyment of that interest.

An 'interest in reversion' arises where the grantor retains a proprietary interest, usually where they fail to exhaust their entire interest when they make their grant. Thus, when the interests they have granted expire, their fee simple will 'revert' to them.

We can see how the different expressions operate if we look at a simple example – for instance, A grants Blackacre to W for life, then to X for life, then to Y for life. A retains the fee simple absolute. W clearly has an interest in possession since W has a present right to occupy and enjoy Blackacre. X has an interest in remainder since, whilst W is alive, she does not have an interest in possession. X will only gain this when W dies and X's interest then 'falls in'. Similarly, Y also has an interest in remainder as his right to occupy Blackacre is deferred until the prior interests of W and X expire. Whilst all the interests of W, X and Y exist, A continues to hold the fee simple absolute but of course he does not hold this 'in possession' because he is subject to the prior interests. When the prior interests expire, a fee simple then 'reverts' to A (or his successors), so he then acquires a fee simple absolute in possession. Let us take the analysis a stage further. The interests of W, X and Y must be equitable interests. Why? It can be seen that life interests are not mentioned in the Law of Property Act 1925 s.1 so they *must* be equitable interests. A's fee simple in reversion must also be equitable. Why? A's interest is not 'in possession' and therefore falls outside of the criteria stated in the Law of Property Act 1925 2.1(1)a and so this must also be an equitable interest. Thus all the interests of W, X, Y and A are equitable interests but where is the legal estate?

We stated in Chapter 2 that there can be no vacuum as to the legal estate in land – there must be a legal estate owner somewhere. Equitable interests must exist behind a trust and therefore the legal estate continues to be held by A, except that he holds it on trust for the prior interests. The position can therefore be summed up diagrammatically as shown in Figure 3.3.

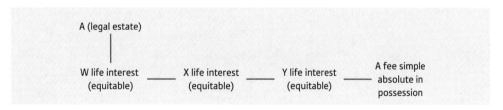

Figure 3.3

When all the life interests 'fall in' and end as W, X and Y die, A now holds a fee simple absolute in possession both at law and equity and therefore he now holds a 'perfect title'.

The expression 'possession' needs further qualification. 'Possession' does not necessarily mean physical occupation. The Law of Property Act 1925 s.205(1)xix provides: '"Possession" includes receipts of rents and profits or the right to receive the same, if any, and "income" includes rents and profits.' Thus, if the owner of the fee simple absolute grants a lease to a tenant for 50 years, even though the tenant occupies the land, the fee simple owner, the landlord, is still 'in possession' of it and would have a legal estate.

Term of years absolute

This is the second type of estate that can exist at law. As we have already seen, this expression is usually called a leasehold estate, as opposed to the fee simple absolute in possession, which is a freehold estate. The relationship of the parties to a lease is one of landlord and tenant or lessor and lessee.

What is the meaning of the expression 'absolute' in this context? In fact, the Law of Property Act 1925 s.205(i)xxvii defines a 'term of years absolute' as a lease that is 'liable to determination by notice, re-entry, operation of law, or by a provision for cesser on redemption, or in any other event'. Thus a lease that is conditional or determinable is encapsulated within the expression 'absolute' and, unlike the same expression in 'fee simple absolute', it appears to have no significant meaning.

As we have already seen in Chapter 2, a lease is a right to occupy and enjoy land for a fixed period of maximum duration, such as a lease for 99 years, or a lease that is capable of being made certain, as in a monthly tenancy where the lease continues from month to month until it is terminated on the giving of notice. The Law of Property Act 1925 s.205(i)xxvii also includes leases for less than a year. It should be noted that leases can be assigned – for example, if L gives T a lease for 99 years, after T has occupied the land for five years she can assign the balance of her lease, i.e. 94 years, to an assignee, who, in turn, can do the same. Clearly, it is not possible to assign a lease for a longer period than the original 99 years – nemodat quod non habet (one cannot give what one has not got!)

It will be noticed that, unlike a fee simple absolute in possession, a term of years can exist in a legal form even if it is not in possession. It is therefore possible for a fee simple owner to give a 20-year lease to a tenant that is to take effect in five years' time. Here the tenant's 20-year lease can still be a legal lease even though he will not be in possession at the date of the grant. There are, however, limitations on the granting of such future leases, thus the Law of Property Act 1925 s.205(i)xxvii provides that a lease must take effect in possession within 21 years of its creation.

Since possession is not required, it is possible not just to assign a lease but also to grant a sub-lease. The effect of this is that there can be several legal leases in existence at the same time – L could grant a lease to T for 99 years; T can grant a sub-lease to ST1 for 50 years; ST1 can grant a sub-lease to ST2 for 25 years; ST2 can grant a sub-lease to ST3 for 5 years, as shown in Figure 3.4.

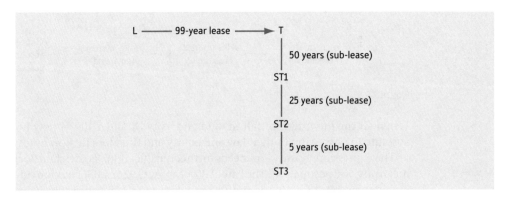

Figure 3.4

All these leases can exist as legal estates, though only ST3 is in physical occupation of the premises. The legislators in 1925 had no objections to legal estates existing concurrently with each other and, indeed, the Law of Property Act 1925 s.1(5) provides that 'a legal estate may subsist concurrently with or subject to any other legal estate in the same land in like manner as it could have done before the commencement of this Act'.

The five legal interests

The Law of Property Act 1925 s.1(2) sets out five 'interests' or 'charges' that are capable of existing at law. Again, the occurrence of such interests or charges does not mean they are necessarily legal – they can exist in equity as well – all the law is saying is that these are the *only* types that can exist in a legal form.

S.1(2)a – Easements, rights and privileges

S.1(2)a refers to:

> An easement, right or privilege in or over land for an interest equivalent to an estate in fee simple absolute in possession or a term of years absolute.

This provision refers to both easements and profits à prendre. An easement confers the right to use the land of another person or, indeed, to prevent it from being used for certain purposes. Typical examples of such easements are rights of way or rights to light. A profit à prendre is a right to take something from the land of another - for instance, fish, peat or wood.

Rights of easement can be very important since the right of way also extends to pipes and electricity cables running over or under the land of another person, without which the ability to live in one's own property would be virtually untenable.

Whilst easements and profits à prendre can exist for various periods of time, s.1(2)a provides that, to exist as legal interests, they must be for a period of either a fee simple absolute in possession or a term of years absolute. An easement for the life of another must then be an equitable easement since this would not fall within the definition set out in s.1(2)a.

Easements provide a good example of the dilemma facing a third party purchaser of land and the vulnerability of the owners of an equitable interest. Let us look at an example.

Example

A owns a piece of land, Blackacre, and decides to sell off two pieces to B and C. The pieces she sells to B and C have no access to the roadway adjoining the property – they are essentially 'landlocked closes', as this arrangement is sometimes described. A grants to B a fee simple absolute in possession and gives him a right of way by way of a driveway over her, A's, land. B therefore has a legal estate with a legal easement attached to it. A, on the other hand, grants to C a piece of land for C's life only and also gives him a right of way to cross A's land. C has an equitable interest since his estate falls outside of the two legal estates contained in s.1(1). His right of way is also an equitable interest since this falls outside of the definition in s.1(2)a, as it is neither for a period of a fee simple absolute in possession nor a term of years absolute. A now decides to sell her remaining piece of land to X. The picture therefore is as shown in Figure 3.5.

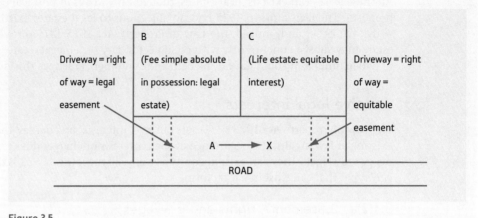

Figure 3.5

To what extent is X bound to allow B and C to make use of their driveways? Can she refuse them access to cross her own land, in doing so, rendering their land possibly valueless? We have already noted that 'legal rights bind the world' and therefore X is bound by B's right of way and must let him pass. What about C? Prior to 1925, if X is a bona fide purchaser of A's legal estate for value without notice of C's right of way then she would take free from C's equitable easement and could stop him using the driveway. Essentially, therefore, C loses his right of access to his property, and whilst he has no rights in them in relation to the land, he does have rights in personam against A, since it was she who promised C that he could have a right of way. If X is not a bona fide purchaser for value without notice – remember, she should have inspected the property as per the rule in ***Hunt v Luck*** [1902] 1 Ch 428 and, no doubt, she would have seen the driveway and therefore should have made inquiries about it and thus be bound by C's right of way. If she has, she will have actual notice of it and, if not, she will have constructive notice of it. It is precisely this type of situation that the 1925 legislation was designed to deal with.

S.1(2)b – Rentcharges

S.1(2)b refers to:

> A rentcharge in possession issuing out of or charged on land being either perpetual or for a term of years absolute.

Do not confuse a rentcharge with rent that is paid as part of a lease; the two are not the same. Essentially, a rentcharge is a periodic payment of money that is charged or secured on the land for a period equivalent to a fee simple absolute in possession or a term of years absolute. A rentcharge for the life of another must therefore be an equitable interest.

In the north of England it is commonly known as a 'chief rent' if secured against freehold land and 'ground rent' if secured against leasehold land. Generally speaking, rentcharges are usually for relatively small amounts of money, say £50 per year, and were often imposed by property developers as a means of securing a future income. Some rentcharges are for merely a few pounds, which can be a nuisance, though that is not to say they should be ignored, since real problems can arise later if the owner of the land wishes to sell it.

The Rentcharges Act 1977 now provides that no new rentcharges can be created since 1977, either at law or in equity, and any attempt to do so is void. Furthermore, all existing rentcharges stand to be extinguished on the expiry of a period of 60 years beginning with the commencement of the 1977 Act or with the date on which the rentcharge in question first became payable, whichever is the later. It is possible to continue to create 'estate rentcharges' which are used to meet or contribute towards the cost of the provision of services, the carrying out of repairs, taking out insurance or other payments for the benefit of the land affected by the rentcharge. Estate rentcharges are therefore very common in flats where there are common areas inside or outside the building that require servicing, such as gardens, repairs to the building, decoration of corridors or the provision of security in a foyer.

S.1(2)c – Mortgages

S.1(2)c refers to:

A charge by way of a legal mortgage.

A mortgage has been explained earlier but a change is now the usual method for creating a legal mortgage since 1925. It will be examined in more detail in Chapter 16.

S.1(2)d – Miscellaneous charges

S.1(2)d refers to:

[Land tax, title rentcharge] and any other similar charge on land which is not created by an instrument.

This legal interest is now virtually moribund as land tax and title rentcharges have all been abolished. The provision originally related to periodical payments which burdened the land at law but not by a conveyance or some other voluntary act of the parties.

S.1(2)e – Right of entry

S.1(2)e refers to:

Rights of entry exercisable over or in respect of a legal term of years absolute, or annexed, for any purpose, to a legal rentcharge.

A right of entry is a right of a landlord to enter the premises and forfeit the tenant's lease if the tenant fails to pay rent or otherwise comply with any covenants that might be contained in the lease. A right of entry may also be exercised for non-payment of a rentcharge.

A right of entry is a legal interest if it is attached to a lease or a rentcharge which is itself legal, otherwise the right of entry must be an equitable interest.

The creation of legal estates and interests

Usually, no conveyance is effective to create a legal estate unless the conveyance is made by deed. The Law of Property Act 1925 s.52(1) provides:

All conveyances of land or of any interest therein are void for the purpose of conveying or creating a legal estate unless made by deed.

The result of the provision is that a grant of either of the two legal estates in a written document which is not a deed will operate to convey an equitable interest only. There are some exceptions to this – for instance, the Law of Property Act 1925 s.54(2) provides that a legal lease taking effect in possession for a term not exceeding three years, whether or not the lessee has a power to extend the term, can be created orally if it is at the best rent reasonably obtainable.

With regards to the creation of legal interests, it can be seen that these are also contained within s.52(1), since this refers to 'any interest therein'. It should be borne in mind that there are exceptions here as well, since it is possible, for instance, for an easement to be implied into a deed by giving it the status of a legal interest even though it is not referred to in the deed.

Equitable interests

So far, we have seen the Law of Property Act 1925 s.1(1) and s.1(2) created two legal estates and five legal interests. The Act goes further and in s.1(3) declares:

> All other estates, interests and charges in or over land take effect as equitable interests.

The protection of equitable interests

The legislators in 1925 recognised the vulnerability of owners of equitable interests to the loss of their interests if the land is sold to a bona fide purchaser of the legal estate for value without notice of the interests. The legislators dealt with this by dividing equitable interests into two types – interests of a 'commercial' nature and interests of a 'family' nature. Interests of a commercial nature became subject to a system of registration under the Land Charges Act 1925, now the Land Charges Act 1972, and interests of a family nature became subject to a process called 'overreaching'. The legislators, however, recognised that it would be more convenient if all interests, legal or equitable, were brought together into a central register so that the interests were easily discoverable and conveyancing would be made a great deal easier. This system was dealt with under the Land Registration Act, now the Land Registration Act 2002.

It is important to understand that in 1925 *two* systems of registration were introduced. The system under the Land Charges Act 1925 (1972) was introduced to be a temporary measure to deal with the immediate need to protect equitable interests, but eventually this would give way to a wider process of land registration under the Land Registration Act 1925 (2002). This dual system of registration gave rise to another way of classifying land – unregistered land under the 1972 Act and registered land under the 2002 Act.

It is absolutely vital not to mix up the two systems of registration, which operate separately. Conveyancers have to identify what system will apply to a piece of land and thus have to know and understand the two different systems of conveyancing. Unregistered land is gradually dying out since, as each piece of unregistered land comes to be conveyed, it is converted to registered land and it is incumbent on the purchasers to undertake this conversion. In recent years, the conversion process has been accelerated so that some 90% of titles have now become registered land. Unfortunately, it will be many years before the process is fully completed – unfortunate since in the meantime land lawyers have to know and understand how the two systems operate! We will deal with registered land in Chapter 5.

The system of registration for unregistered land under the Land Charges Act 1972 amounted to a reform of the doctrine of notice and, as such, had two effects:

(i) Registration of an interest constitutes actual notice of the registered interest: LPA 1925 s.198.

(ii) Non-registration makes the interest void.

Finally, not all equitable interests are registrable as land charges and those that are not covered by this or the doctrine of overreaching are still subject to the 'old' doctrine of notice that we have already examined.

Registrable interests of a commercial nature

Although there are five separate registers in the LCA 1972 that contain matters that will bind transferees, we are mainly concerned with the land charges that are contained within s.2 of the Act.

Land charges

These are divided into six classes, A, B, C, D, E and F, which are defined in s.2 of the Act. Any equitable interest that falls outside of these cannot be registered.

Class A – Charges imposed by statute on application

A Class A land charge is:

> a rent or annuity or principal money . . . which is not a charge created by deed but is a charge upon land . . . created pursuant to the application of some person under the provisions of any Act of Parliament . . .

These types of land charge generally apply to work that is carried out by some public authority in relation to the land, the cost of which is secured against the owner of the land by registration. It can also apply if an Act of Parliament imposes a charge for specific purposes so that a payment can be recovered. Such charges are fairly uncommon since they are discharged once the payment has been made.

Class B – Charges imposed by statute automatically

A Class B land charge is:

> a charge on land (not being a local land charge) . . . created otherwise than pursuant to this application of any person.

The land charges arise automatically by statute in order to recover the repayment of costs or expenses. Thus, if an action is brought to recover property with the assistance of legal aid, the costs of legal aid can be reclaimed should the action be successful.

Class C

Class C land charges are subdivided into four further classes:

C(i) – Puisne mortgage
A puisne (pronounced 'puny') is a legal mortgage not protected by deposit of title deeds relating to the legal estate affected. At this moment, you may well shout, 'Hold on, I thought we are dealing with *equitable* interests here?' It is true that land charges are mainly concerned with equitable interests – however, the puisne mortgage is the exception and is so for a particular reason.

Usually, when a person (the mortgagor) takes a mortgage from a lender (the mortgagee), the mortgagee will take the title deeds to the property - these form their security so that if the borrower or mortgagor fails to pay the mortgage, the mortgagee can use the deeds to sell the property and recover their money. There is no need to register the mortgage here, since if X attempts to sell his land to Z, the fact that X does not have the title deeds will alert

Z to the existence of Y's mortgage. Of course, Z will require X to produce the title deeds and X will only be able to get hold of his title deeds once he has paid off the mortgage with Y, who then hands the deeds back to X.

The position would be different if X has taken out a second mortgage with M. Here M would not have the security of the title deeds since these are with Y. The Land Charges Act 1972 provides M with another means of securing their loan – registration as a C(i) land charge. This is important to Z, our purchaser. We have seen that the absence of the title deeds alerts Z to the existence of the first mortgage, but once the mortgage is paid off and the title deeds are handed back to X by Y, Z has no way of knowing about the existence of the second mortgage with M.

This situation poses a real threat to Z since, because this is a legal mortgage, the principle that 'legal interests bind the world' means that Z will purchase the property subject to the second mortgage. This situation would also cause complication for the second mortgagee, M, if they had to enforce their security to recover their mortgage. Since M is allowed to register their mortgage, the fact of registration will warn Z of the existence of M's mortgage. The Class C(i) land charge is thus a rare example of a legal interest that requires protection by registration. It must be remembered that only a legal mortgage *not* protected by deposit of title deeds is capable of registration.

C(ii) – Limited owner's charge

This is an equitable charge which a tenant for life or some other statutory owner acquires by discharging inheritance tax or other liabilities. For example, we could have a settlement as follows: A for life, B for life, C in fee simple.

When A dies, inheritance tax may be payable. In this situation, B may prefer to pay the inheritance tax personally, rather than allowing the burden of the tax to fall on the settled property, since this may require the property to be sold. In this situation, B is entitled to take out a charge on the property in much the same way as if he had lent money to the estate. This type of charge is registered as a C(ii) land charge.

C(iii) – General equitable charge

This charge includes many different types of equitable charge which:

(a) is not secured by a deposit of documents relating to the legal estate affected;

(b) does not arise, or affect any interest arising, under a trust of land or settlement under the Settled Land Act 1925 (and is therefore overreachable as a family interest – see later);

(c) is not affected in any other class of land charge.

This charge is therefore a 'dustbin' category in that it is a residuary class that captures equitable charges not registrable elsewhere, such as equitable mortgages of a legal estate or an unpaid seller's right to charge the land for unpaid purchase money (known as an 'unpaid vendor's lien'). It also covers certain annuities created after 1925. It does not cover equitable interests arising under a trust of land since these are regarded as 'family interests', as opposed to 'commercial interests', and are dealt with by the process of overreaching.

C(iv) – An estate contract

This is a contract to convey or create a legal estate by a person who either owns the legal estate or is entitled at the date of the contract to have the legal estate conveyed to them. Since the Law of Property (Miscellaneous Provisions) Act 1989 s.2 all such contracts must be in writing, though contracts made up to July 27 1989 could have been made orally, provided they were evidenced by writing or past performance, as provided by the LPA 1925 s.40.

The signing of a contract is an integral part of the process of purchasing a piece of land. Its importance can be seen on estate agents' boards posted outside houses for sale. When a sale is agreed, the sign "Sold Subject to Contract" is often attached to the board. At this point, there is no obligation on the vendor to sell, nor on the purchaser to buy. The position changes, however, once both parties have signed the contracts and these are 'exchanged'. At this point, the vendor *must* sell and the purchaser *must* buy. The signing and exchanging of contracts thus imposes legal obligations and gives the purchaser an interest in the property to the extent that they should insure the property since, should the property be destroyed by fire, for instance, they are still obliged to continue with the purchase.

Since the purchaser now has a proprietary right in the land, as well as a contractual right, they can protect their interest by registering it as a C(iv) land charge. This prevents the vendor from selling the property to another third party since the third party will have notice of the contract with the original purchaser and be aware of that purchaser's interest in the property.

Estate contracts include contracts for the sale of the fee simple but also leases and contracts to mortgages of the legal estate. Such estate contracts, however, go further and include option to purchase, rights of pre-emption and any other similar rights.

An option arises where, for instance, A is selling her land and B would like to consider purchasing the land but has not yet made his mind up. B's position is that he does not want to miss the opportunity of the purchase, which would arise if A sold the land to a third party. In order to keep the deal open, B therefore agrees with A that he will pay A £500 on the understanding that A will not sell the property to someone else within three months. In such a situation, B now has an option to buy the land, which he can register. If A sells the land to a third party in breach of the contract/option with B, B can exercise the option and enforce it against the third party, since registration of the option has given a warning to the third party that he would take the property subject to the option.

As a contract for the disposition of an interest in land, albeit one that is conditional on B's exercise of his option, the contract must comply with the Law of Property (Miscellaneous Provisions) Act 1989 s.2, as described above. It should, however, be noted that an option to purchase has two stages to it: one under which A grants B the option, the other by which B exercises his option. When A grants B the option, a conditional contract comes into existence and when B exercises the option, an unconditional contract arises. Does B have to register both the grant and the exercise of the option? In *Armstrong and Holmes Ltd* v *Holmes* [1994] 1 All ER it was held that this was unnecessary and that the grant and the exercise of it comprised the same entry, so that the registration of the grant of the option was sufficient to protect the contract to grant the option and its subsequent exercise.

Once B has been granted the option, he gains an interest in the land since B then has a right to enforce the option so as to give rise to a contract whereby he acquires the land. If A refuses to enter the contract, she can be compelled to do so by way of an order for specific performance.

As with any contract, this option must be certain; however, if the option fails to mention the purchase price, it was held in *Sudbrook Trading Estate Ltd* v *Eggleton* [1983] 1 AC 444 that there is an implied term that the price should be a fair and reasonable one. Sometimes the parties may provide for a mechanism to determine the price upon the exercise of the option – for instance, the appointment of a valuer. If this is the case, then that process must be followed, but if a party attempts to frustrate that process, then it was held in *Re Malpass* [1985] Ch 42 that the court may determine the price.

Rights of Pre-emption

The Class C(iv) land charge not only includes options but rights of pre-emption. A right of pre-emption is essentially a right of first refusal and, in many respects, is the converse of an option.

An example of a right of pre-emption is where A owns a piece of land but is undecided whether to sell or not. In such a situation, she may agree with B that, if she does decide to sell, she will first offer it to B and the parties then enter into an agreement to this effect.

The difference between an option and a right of pre-emption can thus be clearly seen. In an option it is B, the purchaser, who takes the initiative to effect the sale by exercising the option. In a right of pre-emption, however, it is A who triggers the sale by deciding to sell and then B who has to agree to the sale. The actual sale thus depends entirely on A deciding to sell.

We have seen that an option gives B, the purchaser, an interest in land that he can enforce against A or a third party who has notice of this option. The question therefore arises as to whether the right of pre-emption confers on B an interest in land that he can enforce against a third party who purchases the land from A. On the other hand, if the right of pre-emption confers no interest in land on B, whilst B can sue A for damages for breach of contract, he has no rights against a third party purchaser from A. The difference between these two positions was considered by the Court of Appeal in **Pritchard v Briggs** [1980] 1 Ch 338.

Pritchard v Briggs [1980] 1 Ch 338

> The facts of the case were that A granted B a right of pre-emption to purchase a parcel of land for £3000. The right was agreed to exist until either A or B died. In order to protect his right of pre-emption, B registered it as a Class C(iv) land charge. Later, A gave X an option to purchase the land for £3000 within three months of A's death. X then registered his option as a C(iv) land charge. Subsequently, A sold the land to B for £14,300 and, eventually, A died. The question which arose was whether B purchased the property subject to X's option to purchase the property.

It is clear that X's option was not exercisable until after A's death – that is, after the expiration of the right of pre-emption granted to B. The Court of Appeal also held that the granting of the option by A to X was not an event that converted B's right of pre-emption into an interest in land. This is significant since when A, under the terms of the pre-emption, sold the land to B, B purchased it subject to X's registered option. Equally, when X took the option, he was not subject to B's right of pre-emption since at that time the right of pre-emption was not an interest in land, in that it had not been activated. The result of this was that, once A died, X could exercise his option and compel B to sell him the land for £3000, as B had purchased the land subject to X's option. Clearly, the whole chain of events was a disaster for B, who having purchased the land for £14,300, now had to sell it for £3000. However, the decision demonstrates the stark contrast between the rights of pre-emption and options and further demonstrates the fact that the system of registration of land charges is not without its flaws. As regards rights of pre-emption, however, the case demonstrates that a right of pre-emption, when first created, does not create an interest in land, albeit it is still capable of registration as a land charge. The right only becomes an interest in land once the right is exercised on the vendor deciding to sell. At this point, the right of pre-emption becomes an option and an interest in land; thus Lord Templeman stated:

The grant of a right of pre-emption creates a mere spes which the grantor of the right may either frustrate by choosing not to fulfil the necessary conditions or may convert into an option and thus into an equitable interest by fulfilling the conditions. An equitable interest thus created is protected by prior registration of the right of pre-emption as an estate contract but takes its priority from the date when the right of pre-emption becomes exercisable and the right is converted into an option and the equitable interest is then created . . . It does not seem to me that the property legislation of 1925 was intended to create, or operate to create an equitable interest in land where none existed.

Class D

Class D land charges are sub-divided into three further classes:

D(i) – Inland Revenue charges

When a person dies, their estate is valued and the excess over the personal allowance is subject to inheritance tax. In such a situation, Her Majesty's Revenue and Customs may take a charge against the deceased's property to the extent of the inheritance tax owed. This type of charge can only be taken out against freehold land as it does not apply to leaseholds and undivided shares in land under a trust of land. Once the charge is taken out, it will bind purchasers of the land. In practice, the HMRC rarely take out such a charge since the grant of probate or letter of administration is dependent on the personal representatives paying any inheritance tax due in any event.

D(ii) – Restrictive covenants

Under this land charge, any restrictive covenant may be registered, provided:

● it was entered into after 1925, and

● it was not entered into between lessor and a lessee.

It can immediately be seen that only restrictive covenants in freeholds are capable of registration.

Restrictive covenants entered into prior to 1926 are dealt with under the doctrine of notice, which we have already considered, and are thus binding on everyone except the bona fide purchaser of the legal estate without notice of the restrictive covenant.

D(iii) – Equitable easements

This category of land charge covers any 'easement, right or privilege over or affecting land'. Such a land charge may be registered provided:

● it is merely equitable, and

● it was created or arose after 1925.

Any easement not created by deed, or created for a lifetime, must essentially be equitable and, provided it arose after 1925, is capable of being registered. It would seem the definition also captures profits à prendre, but the expression 'right or privilege' is limited by the context of easements and profits so that rights of entry or interests arising under proprietary estoppel do not fall within this category and fall within the doctrine of notice.

Somewhat perversely, because of the way in which legal easements are created (see Chapter 15), it is often easier to discover equitable easements, which need to be registered as D(iii) land charges than legal easements.

Class E – Annuities

This type of land charge applies to annuities created prior to 1926 but not registered until after 1925. It is highly unlikely that a person granted such an annuity can still be alive and thus, for all intents and purposes, this category of land charge is now obsolete.

Class F – Special rights of occupation

Class F land charges comprise the rights of occupation of the matrimonial home enjoyed by a spouse as conferred by the Family Law Act 1996 Part IV. It has to be stressed that a Class F land charge does not give the spouse an equitable interest in the property. The rights conferred in this land charge arise where the legal title to the matrimonial home lies in the name of the spouse and confers on the other spouse a right not to be evicted from the home except by the leave of the court. This right not to be evicted is registrable as a Class F land charge.

> ### Example
> The title to Blackacre, the matrimonial home, is vested in the name of the husband (H) alone. The Family Law Act 1996 confers on his wife (W) a right to occupy Blackacre. It may be that the marriage between H and W is not going well and W, being aware that the title is in H's name alone, is concerned that H might sell the house to a purchaser (P) without conferring with W. Clearly, W would be extremely concerned at losing her home, particularly if she is living there with children. W therefore registers a Class F land charge which would put P on notice of W's rights of occupation and under normal circumstances he would withdraw from the sale as, usually, purchasers such as P would wish to take the home with vacant possession. Certainly, P would insist that the purchase would not proceed until W cancelled the land charge – something she would not do unless, of course, H offered her alternative accommodation.

It should be noted that it is not necessary for a spouse to be in actual occupation in order to register the Class F land charge. For instance, in the example above, W's marriage might have become so unbearable that she might have left H and the matrimonial home. In such circumstances, it is vital she protects her right to occupy since, if H attempts to sell the property, P might believe the house, for all intents and purposes, to be in the sole occupation of H and would hope to get vacant possession. If W has registered the land charge, then P will be put on notice of her right of occupation. Of course, eventually, a court might give W the right to occupy the home – however, a Class F land charge would protect W's rights even before the court has made such an order.

The registration of a Class F land charge is often regarded as a hostile act on the part of a spouse and it is for that reason unusual for it to arise where the two spouses are living together – it is hardly going to enhance their relationship! It should also be borne in mind that the right of occupation is not an absolute right and it ends when the marriage ends – though in the case of a divorce the court has wide powers to make property adjustment orders. In any event, under the Family Law Act 1996 s.33(6) the court has wide powers to restrict, terminate, prohibit or suspend the right of occupation of either spouse, including the owning spouse. In making any orders, the court has a wide discretion in terms of the factors to take into account, such as the housing requirements of the spouses, the need for any children to have a roof over their head and the financial resources of the spouses. The court may also consider whether the land charge has been registered for some ulterior purpose, such as putting financial pressure on the owning spouse, as held in **Barnett v Hassett** [1981] 1 WLR 1285, and the court can put the land charge on one side in such circumstances.

If a spouse has an equitable interest in the property this would also give the spouse a right of occupation, but this is distinct and separate from the statutory right of occupation conferred in the Family Law Act 1996. It should be remembered that it is a spouse's statutory right of occupation under the Act that is registered, not their proprietary right conferred by the equitable interest in the land.

Registration and the effects of non-registration

The process of registration

The basic concept and process of registration under the Land Charges Act 1972 is very simple since the owner of an interest falling within the Act merely registers their interest in the Register of Land Charges. Once registered, the interest binds all subsequent purchasers. The expression 'purchaser' in this context is rather broader than someone simply purchasing the legal estate. By the Land Charges Act 1972 s.17 a purchaser means 'any person (including a mortgagee or lessee) who, for valuable consideration, takes any interest in land or in a charge on land'.

Previously, we have seen that, in terms of examining the binding nature of legal estates and interests and equitable interests in unregistered land, two rules predominate. The first is that legal estates and interests 'bind the world', irrespective of the third party's notice or knowledge of the interest (with the exception of a puisne legal mortgage – see above). The second rule is that equitable interests also bind the world *except* a bona fide purchaser of the legal estate for value without notice of the interest.

The process of registration under the Land Charges Act 1972 modifies the doctrine of notice by providing that registration in the Register of Land Charges is, by the Law of Property Act 1925 s.198, 'deemed to be actual notice . . . to all persons and for all purposes' of the existence of the land charges. Once registered, the land charge will continue to remain binding, no matter whose hands the legal estate will later pass to, until, of course, the land charge is extinguished.

All land charges are registered in the name of the estate owner whose estate is to be affected by the land charge – the estate owner being the owner of the legal estate. Generally, since it is the estate owner who creates the land charge, this poses no problem but, as we will see later, it can pose a problem when searching the Register of Land Charges.

Registration should be against the estate owner's full and correct name, usually the name that appears on his or her birth certificate. Care should be exercised not to register against the name by which a person is generally known, or a nickname. At the end of the day, it is possible to register a land charge in more than name in case of doubt. As we will see when we look at the process of searching the register, the matter of the correct name not being used either for registration or for searching the register can pose problems.

Effects of non-registration

We have referred already to the fact that registration is deemed to constitute actual notice to all persons for all purposes under the LPA 1925 s.198.

The effect of non-registration as set out in the LCA 1972 s.4 is not the same for all land charges and the effect depends on the individual land charges. There are two main categories:

(i) the land charge may be void against a purchaser for money or money's worth of a legal estate in land; or

(ii) the land charge may be void against a purchaser for value of any interest in the land.

The effect of failing to register a particular type of land charge can be seen in the table below.

If not registered, the land charge does not bind	
Any purchase for value	*Any purchase of the legal estate for money or money's worth*
Class A – Charges imposed by statute on application	Class C (iv) – Estate contracts
Class B – Charge imposed by statute automatically	Class D (i) – Inland Revenue charges
Class C (i) – Puisne mortgages	Class D (ii) – Restrictive covenants created after 1926
Class C (ii) – Limited owner's charge	Class D (iii) – Equitable easements created after 1926
Class C (iii) – General equitable charges	
Class E – Annuities created prior to 1926	
Class F – Spousal rights of occupation	

Void against a purchaser for money or money's worth of a legal estate in land
The expression 'void' means that the land change will have no legal effect whatsoever. It will also be noticed that there is no element of good faith that we saw under the common law rule; thus the state of mind of the purchaser is of no concern. Even if the purchaser had full knowledge of the existence of the land charge, he or she is still not bound by it if the land charge was not registered.

By way of example of the above principles let us have another look at the case of ***Midland Bank Trust Co. Ltd*** v ***Green*** [1981] AC 513 which we first looked at in Chapter 2. It is useful to review the facts of the case.

Midland Bank Trust Co. Ltd v *Green* [1981] AC 513

Here a son was a tenant farmer of a farm owned by his father. The father granted his son an option for 10 years to purchase the farm for a fixed price of £22,500. The son failed to register the option in the Register of Land Charges as a C(iv) land charge. Six years later, father and son had an argument and the father decided he wanted to revoke the option, but, of course, he was bound by the contract for the option he had entered into with his son. The father, however, noticed his son had not registered the option, so he conveyed the land to his wife for a nominal sum of £500 (despite the fact that the land was then worth £40,000), with the clear intention of defeating the option. The son then attempted to enforce the option against his mother, who refused to sell the land to him in accordance with the terms of the option. The son brought an action against his father and the executors of his mother's estate, claiming the option was binding on the mother's estate and for an order of specific performance against his father for the option.

The son (in fact, his executors since in the meantime the son himself had died) brought an action against his father for an order for specific performance for the option and against his mother's estate, claiming the option was binding on the estate as his mother had actual notice of the option when she bought the estate. The consequences for the son's estate would be profound if the action were successful since, when the action reached the courts, the estate was valued at £400,000, and the executors would have been able to compel a sale of the estate at the original price within the option of £22,500.

The mother's executors alleged in defence that the sale to the mother by the father was a bona fide sale and anyway, as a purchaser of a legal estate for money or money's worth, the option as an estate contract was void against the mother. The son's case was based on three factors:

1 The consideration of the £500 paid by the mother did not amount to 'valuable' consideration as it was significantly less than the true value of the estate.

2 The sale to the mother was not a bona fide sale but was entered into with the specific purpose of depriving the son of the option and was in essence a 'sham'.

3 Whilst the option was not registered as a Class C(iv) land charge, the mother nonetheless had actual knowledge of the existence of the option.

At first instance, Oliver J held that the unregistered land charge was not binding on the mother's estate as she was clearly a purchaser of the legal estate for money or money's worth and thus the option as a land charge was void.

In the Court of Appeal, the decision of Oliver J was reversed by a majority decision. Lord Denning MR held that the mother's estate had not given 'money or money's worth' for the purposes of s.4(6) since the mother had paid £500 for a piece of land that was then worth £40,000. He stated that he did not believe that Parliament had intended to protect a purchaser who had paid less than the market value in collusion with a purchaser. Lord Denning acknowledged the normal rule regarding the fact that, in the law of contract, the law makes no inquiry into the adequacy of consideration in a contract. However, he considered this situation to be different and considered that the expression 'money or money's worth' in s.4(6) meant that the consideration had to be a fair and reasonable value and not an undervalue.

Eveleigh LJ concurred with Lord Denning's view. He declined to allow the mother's estate to have the benefit of the LPA 1925 s.199(1)(i). This provides:

A purchaser shall not be prejudicially affected by notice of –

(i) any instrument or matter capable of registration under the provisions of the Land Charges Act 1925, or any enactment which it replaces, which is void or not enforceable as against him under that Act or enactment, by reason of the non-registration thereof . . .

Eveleigh, in examining the definition of a 'purchaser' under this provision, considered the definition set out in the LPA 1925 s.205(1)(xxi) where the term is defined as 'a purchaser in good faith for valuable consideration . . .' and that 'valuable consideration' 'does not include a nominal consideration in money'. Thus Eveleigh LJ judged that, since the mother was not a bona fide purchaser and as the price of £500 amounted to a nominal consideration, she could not invoke the protection of s.199(1)(i). This decision is all the more remarkable since Eveleigh LJ agreed that the definitions contained within the LPA 1925 s.205(1)(xxi) were not capable of being imparted into the Land Charges Act 1972. In any event, the Land Charges Act 1972 s.17(1) also contains a definition of a 'purchaser' which does not include a reference to good faith.

Lord Denning went further than simply deciding the case on the grounds that the mother had not been a purchaser of a legal estate for money or money's worth. He considered that the immunity provided from an unregistered land charge could never protect the purchaser, the mother, where the sale amounts to a fraud on the holder of the estate contract, the son. In arriving at that reasoning he referred back to an earlier decision of his in *Lazarus Estates Ltd* v *Beasley* [1956] 1 QB 702 where he stated at 712:

No court in this land will allow a person to keep an advantage which he has obtained by fraud. No judgment of a court . . . can be allowed to stand if it has been obtained by fraud. Fraud unravels everything. The court is careful not to find fraud unless it is distinctly pleaded and proved; but once it is proved, it vitiates judgments, contracts and all transactions whatsoever . . .

Lord Denning considered that the mother and father had hatched a plot to deprive the son of the benefit of his option and deprived his widow and children of the farm. In Denning's view, neither the mother nor her executors could be allowed to take advantage of the fraud, so that the mother's estate took the property subject to the option. Sir Stanley Rees, who was the dissenting judge in the Court of Appeal, considered that, whilst the mother and father appeared to be acting spitefully and deceitfully to deprive their son of the farm, on the balance of probabilities, the parents believed they were acting in the best interests of the family. He considered that there might well have been a justification for their actions and, as such, this would not amount to fraud. Sir Stanley Rees therefore refused to find that the transaction was a 'sham'. In arriving at his judgment, Sir Stanley Rees referred to the dicta of Lord Cozens-Hardy MR in **Re Monolithic Building Co.** [1915] 1 Ch 643 in which he stated at 663:

> The doctrine of the court in a case of fraud, of course, proceeds upon a different footing, and any security may be postponed if you can find fraud in its inception. But it is not fraud to take advantage of legal rights, the existence of which may be taken to be known to both parties.

Further he referred to Megarry J in **Miles v Bull** [1969] 1 QB 258 in which he stated at 265:

> On the other hand, a transaction is no sham merely because it is carried out with a particular purpose or object. If what is done is genuinely done, it does not remain undone merely because there was an ulterior purpose in doing it.

Sir Stanley Rees concluded that, unless there is fraud or the conveyance is a sham, an unregistered estate contract is void against it. He considered that, if this was not the case, there would be a departure from the 'sound' ordinary rule in contract law that the court will not look into the adequacy of consideration. He also considered that the policy of the Land Charge Act 1925 was to get rid of equitable rights arising from unregistered estate contracts.

One of the difficulties presented by the Midland Bank Trust Co. case is the fact that, whilst the estate contract was not registered, the mother did have actual knowledge of the existence of the option. It has to be considered here in that the whole philosophy behind the LCA 1972 is that, if an interest is registrable but it is not in fact registered, then it is not binding on the purchaser, irrespective of whether the purchaser had constructive or actual knowledge of the interest. This policy was deliberate on the part of the legislators in that they wished to depart from the difficulties presented in attempting to analyse the different states of mind that a third party might possess. These states of mind can progress from carelessness, to recklessness, to wilfully shutting one's eyes to a set of events through to actual notice. The legislators in 1925 cleverly sidestepped the need to examine the purchaser's state of mind. To protect the interest registration is everything and this is borne out by the fact that s.198 of the LPA 1925 provides that registration of a land charge is deemed to be actual notice to all persons for all purposes.

The distinction between actual and constructive notice was conclusively eliminated when the case of **Midland Bank Trust Co. Ltd v Green** finally reached the House of Lords, which unanimously reversed the decision of the Court of Appeal. Their Lordships conclusively held that the LCA 1972 s.4(6) was not qualified by a requirement that a purchaser must have acted in good faith and that the consideration must not be for a nominal amount. The House of Lords held that the mother was a purchaser for money or money's worth and was not bound by the option, which was void for want of registration.

Lord Wilberforce provided the leading judgment and stated that the omission of any requirement of good faith by a purchaser was a deliberate intention of Parliament and provided a reason for the drafting of the Act; thus he stated at 530:

> Addition of a requirement that a purchaser should be in good faith would bring with it the necessity of enquiring into the purchaser's motives and state of mind. The present case is a good example of the difficulties which would exist.

Lord Wilberforce considered that the whole point of the legislation was to place an emphasis on a simple mechanical process without any issues of motive becoming involved. Lord Wilberforce considered that the issue of good faith largely depends on the point of view from which one views the transaction. From the point of view of the son, it was clear that his mother was acting in bad faith to destroy his interest. On the other hand, from the mother's point of view, her motive might not have been to obtain a benefit herself, but to ensure that the property was to be distributed more equally between the son's brothers and sisters. In such a situation, it can be clearly agreed that she was acting in good faith, with the best of intention. Clearly, then, the issues relating to avarice, greed, malice and good faith become so intertwined that it is an extremely difficult task, both in law and in fact, for the courts to separate them. Lord Wilberforce considered it was probably for this reason Parliament removed the need for this to be considered by the courts, thus the presence or absence of good faith was irrelevant.

Lord Wilberforce also rejected Lord Denning's analysis that the consideration provided by the purchaser had to be 'adequate'. He stated:

> The word 'purchaser', by definition [LCA 1972 s.17(1)], means one who provides valuable consideration – a term of art which precludes any inquiry as to adequacy. [LCA1972 s.4(6)] requires money or money's worth to be provided: the purpose of this being to exclude the consideration of marriage. There is nothing here which suggests, or admits of, the introduction of a further requirement that the money must not be nominal.

Thus the fact that the mother was a purchaser for money or money's worth meant that she took the land free from the option and that there was no requirement that she must have acted in good faith or that the sum she paid had to be more than a nominal amount.

Any purchaser for value

Class A, B, C(i), C(ii), C(iii), E and F land charges are by the LCA 1972 s.4(2) and s.4(5) void against a purchaser of the land charged with them or any interest in such land unless the land charge is registered in the register of land charges before completion of the purchase. This category is therefore wider than a 'purchaser for money or money's worth of a legal estate in land'. Thus Class A, B, C(i), C(ii), C(iii), E and F land charges are void against a purchaser of any estate or interest, whether legal or equitable, if not registered.

The expression 'purchaser for value' will therefore protect not only purchasers of a legal estate but also purchasers of legal or equitable interests. Furthermore, the fact that the provisions refer to purchasers for value, as opposed to purchasers for money or money's worth, means that the consideration can also amount to marriage, as in the case of ante-nuptial marriage settlements.

Searching the register of land charges

Searches

It can clearly be seen from the above that, prior to the conveyance of an unregistered estate in land, a prudent purchaser must make a search of the Register of Land Charges in order to discover if any incumbrances in the nature of land charges have been registered. Whilst it is possible to conduct a personal search, searches are invariably conducted by way of an 'official search'. This is done by filling in an appropriate form and sending it to the Land Registry where the staff conduct a search of the registers and enter the details on to a search certificate. If there are no entries entered on the registers then the enquirer will receive a 'clear' certificate. An official search has several advantages, not least the fact that the details are, by the LCA 1972 s.10(4), deemed to be conclusive as to the state of the title.

> ## Example
>
> V contracts to sell Blackacre to X and, to protect his interest, X registers a C(iv) land charge against V's name. Later on V decides, despite the contract, to sell Blackacre to P, who then makes an official search. Unfortunately, the staff at the Land Registry in error issue a clear certificate to P, who now proceeds to purchase Blackacre. In this situation, P will acquire Blackacre 'free' from X's C(iv) estate contract, which is deemed to be void for non-registration as the certificate is deemed to be conclusive. Here X's only remedies will be either against V for breach of contract or against the Land Registry for negligence, or both.

A further advantage is that a prudent purchaser will, shortly before the completion date for the transaction, requisition an official search of the register against the vendor's name. The purpose of doing this is to ensure that no new land charges have been registered and, further, the effect of the official search is to give the purchaser a 15-day priority period. Thus, provided the completion takes place within the 15-working day period, the purchaser will not be subject to any new entries on the register that were unknown to them at the date of signing the contract. If a search did reveal the existence of a newly registered charge, the purchaser can rescind the contract.

Searching against the names of the estate holders

Whilst one would have thought that searches would be conducted against the address of a piece of land or its location, this is not the case. Entries are registered against the name of the holder of the legal estate, as provided by the LCA 1972 s.3(1). Thus if, as we saw earlier, Blackacre was owned by V but, prior to that, it had been owned by X, Y and Z, then the purchaser, P, would have to make a search against the names of X, Y and Z and indeed any other predecessors in title. This, on the face of things, might pose a problem for P since they would need to find out the names of those previous estate owners.

If we have a situation that V bought from Z and Z bought from Y and Y bought from X, then V, Z and Y should all have conducted searches against the previous owners. The earlier search certificates will all form parts of the title deeds appertaining to Blackacre and therefore it is usually unnecessary to go on a scavenging exercise to discover the names. Furthermore, the existence of the prior certificates will save the expense of making additional searches against the names of the predecessors in title.

The process of searching against the names of estate holders can give rise to two problems. Firstly, what happens if a purchaser searches against an incorrect version of a person's name? An example of this can be seen in the case of **Oak Co-operative Building Society v Blackburn** [1968] Ch 730.

Oak Co-operative Building Society v Blackburn [1968] Ch 730

In this case, the name of the estate owner was Francis David Blackburn, who agreed to sell the house to Mrs Caines, who moved into the property. In fact, the house was not legally conveyed to Mrs Caines and therefore the agreement was actually an estate contract, which of course should have been registered as a C(iv) land charge. This was eventually done, but it was registered against the name Frank David Blackburn since Mr Blackburn was always known as 'Frank'. Mr Blackburn then took out a mortgage with the building society which made a search of the land charges register but against the name Francis Davis Blackburn. Not surprisingly, the search did not reveal the existence of the estate contract. The question arose as to whether the building society was bound by the estate contract.

It was held by the Court of Appeal that registration against a version of an estate owner's true name was effective against a purchaser who searched against an incorrect name or who did not search at all.

Another issue that can arise in relation to names is where the owner of a land charge actually registers against an incorrect name but the person making the search does so against the correct name. Such a situation arose in the case of **Diligent Finance Ltd v Alleyne** [1972] 23 P & CR 346.

Diligent Finance Ltd v Alleyne [1972] 23 P & CR 346

In this case, the legal title to a house was in the name of a husband, Erskine Owen Alleyne. His wife registered a Class F land charge against the name Erskine Alleyne. The husband subsequently granted a mortgage to Diligent Finance Ltd, which searched against his full correct name of Erskine Owen Alleyne. The search revealed no land charge on the house. It was held that the incorrect registration by the wife did not fix the finance company with actual notice of the charge, so it took priority over the wife's interest.

The lesson to be learnt from these cases is that one must search against not only the full name but also any names by which a person may be known in order to ensure that the search is effective.

The second potential problem with regards to searching against possible names is that one may not know all the names that one should search against since some of the documents of title since 1925 may have become lost, with the result that the person searching may not know the name of the previous owner. This issue arises out of the process relating to the need for the vendor to prove they have a good title to the property in question. In order to prove their title the vendor must provide an unbroken chain of documents relating to every transaction that has taken place over the years. If one of these documents is lost then the chain is broken and they cannot prove their title to the purchaser. Originally, a vendor had to prove an unbroken chain back at least 30 years and potentially to 1925 in order to provide a 'good root of title'. The problem that arises is that, in order to search for any adverse land charges, a purchaser would have to search against all estate owners after 1925 to ensure that there were no land charges that could bind him or her. For example, it is possible that in 1930 the owner of the freehold might have granted an option to purchase the property that was to last 100 years. If this option was registered as a C(iv) land charge, a purchaser in 2012 could only discover the existence of the land charge by searching against the name of the freeholder owner in 1930. This is fine if there is an unbroken chain of title deeds going back to 1930; however, the Law of Property Act 1969 s.23 provided that a purchaser only had a statutory right to examine the title deeds dating back at least 15 years in order to establish a good root of title. The result of this is that a purchaser may not be able to discover the name of the owner of the freehold in 1930 in order to discover the existence of the C(iv) land charge created in 1930. Despite the problem that the purchaser cannot discover the existence of the land charge, they will nevertheless be bound by it since, as we know, registration is deemed to be actual notice to the purchaser by virtue of the LPA 1925 s.198.

In order to resolve this difficulty, the LPA 1969 introduced a scheme whereby a purchaser who was adversely affected by an undiscoverable land charge could receive compensation, though the purchaser remained subject to the land charge.

Example

Blackacre, an unregistered estate, was conveyed to Alan in 1926 but since then the following transactions have arisen in relation to Blackacre:

Alan conveyed his title to Bill

1936: Bill granted an equitable right of way over Blackacre in favour of Roger, his next door neighbour. Roger correctly registered the right of way (an easement) as a Class D(iii) land charge against Bill's correct name

1947: Bill conveyed Blackacre to Charlotte

1960: Charlotte conveyed Blackacre to David

1972: David conveyed Blackacre to Catherine

1980: Catherine conveyed Blackacre to Frank

1983: Graham, Frank's son, inherited Blackacre on the death of Frank

1988: Graham sold Blackacre to Sarfraz

In 2005 Sarfraz decided to sell Blackacre to Ian. Blackacre is still unregistered land. Sarfraz must prove his title going back to a good root of title – that is, a document which deals with the whole of the legal and equitable interest in the land, which describes the land adequately and contains nothing that casts any doubt on the title, and is at least 15 years old. In order to do this, Sarfraz will need to produce the conveyance from Graham to himself, and the assent from Frank's estate on his death to Graham (an assent is a means of transferring an estate from a deceased person to an heir). These two documents provide the chain of title documents; however Sarfraz must provide a chain *at least* 15 years old so he must also produce the conveyance from Catherine to Frank. Ian may now be able to search the land charges register against all these names but he may not be able to search against any names preceding Catherine since these conveyances do not need to have been kept. It may thus be impossible for Ian to search against the names of Bill, Charlotte and David. Despite the fact that there is no way Ian can discover the D(iii) land charge, he will be bound by it because of the effect of the LPA 1925 s.198. The only recourse open to Ian is to claim compensation under the LPA 1969 s.25, which provides:

(1) Where a purchaser of any estate or interest in land under a disposition to which this section applies has suffered loss by reason that this estate or interest is affected by a registered land charge, then if –

(a) the date of completion was after the commencement of this Act, and

(b) on that date the purchaser had no actual knowledge of the charge, and

(c) the charge was registered against the name of an owner of an estate in land who was not an owner of any such estate, a party to any transaction, or concerned in any event, comprised in the relevant title;

(d) the purchaser shall be entitled to compensation for the loss.

Thus Ian, whilst bound by the charge, will be able to claim compensation provided he had no actual knowledge of the charge – for instance, by seeing any previous search certificates.

The LPA 1969 s.25 does not thereby provide a solution to the problem of undiscoverable land charges. The solution would, of course, have been better if there were some mechanism by which all previous land charges could have been discovered. In 1925 Parliament did provide such a solution in the form of developing a system of registered land but the effect was that there were two systems by which land could be held and conveyed. It is extremely important that these two systems are not mixed up – they both do the same job but in different ways. The advantage of the system of registration of title under the Land Registration Act 1925 is that the need to search through bundles of title deeds is done away with so that (supposedly) all there is to know about an estate in land is found within the registration system, but we will discuss this system in much greater detail later on.

Priority notices

Sometimes a sequence of transactions occurs in rapid succession so that there may be little time to register a land charge in order to bind a successive purchaser. This may mean that, whilst the successive purchaser makes a search of the land charges register, the new land charge has not been registered in time. Reference to an example demonstrates the problem rather more clearly.

Example

V agreed to sell Blackacre to P for £150,000. In order to raise the money for the sale, P arranges a mortgage with B. In the negotiations for the sale of Blackacre, V imposes a restrictive covenant on P that she will use the premises for residential purposes only. The result of this series of transactions is that the restrictive covenant and the mortgage will take effect simultaneously when the transaction is completed. Clearly, P needs to execute the mortgage with B so that P can pay V and, at the same time, V needs to register the restrictive covenant. Here the restrictive covenant cannot be registered before the creation of the mortgage and therefore the restrictive covenant, a D(ii) land charge, will be void for non-registration against B as a purchaser of the legal estate for money or money's worth (remember that B as a mortgagee is regarded as a purchaser).

B will not therefore be subject to the restrictive covenant. This could become important later since, if P fails to pay her mortgage, B could take possession of Blackacre and subsequently sell it to C. In such a situation, B is not bound by the restrictive covenant, nor will C be as B's successor in title. C could therefore operate a business on Blackacre, something which V wanted to guard against.

In order to avoid such a scenario, V can make use of a priority notice under the LCA 1972 s.11. This process requires V to give a priority notice to the registrar at least 15 days before the creation of the restrictive covenant – usually the date on which the conveyance between V and P is to be executed. If V then registers the D(ii) land charge within 30 days of the entry of the priority notice in the land charges register, the registration of the restrictive covenant is deemed to date back to the date of the creation of the restrictive covenant – i.e. the date of the execution of the conveyance between V and P.

By the use of the priority notice, V can ensure that his restrictive covenant will bind B, despite the fact that B may technically create its mortgage over Blackacre prior to the registration of the restrictive covenant. The 15-working day period for the priority advance notice allows for the expiry of the 15-working day protection afforded to purchasers making an official search. If B is a prudent purchaser, and no doubt as a lender of money it will wish to make sure that it is not bound by any new land charge, it will make an official search just prior to the completion date. In the case of a mortgage it is in B's interests to do so since there is always the possibility that P took out another second mortgage with X and B will be most concerned that its mortgage comes before X's second mortgage in order to ensure that its loan is secure.

Interests of a family nature

Interests of a family nature are dealt with by a system of 'overreaching'. Commercial and family interests are mutually exclusive in that family interests can never exist as land charges, nor are commercial interests overreachable.

Previously, we saw that in land law prior to 1925 there were many different types of legal estates, legal interests and equitable interests and that one of the objects of the LPA 1925 and its other co-legislation was to make ownership of land more definable and, importantly, freely alienable – i.e. transferable. We saw that the LPA 1925 s.1 reduced the number of legal estates to two and the number of legal interests to five, while everything else became an equitable interest.

In relation to selling a piece of land, the purchaser needs to make a search of the land charges register to discover land charges of a commercial nature. A purchaser of course has to be particularly careful of purchasing a piece of land in which equitable rights exist. The last thing the purchaser wants is to buy the land and then find some third party has rights in relation to that piece of land. Such a situation could arise where there is a trust of land or a strict settlement. Overreaching is a process where the equitable rights of third parties are swept off the land and essentially destroyed as far as the land is concerned. That is not to say that the third party loses all rights as their equitable interest is now converted into the proceeds of sale. The point is that the purchaser will now own the land with a clear title.

Let us look at an example: Blackacre is held by A on trust for B. A has the legal fee simple and B therefore has an equitable interest, as shown in Figure 3.6.

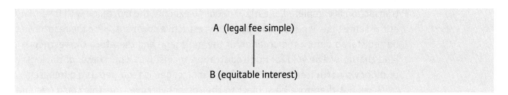

A (legal fee simple)

B (equitable interest)

Figure 3.6

A now decides to sell the legal fee simple to P for £200,000 (Figure 3.7).

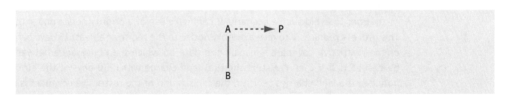

A ------► P

B

Figure 3.7

If P is a bona fide purchaser for value of the legal estate without notice of B's interest, he will take free from it. The problem though is that, if he investigates the title thoroughly and/or inspects Blackacre, he may be deemed to have actual, imputed or constructive notice of B's equitable interest. For instance, if he inspects Blackacre and can see evidence of another third party living there, he *must* make inquiry of A to discover what rights that third party, B, has in relation to Blackacre. If he does not do so he will purchase Blackacre subject to those rights of B – he will no longer be a bona fide purchaser for value of the legal estate *without* notice. Essentially, P will replace A as trustee of Blackacre for the benefit of B (see Figure 3.8).

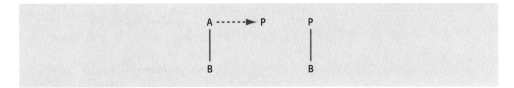

Figure 3.8

In order to avoid this situation, the LPA 1925 s.2(1) and s.27 provide that, if P pays his purchase monies to two trustees or a trust corporation and obtains a valid receipt from them, he will take free of the equitable interests of B even if he is aware of B's interest. Thus, in the example we have been looking at, P must insist that A appoints another trustee, X, before proceeding with the purchase. The picture is now as shown in Figure 3.9.

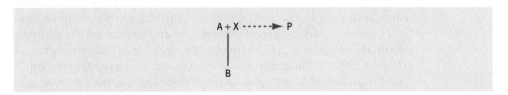

Figure 3.9

P now holds the legal title free from B's interest. Of course the trust in favour of B continues but now it is in the proceeds of sale, not Blackacre (see Figure 3.10).

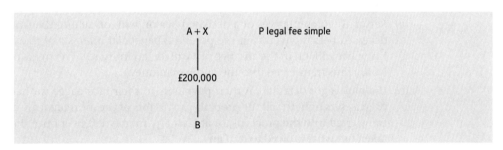

Figure 3.10

It should be emphasised that overreaching does not apply where there is a bare trust, which is the situation where A only holds the legal estate on trust for B, as we saw at the start of our example. There must be two trustees (or a trust corporation) for the process to operate, with the exception of where a sale is made by a sole personal representative administering the estate of a deceased person, who is entitled to give a valid receipt to the purchaser (LPA 1925 s.2 & s.27).

Until 1997, overreaching under the LPA 1925 applied to trusts for sale, either by way of an express trust for sale or by way of an implied trust for sale by reason of beneficial co-ownership. Rather peculiarly, until this date the beneficial rights of third parties were always deemed to be rights in the purchase money into which those beneficial rights would eventually be converted by a future sale. This was because of the equitable doctrine of conversion. Clearly, this was a somewhat artificial position. For instance, if a married couple (H and W) bought a house together, both the legal title and the equitable beneficial title would be in their joint names. Essentially, they both held the legal title on trust for each other, as in Figure 3.11.

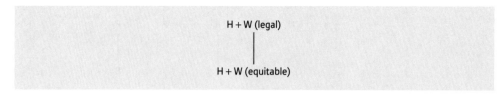

Figure 3.11

The doctrine of conversion meant that their beneficial title was never an interest in land but in the proceeds of sale. Here the law assumed that, as this was a trust for sale of the property, the land in question would be sold in the future. This flies in the face of reality as the married couple have not bought the house to sell it but to live in it!

Since 1997, by virtue of the Trusts of Land and Appointment of Trustees Act ('TOLATA') 1996 s.1, a trust of land is defined as 'any trust of property which consists of or includes land'. Such a trust of land is implied in beneficial co-ownership of land. The definition, however, also includes express trusts for sale and bare trusts of land. Implied trusts for sale are therefore abolished. Furthermore, the doctrine of conversion was also abolished by TOLATA 1996 s.3. The effect of this is that the beneficial rights in the land are now regarded as rights in the land, not rights in pure personalty (i.e. the proceeds of sale) and, indeed, remain rights in land even after the land is sold in the event that further land is purchased with the proceeds of the sale later on. It should be noted that the overreaching provisions contained in the LPA 1925 s.2(1) and s.27 (as amended by TOLATA 1996 Sched. 3 para 4(1) apply equally to trusts of land.

Overreaching can apply in other situations:

(a) Personal representatives of a deceased person will, on selling the land owned by the deceased person, overreach the potential beneficial interests of those entitled under his or her will, or, in the absence of a will, on an intestacy. The rights of the beneficiaries are thus transferred into the purchase money.

(b) If a mortgagor defaults on their payments to their mortgagee so that the mortgagee exercises its right to sell the property, any rights of the mortgagor are overreached and transferred into the proceeds, or at least any money left over once the mortgagee has taken out what is owed to it, if any.

Overreaching is, and remains, an important concept which will arise later on in our studies of land law.

Interests that are not capable of registration under the Land Charges Act 1972

We have seen that the land charges registrable as Class A, B, C, D, E and F land charges are very specific as to the type of interests that are capable of registration. There are, however, categories of interests that do not fall within these interests, either by design or by the fact that they were not considered by the parliamentary draughtsmen when producing the Land Charges Act 1925, which was the forerunner of the Land Charges Act 1972. It remains to be seen therefore how these interests are dealt with in the unregistered land regime.

Legal interests

With the exception of a legal mortgage not protected by deposit of title deeds, which is registrable as a Class C(i) puisne mortgage, legal interests 'bind the world' and bind any subsequent owner of the land. An example of such a legal interest would be a legal lease.

Equitable interests

These interests comprise the following:

(a) Restrictive covenants made prior to 1926 (those made after 1925 are registrable as a Class D(ii) land charge).

(b) Equitable easements made prior to 1926 (those made after 1925 are registrable as a Class D(iii) land charge).

(c) Rights of re-entry – for example, a right reserved on an assignment of a lease whereby an assignor may retain the right to re-enter the land and re-take it where the assignee is in breach of a covenant under a lease: ***Shiloh Spinners Ltd v Harding*** [1973] AC 691. Such a right of re-entry is an equitable interest that is incapable of registration under the Land Charges Act 1972.

(d) Equitable rights established by way of proprietary estoppel. An example of such an equitable interest can be seen in ***ER Ives Investments Ltd v High*** [1967] 2 QB 379.

ER Ives Investments Ltd v High [1967] 2 QB 379

In this case High ('H') purchased a bombed-out site in Norwich and commenced constructing a house on it. P subsequently purchased the site adjoining H's land and built a block of flats on it. The foundations of the flats encroached on to H's land and this constituted a trespass. H objected to the trespass but entered into an agreement with P whereby P could retain the foundations, provided H was given a right of way across P's land so as to give H access to the main road. Later, in 1950, P sold the site to X, who was fully aware of the agreement between H and P and continued to allow H to make use of the right of way. In 1959 H constructed a garage on his land in such a way that it could be accessed by way of the right of way across the land where the flats were constructed. In 1962, the flats were sold to ER Ives Investments Ltd ('I') who were aware of the right of way in that the conveyance stated that the land was conveyed subject to the right of way. I claimed that, if H had an equitable interest in the land, this should have been registered as a Class D(iii) land charge and, since it had not been so registered, it was void against I as a purchaser of the legal estate for money or money's worth as per the LCA 1972 s.4(6).

It was held that, because I's predecessors in title had acquiesced in H's right under the agreement, H had an equitable right of way across the land. Here H's equitable right arose by way of the application of the equitable doctrine of proprietary estoppel in that I was estopped from denying H's right of way. Lord Denning, with Danckwerts LJ concurring, held that equitable easements that fell within a Class D(iii) land charge were those rights which, prior to 1926, were capable of being conveyed or created at common law (i.e. legal interests), but since 1926 could only take effect as equitable interests because of the effect of the LPA 1925 s.1. He considered that, since H's right of way was never capable of existing as a legal right prior to 1926 or afterwards, it was not capable of being registered as a Class D(iii) land charge and thus the failure to register did not prevent H from enforcing his right of way.

(e) Equitable interests arising under a trust. It can be seen from the definition of Class C(iii) (General Equitable Charges) that interests arising under a trust of land or a settlement are not capable of being registrable as a land charge. The reason for this is that equitable interests arising under a trust of land are deemed to be interests of a family nature and these are dealt with by the doctrine of 'overreaching'.

All the equitable interests above, with the exception of interests arising under a trust, are dealt with by the old doctrine of notice and therefore a purchaser will take free from these interests if they can show that they are a bona fide purchaser for value of the legal estate with actual, imputed constructive notice of the prior equitable interest. Clearly, this means that a purchaser must thoroughly search through all the prior title deeds pertaining to the unregistered land in order to discover any such prior interests, otherwise they would be deemed to have constructive notice of the interest. This begs the question as to whether they have to go back through all of the title deeds. The answer to this is 'No' as they are only deemed to have notice of any interests they would have discovered in investigating the vendor's 'good root of title' – i.e. the unbroken chain of deeds that goes back at least 15 years. In practice, any equitable interests that exist prior to this time should be contained in those title deeds anyway and therefore should be discoverable. However, if such an interest is omitted in error then the purchaser would not be deemed to have constructive knowledge of the prior equitable interest.

Local land charges

In addition to the register of land charges under the LCA 1972, local authorities maintain registers of local land charges under the Local Land Charges Act 1975. Generally, local land charges are charges acquired by local authorities by way of statutory provisions, though they can also be imposed by government departments. Local land charges usually relate to public rights, whilst land charges under the LCA 1972 relate to private rights. Rights falling within local land charges are quite disparate and include matters such as tree preservation orders, conditions attached to planning permits, demolition orders for houses, compulsory purchase orders and areas designated as areas of special scientific interest among many others.

Responsibility for the registration of local land charges rests with the relevant local authority. There are significant differences between local land charges and land charges under the LCA 1972. Firstly, local land charges are registered against the address of the property in question so, when searching for the existence of a land charge, only the address need be supplied. Secondly, even if a local land charge is not registered, it will still bind any person who acquires the land. If, however, a purchaser obtains an official search certificate which does not reveal the existence of a local land charge they are entitled to compensation from the relevant authority.

Registered land

Looking back over unregistered land, the process of acquisition of an unregistered piece of land is a complex and somewhat awkward process. The purchaser has to satisfy him/ herself that the vendor has the power to sell the land and that there are no undisclosed incumbrances that affect the property. The purchaser does this by way of physical inspection of the land, searching through the documents of title back to a good root of title (always with the possibility that one of those documents in the bundle of title deeds has gone astray), searching the register of land charges and the register of local land charges. The difficulties associated with unregistered conveyancing were well recognised in 1925 – and indeed prior to that, with a voluntary system of registration of title being enacted as early as 1862. However, it was not until the Land Transfer Act 1897 that a compulsory system of registration of title was set up, though this was confined to London.

In 1925 Parliament enacted the Land Registration Act with the intention of simplifying the conveyancing process and doing away with all the vagaries of the unregistered land processes. The system of registration of title encompasses three principles:

- The 'mirror' principle in that the register should be a mirror of all the estates and interests that affect the land;
- The 'curtain' principle, whereby details of any trusts affecting the land should not be capable of being seen on the title;
- The 'indemnity' principle, by which the state provides a guarantee as to the accuracy of the register and indemnifies for any losses caused by any errors.

The aim behind the Land Registration Act 1925 was that all land would be moved away from unregistered conveyancing. It has taken a long time to get to that point as originally the system was developed in a piecemeal fashion over the whole country, though today it is now compulsory for unregistered land to become registered as and when dealings with unregistered land arise. Today more than 80% of the land in England and Wales comprises registered land but unfortunately for conveyancers (and land law students!) knowledge of the unregistered system of conveyancing is still required, at least for the time being.

Registered land is now governed by the Land Registration Act 2002 (LRA 2002) which replaced the LRA 1925. The LRA 2002 is essentially the same as the LRA 1925 in many respects; however, it made substantial amendments to the way in which the system operates and, crucially, paved the way for the introduction of electronic conveyancing so that the whole process could be expedited more quickly and efficiently. We will look at the system of registered land in much more detail in Chapter 5 but first we will look at an outline of the conveyance process.

Summary

The structure of land law after 1925

- Law of Property Act 1925
- Land Charges Act 1972
- Land Registration Act 1925
- Administration of Estates Act
- Settled Land Act 1925
- Trustee Act 1925

The Law of Property Act 1925 forms the central plank of the 1925 legislative regime. The legislation had two objectives:

(a) to ensure that land was freely alienable, and

(b) to ensure the legal regime could deal with a fragmented title in that it is possible to create different interests in land.

The objectives were achieved by reducing to two the number of legal estates that could exist:

(a) fee simple absolute in possession – LPA 1925 s.1(1)a, and

(b) terms of years absolute – LPA 1925 s.1(1)b.

In addition, by virtue of the LPA 1925 s.1(2) the number of legal interests that could exist was reduced to five:

(a) Easements, rights and privileges – s.1(2)a

(b) Rentcharges – s.1(2)b

(c) Mortgages – s.1(2)c

(d) Miscellaneous charges – s.1(2)d

(e) Rights of entry – s.1(2)e.

All other interests by virtue of the LPA 1925 s.1(3) became equitable interests which were divided into two categories:

(a) Equitable interests of a commercial nature; and

(b) Equitable interests of a family nature.

The protection of equitable interests

Equitable interests were protected in two ways: equitable interests of a commercial nature were protected by a system of registration under the Land Charges Act1925 (1972), whilst equitable interests of a family nature were protected by a process called 'overreaching'.

The system of registration for unregistered land under the Land Charges Act 1972 amounted to a reform of the doctrine of notice and, as such, had two effects:

(a) Registration of an interest constitutes actual notice of the registered interest: LPA 1925 s.198.

(b) Non-registration makes the interest void.

Finally, not all equitable interests are registrable as land charges and those that are not covered by this or the doctrine of overreaching are still subject to the 'old' doctrine of notice.

Registrable interests of a commercial nature

Although there are five separate registers in the LCA 1972 that contain matters that will bind transferees, we are mainly concerned with the land charges that are contained within s.2.

Land charges

These are divided into six classes, A, B, C, D, E and F, which are defined in s.2 of the Act. Any equitable interest that falls outside of these cannot be registered.

(a) Class A – Charges imposed by statute on application

(b) Class B – Charges imposed by statute automatically

(c) Class C land charges are subdivided into four further classes:
    (i)   C(i) – Puisne mortgage
    (ii) C(ii) – Limited owner's charge
    (iii) C(iii) – General equitable charge
    (iv) C(iv) – An estate contract

(d) Class D land charges are sub-divided into three further classes:
    (i)   D(i) – Inland Revenue charges
    (ii) D(ii) – Restrictive covenants
    (iii) D(iii) – Equitable easements

(e) Class E – Annuities

(f) Class F – Special rights of occupation

Registration and the effects of non-registration

The process of registration

The basic concept and process of registration under the Land Charges Act 1972 is very simple since the owner of an interest falling within the Act merely registers their interest in the Register of Land Charges. Once registered, the interest binds all subsequent purchasers.

The process of registration under the Land Charges Act 1972 modifies the doctrine of notice by providing that registration in the Register of Land Charges is, by the Law of Property Act 1925 s.198, 'deemed to be actual notice . . . to all persons and for all purposes' of the existence of the land charges. Once registered, the land charge will continue to remain binding, no matter whose hands the legal estate will later pass into, until of course the land charge is extinguished.

Effects of non-registration

We have referred already to the fact that registration is deemed to constitute actual notice to all persons for all purposes under the LPA 1925 s.198.

The effect of non-registration as set out in the LCA 1972 s.4 is not the same for all land charges and depends on the individual land charges. There are two main categories:

(i) the land charge may be void against a purchaser for money or money's worth of a legal estate in land; or

(ii) the land charge may be void against a purchaser for value of any interest in the land.

Searching the register of land charges

Searches

Prior to the conveyance of an unregistered estate in land, a prudent purchaser must make a search of the register of land charges in order to discover if any incumbrances in the nature of land charges have been registered. Whilst it is possible to conduct a personal search, such searches are invariably conducted by way of an 'official search'. This is done by filling in an appropriate form and sending it to the Land Registry where the staff conduct a search of the registers and enter the details on to a search certificate.

Searching against the names of the estate holders

Oak Co-operative Building Society v *Blackburn* [1968] Ch 730

Diligent Finance Ltd v *Alleyne* [1972] 23 P & CR 346

Priority notices

Sometimes a sequence of transactions occurs in rapid succession so there may be little time to register a land charge in order to bind a successive purchaser. This may mean that, though the successive purchaser makes a search of the land charges register, the new land charge has not been registered in time. In order to avoid such a scenario it is possible to make use of a priority notice under the LCA 1972 s.11.

Interests of a family nature

Interests of a family nature are dealt with by a system of 'overreaching'. Commercial and family interests are mutually exclusive in that family interests can never exist as land charges, nor are commercial interests over reachable.

Overreaching is a process where the equitable rights of third parties are swept off the land and essentially destroyed as far as the land is concerned. That is not to say that the third party loses all rights as their equitable interest is now converted into the proceeds of sale. The point is that the purchaser will now own the land with a clear title.

Interests that are not capable of registration under the Land Charges Act 1972

These are categories of interests that are neither registrable as land charges nor are they interests of a family nature. Again they fall into two types of interest: legal and equitable.

Legal interests

With the exception of a legal mortgage not protected by deposit of title deeds, which is registrable as a Class C(i) puisne mortgage, legal interests 'bind the world' and bind any subsequent owner of the land. An example of such a legal interest would be a legal lease.

Equitable interests

These interests comprise the following:

(a) Restrictive covenants made prior to 1926 (those made after 1925 are registrable as a Class D(ii) land charge.

(b) Equitable easements made prior to 1926 (those made after 1925 are registrable as a Class D(iii) land charge.

(c) Rights of re-entry: ***Shiloh Spinners Ltd v Harding*** [1973] AC 691.

(d) Equitable rights established by way of proprietary estoppel: ***ER Ives Investments Ltd v High*** [1967] 2 QB 379.

(e) Equitable interests arising under a trust.

All the equitable interests above, with the exception of interests arising under a trust, are dealt with by the old doctrine of notice and therefore a purchaser will take free from these interests if they can show that they are a bona fide purchaser for value of the legal estate with actual, imputed constructive notice of the prior equitable interest.

Local land charges

In addition to the register of land charges under the LCA 1972, local authorities also maintain registers of local land charges under the Local Land Charges Act 1975. Generally, local land charges are charges acquired by local authorities and government departments by way of statutory provisions.

Further reading

Harpum, 'Purchasers With Notice of Unregistered Land Charges' (1981) *Cambridge Law Journal* 213

Harpum, 'Midland Bank Trust Co. Ltd v Green' (1981) *Cambridge Law Journal* 213

Thompson, 'The Purchaser as a Private Detective' [1986] 50 *The Conveyancer and Property Lawyer* 283

Thompson, 'The Widow's Plight' [1996] 60 *The Conveyancer and Property Lawyer* 295

Yates, 'The Protection of Equitable Interests Under the 1925 Legislation' (1974) 37 *Modern Law Review* 87

4

An outline of the conveyancing process and unregistered land

Aims and objectives

At the end of this chapter you should be able to:

- Understand the broad principles of the conveyancing process.
- Understand the processes of exchanging contracts for sales or dispositions in land prior to and after 1989.
- Know the requirements for a valid contract for the sale of land.
- Understand the nature of proprietary estoppel and constructive trusts in contracts for the sale of land.
- Know the remedies available for breach of contract.
- Know the processes from contract to completion of the transaction in the purchase of unregistered and registered land.

Introduction

Conveyancing is the process by which land is sold and bought and is, in many respects, a subject in its own right – though, of course, to understand and carry out the process it is necessary to have a knowledge of the underlying principles of land law, which is what this work is about. This is not a book about conveyancing per se; however, it is useful at this juncture to have some understanding of the processes involved, particularly with regards to contracts for the sale of land.

Essentially, conveyancing is concerned with two matters:

(i) Does the vendor have the right to sell the property? To this extent the vendor has to prove their title to the purchaser.

(ii) Are there any third party rights affecting the land which might conflict with the purchaser's eventual use of the land: for instance, restrictive covenants, easements, estate contracts or mortgages operating against the land?

The process by which these two functions differ depends on whether the land is unregistered or registered. We have seen already that unregistered land is governed by the old common law and equity, as amended by the Law of Property Act 1925 and the Land Charges Act 1972.

Registered land is governed by the Land Registration Act 2002. It is therefore absolutely crucial to ascertain which system of conveyancing will apply to the land in question since, whilst approximately 80 per cent of the land in England and Wales is registered, there will be occasions when one will have to deal with unregistered land.

Land has become registered land by different processes within the Land Registration Act 1925 and by various pieces of amending legislation, through to the Land Registration Act 2002. The latter Act did not introduce a new system of registration but largely restated, with amendments, the law existing prior to its enactment. Some of the language and other aspects changed but, essentially, the structures enacted by the Land Registration Act 1925 remain the same.

Under the Land Registration Act 1925 certain areas became areas of compulsory registration so that as a dealing with a piece of unregistered land occurred, it was converted over to the 'new' system. These areas increased incrementally until, on 1 December 1990, the whole of England and Wales became an area of compulsory registration. Not all dealings with a piece of land required compulsory registration since it was considered that this could involve the parties in quite high costs; however, estates in land had to be registered at the time of the first dealing for value of the estate in question once the land fell within an area of compulsory registration (now the whole of the country, as indicated earlier).

As we have just stated, the original 'trigger' point for registration occurred if there was a dealing for value with the estate, either the sale of the freehold or where there was a grant of a long lease over the land. From 1997, the occasions which trigger compulsory registration have been increased to include assents by personal representatives distributing the estates of deceased persons, dispositions by way of gift, mortgages with deposit of title deeds and dispositions by trustees either to beneficiaries or where there is an appointment of a new trustee. These occasions will be looked at in more detail in Chapter 5 – Registered Land. These additional trigger points have resulted in a significant increase in the number of estates coming on to the register.

In addition to compulsory registration, there are also occasions when voluntary registration is possible. For example, an owner of unregistered land might find it convenient to register their title because they wish to develop the land by building houses on it. As the landowner/developer sells each house or plot, it will be easier for their purchasers to purchase the property and thus the initial first registration makes the whole process more convenient and cheaper. Voluntary registration is also available if the landowner of an unregistered title has lost their title deeds and thus registration provides a solution to the problem. In addition, voluntary registration assists an estate owner if they are concerned about the possibility of third parties acquiring title to part of the land by adverse possession since the Land Registration Act 2002 provides safeguards for estate owners in fear of such an occurrence.

Discovering if a title is registered or not

As we have seen, it is quite crucial to discover if a title has been registered or not. To discover this, a prospective purchaser can make an 'index map search' with the Land Registry, which will inform the purchaser if the land is registered or not. Any land not shown on the index map must, of necessity, be unregistered land and the old rules of conveyancing will apply to it.

An index map search will not reveal any other information about the land other than whether it is registered or not; however, from 3 December 1990, the Land Registry was opened up to public inspection. Prior to this date, the consent of the registered proprietor was required. Members of the public are now entitled to inspect the register and obtain copies of any entries on the register.

Purchasing land – the processes outlined

Whilst purchasing a piece of land may appear to be one long process, just as with normal contracts, this process can be broken down into a series of constituent points, some of which require distinct and important formalities.

Pre-contract negotiations

Many of you will be already familiar with the process from a general knowledge point of view. The process often starts with a prospective purchaser visiting an estate agent and looking at properties that fall within his or her budget. The purchaser would then view a particular property and if he or she likes it then they would make an offer on the property. If the vendor accepts the offer, then they will have an agreement. It is vital to understand that, unlike agreements to purchase personal property, there is no binding contract at this stage – this will only arise once contracts have been signed and exchanged.

The pre-contract agreement to purchase a property is really nothing more than a 'gentleman's agreement' and a shake of hands carries with it no legal obligation to buy or to sell. It is during this pre-contract period that 'gazumping' and 'gazundering' are likely to occur. 'Gazumping' arises in a 'rising' market where there is a demand for properties and prices are rising. Here the vendor may receive a higher offer for their property than that made by the previous prospective purchaser. In such a case, the vendor may decide to sell to the new bidder and withdraw from the agreement with the first bidder. Alternatively, they may go back to the first bidder and ask him or her to increase their price, and if they refuse, the vendor would withdraw from the agreement to sell. 'Gazundering' is the opposite of 'gazumping'. Here there is a 'falling' market where demand is slack and prices are dropping. Here the purchaser may go back to the vendor and ask him or her to reduce the price agreed on the threat of the purchaser withdrawing from the agreement.

Gazumping tends to have a bigger impact on a potential sale since in the run-up to signing and exchanging contracts the purchaser will often incur considerable costs. Thus a purchaser would normally employ a surveyor to inspect the property to ensure it is structurally sound and the cost of this may be considerable. In addition, the purchaser's solicitor will also be carrying out other legal work, such as conducting local land charge searches, drafting the written contract and making inquiries regarding such matters as boundary disputes and investigating the title to the property – referred to as 'requisitions'.

'Requisitions' are an important part of investigating the seller's title since normally the contract will contain a clause preventing the purchaser from questioning the seller's title once the contract for sale has been entered into. If the purchaser's solicitor does discover a problem with the seller's title then the purchaser can withdraw from the transaction at this point. The fact remains, though, that the purchaser can incur significant costs at this stage and thus gazumping can have a considerable impact on the purchaser.

The costs incurred by purchasers in the pre-contract stage and the fact that these costs cannot be recovered have been the subject of considerable criticism over the years. In order to address this criticism, the government introduced Home Information Packs ('HIP') by virtue of Part 5 of the Housing Act 2004. HIPs were required before any property could be put on the market with vacant possession. The pack was essentially a set of documents about the property: local authority searches, title documents, answers to standard pre-contract enquiries, planning and building regulation consents, warranties and guarantees for any work carried out, a draft sale contract, information about leasehold property (such as management charges) and an Energy Performance Certificate. It was suggested that such packs would reduce the number of abortive sales and reduce the incidence of gazumping and gazundering. The measure was introduced despite the fact that there was strong opposition from the building industry and estate agents on the grounds that the high cost of preparing the HIPs would deter vendors from putting their houses up for sale. Indeed, it was alleged that the need for such HIPs contributed to the 2007–2009 housing crisis. In the face of this criticism, the need for such packs, with the exception of the Energy Performance Certificate, was suspended with effect from 21 May 2010 by the incoming government and this was confirmed by the Localism Act 2011 s.183.

The threat of gazumping sometimes gives rise to purchasers entering into so-called 'lock-out' agreements with vendors. A lock-out agreement is one in which the vendor agrees with a prospective purchaser that for a specified period – for example, two weeks – they will not accept an offer from another prospective purchaser. In this way, a purchaser seeks to avoid the possibility of being gazumped. Such lock-out agreements do not ensure that the purchaser will get the property and, in fact, the vendor is still free to sell to the highest bidder, though they will be liable for breach of contract. Presumably, however, the threat of having to pay damages will dissuade the vendor from gazumping the prospective purchaser. It should be noted that such contracts are collateral agreements and do not have to comply with the Law of Property (Miscellaneous) Provisions Act 1989 s.2. Such agreements therefore do not have to be in writing as they are not contracts for the Sale of Land and can in fact be created orally, though they are often reduced into writing: *Pitt* v *PHH Asset Management Ltd* [1993] 4 All ER 961.

As with any other contracts, purchasing land is subject to the over-arching principle of caveat emptor and thus the process of registration is an important element in the purchaser investigating the title to the land in question. As we have seen, surveys and searches of the title are central to this process – however, the process often goes further and questions may be asked as regards such matters as curtains, carpets and plants in the garden to determine what is or is not being included in the sale. If the vendor is asked direct questions about the property or any such associated matters, they must reply honestly, though there is no duty of care on the vendor to disclose matters which they are not asked about. They are, however, under a duty of care to disclose any latent defects in the title. So, for instance, in *Sykes* v *Taylor-Rose* [2004] EWCA Civ 299 a vendor was not required to tell the purchaser about a particular gruesome murder that had occurred on the property when no question was asked of him about such matters. On the other hand, the case of *McMeekin* v *Long* (2003) EG 120 provides a salutory lesson.

McMeekin v *Long* (2003) EG 120

In this case, Mr and Mrs McMeekin were purchasing a four-bedroomed detached house in Hampshire. When viewing the property, they asked about the neighbours and were reassured that they were friendly. As part of the pre-contract process their solicitor submitted a 'seller's property information form' ('SPIF') to the Longs' solicitor in which the question was asked, 'Do you know of any disputes about this or any neighbouring property?' and 'Have you received any complaints about anything you have or have not done as owners?' Mr and Mrs Long answered 'No' to both questions. After the McMeekins moved into the house, they heard there had been problems between neighbours, centring on arguments relating to parking in the access road and the dumping of rubbish on nearby land. Whilst concerned, the McMeekins remembered the responses on the SPIF. All was well at first but then the neighbours, Mr and Mrs Cooper, began to object to the Tesco Home Delivery van coming up the access lane. It transpired that there had been a great deal of aggravation between Mr and Mrs Cooper and the other neighbours in the area in the past. Despite trying to resolve the situation, the problem continued and Mr and Mrs McMeekin then sued Mr and Mrs Long for misrepresentation. It was held that Mr and Mrs Long were liable for fraudulent misrepresentation and were ordered to pay £67,500 for the devaluation of the property caused by the dispute (they paid £124,000 for the house!).

Astill J stated:

The truth of the matter is that there was an atmosphere of constant confrontation between Mr and Mrs Cooper and the occupants of the houses on the road . . . This is precisely the kind of information which must be disclosed to a potential purchaser for them to be able to make up their mind whether they wish to buy a property with the running sore of constant disputes and antagonism between the owners.

Astill J commented that the questions on the form were simple to understand and the disputes so obvious that it was 'impossible to conclude other than that [the Longs] must have known that they were not being truthful when they answered those two questions'.

The duty to disclose latent defect in the title, whilst important, needs to be qualified as the vendor is under no obligation to disclose any defects of which the purchaser is aware – 'which is patent' – in which case caveat emptor applies. According to the decision of Sargant J in *Yandle & Sons v Sutton* [1922] 2 Ch 199 at 210, a patent defect is one 'which arises to the eye or by necessary implication from something which is visible to the eye'. Thus interests such as mortgages or restrictive covenants would be regarded as 'latent' incumbrances, whilst a pathway amounting to a right of way (an easement) would be regarded as 'patent'.

It should be noted that in *McMeekin* the claim was pursued on the basis of misrepresentation. However, if a purchaser is induced to enter a contract because of matters disclosed or not disclosed in the draft particulars of sale, the purchaser may also have an action for breach of the contract of which the particulars of sale become part. A breach of the vendor's duty to disclose latent defects in the title is often treated as breach of an implied term of the contract so that the purchaser can repudiate the contract and claim damages. Repudiation is not possible, however, if the non-disclosure of a latent defect is minor or where the defect in title can be removed: *Pips (Leisure Productions) Ltd v Walton* (1980) P & CR 415.

Exchange of contracts

Whilst contracts for the sale of land are just like any other contract in terms of the legal requirements to form a contract – i.e. offer and acceptance, capacity, consideration, etc. – land law requires that certain formalities must be adhered to. The requirements for these formalities changed following the enactment of the Law of Property (Miscellaneous Provisions) Act 1989. The Act addresses contracts entered on or after 27 September 1989 but contracts entered into prior to this date must conform with the provisions of the Law of Property Act 1925 s.40. Whilst these are quite rare, we will consider them later on in this chapter, since you need to be aware of these formalities.

Contracts for the sale or other disposition of an interest in land created after 27 September 1989

Introduction

As already stated, such contracts must comply with the provisions of the Law of Property (Miscellaneous Provisions) Act 1985 s.2, which provides:

1 A contract for the sale or other disposition of an interest in land can only be made in writing and only by incorporating all the terms which the parties have expressly agreed in one document or, where contracts are exchanged, in each.

2 The terms may be incorporated in a document either by being set out in it or by reference to some other document.

3 The documents incorporating the terms, or where contracts are exchanged, one of the documents incorporating them (but not necessarily the same one) must be signed by on or behalf of each party to the contract.

In summary, s.2 contains the following features:

(i) It is not confined to contracts for the sale of estates only but to an 'interest' in land.

(ii) The contract for the sale of land must be in writing.

(iii) It must contain all the terms of the agreement.

(iv) It must be signed by both parties.

We shall now consider each of these features in turn.

Contracts for the sale or other disposition of an interest in land

The effect of this feature is that the provisions do not only apply to freehold and leasehold estates but also to other interests and changes in or over the land in question. The provision therefore applies to contracts for the grants of easements and mortgages.

(a) Options

As we saw in the last chapter, one problematical area as regards contracts for the sale of an interest in land lies with options. It will be recalled that an option arises where an owner of land gives another an option to purchase the land at a later date. Once the purchaser decides to exercise the option, the landowner must sell to him or her, and if the landowner refuses to sell, the purchaser may enforce the contract by way of specific performance. Furthermore, the purchaser may enforce the option against a third party purchaser if that new purchaser has notice of this option – for instance, by way of a C(iv) land charge if the land is unregistered. The point at which the option becomes operative has been open to some debate. Some consider that the conferring of the option must comply with s.2, whilst others consider an option to be an irrevocable offer that only comes into existence when the option is actually exercised. The point was considered in the case of *Spiro v Glencrown Properties Ltd* [1991] All ER 600, where it was stated that, whilst an agreement for an option had to comply with s.2, the exercise of the option did not. Thus Hoffman J stated:

> Section 2 . . . was intended to prevent disputes over whether the parties had entered into a binding agreement or over what terms they had agreed. It prescribes the formalities for recording their mutual consent. But only the grant of the option depends upon consent. The exercise of the option is a unilateral act. It would destroy the very purpose of the option if the purchaser had to obtain the vendor's counter signature to the notice by which it was exercised.

(b) Collateral contracts

Another issue as regards contracts for the sale of interests in land arises with regards to collateral contracts. In such contracts, the parties agree conditions in a separate agreement. Here the collateral contract does not need to comply with s.2, provided the collateral contract is not regarded as being one for the disposition of an interest in land. Thus in *Record v Bell* [1991] 1 WLR 853 it was held that a warranty as to the seller's title made orally was part of a collateral contract and, as such, did not need to be in writing in order to bind the seller to his promise.

Similarly, lock-out agreements, which we looked at earlier, are not contracts for sale of an interest in land and are also outside the scope of s.2: *Pitt v PHH Asset Management Ltd* [1993] 4 All ER 961.

(c) Contracts of sale with third parties

In *Jelson Ltd v Derby City Council* [1999] 3 EGLR 91 there was an agreement between Jelson and Derby City Council by which Jelson was required to transfer part of a site for affordable housing to a housing association nominated by the council. No housing association was, in fact, party to the agreement. The court considered that the effect of the agreement was to compel Jelson to convey the property if certain conditions were met and therefore it was a contract for the sale or disposition within the meaning of s.2 and thus it was void as the proposed housing association had not signed the agreement (see below as regards signatures). The implication of this case was that contracts for the sale of land to a third party must comply with s.2.

The decision in *Jelson* was however questioned by the Court of Appeal in *Nweze v Nwoku* [2004] 2 P & CR 33.

Nweze v Nwoku [2004] 2 P & CR 33

The facts of this case were that Mr and Mrs Nweze agreed to sell their property to their cousin, Mr Nwoku, for £135,000. The parties agreed that Nwoku would pay £100,000 on completion and the balance within six months. The price on the contract falsely showed £105,000 in order to avoid stamp duty. Following completion, Nwoku paid £105,000, as per the contract, and subsequently the Nwezes pressed for the additional £30,000 plus the reimbursement of the deposit they had lent Nwoku.

It was subsequently agreed (a compromise agreement) that the property would be sold with vacant possession at the best market value and, once the mortgage had been discharged, the net proceeds would be passed on to the Nwezes. Nwoku then decided he would not proceed with the sale and the Nwezes sued to enforce the original contract at the agreed price of £135,000 or, in the alternative, to enforce the compromise agreement.

It was argued for Nwoku that the original contract and compromise agreement were void for non-compliance with s.2 since neither was in writing or signed by the parties. The Nwezes, for their part, argued that the compromise was not caught by s.2 since the agreement was not a contract for the sale of the property, nor was it a disposition of an interest in the property. Broadly speaking, it was argued that the compromise agreement was simply an agreement to enter into such a contract if a buyer for the property could be found.

Counsel for Nwoku argued that s.2 did not demonstrate that it was only intended to apply to contracts for the sale of land between two parties. Referring to the Law Commission Report (1987) No. 164 Formalities for Contracts for Sale etc. of Land, it was stated that the purpose of s.2 was to protect the consumer, provide certainty and prevent fraud and that the circumstances of the case meant that the compromise agreement fell within s.2. Counsel also relied on the decision in *Jelson Ltd v Derby City Council*.

The Court of Appeal held that the Law Commission Report supported the Nwezes' position, since the report was clearly only concerned with contracts for the sale or disposition of an interest in land. The court considered that s.2 was concerned with contracts that resulted in a sale between two people and not contracts between two people with a view to effect a sale to a third party. The court stated that the position in English law was that parol contracts were valid and that s.2 was an exception to this principle and should not be construed any more widely than necessary. Walker LJ stated that, whilst the compromise agreement required the buyer (Nwoku) to sell the property to a third party, it did not, of itself, effect a sale of the property. The Nwezes could not be said to be gaining any legal or beneficial interest in the property by virtue of the compromise agreement.

Walker LJ distinguished the case from Jelson and recognised that a contract between two parties, A and B, under which B can call for the property to be transferred to a nominated buyer, C, fell within s.2 where there is a contract for the sale or disposition of an interest in land. Walker LJ questioned the decision in Jelson on the basis that, as far as the requirement of a signature is concerned, it is only the signature of the contracting parties that is required.

The contract for the sale of land must be in writing

Section 2 of the 1989 Act requires the contract to be in writing and nothing else will suffice. Failure to comply with this requirement will render the contract *void*. Care must be exercised to distinguish the requirements under the Law of Property Act 1925 s.40 (1) which applies to contracts prior to 27 September 1989. This requires contracts to be *evidenced* in writing, for instance an exchange of letters, which demonstrates the existence of an oral agreement. The effect of non-compliance is very different here since the contract is *unenforceable*, not void, unless there is some act of performance as set out in s.40(2).

Whilst the absence of writing within s.2 renders the contract void, it is nevertheless possible for the contract to be enforced if an estoppel or a constructive trust can be shown. We will deal with these aspects later.

One exception to the requirement of writing is that s.2 does not apply to contracts made in the course of a public auction. Here a valid contract arises on the fall of the auctioneer's hammer.

The contract must contain all the terms of the agreement

The written document that makes up the contract must incorporate all the terms of the contract, either by setting out all the terms or by referring to another document. From time to time, cases have come before the courts where a party has sought to have the contract declared void, so as to escape their obligation under the contract, because the contract has failed to include a matter agreed by the parties. The approach of the courts to this matter has varied. Some courts have held that the contract is valid because all the required terms for the disposition of an interest in land have been included in the written agreement and the omitted terms form part of a collateral contract which was not a contract regarding land and does not have to comply with s.2 – for example, if the parties had negotiated for carpets and curtains to be included in the sale and this term was not included in the written contract. In other cases, the courts have treated the contract as void because all the terms have not been included in the written agreement. These two approaches can be seen in the following cases:

Record v *Bell* [1991] 1 WLR 853

It was held in this case that a promise made by the seller as to his title was the subject of a collateral contract and, whilst there was no writing supporting the promise in the written contract, its absence did not undermine the validity of the main contract. Essentially, the promise was not in itself a contract for the sale or disposition of an interest in land and therefore did not need to conform with the s.2 requirements and could be created orally.

Tootal Clothing Ltd v *Guinea Properties Management Ltd* [1992] 2 EGLR 80

In this case there were two agreements: one for the grant of a lease and another, the supplemental agreement, whereby the tenant (Tootal) would carry out shopfitting works on the premises within 12 weeks, the premises to be rent-free during this period. On satisfactory completion of the shop-fitting works, the landlord (Guinea Properties) would pay £30,000 towards the cost of the works.

The grant of the lease was subsequently executed and the tenant carried out the works, at which point the landlord refused to pay the £30,000 on the ground that s.2 required that all the terms of a contract for this sale or disposition of an interest in land had to be incorporated into one document and that document had to be signed by both the parties. The landlord argued that the term regarding the £30,000 was part of the consideration for the lease agreement and therefore it should have been in the same document as the lease agreement. Since the terms of the supplemental agreement were not in the lease agreement, it was void and unenforceable.

At first instance, the trial judge 'without any enthusiasm at all' concluded that the arguments of the landlord were sound and that the tenant was barred from recovering the £30,000.

In the Court of Appeal, Scott LJ stated that s.2 is only of relevance to executory contracts and has no relevance once the contract has been concluded. Once the parties had completed the lease agreement, it ceased to be an executory contract and therefore any question as to whether the lease agreement was unenforceable because not all the terms of the contract had been incorporated became irrelevant. Scott LJ stated that the supplemental agreement was not in itself a land contract and therefore, once the lease agreement had been executed by completion, s.2 had no relevance to the contractual enforceability of the supplementary agreement.

Scott LJ went further however and stated:

I am of the opinion, speaking for myself, that even before completion of the lease agreement . . . s.2 would not have prevented the enforcement of the lease agreement. If parties choose to hive off part of the terms of their composite bargain into a separate contract distinct from the written land contract that incorporates the rest of the terms, I can see nothing in s.2 that provides an answer to an action for enforcement of the land contract, on the one hand, or of the separate contract on the other hand. Each has become, by the contractual choice of the parties, a separate contract.

These two cases therefore represent a significant answer where there is an attempt to invalidate an agreement on the basis of non-compliance with s.2, since omitted terms may be treated as a separate contract, provided the terms are not concerned with land.

The mechanism of using a collateral contract to avoid the requirements of s.2 has not been completely accepted by the courts – indeed in **Grossman v Hooper** [2001] EWCA Civ 615 Sir Christopher Staughton considered that if parties were allowed to avoid the effects of s.2 there was little point in Parliament enacting it. He referred to the decision of Brown LJ in *Godden* v *Merthyr Tydfil Housing Association* [1997] 74 P & CR in which Brown LJ stated:

> . . . there was in this case but one single unified agreement – an agreement under which the defendants undertook to purchase from the plaintiff land which in the first place he was to acquire, prepare and develop to their order. It seems to me entirely unreal to attempt to separate that out into two discrete, or even distinct agreements – one involving the disposition of land, the other not. Rather, all the obligations between the parties were integral to each other, part and parcel of a single scheme.

Similarly, in the case of *Wright* v *Robert Leonard (Developments) Ltd* [1994] EGCS 69 one of the terms of sale of a show flat was that the sale would include certain furnishings, but the contract made no mention of this. A dispute arose when the seller removed certain items. The Court of Appeal held that the oral agreement relating to the sale of the contents was part of 'one package' for the sale of the flat and contents and that s.2 applied to the whole agreement. To comply with s.2 the written contract should have referred to the term including the sale of the contents, and so, on the face of things, there was no valid agreement for the sale of the flat. Thus the Court of Appeal in this case did not avail itself of the collateral contract mechanism adopted in *Record* v *Bell*.

It is interesting in this case that the Court of Appeal took another approach to helping the purchaser in that it rectified the written contract so as to incorporate the furnishings term. Rectification is specifically permitted in s.2(4) of the 1989 Act, which states:

> Where a contract for the sale or other disposition of an interest in land satisfies the conditions of this section [s.2] by reason only of the rectification of one or more documents in pursuance of an order of a court, the contract shall come into being, or be deemed to have come into being, at such time as specified in the order.

Clearly, rectification is of great utility in such a situation – however, it does have its limitations since there must be some prior agreement between the parties before the contract is drawn up: *Joscelyne* v *Nissen* [1970] 2 QB 36; *Munt* v *Beasley* [2006] EWCA Civ 370. A contract does not necessarily have to be agreed, but there must be something that objectively demonstrates a common intention. Rectification cannot be used to incorporate into a document matters about which the parties had no intention at all. As stated in *Bidwell* v *Little* [2002] EWHC 2869:

> It is not the function of the court, when exercising its jurisdiction to grant rectification, to re-write documents for parties or to fill gaps about matters to which they have given no thought.

The position from a practical point of view is that the parties should include all terms as part of their contract since otherwise they may well fall foul of the s.2 requirements. Clearly, the recent decisions of the courts have not always seen fit to make use of the *Record* v *Bell* mechanism of the collateral contract.

So far, our examination of the fact that a contract must contain all the terms of the agreement appears to imply that all the terms must be contained within one document and certainly s.2(1) appears to envisage this. Nevertheless, it is possible for the contract to be formed in two or more documents provided that some terms expressed in some other document are expressly referred to in the main contractual document.

It is no longer possible to create contracts by correspondence by virtue of s.2(1) and (3). Prior to the 1989 Act, it was possible for an enforceable contract to come into existence by one party making an offer in a letter and the second party accepting the offer also by way of a letter. This point was considered in relation to the 1989 Act in the case of **Commission for New Towns v Cooper (Great Britain) Ltd** [1995] Ch 259. The facts of the case are complex, but essentially it concerned a passing of letters between the parties that purported to affirm an oral agreement. The Court of Appeal held that an exchange of letters did not constitute an exchange of contracts for the purposes of s.2. The court considered that any agreement reached between the parties had to be reduced into one primary document, signed by both parties, or two documents, signed by each party, which are then exchanged. Offers and acceptances contained within a series of letters or other correspondence are merely stages by which an agreement is reached and that agreement must then be reduced into writing.

The contract must be signed by both parties

An exchange of contracts is normally carried out by each party signing a copy of the contract and those copies are then exchanged – s.2(1) and (3). It is important that a signature means just that; the typing or printing of a name does not constitute a signature. In other words, as held by Denning LJH in **Goodman v J Eban Ltd** [1954] 1 QB 550, for a contract to be 'signed' a person 'must write his name with his own hand upon it'.

Firstpost Homes Ltd v Johnson [1995] 1 WLR 1567

The purchaser had prepared a letter to himself from the seller in which the seller had agreed to sell him land which was identified on a plan. The purchaser signed the plan, but not the letter itself. The letter had the purchaser's name and address on the top of it. The purchaser then sent both the letter and the plan to the seller, who then signed both documents. Following the death of the seller, the purchaser attempted to enforce the contracts against the personal representatives of the seller.

The Court of Appeal held that there was no contract, since the plan did not refer to the letter. Where there are two documents, the first document must refer to the second document, since the requirement of s.2 is that there must be one contractual document or two joined together. In this case, simply enclosing another document with the letter does not make it the same document as the letter. The Court of Appeal held that, since it was the letter that contained the terms of the contract and referred to the plan, it was this document that should have been signed by both parties. It was not sufficient that the purchaser was identified in the letter. The Court considered that merely typing or printing the name and address of one of the parties could not be regarded as a signature and referred to Lord Denning's statement in **Goodman v J Eban Ltd** above. The Court of Appeal therefore held that s.2(3) had not been complied with and that therefore there was no written contract within the requirements of s.2.

With regards to signatures, it should be noted that with the move towards electronic conveyancing, particularly electronic exchange of contracts, the courts have stated that electronic signatures will meet the requirements of the Law of Property (Miscellaneous Provisions) Act 1989 s.2(1).

Whilst it may sound somewhat obvious, the contract must, of course, be signed by the parties to the contract to be enforceable. Surprisingly, cases do sometimes arise that test this point. Thus in **Jelson Ltd v Derby County Council** [1999] 3 EGLR 91, a developer entered into a written contract with the county council to develop a site. Part of this contract required the developer to use part of the site for affordable housing and once this part of the development was completed it would transfer that part of the development to a housing association. The developer subsequently successfully pleaded that this part of the contract was void under s.2 on the basis that the housing association had not signed the contract as the prospective purchaser.

A similar situation arose in *R G Kensington Co. Ltd* v *Hutchinson IDH Ltd* [2003] 2 P & CR 195. Here the developer agreed to sell the developed part of the site to Kensington as the second claimant and the developer again pleaded that, as Kensington had not signed the contract, it was unenforceable. In this case, though, Neuberger J rejected this contention by the developer on the basis that s.2(3) required the contract to be signed by 'each party to the contract', not by each party to the prospective conveyance or transfer. The Court held that, as Kensington was not a party to the contract, there was no requirement for Kensington to sign it. Neuberger J thus distinguished his case from the *Jelson* decision; however, his logic has now been affirmed in *Nweze* v *Nwoku* [2004] 2 P & CR 33.

Exceptions to Law of Property (Miscellaneous Provisions) Act 1989 s.2

Not all contracts for the sale or other disposition of an interest in land have to comply with the requirements set out in s.2(1), (2) and (3). S.2(5) provides for certain contracts to be outside of these provisions. These are:

Short leases
S.2(5) provides that contracts to grant leases that fall within the Law of Property Act 1925 s.54(2) do not have to comply with the principal s.2 provisions under the Law of Property (Miscellaneous Provisions) Act 1989. Normally a *grant* of a lease must be contained within a deed. However, the Law of Property Act 1925 s.54(2) provides that leases for not more than three years can be granted informally by writing or even orally. It can be seen that it would be illogical to require a *contract to grant* such a lease to be in writing when a *grant* of such a lease does not require any formality at all. S.2(5)a therefore reconciles these two situations.

Contracts made in the course of a public auction
These types of contract have their own rules. However, in an auction the contract is concluded at the fall of the auctioneer's hammer and it would therefore be inconsistent with this type of sale for the requirements of s.2 to be imposed.

Contracts regulated under the Financial Services and Markets Act 2000
This exclusion from s.2 covers certain types of investment contract which include interests in land – for example, debentures in a limited company which provide a charge over the company's assets and property. Debentures are similar to mortgages, but it should be noted that regulated mortgage contracts do not fall within this exception and must comply with requirements of s.2.

'. . . and nothing in this section affects the creation or operation of resulting, implied and constructive trusts'
Normally, to create an express trust there must be evidence in writing to comply with the Law of Property Act 1925 s.53(1)b. Some trusts, namely resulting, implied and constructive trusts, are created by operation of law and are specifically excluded from the requirements of s.53(1)b by s.53(2). This is intended to ensure consistency with s.53(2). These types of trust have become an important vehicle for parties who rely on invalid contracts as a means of obtaining the assistance of equity in their transaction.

Contracts created before 27 September 1989 – Law of Property Act 1925 s.40

Prior to 27 September 1989, contracts relating to land could be made in writing or orally; however, the latter was not capable of enforcement unless the contract was *evidenced* by writing or by some act of past performance by virtue of the Law of Property Act 1925 s.40, which states:

1 No action may be brought upon any contract for the sale or other disposition in land or of any interest in land, unless the agreement upon which the action is brought, or some memorandum or note thereof, is in writing, and signed by the party to be charged or by some other person thereunto by him lawfully authorised.
2 This section . . . does not affect the law relating to past performance.

S.40 applied to the same types of transaction as those covered by the Law of Property (Miscellaneous Provisions) Act 1989 s.2 and the written contracts were entered into in broadly the same way – for example, by both parties signing the contract or by the parties each signing a copy and then exchanging them. In addition, however, it was possible for a written contract to come into existence by way of correspondence between the parties, which is no longer possible today.

It was also possible for valid contracts to be created orally prior to 27 September; however such contracts, whilst valid, were unenforceable unless supported by some writing in the form of 'some memorandum or note'. There was thus no prescribed form and all that was required was a written document of some sort that set out the terms of the contract and indicated that an oral contract had been made. It should be noted that there was no requirement that the document had to be signed by both parties as under the Law of Property (Miscellaneous Provisions) Act 1989 s.2; s.40 only required the memorandum or note to be signed by 'the party to be charged'. Thus, if X was enforcing a contract against Y, all he or she had to show was that Y had signed the document and not that X had done so him/herself.

Non-compliance with s.40 rendered the contract unenforceable, not void as now under the Law of Property (Miscellaneous Provisions) Act s.2. This difference could have some important effects, as can be seen in the case of **Low v Fry** (1925) 51 TLR 322 where the parties had entered into an oral contract for the sale of an estate in land. Following the agreement, the purchaser gave the vendor a cheque for part of the payment in land. Later, the purchaser had second thoughts about his purchase and instructed his bank to stop the cheque. Clearly, the vendor could not enforce the contract because of s.40 in that there was no signed memorandum or note and as such the contract was unenforceable, but could he sue on the cheque? It must be remembered that the contract per se is valid but unenforceable and therefore he could sue on the cheque as a promissory note, rather than the cheque representing consideration under the contract.

Just as the Law of Property (Miscellaneous Provisions) Act 1989 s.2 provided a number of exceptions, so too did the Law of Property Act 1925 in the form of past performance in s.40(2). This was originally an equitable doctrine that emerged after the Statute of Frauds 1677 and provides that, even if there was no written evidence of an oral contract, the contract may still be enforced if a claimant could demonstrate that they had nevertheless performed part of their obligation under the contract.

Typically, past performance might arise if, following an oral contract, the vendor allowed the purchaser to enter the land on the strength of the oral contract and make alterations to the property – for instance, install a new kitchen, in anticipation of a written contract being entered into. The vendor would then refuse to enter into the written contract and take the property back, together with the improvements. Since the contract was unenforceable, there was little the purchaser could do about this. It was at this point that equity stepped in since it was considered that such actions were unconscionable on the part of the vendor. Thus if a party to a contract relied on the contract by the promises made by the other party then equity would enforce the contract, despite the fact that no written note or memorandum had been provided.

The equitable doctrine of past performance was specifically preserved in the Law of Property Act 1925 s.40(2). In order to invoke the doctrine, a claimant had to demonstrate that their actions clearly evidenced the existence of a contract; that they had acted on the basis of the contract; and that it would be unfair if the other party reneged on the oral contract when the claimant had relied upon it: *Rawlinson v Ames* [1925] Ch 96.

The Law of Property (Miscellaneous Provisions) Act 1989 was framed against the recommendation of the Law Commission Report on Formalities for Contracts of Sale etc. of Land 1987 (Law Com No. 164) in which the Law Commission recommended that the doctrine of past performance should be abolished. It considered that there were other equitable remedies such as proprietary estoppel and constructive trusts that could provide relief in the circumstances in which past performance formerly operated. That said, the 1989 Act did not formally repeal the doctrine of past performance but merely repealed s.40. The problem is that s.40(2) merely stated that it did 'not affect the law relating to past performance' with the effect that, for some time afterwards, there was uncertainty as to whether the doctrine had survived following the enactment of the Law of Property (Miscellaneous Provisions) Act 1989. It is now recognised that the doctrine was indeed abolished and the courts turned their attention to other ways in which equitable relief could be utilised in the circumstances that were formerly covered by the doctrine of past performance, namely proprietary estoppel and constructive trusts.

Proprietary estoppel and constructive trusts

We have already seen that the Law of Property (Miscellaneous Provisions) Act 1989 s.2(5) specifically preserves the operation of constructive trusts as an exception to the operation of s.2; proprietary estoppel, however, represents a fifth exception to s.2 and arises where a person acts to their detriment on the basis that there is a valid and enforceable contract, although this is an incorrect assumption.

The issue of the application of proprietary estoppel was considered by the Court of Appeal in *Yaxley v Gotts* [2000] Ch 162.

Yaxley v Gotts [2000] Ch 162

In this case, the claimant was a builder who wanted to purchase the freehold of a house in order to refurbish it and convert it into flats. The claimant entered an agreement with a second defendant that the defendant would acquire the property and that the claimant would carry out the necessary work. In return, the claimant was to be given the ground floor of the house. No written contract was entered into. The matters went ahead as agreed. In fact, the property was purchased by the first defendant, who was the son of the second defendant, and the property was registered in his name. The first defendant gave the claimant no interest in the house and when, some years later, the parties fell out, the first defendant excluded the claimant from the property. The claimant sought a declaration that he was entitled to ownership of the ground floor of the house.

At first instance, the judge considered that, on the facts, proprietary estoppel arose and this was to be satisfied by the claimant taking a lease for 99 years rent-free.

The defendant appealed on the basis that the agreement was in fact a contract for the sale or disposition of an interest in land and as such should have complied with the Law of Property (Miscellaneous Provisions) Act 1989 s.2 and should have been made in writing.

Since the agreement had not been reduced into writing, it was void. The defendant also raised a rule of public policy that was referred to by the Court of Appeal in *Godden v Merthyr Tydfil Housing Association* (1997) 76 P & CR D 1 in which it stated that it is a 'cardinal rule that the doctrine of estoppel may not be invoked to render valid a transaction which the legislature has enacted to be invalid'.

Robert Walker LJ in *Yaxley v Gotts* stated at 174 that he had:

> ... no hesitation in agreeing with what I take to be the views of Peter Gibson LJ [in *United Bank of Kuwait v Sahib* [1999] Ch 107], Neil LJ and Morritt LJ (in *McCausland v Duncan Lawrie Ltd* [1997] 1 WLR 38], that the doctrine of estoppel may operate to modify (and sometimes perhaps even counteract) the effect of s.2 of the Act of 1989. The circumstances in which s.2 has to be complied with are so various, and the scope of the doctrine of estoppel is so flexible, that any general assertion of s.2 as a 'no go area' for estoppel would be unsustainable. Nevertheless, the impact of the public policy principle [the 'cardinal rule'] does call for serious consideration.

Robert Walker LJ was clear at 175 that Parliament's intention that the need for certainty as to formation of contracts for the sale and or disposition of an interest in land had to outweigh 'the disappointment of those who make informal bargains in ignorance of the statutory requirement'. He added, 'If an estoppel would have the effect of enforcing a void contract and subverting parliament's purpose it may have to yield to the statutory law which confronts it. . . .' Thus Robert Walker LJ considered that the claimant in this case could not rely on proprietary estoppel to avoid the requirements of s.2; however, he then went on to provide another means by which the claimant could succeed – a constructive trust.

We have seen that, in the exceptions set out in s.2(5), the operation of constructive trusts is expressly preserved and therefore may provide a vehicle for avoiding the requirement of writing in s.2. Whilst we will deal with constructive trusts in more detail later on in this book, it is worth explaining that such trusts arise by operation of law where equity regards a person's conduct to be unconscionable so that he or she is required to hold all or part of his or her property on trust for another person. There are a variety of ways in which constructive trusts can arise – however, one species is based upon what is known as 'common intention'. This arises where there is some agreement or understanding between the parties and one of them has acted to his or her detriment in reliance on the agreement or undertaking – i.e. the 'common intention' originally arrived at by the parties. Robert Walker LJ considered this type of constructive trust to be indistinguishable from proprietary estoppel, stating that equity enforces it because it would be unconscionable for the other party to disregard the claimant's rights. In this way, he sidestepped the rule of public policy argument put forward by the defendants by largely dressing up proprietary estoppel as a form of constructive trust, the operation of which had been expressly contemplated by Parliament in s.2(5), and dismissed the defendant's appeal.

Beldam LJ and Clarke LJ concurred with Robert Walker LJ's judgment though the former relied more on the reports of the Law Commission in justifying his stance. He pointed out that the Law Commission had been clear that its proposals for the 1989 Act were not intended to curtail equitable intervention by way of proprietary estoppel or constructive trusts. Beldam LJ stated at 191–193:

> The Commission's report makes it clear that in proposing legislation to exclude the uncertainty and complexities introduced into unregistered conveyancing by the doctrine of past performance, it did not intend to affect the availability of the equitable remedies to which it referred. The general principle that a party cannot rely on an estoppel in the face of a statute

> depends upon the nature of the enactment, the purpose of the provision and the social policy behind it. This was not a provision aimed at prohibiting or outlawing agreements of a specific kind, though it had the effect of making agreements which did not comply with the required formalities void. This by itself is insufficient to raise such a significant public interest that an estoppel would be excluded. The closing words of s.2(5) of the Act . . . are not to be read as if they merely qualified the terms of s.2(1). The effect of s.2(1) is that no contract for the sale or other disposition of land can come into existence if the parties fail to put it into writing; but the provision is not to prevent the creation or operation of equitable interests under resulting implied or constructive trusts, if the circumstances would give rise to them . . . In my view the provision that nothing in s.2 of the Act of 1989 is to affect the creation or operation of resulting, implied or constructive trusts effectively excludes from the operation of the section cases in which an interest in land may equally well be claimed by relying on a constructive trust or proprietary estoppel.

Thus Beldam LJ considered that, whilst the case could be decided on a finding of a constructive trust, there was equally no reason why a similar decision could not also be reached on the basis of proprietary estoppel, as the trial judge had, in fact, done. On this basis, Beldam LJ seems to be blurring the distinction between constructive trusts and proprietary estoppel and certainly the decision has been criticised on this basis. However, we will come back to this matter later on in this work.

Despite the effect of the decision in *Yaxley* v *Gotts*, it would be wrong to think in terms of past performance and proprietary estoppel or constructive trusts being the same thing; they are not, since the effects may be very different. Past performance formerly operated to enforce an oral contract against the other party. Proprietary estoppel or constructive trusts have a less certain effect. A court is likely to view the oral agreement and the circumstances in which proprietary estoppel operates as providing a means of enforcing an equity on a party despite the fact that the contract is void. The court is not, however, always going to enforce the oral contract made between the parties, though it is within its discretion to do so. This discretion may also operate to give a party a very different interest from what was intended under the contract – which, of course, was the situation in *Yaxley* v *Gotts* itself. This principle can also be seen in *Ottey* v *Grundy* [2003] EWCA Civ 1176 where Arden LJ stated that:

> . . . the purpose of proprietary estoppel is not to enforce an obligation which does not amount to a contract nor yet to reverse a detriment which the claimant has suffered, but to grant an appropriate remedy in respect of unconscionable conduct.

The boundaries between constructive trusts and proprietary estoppel are very unclear. S.2(5) refers to constructive trusts but not to proprietary estoppel and thus the question arises as to whether, in considering constructive trusts, one is, by implication, also including proprietary estoppel. But can proprietary estoppel also exist as an exception to s.2(1) in its own right? As we have seen in *Yaxley* v *Gotts*, both Beldam LJ and Clarke LJ supported this view. In a number of cases following *Yaxley* v *Gotts* – for example, *Shah* v *Shah* [2002] QB 35 – this view was also supported. However, in *Kinane* v *Mackie-Conteh* [2005] EWCA Civ 45 it was stated that estoppel could only apply in circumstances that also gave rise to a constructive trust, thus bringing proprietary estoppel inside the s.2(5) exception, but that proprietary estoppel in its own right could not amount to an exception. This point was considered by the House of Lords in *Cobbe* v *Yeoman's Row Management Ltd* [2008] 1 WLR 1752.

Cobbe v *Yeoman's Row Management Ltd* [2008] 1 WLR 1752

The claimant was a property developer and the defendant was the owner of a property that was ripe for development. The parties entered into an oral agreement that the claimant would obtain the necessary planning permissions and the defendant would then sell him the property. The developer would then carry out the requisite work and, once the units in the property were sold, both parties would receive sums from the sales.

The developer spent a considerable amount of time and money and eventually obtained the requisite planning permission. The defendant then went back on his word and demanded a considerably higher price from the developer. The developer refused to pay. However, since there was no written contract within the Law of Property Act (Miscellaneous Provisions) Act 1989 s.2(1), the agreement was void and the developer could not enforce the contract. The developer brought an action claiming that there was either a proprietary estoppel or a constructive trust in operation that gave him rights in the property. The developer also claimed undue enrichment and restitution on the basis of quantum meruit.

At first instance, and in the Court of Appeal, the developer's claim was upheld on the basis of proprietary estoppel, even though both the parties were fully aware that the oral agreement was not binding and that a written agreement would only be entered into in the future. The House of Lords reversed the decision of the Court of Appeal, addressing each claim put forward by the developer:

Proprietary estoppel

Lord Scott considered that proprietary estoppel could not arise where there was uncertainty as to what interest the developer believed he would acquire in the property. The requirement for proprietary estoppel is that there must be an expectation that a claimant would acquire 'a certain interest in land' and in this case this was not defined and was to arise out of further negotiations which would eventually culminate in a written binding contract. Until this had taken place, there was no certainty as to what interest the claimant would acquire. Secondly, proprietary estoppel arises where a person, the developer, claims rights in another's property, the owner's, and asserts that that person is barred from presenting 'some fact or facts, or sometimes, something that is a mixture of fact and law, that stands in the way of some right claimed by the person entitled to the benefit of the estoppel'. The House of Lords considered that the developer had not demonstrated what it was the owner was estopped from asserting or denying. Clearly, the owner cannot be estopped from asserting that the agreement was unenforceable for want of writing, since the developer did not claim that the agreement was enforceable anyway. Similarly, the owner cannot be estopped from denying that the agreement covered all the terms that needed to be agreed between the parties, since the developer did not claim that it did so. Thus Lord Scott considered that the content of the estoppel had not been identified. In the Court of Appeal, the conclusion in favour of proprietary estoppel was justified on the basis of unconscionable behaviour and, whilst Lord Scott considered that this might lead to a remedy, 'proprietary estoppel cannot be the route to it unless the ingredients for a proprietary estoppel are present'.

Thirdly, it was clear that the developer was fully aware that the agreement was not of a legally binding nature and, indeed, understood that the owner regarded himself as bound in honour only to enter into a formal written contract if planning permission was granted.

Both parties were experienced in property matters and knew perfectly well that neither was legally bound by the agreement. Lord Walker pointed out the principle laid down by the House of Lords in **Ramsden v Dyson** (1866) LR 1 HL 129 where Lord Cranworth stated at 145:

> If any one makes an assurance to another, with or without consideration, that he will do or will abstain himself from doing a particular act, but refuses to bind himself, and says that for the performance of what he has promised the person to whom the promise has been made must rely on the honour of the person who has made it, this excludes the jurisdiction of the courts of equity no less than the Courts of Law.

Thus an arrangement which is regarded as a 'gentleman's agreement' is not capable of giving rise to an estoppel.

Constructive trust

Lord Scott also considered whether, independently of a claim based on a proprietary estoppel, a constructive trust arose in relation to the owner's freehold land. Such trusts arise in many different types of situation; however, Lord Scott stated that simple unconscionable conduct by the owner is not sufficient to give rise to a constructive trust and thus give the developer a beneficial interest in the property. Lord Scott considered that, in order to achieve such an outcome, the developer would have to bring the case within a particular type of constructive trust where there is a joint venture. Such a situation arises if two or more persons agree to embark on a joint venture to acquire an identified piece of land in order to subsequently exploit it for the purposes of a joint venture. If one of the parties to the venture subsequently acquires the land in his or her own name, but with the agreement of the other parties who believe he or she is acting on behalf of the joint venture, then he or she will be regarded as holding the land on trust for all the members of the joint venture. Lord Scott, with reference to the decisions in **Pallant v Morgan** [1952] Ch 43 and **Banner Homes Group plc v Luff Developments Ltd** [2000] Ch 372, considered that these principles could not help the developer. He stated that joint venture constructive trusts arise where A *acquires* property as part of a joint venture with B. Thus a constructive trust cannot arise where B seeks to impose a trust on A where A held the property *prior* to the joint venture agreement.

Restitution/unjust enrichment

The House of Lords did not allow the developer to go away empty-handed, despite the fact he could not establish a proprietary claim in either proprietary estoppel or a constructive trust. Lord Scott considered that the developer was entitled to succeed with his in personam claims for unjust enrichment, for quantum meruit and for a restitutional remedy arising out of a total failure of consideration. Lord Scott considered the developer had established his claim on the basis of each of these, though he did not elaborate on the relationship between them. With regards to unjust enrichment, he did not consider that this was to be measured by the difference between the market value of the property without planning permission and the property with it. The planning permission did not create the development potential of the property, but merely unlocked it. The owner was unjustly enriched because it obtained the developer's services without having to pay for them. Lord Scott used the analogy of a locked cabinet with treasures inside it but with no key. The cabinet was valuable, so the owner did not want to destroy it and therefore he engaged the services of a locksmith. The locksmith then unlocked the cabinet to reveal the treasures within. Whilst the locksmith had hoped to be rewarded with a share of the contents, there was no agreement between the parties to this effect and, indeed, the owner hoped to reward him with a mere statement of gratitude. The owner, however, has been enriched by the locksmith's work – some would say unjustly so, since why should the locksmith work for nothing? The extent of this enrichment is no more than the value of the locksmith's services and everything else in the cabinet belongs to the owner. So too with the owner in this case, so the developer would receive no more than the price of his services. To this extent, the developer's reward is based on quantum meruit – that is, he gets as much as he deserves. Lord Scott stated that the developer had a total failure of consideration claim: 'where an agreement is reached under which an individual provides money and services in return for a legal but unenforceable promise which the promissor, after the money has been paid and the services provided, refuses to carry out, the individual would be entitled, in my opinion, to a restitutionary remedy'. The result of this is that the developer, rather than being awarded £2 million for the increase in the value of the property arising from the grant of the planning permission, was awarded £150,000 for his services in securing that permission.

Enforcement of contracts

Once the contract has been signed, the purchaser becomes the real and beneficial owner of the land and, of course, becomes liable to pay the purchase money when completion takes place. Virtually all contracts for the sale of land are specifically enforceable. This is based on the maxim that 'equity treats that as done which ought to be done' and, following the signing of the contract, that which 'ought to be done' is the completion of the sale, either by deed (in unregistered land) or by transfer and registration of it (in registered land). Equity thus treats the purchaser as having the benefit of the completion at that point. Of course they are not the *legal* owner since their name is not yet on the title, but they are the equitable or beneficial owner. Essentially, there are two owners at this point: the legal owner and the beneficial owner. In other words, the vendor, the legal owner, holds the property on trust for the purchaser, the beneficial owner.

The vendor, as trustee of the property for the purchaser, has certain obligations with regards to the purchaser. The vendor is bound to take reasonable care of the property and is liable if they damage the property or fail to safeguard the property with regards to the actions of third parties or natural events, such as flooding. The vendor is entitled to retain possession until completion but some other powers they would normally have are suspended so that if the property has a tenant in it the vendor is not allowed to change the tenancy, as held in *Rafferty v Schofield* [1897] 1 Ch 937.

As regards the purchaser, once the contract is signed, the risk in the property passes to them. Thus if the house is destroyed by a flood then the purchaser is still obliged to complete the purchase and pay the contract price: *Lysaght v Edwards* (1876) 2 Ch D 499. The result of this is that it is vital that the purchaser insures the property from the date of signing the contract, since at this point they bear the risk. It should be pointed out that under the Standard Conditions of Sale the vendor normally retains the risk until completion; however, it should be noted that the vendor is under no obligation to the purchaser to insure the property and therefore the purchaser should always arrange for the property to be insured.

Another subtle change that takes place on the signing of the contract is that the vendor, whilst still being the legal owner, no longer has an interest in realty, but in personalty. In contrast, the purchaser, while being the beneficial owner and having a personal interest in the form of their purchase money, now has an interest in real property, though the distinction between these different forms of property is not that relevant today.

If either party fails to carry out their obligations under the contract then a variety of remedies may be available to them.

Damages

Here the normal common law remedy for breach of contract applies. The usual measure is the foreseeable loss which the claimant has suffered as a result of not completing the transaction or if there has been some misrepresentation, subject to the requirement that the claimant might mitigate their loss.

Specific performance

This is an equitable remedy and, as such, is discretionary. The usual maxims and principles of equity apply so that, for instance, a court would not make an award if one party has 'dirty hands' as per the maxims that 'he who seeks equity must do equity' and 'he who seeks equity must come with clean hands'. Specific performance is only available if the subject of the contract, in this case the land, is unique. Otherwise an award of damages would be made. Equity, however, considers that every piece of property is unique – it would not be possible to go into the market place and buy a piece of land that is exactly the same as the one contracted for, as with a car, for instance. The remedy may be used to compel a defaulting party to carry out the terms of the contract.

Injunction

Again this is an equitable remedy and would be used to restrain a threatened breach of contract.

Rescission

Rescission is used where a party breaks a term of the contract that is a condition precedent. As we have seen, the vendor must prove that they have good title to the property and if they are unable to provide this then the purchaser may rescind the contract and withdraw from it. Rescission is a remedy that a party elects to take; they may wish to proceed with the contract and claim damages instead. The same principles apply as with any other type of contract and as such rescission is only available if restitutio in integrum is possible so that the parties are able to return to their original positions before the contract was entered into.

Rectification

This is the correction of an inaccurate written record of a parol (oral) agreement. Courts are reluctant to provide such a remedy as the parol evidence rule normally provides that evidence will not be admitted which seeks to add, vary or contradict the terms of a written contract. The use of the word 'parol' is somewhat deceptive since it applies not only to oral evidence but to any extrinsic evidence that seeks to have the above effect: *Joscelyne* v *Nissen* [1970] 2 QB 86. The rule in fact reinforces the objective nature of the modern contract in that the law is not so much concerned with the actual intentions of the parties as with their manifest intentions as expressed within the four corners of the contractual documents. Such reticence by the courts is understandable for two reasons. Firstly, if the parties have gone to considerable lengths to negotiate and reduce the contract into writing then why has the term in question been omitted? Secondly, if terms can be added to, removed or varied this would introduce uncertainty in the agreement so that it would not be possible for the parties (and third parties) and the courts to rely on the written contract.

Declaration

A declaration is a process whereby the parties might ask for the court to adjudicate on a meaning of a term of the contract or as to whether the vendor has proven a good title or not.

Contract to completion

Whilst this book is about land law, as we have already seen, this has a close association with conveyancy and all conveyancers have to have a sound knowledge of land law. It is worthwhile at this stage, before going on to look at the final stage of completion, to briefly consider the activities that conveyancers undertake once a contract has been signed. The primary aim at this stage is for the purchaser's solicitor to conduct various searches to discover if the vendor has a good title to the land and to discover if there are any third party rights – 'encumbrances' – affecting the property, such as easements, restrictive covenants, mortgages, etc. The steps taken to prove the title vary depending on whether the land is unregistered or registered, the process being rather more complex in the case of the former.

Unregistered land

As we have already seen, in order to prove title in unregistered land one has to go back to a good root of title which, by the Law of Property Act 1925 s.23, is a documentary root going back at least 15 years. The vendor must produce all the documents dealing with the title going back at least 15 years, though it could be considerably older than this. In the past, the purchaser had to produce an 'abstract of title', which is really a summary of the documents provided, along with a recital of various events that have occurred over this period, such as births and deaths that affect the title. It is, however, true to say that abstracts of title are now quite rare since, with the development of photocopying, instead of an abstract of title being provided, an 'epitome' of title is produced instead. An epitome of title is simply a list of all the relevant documents going back to the good root of title, to which photocopies of the various documents are attached.

On receipt of either the abstract or epitome of title, the purchaser's solicitor will examine these documents and consider the validity of the title conferred. Where an abstract of title is produced, the solicitor will not be able to confirm the title until completion, since it is then that the actual documents are produced representing the title deeds. Where an epitome of title is produced, the solicitor will generally be able to confirm the title at that point, since photocopies of the relevant documents will be produced at the same time.

The types of document that must be produced to support an abstract or epitome of title are conveyances on sale and by gift, death, grants or representation to deceased owners' estates, mortgages, discharge or legal mortgages, leases, documents arising prior to the good root of title that contain details of any restrictive covenants affecting the property, etc. It is well to remember that the process of producing all these documents going back to the good root of title is based on the fiction that the conveyancer at the time of the good root of title and all conveyancers subsequently have properly investigated the title. The good root of title therefore represents the long stop with regard to the investigation of the title. By virtue of the Law of Property Act 1925 s.44, a purchaser is bound by matters that would be revealed by the good root of title, but not by any matters that occurred before that root of title. Thus there are real dangers involved in not tracing the title back to the root since one would be bound by any encumbrances that are not revealed. If the purchaser's solicitor has any questions that are raised regarding the title, they will ask for clarification by way of 'requisitions on title' from the vendor.

As we saw in the previous chapter, the purchaser's solicitor will also make various other searches, such as in the Register of Local Land Charges and water and drainage enquiries. Most importantly, the solicitor will conduct a search of the Land Charges Register. Whilst the latter search is often conducted prior to the exchange of contracts in order to discover any potential problems that might arise, such as a seller's bankruptcy, Family Law Act 1996 rights and such issues as estate contracts, it should also be carried out again just prior to completion, so as to take advantage of the priority period of 15 working days. As we have seen, this protects the buyer against any further entries that may be made after the date of the search but before completion takes place. If it turns out that completion cannot be carried out during this priority period then the search will have to be repeated so that another priority period is obtained. The date on the search certificate setting out the priority period and the date on which it ends are of vital importance.

Registered land

If the land is registered then the proof of the title can be found in the Land Registry entry for that land. As we shall see in Chapter 5, registered title is a government-guaranteed title, so there is no need to perform the type of investigations required with unregistered land. The result is that, subject to restrictions on the title, the registered proprietor can provide conclusive proof of ownership of the legal estate that they hold in the land. That is not to say that the purchaser can simply accept that position as there are inquiries that have to be made.

Nowadays, the register can be searched by anyone, since, by virtue of the Land Registration Act 1988 s.1, from 3 December 1990 the land register has been open to public inspection, with the right to obtain copies of it. Prior to that, the purchaser was required to obtain the consent of the registered proprietor to inspect the register – though, on the sale or other disposition of the land, the registered proprietor was obliged to give the purchaser the authority to inspect the register. It should be noted, though, that even prior to 1990 it was possible for a member of the public to examine the index map, parcels index and the register of pending registration applications in order to discover whether the land was indeed registered land or not. Registration is therefore a very convenient process in the purchasing of land. However, there is a proviso here in that, if the land merely has a possessory or qualified title, then the title has to be investigated as for unregistered land. Furthermore, the title has to be investigated in order to discover any interests that override registration, such as adverse possession claims, but subject to these there is no need to examine the past history relating to the estate.

In registered conveyancing there is still a requirement for the purchaser to raise requisitions on title if their official search reveals matters that require further investigation, such as cautions. The purchaser will also be anxious to see the registered proprietor's response to any enquiries they may have raised as regards matters on the draft contract.

Finally, a few days prior to completion, the purchaser will make an official search of the register to ensure that no new entries have been entered since the initial perusal of the register. The official search certificate provides the purchaser with a priority period – that is, a period of 30 working days after the application for the search. This protection provides that, if the purchaser's application for registration of title for the property is delivered to the Land Registry during that period, any new entries are said to be postponed to him. The purchaser is thus protected from any last-minute entries that might appear on the register.

Completion

The final stage of the conveyancing process is completion, which is the formal process of transferring the legal title in the land from the vendor to the purchaser. In order to transfer the legal estate a deed is required. This requirement was set out in the Law of Property Act 1925 s.52(1), which states:

> All conveyances of land or any interest therein are void for the purpose of conveying or creating a legal estate unless made by deed.

Originally, a deed had to be 'signed, sealed and delivered' in order to be effective. Sealing formerly required hot wax to be dripped on the document, into which a seal or seal ring was impressed. The process was all very dramatic and added importance to the document, though for many years until 1990 the seal was simply a wafer of red paper that was glued on to the bottom of a document. The process of sealing was abolished by the Law of Property (Miscellaneous Provisions) Act 1989 s.1 which states:

(1) Any rule of law which:
  (a) restricts the substances in which a deed may be written;
  (b) requires a seal for the valid execution of an instrument as a deed by an individual; or
  (c) requires authority by one person to another to deliver an instrument as a deed on his behalf to be given by deed, is abolished.
(2) An instrument shall not be a deed unless:
  (a) it makes it clear on its face it is intended to be a deed by the person making it or, as the case may be, by the parties to it (whether by describing itself as a deed or expressing itself to be executed or signed as a deed or otherwise); and
  (b) it is validly executed as a deed by that person or, as the case may be, one or more of those parties.
(3) An instrument is validly executed as a deed by an individual if and only if:
  (a) it is signed:
    (i) by him in the presence of a witness who attests the signature; or
    (ii) at his discretion and in his presence and the presence of two witnesses who each attest the signature; and
  (b) it is delivered as a deed by him or a person authorised to do so on his behalf.

The requirement now is that the instrument only has to be signed as a deed by the person making it. Physical delivery of the document is no longer necessary; now once the instrument has been executed it is regarded as being legally binding.

It can be seen that the Law of Property (Miscellaneous Provisions) Act 1989 s.1(3) requires the deed to be signed by an individual for it to be validly executed and it must be signed in the presence of a witness who attests the signature. In some situations, however, an individual is not able to sign the deed personally – for instance, if he or she is too ill to sign. In these circumstances, the individual can direct or authorise someone to sign on his or her behalf and this will be equally valid, provided it is done in the presence of the individual and also in the presence of two witnesses who must each attest the signature.

As we will see later, the development of e-conveyancing will eventually end the requirement for a deed entirely, as the Land Registration Act 2002 s.91(5) provides that, where a document in an electronic form falls within the criteria set out in s.91(1)–91(4), the document will be regarded as a deed.

The completion process varies, depending on whether the land in question is unregistered or registered land.

Unregistered land

Once the purchaser has made all the necessary enquiries, as discussed above, it remains for the completion process to be finalised. Clearly, the purchaser must have made the appropriate arrangements for the payment of the purchase price, either from his or her own resources or by way of a mortgage. The vendor will then execute the deed in the format required above. Once payment has been received and cleared by a bank, unless a banker's draft is used (in these days of money laundering regulations cash is not acceptable), the keys will be handed over, along with the title deeds to the property. In the past that would have been the end of the transaction and, indeed, for the vendor it is. The purchaser, however, has some more work to do, since it is the purchaser's responsibility to convert the unregistered land into registered land. This work is compulsory when a freehold estate or a lease with more than seven years unexpired is sold, transferred by way of gift or mortgaged by way of first legal mortgage: Land Registration Act 2002 s.4(1). The need for first registration is also triggered where a person dies and the personal representatives of the deceased transfer the land to a beneficiary by way of an assent: Land Registration Act 2002 s.4(1)(a)(ii).

We have already seen that nowadays the whole country is an area of compulsory registration. It is vital that the purchaser undertakes this work since, by the Land Registration Act 2002 s.6 and s.7, if a purchaser fails to do this within two months of the date of the execution of the conveyance/deed, then the conveyance will be deemed to be void. This has the unfortunate effect that the legal estate will revert back to the vendor! The vendor, in such circumstances, will hold the property on a bare trust for the purchaser.

Registered land

Again, once the purchasers are satisfied with their enquiries, they must pay the purchase price and at this point the vendor will execute a transfer, using the appropriate Land Registry form (Form TR1). There are, of course, no title deeds in the case of registered land, so these do not need to be transferred to the purchaser. The main difference between completion in the case of unregistered land and completion in registered land is that, in the latter, by the Land Registration Act 2002 s.27(2), the transfer does not have the effect of conveying the legal title to the purchaser. To effect this, the purchaser must register the transfer at the appropriate District Land Registry within two months of purchase (Land Registration Act 2002 s.6) and until this is done the vendor remains the legal owner, albeit he holds the legal estate on a bare trust for the purchaser, in the case of freehold land or in the case of a lease for more than 7 years, as contract for a lease: Land Registration Act 2002 s.7(2) – just as he has since the contract was signed. Thus in registered land it is a deed plus registration that fully completes the transaction.

A word of warning needs to be given here. We have mentioned very briefly that the onset of e-conveyancing will soon be upon us to speed up the whole process of conveyancing. Under the proposals set out in the Land Registration Act 2002 s.93, a disposition of a registered estate or charge, or an interest which is the subject of a notice in the register will only have effect if it is made by means of a document in electronic form and if, when the document takes effect, it is electronically communicated to the registrar and the relevant registration requirements are met. The effect of this is that neither the equitable nor legal title will pass to the purchaser unless these formalities are carried out. It is intended that this process will remove what is termed the 'registration gap' which currently exists between execution of the transfer and registration.

As we have seen, we currently have a registration gap; however, a failure to register the transfer, apart from failing to transfer the legal estate, carries with it other very real dangers.

Registration of a disposition provides priority over certain earlier and all subsequent rights and thus failure to register may mean that such priority is lost. Additionally, failure to register the disposition invariably means that the name of the previous registered proprietor continues on the register and thus they remain capable to create rights on the land. Whilst these rights are, of course, subsequent rights to the registrable disposition, these rights of themselves may be registrable dispositions and thus take priority over the original registered disposition. An example of the dangers associated with the registration gap can be seen in the case of *Barclays Bank plc v Zaroovabli* [1997] Ch 321 where a bank was granted a mortgage in 1988 by the registered proprietor. The bank failed to register this change until 1994, with the effect that the bank had the mortgage in equity only. The mortgage contained a term that the registered proprietor, the mortgagor, should not grant a lease over the property without the bank's consent. In fact, the mortgagor did grant a lease over the property some two months after the creation of the mortgage, without obtaining the relevant consent. Later, in 1995, the mortgagor was unable to pay the mortgage and the bank sought possession of the property as a precursor to selling it in order to realise its security in the property. The question arose as to whether the bank was bound by the lease that had been granted by the mortgagor. It was held that the restriction on the mortgagor's ability to grant a lease only operated if the mortgage was a legal mortgage and since the bank only had an equitable mortgage the lease was valid. The bank was therefore bound by the lease when it eventually registered its mortgage as the lease had been granted prior to the legal mortgage being completed by registration.

The effect of non-registration had a profound effect on the bank in Zaroovabli since the tenant, as a Rent Act-protected tenant, was entitled to remain in the premises. The result was that the bank could not sell the property with vacant possession and that the value of the property was thereby substantially reduced. The principles that applied in the Zaroovabli case apply equally to situations that concern registered freehold and leasehold estates so that the failure to register allows the vendor's name as registered proprietor to remain on the title, with the result that, if he or she subsequently takes out a mortgage, say, on the property prior to the purchaser registering his or her title, the purchaser will be bound by that mortgage. This problem is likely to disappear with the onset of e-conveyancing since the process envisages that the transfer and registration of the transfer will take place at the same time so that the 'registration gap' will disappear.

Another interesting issue with non-registration of title on the purchase of a legal freehold or leasehold only providing the purchaser with an equitable interest arises where a competing equitable interest has been created in the 'registration gap'. As we have already seen previously, the rule is that 'where the equities are equal, the first in time prevails'. It will be recalled that this rule does not operate if the holder of the earlier equitable interest has acted inequitably. The Land Registration Act 2002 s.28, however, removes this latter principle, so that the issue of the conduct of the earlier equitable interest is now irrelevant, priority being determined simply by the date of creation: *Halifax plc and Bank of Scotland v Curry Popeck* [2008] EWHC 1692 (Ch).

Electronic conveyancing

The Land Registration Act 2002 replaced the Land Registration Act 1925 and heralded a new era in land law and the conveyancing process. The 2002 Act was a product of the Law Commission Report No. 271, *Land Registration for the Twenty-First Century: A Conveyancing Revolution*. Whilst the new Act retained many of the original features of the 1925 Act, it did make some profound changes, which we will look at more fully in the next chapter. The most radical change, however, is the introduction of e-conveyancing that is intended to speed up and make the conveyancing not only paperless but also more efficient. No doubt this is in response to the criticism often levelled at the conveyancing process that it takes far too long to expedite what should be a fairly routine process. E-conveyancing will be rolled out gradually but it will provide a radical and fundamental break with the past when fully implemented.

The provisions for the operation of e-conveyancing are set out in the Land Registration Act 2002 Part 8 ss.91–95. However, these are simply broad principles and the detailed rules for its operation will be installed by various Land Registry Rules.

The central plank of e-conveyancing lies in the establishment of a Land Registry communications network by the registrar for such purposes as he or she thinks fit relating to land registration or the carrying on of transactions which involve registration and are capable of being effected electronically. Schedule 5 of the 2002 Act sets out the regime for the operation of the Land Registry Network with regard to access for conveyancers, lenders, etc.

Summary

Introduction

- Conveyancing is the process whereby land is sold and bought and essentially, therefore, it is concerned with two matters:
  (a) Does the vendor have the right to sell the land? (To this extent the vendor has to prove their title to the purchaser)
  (b) Are there any third party rights affecting the land which might conflict with the purchaser's essential use of the land – for instance, restrictive covenants, easements or mortgages?

- The process is governed by two systems, unregistered and registered land:
  (a) Unregistered land is governed by the old rules pertaining to the common law and equity, as amended by the Land Registration Act 1925 and the Land Charges Act 1972.
  (b) Registered land is governed by the Land Registration Act 2002.

It is therefore essential to identify which system of conveyancing will apply to the land in question. Since 1 December 1990 the whole of England and Wales has become an area of compulsory registration under the Land Registration Act 2002. From 1997 the occasions which trigger compulsory registration have been increased and, where these arise, it is the duty of the seller to convert any unregistered land into a registered title.

Purchasing land – the processes outlined

Pre-contract negotiations

- This is the process where the parties meet for the first time and an agreement to buy and sell arises. This agreement is largely unenforceable and is merely a 'gentleman's agreement' from which either party can withdraw at anytime – hence the phenomena of 'gazumping' and 'gazundering'.

- As in any contract, the purchaser of land is subject to the overarching principle of 'caveat emptor'; however, if the vendor is asked any direct questions about the property they must answer honestly, though they are under no duty of care to disclose matters about which they are not asked: *McMeekin* v *Long* (2003) EG 120.

Exchange of contracts

- Whilst contracts for the purchase of land are just like any other contract, certain formalities are required to create an enforceable contract for the sale of land.
- Contracts entered into on or after 27 September 1989 must comply with the requirements of the Law of Property (Miscellaneous Provisions) Act 1989. Contracts entered into before this date must comply with the Law of Property Act 1925 s.40.

Contracts for the sale or other disposition of an interest in land created after 27 September 1989

- Such contracts must comply with the Law of Property (Miscellaneous Provisions) Act 1989 s.2 which requires that any sale or other disposition of an interest in land must be made *in writing*, contain all the terms of the agreement and be signed by both parties.
- Exceptions to the Law of Property (Miscellaneous Provisions) Act 1989 s.2 are:
  - Short leases: Law of Property Act 1925 s.54(2): leases for not more than three years.
  - Contracts made in the course of a public auction.
  - Contracts regulated under the Financial Services and Markets Act 2000.
  - The creation of resulting, implied and constructive trusts: these are excluded from the requirements or formality under s.53(1)b by s.53(2).

Contracts created prior to 27 September 1989

- Such contracts are required to be *evidenced in writing* by virtue of the Law of Property Act 1925 s.40:
  - *Low* v *Fry* (1935) 51 TLR 322.
  - Note the exception contained in the Law of Property Act 1925 s.40(2) which preserved the equitable doctrine of part performance: *Rawlinson* v *Ames* [1925] Ch 96.

Proprietary estoppel and constructive trusts

- Proprietary estoppel represents a fifth exception to the requirements of the Law of Property (Miscellaneous Provisions) Act 2002 s.2.
- Proprietary estoppel arises where a person acts to their detriment on the basis that there is a valid and enforceable contract, albeit their reliance is based on an incorrect assumption based on the representations of the other party: *Yaxley* v *Gotts* [2000] Ch 162; *Cobbe* v *Yeoman's Row Management Ltd* [2008] 1752.
- Enforcement of contracts: Virtually all contracts for the sale of land are specifically enforceable on the basis that 'equity treats that as done which ought to be done'.
- A vendor is bound to take reasonable care of the property and is liable in damages if they fail to do so.
- Once a contract is signed, the risk in the property passes to the purchaser: *Lysaght* v *Edwards* (1876) 2 Ch D 499.
- If either party fails to carry out their obligations under the contract then a variety of remedies may be available, such as: damages, specific performance, injunction, rescission, rectification or declaration.

Contract to completion

Unregistered land

- In order to prove his or her title the vendor must produce a documentary root of title going back at least 15 years: Law of Property Act 1925 s.23.
- A purchaser is bound by matters that would be revealed by the good root of title but not any matters that occurred before that root of title: Law of Property Act 1925 s.44.

Registered land

- If the land has a registered title then proof of the title can be found in the Land Registry entry for that land. The result is that, subject to restrictions on the title, the registered proprietor/vendor can provide conclusive ownership of the legal estate they hold in the land.

Completion

- In order to transfer the legal estate a deed is required: Law of Property Act 1925 s.52(1).
- The deed must be signed in the presence of a witness to be validly executed.
- With the development of e-conveyancing, the requirement for a deed as such will end: Land Registration Act 2002 s.91.

Unregistered land

- Once the completion process is finalised, the purchaser will have to convert the land into a registered title if a freehold estate or a lease with more than seven years unexpired is sold or transferred by way of gift or mortgaged by way of a first legal mortgage.

Registered land

- Here the vendor will execute a transfer using the appropriate Land Registry form (TR1).
- The transfer in registered land does not have the effect of conveying the legal title to the purchaser. To do this, the purchaser must register the transfer at the Land Registry within two months of the purchase: Land Registration Act 2002 s.6. Until this is done the vendor remains the legal owner, albeit on a bare trust for the purchaser: Land Registration Act 2002 s.7(2).

Electronic conveyancing

- The most radical change contained in the Land Registration Act 2002, following the Law Commission Report No. 217, is to make provisions for the introduction of e-conveyancing.
- The provision for e-conveyancing is set out in the Land Registration Act 2002 Part 8 ss.91–95.
- The Land Registration Act 2002 Schedule 5 sets out the regime for the operation of the Land Registry Network with regard to access for practitioners.

Further reading

Dixon, 'The Reach of Proprietary Estoppel: A Matter for Debate' [2009] 73 *The Conveyancer and Property Lawyer* 85

Fetherstonhaugh, 'Proprietary Estoppel and s.2 – Where Are We Now?' (2009) *Estates Gazette* 98

Griffiths, 'Proprietary Estoppel – The Pendulum Swings Again?' [2009] 73 *The Conveyancer and Property Lawyer* 141

Griffiths, 'Part Performance – Still Trying to Replace the Irreplaceable?' [2002] 66 *The Conveyancer and Property Lawyer* 216

Howell, 'Informal Conveyances and Section 2 of the Law of Property (Miscellaneous Provisions) Act 1989' [1999] 54 *The Conveyancer and Property Lawyer* 441

McFarlane, 'Proprietary Estoppel and Failed Contractual Negotiations' [2005] 69 *The Conveyancer and Property Lawyer* 501

Moore, 'Proprietary Estoppel, Constructive Trusts and s.2 of the Law of Property (Miscellaneous Provisions) Act 1989' (2000) *Modern Law Review* 912

Pawlowski, 'Oral Agreements, Estoppel, Constructive Trusts and Restitution' (2008) 12 *Landlord and Tenant Review* 163

Smith, 'Oral Agreements for the Sale of Land: Estoppels and Constructive Trusts' (2000) 116 *Law Quarterly Review* 11

Tee, 'A Merry-Go-Round for the Millennium' (2000) *Cambridge Law Journal* 23

Thompson, 'Oral Contracts for the Sale of Land' [2000] 64 *The Conveyancer and Property Lawyer* 245

5

Registered land

Aims and objectives

At the end of this chapter you should be able to:

- Know the historical basis on which registered land stands.
- Understand the principles on which registered land is founded.
- Recognise the form of the registers in registered land.
- Recognise and understand the classification of interests in registered land.
- Know and understand how the system of land registration operates.
- Understand the process by which the register may be altered.

Introduction

Historical perspective

Historically, as we have seen in relation to unregistered land, there has never been a central register as to who owns what in relation to land. Title to land was evidenced by the title deeds pertaining to a particular piece of land and it is these which described the type of estate held by the owner, or owners since a piece of land can have different types of owner, depending on the estate held and the encumbrances affecting the land, though even here some encumbrances did not appear within the title deeds. The main problem with proving title by reference to the deeds was the very real risk of one of the deeds becoming misplaced or lost, thereby breaking the links to providing good title. Even where all the deeds were, in fact, present, investigating the title and discovering encumbrances could be a complex and lengthy process in which persons dealing with the property relied on the accuracy of the previous conveyances. Thus not only was buying and selling property slow, it was also expensive and for many years the whole process had been subject to sharp criticism.

The answer to the criticisms levelled at unregistered conveyancing lay in the need to have a system of registered land. A variety of attempts can be traced, going back some 300 years, though the first meaningful attempts began with the Land Registry Act 1862 and the Land Transfer Act 1875 – the latter introducing the idea of a single land register. The system of registration introduced by these Acts was voluntary and so, unsurprisingly, there was little take-up by the estate owners. It was only with the Land Transfer Act 1897 that a compulsory system of registration emerged, though this only covered dealings in land in London. It was not until the passing of the Land Registration Act 1925 that a coherent system of compulsory registration for title to land emerged. This Act was poorly drafted and so a series of amending Acts were passed, which were themselves supplemented by Land Registration Rules. All these Acts have now been repealed by the Land Registration Act 2002 which will, no doubt, be also supplemented by the passing of Land Registration Rules from time to time. The result of these developments is that registered conveyancing is now the predominant means of conveying property. Though there remains a significant amount of unregistered land, this is quickly becoming rarer, though unfortunately anyone involved in conveyancing has to know this means of conveying property.

The basis of registered land

Registered land has two broad principles:

(i) to replace investigation of title with a state guaranteed title, and

(ii) to create a single register whereby a prospective purchaser can discover whether the vendor has the right to sell the title to the land and to discover what encumbrances affect the land.

Whilst these broad principles have been largely achieved, it is also true to say that not all encumbrances affecting a piece of land can be found on the register. The fact remains that the complexity of rights that can affect a piece of land are such that it is impossible to make provision for these on the register and thus these have to be investigated in much the same way as they are for unregistered conveyancing. Nevertheless, the system of land registration goes a long way towards encompassing the vast majority of interests.

Land registration is built around three principles:

The mirror principle

This means that the register of land ownership is intended to be an accurate and conclusive reflection of the ownership of title and the range of interests affecting the land in question. The corollary of this is that if rights that can exist in land are not registered – either because they cannot or do not need to be – then the register does not present an accurate reflection of the title to the land.

The curtain principle

Rights which a purchaser does not need to be concerned with are hidden behind the 'curtain' of registration. For instance, whilst a purchaser may be interested as to whether a trust affects the land, the purchaser is not concerned with the names of the beneficiaries within the trust and these are not therefore revealed on the register.

The insurance principle

The accuracy of the register is guaranteed by the state so that, if loss arises because of an inaccuracy on the register, compensation will be paid to the person who has suffered loss by relying on this register.

The land register is maintained by the Chief Land Registrar and, whilst there is one central Land Registry in London, there are also 18 district land registries. As we stated earlier, the register is, by the Land Registration Act 2002 s.66, open for inspection by the general public. Inspections are aided by the presence of an index, including an index map, that makes it possible to discover if a piece of land has a registered title or not: Land Registration Act 2002 s.68.

The form of the register

Whilst one talks of the 'register' in the Land Registration Act 2002, the expression can be something of a misnomer. Whilst it can refer to the entire register that is maintained by the Land Registry, it can also be used to describe the separate parts of the register, as well as the register for each individual title. This excessive use of the word can be confusing and it is well to be aware of the different contexts in which the expression is used.

It must be remembered too that it is not the land per se that is registered at the Land Registry, but the estate affecting the land. Thus a piece of land may have two or more entries – for instance, a piece of land, Blackacre, may have the freehold registered but it could have a number of leases affecting Blackacre also registered. Each individual estate is given an individual title number.

The entry for each individual estate that is 'entered' on to the land register is sub-divided into three individual sections, or registers, that provide different details, depending on which aspects of the land each register relates to. These registers are reflected in the format of the 'title information document' (see Figure 5.1).

The property register

This register identifies the estate to which the registration is made, thus it refers to either a freehold or leasehold estate. Whilst the entry provides a verbal description, it also refers to an index map. It should be borne in mind that any boundary descriptions are regarded as general only and do not provide exact boundary lines: Land Registration Act 2002 s.60. This register may also refer to any rights which *benefit* the land, such as restrictive covenants and easements that the registered proprietor enjoys over other land to which the registered estate is the dominant tenement. In the case of registered leasehold estates, the property register also provides a brief description of the lease.

The proprietorship register

This contains the name of the owner of the estate that is registered. In registered land the owner is described as the 'registered proprietor' – a useful way of distinguishing registered land from unregistered land. The proprietorship register also provides a description of the quality of the estate that the registered proprietor owns but we shall see more on this later. The proprietorship register also details any 'restrictions' that may be placed on the ability of the registered proprietor to dispose of the estate. Commonly, a restriction will limit or restrict the ability of the registered proprietor to dispose of the estate without the consent of a named individual or beneficiaries under a trust.

The charges register

This register contains details of any third party rights which *burden* the land – for instance, details of any mortgages over the property, easements which third parties enjoy over the property (e.g. rights of way) or restrictive covenants that limit the use of the land (e.g. a covenant not to use the property for commercial purposes). Not all third party rights are capable of being entered in the charges register and thus it is not possible to detect what these are by examining the register. In such circumstances, it may be necessary to physically inspect

Land Registry

Official copy of register of title

Title number XX231786 Edition date 28.09.2001

- This official copy shows the entries on the register of title on 24 APR at 09:42:40
- This date must be quoted as the "search from date" in any official search application based on this copy.
- The date at the beginning of an entry is the date on which the entry was made in the register.
- Issued on 24 Apr 2013.
- Under s.67 of the Land Registration Act 2002, this copy is admissible in evidence to the same extent as the original.
- For information about the register of title see Land Registry website www.landregistry.gov.uk or Land Registry Public Guide 1-*A guide to the information we keep and how you can obtain it.*
- This title is dealt with by Land Registry, Fylde Office.

A: Property Register

This register describes the land and estate comprised in the title.

GREATER MANCHESTER : SALFORD

1   (28.09.2001) The Freehold land shown edged with red on the plan of the above Title filed at the Registry and being 5 Spring Street, Eccles, (HD24 8SL).

2   (28.09.2001) The mines and minerals together with ancillary powers of working are excepted.

3   (28.09.2001) A Conveyance of 3 Spring Street dated 12 October 1960 made between (1) Henry Pennington and (2) John Torr contains the following provision:-

"IT IS HEREBY AGREED AND DECLARED

All drains gutters eaves and other apparatus used in common by the property hereby conveyed and the adjoining property numbered 1 5 and 7 Spring Street Eccles aforesaid shall be maintained at the joint expense of the owners thereof for the time being and the walls or fences separating the property hereby conveyed from the adjoining property Numbered 1 and 5 Spring Street aforesaid are hereby declared to be party walls and fences and shall be maintained and repaired at the joint expense of the respective owners thereof for the time being"

4   (28.09.2001) A Transfer of the land of 7 Spring Street dated 24 February 1986 made between (1) Kathleen Smith and Vera Margaret Jones and (2) Teresa Anna Thomas contains the following provision:-

"IT IS HEREBY AGREED AND DECLARED:-

All drains gutters eaves and other apparatus used in common by the property hereby transferred and the adjoining property Numbered 5 Spring Street, Eccles aforesaid shall be maintained at the joint expense of the owners thereof for the time being and the walls or fences separating the property hereby transferred from the adjoining property numbered 5 Spring Street aforesaid are hereby declared to beparty walls and fences and shall be maintained and repaired at the joint expense of the respective owners thereof for the time being."

Figure 5.1 Reproduced with kind permission of Land Registry, © Crown copyright 2001 Land Registry.

B: Proprietorship Register

This register specifies the class of title and identifies the owner. It contains any entries that affect the right of disposal.

Title absolute

1   (28.09.2001) PROPRIETOR: KATHLEEN SMITH of 3 Cornfield Road, Davyhurst, Manchester M60 5XD and JOHN MARTIN JONES of 2 Barley Road, Bluefield, Oldhampton OX3 7PW and ANTHONY NORMAN JONES of 8 Wheat Lane, Redfield, Rainhurst, Merseyshire WX1 7QW and PHILLIP HENRY JONES of 18 Grass Lane, Holmforth, Hudderstown HT39 7TX.

2   (28.09.2001) RESTRICTION: No disposition by a sole proprietor of the land (not being a trust corporation) under which capital money arises is to be registered except under an order of the registrar or of the Court.

3   (28.09.2001) The value as at 28 September 2001 was stated to be under £40,000.

C: Charges Register

This register contains any charges and other matters that affect the land.

1   (28.09.2001) The land in this title with other land is subject to a yearly rentcharge of £15.14s.0d. created by a Conveyance dated 10 October 1876 made between (1) The Honourable Egerton Algernon (2) The Right Honourable Francis Charles Granville and (3) William Hirst.

     The said Deed also contains covenants.

     NOTE:-Abstract issued with Certificate. Abstract filed under LX26891011. Rentcharge registered under YY275943.

     By the Conveyance dated 2 December 1876 referred to below the land conveyed was informally exonerated from this rentcharge.

2   (28.09.2001) The land in this title with other land is subject to a perpetual yearly rentcharge of £8.8s.0d. created by a Conveyance dated 3 October 1911 made between (1) Henry Hirst and Thomas Ball (2) Henry Hirst and others and (3) Henry Jones.

     The said Deed also contains covenants and reservations.

     NOTE 1:-Abstract issued with Certificate. Original filed.

     By a Conveyance of 3 to 9 (odd) Spring Street dated 6 November 1912 made between (1) Henry Jones the Elder (2) Henry Jones the Younger and (3) Fred Jones this rentcharge was informally apportioned as to £4.4s.0d. to the land thereby conveyed.

     By a Conveyance of 9 Spring Street dated 16 August 1984 made between (1) Kathleen Smith and Vera Margaret Jones and (2) Graham Arrowsmith and Eileen Grouch the said apportioned rent of £4.4s 0d. became exclusively out of the land thereby conveyed in informal exoneration of the land in this title and other land affected thereby.

Figure 5.1 (*cont'd*)

the land or to make inquiries of the registered proprietor. Such unregistrable charges clearly demonstrate that land registration does not provide the 'mirror' referred to earlier.

Prior to the Land Registration Act 2002, a copy of the above registers was included in a document called a 'land certificate' which was given to a registered proprietor as a record of his or her title. This document was not a title deed as with unregistered land but was simply evidence of the proprietor's title. It is the record of the official entry on the register that proves ownership of the land. Since the passing of the Land Registration Act 2002, land certificates are no longer issued and have been replaced by a 'title information document', which is an official copy of the register, and an official copy of the title plan. Again, these documents simply provide evidence of the proprietor's title. When there is a change to the title, the Land Registry supplies an 'official copy of register of title', which provides an up-to-date statement of the registers since it is quite possible that changes, such as additional mortgages, might have taken place after the registered proprietor took ownership of the property. Thus it is the official entry of the register that proves ownership.

Similarly, prior to the Land Registration Act 2002, if the land was subject to a mortgage, the Land Registry would issue a 'charge certificate' to the lender. To all intents and purposes, this was the same as the land certificate, apart from the heading on the top of the document. Charge certificates have now also been abolished under the Land Registration Act 2002.

It can be seen that the abolition of land certificates and charge certificates is in keeping with the drive towards e-conveyancing and electronic records.

The doctrine of notice and registered land

When we examined unregistered land, we saw that the doctrine of notice played an important role in dealings with the property as regards equitable interests. It is important at this stage of our examination of registered land to note that the doctrine of notice has no place in registered conveyancing and that the only kind of notice that is recognised is entry on the register. Thus if a right is capable of registration but it has not been so registered, it will not take effect so as to bind a purchaser for valuable consideration – unless it takes effect as an overriding interest. This will be discussed later.

The effect of abandoning the doctrine of notice is that the distinction between legal and equitable interests has now largely been discarded. The Land Registration Act 2002 provides four distinct categories of proprietary interest and it is more important to be able to discern into which of these four categories a person's interest falls. The Land Registration Act 2002 does sometimes make use of the legal/equitable distinction to determine the appropriate category, but it is the nature of the category that is important rather than the actual legal or equitable nature of the right per se.

The classification of interests under the Land Registration Act 2002

As we have referred to above, the Land Registration Act 2002 operates a different means of classifying interests from unregistered land where we identified legal estates, legal interests, commercial equitable interests capable of protection under the Land Charges Act 1972, family equitable interests that were capable of being overreached and equitable interests that may be 'protected' by the doctrine of notice. In registered land interests are divided into:

- registrable estates;
- interests created by a registrable disposition;
- interests capable of protection by registration;
- interests which override.

Registrable estates

Registrable freehold and leasehold estates

The Land Registration Act 2002 s.3 and 4 provides for registration of ownership of two legal estates and certain legal interests.

Registrable estates are interests that are capable of being substantively registered, by which we mean that they will each have their own entry in the Land Registry. Generally speaking, these correspond with those estates which are found within the Law of Property Act 1925 s.1(1) – that is, legal fee simple absolute in possession and the legal term of years absolute. The latter estate is cut down somewhat in the Land Registration Act 2002 since a term of years absolute is only registrable if it has more than seven years unexpired on the lease. The reason for the time period with regard to leases is that there can be so many short leases on a piece of land that the register would become overcrowded. In any event, the limited lifespan of short leases means that registration of title for such leases is largely irrelevant. Furthermore, the work involved in registering and then removing them was regarded as undesirable. Originally, in the Land Registration Act 1925, the period was, in fact, 21 years but the advent of computers and the introduction of e-conveyancing have meant that this period could be reduced to seven years. As e-conveyancing becomes more common, it is possible that the period could be reduced still further in the future.

In addition to the above estates, the Land Registration Act 2002 provides that certain leases, irrespective of their length, are capable of registration. Such leases are:

(i) leases to take effect in possession more than three months after the date of the grant of the lease – Land Registration Act 2002 s.4(1)d; and

(ii) leases to which the right to possession is discontinuous – Land Registration Act 2002 s.3(4).

The reason why the Act allowed for these two estates to be registered is that, because the tenant may not be physically in possession, it may be possible for the landlord to sell his or her estate to a purchaser who is unaware of the existence of the lease. The second type of lease above tends to relate to timeshare arrangements. The registration of such leasehold titles is made against the landlord's estate irrespective of the period of the lease.

Registrable legal interests

In s.2(a) the Act also makes provision for unregistered legal estates, which are interests of the following kinds:

(a) rentcharges;

(b) franchises;

(c) profits à prendre in gross;

(d) any other interests or charges which benefit or burden any registered estate.

The effect of the above is that owners of the above legal interests, such as profits à prendre, easements or charges by way of a legal mortgage, can be registered in the same way as the legal estates we have previously examined. It can be seen that the notion of a legal estate is much wider than that seen in unregistered land. This blurring effect is a consequence of the system of registration rather than a change in classification of such interests in land law itself. This process is a repeat of what was originally seen in the Land Registration Act 1925; however, it has two new additions: franchises and profits à prendre in gross.

A franchise in this context means a privilege granted by the Crown – for instance, to collect tolls on a toll bridge.

We have already seen that a profit à prendre is a right to take something from another's land – for example, wood or fish. Rights such as these can be 'appurtenant' to the land in question; that is, the benefit is owned by an adjacent property to the burdened land. On the other hand, such rights can exist 'in gross'; that is, the right stands alone and is not owned for the benefit of the adjacent property. For example, it is possible for an individual to own fishing rights over a piece of land even though he or she may live many miles away and hence their right to fish is held 'in gross'. Clearly, salmon fishing rights can be of great value but until the 2002 Act these were not capable of registration unless they were appurtenant to the burdened land.

Interests created by registrable disposition

The limited number of registrable estates seen above is supplemented by some subsidiary interests in land that are only capable of being created at law by registration. These rights, which are to be found in the Land Registration Act 2002 s.27, arose by way of a registrable disposition. The most important of these are charges by way of a legal mortgage and express legal easements. Thus a disposition (or transaction) in relation to these interests must be completed by registration. It should be noted that, unlike the registrable estates, the creation of these rights does not create a separate title on the register but involves the making of an entry on the register of title of the estate that is to be burdened or benefited by the relevant disposition.

Interests capable of protection by registration

This third category comprises those interests that do not have to be created by way of a registered disposition. Previously, under the Land Registration Act 1925, such interests were known as 'minor interests' which was probably a less confusing collective term for such interests; however; the Land Registration Act 2002 does not refer to them in this way. Most of these interests are equitable interests and loosely correspond with those equitable interests that were protected by registration as land charges under the Land Charges Act 1972 in unregistered land. This type of interest therefore covers restrictive covenants, equitable easements, estate contracts, etc. These types of interest may be protected by either a 'notice' or a 'restriction' so as to protect third party rights, though some types of interest must be protected in this way. By registering an interest in one of these ways, the Land Registration Act 2002 guarantees that the right will have priority over any rights subsequently created.

Example

Alfred is the registered proprietor of Blackacre, which he has agreed to sell to Alison. Alison now has an equitable interest arising from an estate contract – a specifically enforceable contract. Alison should now protect this right by an entry on the register. In this way, if Alfred subsequently sells the land to Richard then Richard will have notice of the entry and will know that he will be purchasing Blackacre subject to Alison's estate contract. On the other hand, if Alison does not protect her estate contract then Richard will not be bound by Alison's interest.

The Land Registration Act 2002 made some amendments to the types of interest that are capable of being registered, thus rights of pre-emption, which we saw in an earlier chapter were not classified as equitable interests, are now capable of being entered on the register. Remember, in registered land, the notion of whether an interest is legal or equitable is of less interest as the central purpose of the system is to reflect what interests affect the property (the 'mirror' principle). Similarly, some rights which were formerly dealt with by the doctrine of overreaching are now capable of being entered on the register.

Interests which override

Formerly, under the Land Registration Act 1925, interests which override were known as 'overriding interests' – a rather less clumsy title. Whilst we saw in the category above that the idea of entering interests on the register was to reflect the interests that affect the land, interests that override provide a significant crack in the so-called 'mirror' principle. The reason for this is that they are not capable of being entered on the register, yet nevertheless bind the land and purchasers of it. Undoubtedly, overriding interests (which we will call them despite the Act) present many problems to the system of land registration, particularly in the move towards e-conveyancing, since the only way they can be discovered is by making enquiries and/or inspecting the property itself. Overriding interests are contained in Schedules 1 and 3 of the Land Registration Act 2002.

Having summarised how the Land Registration Act 2002 classifies interests that arise under the registered land scheme, it remains for us to see how the system actually operates. We will come back to the interests above in more detail later on in this chapter, but for the moment it is sufficient that you have a broad idea of the building blocks on which the system of land is based.

How the system of land registration works

In considering how the system of registration under the Land Registration Act 2002 works, we will look at two aspects: when the land is first registered, and dealings with the land when it has already been registered.

First registration

Preliminary considerations

First registration arises where unregistered land is brought within the land registration system, the aim being to eventually bring all land within this system. First registration can arise in two ways: where the land is voluntarily brought within the system and where compulsory registration is required.

Voluntary registration

This arises under the Land Registration Act 2002 s.3 and arises where an owner desires to register their title though not obliged to do so at that moment in time. There are some advantages in electing for voluntary registration since there is a 25 per cent reduction in fees; there is a degree of protection offered to a registered proprietor from rights of adverse possession being established by a squatter; and, finally subsequent dealings with the property are easier when land is registered.

Section 3 of the Land Registration Act provides:

(1) This section applies to any unregistered legal estate which is an interest of any of the following kinds –
   (a) *an estate in land,*
   (b) *a rentcharge,*
   (c) *a franchise, and*
   (d) *a profit à prendre in gross.*

(2) Subject to the following provisions, a person may apply to the registrar to be registered as the proprietor of an unregistered legal estate to which this section applies if –
   (a) *the estate is vested in him, or*
   (b) *he is entitled to require the estate to be vested in him.*

(3) Subject to subsection (4), an application under subsection (2) in respect of a leasehold estate may only be made if the estate was granted for a term of which more than seven years are unexpired.

(4) In the case of an estate in land, subsection (3) does not apply if the right to possession under the lease is discontinuous.

(5) A person may not make an application under subsection (2)(a) in respect of a leasehold estate vested in him as a mortgagee where there is a subsisting right of redemption.

(6) A person may not make an application under subsection (2)(b) if his entitlement is as a person who has contracted to buy under a contract.

As can be seen from s.3(1) above it is possible to register not only a freehold or leasehold with at least seven years to run but also rentcharges, franchise and profits à prendre. It should be noted that there is no place for a purchaser of property to voluntarily register since such a person is compulsorily required to register in any event – s.3(6).

Compulsory registration

This arises under the Land Registration Act 2002 s.4 and provides that, when certain 'triggers' arise, the owner is obliged to convert the unregistered title into a registered title. Section 4 is quite a long section but it identifies three broad areas in which the 'trigger' event occurs:

(i) Where there is a transfer of the 'qualifying estate' for valuable or other consideration, by way of gift or as a result of a court order (s.4(1)(a)(i)) where there is a transfer by way of an assent – that is, where a personal representative transfers the estate to a beneficiary either under a will or by intestacy (s.4(1)(a)(ii)).

(ii) Where there is a grant of a lease out of a qualifying estate for a term of years absolute of more than seven years from the date of the grant for valuable or other consideration, by way of gift or as a result of a court order (s.4(1)(c)(i) and (bb)) where there is a grant out of a qualifying estate of an estate in land for a term of years absolute to take effect in possession after the end of a period of three months from the date of the grant (s.4(1)(d)).

(iii) On the creation of a first legal mortgage of a qualifying estate protected by deposit of title deeds.

By virtue of s.4(2) a 'qualifying estate' is an unregistered legal estate which is a freehold estate or a leasehold estate for a term which, at the time of transfer, grant or creation, has more than seven years to run.

One feature of the criteria for compulsory registration is that it is not only sales of qualifying estates for value that are caught by the requirement of compulsory registration, but also gifts of such estates and court orders. Equally, compulsory registration applies to assents by personal representatives to beneficiaries under a will, or an intestacy, but also where trustees pass the property to a person entitled under a Settled Land Act settlement. Furthermore, if a vesting order is made to a new trustee so that the new trustee becomes a legal owner of the land, compulsory registration must take place. Finally, where there is co-ownership of land and the trustees decide to partition the land between the different co-owners, compulsory registration must also take place.

The duty to apply for first registration

By s.6(3) if the requirement to register arises out of a transfer or a grant, the person responsible for ensuring that registration takes place is the new owner (i.e. the new purchaser or new tenant) and that person or persons will then become the registered proprietor: s.6(1).

Where the triggering event is the creation of a mortgage, the person normally responsible for the application for first registration is the mortgagor, as the owner of the mortgaged estate. By s.6(6) a mortgagee (i.e. the lender) is entitled to register the estate if the mortgagor does not do so. The mortgagee may do this whether or not the mortgagor consents.

The period for registration is two months, beginning with the date on which the relevant event occurs or such larger period as the registrar may provide. The registrar may extend the period if an interested person applies for an extension and the registrar is satisfied that there is good reason to grant one: s.6(4) and (5).

Effect of non-compliance with the requirement to register

It is vital that estate owners apply for registration within the two-month time limit set out in s.6(4) as s.7(1) provides that failure to do so will render the transfer or grant of the estate void. In such a situation, where the triggering event is a transfer, the estate will revert to the transferor, who will hold it on a bare trust for the transferee – s.7(2)a. Where the event is the grant of a lease or the creation of a mortgage, the grant or creation will take effect as a contract made for valuable consideration to grant or create the legal estate in question (i.e. an estate contract) – s.7(2)b. If the failure is one of registering a transfer to a new trustee, the title to the legal estate reverts to the person in whom it was vested immediately prior to the transfer – s.7(2)aa. The effect of these provisions is that the transactions in question will only take effect in equity.

We have seen that a freehold is technically a fee simple absolute in possession and the reverter arising in s.7(2)a could potentially have the effect of converting this into a determinable fee simple. This matter is addressed by s.7(4), which provides that the reverter in s.7(2)a is to be disregarded for determining whether the fee simple is a fee simple absolute.

It can thus be seen that failure to register can have serious consequences – not least the fact that the person responsible for applying for the registration will be liable to the other party for all the costs incurred in the re-transfer, re-grant or re-creation of the legal estate – s.8(a). Furthermore, the person responsible will be liable to indemnify the other party in respect of all liability reasonably incurred because of the failure to comply with the requirement of registration.

Failure to register can also have other consequences, as can be seen in the case of ***Sainsbury's Supermarkets Ltd*** v ***Olympia Homes Ltd*** [2006] 1 P & CR 17.

Sainsbury's Supermarkets Ltd v *Olympia Homes Ltd* [2006] 1 P & CR 17

In this case, the first defendant, Hughes, purchased an unregistered estate but failed to comply with the requirements for first registration as required by the Land Registration Act 2002 s.6(1) and (4). As per the operation of s.7(1) and (2), the legal estate then reverted to the vendor of the land. The effect of this was that the vendor held the legal title on a bare trust for Hughes, who consequently only had an equitable interest in the property. At this point, because the transfer was void, the land remained as unregistered. Hughes then granted an option to sell the land to Sainsbury's Supermarkets Ltd ('Sainsbury's') who, because the land is unregistered, should have protected this as a C(iv) land charge under the Land Charges Act 1972, but failed to do so. Later, Hughes found himself in financial difficulties and, following an application by one of his creditors, an order of sale of the land was ordered by the court. The land was then bought by Olympia Homes Ltd ('Olympia Homes') believing it was acquiring a legal estate though in fact it only acquired an equitable interest since this was all Hughes had. Olympia Homes then applied for and was granted first registration from the original vendor so that the legal estate became vested in Olympia Homes as the registered owner. Sainsbury's then attempted to enforce its option against Olympia Homes. The issue was that, if Olympia Homes had purchased the legal estate it would, as a purchaser of the legal estate for money or money's worth under the Land Charges Act 1972 s.4(6), have taken the estate free from Sainsbury's option. However, Olympia Homes had not acquired the legal estate but only the equitable interest held by Hughes. The effect of this was that s.4(6) had no application, Olympia Homes took subject to Sainsbury's option and the court ordered that a notice should be entered on the register protecting Sainsbury's option.

Cautions against first registration

If a person has an interest in unregistered land they may consider that their interest might be adversely affected by first registration of title and on this basis they may wish to oppose the application for first registration. It would be unusual to take such a course of action and really what they desire is for their interest to be protected on the register of title. Normally, if their interest is protected as a land charge under the Land Charges Act 1972 this would be discovered when the application for first registration is made and it would then be protected by an entry on the register of title under the Land Registration Act 2002.

The Land Registration Act 2002 (like its predecessor the Land Registration Act 1925) provides for additional protection for the person with the interest in unregistered land. By s.15 it is possible for the owner of the interest to enter a 'caution against first registration'. Such a caution has no substantive effect on the validity or priority of the interest claimed but rather it allows the owner of the interest an opportunity to substantiate their claim. Section 16 provides that, on receipt of the application for first registration, the registrar must give the owner of the interest (or cautioner) notice of the application and their right to object to it.

The process of registration

It has been stated already that one of the aims of the land registration system is to provide a state guaranteed title to the registered estate. In achieving this aim, the system requires the estate owner to prove their title – much as if the Land Registry itself were purchasing the land – and during this process the Land Registry will award a class of title, which is a measure of the quality of the estate. We will consider the issue of the quality of the estate in the next section but here we will briefly consider the process the estate owner has to go through in proving their title.

Clearly, once the title or estate has been registered, the registered owner may wish to sell the property at some point in the future and the purchaser at this time needs to be sure that the vendor's title is a good one and that they can rely on the entries in the register. In order to achieve this, the Land Registry will need to be satisfied that the estate owner actually owns the property in question and that it is free from any encumbrances or third party rights, other than those already disclosed. To achieve this, the process of registration is the same as if the Land Registry were actually purchasing unregistered land, so it will look for a good root of title going back at least 15 years, scrutinise all the appropriate title deeds and make all the relevant searches associated with unregistered conveyancing. It is highly likely that the Land Registry will be even more scrupulous in carrying out this process since it will henceforth be guaranteeing the title and will be liable to pay compensation for any losses suffered by a subsequent purchaser if it makes a mistake. Once the process is completed, the Land Registry will register the title and award a class or grade of title which informs a future purchaser of the quality of the estate that they are acquiring.

The classes of title

As we have already seen, the register of title is subdivided into three separate registers – the property register, the proprietorship register and the charges register. The first two registers tell a purchaser about the nature of the estate and who owns it. They will tell the purchaser whether he or she is acquiring a freehold or a leasehold estate, together with what rights benefit the estate in terms of easements, etc. As indicated in the previous section, the register will also disclose the class or grade of title awarded on first registration and thus provides an indication of the reliability of the title. Some titles may be regarded as sound, but others may be less so and may indicate technical defects whilst others may indicate that the title should be considered unreliable – for instance, if it is based on rights by adverse possession or squatter's rights.

The Land Registration Act 2002 s.9 and s.10 specify seven classes of title – three freehold clauses and four leasehold clauses – which we will now consider in turn.

Classes of freehold title

Absolute freehold title

The Land Registration Act 2002 s.9(2) states that a person may be registered with an absolute title if the registrar is of the opinion that the person's title to the estate is such as a willing buyer could be properly advised by a competent professional adviser to accept. This is not to say that the registrar may disregard any defects in the title if he or she is of the opinion that the defect will not cause the holding under the title to be disturbed. This provision provides a major advantage to the registered proprietor since registration has a curative effect of eliminating unimportant or technical defects on the title which future purchasers do not have to concern themselves with.

The effect of registration with absolute title is set out in s.11(3) and (4). Section 1(3) provides that the estate is vested in the proprietor, together with all interests that benefit the estate – such as easements which might give such things as rights of drainage or rights of way – in other words, rights over neighbouring land. On the other hand, s.11(4) provides that the proprietor takes the absolute title free from encumbrances except for:

- interests which are entered in the register;
- unregistered interests that override first registration ('overriding interests');
- interests acquired under the Limitation Act 1980 of which the proprietor has notice – that is, squatter's rights;
- rights of beneficiaries.

In addition, under s.11(5), if the registered proprietor is not entitled to the estate for their own benefit, i.e. they act as a trustee, or is not entitled solely for their own benefit, then they take subject to the rights of the beneficiaries under the trust.

It is worth looking at each of these different types of encumbrance in more detail.

Interests which are entered on the register The registrar, when he or she examines the title of the property on first registration, will note any encumbrances he or she comes across in the charges register so as to provide a complete statement of the encumbrances to which the property is subject. Depending on the nature of the encumbrance, these will be noted either as a 'notice' or as a 'restriction'. Under the Land Registration Act 1925, such interests were known as 'minor interests', but this expression is not used in the 2002 Act and, strictly speaking, should not be used. However, in order to identify these interests more readily, we will use this expression when we come to look at them in more detail, but bear in mind this proviso when we come to examine them. Broadly speaking, these are the types of interest that were formerly registrable as land charges under the Land Charges Act 1972 but there are others which we will consider in more detail later.

Unregistered interests that override first registration These encumbrances are to be found in the Land Registration Act 2002 Schedule 1 and comprise interests that will bind the registered proprietor despite the fact that they do not appear on the register at all and are therefore a potentially 'dangerous' form of interest. The list in Schedule 1 includes:

- leases for a term not exceeding seven years;
- interests of persons in actual occupation;
- legal easements or profits à prendre;
- customary and public rights;
- local land charges;
- mining and mineral rights;
- miscellaneous other rights, e.g. manorial rights.

Whilst these interests bind the registered proprietor even if they do not appear on the register, they may be entered on the register if the registrar is aware of them. It should be borne in mind that by s.7i(a) and the Land Registration Rules 2003 r.28 there is a duty on the applicant for first registration to inform the registrar if they are aware of them.

Interests acquired under the Limitation Act 1980 Generally, these are colloquially known as 'squatter's rights'. They arise if the owner loses possession of the property for whatever reason. In these circumstances, the owner of the unregistered land has a period of 12 years to bring an action to recover their land and if they fail to do so the squatter will be regarded as the legal owner and could register their legal title with the Land Registry – another reason why voluntary registration may be desirable. Originally, it was possible for the squatter to go out of possession and retain ownership of the land; however, the Land Registration Act 2002 has tightened up on the overriding effect of squatter's rights so that if the squatter is not in actual occupation of the land their 'rights' will not override first registration unless the proprietor has notice of them.

Rights of beneficiaries If the first registered proprietor is a trustee, he or she is bound by the rights of the beneficiaries within the trust of which he or she has notice.

Qualified freehold title
These are extremely rare and s.9(3) provides that an estate will attract such a class of title if the registrar is of the opinion that the person's title to the estate has been established only for a limited period of time – for instance, it may have a good root of title which is 10 years old instead of 15 – or if the title is subject to reservations which cannot be disregarded under s.9(3) – see above. Section 11(6) provides that registration with a qualified title has the same effect as registration with an absolute title, except that 'it does affect enforcement of any estate, right or interest which appears from the register to be excepted from the

effect of registration'. Thus if an applicant for first registration has indeed only investigated the title back 10 years, a subsequent purchaser of the title will be aware that there is a possibility that the title may be subject to defects in the title that were not discovered by the limited investigation conducted by the original applicant for first registration.

Possessory freehold title

Section 9(5) provides that a person may be registered with a possessory title if the registrar is of the opinion that the applicant is in possession of the land (or in receipt of the rents and profits of the land) by virtue of the estate and that there is no other class of title with which he or she may be registered. Such a situation could arise if all the title deeds are destroyed in a fire or lost and therefore there are no documents available for the registrar to be able to investigate the title. The problem with a possessory title for a purchaser is that there is always a danger of someone with a better claim to the property coming forward at a later date.

Classes of leasehold title

Absolute leasehold title

As with absolute freehold titles, s.10(2)a provides that a person may be registered with an absolute leasehold title if the registrar is of the opinion that the person's title to the estate is such as a willing buyer could properly be advised by a competent professional adviser to accept. Leasehold titles have an extra dimension, however, since a purchaser needs to be assured that the landlord (lessor) who granted the lease in the first place was actually entitled to grant the lease. The purchaser therefore needs to investigate the superior title held by the lessor to check that they have a good title to that superior estate. Thus s.10(2)b provides that the registrar also approves the lessor's title to grant the lease. If the lessor holds a registered freehold with title absolute, this should not pose a problem. On the other hand, if the lessor holds an unregistered freehold estate, they will have to make all the investigations appropriate to proving the lessor's estate and, if they are unable to satisfy the registrar, they will only be able to register their lease with a 'good leasehold title'.

By s.12(3) an absolute leasehold title vests the registered proprietor with a leasehold estate, together with all interests that subsist for the benefit of the estate. In addition, by s.12(4) the estate is vested subject to the following interests affecting the estate at the time of registration:

- implied and express covenants, obligations and liabilities;
- interests which are the subject of an entry in the register in relation to the estate ('minor interests');
- unregistered interests which override first registration ('overriding interests');
- interests acquired under the Limitation Act 1980 of which the proprietor has notice – that is, squatter's rights.

These are the same as those we looked at under the classes of freehold title.

The effect of this is that the owner of the absolute leasehold title is not only subject to express and implied covenants imposed by the lease but they are also subject to any encumbrances that affect the freehold title. Thus the lease is also subject to covenants that bind the superior title as well as the lease.

By s.12(5) if the registered proprietor is not entitled to the estate for their own benefit (i.e. they act as a trustee), or not entitled solely for their own benefit, then they take subject to the rights of the beneficiaries under the trust.

Good leasehold title

By s.10(3) good leasehold title is awarded if the registrar is of the opinion that the person's title to the estate is such as a willing buyer could be properly advised by a competent professional to accept. In this regard then a good leasehold title is the same as an absolute leasehold title – s.12(3); however, in the case of a good leasehold title there is no evidence as to the quality of the superior title which the registrar can approve. This has the effect that there can be no certainty that the landlord has the power to award a lease out of their own superior title.

Qualified leasehold title

By s.10(5) a person is registered with a qualified leasehold title if the registrar is of the opinion that the person's title to the estate, or the lessor's title to the superior title, has been established only for a limited period or is subject to such reservations that the registrar is unable to disregard them as being unlikely to disturb the title: s.10(4). Just as with qualified freehold title, these are extremely rare.

Possessory leasehold title

By s.10(6) a person is registered with such a title if the registrar is of the opinion that the person is in actual possession of land (or in receipt of the rents and profits of the land) by virtue of the estate and there is no other class of title with which they may be registered. As with possessory freehold title, this is likely to arise if the title deeds have been lost or destroyed and the only evidence of the estate arises from the applicant's possession of the land. Again these are extremely rare and virtually unheard of.

Upgrading the class of title

Freehold estates

It is possible for qualified and possessory freehold titles to be upgraded to an absolute title. By s.62(1) the registrar may enter a qualified or possessory title as an absolute if he or she is satisfied as to the title of the estate. In the case of qualified title, it may be that any defect on the title has been resolved. In the case of a possessory title, if the title deeds were lost the registrar may upgrade the title if the title deeds are subsequently found. Further, in the case of a possessory title, one should not ignore the potential of the limitation period under the Limitation Act 1980 'curing' the title. Thus if the registered proprietor under a possessory title is in possession of the property for 12 years without challenge, then any subsequent claim would become extinguished. In such circumstances, the registrar might upgrade the title to an absolute one.

Leasehold estates

It is possible for a good leasehold title to be upgraded to an absolute leasehold title if the registrar subsequently becomes satisfied as to the validity of the superior title. This is likely to occur if the superior title subsequently becomes registered – s.62(2). Thus registration of the superior title can have a curative effect on the leasehold title.

In the case of qualified and possessory leasehold titles, the registrar may upgrade these titles to a good leasehold title if he or she subsequently becomes satisfied as to the title of the estate – s.62(3)a. The registrar by s.62(3)b may upgrade these titles to an absolute leasehold title if he or she becomes satisfied both as to the title of the estate and as to the superior title.

As with freehold titles, in the case of a leasehold estate with possessory leasehold title that has been entered in the register for at least 12 years, the registrar may enter it as a good leasehold title if the registrar is satisfied that the proprietor is in possession of the land. This again displays the curative effect of the Limitation Act 1980 in that any claim to the land is extinguished once the 12-year limitation period has expired without any claim or challenge being made.

Subsequent dealings with a registered estate

So far it should have been noted that it is not the land itself that is registered but each individual estate appertaining to that land. Of course, there can be only one freehold registered, but this is not the case with leaseholds, provided they are created for more than seven years' duration. It is, however, possible for there to be a registered leasehold estate but no registered freehold estate – for instance, if the owner of the unregistered freehold granted a lease of, say, 10 years' duration.

It is possible for a registered estate to drop out of the system of land registration. This is likely to happen where a lease of 10 years comes to the end of its term. Thus, once a lease terminates, on the expiry of the terms it would cease to be a registered interest.

Generally speaking, once the freehold becomes registered, all subsequent dealings that derive from that freehold estate will also be registered – provided, of course, they are registrable interests. A lease of five years would, for example, not become a registered estate.

The Land Registration Act 2002 does nothing to curtail the powers of the owner of the registered land. Indeed, the powers of the owner are expressly preserved by the Land Registration Act 2002 s.23, which stated that the registered proprietor has:

> power to make a disposition of any kind permitted by the general law in relation to an interest of that description . . .

These powers are also extended to persons entitled to be registered as the proprietor by way of the Land Registration Act 2002 s.24.

The only limit set by s.23 is that the registered proprietor, whilst able to change the estate by way of a legal mortgage, is not able to create a mortgage by 'demise or sub-demise'. We will discuss this later when we deal with mortgages in Chapter 16.

Once an estate has been registered, dealings with it fall to be governed by the registered land rules if they are to be legally effective. Thus whilst the registered proprietor must use a deed as required by the Law of Property Act 1925 s.52(1) if he or she decides to sell it, lease it, grant easements or mortgages, compliance with the requirements set out in the Land Registration Act 2002 s.27 must be adhered to.

Registrable dispositions

The Land Registration Act 2002 s.27 sets out a list of dispositions that must be completed by registration. This list includes the following:

(a) A transfer of the registered estate (s.27(2)a).

(b) Newly granted leases (s.27(2)b& c) if they are:

- for more than 7 years; or
- to take effect in possession more than three months from the date of their grant; or
- they are for discontinuous periods; or
- they fall within certain provisions of the Housing Act 1985 (the right to buy); or
- they are leases of a franchise or a manor.

(c) Express creation of interests falling within the Law of Property Act 1925 s.1(2)a, b or e (s.27(2)d& e), that is:

- a legal easement or profits
- a legal rentcharge;
- a legal right of re-entry.

(d) Charges by way of a legal mortgage (s.27(2)f).

Failure to register a disposition above will mean that the dispositions will not take effect at law until the registration requirements are met and thus the unregistered disposition only creates equitable rights: s.27(1). There are often consequences, however, since registration of a disposition gives it priority over some earlier rights and thus a failure to register will mean that this priority will be lost. Similarly, registration of the disposition confers priority over all subsequent rights and thus failure to register will mean the loss of that priority.

It should be noted that once e-conveyancing becomes fully operational then by s.93(2) a disposition will only take effect when it is electronically communicated to the registrar and the relevant registration requirements are met. This means that the disposition will not even take effect in equity until the registration requirements are met.

The registration requirements

Registration takes effect by way of the appropriate entry in the registered estate concerned or, where necessary, the creation of a new registered estate or title. These requirements are set out in the Land Registration Act 2002 Schedule 2 as follows:

Transfer of the registered estate	The transferee must be entered as the registered proprietor.
Transfer of part of the registered estate	Details of the transfer must be entered in the register in relation to the registered estate out of which the transfer is made.
Grant of a lease	The grantee must be entered as the registered proprietor of the lease. In appropriate cases, this may also involve the creation of a new registered estate if the lease is a new one for more than seven years. Leases for less than seven years take effect as overriding and do not need to be registered. In addition a *notice* is entered in the charges register of the grantor's title.
Legal charges (mortgages)	These do not require a separate register, do not have their own titles and can only be entered on an existing registered title. They are registered in the charges register of the estate which they bind.
Legal easements and profits	Like charges, these do not have their own titles. If legal, they are registered on the title of the land that is *benefited* by the easement in the Proprietorship Register. In addition, a *notice* is entered on the title to be *burdened* by the easement in the charges register.
Legal rentcharges	In the case of a rentcharge granted for seven years or more, registration requires the creation of a new registered estate (like leases). If the rentcharge is for a period of less than seven years, registration is completed by entering of notices on the grantor's title in the charges register.

Interests which bind subsequent registered proprietors

The Land Registration Act 2002 s.29(1) provides:

> If a registrable disposition of a registered estate is made for valuable consideration, completion of the disposition by registration has the effect of postponing to the interest under the disposition any interest affecting the estate immediately before the disposition whose priority is not protected at the time of disposition.

It can be seen that the effect of s.29(1) on the priority of a registered estate over existing interests that affect the estate immediately prior to the disposition is dependent on a number of factors:

(a) The disposition must be made for valuable consideration and the registration requirements for completion of the disposition complied with.

(b) The priority of the existing interest will only be postponed (i.e. not enforceable) against the new registered proprietor if the existing interest is not protected at the time of the registration of the registrable disposition.

(c) If the owner of the existing interest has protected that interest at the time the registrable disposition is registered then the existing interest will be enforceable against the new registered proprietor.

Section 29(2) goes on to identify four categories of interest that a registered disposition will take subject to. Thus s.29(2) states:

> For the purposes of subsection (1), the priority of an interest is protected –
>
> (a) in any case, if the interest –
> (i) is a registered charge or the subject of a notice in the register
> (ii) falls within any of the paragraphs of Schedule 3, or
> (iii) appears from the register to be excepted from the effect of registration, and
> (b) in the case of a disposition of a leasehold estate, if the burden of interest is incident to the estate.

S.29(2)(a)(i) refers to registered charges (i.e. legal mortgages) that appear in the charges register and to interests protected by notice on the register (i.e. those that were formerly 'minor interests'). S.29(2)(a)(ii) refers to interests that fall within Schedule 3 (i.e. overriding interests). Both interests are protected by notice on the register and overriding interests will be discussed in more detail below.

S.29(2)(a)(iii) refers to interests that are precluded from registration with an absolute title (i.e. absolute freehold titles and absolute leasehold titles) in that they suffered from a disability that could interfere with the title or proprietor and therefore the proprietor could only be registered with a qualified or possessory title.

S.29(2)b refers to particular issues that affect leasehold titles. This provision talks about the burden of the interest being incident to the estate and would include such interests as restrictive covenants. In the case of a leasehold estate, the burden of a restrictive covenant cannot be registered by the entry of a notice. Usually, such restrictive covenants will be revealed when the lease is examined when the title is investigated and is thus given protection.

Certain leases are given additional protection in s.29(4). We have seen that leases not exceeding seven years are not registrable dispositions. S29(4) provides that the grant of such leases (i.e. legal leases) is to be treated as if the grant was a registrable disposition and the disposition was registered at the time of the grant, so providing an exception to the general rule in s.29(1).

By s.28 any disposition not made for valuable consideration will render the new registered proprietor subject to all pre-existing interests.

Having seen how the system of land registration works in terms of the registration of registrable dispositions, we now need to examine the various interests that will bind the registered title. As we have seen above, this falls into two broad categories:

- interests protected by entry on the register; and
- unregistered interests which override dispositions.

Interests protected by entry on the register

So far in our examination of registered land we have examined registrable estates that are required to have their own registers of title, although leasehold estates must also be protected by entry in the charges register of the title affected by the lease. We have also considered interests which, whilst not generating their own register of title, must nevertheless be entered on the Property Register of the estate to be benefited by the interest and also entered in the charges register of the estate to be burdened by the interest.

We are now going to move on to a third category of interest that must be protected by entry on the register. Broadly, these correspond with those interests which under the Land Registration Act 1925 were classed as 'minor interests' and in the context of unregistered land were protected as land charges under the Land Charges Act 1972. This was a concept that was found in the Land Registration Act 1924 s.70(1)g; however, the provision in the Land Registration Act 2002 gives no protection to persons who are in receipt of rents and profits since they are not necessarily in actual occupation of the land. Failure to register these 'minor interests' will result in a loss of priority and the interest being postponed to a subsequent disposition of the registered estate. Registration is thus extremely important if the interest is to be enforced against a new registered proprietor.

There are two ways in which third party rights can be entered on the register to provide protection for such rights:

- notices;
- restrictions.

Notices

This form of registration is used to protect those interests which under the Land Charges Act 1972 were protected as land charges, however it also includes a wider category of interests in registered land. The Land Registration Act 2002 s.32(1) thus states that 'notice is an entry in the register in respect of the burden of an interest affecting a registered estate or charge'. The approach of the Land Registration Act 2002, however, is not to provide a list of interests that must be protected by notice but rather to provide a list of interests that are *not* capable of being protected by the entry of a notice in the charges register. The most important of these excluded interests set out in s.33 are as follows:

1 Interests under a trust of land or a settlement under the Settled Land Act 1925. These are protected as 'restrictions', which we will discuss later.

2 Leases for a term of three years or less from the date of the grant, the title for which is not required to be registered.

3 Restrictive covenants made between a lessor and lessee, so far as relating to the demised premises.

By s.32(3) it should be noted that an interest that is the subject of a notice is not necessarily valid. What a notice does mean is that if the interest is valid then its priority is protected, so it will bind any purchaser for valuable consideration. Of course, the notice provides the purchaser with knowledge of the interest prior to taking the estate. In this way, the interest is enforceable against a subsequent registered proprietor – s.29(1), s.29(2)(a)(i), s.30(1) and s.30(2)(a)(i).

A notice may be entered by way of either an 'agreed notice' or a 'unilateral notice'. An agreed notice by s.34(3) may only be approved for entry by the registrar if it is made with the consent of the registered proprietor and the registrar is satisfied as to the validity of the applicant's claim. Such notices are usually entered if the registered proprietor has personally created the interest – such as an equitable mortgage or a restrictive covenant.

A 'unilateral notice' is entered without the consent of the registered proprietor – for instance, if he disputes the claim to the interest. If the registrar enters such a unilateral notice he must, by s.35(1), give notice of the entry to the registered proprietor. It should be noted that a unilateral notice must indicate that it is, in fact, a unilateral notice and it must indicate who the beneficiary of the notice is. The registered proprietor may then apply for the notice to be cancelled. Here the beneficiary of the notice must be notified of the application to cancel and informed of their right to object to the cancellation. If there is an objection to the application for cancellation by the beneficiary of the interest and the matter cannot be resolved, the registrar by virtue of s.73(7) must refer the matter to an adjudicator, who will then determine whether to cancel the notice or, if the beneficiary establishes a correct claim to the interest, that an appropriate entry be made on the register.

Entering a unilateral notice should not be considered lightly, since there is a real danger that such a notice that is subsequently cancelled could do real harm to the registered proprietor. This is recognised by the Land Registration Act 2002 s.77(1): a person must not enter a notice (or a restriction – see below) without reasonable cause. By s.77(2) a duty is owed to any person who suffers damage as a result.

Restrictions

The Land Registration Act 2002 s.40(1) defines the nature of a restriction as 'an entry in the register regulating the circumstances in which a disposition of a registered estate or charge may be the subject of an entry in the register'. A restriction therefore is entered on the Proprietorship Register of the affected title and indicates any limitations on the powers of the registered proprietor to deal with the registered estate. When a restriction is placed on the register, the registrar will not allow any entry in respect of a disposition otherwise than in accordance with the terms of the restriction, or modify the terms of the restriction: s.41(2).

Restrictions can apply in varying degrees. They can impose a complete prohibition on any disposition or may impose conditions on the kind of dispositions that can be made. A restriction can prohibit the making of a disposition indefinitely, or for a specified period, or until the occurrence of a specified event: s.40(2)b. The Land Registration Act 2002 does not specify the type of events that can be imposed but s.40(3) provides that, without prejudice to the generality of s.40(2)b, the events that may be specified include: the giving of notice, the obtaining of consent, and the making of an order by the court or registrar. Commonly, restrictions are used to ensure that if the registered estate is held in trust then, if the trustees decide to sell the property, they must first obtain the consent of the beneficiaries.

A restriction therefore informs a purchaser of any conditions that he or she must comply with in order to become a registered proprietor of the property. A restriction is therefore required with regards to the interests of beneficiaries under a trust of land or a strict settlement. Here the restriction provides that no registration of a registered disposition can take place unless any capital money is paid to two trustees or to a trust corporation. In this way, the disposition of the registered estate will ensure that any equitable interests under a trust are overreached so that the purchaser is assured that he or she will take free of those equitable interests when the disposition is registered.

The registrar has the power to enter a restriction under circumstances set out in s.42(1). Thus the registrar has the power to enter a restriction:

If it appears to him that it is necessary or desirable to do so for the purpose of –

(a) preventing invalidity or unlawfulness in relation to dispositions of a registered estate or charge,
(b) securing those interests which are capable of being overreached on a disposition of a registered estate or charges are overreached, or
(c) protecting a right or claim in relation to a registered estate or charge.

The registrar has the power to make an entry for a restriction on his or her own initiative. Notwithstanding this, a person may apply for the entry of a restriction under s.42(1) if:

(a) he is the relevant registered proprietor, or a person entitled to be registered as such proprietor,
(b) the relevant registered proprietor, or a person entitled to be registered as such proprietor consents to the application, or
(c) he otherwise has a sufficient interest in the making of the entry. (s.43(1))

If the registrar makes an entry under this provision without the consent of the registered proprietor, the registrar must notify the registered proprietor of the application and the registered proprietor's right to object to the entering of the restriction: s.45.

In some circumstances, the registrar is under an obligation to enter a restriction. Thus if the registrar enters two or more persons as registered proprietors, he or she must enter a restriction to ensure that the interests of the persons are overreached since in a co-ownership situation like this a trust of land arises automatically: s.44(1).

By s.46 a court may make an order requiring the registrar to enter a restriction if it appears to the court that it is necessary or desirable to do so for the purpose of protecting a right or a claim in relation to a registered estate or charge.

Finally, the Land Registration Act 2002 does not allow for any crossover between restrictions and notices. Thus s.42(2) and s.46(2) provide that no restriction may be entered for the purpose of protecting the priority of an interest which is, or could be, the subject of a notice.

Unregistered interests which override a registered disposition

Introduction

As we saw earlier under the Land Registration Act 1925, such interests were known as 'overriding interests' and it is still useful to use this expression in the vernacular, though they are not referred to as such in the Land Registration Act 2002. These types of interest can pose problems for a system that is supposedly based on registration since, despite the fact that they do not appear on the register, they will still bind a person taking title under a registered disposition, whether or not they are a purchaser for valuable consideration. The existence of such interests amounts to a significant crack in the mirror principle that the register should reflect the variety of interests that pertain to a registered estate.

The truth of the matter is that overriding interests under the Land Registration Act 1925 provided a vehicle which rendered the system of registration to a large degree unreliable, largely helped by judicial intervention. Thus it became possible for unregistered minor interests to re-emerge as overriding interests and binding, despite the fact they were unregistered, principally through the Trojan horse of the Land Registration Act 1925 s.70(1)g overriding interest by way of the rights of persons in actual occupation of the property. Some of these interests were enforceable, despite the fact that there had been an inspection of the land and significant enquiries made by a purchaser. It therefore comes as little surprise that Cross J in *National Provincial Bank Ltd* v *Hastings Car Mart Ltd* [1964] Ch 9 stated at 15:

> Overriding interests are, speaking generally, matters which are not usually shown on the title deeds or mentioned in abstracts of title and as to which, in consequence, it is not possible to form a trustworthy record on the register. As to such matters, persons dealing with registered land must obtain information outside the register in the same manner and from the same sources as people dealing with unregistered land would obtain it.

Clearly, the existence of overriding interests provided a significant hurdle to the Law Commission in its report *Land Registration for the Twenty-first Century: A Conveyancing Revolution*, (Law Com No. 271) in achieving its objective of designing a register that would be a 'complete and accurate reflection of the state of the title to the land at any given time, so that it is possible to investigate title to land online, with the minimum of additional enquiries and inspections'. Indeed, the presence of overriding interests posed a particular problem to the aspiration of the development of e-conveyancing that was meant to streamline and speed up a conveyancing process that had become notoriously slow and cumbersome, despite the presence of registered land under the Land Registration Act 1925.

The truth of the matter was that the existence of overriding interests brought the avowed original aims of a system of registered land into almost disrepute, to the extent that there were many calls for their abolition. On its part, the Law Commission gave such an approach serious consideration, but at the end of the day had to concede that this would not be possible, stating:

> The way in which the law on overriding interests has developed over the last seventy-two years has demonstrated that overriding interests are by no means only 'minor liabilities' . . . Most overriding interests do appear to have one shared characteristic, however, that is related to the orthodox explanation of them, namely that it is unreasonable to expect a person who has the benefit of the right to register it as a means of securing its protection.

Having conceded that it would not be possible to abolish overriding interests completely, the Law Commission embarked on a wholesale reform of this type of interest so as to minimise their impact. In order to achieve this objective the Law Commission adopted a number of strategies:

1 The number of rights that could exist in overriding interests were reduced and some rights reformed. So rights by adverse possession would not survive first registration unless the first registered proprietor had notice of them. At the same time, adverse possession was subject to reform where the title to the land was registered. Thus rights of squatters by adverse possession could no longer be binding as an overriding interest.

2 A number of overriding interests would be phased out after 10 years from the enactment of the Land Registration Act 2002. These interests are set out in paragraphs 10–14 of Schedule 1 and 3 of the Land Registration Act 2002 and include franchises, manorial rights, rents reserved to the Crown, non-statutory rights in respect of an embankment, or sea or river wall, and payments in lieu of titles. During this 10-year period s.117 provides that the beneficiary of the overriding interest could apply for their interest to become a caution against first registration if the land were unregistered or, if the land were registered, for the interest to be protected by an entry as a notice.

These interests cease to be overriding interests as from 13 October 2014 (10 years after the Land Registration Act 2002 came into force). The reason why a period of 10 years was selected was because there were fears that simply removing them would contravene the Human Rights Act 1998 in depriving the owner of their interest.

It should be noted that paragraph 16 rights in respect of the repair of a church chancel were added to the list of time-limited overriding interests by the Land Registration Act 2002 (Transitional Provisions) (No. 2) Order 2003.

3 Some overriding interests, whilst retaining their status as overriding interests, have been narrowed down and redefined. Overriding interests that fall within this group are to be found in paragraphs 1–3 of Schedule 3 and consist of short leases, interests of persons in actual occupation and easements and profits. We will focus mainly on these when we come to examine Schedule 1 and Schedule 3.

4 As we have already seen in the Land Registration Act 2002 s.71(a), a person applying for first registration of a subsequent registrable disposition must provide the registrar with information about any interest falling within Schedule 1. Similarly by s.71(b) a person applying for registration of a subsequent registrable disposition must provide the registrar with information about any interest falling within Schedule 3. In both these instances the registrar may then enter a notice on the register with respect of the interest falling within Schedules 1 and 3. In this way the unregistered nature of the overriding interests will cease.

5 On the arrival of e-conveyancing, most interests that are created will be conditional on their being simultaneously registered.

The anticipated overall effects of these strategies will significantly reduce the number of unregistered overriding interests. In the Law Commission Report at paragraph 2.27 it identified a much reduced number of overriding interests that were likely to survive. They are likely to comprise:

(1) Most leases granted for 3 years or less;
(2) The interests of persons in actual occupation where –
    (a) that actual occupation is apparent; and
    (b) the interest –
        (i) is a beneficial interest under a trust; or
        (ii) arose informally (such as an equity arising by estoppel);
(3) Legal easements and profits à prendre that have arisen by implied grant or reservation or by prescription;
(4) Customary and public rights;
(5) Local land charges; and
(6) Certain mineral rights.

The guiding principle in determining these is that interests should only exist as overriding interests if it is unreasonable to expect them to be protected in the register.

Interests that are overriding

The Land Registration Act 1925 provided one list of overriding interests that were contained in s.70(1). In that Act no distinction was made between overriding interests that arose on first registration and those that arose in subsequent dealings. Under the Land Registration Act 2002 this distinction is made and, although there is a great deal of commonality between the different overriding interests, there are also significant differences between them with regards to certain interests.

The Land Registration Act 2002 therefore provides two sets of overriding interests contained in Schedules 1 and 3. Schedule 1 contains interests that override first registration and Schedule 3 contains those overriding interests that override subsequent dealings with the registered estate. We will now proceed to examine both of these schedules.

Schedule 1 – Unregistered interests which override first registration

The reason why Schedule 1 is included in the Land Registration Act 2002 is that the applicant for first registration already has the legal estate vested in them as part of the unregistered land conveyancing process and is therefore already subject to those interests. First registration is only intended to bring the legal estate within the system of land registration and is not intended to affect the enforceability or priority of interests that have been established by the unregistered land process. This is, of course, not the case with subsequent registered land dispositions where there are issues of enforceability and priority possibly arising in relation to a new owner of the title. A further reason for this list is that it would be clearly incorrect to allow an owner to avoid an interest by applying for registration (either voluntarily or compulsorily) by way of the operation of s.29 (see above).

In Schedule 1 the overriding interests are set out in paragraphs 1–16. These comprise:

Para 1 – Leasehold estates granted for a term not exceeding seven years from the date of the grant.

Para 2 – An interest belonging to a person in actual occupation so far as relating to land of which they are in actual occupation, except for an interest under a settlement under the Settled Land Act 1925.

Para 3 – A legal easement or profit.

Para 4 – A customary right.

Para 5 – A public right.

Para 6 – A local land charge.

Para 7 – An interest in any coal or coal mine.

Para 8 – In the case of land to which title was registered before 1898, rights to mines and minerals created before 1898.

Para 9 – In the case of land to which title was registered between 1898 and 1925 inclusive, rights to mines and minerals created before the date of registration of the title.

Para 10 – A franchise.

Para 11 – A manorial right.

Para 12 – Crown rents.

Para 13 – A non-statutory right in respect of an embankment, sea or river wall.

Para 14 – Payments in lieu of titles.

Para 15 – A right acquired under the Limitation Act 1980.

Para 16 – A right in respect of the repair of a chancel.

As we have already seen, those interests in paragraphs 10–14 (in both Schedule 1 and 3) ceased to be overriding as from 13 October 2013. It should be noted that these interests will nevertheless continue to be binding if they are protected in the appropriate manner (see above). We will consider para 15, rights acquired under the Limitation Act, in each schedule separately.

The overriding interests that arise in Schedule 3 largely duplicate the interests contained within Schedule 1; however, there are significant differences with regards to the interests contained in paragraphs 1–3 and therefore we will look at these in Schedule 1 before considering the Schedule 3 interests.

Paragraph 1 – Leasehold estates granted for a term not exceeding seven years from the date of the grant

One key word here is 'grant' and thus this provision means that *legal* leases granted for a term not exceeding seven years will override first registration. The paragraph provides three exceptions to the overriding status of short leases. These are contained in s.4(1)(d), (e) or (f); that is, a grant of a lease out of unregistered land that is to take effect in possession after more than three months from the date of the grant; the grant of a lease out of unregistered land in pursuance of Part 5 of the Housing Act 1985 under the 'right to buy' provisions; and the grant of a lease out of unregistered land in circumstances where, in the private sector, the lease is granted to the landlord where the tenant's right to buy is preserved within the ambit of s.171A of the Housing Act 1985.

This provision has no application to equitable leases that are not created out of deed by signed writing although such equitable leases may be caught by paragraph 2 below if the tenant is in actual occupation of the premises at the relevant time. Legal leases that are created for three years or less and take effect in possession within the exception contained in the Law of Property Act 1925 s.54(2) will also override first registration even if created orally.

Paragraph 2 – An interest belonging to a person in actual occupation

Paragraph 2 states:

> An interest belonging to a person in actual occupation, so far as relating to land of which he is in actual occupation, except for an interest under a settlement under the Settled Land Act 1925.

This is an extremely important category that provides that the interests of persons who are in actual occupation of the land are overriding interests. This was a concept that was found in the old Land Registration Act 1925 s.70(1)g; however, the provision in the Land Registration Act 2002 gives no protection to persons who are in receipt of rents and profits since they are not necessarily in *actual* occupation of the land. Thus the land must actually be occupied by the holder claiming the overriding interest.

It is very important to understand that it is not actual occupation per se that gives rise to the overriding interest. The person claiming the overriding interest must prove that he or she has a proprietary interest in the land at first registration and that he or she is in actual occupation at the relevant time. Thus to claim the overriding interest there *must* be:

An Interest in Land + Actual Occupation = Overriding Interest

> ## Example
>
> A purchases Blackacre for £200,000. She is helped in gathering the purchase price by her son, X, who contributes £50,000. Blackacre is conveyed into A's name alone but, rather than live there herself, she allows X to live there with his girlfriend, Y. All goes well until, five years later, X and Y have an argument and X leaves. Since A's intention was to buy Blackacre for the purposes of providing a home for X and Y to live in, and since X and Y have now broken up, A decides to sell the property to B. X and Y attempt to establish an overriding interest against B. In this situation, X will not be able to establish an overriding interest because, whilst he has an interest in the property by virtue of his contribution to the sale price, he is not in actual occupation of Blackacre. Y will also not be able to claim an overriding interest since, whilst she is in occupation of Blackacre, she has no interest in the property. B can therefore take Blackacre free from any claims of X and Y.

Much of the debate about overriding interests arising out of an interest belonging to a person in actual occupation arose out of the application of the Land Registration Act 1925 s.70(1)g.

The Land Registration Act 1925 s.70(1)g defines the category of overriding interest as:

> The right of every person in actual occupation of the land or in receipt of the rents or profits thereof, save where enquiry is made of such a person and the rights are not disclosed.

In this respect, Schedule 1 paragraph 2 is little different from this provision. In examining the rights of a person in actual occupation, we need to look at the two components set out above in more detail.

An interest in land

The interest in land must be a proprietary right in land. A personal right, such as a licence to occupy the land, will *not* suffice. The position was first set out by Russell LJ in **National Provincial Bank Ltd v Hastings Car Mart Ltd** [1964] Ch 665, where he stated at 696:

> Section 70 in all its parts is dealing with rights in reference to land which have the quality of being capable of enduring through different ownerships of land, according to normal conceptions of title to real property.

That view of Russell LJ was confirmed in **National Provincial Bank Ltd v Ainsworth** [1965] AC 1175. In that case, the House of Lords decided that a wife, who was not entitled to a share of the ownership of the matrimonial home, did not have the right to occupy the home merely because of her status as a wife. Since she had not established a share of the ownership, she was incapable of establishing an overriding interest. Lord Denning had argued that she should have the protection of s.70(1)g based on a 'deserted wife's equity' in the property. This argument was rejected and Lord Wilberforce made it clear that s.70(1)g did not extend to all rights, irrespective of whether they were of a personal nature or not. Lord Wilberforce stated at 1261:

> To ascertain what 'rights' come within this provision, one must look outside the Land Registration Act and see what rights affect purchasers under the general law. To suppose that the subsection makes any right, of howsoever a personal character, which a person in occupation may have, an overriding interest by which a purchaser is bound, would involve two consequences: first that this Act is, in this respect, bringing about a substantive change in real property law by making personal rights bind purchasers; second, that there is a difference as to the nature of the rights by which a purchaser may be bound between registered and unregistered land; for purely personal rights including the wife's right to stay in the house (if

my analysis of this is correct) cannot affect purchasers of unregistered land even with notice. One may have to accept that there is a difference between unregistered land and registered land as regards what kind of notice binds a purchaser, or what kind of inquiries a purchaser has to make. But there is no warrant in the terms of this paragraph or elsewhere in the Act for supposing that the nature of the rights which are to bind a purchaser is to be different, excluding personal rights in one case, including them in another.

What follows from this is that it is only proprietary rights that are capable of becoming the subject of overriding status under the Land Registration Act 1925 s.70(1)g. Personal rights, such as licences, are incapable of having an overriding status. The principle can be seen in the case of **Strand Securities v Caswell** [1965] Ch 958.

Strand Securities v Caswell [1965] Ch 958

In this case, a sub-lessee of a flat, who had not registered his interest, allowed his stepdaughter to live in the flat rent free. The landlord then sold the flat, subject to the sublease. The sub-lessee then applied for registration of the sublease. The plaintiffs then applied for registration of the transfer to themselves, claiming that they took the flat free from the sublease. Their claim was based on two grounds: firstly, the application for registration of the sublease was void for failure to comply with the relevant formalities; and, secondly, the sub-lessee had no overriding interest under s.70(1)g.

With regards to the latter point, it was clear that the sub-lessee, Caswell, had a proprietary interest in the land; however, he was not in actual occupation. Nor could he establish occupation by reason of being 'in receipt of rents and profits' within s.70(1)g since his stepdaughter lived there rent-free – she was a mere licensee. On the stepdaughter's part, whilst she was in actual occupation of the flat, she had no proprietary interest. Thus the sub-lessee had the 'right' and the stepdaughter had the 'actual occupation' but neither had both the 'right' *and* the 'actual occupation'.

Many different types of interest can be sufficient, with actual occupation, to turn them into overriding interests. Options to purchase land qualify (**Webb v Pollmount** [1966] Ch 584); the right to rectify, i.e. alteration, of the register (**Malory Enterprises Ltd v Cheshire Homes (UK) Ltd** [2002] EWCA Civ 151) and a beneficiary's interest under a trust of land (**Hodgeson v Marks** [1971] Ch 892) all provide examples. Another important category of proprietary rights is those arising under resulting or constructive trusts as seen in **Williams & Glyn's Bank plc v Boland** [1981] AC 487, even though these rights are potentially overreachable. Having said this, once the right is actually overreached it ceases to be an interest in land: **City of London Building Society v Flegg** [1988] AC 54. The case of **Williams & Glyn's Bank plc v Boland** [1981] AC 487 is the seminal case on s.70(1)g and is therefore worthy of a closer look.

Williams & Glyn's Bank plc v Boland [1981] AC 487

In this case a husband and wife purchased a property with registered title together and, whilst both made contributions to the purchase price, the house was registered in the husband's name alone. The effect of this was that the husband had the legal title on trust for himself and his wife, in equal shares, as shown in Figure 5.2.

The husband then mortgaged the house to Williams & Glyn's Bank plc (the 'bank'). He did not consult with his wife, nor was she involved in any of the negotiations, the reason being that, as a beneficial owner only, she had no rights in this regard.

The husband then defaulted on the mortgage repayments and the bank sought possession of the property in order to realise their security.

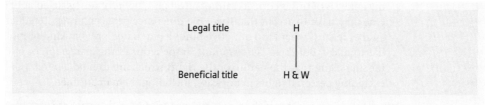

Figure 5.2

> The wife resisted the bank's claim on the basis that her equitable interest arising from her contribution to the purchase, coupled with her actual occupation, gave her an overriding interest under s.70(1)g and that the bank took subject to her interest. If that was the case, the bank could not exercise its statutory right to sell the property as to do this it would need vacant possession – which, of course, it could not get because of the wife's overriding interest.

The bank's arguments were formidable indeed since it argued that the three types of interest within the Land Registration Act 1925 – registered interests, minor interests and overriding interests – were all mutually exclusive. The bank argued that, if the wife had an interest, it was a minor interest, which was defined by the Land Registration Act 1925 s.3(xv) as an interest under a trust of sale (as it then was) that was capable of being overreached. If the wife had a minor interest, this was not capable of being an overriding interest and, furthermore, this minor interest should have been protected by an entry on the register. Since the interest had not been so protected, the bank argued it took free from it. The issue of actual occupation therefore did not arise at all.

It should be noted that, under a trust for sale, the wife's interest was not in the land but in the proceeds of sale, since under the doctrine of conversion (prior to its abolition by the Trusts of Land and Appointments of Trustees Act 1996), the presumption was that the property would be sold and so the interest was never in the land but always in the proceeds of sale. There was therefore no interest in land for the purpose of s.70(1)g.

The House of Lords held that, whilst Mrs Boland's interest under a trust for sale was a minor interest, one also had to look at her interest pending sale since this included a right to occupy the land. Mrs Boland therefore had two interests – her right in relation to the proceeds of sale, which was a minor interest, and her right of occupation, which was – or could be – an overriding interest. Once her minor interest became coupled with actual occupation, the wife's right became an overriding interest and thus bound the bank. As Lord Wilberforce stated at 507:

> It is clear, at least, that the interests of the co-owners under the 'statutory trusts' are minor interests – this fits with the definition in s.3(xv). But I can see no reason why, if these interests, or that of any one of them, are or is protected by 'actual occupation' they should remain merely as 'minor interests'. On the contrary, I see every reason why, in that event, they should acquire the status of overriding interests.

In Boland the wife's enforceability of her overriding interest by way of her equitable interest arose because the bank (remember the bank is a purchaser) failed to trigger the overreaching provisions by paying the loan money to two trustees. If it had done this then the doctrine of overreaching would mean that the equitable interests would be 'swept' off the land and into the proceeds of sale. The bank would take free of the equitable interests, which would cease to exist as equitable interests in the land. In such a case, whilst there may have been actual occupation, there would be no interests in land for the purpose of founding an overriding interest. The case of *City of London Building Society* v *Flegg* [1988] AC 54 illustrates the principle.

City of London Building Society v Flegg [1988] AC 54

In this case, Mr and Mrs Maxwell-Brown ('MB') were the registered proprietors of Bleak House and beneficial joint owners. The purchase price of the house was £34,000 of which £16,000 was raised by Mr and Mrs MB by way of a loan secured by a legal charge over the property. The other £18,000 was provided by Mr and Mrs Flegg, who were the parents of Mrs MB. The Fleggs occupied the house with their daughter and son-in-law. By virtue of their contribution to the purchase of the house, the Fleggs had a beneficial interest in the property. The position therefore looked like this:

Legal Title   Mr MB – Mrs MB
Equitable Title   Mr MB – Mrs MB and Mr F – Mrs F

Mr and Mrs MB subsequently created two further legal charges over the property and later created another legal charge in favour of the City of London Building Society with which they paid off the earlier two legal charges. Mr and Mrs MB then defaulted on the repayments to the building society, which then sought possession of the property. The Fleggs sought to rely on the decision in *Williams & Glyn's Bank* v *Boland* and claimed they had an overriding interest under s.70(1)g.

The House of Lords distinguished the case from the decision in *Boland* in that, since the building society had paid the mortgage to Mr and Mrs MB as trustees, all the beneficial interests were swept off the land into the proceeds of sale and the building society could take vacant possession of Bleak House free from the beneficial interests. The beneficial interests of the Fleggs were thus converted into the proceeds left over once the property had been sold and the building society had taken what was owed to it. In other words, they had no equitable interest in Bleak House that could form the basis of an interest in land for the purposes of s.70(1)g.

There is nothing to suggest that the law contained in Schedule 1 paragraph 2 has changed from the principles set out above.

Actual occupation

As we saw in relation to interests in land, there is nothing to indicate that the notion of actual occupation is any different in Schedule 1 paragraph 2 from that contained in s.70(1)g. This seems to have been confirmed in *Thompson* v *Foy* [2009] EWHC 1076 (Ch) by Lewison J and by the Court of Appeal in *Link Lending Ltd* v *Bustard* [2010] EWCA Civ 1754. Nevertheless, the concept of what constitutes actual occupation has been a somewhat troublesome one for the courts over the years.

In *Boland* the bank contended that, even if Ms Boland was capable of having an interest in the land that fell within s.70(1)g, she was, in any event, unable to claim an overriding interest as she was not in actual occupation of the premises – it was her husband who was in actual occupation.

The bank raised three arguments in attempting to demonstrate that the wife was not in actual occupation. Firstly, it alleged that, if the vendor (the husband) is in occupation, this excludes the possibility of occupation by others. Lord Wilberforce rejected this proposition in that, whilst such a proposition might be convenient for purchasers and intending mortgagees, there was no doctrine that the presence of a vendor with occupation excludes the possibility of occupation by others. Secondly, the bank suggested that the wife's occupation was nothing but a 'shadow' of the husband's. This was a somewhat archaic doctrine based on a doctrine of unity of husband and wife. The principle harks back to a time when the husband was the head of the household and the wife's position was 'tucked in' behind that of her husband. Lord Wilberforce considered such a doctrine to be 'heavily obsolete'. Finally, the bank suggested that, to come within s.70(1)g, the occupation in question must be inconsistent with or adverse to the title of the vendor. The bank suggested that this argument must exclude the wife from s.70(1)g since her occupation is accountable for by the presence of the husband. Again, this was rejected by Lord Wilberforce, who stated at 505:

> The appellant's main and final position became in the end this: that, to come within the paragraph, the occupation in question must be apparently inconsistent with the title of the vendor. This, it was suggested, would exclude the wife of a husband-vendor because her apparent occupation would be satisfactorily accounted for by his. But, apart from the rewriting of the paragraph which this would involve, the suggestion is unacceptable. Consistency, or inconsistency, involves the absence, or presence, of an independent right to occupy, though I must observe that 'inconsistency' in this context is an inappropriate word. But how can either quality be predicated of a wife, simply qua wife? A wife may, and everyone knows this, have rights of her own, particularly, many wives have a share in a matrimonial home. How can it be said that the presence of a wife in the house, as occupier, is consistent or inconsistent with the husband's rights until one knows what rights she has? and if she has rights, why, just because she is a wife (or in the converse case, just because an occupier is the husband), should these rights be denied protection under the paragraph? If one looks beyond the case of husband and wife, the difficulty of all these arguments stands out if one considers the case of a man living with a mistress, or of a man and a woman – or for that matter two persons of the same sex – living in a house in separate or partially shared rooms. Are these cases of apparently consistent occupation, so that the rights of the other person (other than the vendor) can be disregarded? The only solution which is consistent with the Act (s.70(1)g) and with common sense is to read the paragraph for what it says. Occupation, existing as a fact, may protect rights if the person in occupation has rights. On this part of the case I have no difficulty in concluding that a spouse, living in a house, has an actual occupation capable of conferring protection, as an overriding interest, upon rights of that spouse.

Lord Wilberforce concluded that the words 'actual occupation' are 'ordinary words of plain English and should, in my opinion, be interpreted as such . . . Given occupation, that is presence on the land, I do not think that the word "actual" was intended to introduce any additional qualification, certainly not to suggest that possession must be "adverse": it merely emphasises that what is required is physical presence not entitlement in law.'

The expression 'actual occupation' seems to suggest, according to Lord Wilberforce, that a physical presence is required on the land; however, this does not necessarily mean that personal presence is required. Essentially, actual occupation is a question of fact and, indeed, in ***Abbey National Building Society v Cann*** [1991] 1 AC 56 it was stated that ' "occupation" is a concept which may have different connotations according to the nature and purpose of the property which is claimed to be occupied' (per Lord Oliver).

Abbey National Building Society v *Cann* [1991] 1 AC 56

In this case, a mother attempted to claim a s.70(1)g overriding interest in her son's house by way of her rights under the 'right to buy' legislation. Clearly, she needed to prove that she was in actual occupation on the day she moved into the house, but in fact she was abroad on holiday on that day. Her belongings were moved into the house some 35 minutes before completion took place. The question was whether this very short period of actual occupation was sufficient to set up an overriding interest.

The House of Lords held that her period of occupation was not sufficient to support her claim of actual occupation so as to give her priority over the mortgagees. Lord Oliver, in particular, stated that actual occupation had to 'involve some degree of permanence and continuity which would rule out mere fleeting presence'. Thus, for instance, measuring up for new curtains or carpets could not amount to actual occupation.

Lord Oliver in *Cann* did, however, say that actual occupation did not necessarily require the physical presence of the person claiming the right. Thus, for instance, in *Kling v Keston Properties Ltd* (1983) 49 P & CR 212 it was held that actual occupation can arise by the parking of a car in a garage on a regular basis. Similarly in *Chhokar v Chhokar* [1984] FLR 313 it was held that, when a wife went into hospital for the delivery of her new baby, she was nevertheless in actual occupation when her husband sold the family home and left the country with the proceeds of sale. Temporary absence will not therefore prevent actual occupation from arising, even if the person is away from the premises on a repeated and regular basis, though there must be at least some evidence of the person's actual occupation by way of personal belongings or furniture. In *Kingsnorth Finance Ltd v Tizard* [1986] 1 WLR 783, a wife who had left the family home but visited on a regular basis to look after her children who remained with her husband could still establish an overriding interest by way of actual occupation.

What is important in establishing actual occupation is that there must be a sufficient degree of continuity and permanence. The presence of furniture is not per se sufficient to prove this; however, it would provide evidence of such continuity and permanence. Thus in *Link Lending Ltd v Bustard* [2010] EWCA Civ 1754 the claimant was detained for various lengthy periods in a residential home for psychiatric treatment, but was still able to claim actual occupation by virtue of the fact that the house was nevertheless her permanent home, containing all her furniture and belongings, and the fact that she continued to pay all the bills.

Coupled with the requirement of continuity and permanence is that there must be an ongoing intention to remain in the property. For this reason one does not lose the right of actual occupation by going on holiday for two weeks. What is not clear, however, is at what point a period of absence brings actual occupation to an end. In *Stockholm Finance Ltd v Garden Holdings Inc.* [1995] NPC 162 it was held that a claimant who was on holiday with her mother and absent from her fully furnished home for 14 months was not in actual occupation.

It would seem that actual occupation can also arise by way of an agent as discussed in *Lloyds Bank plc v Rosset* [1989] Ch 350.

Lloyds Bank plc v Rosset [1989] Ch 350

A husband and wife decided to purchase a property that was in a semi-derelict state. The property was not inhabitable until a certain amount of building work had been done. The vendors allowed the couple to start the renovation work before the contracts had been exchanged and so the couple engaged builders, who commenced work on the site. The work was supervised by Mrs Rosset, who made frequent visits to the site to undertake the management of the project. On completion, the property was mortgaged to the bank and the title was conveyed into the husband's name alone. The husband later defaulted on the mortgage repayments and the bank sought possession of the property.

Mrs Rosset resisted the claim on the basis that she had a beneficial interest in the house by virtue of a common intention with her husband and that this beneficial interest bound the bank by virtue of her 'actual occupation' at the date of the mortgage.

It was held at first instance that she would have an overriding interest under s.70(1)g. The bank then appealed to the Court of Appeal, which concurred with the decision at first instance. The majority of the court stated that there was no reason why a semi-derelict house could not be capable of actual occupation since, although no one had commenced living in the premises, the physical presence of the wife in supervising the building work amounted to actual occupation. In any event, the court expressed the view that the builders, either as agents or employees of the couple, were sufficient to establish Mrs Rosset's actual occupation. It should be noted that the House of Lords reversed the judgment of the Court of Appeal though, on the basis that Mrs Rosset had not established a beneficial interest in the property. Thus the decision of the Court of Appeal appears to be sound as regards actual occupation through agents or employees and, indeed, applied in the case of **Thomas v Clydesdale Bank plc** [2010] EWHC 2755.

In the **Rosset** case the property was uninhabitable without renovation work being carried out; however, the mere fact that a property is derelict or unusable is not necessarily a bar to the establishment of rights of actual occupation. In **Malory Enterprises Ltd v Cheshire Homes (UK) Ltd** [2002] Ch 216 it was held that the claimant could establish actual occupation by putting a fence around some derelict property.

It is not possible for a minor to be a person in actual occupation of premises, as held in **Hypo-Mortgage Service v Robinson** [1997] 2 FLR 271, where Nourse LJ stated:

> The minor children are there because their parent is there. They have no right of occupation of their own. As Templeman J put it in Bird v Syme-Thomson [1979] 1 WLR 440 '... they are there as shadows of occupation of their own parent ...'.

Even if the minor children are present in the property on their own for lengthy periods, this does not give them rights of occupation of the premises. There does not appear to be any consideration of children who get married at the ages of 16 or 17, however.

Prior to the passing of the 2002 Act, it was held by the Court of Appeal in **Wallcite Ltd v Ferrishurst Ltd** [1999] 1 All ER 977 that the claimant, who held part of the land as an underlessee but had an option to purchase the entire landholding held by the owner of the superior lease, could claim an overriding interest over the whole parcel of land. Schedule 1 paragraph 2 no longer allows the overriding interest to operate over the whole of the land, but only that under actual occupation. This represents a significant change from s.70(1)g in that a person's claim to an overriding interest under Schedule 1 paragraph 2 is limited 'so far as relating to the land of which he is in actual occupation'. Thus the overriding interest only relates to land actually occupied by the claimant, thereby reversing the decision of the Court of Appeal in **Wallcite Ltd v Ferrishurst Ltd** [1999] 1 All ER 977.

Suffice it to say that, as far as Schedule 1 paragraph 2 is concerned, the overriding interest claimed must be in existence immediately before the owner makes first registration of the title at the Land Registry. If the owner can establish that the overriding interest did not exist at the time of first registration then the Land Registration Act 2002 cannot be used to revive that interest. In that regard it should be remembered that there is no 'registration gap' on first registration – the applicant is merely registering what he or she already owns and thus if the overriding interest is not established before the application it can clearly have no effect on the applicant.

We saw earlier that Schedule 1 paragraph 2 removes the possibility of someone who is merely in receipt and profits from establishing occupation; however, the Land Registration Act 2002 also places other restrictions on the establishment of an overriding interest under this head. Thus a person claiming an overriding interest cannot establish a Schedule 1 paragraph 2 overriding interest in respect of an interest under a settlement governed by the

Settled Land Act 1925. In the case of such interests, the proper method of protection is by way of a restriction under s.40. It should be noted that, by s.33(a)(ii), such interests are prohibited from being entered as a notice.

There are other excluded interests that cannot be overriding interests under this head. These are set out in Schedule 11 and include, inter alia, a spouse's rights of occupation of the matrimonial home under the Family Law Act 1996; rights arising under the Landlord and Tenant (Covenants) Act 1995; rights conferred on a person by or under an access order under the Access to Neighbouring Land Act 1992.

Other than the excluded interests above, *any* proprietary right is capable of being an interest for the purpose of Schedule 1 paragraph 2. Often such interests will be a beneficiary's interest under a trust of land or equitable leases but really any proprietary right will suffic – but NOT personal rights, for example a licence over land.

Paragraph 3 – A legal easement or profit

Such rights will override first registration since, being legal rights and being in existence prior to registration, they follow the maxim 'legal rights bind the world'. Such rights on first registration will inevitably cease to be overriding interests as they will be entered in the register – the burden being registered against the burdened or servient land and the benefit being registered against the benefited or dominant land. The reason for this is that the registrar, in investigating the title prior to first registration, will detect the existence of such rights from the title deeds and then make the appropriate entries in the registers.

Equitable easements or profits cannot amount to overriding interests with respect to first registration. As with paragraph 2, the issue here is that the equitable easement should already be in existence and binding on the owner applying for first registration at the time of application. For an equitable easement to be binding on the owner, it should have been registered as a D(iii) land charge under the Land Charges Act 1972 s.2(5)iii. This would have been revealed to the registrar when investigating the title prior to first registration and on discovery he or she would have protected the equitable easement or profit as a notice on the newly registered title. If the equitable easement had not been registered as a land charge then it would be void in any event and could not be revived by way of first registration in the form of an overriding interest.

A word of warning is required here since interests that were overriding prior to the Land Registration Act 2002 will continue to be so. The impact of this in terms of equitable easements means that, following the case of *Celsteel Ltd* v *Alton House Holdings* [1986] 1 WLR 512, such easements could derive overriding status under the old law and as such will have the same effect here. In *Celsteel* it was held that if an equitable easement was 'openly exercised and enjoyed' at the time the servient land was transferred then it would fall within the LRA 1925 s.70(1)a and bind a purchaser. This decision, whilst widely criticised, was upheld by the Court of Appeal in *Thatcher* v *Douglas* [1996] 146 NLJ 242.

Schedule 3 – Unregistered interests that override subsequent dealings

As already indicated, these interests are fairly similar to unregistered interests that override first registration; however, there are some important differences with regards to the rights of persons in actual occupation (Schedule 3 paragraph 2) and easements and profits à prendre (Schedule 3 paragraph 3). As with our examination of Schedule 1, we will focus on paragraphs 1–3.

The other 'permanent' overriding interests found in Schedule 1 remain the same in Schedule 3 – customary rights (paragraph 4); public rights (paragraph 5); local land charges (paragraph 6) and rights to mines and minerals (paragraphs 7–9). As indicated earlier, paragraphs 10–14 and 16 are time-limited and by s.117 ceased to exist when the schedule came into force on 13 October 2013. Since this date they must be entered as a notice in the burdened registered title. We will consider paragraph 16, rights of adverse possession, separately. Thus the aim of the Law Commission and the Land Registration Act 2002 of reducing the number of overriding interests and eliminating overriding interests that are undiscoverable is upheld.

Before proceeding with the examination of the first three paragraphs of Schedule 3, it is important to remember the effect of s.29 in that, where the land is transferred to a new registered proprietor for valuable consideration, the priority of an existing interest will be postponed to him or her unless it is registered as a notice or it is an overriding interest under Schedule 3. Where the newly registered proprietor has not given valuable consideration, then that person takes subject to all existing interests: s.28.

Paragraph 1 – Leasehold estates granted for a term not exceeding seven years from the date of the grant

This provision is virtually analogous to that contained in Schedule 1 so that a legal lease granted for a term not exceeding seven years will override a registered disposition. Note that, by virtue of s.29, these leases automatically bind the new registered proprietor.

Legal leases for a longer period than seven years will be substantively registrable with their own title. The period of seven years is a significantly reduced period compared with that formerly contained in the Land Registration Act 1925 s.70(1)k, which applied to leases not exceeding 21 years. However, computerisation and structural changes in the Land Registry have meant that it can deal with more leasehold titles than previously entered on the register. In s.118 there is a provision to allow for the period of seven years to be reduced still further in the future.

Just as in Schedule 1 paragraph 1, certain types of lease are excepted. These are set out in s.4(1)d, (e) or (f), as before. In addition, paragraph 1(b) includes an extra class of excepted lease being a 'lease the grant of which constitutes a registered disposition' – that is, by s.27(2)c a lease granted out of a registered franchise or manor.

Equitable leases, just as in Schedule 1, do not fall within this provision and must be protected by a notice on the register, unless caught by paragraph 2 below – actual occupation. Similarly, leases for three years or less that are created may be legal leases even if made orally and, as such, are overriding interests within this paragraph.

Paragraph 2 – An interest belonging to a person in actual occupation

Paragraph 2 states:

> An interest belonging at the time of the disposition to a person in actual occupation, so far as relating to land of which he is in actual occupation, except for
>
> (a) an interest under a settlement under the Settled Land Act 1925;
> (b) an interest of a person of whom inquiry was made before the disposition and who failed to disclose the right when he could reasonably have been expected to do so;
> (c) an interest –
>   (i) which belongs to a person whose occupation would not have been obvious on a reasonably careful inspection of the land at the time of the disposition, and
>   (ii) of which the person to whom the disposition is made does not have actual knowledge at that time;

(d) a leasehold estate in land granted to take effect in possession after the end of the period of three months beginning with the date of the grant and which has not taken effect in possession.

It is clear that paragraph 2 under Schedule 3 is a great deal more restrictive than its counterpart in Schedule 1. Certain things remain the same, thus:

- the meaning of 'actual occupation';
- the claimant must have a proprietary interest in the land occupied;
- 'actual occupation' only extends to land actually occupied by the claimant;
- persons who are in receipt of rents and profits have no protection;
- a person cannot claim an overriding interest in respect of an interest under a settlement under the Settled Land Act 1925 nor the other excluded interests set out in Schedule 11.

Despite these similarities, there are a number of matters that require further examination in evaluating the operation of Schedule 3 paragraph 2.

The time of actual occupation

The Land Registration Act 2002 s.74 provides that an 'application for registration in relation to a disposition [is] required to be completed by registration'. Thus registration is effective from the date of registration, not the date of completion of the transaction. The effect of this is that notices or restrictions are still capable of being protected, even after the date of completion. Pre-2002 Act, this date was also adopted for the validity of overriding interests by the House of Lords in *Abbey National Building Society v Cann* [1991] 1 AC 56 and it has now been embodied in the Land Registration Act 2002 s.29.

In relation to overriding interests as regards actual occupation, however, *Cann* held that the date for establishing actual occupation was the date of completion. This obviously made sense, since a person purchasing property would only make inquiries as to adverse interests affecting the property up until this date, since the transaction, for all intents and purposes, would have been settled, bar registration, at this date. If an overriding interest were to occur after this date, the new owner would have no means of controlling this, despite being fully committed to the transaction by paying for the property. This is the so-called 'registration gap' which we examined previously. Schedule 3 paragraph 2 now makes it clear that actual occupation must exist at the date of completion (i.e. 'disposition') for the overriding interest to arise. In *Thompson v Fog* [2010] 1 P & CR 308 Lewison J considered that the actual occupation must also continue until the time of registration. Some commentators reject such a view as it makes little sense, since a purchaser is most unlikely to make further inquiries once completion has taken place and the transaction has fundamentally been executed. In any event, this problem will disappear with the onset of e-conveyancing since the deed of transfer will be prepared and actuated electronically, with transmission to the land registry for registration taking effect simultaneously, thus eliminating the 'registration gap'.

Discoverability

We have already seen that in Schedule 1 actual occupation has to be proven as a fact and that this is found by looking at all the circumstances surrounding the case. The same principles apply to actual occupation in Schedule 3. Schedule 3, however, goes further and places certain restrictions on the ability of the holder of an interest to claim an overriding interest that will override a registered disposition. We have seen that, as far as possible, adverse rights were to be brought onto the register. Clearly, overriding interests do not fall within such a category of rights. The Law Commission therefore wanted to ensure that any adverse rights that were not on the register should be easily discoverable, which would be extremely important as the movement towards e-conveyancing gained pace. In attempting to achieve this objective, the Law Commission introduced two conditions on the ability of an interest holder in actual occupation to claim an overriding interest.

The first condition in paragraph 2(b) states that the interest holder cannot claim an overriding interest where inquiry was made of the interest holder 'before the disposition and . . . [the interest holder] failed to disclose the right when he could reasonably have been expected to do so'. This therefore provides the transferee/purchaser with a statutory defence, however; the inquiry must be made of the holder of the interest and it is that person's responsibility to disclose their interest. This defence places a responsibility on the purchaser to inquire of the vendor as to who is in actual occupation and then the purchaser must make inquiries of those persons as to what interests they have. Some care is required here since it is the *interest* that must be declared, not why that person is in occupation. The reason for this can be seen in the case of **Webb v Pollmount** [1966] Ch 584 where a tenant had a lease which gave him an option to purchase the reversion from his landlord. Hence the actual occupation arose out of his lease but it was the option that provided the interest for the overriding interest to arise. It should be noted that if the *vendor* declares the interest of a person in actual occupation this will not prevent the holder of the interest from claiming the overriding interest. For example, if a property is in the name of the husband and he declares the interest of his wife, who is in actual occupation, the wife could still claim the overriding interest. This provision also assumes that the holder of the interest is actually able to identify that they have an interest. To that extent, the condition provides that the holder of the interest is only bound to disclose their interest if they 'could reasonably be expected to do so'. But how is the expression 'reasonably' to be interpreted? Would it be reasonable to expect Mrs Bustard in **Link Lending Ltd v Bustard** [2010] EWCA Civ 1754 to declare her interest when she was undergoing psychiatric treatment? Would it be reasonable to expect the potential interest holder to even recognise that they had a proprietary interest? The full extent of the defence will only be known once there is an overlay of judicial impression from the courts.

The second condition, unlike the first, is completely new and had no basis within s.70(1)g. As we have seen, this arises in paragraph 2(c)(i) and (ii) and provides that a person will not have an overriding interest by way of actual occupation if the interest belongs to a person whose occupation would not have been obvious on a reasonably careful inspection of the land at the time of the disposition and of which the person to whom the disposition is made does not have actual knowledge at that time. The effect of this is to place a limitation by which unregistered (i.e. overriding) interests can override a disposition. As can be seen this limitation arises if two conditions are met:

(i) If an interest belongs to a person whose *occupation* is not obvious from a reasonably careful inspection of the land at the time of the disposition. It is clear that it is the occupation that must be obvious, *not* the interest. Furthermore, the test is not one requiring a reasonable inquiry about the fact of occupation – it must be obvious; and

(ii) The *interest* is one which the transferee does not have actual knowledge of at the time of the disposition. Thus if the transferee has actual knowledge of the interest, the interest is still capable of being an overriding one and will bind the transferee.

It must be emphasised that both conditions must be present for the limitation to apply. Thus if the transferee has actual knowledge of the interest, but the occupation is not obvious, the overriding interest will bind the transferee. On the other hand, if the occupation is obvious but the transferee does not have actual knowledge of the interest, the overriding interest will still bind the transferee.

Usually, a transferee, on discovering that a person is in actual occupation, will make further inquiries of what interests that person may claim and indeed this has become common practice since *Williams & Glyn's Bank* v *Boland* [1981] AC 487.

Reversionary leases

A further limitation on overriding interests by way of actual occupation arises in paragraph 2(d) so that the holder of a reversionary lease, that is a lease taking effect in possession three months from the date of the grant, who has not taken effect in possession at the date of the disposition is excluded from being capable of forming an overriding interest by actual occupation.

Paragraph 3 – A legal easement or profit

Schedule 3 paragraph 3 relating to legal easements and profits essentially replaces s.70(1)a of the Land Registration Act 1925. We have already seen how the equivalent in Schedule 1 paragraph 3 operates in relation to first registration; however, the equivalent provision in relation to registered dispositions is not clear cut. The drafting of the provision is clearly aimed at the overall policy set out by the Law Commission to cut down the number of, in this case, legal easements and profits that do not appear on the register – it should be noted that no equitable easement or profit can become an overriding interest.

Only certain legal easements and profits are capable of becoming overriding interests since the others, as we saw earlier, have now become registrable dispositions within s.27(d) and are required to be completed by registration in order to exist as a legal interest. To be legal they are registered in the proprietorship register on the title to be benefited by the easement or profit, and are entered in the charges register as a notice on the title to be burdened by the easement or profit.

In order to discover which legal easements and profits can exist as overriding interests, one therefore has to look 'behind' the overall land registration scheme to discover the types that fall within Schedule 3 paragraph 3. Clearly, if an estate is registered, then the legal easement or profit is registered as per s.27 above. As we know, some estates are not substantively registered and here we look to leases of seven years or less. In such leases, there is no substantive title to register the legal easement or profit. In addition, there are also legal easements and profits that can be created by way of an implied grant by way of necessity. The operation of the Law of Property Act 1925 s.62, common intention, the rule in *Wheeldon* v *Burrows* or prescription will be discussed more fully in Chapter 15. Even in these cases a legal easement or profit may not amount to an overriding interest unless it meets the additional conditions set out in paragraph 3.

The conditions set out in paragraph 3 provide that a legal easement or profit is an overriding interest if, at the time of the disposition, *one* of the following conditions applies:

- if the legal easement or profit is within the actual knowledge of the purchaser; or
- if the purchaser did not know about the easement or profit but it is obvious on a reasonably careful inspection of the land over which the easement or profit is exercisable; or
- the person entitled to the legal easement or profit proves that it has been exercised in the period of one year ending with the date of the disposition; or

● the legal easement or profit is registered under the Commons Act 2006. This refers to certain specialist easements or profits that apply in relation to common land. Generally, those rights include the right to graze stock, rights of turbary (to cut peat), rights of piscary (to fish), etc.

It should be noted that the legal easement or profit may arise by way of grant or by way of reservation.

Alteration of the register

Introduction

On a number of occasions when evaluating the structure and operation of registered land it has been stated that the avowed aim of the Law Commission was to have as much information as possible about a parcel of land entered on the register so that it is as true a reflection of the interests that affected the land as possible. It is obviously vital therefore in a system of registration that the register should be as accurate as can be achieved. Even with the best of intentions, however, errors occur, sometimes because of incomplete or inaccurate information being available at the time of registration and, at other times, because of fraudulent or negligent behaviour by the participants in the system.

Whilst the register is largely very robust, there are circumstances when individual registered proprietors may find their title disturbed. As we have seen, there are various grades of registered title, which should give a prospective purchaser some idea of the quality of title they are acquiring. The truth of the matter, though, is that, even with an owner having an absolute title, this is not necessarily a complete guarantee since it is possible for a title to be altered.

The system of land registration provides a state-guaranteed title which is administered by way of an indemnity scheme from a central fund where a person suffers loss due to the register being altered. This state-guaranteed title does not, however, extend to all cases where alteration takes place and, indeed, surprisingly little is paid out of the indemnity fund in respect of errors. In the Land Registry Annual Report and Accounts for 2011/12 indemnity payments (inclusive of cost) amounting to £9,266,959 were paid out in respect of 935 claims from a fund amounting to £26.8 million. Fraud and forgery formed by far the biggest proportion of the indemnity paid out, amounting to £7,190,094 (including costs) from 52 cases. On the other hand, indemnity in respect of losses from 'errors in/omissions from register entries' amounted to £521,340 from 154 claims. In respect of 'lost documents and administrative errors', which formed the greater number of claims (366 cases), only £29,413 was paid out of the indemnity fund. The 'insurance' principle which we examined at the commencement of this chapter is not an all-embracing one.

The Land Registration Act 2002 established a scheme for altering the register and correcting mistakes within it in Schedule 4 and s.65 of the Act. These provisions are supplemented by Schedule 8, which provides an indemnity where a person suffers loss by reason of a mistake in the register, whether caused by clerical error or fraudulent conduct.

The Act makes significant changes and reforms to what was originally termed 'rectification' under the Land Registration Act 1925. The Law Commission considered that the expression 'rectification' operated far too widely since it ranged from minor errors on the register to those that could have a significant impact on the property rights relating to a registered title. Other changes that fell within rectification could also be the removal of clerical errors or the removal of entries that, by time or circumstance, had become obsolete. In the Land Registration Act 2002, whilst the expression 'rectification' is still used, by virtue of Schedule 4 para 1, it is given a rather narrower meaning; thus 'rectification' is now a type of alteration which:

(a) involves the correction of a mistake, and
(b) prejudicially affects the title of the registered proprietor.

The circumstances in which the register can be altered

Schedule 4 provides the circumstances in which the register can be altered. Schedule 4 paragraphs 2 and 5 provide that either the court or the registrar can alter the register with a view to:

(a) correcting a mistake,
(b) bringing the register up to date, or
(c) giving effect to any estate right or interest excepted from the effect of registration.

In addition, in Schedule 4 paragraph 5(d), the registrar may alter the register 'for the purpose of removing a superfluous entry'. Sub-paragraph (b) is an alteration that reflects changes on the basis that the register no longer reflects the legal position of the property; for example, there may be a short lease noted on the register, which has now expired. Another example might be the existence on the register of an option which is no longer current or, perhaps unusually, has been declared to be invalid or unenforceable by a court. In contrast to expired rights, it may be necessary to alter the register to reflect new rights which are either for the benefit of the land or to burden the land but which are not currently reflected on the register: for instance, a prescriptive right to light.

Sub-paragraph (c) allows the registrar to make an alteration – for instance, in the case of 'qualified' or 'possessory' titles. If the registered proprietor has been registered with these grades of titles rather than an 'absolute' title, it is possible for the grade to be subsequently upgraded if the defect on the title is cured at some point in the future – for instance, if the title deeds which were lost came to light.

Sub-paragraph (d) allows the registrar to alter the register if, for example, an interest is entered on the register more than once or where the powers of the registered proprietor are subject to a restriction which no longer applies.

It can be seen that sub-paragraph (a) – 'correcting a mistake' – provides the only substantive ground for alteration that essentially changes the legal position that existed prior to alteration. It applies in two circumstances: firstly, where the alteration does not prejudicially affect the title of the registered proprietor and, secondly where it does so affect the title of the registered proprietor.

Where sub-paragraph (a) does not prejudicially affect the title of the registered proprietor an alteration is likely to be of an administrative nature, similar to the other three paragraphs. In such a situation, the registrar *may*, by virtue of paragraph 5, make an appropriate alteration. In the case of such an alteration being made by the court, the court *must* make the alteration 'unless there are exceptional circumstances which justify its not doing so' (paragraph 2).

Where sub-paragraph (a) does prejudicially affect the title of the registered proprietor this falls within rectification, as indicated in paragraph 1. This is of a much more fundamental and serious nature which we will now examine.

Rectification

Unlike relatively simple administrative alterations of the register, rectification is subject to special provisions. Both the court and the registrar have discretion to order rectification of the register; however, in any proceedings in which the court or the registrar has the power to make an order then they *must* do so unless there are exceptional circumstances which justify their refusal to do so.

It is important that, for rectification to be possible, there must be a 'mistake' *and* any alteration must 'prejudicially affect the title of the registered proprietor' (Schedule 4 paragraph 1).

What constitutes a 'mistake' is not prescribed by the Land Registration Act 2002, though it is considered that the expression will be construed widely. One reason for this is that it is only possible to obtain an indemnity where rectification arises and thus if 'mistake' is construed narrowly it will put an indemnity out of reach of a claimant. The wide construction of 'mistake' therefore means that it can arise irrespective of the fault of a party or the Land Registry itself – indeed, it can arise even if a person is a registered proprietor albeit their conduct was entirely innocent. An example can be seen in the case of ***Baxter v Mannion*** [2011] 1 WLR 1594.

Baxter v Mannion [2011] 1 WLR 1594

In this case Mr Mannion ('M') was the registered proprietor of a field of which Mr Baxter ('B') had applied to the Land Registry to be registered as owner on the basis of adverse possession. B was registered as the proprietor of the property. M applied for rectification of the register under Schedule 4 paragraph 5 of the Land Registration Act 2002, on the basis that B was not entitled to be the registered proprietor as he had not satisfied the requirements to establish such a right by adverse possession in that he had not completed 10 years in adverse possession. M therefore claimed there had been a mistake in B being registered as the proprietor. B argued that the only mistake was that M had failed to serve a counter notice to his application and that there was no procedural mistake in his registration.

The Court of Appeal held that rectification for mistake was not limited to procedural errors and, indeed, in this case the rules of registration had been complied with correctly. The court considered that the registration of B as registered proprietor when he had clearly not satisfied the requirements to satisfy a claim by adverse possession was a mistake and that putting the register back to where it was would correct the mistake.

The decision makes it clear that correcting a mistake is not confined to clerical errors, nor is it limited to correction by the Land Registry. The court considered that to be confined in this way would be an invitation to fraud and one can see the issue here in the judgment of Jacob LJ when he stated at 1596:

> . . . can a man who has got his name registered as proprietor of a parcel of land by wrongly claiming that he had been in adverse possession for ten years hang on to that title if the original proprietor, within 65 days of its being posted to him, failed to fill up and return a form posted to him by the Land Registry? Or can the original proprietor apply to the registrar to have the title rectified by 'correcting a mistake'? Does the machinery of the Land Registration Act 2002 allow a party to take someone else's land by operation of a bureaucratic machinery which trumps reality?

The second requirement of Schedule 4 paragraph 1 is that, for rectification to be applied, any alteration must prejudicially affect the title of the registered proprietor. Clearly, not every alteration will have such an effect on the registered proprietor – though, broadly, alterations that affect the value of the property will be prejudicial. Similarly, an alteration which results in a registered proprietor being removed from the register and/or a new registered proprietor being added to the register will also be prejudicial within this provision. Some care needs to be exercised here since some alterations which might be thought prejudicial are not considered as such at all. An example here would be where the alteration gives effect to an interest which overrides registration, since here the overriding interest already binds the registered proprietor.

This was the case in *Drake v Fripp* [2011] EWCA Civ 1279 where there was a discrepancy regarding the boundary of the property on the title plan of the register. On the property there were two boundaries marked, one a wire and post fence, and the other an ancient 'Cornish' hedge. The question raised related to which of the two boundary lines provided the correct line. Once this decision was reached, the question arose as to how the title plan could be corrected to give effect to the decision. If the alteration of the register fell within rectification, would the correction prejudicially affect the registered proprietor, who would lose a proportion of his property as a result of the correction? This was important since, if the alteration was prejudicial, that party could get an indemnity. The Court of Appeal held that the boundaries on the title plan do not 'determine the exact line of the boundary' (Land Registration Act 2002 s.60) and that the boundary on the title plan only represented 'a general boundary'. Once the title plan was altered, it would still only represent a 'general boundary' and, as such, the alteration did not prejudicially affect the registered proprietor; thus the direction to the Land Registry to alter the title plan did not amount to rectification.

Simply because the conditions set out in Schedule 4 paragraph 1 are met does not mean that rectification will follow automatically. The Land Registration Act 2002 provides that rectification is only available against a registered proprietor in possession. It is clear from the Land Registration Act 2002 s.131(1) that the expression 'possession' refers to a registered proprietor who is physically in possession of the land. It is possible, though, for possession to take place through the agency of others, thus s.131(2) provides that possession may only take place through the registered proprietor's tenant, mortgagee, licensee or beneficiary. It is not, however, possible for possession to take place where the entitlement to possession arises through adverse possession by virtue of s.131(3).

Alteration against a registered proprietor in possession is only available if certain conditions are met, as set out in paragraphs 3(2) and 6(2). There are three such conditions:

(i) Rectification is available against a registered proprietor in possession if he consents to the alteration; or,

(ii) Rectification is available without the registered proprietor's consent if he has by fraud or lack of proper care caused or substantially contributed to the mistake; or,

(iii) Rectification can be ordered without the registered proprietor's consent if it would for any other reason be unjust for the alteration not to be made.

The notion of what is 'unjust' is somewhat vague. In *Baxter v Mannion* [2011] 1 WLR 1594 it was held that, where it was necessary to correct a mistake, this was done as a matter of 'simple justice'. A mere mistake, however, does not of itself represent an injustice. To imply such a meaning would be to introduce a general power to alter the register and clearly this would contradict the overall philosophy of registered land. It is for the person applying for rectification to demonstrate to the court or registrar that it would be unjust *not* to rectify the register. For instance, it might be regarded as unjust if there was a mistake in not entering a registered interest on the register, particularly if any claim to compensation would not adequately compensate for the lack of registration of the interest.

Finally, in considering rectification it is important to note that once the case for rectification has been established in paragraphs 2 and 5, under paragraphs 3 and 6 of Schedule 4 the court or registrar *must* make an order for rectification provided the rectification is being made against a registered proprietor not in physical possession or otherwise where the three conditions above apply.

Indemnity

The power to alter or rectify the register inevitably means that a person may suffer loss and the Land Registration Act 2002 makes provision in Schedule 8 for the payment of compensation by way of an indemnity in response to such a situation. An indemnity is not payable in all situations where there has been an error or where the register is inaccurate. Thus Schedule 8 paragraph 1 provides:

(1) *A person is entitled to be indemnified by the registrar if he suffers loss by reason of –*
  (a) rectification of the register,
  (b) a mistake whose correction would involve rectification of the register,
  (c) a mistake in an official search,
  (d) a mistake in an official copy,
  (e) a mistake in a document kept by the registrar which is not an original and is referred to in the register,
  (f) the loss or destruction of a document lodged at the registry for inspection or safe custody,
  (g) a mistake in the cautions register, or
  (h) failure by the registrar to perform his duty under section 50.

The two principal grounds for payment of an indemnity fall within paragraphs 1(1)(a) and (b) and these are subject to further qualifications contained in paragraphs 1(2) and (3).

We have already seen that Schedule 4 paragraph 1 provides that rectification arises where the alteration of the register involves the correction of a mistake that prejudicially affects the title of the registered proprietor. It should therefore come as no surprise that Schedule 8 paragraph 1 provides that the right to an indemnity is available where rectification arises or where there is a mistake whose correction involves rectification of the register. Schedule 8, however, provides for other criteria that must be met before an indemnity becomes payable:

(i) A person is only entitled to be indemnified by the registrar if he or she suffers loss because of the correction of the register. It is thus not the mistake that must cause the loss but the correction of the mistake.

(ii) A person may claim an indemnity where there has been a mistake but nevertheless the register is not rectified. Even if the register is rectified, it is still possible for a person to suffer loss because of the prospective nature of the rectification itself. For instance, if there is an error so that a registered charge is deleted, then any subsequent charge that is created and registered will gain priority over the first charge, even if it is reinstated by the register being rectified. It should be noted, though, that by Schedule 8 paragraph 3 no indemnity is payable until a decision has been made as to whether to alter the register for the purpose of correcting the mistake. Any loss suffered as a consequence of the mistake is then determined in the light of that decision.

Even if a claimant can establish a ground for an indemnity they may still not be able to claim since there are further limitations that may extinguish or limit their claim. These limitations are:

(i)   Schedule 8 paragraph 5(1)(a) – No indemnity is payable on account of any loss suffered by a claimant wholly or partly as a result of their own fraud.

(ii) Schedule 8 paragraph 5(1)(b) – No indemnity is payable on account of any loss suffered by the claimant wholly as a result of their own lack of proper care.

(iii) Schedule 8 paragraph 5(2) – Where any loss is suffered by a claimant as a result of their own lack of proper care, any indemnity payable to them may be reduced to the extent as is fair having regard to the person's share in the responsibility for the loss.

(iv) Schedule 8 paragraph 8 – A limitation period of six years applies to the right to apply for an indemnity, after which the right lapses. The limitation period begins to run when the claimant knows, or but for their own default might have known, of the existence of the claim.

(v)   Schedule 8 paragraph 2 – No indemnity is payable on account of any mines or minerals, or the existence of any right to work or get mines or minerals unless it is noted in the register that the title to the registered estate includes the mines or minerals.

The amount of the indemnity awarded, if any, is normally the amount the claimant has lost. However, where the indemnity is in respect of the loss of an estate, interest or charge, the amount of the loss will not exceed its value immediately before rectification in respect of an indemnity falling within Schedule 1 paragraph1(1)(a). In the case of a claim under Schedule 1 paragraph 1(1)(b), the amount of the indemnity will not exceed the value of the estate, interest or charge at the time of the mistake which caused the loss – i.e. the time at which the mistake was not rectified.

Summary

The objectives of land registration

The basis of land registration has two broad objectives:

(a) to replace investigation of title with a state guaranteed title, and

(b) to create a single register whereby a prospective purchaser can discover whether the vendor has the right to sell the title to the land and to discover not all encumbrances affecting a piece of land can be found on the register.

The principles of land registration

Land registration is built around three principles:

(a) the mirror principle;

(b) the curtain principle;

(c) the insurance principle.

The form of the register under the Land Registration Act 2002

(a) The property register – identifies the estate to which the registration is made and refers to rights which *benefit* the land.

(b) The proprietorship register – identifies the owner of the estate – the 'registered proprietor'. This register contains any 'restrictions' placed on the ability of the registered proprietor to dispose of the land.

(c) The charges register – identifies third party rights that *burden* the land.

The details of the different registers are contained in a 'title information document'.

The doctrine of notice and registered land

The doctrine of notice has no part to play in registered conveyancing and the only type of notice is that recognised by entry on the register. The effect of this is that the distinction between legal and equitable interests has now largely been discarded.

Classification of interests under the Land Registration Act 2002

In registered land the land interests are divided into:

- registered estates;
- interests created by a registrable disposition;
- interests capable of protection by registration;
- unregistered interests which override.

Registrable estates

The Land Registration Act 2002 s.3 and s.4 provides for registration of ownership of two legal estates and certain legal interests.

1 Registrable freehold and leasehold estates
   - Legal fee simple absolute in possession
     Term of years absolute with more than seven years unexpired on the lease.
2 Registrable legal interests

By s.2(a) the Act makes provision for unregistered legal interests which are interests of the following kind:

(a) rentcharges;

(b) franchises;

(c) profits à prendre in gross;

(d) any other interest charge which benefits or burdens any registered estate.

The effect of this is that such interests can be substantively registered in the same way as the legal estates above.

Interests created by registrable dispositions

The limited number of registrable estates is supplemented by some subsidiary interests in land that are only capable of being created at law by registration. These are found in the Land Registration Act 2002 s.27 and arise by way of a registrable disposition. The most important of these are charges by way of a legal mortgage and express legal easements.

Note: Unlike registrable estates, the creation of these rights does not create a separate title on the register but involves the making of an entry on the register of title of the estate to be burdened or benefited by the relevant disposition.

Interests capable of protection by registration

Most of these interests are equitable interests and loosely correspond with those equitable interests that were protected by registration as land charges under the Land Charges Act 1972 in unregistered land, e.g. restrictive covenants, equitable easements, estate contracts, etc.

These types of interest may be protected by either a 'notice' or a 'restriction' so as to protect third party rights, though some types of interest must be protected in this way. A 'notice' is 'an entry in the register in respect of the burden of an interest affecting a registered estate or charge'. The Land Registration Act 2002 does not provide a list of interests that must be protected by notice but instead provides a list of interests that are *not* capable of being protected by a notice in the Charges register. The most important of these are contained in s.33.

A notice may be entered either as:

- an agreed notice, or
- a unilateral notice.

A 'restriction' is an entry in the register regulating the circumstances in which a disposition of a registered estate or charge may be the subject of an entry in the Proprietorship Register. A restriction indicates any limitations on the powers of the registered proprietor to deal with the registered estate.

Registration guarantees that the right will have priority over any rights subsequently created.

Interests which override

These types of interest are not capable of being entered on the register but nevertheless bind the land and the purchasers of it. The existence of such interests amounts to a significant crack in the mirror principle that the register should reflect the variety of interests that pertain to a registered estate (***National Provincial Bank Ltd v Hastings Car Mart Ltd*** [1964] Ch 9).

Overriding interests are contained in Schedules 1 and 3 of the Land Registration Act 2002. Schedule 1 overriding interests are those which override first registration, whilst Schedule 3 overriding interests are those that override subsequent dealings. Whilst there are some important differences between the two in broad terms they comprise the following:

- leasehold estates granted for a term not exceeding seven years from the date of its grant;
- an interest belonging to a person in actual occupation so far as relating to land of which they are in actual occupation;
- legal easements or profits à prendre;
- customary rights;
- public rights;
- local land changes;
- rights to mines and minerals.

How the system of land registration works

First registration

Parliamentary considerations

These arise when an unregistered estate is brought within the land registration system. They arise in two ways:

Voluntary registration

This arises under s.3 and occurs where an owner desires to register his title though not obliged to do so.

Compulsory registration

This arises under s.4 and provides that, when certain 'triggers' arise, the owner is obliged to convert an unregistered title into a registered title. The 'triggers' are divided into three broad areas:

- where there is a transfer of a 'qualifying estate' for valuable or other consideration, by way of gift or court order: s.4(1)(a)(i);
- where there is a grant of a lease out of a qualifying estate for a term of years of more than seven years from the date of the grant for valuable or other consideration by way of gift or court order: s.4(1)(c)(i);
- on the creation of a first legal mortgage of a 'qualifying estate' by deposit of title deeds.

A 'qualifying estate' is by s.4(2)a an unregistered legal estate which is a freehold estate or a leasehold estate for a term, at the time of transfer, grant or creation that has more than seven years to run.

The duty to apply for first registration

By s.6(3) if the requirement to register arises out of a transfer or a grant, it is the new owner who is responsible for ensuring registration takes place.

By s.6(2) if the triggering event is the creation of a mortgage, the person normally responsible is the owner of the mortgaged estate, i.e. the mortgagor. By s.6(6), however, if the mortgagor does not register then the mortgagee is entitled to do so.

The period for registration is two months beginning with the date on which the relevant-event occurs or such longer period as the registrar may provide – s.6(4).

Effect of non-compliance with the requirement to register

Failure to register within the two-month time limit renders the transfer or grant of the estate void: s.7(1). Similarly, any creation of a mortgage will also become void. An example of some of the consequences of failure to register can be seen in **Sainsbury's Supermarket Ltd v Olympia Homes Ltd** [2006] 1 P & CR 17.

Cautions against first registration

By s.15 it is possible for a person with an interest in unregistered land to apply a 'caution against first registration'. This has no substantive effect but allows the owner of the interest to substantiate their claim. By s.16 the registrar must give the cautioner notice of the application and their right to object to it.

The classes of title

On first registration, the title is awarded a class of title which provides an indication of the reliability of the title. The Land Registration Act 2002 s.9 and s.10 specify seven classes of title – three freehold classes and four leasehold classes:

Freehold classes:

Absolute freehold title
Qualified freehold title
Possessory freehold title

Leasehold classes:

Absolute leasehold title
Good leasehold title
Qualified leasehold title
Possessory leasehold title

It is possible for these titles to be upgraded.

Subsequent dealings with the registered estate

There can only be one freehold title but any number of registered leasehold titles, provided they are created for a term exceeding seven years.

Note: It is possible for there to be a registered leasehold title but no registered freehold title.

The Land Registration Act 2002 s.27 sets out a list of dispositions that must be completed by registration. Failure to register will mean that the dispositions will not take effect at law until the registration requirements are met. These requirements are set out in Schedule 2.

Alteration of the register

Whilst the land register is largely robust, there are circumstances when registered proprietors may find their title disturbed by an alteration either by the court or by the registrar. The scheme for altering the register and correcting mistakes is found in Schedule 4 and s.65 of the Land Registration Act 2002. In addition, these provisions are supplemented by Schedule 8, which sets out a scheme to provide an indemnity where a person suffers loss by the register being altered or subject to rectification.

Further reading

Brown, 'E-conveyancing: Nothing to Fear' (2005) 155 *New Law Journal* 1389

Dixon, 'Registration, Rectification and Property Rights', 46 *Student Law Review*, Autumn

Dixon, 'The Reform of Property Law and the Land Registration Act 2002: A Risk Assessment' [2003] 67 *The Conveyancer and Property Lawyer* 136

Law Commission (2001) *Land Registration for the Twenty-First Century: A Conveyancing Revolution*, Law Com No. 271

Law Commission/HM Land Registry (1998) *Land Registration for the Twenty-First Century: A Consultative Document*, Law Com No. 254

Tee, 'The Rights of Every Person in Actual Occupation: An Enquiry into Section 70(1)g of the Land Registration Act 1925' (1998) *Cambridge Law Journal* 328

Part 2

The estates in land

6

Leasehold estates in land

Aims and objectives

At the end of this chapter you should be able to:

- Know and understand the terminology attached to leasehold estates.
- Recognise the characteristics of a lease.
- Understand how legal and equitable leases are created.
- Recognise the different types of lease.
- Know and understand the differing covenants and the obligations of landlord and tenant.
- Know and understand how leases are terminated.
- Understand the remedies of landlord and tenant for breach of covenant.

Introduction and terminology

A lease or 'term of years absolute' is one of the two estates that can now exist at law under the Law of Property Act 1925 s.1(1)b; however, as we will see, they are also capable of existing in an equitable form as well. Undoubtedly, leases are a very flexible form of land-holding and this is borne out by the flexible language that is often used to describe this type of interest. Thus in a legalistic form leases are described as 'terms of years absolute'; they can also be described simply as 'leases' or 'tenancies'. The term 'lease' is usually used for relatively long periods, whilst the expression 'tenancy' is used for short periods – for instance, a 'yearly lease' or a 'weekly tenancy'. Thus the expressions 'terms of years absolute', 'leases' and 'tenancies' are synonymous. This was not always the case since, prior to 1926, it was possible to have a lease for life, but these are now very rare and it would be highly unusual to come across such an interest.

The expressions that describe the parties to a lease also have variations, though commonly the expressions 'landlord' and 'tenants' are used. The grantor of a lease will be the landlord, but in a legal form he or she is described as the 'lessor'. On the other hand, the person to whom the lease is being granted, the grantee, will be a tenant but, again, in the legal form, he or she is described as the 'lessee'.

We have already seen that there can only be one freehold estate in relation to a piece of land; however, with regards to leases there can be any number of leases of various duration applying to a piece of land. Thus a freeholder ('L') could grant a lease for 999 years to a tenant ('T1') and, in turn, that tenant could grant a sub-lease for 99 years to a sub-tenant ('T2'). In this situation, the freeholder (L) is the landlord to the tenant (T1) and, equally, T1 is the landlord for the sub-tenant (T2). Both L and T1 have a 'reversion' – that is, at the end of the lease, the property will revert to them. So, at the end of the 99-year lease, the property reverts to T1 and, in turn, at the end of the 999-year lease, the land reverts to L as the freeholder (see Figure 6.1).

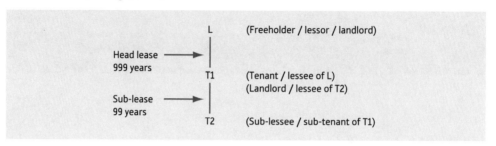

Figure 6.1

Clearly, there is an opportunity for some confusion here, so it is advisable to refer to the landlord as the person who grants the first lease or 'head lease'. In turn, T1 should be described as the 'tenant' or 'lessee' when referring to his relationship with L. On the other hand, when referring to T1's relationship to T2, he should be described as the 'sub-lessor' and T2 as the 'sub-lessee'.

In the example above, it is highly unlikely that T1 will live for 999 years and, equally, it is unlikely that T2 will survive more than 99 years. It is therefore possible (providing there is no prohibition in the lease) for T1 or T2 to assign or transfer their leases to someone else, an assignee who will take over the respective positions of their assignors, as shown in Figure 6.2.

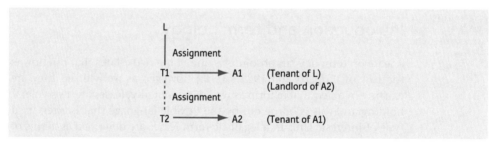

Figure 6.2

Both A1 and A2 will be assigned the lease but of course they would not be able to enjoy the whole term of the lease. Thus, if T1 had been in occupation of the lease for 9 years he would assign his lease, the balance of which is 990 years, to A1. Similarly, if T2 had occupied the lease for 20 years, she could only assign the balance of her lease to A2 – that is, 79 years.

Of course, with leases extending for as long as 999 years there will undoubtedly be many assignments, but this will not detract from the principles set out above.

With regard to the granting of sub-leases, it must be remembered that a tenant or sub-tenant can never grant a sub-lease that is longer than the lease that they actually have themselves. For instance, T1 could never grant a sub-lease of 2000 years to T2, since he only has a 999-year lease himself – nemo dat non quod habet (no one can give what they have not got!).

It is important to remember that all the above participants have a proprietary interest in the land. The tenants have a lease which they purchase by way of rent, whilst the landlords all have reversionary interests.

The relationships between the various landlords/ tenants/ sub-lessors/ sub-lessees are generally governed by a set of conditions contained within the lease called 'covenants'. We will discuss how these are enforceable between the parties in a later chapter – however, it is as well to note that covenants generally fall into three discrete types.

- Express covenants are literally covenants that the landlord and tenant agree should be set out in the lease.
- 'Usual' covenants are covenants of a type that, whilst not expressly included in the lease, commonly reflect the relationship between a landlord and tenant so that they are implied into a lease unless expressly excluded. Examples of such covenants are a covenant to provide the tenant with 'quiet enjoyment' by the landlord, or a covenant by the tenant to pay rent to their landlord.
- Some covenants are implied by law: for instance, under the Landlord and Tenant Act 1985 s.11(1)a a landlord has an obligation to keep the structure and exterior of the property in a state of proper repair.

Before proceeding to look at the nature of a lease, one rider must be considered. The relationship between landlords and tenants over the last 200 or more years has not often been a happy one. There is a wealth of material recounting bad practices by landlords along the lines of extortion and exploitation of tenants of dilapidated slum property. As a result of these practices, there is a whole raft of statutory protection that overlays the landlord and tenant relationship. Consideration of this statutory overlay is outside the scope of this book as this is a separate subject in its own right.

The nature of a lease

Definition

A definition of a lease or term of years absolute is given in the Law of Property Act 1925 s.205 (xxvii):

> Term of years absolute means a term of years (taking effect either in possession or in reversion whether or not at a rent . . . either certain or liable to determination by notice, re-entry, operation of law . . . and includes a term for less than a year, or for a year or years and a fraction of year or from year to year

Leases have also been defined at common law, most famously by Lord Templeman in *Street v Mountford* [1985] AC 809 in which he stated at 816:

> The traditional view that the grant of exclusive possession for a term at a rent creates a tenancy is consistent with the elevation of a tenancy into an estate in land.

From these definitions we can discern a number of elements that are required in order to create a valid lease. These are:

- premises must be sufficiently defined;
- a term of certain duration;
- exclusive possession;
- rent.

We will consider each one of these elements in turn, though the issue of formalities will be considered separately.

Premises must be sufficiently defined

Whilst this requirement is not specifically referred to in the definition above, it is nevertheless clear that a lease can only exist in relation to premises that are sufficiently defined. For instance, in **Interoven Store Co. Ltd v Hibbard** [1926] 1 All ER 263 it was held that a lease of unspecified storage facilities in a warehouse could not give rise to a lease. The owner of the goods could not point to a defined area that was under his control. Furthermore, the owner of the warehouse was free to select a location for the goods and, indeed, move them to other parts of the warehouse at his discretion.

A term of certain duration

Blackstone in his *Commentaries on the Law of England*, 2nd edn (1766) Vol. 11 stated:

> Every estate which must expire at a period certain and prefixed, by whatever words created, is an estate for years. And therefore this estate is frequently called a term, terminus, because its duration or continuance is bounded, limited and determined: for every such estate must have a certain beginning, and certain end.

There are two aspects to this requirement – commencement and termination. A term of years must commence at a certain time and must have a certain end. Commencement is either expressly agreed by the parties or at least it must be readily identifiable before the start of the term. Leases do not necessarily have to start immediately (i.e. in possession), they can exist as 'reversionary' leases – that is, start at some time in the future. Having said that, the Law of Property Act 1925 s.149(3) provides that a lease to take effect more than 21 years after the instrument creating it is void.

Providing that the maximum duration of a lease is ascertainable, a lease can be of any length of time. This, of course, ties in with the definition of a lease contained in the Law of Property Act 1925 s.205 (xxvii) where it talks about the term being 'for less than a year, or year'. It is possible for leases to cover very extensive periods of time and, indeed, in the context of creating certain types of mortgage, leases of 3000 years are not unknown. It is common for residential leases to be for 999 years, though in relation to many tenancies of terraced houses and flats, terms of 99 years are equally common. From the outset, however, the finite point for the termination of a lease must be expressed or be implied, or it must at least be for a term that is capable of being made certain. We will consider the latter point more fully when we look at types of lease later on, but for the moment it is useful to look at an example of a lease for a periodic tenancy. Such a lease may be a monthly tenancy. Here the lease is for a period of one month from month to month. On the face of things, such a lease appears to continue indefinitely; however, the term is capable of being made certain by the landlord or tenant giving one month's notice to quit and thus the lease is of a term capable of being made certain.

It is clearly not possible for a lease to be created for an uncertain period. Thus in **Lace v Chantler** [1944] KB 368 the Court of Appeal held that no lease was granted where it was given 'for the duration of the war'.

Whilst there have been attempts to depart from this ancient principle regarding the need for the maximum duration of a lease to be ascertainable, the principle was re-affirmed by the House of Lords in the case of **Prudential Assurance Co. Ltd v London Residuary Body** [1992] AC 386.

Prudential Assurance Co. Ltd v London Residuary Body [1992] AC 386

In this case, the London County Council granted a lease in 1920 of a strip of land fronting a highway for £30 per annum. The tenancy was expressed to continue until the land was required by the council for the purpose of widening the highway. Later, the council abandoned its intentions to widen the highway. Eventually, when the London County Council was abolished the freehold reversion of the land passed to the London Residuary Body, which was not a highway and had no road marking powers. In the intervening years, shop premises were erected by the occupier on the strip of land. Valuers acting on behalf of both the parties considered that the likely current commercial rate for the rental of the land would be in excess of £10,000 per annum. The London Residuary Body claimed that the tenant only held a yearly tenancy and that this could be terminated by giving half a year's notice. The tenant argued that the original agreement entitled it to stay for an indefinite period of time at a rent of £30 per annum and that the lease could only be determinable in the event of a proposal to widen the road.

The House of Lords held, affirming the orthodox common law approach, that a lease for an indeterminate period of time could never amount to a legally recognisable term of years. Lord Templeman stated that 'principle and precedent dictate that it is beyond the power of the landlord and tenant to create a term which is uncertain'. The consequence of this was that the tenant only held a yearly tenancy which could be terminated by half a year's notice to quit. The other judges of the House of Lords were clearly reluctant to endorse the principle – not only on the basis that the principle overturns the contractual relationship, but also on the grounds that the effect of the decision left the parties with a piece of land that neither could use. Lord Browne-Wilkinson considered the rule to be archaic and urged that the Law Commission should examine the rule in order to 'see whether there is in fact any good reason now for maintaining a rule which operates to defeat contractually agreed agreements between the parties (of which all successors in the title are aware) and which is capable of producing such an extraordinary result as that in the present case'. Certainly, if the decision of the House of Lords only had a prospective effect (as opposed to a retrospective effect under the declaratory theory of the common law) it is highly unlikely that they would have departed from precedent and overturned the principle.

Exclusive possession

In *Street* v *Mountford* [1985] AC 809 Lord Templeman stated at 816:

The traditional view that the grant of exclusive possession for a term at a rent creates a tenancy is consistent with the elevation of a tenancy into an estate in land. The tenant possessing exclusive possession is able to exercise the rights of an owner of land, which is in the real sense his land albeit temporarily and subject to certain restrictions. A tenant armed with exclusive possession can keep out strangers and keep out the landlord unless the landlord is exercising limited rights reserved to him by the tenancy agreement to enter and view and repair.

Exclusive possession is therefore an essential component of a lease and without it there can be no lease. Exclusive possession means just that – it is the right to use and occupy the premises to the exclusion of all others, including the landlord. The tenant therefore has effective control of the premises in terms of who can enter the premises and, of course, who can be excluded. This is not to say the landlord cannot enter the premises at all and invariably in the lease, as Lord Templeman indicates, there will be provision for the landlord to enter the premises to view it and, if necessary, carry out repairs they are responsible for. What the landlord cannot do is to enter at will. Such a right must generally be exercised after giving the tenant notice of their intention to visit and enter the premises. Even then, such visits by the landlord have to be exercised in a reasonable manner – for instance, it would not be appropriate for the landlord to enter at one o'clock in the morning! A landlord who did not exercise their rights in a reasonable manner would become a trespasser.

Some care needs exercising here. Whilst exclusive possession is a necessary ingredient for a lease, it does not invariably mean that a person with exclusive possession actually has a lease, since it is possible that the occupier is a mere licensee. A licensee has no proprietary interest in the property, has no security of tenure in the property and is present only with the permission of the owner of the property. The difference is that, whilst a licensee may be in exclusive *occupation* of the premises, they are not in exclusive *possession*. Another crucial difference between a lease and a licence is that a licence, unlike a lease, does not bind third parties.

Whilst the distinction between a lease and a licence appears to be clear, it is anything but, and for many years the courts have struggled with the concept of exclusive possession in terms of deciding whether a lease or a licence exists over a property. In the latter part of the twentieth century, many landlords attempted to create licences rather than leases in residential premises because landlord and tenant legislation imposed heavy burdens on landlords. By giving a 'tenant' a licence rather than a lease, a landlord could sidestep the legislation. Thus many licences were a 'sham' that provided a licensee with no security of tenure or other protection under the landlord and tenant law. The courts found themselves having to adjudicate on these arrangements and exclusive possession often formed the central issue in these cases so that an extensive body of case law developed. We will look at these cases in more detail in Chapter 8; however, some aspects are worthy of consideration here.

Examples of cases where exclusive possession may arise

Retention of keys by the landlord

Just because a landlord retains keys to enter the premises this does not necessarily mean that a licence arises. The retention of keys may allow the landlord to enter the premises. They may have good reason for doing so, such as making repairs or inspecting the premises as part of the terms of the lease, but would still have to obtain the consent of the tenant to enter the premises. In *Aslan v Murphy* [1990] 1 WLR 766, the owner entered a licence agreement under which he would retain the keys and have an unconditional right of entry to the premises. The Court of Appeal held that the retention of keys did not prevent a tenancy from arising. Donaldson MR stated at 773:

> Provisions as to keys, if not a pretence, which they often are, do not have any magic in themselves. It is not a requirement of a tenancy that the occupier shall have exclusive possession of the keys to the property. What matters is what underlies the provisions as to keys. Why does the owner want a key, want to prevent keys being issued to the friends of the occupier or want to prevent the lock being changed?
>
> A landlord may well need a key in order that he may be able to enter quickly in the event of emergency – fire, burst pipes or whatever. He may need a key to enable him or those authorised by him to read meters or to do repairs which are his responsibility. None of these underlying reasons would of themselves indicate that the true bargain between the parties was such that the occupier was in law a lodger. On the other hand, if the true bargain is that the owner will provide genuine services which can be provided only by having keys, such as

frequent cleaning, daily bed-making, the provision of clean linen at regular intervals and the like, there are materials from which it is possible to infer that the occupier is a lodger rather than a tenant. But the inference arises not from the provisions as to keys but from the reason why those provisions formed part of the bargain.

On the facts of this case, the argument based upon the provision as to keys must and does fail, for the judge found that 'during the currency of the present agreement virtually "no services" had been provided'. These provisions may or may not have been pretences, but they are without significance in the context of the question which we had to decide.

Sharing of premises

If a number of people live in and occupy the same premises this does not, of itself, indicate that they do not have exclusive possession. They may have joint occupation of the premises and enjoy joint exclusive possession of the premises. In such a situation, a court would have to decide if there was, in fact, joint occupation of a tenancy or whether they each individually have a licence to occupy. Such a case arose in the case of *Antoniades* v *Villiers* [1990] 1 AC 417, where a couple occupied a flat and enjoyed exclusive occupation of it. In order to avoid the granting of tenancy, the owner required them both to enter into separate agreements, described as licences. Each had to pay half the rent. The licence gave the owner the right to enter into occupation of the flat with the couple, or, indeed, to allow others to occupy the premises. The House of Lords held that the two agreements being interdependent gave the couple joint ownership of a lease. Their Lordships considered that the landlord never had any intention of occupying the premises, nor, indeed, of imposing any third parties on the couple. The arrangement was therefore held to be a 'sham' and the couple were not licensees but tenants.

In comparison, the House of Lords came to a different decision in *AG Securities* v *Vaughan* [1990] AC 417, which was decided at the same time as the *Antoniades* case above. Here the owner of a four-bedroomed flat entered into separate agreements with four separate occupiers. Each of the agreements was expressed to be a licence. The occupiers had the sole use of a bedroom but shared the use of the lounge, bathroom and kitchen. The occupiers had entered the agreements at different times and had a licence for different periods, paying differing rents. The flat remained fully occupied over a period of time; as one person left another would be granted a licence. The House of Lords held that the occupiers were licensees and not joint owners of a lease, as the four unities of time, interest, possession were not present for the establishment of a joint tenancy. Lord Templeman stated at 460:

> In the present case, if the four [occupiers] had been jointly entitled to exclusive occupation of the flat then, on the death of one of [them] the remaining three would be entitled to joint and exclusive occupation. But, in fact, on the death of one [occupier] the remaining three would not be entitled to joint and exclusive occupation of the flat. They could not exclude a fourth person nominated by the [owner].

Premises for employees

Generally speaking, if a person occupies premises by reason of their employment then a licence arises, not a lease. Thus, for example, a farm worker who occupies a cottage on a farm will be regarded as a licensee, not a tenant, since here they are required to occupy the cottage in order to better perform their services on the farm. On the other hand, if the nature of the employee's work does not require them to be in occupation then it is more likely that a tenancy will be found to exist. The principle can been seen in *Facchini* v *Bryson* [1952] 1 TLR 1386, where a manufacturer of ice cream allowed his assistant to occupy a house in return for a weekly payment. Even though the parties referred to the agreement as a licence, the court found for a tenancy since the use of the premises was not necessary for him to perform his work.

Limitation of use and the provision of services

Sometimes an agreement suggests that the occupier does not have exclusive possession and limits the period of occupation. Such a situation could be seen in the case of ***Crancour Ltd v Da Silvaesa*** (1986) 1 EGLR 80, where the parties entered into an agreement called a 'licence'. The occupiers were allowed to use a room in a house 'on each day between the hours of midnight and 10.30 am and between noon and midnight but at no other times for a period of 26 weeks . . . for the purpose of temporary accommodation for the licensees' personal use only . . .'. Other clauses reserved to the 'licensor' possession, management and control of the room, and gave him an absolute right of entry at all times for the purpose of providing attendances and enabled him to remove furniture from the room without having an obligation to replace it. The licensor was also to provide, inter alia, a housekeeper, window cleaning, cleaning of the room, collection of rubbish and provision and laundering of bed linen. When the agreement ended, the housekeeper asked the occupants to leave and, when they refused to do so, proceedings for possession were started.

At first instance, it was considered that the agreement was a 'lodger-type' licence and an order for possession was made. In the Court of Appeal it was considered whether a 'lodger-type' licence had been created or whether there was evidence of a 'sham'. Gibson LJ stated that the obligation to provide attendance and services was not conclusive of a licence. He stated that the 'question to be answered is whether in all the circumstances having regard to the landlord's obligation it is clear that the landlord requires unrestricted access and has reserved the right to exercise such access to look after the house and the furniture'. Both Gibson LJ and Nicholls LJ agreed that the agreement on this basis resulted in the occupants being licensees, not tenants.

Gibson LJ and Nicholls LJ went further, however, and considered that the provision to restrict the times when the occupants could stay in the room and the proviso that allowed the landlord to remove the furniture was evidence of a sham. In examining this, they referred to the case of ***Snook v London and West Riding Investments Ltd*** [1967] 1 All ER 518 where Diplock LJ stated:

> . . . this popular and perjorative word [i.e. 'sham'] . . . means acts done or documents executed by the parties to the 'sham' which are intended to give third parties or to the court the appearance of creating between the parties legal rights and obligations different from the actual legal rights and obligations (if any) which the parties intend to create.

Both Gibson LJ and Nicholls LJ considered that the limited access and removal of furniture clauses were 'astonishingly extreme' and indeed had never been enforced. Both judges considered that these clauses provided evidence of a 'sham' and that the agreement has 'an artificial contrivance intended to mislead'.

Examples of cases where exclusive possession may not arise

Lodgers/hotel residents

Where a person shares occupation of premises with the owner – for example, a student living in 'digs' – that person does not enjoy the rights of a tenant. Thus Lord Templeman stated at 818 in ***Street v Mountford***:

> The occupier is a lodger if the landlord provides attendance or services which require the landlord or his services to exercise unrestricted access to and use of the premises. A lodger is entitled to live in the premises but cannot call the place his own.

Thus the student in the example above, whilst entitled to enter the premises, is unable to refuse access to the premises to the owner, who remains entitled to enter their room at will.

Similar principles apply to persons who occupy a room in a hotel and do not have a tenancy in relation to the room. In such a situation, cleaners, hotel management, etc. have rights of entry to the room to clean the room, change linen, or to inspect it and such entry is inconsistent with the granting of a tenancy: *Appah v Parncliffe Investments Ltd* [1964] 1 WLR 1064.

In these types of situation, which would also apply to hostel accommodation, as in *Westminster City Council v Clarke* [1992] 2 AC 288, the occupier merely has rights of exclusive occupation and has no tenancy. Similar principles also apply to care homes for the elderly where residents also do not enjoy a tenancy. In *Abbeyfield (Harpenden) Society v Woods* [1968] 1 WLR 374 it was held that an 85-year-old man who occupied a room for a weekly payment was a licensee, despite the fact that he was entitled to 'sole occupation' of his room. The society provided him with meals, lighting, heating and the services of a resident housekeeper. The Court of Appeal held that the arrangement was of a purely personal nature and this, together with the provision of services, rendered the arrangement to be a licence.

Acts of friendship and family relationships

Occupation based on an act of friendship will generally negate a finding of a tenancy, on the basis that there is no intention to enter into a legal relationship. Thus in *Rhodes v Dalby* [1971] 2 All ER 1144, where a teacher was allowed by a farmer to live in a cottage on the farm on the basis of a 'gentleman's agreement', the court held that no tenancy had been created.

Where occupation arises by way of a family relationship, again the absence of an intention to create legal relations normally negates the finding of a tenancy. Thus in *Cobb v Lane* [1952] 1 TLR 1037 an owner allowed her brother to occupy a house rent-free. It was held by the Court of Appeal that there was no intention to create a legal relationship, no intention to create a lease, and therefore the brother had a mere licence.

This does not always follow, however, and the overall circumstances will be considered by a court, as in *Nunn v Dalrymple* (1990) 59 P & CR 231. In this case, a son-in-law agreed to renovate a lodge on the estate owned by his wife's parents. On completion of the renovation, he moved into the lodge and began paying rent. The Court of Appeal held that he had exclusive possession of the lodge and that he had a tenancy. No doubt the fact that he gave up the tenancy of a council house in order to move to the lodge was an important factor in the court arriving at that decision.

Charity

Consistent with the category above, if occupation is granted as a matter of charity or generosity, this tends to suggest that there was no intention to create a tenancy. The principle can be seen in the case of *Marcroft Wagons Ltd v Smith* [1951] 2 KB 497, where a daughter lived with her mother who was a statutory protected tenant of a house under the Rent Acts. On the death of the mother, the daughter requested the landlord to transfer the tenancy of the house to her. The landlord asserted she had no rights to become a statutory protected tenant by succession under the Rent Act. The landlord nevertheless accepted rent from the daughter while they were considering the position. The landlord then applied for possession and proved that the daughter was not a statutory tenant and that the money paid by the daughter was not a rent but a mesne profit. The Court of

Appeal held, with some hesitation, that the landlord had never accepted the daughter as a tenant and never intended to contract with her despite the six-month delay before applying for possession. In the judgment Roxburgh stated at p. 507:

> Generally speaking, when a person, having a sufficient estate in land, lets another into exclusive possession, a tenancy results, and there is no question of a licence. But the inference of a tenancy is not necessarily to be drawn where a person succeeds on a death to occupation of rent-controlled premises and a landlord accepts some rent while he or the occupant, or both of them, is or are considering his or their position. If this is all that happened in this case, then no tenancy would result.

In addition, Lord Evershed MR in particular was reluctant to find for a lease when the arrangement was made out of an act of kindness. He considered it was wrong to disincentivise landlords from acting out of 'ordinary human instincts of kindliness and courtesy', lest they be saddled with a tenant they were unable to remove.

It can be seen from the above examples that 'exclusive possession' can be a difficult concept to define and indeed in **Street v Mountford** Lord Templeman alluded to this towards the end of his judgment when he stated at 826:

> Sometimes it may be difficult to discover whether, on a true construction of an agreement, exclusive possession is conferred. Sometimes it may appear from the surrounding circumstances that there was no intention to create legal relationships. Sometimes it may appear from the surrounding circumstances that the right to exclusive possession is referable to a legal relationship other than a tenancy . . . But where . . . the only circumstances are that residential accommodation is offered and accepted with exclusive possession for a term at a rent, the result is a tenancy.

Thus if an agreement satisfies all the requirements of a tenancy, then the agreement produces a tenancy and the parties are unable to alter the effect of that agreement by insisting that only a licence has been created. Thus Lord Templeman famously stated at p. 819:

> The manufacture of a five pronged implement for manual digging results in a fork even if the manufacturer, unfamiliar with the English language insisted that he intended to make and has made a spade.

The objective test adopted in **Street v Mountford** is, however, no 'magic bullet' for determining the existence of a lease or a licence. Clearly, the focus has to be on the factual position of the parties and not what is contained within the agreement but, whilst the legal concept of exclusive possession appears robust, the *factual* notion of the concept is often blurred against the background of exclusive occupation. Applied extremely, it can have some surprising consequences, as seen in the case of **Bruton v London and Quadrant Housing Trusts** [2000] 1 AC 406.

Bruton v London and Quadrant Housing Trusts [2000] 1 AC 406

In this case, the trust held several properties on licence (prior to obtaining a lease) from Lambeth Borough Council. They used the properties to provide short-term housing for the homeless, who were all provided with licence agreements. Bruton was one of the these licensees and he sought to compel the trust to carry out repairing obligations set out in the Landlord and Tenant Act 1985 s.11. This Act did not apply to licensees and therefore Bruton sought to demonstrate that he was not a licensee but a tenant and fell within the legislation. The trust asserted that it was not capable of granting a leasehold estate to Bruton and that the nemo dat quod non habet principle applied.

Obviously, the assertion by the trust accords with the principle. As we stated earlier, it is not possible to 'carve' a greater interest out of a smaller one. As the trust had a mere licence, on principle it should not be able to grant a lease, a proprietary interest, since it did not have such a proprietary interest itself – nemo dat non quod habet. Mr Bruton asserted that he was a tenant using the principles in **Street v Mountford** and that the trust was estopped from denying he had a tenancy. Bruton was therefore using two devices to establish his tenancy – **Street v Mountford** and tenancy by estoppel.

A tenancy by estoppel arises where a person purports to grant a tenancy and is not permitted to deny he has done so by asserting his own want of title. If he has no title then his grant becomes a tenancy by estoppel. The Court of Appeal held that Bruton could not establish a tenancy by estoppel since the trust did not purport to grant a tenancy in the first place as it was aware that it did not have title itself – hence the fact that the occupiers, including Bruton, were only given licences.

The House of Lords reversed the decision of the Court of Appeal and held that a lease had been created since Bruton was indeed in exclusive possession of the property for a term at a rent. The House of Lords considered that the fact that the trust was a charity and held no lease itself did not take it outside of the principle in **Street v Mountford**.

At this point you may be forgiven for feeling bewildered – how can the trust create a lease when it has no estate in land? Lord Hoffman gave the leading judgment in the House of Lords, explaining that it is the agreement between the parties that creates a lease, whether or not the landlord is able to grant an estate. He stated that, whilst an estate is often created from an agreement, that is not a necessary consequence of the agreement. He stated at 415:

> . . . the term 'lease' or 'tenancy' describes a relationship between two parties who are designated landlord and tenant. It is not concerned with the question of whether the agreement creates an estate or other proprietary interest which may be binding on third parties. A lease may, and usually does, create a proprietary interest called a leasehold estate or, technically, a 'term of years absolute'. This will depend upon whether the landlord had an interest out of which he could grant it. Nemo dat quod non habet [no-one can give what he has not got]. But it is the fact that the agreement is a lease which creates the proprietary interest.

The position therefore is that, once Bruton could establish that his agreement with the trust fell within the **Street v Mountford** principle, this had the legal effect of creating a landlord and tenant relationship and it was not necessary for him to establish that he then had a proprietary title good against the whole world.

The effect of the judgment is that there now appear to be two types of lease – a proprietary lease, which has been recognised for centuries, and a contractual or non-proprietary lease. The whole purpose, however, of Lord Templeman's test of exclusive possession in **Street v Mountford** is to establish a proprietary right that gives exclusive control of the premises to the exclusion of all others, including the landlord. If a contractual or non-proprietary lease does not give this control then it is not a lease but a licence! Indeed in **Kay v London Borough of Lambeth** [2006] UKHL 10, the House of Lords was clear that so-called 'Bruton tenancies' had no proprietary interest at all.

The case of **Kay v London Borough of Lambeth** [2006] UKHL 10 was an interesting follow-on from **Bruton**. After the **Bruton** case, each of the occupiers from the trust became a tenant of the trust. Lambeth Borough Council then gave notice to the trust terminating the lease it had granted to the trust following the initial licence agreement. After granting the notice to the trust, Lambeth City Council notified the occupiers that they were, or would soon become, trespassers vis-à-vis Lambeth City Council and commenced possession proceedings against them. The occupiers responded that, as a result of the **Bruton** case, they had become tenants of the trust and that, when Lambeth terminated the trust's lease, they had become tenants of the Lambeth Borough Council.

In order to establish this claim, the occupiers relied on a principle established in **Mellor v Watkins** (1874) LR 9 QB 400. This principle states that if A has granted a tenancy to B and B has granted a sub-tenancy to C, a surrender by B to A of B's tenancy does not determine C's tenancy but has the effect that A becomes C's landlord: that is, C holds his or her tenancy directly from A.

The House of Lords held that the principle in **Mellor v Watkins** has no application to a case in which a tenancy has been granted by someone without any estate in the land in question. All the Bruton tenancies were of this nature in that they were granted at a time when the trust merely had a licence from Lambeth Borough Council. The tenancies were not granted by Lambeth and were not carved out of an estate that Lambeth Borough Council had granted to the trust. In other words, the tenancies of the occupiers were not derivative estates and so, once the licence/lease of the trust had been terminated, the occupiers became trespassers to Lambeth Borough Council.

The decision therefore sets out the limits of Bruton tenancies in that they are clearly not of a proprietary nature in that they bind third parties and indeed do not accord with the normal principles associated with conventional proprietary leases and are essentially licences in that sense. It is suggested that what the House of Lords in **Bruton** created was a relationship between the tenant and the trust that was in the *nature* of a landlord and tenant relationship, so that the tenant could avail himself of the provisions of the Landlord and Tenant Act 1985 for the purpose, in that case, of compelling the trust to carry out the repair obligations in s.11. Thus the decision in the **Bruton** case is confined to very specific parameters.

Rent

Whilst Lord Templeman considered that rent is an essential element of a lease, the Court of Appeal in **Ashburn Anstalt v W J Arnold & Co.** [1989] Ch 1 stated that a lease could arise even where there was exclusive possession for a term at no rent. This is consistent with the definition contained in the Law of Property Act 1925 s.205(xxvii) where a term of years means 'a term of years (taking effect either in possession or in reversion whether or not at a rent)'.

The creation of leases

We have already seen that leases or terms of years absolute are one of the two estates that can exist in a legal form by virtue of the Law of Property Act 1925 s.1(1). In order to exist in a legal form the creation of a *legal lease* must comply with certain formalities, otherwise the lease will exist as an *equitable lease*. We will look at each of these in turn to see how they are created.

Legal leases

Creation

To create a legal lease a conveyance is required which transfers the leasehold estate to a tenant. This requirement is set out in the Law of Property Act 1925 s.52(1) which states:

> All conveyances of land or any interest therein are void for the purpose of conveying or creating a legal estate unless made by deed.

The Law of Property Act 1925 s.52(2)d, however, provides for certain leases which do not have to be made in writing. Such a lease is found in the Law of Property Act 1925 s.54(2) which provides that:

> Nothing in the foregoing provisions of this Part of the Act shall effect the creation by parol of leases taking effect in possession for a term not exceeding three years (whether or not the lessee is given the power to extend the term) at the best rent which can be reasonably obtained without taking a fine.

The effect of this provision is that an oral ('parol') grant of a lease for a period of less than three years will therefore create a legal term of years within the auspices of the Law of Property Act 1925 s.1(1) provided it is at the best rent reasonably obtainable 'without taking a fine'.

Two points emerge here. 'Best rent' has been held in *Fitzkriston LLP v Panayi* [2008] EWCA Civ 283 by the Court of Appeal to be the 'market rent'. A 'fine' is a premium or a lump sum that is paid at the commencement of a lease. 'Fines' are highly exceptional today in short leases.

The exception under s.54(2) only applies if the lease is for a term not exceeding three years; however, it is possible to create a lease within the exception if, for example, A gives B a two-year lease with an option to renew it for another two years, since the provision states 'whether or not the lessee is given a power to extend the term'. The provision makes no reference to periodic tenancies (i.e. weekly, monthly or yearly tenancies). Technically, these can, and do, exist for many years since they exist from week to week, month to month and year to year. These types of leases are originally granted for the term specified in the grant-lease ('conveyance') – that is, a week, month or year – and are therefore well within the three-year rule.

The final point that should be noted about the exception is s.54(2) in that it must take effect in possession. This is different from leases outside of the exception – for instance, the term of years stated in s.1(1) mentions a 'terms of years absolute'. It does not have to be in possession and can be a reversionary lease – that is, a lease that takes effect in the future. Thus, in the s.54(2) exception, the lease must take effect immediately in possession. A reversionary lease – even one for two years, say – can only take effect if it is made by deed within s.52(1).

Registration

Whilst we discussed the registration requirements of leases in the Chapter 5, it is worth reminding ourselves of these requirements.

Registered land

(i) Where a lease is granted (i.e. made by deed out of a registered title – that is, where the freehold or the Superior lease is a registered title), and it is for a term of *more* than seven years, then the lease must be substantively registered at HM Land Registry. Substantive registration means that the lease will have its own entry and title number. If the lease is not registered, it will not by the Land Registration Act 2002 s.27(1) take effect as a legal lease but only as an equitable lease. It should also be noted that, if the lease is not registered and is only effective in equity, the lessee is not able to grant a legal sub-lease since they do not have a legal lease from which to carve out the new lease. Once registered, the lease will be entered as a notice on the registered title of the landlord. If the lease is one for seven years or less and is for a period of not less than three years, there is no requirement for the lease to be substantively registered and it will take effect as an interest that is overriding under the Land Registration Act 2002 Schedule 3 Paragraph 1. It should be noted that the Land Registration Act 2002 makes provision for leases of seven years or less to become substantively registered at some time in the future. This has not yet been activated but, no doubt, as e-conveyancing becomes fully operational, such leases will require substantive registration so that the register will provide a more complete reflection of the interests that affect the land in question.

(ii) Where a lease is granted out of an unregistered title – that is where the freehold or superior lease is *not* a registered title and, again, the lease is for a term of more than seven years, the title must be compulsorily registered at the HM Land Registry by virtue of the Land Registration Act 2002 s.4(1), since this is regarded as a 'trigger' event. Failure to register results in the lease only taking effect in equity. There are certain other leases that fall within s.4(1) and require registration, such as timeshare leases. Again, it is likely that the seven-year period will be shortened to three years, as in (i) above.

Unregistered land

If the lease is for seven years or less and arises out of unregistered land then, because this is not a 'trigger' event, all that is required is a grant by way of a deed to give the tenant a leasehold estate in the land. Such a lease as a legal estate 'will bind the whole world', including any purchasers of the landlord's reversion, whether the freehold or the superior leasehold. When the purchaser of the landlord's reversion registers the estate on the basis of compulsory first registration then the lease will be an interest that is overriding by virtue of the Land Registration Act Schedule 1 Paragraph 1.

Equitable leases

Creation

As we have seen, to create a legal lease for a term of more than three years a deed is required. Leases for three years or less qualify as legal estates under the s.54(2) exception. Where the lease is for more than three years and no deed is used then an equitable lease will arise, provided there is a valid contract to create the lease under the Law of Property (Miscellaneous Provisions) Act 1989 s.2(1). This provision requires that:

- the contract be in writing; and
- incorporate all the terms the parties have expressly agreed in one document or, where documents have been exchanged, in each; and
- the document must be signed by all the parties.

The common law would clearly not recognise the transaction as conveying a legal estate without a deed; however, the stance of equity was very different and under the principle in *Parker* v *Taswell* (1858) 2 De G & J 559 would treat the imperfect grant of the lease as a *contract* to grant the lease and thus gave the lessor and lessee all the rights and obligations contained in the contract. The underlying concept that equity used to enforce the contract was based on the maxim 'equity treats that as done which ought to be done'. Equity would look at the transaction and see that there was a valid contract to create a lease, including the granting of a deed but, whilst this had not been done, it would enforce the contract as if a deed had been granted. If a dispute arose between the parties, equity would then enforce the contract by way of a decree of specific performance and compel the landlord to give the tenant a deed and at this point a legal lease is created.

Example

L agrees to give T a lease for seven years and they both sign a contract to that effect. No deed is executed. L then attempts to go back on his word and refuses to execute the deed. If T now went to the common law courts for help, the courts would refuse, on the basis that there was no deed, and would not recognise the arrangement or T's rights. T would then take her case to equity, the Court of Chancery. The court would decide the case as a matter of conscience and, if it considered that L had acted unfairly or against his conscience, it would enforce the contract by way of decree of specific performance, and compel L to grant the deed. T would then end up with what she wanted – a legal lease for seven years.

The classic case that illustrates the operation of the court of equity is that of **Walsh v Lonsdale** (1820) 21 Ch D 9.

Walsh v Lonsdale (1820) 21 Ch D 9

In this case Walsh ('W') and Lonsdale ('L') entered into an agreement under which L would give W a seven-year lease of a mill. The contract provided that the lease would state that rent should be payable one year in advance, on L's demand. Whilst L did not execute a deed, he nevertheless allowed W to go into possession of the mill and pay his rent for one year in arrears. Shortly after the first year, L demanded a year's rent in advance, as per the contract. W refused to pay the rent and therefore L exercised his right as a lessor and 'distrained' for the rent. Distress ('distraint') is an ancient remedy that allows a landlord to enter premises and seize goods of a value equivalent to the rent owed. W claimed that L had no right to demand a year's rent in advance and that therefore the distraint was wrongful. He therefore sued L. Was the landlord entitled to a year's rent in advance? If he was, then his distraint was lawful; if not, it was wrongful.

W's case was that, at common law, once he had been let into possession without the deed being executed giving him the seven-year lease, he became a yearly tenant by virtue of the fact that he had paid and L had accepted one year's rent. Remember, a legal lease for a period not exceeding three years can be created orally. W argued, therefore, that he had a *legal* yearly periodic tenancy. At common law, if he had a yearly periodic tenancy, he was not obliged to pay his rent in advance and, that being the case, he was not obliged to pay his rent until the end of the second year of his tenancy. It followed from this that L had exercised his right to levy distress wrongfully.

Equity, however, takes a very different view of the transaction since it recognised the contract for the seven-year lease. As L had contracted to grant the lease, it would recognise the lease and therefore an equitable lease for seven years would arise that was on the same terms as those set out in the contract – that is, equity treats that as done which ought to be done. On that basis, W was obliged to pay his rent in advance when L demanded it and therefore L's levying of distress was lawful.

We can therefore see that there is a clear conflict between common law and equity. The Judicature Act 1873 s.25(11) provides that, where there is a variance between the rules of equity and common law, the rules of equity prevail and therefore an equitable seven-year lease arises. If the court eventually ordered a decree of specific performance then this would compel the landlord (W) to provide a deed and this in turn would then result in a *legal* seven-year lease being created. The principle in **Parker v Taswell** (1858) 2 De G & J 559, as illustrated in **Walsh v Lonsdale** (1820) 21 Ch D 9, is dependent upon the willingness of equity to grant the discretionary remedy of specific performance. The conditions attached to the granting of this remedy, such as the need for damages to be an inadequate remedy, also apply. In addition, and importantly, the person seeking to enforce an equitable lease must 'come to equity with clean hands'.

Coatsworth v Johnson (1886) 55 LJQB 220

In this Johnson ('J') entered into a contract to lease a farm to Coatsworth ('C') for 21 years. The contract contained a clause that C was to manage the farm 'in good and husband-like manner'. C entered into possession of the farm without a deed being executed. Soon after moving in, C had allowed the condition of the land to deteriorate badly and J took the step of evicting C from the farm. C then sued for wrongful eviction and alleged that the contract provided him with an equitable lease for 21 years.

Held: In order to establish his lease, C had to establish that the remedy of specific performance would be available to him. The fact that he had let the farm deteriorate meant that he was in breach of a substantial term of the contract. This meant that C had come to equity with 'unclean hands' and therefore he would be denied the remedy. C was therefore evicted from the farm.

So what happens if specific performance is not available? In these circumstances, the court will fall back on the common law principles so that, for example, if the tenant has been let into possession and is paying rent, then that will give rise to a periodic tenancy. Since a periodic tenancy is usually for less than three years – being either a weekly, monthly, or yearly periodic tenancy – this will fall within the s.54(2) exception and thus be a *legal* periodic tenancy. Thus in **Walsh v Lonsdale** (1820) 21 Ch D 9 if there had been no finding of an equitable lease for seven years Walsh would have had a legal yearly periodic tenancy.

So far, we have seen that equitable leases can arise where there is an enforceable contract but no deed to convey a legal lease. However, equitable leases can arise in other situations, even if there is a deed – for example:

(a) Where there is an attempt to grant a lease to a minor. A minor is not entitled to land or legal estate in land by virtue of the Law of Property Act 1925 s.1(6), therefore any interest held by the minor must be equitable, with the legal title being held in trust for him or her.

(b) Where a legal lease is conveyed to trustees, to be held on trust for a beneficiary, the beneficiary will hold an equitable lease.

(c) Where the owner of a legal lease declares that he or she holds it on trust for a beneficiary, the beneficiary will hold an equitable lease.

(d) Where a lease is granted by a person who holds an interest that is already equitable, such as where the grantor holds an equitable fee simple or where the superior lease is itself equitable.

The effect of equitable leases on third parties

The main problem with equitable leases is that, being equitable, they suffer from the same frailties as all equitable interests in that they do not necessarily bind third party purchasers from the landlord.

Example

L enters into a contract with T to grant T a lease for seven years, the lease being an equitable lease. L then agrees to sell his legal fee simple or his superior legal reversion to X. Will X take subject to T's equitable lease?

The answer to the above question differs, depending on whether the lease is unregistered or registered.

Unregistered land

Since an equitable lease is effectively an enforceable contract to grant a lease then this amounts to an estate contract. As an estate contract, the equitable lease must be registered as a C(iv) land charge against the name of the estate owner (L). If the C(iv) land charge is unregistered it will be void against such a third party purchaser, with the result that the owner of the equitable lease can be evicted from the premises on the sale of a superior title such as a legal fee simple or a superior legal lease.

Registered land

Equitable leases can be protected by the entering of a notice on the register of title of the land over which they take effect. By virtue of the Land Registration Act 2002 s.28 and s.29 registration of the notice gives protection for the holder of the equitable lease against later transferees of the reversion, either the legal fee simple or the superior legal lease.

Even if the holder of the equitable lease fails to register their notice, they can claim to have an interest that is overriding since the holder of the equitable lease will almost certainly be in actual occupation of the land and thus gain the protection of the Land Registration Act 2002 Schedule 3 Paragraph 1. The effect of the above is that the holder of an equitable lease is almost certain to have protection in one way or the other.

The difference between legal and equitable leases

Apart from the difference between legal and equitable leases as regards third parties, as discussed, there are other differences.

Easements

By virtue of the Law of Property Act 1925 s.62 on a conveyance certain easements may be implied into the conveyance. Clearly, an equitable lease is created by a written contract, not by a deed of conveyance, and therefore s.62 has no application here.

The running of covenants

There is clearly a privity of contract between between the parties to the contract for a lease so that they are bound by the covenants within the contract. Both parties take the benefit and burden of the covenants. (See Figure 6.3.)

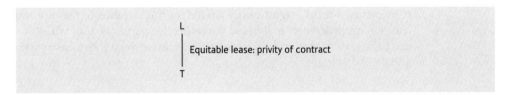

L

Equitable lease: privity of contract

T

Figure 6.3

Where the landlord (L) assigns his reversion to another (R) and the tenant (T) assigns her lease to an assignee (A) the position is very different. The broad principle in English law is that one can assign the benefit of any covenants in a contract but not the burden of any covenants. Thus an assignee of the landlord (R) and an assignee of the tenant are able to enforce the benefits of the covenants against the original parties to the contract, as shown in Figure 6.4.

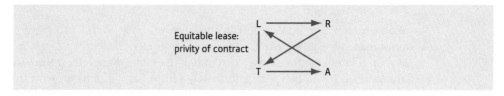

Figure 6.4

The same is not true in relation to the burdens of covenants. Thus L could not enforce the covenants against A, nor could T enforce the covenants against R. Thus assignees are not bound by the covenants as the burden of a contract does not bind the assignees.

The position is not the same with a legal lease, since here there is said to be 'privity of estate' between L and T (see Figure 6.5).

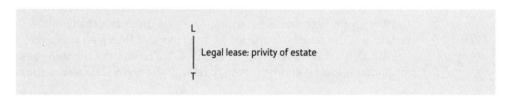

Figure 6.5

Where the original parties assign their interests, the assignees also have privity of estate so that the benefits and burdens are enforceable (see Figure 6.6).

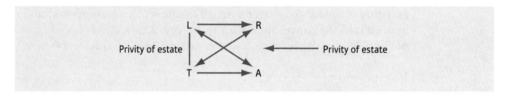

Figure 6.6

The above principles are only summaries of the respective positions of the parties. In any event, the principles only apply to pre-1995 leases since the Landlord and Tenant (Covenants) Act 1995 significantly altered the rules relating to the running of covenants in leases. A more detailed analysis of the respective parties is dealt with later on; however, it can be seen that there are significant differences between the running of covenants in legal and equitable leases.

Types of lease

The different classifications of leases

Leases for a fixed period of time

Leases can be granted for any period of time of certain duration, no matter how long or short. Thus a tenancy for a week is just as valid as a lease for 3000 years. As we have already seen when discussing the nature of leases, it is important that the period of the lease is for a term of certain duration and any departure from the principle will normally render the lease void: *Lace v Chantler* [1944] KB 368.

We have already briefly mentioned reversionary leases – that is, leases to take effect in the future. It will be recalled that, by the Law of Property Act 1925 s.149(3) a lease to take effect more than 21 years after the instrument creating it is void. It should be noted, however, that this provision does not catch *contracts* to grant leases more than 21 years from the date of the contract. Thus, for example, a contract in 2013 to grant a lease for 99 years to take effect in 2043 is perfectly acceptable, since here the lease is not a reversionary one.

The general rule is that leases for a fixed period automatically end (or determine) when the fixed period expires, though there are some statutory modifications that can apply, such as those that are found in the Landlord and Tenant Act 1954.

Periodic leases

Examples of periodic tenancies are weekly, monthly, quarterly or yearly tenancies. A periodic tenancy is one that continues indefinitely until it is brought to an end by the giving of proper notice. The length of the notice depends on the period of the tenancy, subject to contrary agreement and statutory intervention – see below. Potentially, a periodic lease could continue forever since, if the landlord dies, then their reversion will pass by way of their will or according to the rules on intestacy. The same applies if the tenant dies. On the face of things, this appears to run contrary to what was said earlier with regards to the certainty of duration under the nature of the lease. It will be recalled, however, that such a term is capable of being rendered certain by the giving of the appropriate notice. Thus a yearly tenancy runs from year to year, and a monthly tenancy runs from month to month and so on.

Periodic tenancies can arise in a number of ways. Firstly, they can arise expressly where a term is expressed as a 'yearly tenancy'. Secondly, they can arise where reference is made to the notice period required to terminate the tenancy: for example, a lease to T that is determinable on the giving of one month's notice creates a monthly tenancy. Thirdly, they can be implied where there are no express words or other means of inferring the type of lease. In these circumstances, if a lease is given to T at £800 a month then a monthly tenancy arises. If the lease is given to T at £200 per week then a weekly tenancy arises, etc. Thus the period of the tenancy is determined by the period by which the payment of rent is measured. A word of caution is required here. The period of the tenancy is determined by the period by which the payment of rent is measured, despite the fact that the rent is actually payable at some different interval. For example, if there is a lease 'to T at a rent of £5200 per year payable weekly', this does *not* create a weekly tenancy but a yearly tenancy as the tenancy is referable to the interval at which the rent is measured: *Adler v Blackman* [1953] 1 QB 146. Finally, a periodic tenancy may arise where a lease for a fixed period of time expires and the tenant continues in possession of the land, paying rent at a periodic rate which the landlord accepts. For example, the landlord, L, gives a tenant, T, a lease for 10 years at a rent of £700 per month. At the end of this period T remains in possession and continues to pay rent at the rate of £700 per month, which the landlord accepts. Providing there are no circumstances to the contrary, by implication T now holds the property on a monthly tenancy. One point to note here is that, subject to statutory modification, the terms of the monthly tenancy here are on the same terms as those of the 10-year fixed lease, except insofar as the terms of the 10-year lease are inconsistent with the monthly tenancy. For instance, if the 10-year lease requires the landlord to paint the outside of the premises every five years, this term is clearly inconsistent with that of a monthly tenancy.

Whilst periodic tenancies are made certain by the giving of the appropriate notice and this is determined by the period over which the rent is measured, the actual period of notice required is not necessarily that period, though it is true that the period depends on the form of the lease. In the case of a yearly tenancy at common law, subject to contrary agreement, this must be determined on the anniversary of its commencement. In order to give such notice, either party must give the other at least half a year's notice of determination expiring at the end of a completed year of the tenancy. Half a year's notice depends on the date on which the tenancy began; however, traditionally some leases begin on one of the usual 'quarter days'. The 'quarter days' are Lady Day (25 March), Midsummer Day (24 June), Michaelmas Day (29 September) and Christmas Day (25 December). Since medieval times these have traditionally been the days when accounts were settled. The quarter days are actually four festivals in the religious calendar: the Feast of the Annunciation (25 March), the Feast of St John the Baptist (24 June), the Feast of St Michael and All Angels (29 September), and the Feast of the Nativity (25 December). In modern leases the quarter days now being adopted are 1 January, 1 April, 1 July and 1 October. Half a year's notice means 'two quarters'; otherwise 'half a year' means 182 days.

In the case of weekly, monthly and quarterly periodic tenancies at common law the period of notice required to determine the tenancy was a full period's notice, unlike a yearly tenancy, where the period of notice was a half a year's notice. Thus, originally, a week's, a month's or a quarter's period of notice was required. This has now been subject to modification so that, under the Protection of Eviction Act 1977 s.5, where premises are let as a dwelling, at least four weeks' notice is required and the forfeiture of the lease must be conducted through court proceedings.

Tenancies by sufferance

Technically, a tenancy by sufferance is not a tenancy. It occurs where a tenant holds over once their lease has expired, without the landlord's consent or dissent. The separating factor from otherwise becoming a trespasser is that the tenant's original occupation of the land was lawful. Under a tenancy at sufferance, the landlord can claim possession at any time and has a claim against the tenant for their use and occupation of the land. If the tenant pays rent and this is accepted by the landlord then a periodic tenancy arises, based on the principles that have already been discussed. Strictly speaking, there is no relationship of landlord and tenant here at all and the expression 'tenancy by sufferance' seems to arise from the fact that the parties were originally landlord and tenant.

Tenant at will

A tenancy by will arises where the landlord consents to the tenant occupying the land on terms that allow either party to determine the tenancy at any time. The most common situation in which such a tenancy arises is where, on the sale of a property, the vendor allows the purchaser to enter the premises prior to completion. Usually, the tenant pays no rent, but if they do and this is accepted by the landlord then a periodic tenancy may arise by implication on the basis of the principles already discussed – unless, of course, the parties make it clear that only a tenancy at will should subsist.

Since a tenancy at will is essentially one of a personal relationship between the landlord and tenant, it ends if either party dies or assigns their interest in the land.

Tenancies by estoppel

It is a principle of land law that a tenant cannot deny their landlord's title and vice versa. Both parties are said to be estopped from denying the other's title, even if the landlord in fact had a defective title.

> ## Example
>
> L has contracted to purchase Blackacre; however, completion has yet to take place. Whilst this process is ongoing, she leases Blackacre to T for 10 years. Even if it is clear that L's title is defective in terms of creating a lease, both L and T (and their successors in title) will be estopped from denying that the grant of the lease was effective to create the lease/tenancy.

The position was summed up by Lord Denning in *Industrial Properties (Barton Hill) Ltd* v *AEI Ltd* [1977] QB 850 when he stated at 596:

> If a landlord lets a tenant into possession under a lease, then, so long as the tenant remains in possession undisturbed by any adverse claim – then the tenant cannot dispute the landlord's title. Suppose the tenant (not having been disturbed) goes out of possession and the landlord sues the tenant on the covenant for rent or for breach of covenant to repair . . . The tenant cannot say to the landlord: 'You are not the true owner of the property'.

Traditionally, one effect of this rule is that, if a landlord has no estate in land and consequently no actual estate can be conferred on the tenant, it is nevertheless good as between the parties to it and their successors in title. In *Bruton* v *London and Quadrant Housing Trust* [2000] 1 AC 406, the facts of which we have already seen, the House of Lords found that, although the trust merely had a licence, it was nevertheless able to pass a tenancy to Bruton since he had exclusive possession of the property within *Street* v *Mountford*. The House of Lords rejected the decision in the Court of Appeal that Bruton could not establish a tenancy by estoppel since the trust never purported to give him a tenancy in the first place – only a licence, since it only had a licence itself. Millett LJ stated that an estoppel depended upon the grantor having purported to grant a lease and that the trust had not done so.

Lord Hoffman, however, was of a different opinion. He stated at 415:

> . . . I think that Millett LJ may have been misled by the ancient phrase 'tenancy by estoppel' into thinking that it described an agreement which would not otherwise be a lease or tenancy but which was treated as being one by virtue of an estoppel. In fact, as the authorities show, it is not the estoppel which creates the tenancy, but the tenancy which creates the estoppel. The estoppel arises when one or other of the parties wants to deny one of the ordinary incidents or obligations of the tenancy on the ground that the landlord had no legal estate. The basis of the estoppel is that having entered into an agreement which constitutes a lease or tenancy, he cannot repudiate that incident or obligation.

It is important to remember that tenancies by estoppel do not bind third parties that have a better title to the land than the person creating the lease. However, it is possible to transfer a tenancy in the same way as any other lease or tenancy.

Feeding the estoppel

Where a tenancy is created by a person who lacks the legal title and that person, the landlord, subsequently acquires the legal title, then the tenancy is said to be fed. Once this occurs, the tenant automatically acquires a tenancy based upon the newly acquired legal title instead of their tenancy by estoppel. Thus, in the example above, if the transfer of Blackacre to L is completed then T's 10-year lease becomes effective and the tenancy by estoppel is extinguished.

It should be noted that if estoppel arises by deed – that is, the landlord has legal title but denies it – they will be estopped from doing so. In such a case, no tenancy by estoppel will arise since the landlord does, in fact, have legal title (as opposed to an equitable interest) and therefore the tenancy granted will arise in the normal way (see the first example below). However, if the lease granted to the tenant is greater than the legal estate vested in the landlord then the grant of the lease will operate as an assignment of the landlord's legal estate (see the second example below).

> ### Example
> L has a 99-year legal lease of Blackacre and grants T a 10-year lease; no tenancy by estoppel arises.

> ### Example
> L has a 99-year legal lease of Blackacre and grants T a 999-year lease. Clearly L's legal lease is smaller than the lease granted to T. Here L's grant to T will operate as an assignment of his own 99-year legal lease.

Similar principles also apply to the granting of sub-leases. For example, L grants T a lease of Blackacre for seven years in 2010. Three years later, T grants a sub-lease to X for 5 years. Clearly, the sub-lease is greater than the term held by T. In such situations, the grant by T operates as an assignment of his own leases so that now X becomes a direct tenant of L.

Statutory modifications to leases

We have seen that lease can be created for varying degrees of time, whether long or short. However, in some situations Parliament has intervened to make modifications to the term of the lease.

Perpetually renewable leases

These types of lease are very rare today and when they do arise it is usually the result of inept drafting. A perpetually renewable lease arises where a lease is granted with an option to renew the lease on the same terms.

> ### Example
> L grants a lease of Greenacre to T for 10 years with an option to renew the lease for another term of 10 years on the same terms as the original lease.

In such a situation, at the end of the original 10-year lease T can renew her lease for another 10 years. However, this renewal is on the same terms as the first period, so that at the end of the second period of 10 years she has another right to renew it. In such a situation, a perpetually renewable lease is created, even though the parties might have had no intention of doing so.

By virtue of the Law of Property Act 1922 s.145 and Schedule 15 a perpetual renewable lease is converted to a 2000-year term on the same terms as the original lease. The tenant is able to terminate the lease on any date it would have expired on, barring the conversion to a 2000-year term, provided they give at least 10 days' notice. This concession is not available to the landlord.

Another unusual feature of such leases is that, once the tenant assigns the lease, they are no longer liable for any future breaches committed after the assignment. In leases created prior to 1996, the general rule is that a tenant is liable for all breaches throughout the term of the lease.

The courts tend to lean against perpetually renewable leases and in ***Caerphilly Concrete Products Ltd v Owen*** [1972] 1 WLR 372 it was held that a lease that contained a covenant to renew along the lines set out above merely gave the tenant the ability to renew the lease on two further occasions, rather than a 2000-year term as for a perpetually renewable lease.

Leases for life or until marriage

A lease that is created for the duration of the life of a person, or for a term of years determinable on the death of the lessee, or on the marriage or civil partnership of the lessee, at a rent or a fine (premium), is converted into a term of 90 years by virtue of the Law of Property Act 1925 s.149(6).

Example

(a) A lease granted by L to T for life at a rent of £100 per week
(b) A lease granted by L to T for 5 years if T so long lives at a rent of £600 per month
(c) A lease granted by L to T for 25 years for £10,000 if he remains a bachelor.

It can be seen that leases for life are very similar to life estates, which are a type of freehold estate. Such freehold estates, because they are outside the Law of Property Act 1925 s.1(1), can only exist as equitable interests behind a trust on settlement. Leases for life are therefore a type of hybrid. Leases for life, however, are of a commercial nature, whereas life estates are of a family nature and covered by the overreaching provisions we examined earlier. The intention behind the Law of Property Act 1925 s.149(6) is to bring a lease for life within the 1925 property scheme. On the other hand, life estates, which must be equitable, are governed by the Trusts of Land and Appointment of Trustees Act 1996 and exist behind a trust of land. Life interests created prior to 1996 are governed by the Settled Land Act 1925.

Reversionary leases

As we have already seen, any lease created to commence more than 21 years from the instrument creating it is void: Law of Property Act 1925 s.149(3).

Covenants and the obligations of landlord and tenant

Introduction

Most leases contain provisions that impose rights and obligations on the parties to the lease, although in short leases these provisions may be very limited or non-existent – the latter situation being quite common in leases that have been created informally. In long leases or commercial leases, the provisions may be very long and, indeed, extraordinarily complex. These types of provision are, of course, express covenants – however, overlaying the lease may be implied what are termed the 'usual' covenants. It should also be borne in mind that there is a raft of obligations imposed by statute. For the most part, we will not be concerning ourselves with the detailed statutory provisions that relate to landlord and tenant since this is a subject in its own right.

Whilst referring to provisions in leases as 'covenants', one must also distinguish between these and 'conditions'. Covenants tend to be provisions in leases where a 'covenantor' makes a promise to another, the 'covenantee'. Such provisions contained in a deed are referred to as 'conditions'.

It should be remembered that leases are essentially contracts and the principles applying to the law of contract may be equally applicable to a lease. Conditions are regarded as major terms of a contract that allow a party to terminate the contract and claim damages. Conditions tend to be obligations imposed on the tenant by the landlord, breach of which entitles the landlord to terminate the lease. In other words, the granting of the lease is conditional upon the tenant complying with the condition. A breach of covenant, in contrast, does not automatically provide the landlord with the right to terminate the lease. Whether the parties intend a provision to be a covenant or a condition is dependent on the intentions of the parties. Generally speaking, the courts tend to view provisions in leases as covenants rather than conditions but it is well to bear in mind that some important provisions will be treated as covenants as opposed to conditions.

In examining covenants one should remember that these are reciprocal provisions between the landlord and tenant and therefore, in examining the rights and obligations of the parties, we will be looking in turn at the landlord's obligations and the tenant's obligations. In examining these obligations we shall look at covenants that are express, implied and 'usual' in turn.

Express covenants

As this suggests, these are covenants that the landlord and tenant have expressly agreed in the lease they have entered into. Clearly, there could be a wide variety of such covenants and therefore the focus will be on the more important types that are commonly included in leases. Since it is the landlord who will normally draft the lease and its provisions, it should be noted, as in the law of contract, that the contra proferentem rule applies here and the covenants will be construed against the landlord.

Landlord's covenants

Quiet enjoyment
This will be considered under implied covenants below.

No derogation from grant
This will be considered under absolute and qualified covenants below.

Fitness of premises and covenants to repair
The vast majority of leases contain covenants that regulate the obligations of the landlord to maintain the premises in a fit and habitable state and to carry out repairs. In very long leases (for example, 999-year leases), the obligations of the landlord may be very limited or even non-existent and it is the responsibility of the tenant to maintain the premises. In shorter leases, it is often the case that the tenant is responsible for internal repairs and decorating the premises; whilst the landlord is responsible for external and structural repairs to the premises.

Usually, the landlord's covenant to repair is coupled with a right of entry to inspect the premises and carry out repairs. This right of entry has to be carried out reasonably and normally the lease will provide that the landlord has to give notice of his or her intention to inspect and enter the premises. This, of course, accords with the right of the tenant to have exclusive possession and to quiet enjoyment of the premises. If there is no express provision for entry by the landlord then this is, in any case, implied.

Covenant to insure the premises

Whilst the lease may require the landlord to insure the premises, in longer leases, such a covenant may be applied against the tenant instead. Some careful thought is required when inserting such an express covenant since, in order to insure the premises, one needs an insurable interest before an insurance company will enter into such a contract. In short leases, the landlord will clearly have such an insurable interest; however, this is less likely in a long lease.

Tenant's covenants

Covenant to pay rent

Whilst we have already seen that the payment of rent is an unnecessary requirement for the existence of a lease, it is rare for a lease not to contain such an express covenant. The rent must be a certain sum; however, some leases will contain a clause providing for a mechanism for determining the rent to be paid. In commercial leases, it is also common for the lease to contain a clause allowing the rent paid to be reviewed at certain periods and, again, such leases also provide a mechanism for determining the amount to be paid.

In the absence of an agreement to the contrary, rent is normally paid in arrears.

One particular problem that applies to the covenant to pay rent is that the obligation continues even if the premises are destroyed: for instance, by fire, bomb damage or by a heavy goods vehicle. In many respects, the logic is correct since, whilst the layperson may think in terms of renting a house, flat, office or factory, the lawyer knows that one is actually leasing the land. The result of this is that, even if the building is completely destroyed, the tenant still has to pay the rent, regardless of the fact that the premises now comprises a burnt-out shell or a hole in the ground. The doctrine of frustration as seen in the law of contract can rarely apply to a lease. The principles can be seen in the case of *Cricklewood Property & Investment Trust Ltd* v *Leighton's Investment Trust Ltd* [1945] AC 221.

Cricklewood Property & Investment Trust Ltd v *Leighton's Investment Trust Ltd* [1945] AC 221

In this case, a plot of land was let in 1936 to the lessees for 99 years in order that they could build shops on the property. Before the lessees could begin construction, the war broke out and the government subsequently passed the regulations restricting such development. The effect was that the lessees could not build the shops they had covenanted to build and they thus claimed that the lease was frustrated. The House of Lords held that the doctrine of frustration did not apply, basing their decision on the fact that the restrictions would only delay building for a comparatively short period when balanced against the full extent of the 99-year lease. Their Lordships were of divided opinions as to whether frustration could ever apply to leases. Lord Simon and Lord Wright considered it could, but only in the rather extreme circumstance where the land is engulfed by the sea and therefore the very land itself is destroyed. Lord Russell and Lord Goddard considered that frustration could never apply, while Lord Porter declined to express an opinion.

The position not to allow frustration in leases is, however, more than just a little illogical since, if one rents a property for a particular purpose, then surely, if that purpose becomes impossible, the doctrine should apply. Certainly, frustration does exist in the case of a contractual licence to hold land since it was fully accepted in the case of **Krell v Henry** [1903] 2 KB 740 where the contract to rent a room for the coronation procession was held to be frustrated when the procession was cancelled. From here the argument can be taken to the point that the law would have to make a distinction between a legal lease and an equitable lease. The latter takes effect as a contract to grant a lease under the doctrine of **Walsh v Lonsdale** (1882) 21 ChD 9, and it could therefore be discharged by frustration, while a legal lease could not.

The issue relating to frustration and leases would seem to be now decided by the case of **National Carriers Ltd v Panalpina (Northern) Ltd** [1981] AC 675 where the House of Lords decided that frustration could apply to leases. They expressed the view, however, that its occurrence would be rare and probably confined to the situation where there was a joint intention that the property was to be released for a particular purpose, and that the purpose had become impossible because of events beyond the control of the parties. Lord Wilberforce stated at 694:

> if the argument is to have any reality, it must be possible to say that frustration of leases cannot occur because in any event the tenant will have that which he bargained for, namely, the leasehold estate. Certainly this may be so in many cases . . . But there may also be cases where this is not so. A man may desire possession and use of land or buildings for, and only for, some purpose in view and mutually contemplated. Why is it an answer, when he claims that this purpose is 'frustrated' to say that he has an estate if that estate is unusable and unsaleable? In such a case the lease, or the conferring or an estate, is a subsidiary means to an end, not an aim or end of itself.

The result in the case, however, was that a lease for a warehouse which had four and a half years to run was not frustrated by a street closure order that prevented the warehouse from being used for 18 months.

If the tenant fails to pay their rent, the landlord may sue for their money or 'levy distress', as we saw earlier. Distress gives the landlord the right to enter the premises and enforce payment by seizing any goods on the premises to the value of the rent owed. The right is exercisable without a court order, though it is usually executed by a bailiff. The landlord can also take indirect action by way of forfeiture, provided the lease contains such a clause.

Obligations to pay rent are often framed as conditions rather than covenants – hence the fact that the lease can be forfeited without a forfeiture clause. Thus a tenant who fails to pay their rent is in danger of rendering their lease voidable at the option of the landlord. Clearly, it can be seen that a disgruntled tenant who decides to go on a 'rent strike' could lose the very thing they want to keep, their home.

Not to assign, underlet or part with possession

Since the tenant has a legal estate in land, they are entitled to assign, underlet or part with possession of the leased premises without the landlord's consent. It is quite common, however, for a landlord to restrict a tenant's rights by including a covenant against the tenant assigning, underletting or parting with possession of either the whole or part of the premises. Should the tenant assign or underlet the premises, then the assignment or the underlease will be valid, though the landlord will have a right to claim damages or even forfeit the lease. It is clearly in the landlord's interest to include such a covenant since many wish to know who is in the property and whether they are likely to default on paying the rent or cause waste to the property, etc.

Covenants against assigning, underletting or parting with possession have two forms – absolute covenants and qualified covenants.

Absolute and qualified covenants

An absolute covenant prohibits the tenant from assigning, etc., whereas a qualified covenant prohibits the tenant from assigning, etc. without the landlord's consent. Clearly, a breach of an absolute covenant to assign, etc. is an automatic breach of the covenant, though the landlord may choose to waive the breach if they so wish. The landlord is under no obligation to do so even if refusal is completely unreasonable.

With regard to qualified covenants not to assign, etc. without consent, the Landlord and Tenant Act 1927 s.19(1)a provides that, notwithstanding any contrary agreement, such covenants are subject to the proviso that the consent of the landlord must not be withheld unreasonably. If the tenant does, in fact, assign, etc. without the landlord's consent, then they are in breach of the covenant, even if the landlord would not have withheld their consent if the tenant had asked for that consent. On the other hand, if the tenant does ask for the landlord's consent and it is withheld unreasonably, then the tenant is free to assign, grant an underlease/sub-lease or part with possession of the premises.

The Landlord and Tenant Act 1927 created some significant problems for tenants, not least the fact that delays by landlords became a matter of great frustration to tenants wanting to assign, etc. In response to this and the recommendations of the Law Commission, the Landlord and Tenant Act 1988 was passed to provide some relief for tenants from the actions or inactions of evasive or dilatory landlords. By virtue of s.1(3) of the Landlord and Tenant Act 1988, once a landlord has received a written request for consent from the tenant, the landlord has a duty to give their consent within a reasonable time unless it is reasonable to withhold that consent. If the landlord does withhold their consent or gives it subject to conditions then they must serve a notice on the tenant giving their reasons. Any conditions that a landlord makes if they do choose to give consent must be reasonable. If a landlord is in breach of their obligations under the Act then s.4 provides that the landlord will be liable in tort for breach of their statutory duty. With regard to the award of damages, it should be noted that in **Design Progression Ltd v Thurloe Properties Ltd** [2004] EWHC 324 (Ch) it was held that a landlord that sought to profit by the unreasonable withholding of its consent was liable for exemplary damages.

The Landlord and Tenant Act 1988 does not define what is a reasonable time – though, of course, the statutory point will always be the time and date on which the tenant applies for consent from the landlord. In **Go West Ltd v Spigarolo** [2003] EWCA Civ 17 it was held that one had to have regard to all the circumstances surrounding the individual case and the negotiations between the parties prior to the landlord making their decision. In that case, Munby J considered that a reasonable time should be measured in weeks rather than months. Another matter that should be recalled in the **Go West** case is that the tenant had applied for consent and the landlord refused, giving reasons. Following that refusal, the parties continued their negotiations prior to the tenant bringing proceedings for a declaration that the refusal was unreasonable. The Court of Appeal held that the refusal notice by the landlord effectively brought to an end the period of 'reasonable' time. The landlord could not thereafter seek to reconsider the application during the remainder of what might have otherwise been a reasonable period.

By s.1(6) it is for the landlord to establish that their response to the tenant is given within a reasonable time, that their refusal is reasonable or that any conditions imposed on their giving consent are reasonable. Furthermore, it was held in **Norwich Union Life Insurance Co. Ltd v Shopmoor Ltd** [1991] 1 WLR 531 that a landlord who argues that their refusal to consent is reasonable can only rely on those grounds that existed at the end of the reasonable time from the making of the original request by the tenant.

What is a reasonable withholding of consent largely depends on the facts of each case. In **Ashworth Frazer Ltd v Gloucester City Council** [2001] 1 WLR 2180, [2001] UKHL 59, it was the view of Lord Bingham that in considering whether a refusal of consent is reasonable, the expression should be given 'a broad sense meaning'. Some broad guidance can be discerned from the cases, however. For instance, it was held in **International Drilling Fluids Ltd v Louisville Investments (Uxbridge) Ltd** [1986] Ch 513 that a landlord is not entitled to refuse consent on grounds which have nothing to do with the relationship of landlord and tenant in regard to the subject matter of the lease. It is not necessary for the landlord to prove that the conclusions on which their refusal was based were justified, provided they were conclusions which might be reached by a reasonable person in the circumstances. A landlord need only consider their own relevant interests. However, in the above case it was stated that the authorities appear to indicate that there may be circumstances in which the benefit to the landlord and the detriment to the tenant by the landlord withholding their consent are so disproportionate that it is unreasonable for the landlord to withhold their consent.

Originally, it used to be the case that a landlord could not refuse to give consent on the grounds that the intended use by the assignee would be a breach of covenant, as in **Killick v Second Covent Garden Property Co. Ltd** [1973] 2 All ER 237 CA. The House of Lords in **Ashworth Frazer Ltd v Gloucester City Council** [2001] 1 WLR 2180, [2001] UKHL 59 overruled **Killick** and held that a refusal of consent in these circumstances is not automatic. The House of Lords held that the question to be asked is what a reasonable landlord would do in the circumstances of the particular case. It stated that the court cannot and should not formulate strict rules as to how a landlord should exercise their power of refusal. Having said this, it should be noted that, under the Landlord and Tenant (Covenants) Act 1995 s.22 (which applies to leases created on or after 1 January 1996), a landlord and tenant are able to enter into an agreement that specifies the circumstances in which a landlord may refuse to give their consent or the conditions on which they will give consent. If a landlord subsequently refuses to give consent on grounds outside of the agreement, then they will be regarded as acting unreasonably. The agreement between the landlord and tenant does not necessarily need to be contained within the body of the lease itself. The agreement can be ex post facto the lease and made at any time up to the point the tenant makes their request for consent.

Where consent is refused, the tenant could, of course, continue to assign, underlet or part with possession and such dispositions will be effective, although, as stated earlier, the landlord may be able to pursue an action for damages or forfeit the lease. On a more pragmatic level, however, it would be unlikely for potential assignees of the tenant to proceed with the transaction without the consent of the landlord being forthcoming.

If the landlord refuses to give consent, a tenant may also pursue an action for damages for the landlord's breach of statutory duty under the Landlord and Tenant Act s.4 and, as we have noted, the tenant can claim exemplary damages if the landlord unreasonably withholds their consent: **Design Progression Ltd v Thurloe Properties Ltd** [2004] EWHC 324 (Ch).

Probably the safest course of action for the tenant is to initially apply to the court for a declaration as to the reasonableness of the landlord's grounds for refusal or the unreasonableness of any conditions they have imposed in return for their consent.

Implied covenants

Landlord's covenants

Quiet enjoyment

Such a covenant by the landlord is automatically inferred by the landlord and tenant unless replaced by an express covenant. The covenant is not about 'noise', as its name may suggest, but means that the landlord promises that the tenant will be free from disturbance by any adverse claims to the property. The covenant is therefore broken if the landlord, or indeed anyone claiming under the landlord, performs any act that interferes with the tenant's possession or title to the land or with their ordinary enjoyment of the property. It is possible therefore that interference is of a physical, direct nature. Indeed, it may be the case that excessive noise committed by the landlord or another tenant of the landlord could result in a breach of the covenant, as in *Southwark London Borough Council v Tanner* [2001] 1 AC 1. One point that should be noted here is that the covenant relates to future conduct and any pre-existing conditions to the lease coming into operation would not constitute a breach of the covenant. Thus if there was a workshop next door to the premises which created a great deal of noise or vibration and this activity existed prior to the tenant moving in, this would not be a breach of the covenant.

Other examples of a breach of such a covenant are where the landlord persistently intimidates the tenant with a view to making the tenant leave (*Kenny v Preen* [1963] 1 QB 499); creating a right of access across the tenant's property without his or her consent (*Branchett v Beaney* [1992] 3 All ER 910); erecting scaffolding across the tenant's shop premises, causing the tenant to suffer a loss of business (*Owen v Gadd* [1956] 2 QB 99).

No derogation from grant

This means that one cannot give with one hand and take away with the other. The principle is a fundamental one in property law. An example can be seen in the case of *Harmer v Jumbil (Nigeria) Tin Areas Ltd* [1921] 1 Ch 200 where land was leased with the express purpose of storing explosives. The grant of the licence for this activity specifically stated that it was a condition that there were to be no buildings nearby. The landlord owned nearby land which had been used for tin mining, but it was assumed that the mines had been worked out. Later, the landlord's successor in title granted a lease of the land to a tenant who started to work the mines. As part of that activity, the tenant proposed to erect buildings on the land that were so close to the explosives store as to breach the terms of the licence. The original tenant was granted an injunction to prevent the building work during the currency of his licence on the basis that this would be a breach of covenant not to derogate from the grant.

In order to fall within this covenant, the actions of the landlord must make the premises less fit for the purposes for which they were let. It follows from this that the tenant must have made the landlord aware of the purposes they were going to use the premises for at the time of the granting of the lease: *Robinson v Kilvert* (1889) 41 Ch D 88.

There is no breach of the covenant if the landlord lets adjacent premises for the same purpose as the original lease. This may cause additional competition for the original tenant; however, his or her premises are still capable of being used for their original purpose. Such a situation occurred in the case of *Port v Griffith* [1928] 1 All ER 295 where a landlord, having let premises to a tenant to be used as a wool shop, then let other adjoining premises for the same purposes. It is therefore not a derogation from grant to act in a way that places leased property at an economic or commercial disadvantage. It is only if the demised premises are rendered materially less fit that there is a breach of the covenant: *Romulus Trading Co. Ltd* v *Comet Properties Ltd* [1996] 2 EGLR 70.

A landlord is also liable for any actions of persons deriving title from under him or her. Thus it was held in *Chartered Trust plc* v *Davies* [1997] 2 EGLR 83 that the landlord of a shopping mall was under obligation to prevent the tenant of one unit from committing acts of nuisance in relation to the tenant of another unit.

Fitness of the premises and covenants to repair

In terms of implied obligations there is no implied undertaking by landlords as to the fitness of the premises or their liability to keep them in repair in the absence of express covenants to this effect. In these circumstances, as Lord Hoffman indicated in *Southwark London Borough Council* v *Mills* [2001] 1 AC 1, the principle is one of 'caveat lessee' (or tenant beware). This general principle is too simplistic and indeed it is subject to various qualifications at common law and by statute.

Implied contractual terms

The courts may imply a covenant by the landlord in appropriate circumstances. They imply such covenants very much on the basis of normal law of contract principles. Covenants may be implied as a matter of fact emanating from the implied common intention of the parties. In order for a covenant to be implied it must be one that is obvious and necessary to give business efficacy to the contract for the lease. In *Attorney General of Belize* v *Belize Telecom Ltd* [2009] UKPC 10 Lord Hoffman in his landmark judgment at para 21 considered there was only one question that determines the implication of a term as a matter of fact, thus:

> . . . in every case in which it is said that some provision ought to be implied in an instrument, the question for the court is whether such a provision would spell out in express words what the instrument, read against the relevant background, would reasonably be understood to mean.

In addition to implying terms or covenants as a matter of fact, the courts may also imply terms as a matter of law in response to a particular type of agreement. An example of this can be seen in the case of *Liverpool City Council* v *Irwin* [1976] 2 All ER 39.

Liverpool City Council v *Irwin* [1976] 2 All ER 39

The council had let flats in a tower block to the tenants. While the tenancy agreements imposed obligations on the tenants, they were silent as to the obligations of the council as regards the maintenance of the building. Lifts regularly broke down and rubbish chutes became blocked, with the result that the appellant decided to withhold his rent as a protest against the council's failure properly to maintain the building. The council brought an action to seek possession of the appellant's flat, and he counter-claimed that the council were acting in breach of an implied obligation properly to maintain the building. The term could not be implied as a matter of fact since it did not satisfy the officious bystander test, nor was it reasonably necessary to give business efficacy to the contract. However, the House of Lords implied the term as a matter of law. There was a duty on a landlord 'to take reasonable care to keep in reasonable repair and usability' the common areas of the building, such as lifts, stairways, corridors and rubbish chutes, and so on. Lord Cross thought that the test to be applied in making a decision to imply a particular term into all contracts of a specific type was whether, in the general run of such cases, the term in question would be one which it would be reasonable to insert.

In order to imply a term as a matter of law, the courts will have regard to duties which prima facie occur in certain types of contract. The courts will therefore often be guided by matters of policy that affect particular types of contracts and, to this extent, issues of fairness and reasonableness may be examined in considering whether to imply a term or not.

Short leases of dwellings

The Landlord and Tenant Act 1985 s.11, as amended by the Housing Act 1988 s.116, provides that in any lease of a dwelling house granted on or after 24 October 1961 for a term of less than seven years there are implied covenants that the landlord shall keep in repair the structure and exterior of the dwelling house (including drains, gutters and external pipes); keep in repair and proper working order the installations in the dwelling house for the supply of water, gas and electricity and for sanitation (including sinks, baths and toilets); and keep in repair and proper working order the installation in the dwelling house for space heating and heating water.

The provisions apply whatever the value of the rent or rates/council tax. The provision also applies if the lease is for more than seven years, but is determinable at the option of the landlord before the expiration of seven years from the commencement of the term and is treated as a lease for less than seven years (s.13(2)b). It should, however, be noted that a lease is not treated as a lease for less than seven years if the lease confers on the tenant an option for renewal which, together with the original term, amounts to more than seven years (s.13(2)c). The landlord and tenant are not allowed to contract out of the premises.

Furnished lettings

Where a dwelling is let in a furnished state, there is an implied term of the lease that the landlord undertakes that it is fit for human habitation when it is let. Essentially, this amounts to a condition as in a contract, since breach of this undertaking entitles the tenant to repudiate the contract and claim damages for any loss suffered.

Houses at low rents

By virtue of the Landlord and Tenant Act 1985 s.8, if a house is let for human habitation, there is an implied condition that, at the commencement of the letting, the house is fit for human habitation and that the landlord undertakes to keep the premises fit for human habitation during the tenancy. The provision is of very limited value, however, since it only applies to tenancies where the rent in London does not exceed £80 per annum, and elsewhere does not exceed £52 per annum.

Statutory duty of care

By virtue of the Defective Premises Act 1972 s.4(1), where the premises are let under a tenancy in which the landlord has an obligation to the tenant for the maintenance or repair of the premises, the landlord owes a duty of care to all persons who might reasonably be expected to be affected by a defect in the state of the premises. The landlord must ensure that such persons are reasonably safe from personal injury or from damage to their property. The duty arises if the landlord knows, whether being notified by the tenant or otherwise, or if he or she ought to have known, of the defect in the premises. By s.6 any term of an agreement which purports to exclude or restrict this statutory duty of care is void.

Tenant's covenants

Liability for damage or repair

A tenant is not under an implied obligation to repair the premises; however, a tenant is prohibited from committing 'waste'.

Not to commit 'waste'

It is quite common for leases to contain express covenants not to commit waste; nevertheless, in the absence of an express covenant, a tenant has an implied duty not to commit waste. 'Waste' in this context means that a tenant must not do anything or fail to do anything that results in the premises being changed permanently by virtue of their actions or neglect of the premises. Waste is usually divided into two categories. 'Voluntary' waste involves a tenant doing a positive act, such as knocking down an internal wall. 'Permissive' waste arises where a tenant fails to do something, such as stopping a pipe from leaking and causing damage to the property. It can be seen that, in the case of permissive waste, the covenant is analogous to a repairing covenant.

Liability for the different types of waste depends very much on the type of tenancy that is held by the tenant, thus:

(i) Tenancy by sufferance – A tenant by sufferance is probably not liable for permissive waste though they are liable for voluntary waste.

(ii) Tenancy at will – A tenant at will is liable for voluntary waste. Such an action causes their tenancy to terminate and they will be liable in damages for the damage caused.

(iii) Weekly/monthly tenancies – A weekly or monthly tenant is not liable for permissive waste and, in our example, can continue to allow the pipe to leak. This is tempered, though, by their obligation to keep the premises in a 'tenant-like manner': *Warren* v *Keen* [1954] 1 QB 15. The precise obligations of a tenant here are somewhat obscure; however, Lord Denning in *Warren* v *Keen* held that they must 'do little jobs around the property which a reasonable tenant would do'. For instance, the tenant should not dispose of material that is likely to block the drains. The tenant should also ensure that their family and guests do not wilfully or negligently damage the property. A weekly or monthly tenant may be liable for voluntary waste.

(iv) Yearly tenancies – The obligations of a yearly tenant are similar to those of a weekly and monthly tenant, though such a tenant is also under obligation to ensure that the premises are wind- and water-tight: *Wedd* v *Porter* [1916] 2 KB 91.

(v) Fixed-term tenancies – A tenant for fixed term is liable for both voluntary and permissive waste. At one time, there was some doubt as to the liability of such a tenant for permissive waste; however, in *Dayani* v *Bromley London Borough Council* [1999] EGLR 144 it was held that a tenant on a fixed-term tenancy could be liable for permissive waste.

One qualification to liability for waste is that a tenant is not liable for damage caused by 'fair wear and tear'. A tenant is therefore not liable for damages to curtains or fixtures and fittings *provided* they behave in a tenant-like manner.

Not to assign, underlet or part with possession

Such covenants are generally express covenants, breach of which will usually give rise to the right of the landlord to forfeit the lease or claim damages. In the absence of such an express covenant, the tenant is entitled to assign, underlet or part with possession of the premises without the landlord's consent.

To pay rates and other taxes

Unless a landlord is made expressly liable for rates and other taxes, it is an implied obligation of the tenant to pay them. A tenant should make enquiry on taking a lease as to whether their rent includes or excludes items such as water rates and council tax; otherwise, if they are excluded, the tenant will be responsible to pay these in addition to their rent.

To allow the landlord entry to the premises

Whilst we have seen that a tenant must have exclusive possession and is entitled to quiet possession, if the landlord has a duty to repair the premises, the tenant must allow him or her access to the premises to inspect and carry out any necessary repairs. Such an obligation is implied, particularly where the landlord is required by statute to maintain the property.

The 'usual' covenants

We have seen that the landlord and tenant will often have obligations expressly set out in the lease and, in the absence of such express obligations, covenants may be implied, either by the courts or by statute. Sometimes, however, they use a form of shorthand and state that they enter into the lease on the 'usual' covenants. Similarly, if the parties enter into a lease that contains no covenants which normally it should contain, then the lease is deemed to contain whatever covenants are 'usual' in the circumstances. It is clear then that what is 'usual' can vary from lease to lease. Thus what is usual in residential premises may be very different in commercial premises. Generally, when one enters into a contract for a lease it is an implied term of the contract that the lease that is finally entered into will contain the usual covenants. If the lease does not contain such covenants then it may be rectified so as to include any covenants or conditions that are usual.

Whilst the usual covenants may vary according to the different circumstances in which the lease stands, the following covenants and conditions are always regarded as usual:

1 Landlord's obligations

   (a) Covenant for quiet possession.

2 Tenant's obligations

   (a) To pay rent.
   (b) To pay rates and taxes.
   (c) Liability for damage or repair and to deliver the premises up in this condition, save for fair wear and tear.
   (d) To allow the landlord entry on to the premises to inspect and carry out repairs.
   (e) A condition of re-entry for non-payment of rent.

Termination of leases

A lease may terminate in a variety of ways and, when this occurs, the land will return to the freeholder or, in the appropriate cases, to the owner of the head lease.

By expiry of the term

A lease for a fixed period of time will come to an end automatically when the term of the lease comes to an end. It may, however, be the case that there is provision for the lease coming to an end when a specified event occurs and, in such a lease, when the event occurs, the lease terminates automatically. Equally, a tenant may be able to extend their lease at the end of the term under various statutory provisions – for instance, the Housing Acts, the Landlord and Tenant Act 1954, the Agricultural Holdings Act 1986 and the Rent Act 1977.

By notice

Often leases will allow either the landlord or tenant to terminate the lease before the end of the term by the giving of notice. Such 'break' clauses are very common in business leases. As we have already seen in the case of periodic tenancies, these continue indefinitely until one of the parties gives the appropriate period of notice to the other. Having said this, however, there are restrictions on the length of notice that must be given in relation to dwellings. We saw earlier that, in relation to a weekly tenancy, it is possible at common law to end the tenancy by the giving of a week's notice, though this is subject to the operation of the Protection of Eviction Act 1977. By s.5 of this Act, the landlord must give the tenant at least four weeks' notice, unless both the landlord and tenant agree to some shorter period. It should be noted that the protection also extends to licensees as opposed to tenants.

In the case of periodic tenancies where there are joint landlords or joint tenants, the tenancy will come to an end if even one of the joint owners serves notice to quit, irrespective of the wishes of the other co-owner(s). The reason for this is that such tenancies expire at the end of the tenancy unless all the parties concur with the continuation of the tenancy: *Hammersmith and Fulham LBC v Monk* [1992] 1 AC 478. The Law Commission in its report *Renting Homes* (Law Com No. 284 (2003)) recommended that a joint owner should be able to terminate his or her interest in a joint agreement without bringing the whole of the agreement to an end. Thus notice on the basis of this recommendation would only have the effect of bringing to an end the interest of the party giving notice.

By surrender

A tenant may surrender their lease to their landlord and, if the landlord accepts the surrender, the lease will be terminated, as it then merges into the landlord's reversion. The landlord must consent to the surrender. This can be established by way of a letter of consent, the landlord applying to the Land Registry to close the registered leasehold title and/or cancel the notice of the lease from the registered reversionary title, or a deed being executed by both the landlord and the tenant (see below). Surrender may arise either expressly or by operation of law – see Figure 6.7.

In order for an express surrender to take place, it must be contained in a deed by virtue of the Law of Property Act 1925 s.52. Nevertheless a contract to surrender made for value

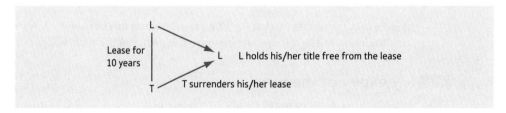

Figure 6.7

between the parties would have the same effect in equity, though it must, of course, comply with the Law of Property (Miscellaneous Provisions) Act 1989 s.2 as it amounts to a disposition of an interest in land. One proviso here is that, if the tenant gives up possession and this is accepted by the landlord, it was held in **Oastler v Henderson** (1877) 2 QBD 575 that the parties will be estopped from denying the occurrence of a surrender by the tenant. Examples of surrender by operation of law:

(i) The landlord grants a new lease of the same premises to the existing tenant. Here the 'old' lease is extinguished.

(ii) The tenant gives up possession of the premises to the landlord and possession is then accepted by the landlord.

(iii) The tenant gives up possession of the premises to the landlord and the landlord then grants a new lease of the premises to a third party with the tenant's consent.

By merger

Essentially, this is the opposite of a surrender. It occurs where the tenant acquires the interest of their landlord. In such a situation the tenant's lease 'merges' into the reversion – see Figure 6.8.

The rule makes sense as one can clearly not hold a lease from oneself.

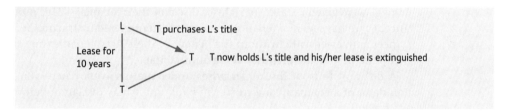

Figure 6.8

Example

L, who has the freehold of Blackacre, gives T a lease for 20 years. After 5 years, T purchases the freehold from L. In this situation, T now has the freehold and her lease ends as it merges into the freehold.

For a merger to arise there must be an *intention* to merge the estates. 'Intention' can be established by the tenant applying to the Land Registry for either:

● closure of the registered leasehold title;

● cancellation of the notice of the lease; or

● merger of an unregistered leasehold estate as part of an application for first registration of the reversionary estate.

By frustration

As we saw earlier in the case of **National Carriers Ltd v Panalpina (Northern) Ltd** [1981] AC 675, the doctrine of frustration can apply to leases, though the circumstances in which it may arise are very rare. Essentially, the very land itself would have to be destroyed, as in the case of a flood, though in that case it was stated that frustration might arise where there was a joint intention that the property was released for a particular purpose and that purpose had become impossible because of circumstances beyond the control of either party.

By enlargement

By virtue of the Law of Property Act 1925 s.153, where a tenant has a lease for more than 300 years, of which more than 200 years are left to run, the tenant has the right to enlarge their lease into a freehold, provided the lease contains no forfeiture clause for breach of covenant, and no rent is reversed or the rent is merely a peppercorn. It is not certain if enlargement actually extinguishes the freehold of the landlord – indeed the Land Registry, rather than close the title of the landlord's freehold, allows it to remain open whilst registering the freehold title of the tenant. Rather peculiarly, this results in there being two freehold titles registered against the land.

By disclaimer

The expression 'disclaimer' is used to describe repudiation of a tenancy where a tenant denies the landlord's superior title to the land.

Disclaimer may also arise by way of statute: for instance, under the Landlord and Tenant (War Damage) Acts 1929 and 1941, tenants whose property was rendered unfit by war damage were given a statutory right to disclaim their tenancies. This process was needed since, as we have seen, a tenancy could not be terminated by frustration in such circumstances and, essentially, without the benefit of these Acts, tenants were still liable to pay their rent, despite the premises being uninhabitable.

A different form of disclaimer arises under the Insolvency Act 1986, under which a liquidator of a company or a trustee in bankruptcy may disclaim onerous property such as a lease.

By repudiation

Since leases are essentially contracts, a party to a lease can repudiate the contract where there has been a fundamental breach of an obligation under the contract, just as in the normal law of contract. At one time, remedies for breach of contract were not applied in the case of leases. In *Chartered Trust plc v Davies* (1998) 76 P & CR 396 the Court of Appeal held that, where a landlord had derogated from their grant in allowing a nuisance to take place in relation to the tenant's premises, the tenant was entitled to disclaim the tenancy and repudiate the lease.

By forfeiture

Generally

Undoubtedly, the most powerful means by which a landlord can terminate a tenant's lease is by way of forfeiture. Unless the lease contains a forfeiture clause, the landlord is limited to an action for damages with regard to a breach of covenant by the tenant, though in some rare circumstances a landlord might be able to obtain specific performance. It is not surprising, therefore, that most leases contain forfeiture clauses and, in any event, following *Shiloh Spinners Ltd v Harding* [1973] AC 691 rights of re-entry are implied in equitable leases.

Essentially, forfeiture gives the landlord the right to re-enter the premises and determine the lease, either because the tenant has not paid their rent or has breached some other covenants within the lease. Since forfeiture is somewhat drastic in operation, it has consistently attracted the attention of the courts. The result is that forfeiture has developed into a complex set of rules, principally designed to protect tenants. It should be noted that forfeiture is a right of the landlord only.

In exercising their right to re-enter the premises under a forfeiture clause a landlord may proceed in two ways: peaceable re-entry or proceedings for possession.

Peaceable re-entry

In *Billson* v *Residential Apartments Ltd* [1992] 1 AC 494 Lord Templeman stated at 536 that peaceable re-entry was a 'dubious and dangerous method of determining a lease'. 'Dangerous' indeed, since, where premises are let as a dwelling, it is unlawful to exercise a right of re-entry otherwise than by court proceedings: Protection of Eviction Act 1977 s.2. Furthermore, a landlord entering such premises without lawful authority is regarded as a trespasser and may incur criminal liability under the Criminal Law Act 1977 s.5. The effect therefore is that forfeiture by this method is not only without legal effect but might also incur criminal liability on summary conviction with a potential term of imprisonment not exceeding six months.

Even in the case of commercial premises, the landlord must make sure that the exercise of the right of re-entry is peaceable and without force: Criminal Law Act 1977 s.6. To that extent, in commercial premises, the right of re-entry is still frowned upon and the House of Lords was critical of its use in *Billson* v *Residential Apartments Ltd* [1992] 1 AC 494.

In order to exercise peaceable re-entry, the landlord must demonstrate an intention to take possession: for instance, by changing the locks or granting a new tenancy to a third party. If the landlord merely accepts rent from a third party, this is not sufficient to demonstrate an unequivocal act of taking possession: *Cromwell Developments Ltd* v *Godfrey* [1998] 2 EGLR 62. Similarly, if a landlord exercises their right to enter the premises to carry out repairs under the terms of the lease, this also is not regarded as an unequivocal act of taking possession: *Charville Estates Ltd* v *Unipart Group Ltd* [1997] 2 EGLR 83.

Proceedings for possession

As already seen, there are significant difficulties and dangers involved in peaceable re-entry and thus the only really acceptable method of seeking possession is by obtaining a court order for possession. In the case of residential premises, because of the Protection of Eviction Act 1977 s.2, this is the only lawful method of obtaining possession.

Once a landlord has commenced proceedings for possession, this is regarded as an unequivocal claim to possession and, at that point, they are deemed to have elected to treat the lease as forfeited; however, the lease is only formally terminated once the landlord obtains judgment for possession. Whilst there is some disagreement as to the status of the landlord and tenant relationship until judgment is obtained, the fact remains that the landlord is entitled to treat the tenant as a trespasser. The effect of this is that any payments made by the tenant are not payments of rent but as 'mesne profits' that are merely regarded as compensation until the landlord obtains possession. Another effect of the tenant becoming a trespasser is that the landlord is unable to enforce any covenants under the lease. On the other hand, if the tenant does not accept the proceedings or termination of the lease, they are free to enforce the covenants against the landlord. If the tenant does, however, accept the forfeiture proceedings, they are relieved of all future rights and liabilities under the lease.

Apart from the Protection of Eviction Act 1977 and the Criminal Law Act 1977, there are other statutory controls on the use of forfeiture as a remedy. The Commonhold and Leasehold Reform Act 2002 ss.167–169 provides that a landlord under a long lease of a dwelling may not exercise a right of re-entry or forfeiture for failure of a tenant to pay rent, service charges or administration charges (or combinations of them) unless the unpaid amount exceeds the prescribed sum or it has not been paid for a prescribed period (currently three years). By s.167(2) the prescribed sum is specified as £350 (The Rights of Re-entry and Forfeiture (Prescribed Sum and Period) (England) Regulations 2004). The Act therefore appears to prevent forfeiture for small sums. A long lease is defined in s.76 as a lease granted for a term exceeding 21 years, whether or not it is terminable before the end of the term by notice given by or to the tenant, by re-entry or forfeiture or otherwise.

Waiver

If a landlord attempting to forfeit a lease is found to have waived the breach then they will not be able to proceed for forfeiture of the lease. Essentially, a waiver arises if the landlord has affirmed the confirmation of the lease, either impliedly or expressly. A waiver does not have to be contemporaneous with the landlord treating the lease as forfeited – it can arise either before or after the landlord decides to forfeit the lease.

For a waiver to arise the landlord must be aware of the tenant's actions or omissions that give rise to forfeiture and the landlord must perform some unequivocal act that demonstrates the continued existence of the lease. The most common way in which waiver arises is if the landlord or their agent demands, sues for or accepts rent falling due after the occurrence of the breach by the tenant. This principle applies even if the rent was demanded or accepted due to a clerical error on the part of the landlord or their agent: *Greenwich London Borough Council* v *Discreet Selling Estates Ltd* (1990) 61 P & CR 405.

A waiver of a breach of covenant or condition only applies to a particular breach and does not amount to a general waiver of that and all future breaches. Where the breach is a continuing breach, as may be the case where there is a breach of a covenant to repair by the tenant, the waiver only applies in respect of the initial breach and not in respect of any further continuing breaches of the covenant.

The forfeiture process

In examining the processes which govern actions for forfeiture there is a marked difference between forfeiture for non-payment of rent and forfeiture for breach of other covenants or conditions under the lease.

Forfeiture for non-payment of rent

In order to exercise a right of forfeiture, whether by re-entry (where appropriate) or by possession proceedings, there must be a forfeiture clause in the lease and the landlord must make a formal demand for the exact sum owed on the day it falls due. Forfeiture clauses often provide that a formal demand is unnecessary and, in such instances, the landlord is exempted from making a formal demand. Even if the lease contains no such exemption, a landlord does not need to make a formal demand if more than half a year's rent is in arrears: Common Law Procedure Act 1852 s.210. The provisions of the Commonhold and Leasehold Reform Act 2002 s.167, as already referred to, must also be adhered to.

Once the above requirements have been complied with, the landlord may proceed to forfeiture, usually by possession proceedings in the county court. The process is not clear-cut and this provides a significant qualification to the rights of the landlord to exercise forfeiture.

Forfeiture for breach of other covenants

The procedure for forfeiture for breach of covenants, other than a breach of a covenant to pay rent, is set out in the Law of Property Act 1925 s.146. The principle behind the provision is to allow the tenant the opportunity to remedy his or her breach and save him/herself from the sanction of forfeiture. The process set out in s.146 must be strictly adhered to and a landlord must serve a notice on the tenant, providing prescribed information. A s.146 notice must therefore:

(i) specify the breach that the landlord complains of;

(ii) request that the breach be remedied, if it is capable of being so;

(iii) request that the tenant pays compensation, if desired by the landlord;

(iv) where appropriate, inform the tenant of his/her rights under the Leasehold Property (Repairs) Act 1928, whereby, if the lease is of seven years or more and has three years or more unexpired, the tenant may serve a counter-notice on the landlord so that no forfeiture may take place without a court order.

It should be noted that tenants have additional protection from forfeiture in the form of the Commonhold and Leasehold Reform Act 2002 s.168. This provides that a landlord of a long lease (i.e. a lease for more than 21 years) may not serve an s.146 notice in respect of a breach of covenant or condition unless the tenant has either admitted the breach or a court or tribunal (Leasehold Valuation Tribunal) has determined that a breach has taken place and that a period of 14 days from the date of the determination by the court or tribunal has passed.

Failure to comply with the above requirements renders any attempt at forfeiture void: *Billson v Residential Apartments Ltd* [1992] 1 AC 494. Clearly, the requirement in point (i) above is always required, but point (iii) is optional if the landlord does not require compensation. In relation to point (ii), the landlord might consider the breach to be irremediable – in which case, they only need specify the breach in their notice and then proceed to forfeit the lease. It is this latter point that has caused the most difficulty since, if a court considers that the breach is capable of being remedied, then the landlord will not be able to proceed to forfeit the lease and the s.146 notice will be invalid.

It is the 'capable of remedy' issue that also determines the pace at which forfeiture may take place. If the breach is capable of remedy, the landlord must give the tenant a reasonable period of time – one to three months – in which to carry out the remediable action. The landlord is not entitled to forfeit the lease, either by court action for possession or by physical re-entry, during this period. If the tenant does take the required remediable action to remedy the breach of covenant, then the forfeiture proceedings end at that point, though a landlord may still claim damages for the previous breach or breaches of covenant. If the breach is not capable of remedy, the landlord can proceed to forfeit the lease, either by action for possession or by physical re-entry, usually after 14 days.

In determining whether a breach is capable of remedy or not, the courts formerly tended to focus on the fact of the breach by the tenant and did not consider the damage that the breach might cause to the landlord. Many of the earlier decisions and the criteria employed by the courts could produce some baffling decisions. The case of *Expert Clothing Service and Sales Ltd v Hillgate House Ltd* [1986] 1 Ch 340 provided a major change in the way a breach of covenant could be regarded as being 'capable of remedy' or not.

In *Expert Clothing* the Court of Appeal considered that a breach of covenant was capable of remedy if it was possible to correct the *damage or harm* the breach of covenant had caused. In this case, the tenant was in breach of a covenant to reconstruct the premises within a prescribed period of time. When the tenant failed to comply with the covenant, the landlord sought forfeiture of the lease. The Court of Appeal held that the breach was capable of remedy by the tenant undertaking the work out of time and compensating the landlord as the landlord would not suffer irretrievable damage in such a situation. In principle, breaches of positive covenants were capable of remedy since the tenant could simply carry out what they were required to do under the covenant. For example, if the tenant was required to maintain the garden, then they could remedy the breach by arranging for the garden to be tidied.

Where the breach of covenant was a breach of a restrictive/negative covenant, the accepted thought was that a breach was irremediable, allowing forfeiture to take place. This accorded with the decision in *Rugby School (Governors) v Tannahill* [1934] 1 KB 695, where MacKinnon J stated:

> A promise to do a thing, if broken, can be remedied by the thing being done. But breach of a promise not to do a thing cannot in any true sense be remedied; that which was done cannot be undone.

To regard all breaches of restrictive covenants as being irremediable is, however, too simplistic and the ability to apply for forfeiture for such a breach rests on whether the breach is one that is 'once and for all' or a continuing breach. A 'once and for all' breach may arise where the breach is irrecoverable – for instance, where the premises are used for illegal or immoral purposes. Thus in *Rugby School (Governors) v Tannahill*, the premises had been used for prostitution in breach of a covenant that the premises should not be used for illegal or immoral purposes. It was held that, as the breach would be known locally and thus the value of the premises would be affected, the breach was incapable of being remedied. Having said this, the principle does not seem to apply where a tenant is unaware of a breach by his sub-tenant and then takes prompt action to limit or prevent damage to the landlord's reputation, as held in *Glass v Kencakes Ltd* [1966] 1 QB 611, where Paull J held that immorality does not itself render the breach automatically incapable of being remedied. Paull J considered that all the circumstances must be taken into account, 'for example, if the notice is not the first notice which has had to be served, or if there are particularly revolting circumstances or great publicity, then it might well be that the slate could not be wiped clean'.

Where a breach is a continuing breach, however, the breach could be remedied by ceasing the activity and giving an undertaking about future conduct.

Clearly, the distinction between positive and restrictive covenants seems illogical, as in the distinction between 'once and for all' and continuing breaches. Both approaches tend to focus on remedying the breach – i.e. putting the parties in the same position they were in prior to the breach. The Court of Appeal in *Expert Clothing* moved away from such a concept by focusing on the harm that had been done to the landlord. Thus if the s.146 notice ensures that the tenant complies with the covenant and provides compensation to the landlord in financial terms then the harm the landlord has suffered accords with the principle behind the s.146 process. The test set out in *Expert Clothing* therefore allows a court to look at each case on its own merits.

In *Savva v Hussein* [1997] 73 P & CR 150 the Court of Appeal again considered the issue of covenants being remedied and confirmed the approach adopted in *Expert Clothing*.

Whilst the merits of each case are considered on their facts there are some situations where a breach, whether of a positive or restrictive covenant, will be incapable of remedy. The Court of Appeal in *Expert Clothing* provided two examples. Firstly, where there is a breach of a covenant to insure against fire, this would be incapable of remedy if there actually was a fire that burned the premises down. Secondly, where there is a breach of a covenant to maintain and repair the premises, this would be incapable of remedy if there was insufficient time to carry out the repairs before the end of the lease.

A further example of an irremediable breach arises where a tenant is in breach of a covenant against assigning or underletting, despite the fact that a tenant may be capable of correcting the harm done to the landlord. Thus in *Scala House and District Property Co. Ltd v Forbes* [1974] QB 575 it was held that, where a tenant was in breach of such a covenant by the granting of a sub-lease, the breach could not be remedied even if the tenant managed to secure the surrender of the sub-lease.

The Court of Appeal in *Scala House* was openly criticised in *Expert Clothing* by O'Connor LJ. Nevertheless, the Court of Appeal was bound by the previous decision in *Scala House* and found itself unable to apply the wider view of remediability now seen in *Expert Clothing*. More recently, in *Akici v LR Butlin Ltd* [2006] 1 WLR 201 Neuberger LJ stated at 216 that 'the reasoning . . . is . . . at least in part, demonstrably fallacious and inconsistent with common sense . . .'. Neuberger LJ, like the Court of Appeal in *Expert Clothing* and *Savva*, attempted to limit the scope of the *Scala House* decision to covenants against assigning and underletting and distinguished such a covenant from a covenant against parting with possession. Thus the *Scala House* decision is limited to instances where a tenant creates or assigns a legal interest in the property.

Given that it is far more likely that a breach of a covenant will be regarded as capable of being remedied, it is important that the landlord makes it clear in their s.146 notice what a tenant must do to remedy the breach. Failure to do so will mean that the notice is invalid and the tenant can frustrate an attempt by a landlord to forfeit the lease, although realistically this will only amount to a delaying tactic until a new notice is issued. The notice must specify the breach in clear terms and set out with reasonable certainty what the tenant has to do.

Relief against forfeiture

Even if a ground for forfeiture exists and the landlord has not waived the breach, it is by no means certain that a landlord will be successful in recovering the property. Both equity and, as we have seen, legislation have intervened to provide tenants with relief against forfeiture so as to allow them to keep their tenancies. The divisions between the various forms of relief generally fall into two categories – forfeiture for non-payment of rent and forfeiture for breach of other covenants.

Relief for non-payment of rent

When considering relief for non-payment of rent, one has to consider that the rules developed very differently from relief for other breaches of covenant and arose within the old Courts of Chancery. The result of this is that relief for breaches for non-payment of rent is based in equity rather than statute, though it should be stated that the equitable rules are overlaid by statutory intervention. Where a tenant pays their arrears of rent and the landlord's costs before trial, the Common Law Procedure Act 1852 s.212 confers an automatic and absolute right to relief, provided the tenant is at least half a year's rent in arrears (s.210).

One difficulty with relief in this area is that different rules apply when the action is heard in the County Courts as opposed to the High Court. In the County Court, a tenant can stop the possession proceedings if they pay all the rent due and the costs of the action at any time up to five days before trial by virtue of the County Courts Act 1971 s.138(2). If the possession proceedings take place and the tenant fails to pay the sum due by the date specified by the court, then the court will order that possession of the land be given to the landlord not less than four weeks from the date of the order, as the court thinks fit, unless the tenant pays into court all rent in arrears and the costs of the action. However, the relief available to the tenant does not cease at that point since, by s.138(a)a (as inserted by the Administration of Estates Act 1985 s.55), if the landlord recovers possession of the land, the tenant may, at any time within six months from the date on which the landlord gains possession, apply to the court for relief. The court then has discretion to provide relief on such terms and conditions as it thinks fit.

In the High Court, the court will exercise its equitable jurisdiction, provided the landlord has obtained judgment for possession and the tenant has sought relief within six months of the execution of the judgment. It appears that this limitation does not apply if the landlord has brought no action but has entered into possession by peaceable re-entry: *Thatcher v CH Pearce & Sons (Contractors) Ltd* [1968] 1 WLR 748.

Since the courts exercise equitable jurisdiction, delay in applying for relief will 'defeat equity', though a disposition to a third party will not necessarily prevent relief from being granted: *Ashton v Sobelman* [1987] 1 WLR 177. The effect of relief being granted to a tenant is that they will continue to hold their original lease and, in any event, the overall object of a court is to place the parties in the same position as if forfeiture had not been claimed.

Relief for breach of other covenants

The Law of Property Act 1925 s.146(2) provides that where a landlord 'is proceeding by action or otherwise, to enforce . . . a right of re-entry, the lessee may apply to the court for relief'. In *Billson v Residential Apartments Ltd*, the House of Lords interpreted s.146 as providing that, where a landlord proceeds to forfeiture by way of a court order, the tenant can apply for relief until such time as the landlord actually takes possession. It should be noted that the tenant's ability to obtain relief does not cease when the landlord has obtained judgment since they are still regarded as 'proceeding' until they actually take possession.

The position, however, is not the same where a landlord embarks on forfeiture by way of peaceable entry since here they are still regarded as 'proceeding' so that a tenant may apply for relief even after the landlord has entered the property. Clearly, therefore, it is not in the interests of a landlord to proceed to forfeiture without a court order since they are always open to the court exercising its inherent equitable jurisdiction once they have obtained possession and for a reasonable time thereafter. This is consistent with the approach taken in *Billson* so as to provide an incentive to landlords to proceed by way of action in the courts.

It has been agreed that the inherent equitable jurisdiction of the court to grant relief following peaceable re-entry did not survive the passing of s.146. As we have already seen in the case of breach of covenant to pay rent, the equitable jurisdiction still remains: *Thatcher v CH Pearce and Sons (Contractors)* [1968] 1 WLR 748. In the case of breaches of other covenants, however, equitable relief is not, strictly speaking, available since here relief is founded in statute and not within the equitable jurisdiction of the court. Nicholls J in *Abbey National Building Society v Maybeech Ltd* [1985] Ch 190, however, stated obiter that equitable relief did indeed survive the passing of s.146, that it was not intended that s.146 would provide a code for the granting of relief and that all applications had to fall within the terms of this provision. It therefore seems that there are circumstances, largely involving persons having derivative interests, where equitable relief may be available for breaches of covenants other than non-payment of rent.

Derivative interests and relief against forfeiture

Derivative interests are interests of sub-tenants and mortgagees of a tenant who derive title from the tenant. Clearly, if a lease is forfeited it comes to an end and this can have a profound effect on a sub-tenant whose lease is founded upon the tenant's head lease and a mortgagee who will lose the security for the mortgage. This is particularly important if the tenant does not apply for relief or where the derivative interests are not even aware of forfeiture taking place until very late in the day. The question therefore arises as to whether relief is available to the holders of derivative interests if the tenancy is forfeited. Again, it is convenient to examine the relief available to derivative interests in the context of non-payment of rent and breaches of other covenants.

Relief for non-payment of rent

As we have already seen, the normal equitable jurisdiction of the High Court applies equally to sub-lessees and mortgagees as well as the tenant, subject to the provisions set out in the Chancery Law Amendment Act 1852 s.210 and s.212 above. If the head lease has already been determined, the original tenant and the last assignee of the tenancy have to be joined into the proceedings since the granting of relief will have the effect of reviving the original tenancy and the consequent re-imposition of liability on the original tenant and the last assignee. The wider liability of such individuals is considered in Chapter 13. The second mode of relief for non-payment of rent arises in both the High Court and County Court and is provided by s.146(4) – this is the only part of s.146 that applies to non-payment of rent. Relief under this provision involves the granting of a completely new tenancy to the applicant. The effect of this is that there is no need to join the original tenant and last assignee of the tenancy into the proceedings. One problem with using this provision is that the application for relief must be made before the landlord actually gains possession, for the reasons already considered above. It seems proceeding would appear to have the same interpretation in s.146(4) as it does in s.146(2). Thus in *Hammersmith and Fulham London Borough Council* v *Tops Shop Centres Ltd* [1990] Ch 237 it was held that a landlord which received rent payable under an underlease was not asserting a right of re-entry. The result was that the underlessees were still entitled to apply for relief under s.146(4) on the basis that the landlord was still 'proceeding'. On the other hand, if the landlord proceeds by peaceable re-entry it would seem logical that a sub-tenant and a mortgagee would also be able to apply for statutory relief, just like the tenant, though there is no authority for this as yet. The House of Lords in *Billson* at least seems to suggest that statutory relief will not be precluded where there is actual re-entry by the landlord.

Relief for breach of other covenants

As we saw above, the normal route for relief lies in s.146(4) – which applies to both breaches for non-payment of rent and breaches for other covenants. The provision applies to applications 'made by any person claiming as underlessee any estate or interests in the property comprised in the lease'. The provision therefore specifically relates to sub-tenants, but also mortgagees. The provision also relates to forfeiture by the landlord by way of court order or by way of peaceable re-entry. Mortgagees are, however, vulnerable here since it is possible they may not be aware of the forfeiture proceedings being brought by a landlord and, once the landlord actually takes possession, a mortgagee loses its right to relief under s.146(4). This was approved of in *Billson*, though it means that a mortgagee is likely to be left without any prospect of relief. The only way forward for a mortgagee is to persuade a court to allow it to submit a claim and to revisit the original court order; however, in

Rexhaven v *Nurse* (1995) 28 HLR 241 it was stated that this is unlikely to succeed if the mortgagee has notice of the landlord's claim.

The same vulnerability is unlikely to affect a sub-tenant since a sub-tenant is likely to be in possession of the property and therefore aware of the action being taken by the landlord.

It is possible that a second route for relief for sub-tenants and mortgagees has emerged following the case of *Escalus Properties Ltd* v *Robinson* [1996] QB 221, which suggests that s.146(2) is also available to sub-tenants and mortgagees. The effects of this decision have still to be developed to their full extent; however, one aspect is worth noting. Unlike under s.146(4), relief is granted in the form of the original lease continuing and, as such, the effect is retrospective and therefore could be beneficial to the interests of both sub-tenants, who might otherwise lose their sub-tenancy or security.

As indicated, relief under s.146(4) involves the creation of a new lease. This can have the rather bizarre effect of providing the tenant with relief the tenant has not claimed or is unable to claim – for instance, if the tenant's breach is irremediable, as may be the case in an immorality/stigma-related breach.

Where a new lease is created, it is usually on the same terms as the original lease – at least as far as the relief is claimed by mortgagees. The effect of this is that the new lease is used as security against the mortgage loan. Again, this is favourable to the tenant as they will hold the equity of redemption until such time as the mortgage is paid off.

The creation of a new lease for a sub-tenant is more problematical. S.146(4) provides that a sub-tenant is not entitled to a longer lease than they held under their original sub-lease. The section provides no guidance as to the terms of the new sub-lease and it appears that this is left to the discretion of the court. In terms of the rent to be paid by the sub-tenant, the landlord is entitled to the higher of the rents between the original head lease and the sub-lease: *Ewart* v *Fryer* [1901] 1 Ch 499.

Where the sub-lease relates to only part of the building – for instance, the sub-lease relates to a single apartment in a block of apartments – then the relief only relates to that apartment. This is important since the sub-tenant is required to remedy the breaches of the tenant. Thus a sub-tenant will be required to make good the tenant's rent arrears to the landlord. If the tenant was required to make good the breaches for the entire block of apartments this would obviously be unfair, hence the relief for the sub-tenant is limited to that part of the building to which their sub-lease relates: *Chatham Empire Theatre (1955) Ltd* v *Ultrans Ltd* [1961] 1 WLR 817.

Breaches of covenants to repair

Whilst relief for breaches of covenants other than breaches for non-payment of rent applies equally for breach of a covenant to repair, special protection for relief is afforded to these types of breach. The need for this protection arises from the fact that property developers, for instance, may buy out the landlord's reversion and then use what may amount to minor breaches of a covenant to repair to evict the tenant. The effect of this is that the new owner may be able to make a windfall profit either from the property itself or by a re-development scheme. In order to prevent this scenario from materialising, the Leasehold Property (Repairs) Act 1928 was passed. The Act applies to repairing covenants in leases exceeding seven years with more than three years unexpired (excluding agricultural leases). The effect of the Act is that a landlord must inform the tenant in the s.146 notice of his right to serve a counter-notice on the landlord. Once the counter-notice is served on the landlord, the forfeiture proceedings are then stopped, so that the landlord may not forfeit without the permission of the court. The permission of the court is only granted if one of five grounds set out in s.1(5) is established – for instance, where the court thinks it just and equitable to do so, or where the remedying of the breach is necessary to prevent substantial diminution of the value of the reversion.

Reform of forfeiture

Perhaps not surprisingly, the complexity of the rules regarding forfeiture and the relief available has attracted a great deal of criticism. There is no doubt that forfeiture has been used by some landlords as a very significant sledgehammer to intimidate vulnerable tenants, particularly with the use of forfeiture by way of re-entry. Whilst technically the re-entry is by peaceable means, the process is highly intimidating. The result of this is that the Law Commission in its report *Termination of Tenancies for Tenant Default* (No. 303, 2006) proposed that forfeiture should be abolished in favour of a statutory scheme.

Under the proposed scheme, the termination of leases could only be carved out under a court order on the ground of a breach of covenant where the breach is a 'tenant default' by means of a 'termination action'. The difference between breaches for non-payment of rent and breaches of other covenants will disappear. There would be no need for a lease to reserve a right of re-entry. 'Termination actions' would be by way of the landlord making a 'termination claim' or by way of a 'summary termination procedure', which provides the landlord with an accelerated means of terminating a tenancy outside of the court process. The latter process would be available where there is a tenant default and where, on a termination claim, the tenant would have no realistic prospect of a court refusing a termination order, and there is no other reason why a trial of the claim will take place. No doubt this process will be invaluable to landlords where a tenant has simply abandoned the premises.

The two forms of termination action cannot run concurrently in relation to the same tenant default and it is for the landlord to elect which one to follow. In either case, the landlord must serve notice on the tenant and on holders of 'qualifying interests' – i.e. derivative interests of which he or she has knowledge. The landlord will be deemed to have notice of qualifying interests where he or she has been notified by the tenant in writing of the interest or where the interest is in the register of title, in the appropriate local land charges register, or in the register of charges kept by the Registrar of Companies. Whether or not a tenant chooses to defend a termination claim, the holder of a qualifying interest may apply to the court for any order, other than a termination order.

A 'tenant default' is a breach of a covenant of the tenancy but it also includes a breach of covenant by a previous tenant (where there has been an unlawful assignment) or a breach of covenant by a guarantor of the obligations of the tenant under the lease. Where there has been a tenant default, the landlord wishing to terminate the lease must serve the tenant with a 'tenant default notice'. The notice sets out the details of the tenant default and the response the landlord requires of the tenant. It may require the tenant to make good the default (including the payment of financial compensation). The notice must set a deadline by which the remedial action should be completed. The deadline imposed by the landlord must be reasonable in all the circumstances but, in any event, it cannot be for less than seven days after the service of the tenant default notice.

The tenant default notice must be given within six months of the day on which the landlord first knew of the facts of the default , though this 'default period' can be extended by the written agreement of the parties. The time limit is intended to displace the current doctrine of waiver.

Once a court is satisfied that a tenant default has occurred, the court has discretion to make such an order as it thinks would be appropriate and proportional in the circumstances set out in the new scheme. The scheme does not limit the range of orders a court can make, though it does introduce six orders in particular: a termination order; a remedial order; an order for sale; a transfer order; a new tenancy order; and a joint tenancy adjust-ment order. It should be noted that a termination order will bring the tenancy and any derivative interests to an end. Once such an order is made, a tenant or a derivative interest holder has no further recourse to the court under the statutory termination scheme. Where a tenant appeals, however, the tenancy will continue.

Clearly, the new scheme is a good deal more transparent than the current regime and appears to provide good protection for the tenant, landlord and holders of derivative interests. To date, the legislation to enact the scheme has not been passed, though it appears the new scheme has widespread support.

Remedies for breach of covenant

Remedies of the landlord

Apart from the landlord being able to forfeit a tenant's lease or treat a breach as a regulatory breach of the lease (both of which we have already considered), more conventional remedies are also available to the landlord.

Damages A landlord may sue for damages for breach of any covenant, other than non-payment of rent. Damages are assessed on a contractual basis so as to place the landlord in the same position as if the breach had not occurred. The exception to this is where there is a breach of a covenant to repair the premises since here the recovery of damages is con-trolled by the Landlord and Tenant Act 1927 s.18. This provides that a landlord's ability to recover damages is limited to the amount by which the landlord's reversion has been diminished in value by the tenant being in breach of the covenant to repair. It is not certain that a landlord would be able to recover the amount necessary to carry out the repairs, since it all depends on the amount by which reversion is diminished. Indeed, it is possible that if the landlord's intention was to demolish the premises on the expiry of the lease, he or she might not get anything at all. It will also be recalled that, under the Leasehold Property (Repairs) Act 1928, with regard to repairing covenants in leases exceeding seven years with more than three years unexpired (excluding agricultural leases), there are specific procedures that need to be followed before damages may be recovered.

Action for recovery of rent By virtue of the Limitation Act 1980 s.19, the ability to recover rent arrears or damages in respect of rent arrears ends after the expiration of six years from the date on which the arrears became due. Essentially, this means that a maximum of six years' rent is recoverable, though it would be a tardy landlord indeed who failed to take action within the limitation period. It should be noted that the amount of rent that is recoverable may be reduced by the tenant applying a 'set-off' against any repairs they have made to the property due to the landlord failing to carry out the repairs.

Specific performance and injunctions As with all equitable remedies, the award of specific performance or an injunction is subject to the discretion of the court and therefore matters such as a landlord delaying in making an application will result in no order being made. More particularly, these orders are not made where enforcement requires the constant supervision of the court. Thus in the case of the *Co-op Insurance Society* v *Argyll Stores* [1997] 2 WLR 898 the court refused to make an order of specific performance with regard to a breach of covenant by the tenant to keep open the premises for retail trade when the store owned by Argyll Stores closed down. Various reasons were provided by the House of Lords, with Lord Hoffman providing the leading judgment. Lord Hoffman considered that this was a case where damages would be an appropriate remedy, but there were other considerations. Firstly, it was settled practice that no order would be made to compel someone to run a business. Second, enormous losses would result from being forced to run a trade. Third, framing the order would be unduly difficult. Fourth, wasteful litigation over compliance would result. Fifth, it was oppressive to have to run a business under threat of contempt of court. Sixth, it was against the public interest to require a business to be run if compensation was a plausible alternative.

Whilst the reasons above can be applied in any number of variations, it does not mean that specific performance, for instance, can never be awarded. So if the landlord had no other remedy, the order could be adequately supervised and could be framed in terms that were certain, then a court might issue such an order.

Distress and commercial rents arrears recovery We first came across distress in the case of ***Walsh* v *Lonsdale*** where we saw that the remedy allows a landlord to enter the premises of their tenant in order to seize goods with a view to selling them in order to compensate for arrears of rent. The remedy is a feudal one that requires no court proceedings, though it is subject to restrictions, some of which arise at common law and others within statutory controls dating from The Distress for Rent Act 1689. The distress must be 'levied' between the hours of sunrise and sunset and a bailiff is not entitled to seize certain goods, more particularly a tenant's 'tools of the trade'. Clearly, distress is a matter which arises in insolvency cases, but in the area of landlord and tenant levying distress operates as confirmation by the landlord that the tenancy is continuing. From that point of view, therefore, distress operates as a waiver so that a landlord cannot then apply for forfeiture of the lease.

Levying distress is highly intrusive and, to that extent, it has been highly criticised and the view expressed that the use of this remedy is a violation of Article 8 of the European Convention of Human Rights (the right to respect for private life) and Article 1 of the First Protocol (the right to peaceful enjoyment of one's possessions). In ***Fuller* v *Happy Shopper Markets Ltd*** [2001] EWHC Ch 702 Lightman J considered that, in the light of these rights, a landlord should have the human rights implications of levying distress at the forefront of their mind before they take this step.

The Law Commission in its report *Landlord and Tenant: Distress for Rent* (Law Com No. 194) (2001) considered the remedy to be 'arbitrary and artificial' and that there was a lack of controls on the landlord when distraining in person and limited controls on bailiffs. The Law Commission pointed out that its use can be totally unexpected by the tenant. The Law Commission considered that the remedy was 'wrong in principle' because 'it offers an extra-judicial debt enforcement remedy in circumstances which are, because of its intrinsic nature, the way in which it arises and the manner of its exercise, unjust to debtors, to other creditors and to third parties'.

In May 2001 the Lord Chancellor's Department published a consultation paper, *Enforcement Review Consultation Paper No. 5: Distress for Rent* and following this the Tribunals, Courts and Enforcement Act 2007 Part 3 and Schedule 12 made provision for the reform of the law on distress. Whilst the Act abolishes distress, this is for leases of commercial premises only. The Act introduces a new statutory process known as 'commercial rent arrears recovery' ('CRAR'). The process covers both legal and equitable leases but is not available for premises which are wholly or partly let as residential premises. Essentially, CRAR is a modified form of distress in that landlords will still be able to take extra-judicial action for taking the tenant's goods for the purpose of selling them to recover rent arrears, thus allowing landlords, or their bailiffs, to enter premises to seize goods either by taking possession of them or by securing them at the premises. Undoubtedly, the CRAR system will be of most importance if the landlord suspects a tenant is about to become bankrupt or insolvent so as to pre-empt a tenant's assets becoming available to the tenant's general creditors.

The procedure for CRAR is set out in Schedule 12 of the Act and provides safeguards which were otherwise unavailable under the common law process. The process requires the tenant to be given notice of the intention to levy distress and the landlord or bailiff may use reasonable force to enter the premises. There are other provisions regulating the sale of any goods sold following seizure so that the landlord or bailiff must sell or dispose of the goods at the best price that can reasonably be obtained.

Part 3 of the Act is not yet in force and it remains unclear as to when this will occur so that at present the common law remedy of distress remains for both residential and commercial leases.

The tenant's remedies

Generally, a tenant's remedies for breach of contract by the landlord revolve around the usual remedies available under the law of contract. To that extent a tenant has fewer options available to them.

Damages A tenant under normal contractual rules is entitled to such damages as to put them in the same position as if the breach had not occurred: *Johnson* v *Agnew* [1980] AC 367. In the case of an award of damages for breach of the repairing covenants of a landlord, it was recognised in *Calabar Properties Ltd* v *Stitcher* [1984] 1 WLR 287 that, where a tenant wishes to remain in occupation of the premises, the diminution in value occasioned by the landlord's breach for which the tenant is entitled to be compensated is the personal discomfort and inconvenience the tenant has experienced as a result of the want of repair. Further, in *Wallace* v *Manchester City Council* [1998] EWCA Civ 1166 Morritt LJ in the Court of Appeal stated that the amount of damages to be awarded may be calculated 'by reference to the rent payable for the period equivalent to the duration of the landlord's breach of covenant'.

Rent strikes One sometimes hears of tenants threatening to go on a 'rent strike' until a landlord has carried out their repairing obligations. This is a highly precarious course of action and a breach by a landlord does not entitle a tenant to not perform their own obligations. In any event, the payment of rent is usually expressed as a condition, breach of which would entitle the landlord to forfeit the lease for non-payment of rent. A tenant's best way forward here is to have the repairs carried out and then deduct the cost from future payments of their rent: *Lee-Parker* v *Izzet* [1971] 1 WLR 1688. It should be noted that this right does not mean that the amount spent on the repairs is treated as rent. Thus Goff J stated at 1693:

> I do not think this is bound up with technical rules of set off. It is an ancient common law right. I therefore declare that as far as the repairs are within the express or implied covenants of the landlord, the . . . defendants are entitled to recoup themselves out of future rents and defend any action for payment thereof. It does not follow however that the full amount expended by the . . . defendants on such repairs can properly be treated as payment of rent. It is a question of fact in every case whether and to what extent the expenditure was proper. . . .

Of course, the use of the ancient common law right by tenants is limited by the ability of the tenant to actually pay for the repairs themselves and, anyway, in the case of an apartment or office in a large building, the ability of a tenant to carry out the repairs may be extremely limited.

Injunctions and specific performance As we have already seen in relation to the landlord's remedies, the award of an injunction is an equitable remedy and therefore is subject to all the limitations that relate to a court's exercise of its discretion in making such an award. Notwithstanding these limitations, a tenant may apply for an injunction to restrain a landlord from breaching or threatening to breach a covenant.

The ability of a tenant to claim for specific performance is founded both in statute and in the supervisory jurisdiction of the courts.

In relation to statute, the Landlord and Tenant Act 1985 s.17(1) provides:

> In proceedings in which a tenant of a dwelling alleges a breach on the part of his landlord of a repairing covenant relating to any part of the premises in which the dwelling is comprised, the court may order specific performance of the covenant whether or not the breach relates to a part of the premises let to the tenant and notwithstanding any equitable rule restricting the scope of the remedy, whether on the basis of a lack of mutuality or otherwise.

In addition to this statutory means of obtaining specific performance, a tenant may rely on general equitable principles under the supervisory jurisdiction of the court. An example of this can be seen in *Jeune* v *Queens Cross Properties Ltd* [1974] Ch 97, where a tenant obtained relief by way of specific performance requiring a landlord to repair a defective balcony. Similarly, in *Posner* v *Scott-Lewis* [1987] 3 All ER 513 the court granted an application for specific performance of a landlord's covenant to employ a resident porter. It should be noted that this was not an award to compel the provision of personal service; this would clearly have required the constant supervision of the court, which would have precluded an award being made. In this case, the award was made merely for the execution of an agreement for the provision for such services.

A tenant has always had greater access for specific performance relief, than a landlord. Until *Rainbow Estates Ltd* v *Tokenhold Ltd* [1999] Ch 64, landlords had no access to such relief on the basis that there was no 'mutuality' in that, since tenants were not entitled to relief from forfeiture, landlords should not be able to claim specific performance: *Hill* v *Barclay* (1810) Vesey Junior 402. However, the ability of a tenant to obtain specific performance should be viewed guardedly since the courts are reluctant to apply the remedy for breach of covenant. In *Newman* v *Framewood Manor Management Co. Ltd* [2012] EWCA Civ 159 the claimant sought an award of specific performance to compel a landlord to comply with a covenant to keep 'certain recreational facilities, including an indoor swimming pool and a whirlpool in good order and repair'. In fact, there was no whirlpool but a jacuzzi, but it was common ground that these were the same thing. When the landlord removed the jacuzzi, substituting it with a sauna, the cost of which would be £30,000, the claimant sought specific performance to compel the landlord to reinstate the jacuzzi, arguing that replacing it with a sauna was not appropriate and that its installation would give rise to a loss of amenity. Arden LJ in the Court of Appeal agreed with the judge at first instance and refused to make an award of specific performance. He stated that, given the cost, to compel the installation of a jacuzzi would be 'excessive and disproportionate when compared with the loss of amenity'. In arriving at this decision, he referred to the case of *Ruxley Electronics and Construction Ltd* v *Forsyth* [1996] AC 344. In that case the House of Lords refused an award of substantial damages for the construction of a new swimming pool with a depth of 7ft 6 in, as contracted for, to replace the one with a depth of 6ft which had actually been constructed. Instead, the House of Lords made an award for loss of amenity as the cost of the new constructions was wholly disproportionate to the loss of amenity.

On the basis of the above, whilst specific performance is clearly accessible as a remedy for breach of a covenant by a tenant, the award is very much discretionary and tenants have to take into account the wider circumstances in which the breach arises. Further, to claim the remedy there must be sufficient definition as to what is required to be done in order to ensure compliance with the order by the landlord. 'Certainty and clarity of a court order will in turn result in the court simply confirming compliance on completion of the works rather than continual supervision of it' (Hatfield, 2012).

Summary

The nature of leases/term of years

Defined in the Law of Property Act 1925 s.205 (xxvii) as follows:

> 'Term of years absolute' means a term of years (taking effect either in possession or in reversion whether or not at a rent) . . . either certain or liable to determination by notice, re-entry, operation of law . . . and includes a term for less than a year, or for a year or years and a fraction of a year or from year to year.

In *Street* v *Mountford* [1985] AC 809 Lord Templeman described the nature of a lease in the following terms:

> The traditional view that the grant of exclusive possession for a term at a rent creates a tenancy is consistent with the elevation of a tenancy into an estate in land.'

The essential qualities of a lease are that a lease:

(i)   provides a right of exclusive possession;

(ii) for a certain term whether for years, year or other periodic tenancies;

(iii) is at a rent, though as a matter of law this is not necessary; and

(iv) that the premises must be sufficiently defined.

It follows that leases do *not* arise in the cases:

- of lodgers/hotel residents;
- where there are acts of friendship;
- where there is an arrangement by way of an act of charity;
- where there is a licence: *Bruton* v *London and Quadrant Housing Trust* [2000] 1 AC 406.

The creation of leases

Leases may be either legal or equitable.

Legal leases

To create a legal lease a conveyance is required, as set out in the Law of Property Act 1925 s.52(1):

> All conveyances of land or of any interest therein are void for the purpose of conveying or creating a legal estate unless made by deed.

The Law of Property Act 1925 s.52(2)d provides that certain leases do not have to be in writing. Such leases are to be found in the Law of Property Act 1925 s.54(2):

> Nothing in the foregoing provisions of this Part of the Act shall effect the creation by parol of leases taking effect in possession for a term not exceeding three years (whether or not the

lessee is given the power to extend the term at the best rent that can be reasonably obtainable without taking a fine.

Thus such a lease can be created orally but it must take effect in *possession* and thus 'reversionary' (future) leases cannot be created under this provision.

Protection of legal lease

Registered land

- Where a lease is made by deed out of a registered title and it is for a term of more than seven years, the lease must be substantively registered at the HM Land Registry. Failure to do so means the lease only takes effect in equity: Land Registration Act 2002 s.27(1).

- Where the lease is one for seven years or less and is for a period of not less than three years, there is no requirement for the lease to be substantively registered and it will take effect as an interest that is overriding under the Land Registration Act 2002 Schedule 3 para 1.

- Where a lease is made by deed out of an unregistered title and it is for a term of more than seven years, the title must be compulsorily registered at the HM Land Registry since, by virtue of the Land Registration Act 2002 s.4(1), the grant of the lease is a 'trigger event'. Failure to register the lease means that the lease will take effect in equity only.

Unregistered land

- If the lease is for seven years or less this is not a trigger event within the Land Registration Act 2002. Provided the lease is made by way of a deed, it takes effect as a legal estate and, as such, 'binds the whole world'. When a purchaser of the landlord's reversion, whether the freehold or the superior leasehold title, registers their estate on the basis of compulsory first registration, then the lease will become an interest that is overriding by virtue of the Land Registration Act 2002 Schedule 1 para 1.

Equitable leases

Where a lease is for more than three years and no deed is used, then an equitable lease will arise *provided* there is a valid contract within the terms of the Law of Property (Miscellaneous Provisions) Act 1989 s.2(1). This requires the contract:

- be in writing; and
- incorporate all the terms agreed in one document or, where documents have been exchanged, in each; and
- be signed by all the parties.

  (*Parker* v *Taswell* (1858) 2 De G & J 559)

  (*Walsh* v *Lonsdale* (1820) 21 Ch D 9)

The principle in the above two cases is dependent on the willingness of equity to grant specific performance and, as such, a person seeking to enforce an equitable lease must 'come to equity with clean hands'.

  (*Coatsworth* v *Johnson* (1886) 55 LJQB 220)

If specific performance is unavailable then a court will fall back on the common law principles so that if a tenant has been let into possession and is paying rent, then that will give rise to a *legal* periodic tenancy based on the period by which the rent is payable.

Protection of equitable leases

Registered land

- An equitable lease may be protected by the entering of a notice on the register of title of the land over which it is to take effect. By virtue of the Land Registration Act 2002 s.28 and s.29 registration of the notice gives protection against later transferees of the reversion, either the legal fee simple or the superior legal lease.

- If the holder of the equitable lease fails to register their notice then they may claim an interest that is overriding by virtue of their actual occupation under the Land Registration Act 2002 Schedule 3 para 1.

Unregistered land

Since an equitable lease is an enforceable contract or lease, it will amount to an *estate contract*. As an estate contract, the equitable lease must be registered as a C(iv) land charge under the Land Charges Act 1972 s.2(4). Such a land charge will bind a purchaser of a legal estate for money or money's worth. If the C(iv) land charge is unregistered, it will be void against a third-party purchaser.

Difference between legal and equitable leases

An agreement or contract for a lease is not as good as a legal lease since:

- It is dependent on the willingness of the court to grant specific performance.
- The Law of Property Act 1925 s.62 only applies to conveyances, so legal easements cannot be implied.
- There is no privity of estate between the landlord and assignee of an equitable lease for the purposes of running of the covenants.

Types of lease

Leases may exist as:

- a lease for a fixed period of time;
- a periodic tenancy;
- a tenancy by sufferance;
- a tenancy at will;
- a tenancy by estoppel.

Statutory modifications to leases

- Perpetually renewable leases: Converted to a 2000-year term by the Law of Property Act 1922 s.145 and Schedule 15

- Leases for life or until marriage: Converted to a 90-year term by the Law of Property Act 1925 s.149(6)

- Reversionary leases: A lease created to commence more than 21 years from the instrument creating it is void: Law of Property Act 1925 s.149(3)

Covenants and obligations of landlord and tenant

Distinction between covenants and conditions

- A covenant is a provision where a 'covenantor' makes a promise to a 'covenantee'. In a deed, such promises are described as covenants.

- Leases are essentially contracts to which the normal laws of contract apply. The lease may therefore contain a term that is expressed as a 'condition'. Such a term is regarded as a major term, breach of which entitles a party to terminate the contract/lease and claim damages.

Types of covenant

Covenants may be express, implied or usual.

Express covenants

These are covenants that the landlord and tenant have expressly entered into.

Landlord's covenants

- Quiet enjoyment.
- No derogation of grant.
- Fitness of premises and covenants to repair.
- Covenant to insure the premises.

Tenant's covenants

- Covenant to pay rent:

  Cricklewood Property and Investment Trust Ltd v *Leighton's Investment Trust Ltd* [1945] AC 221.

- Not to assign, underlet or part with possession.

Implied covenants

Except where a lease provides otherwise, by way of an express covenant, the position of the parties is as follows by way of implied covenants.

Landlord's covenants

- Quiet enjoyment.
- No derogation from grant:
  Harmer v *Jumbil (Nigeria) Tin Areas Ltd* [1921] 1 Ch 200.
- Fitness of premises and covenants to repair:
  Southwark London Borough Council v *Mills* [2001] 1 AC 1
  Attorney General of Belize v *Belize Telecom* [2009] UKPC 10
  Liverpool City Council v *Irwin* [1976] 2 All ER 39.
- Statutory duty of care:
  Defective Premises Act 1972 s.4(1).

Tenant's covenants

- Liability for damage or repair.
- Not to commit 'waste'.
- Voluntary waste: where the tenant commits a positive act that changes the premises permanently – for example, knocking down a wall.
- Permissive waste: where a tenant fails to do something – for example, failing to stop a leak that damages the property.
- Note: Liability for the different types of waste depends on the type of tenancy held by the tenant.
  - Not to assign, underlet or part with possession.
  - To pay rates and other taxes.
  - To allow the landlord entry to the premises.

The 'usual' covenants

Where a lease contains no covenants that such a lease would normally contain then the lease is deemed to contain the covenants that are 'usual' in the circumstances.

Landlord's covenants

- Quiet possession.

Tenant's covenants

- To pay rent.
- To pay rates and taxes.
- Liability for damages or repair.
- To allow the landlord entry onto the premises to inspect and carry out repairs.
- A condition of re-entry for non-payment of rent.

Termination of leases

A lease may terminate in a variety of ways

- By expiry of the term.
- By notice.
- By surrender.
- By merger.
- By frustration:

  National Carriers Ltd v *Panalpina (Northern) Ltd* [1981] AC 675.

- By enlargement – by the Law of Property Act 1925 s.153 where a tenant has a lease for more than 300 years with more than 200 years unexpired, the tenant has a right to enlarge their lease into a freehold.
- By disclaimer.
- Repudiation for breach of contract.
- By forfeiture – this gives the landlord the right to enter the premises because the tenant has not paid their rent or is otherwise in breach of some other covenant (*Billson* v *Residential Apartments Ltd* [1992] 1 AC 494). Re-entry may be by way of:
  - Proceedings for possession.
  - Law of Property Act 1925 s.146 notices.

Remedies for breach of covenant

Landlord's remedies

- Landlords are able to sue for damages for breaches of covenant by the tenant, the measure of damages being that which will place the landlord in the same position as if the covenant had not been broken. There are, however, further statutory controls on this, so that under the Landlord and Tenant Act 1927, where a tenant is in breach of a covenant to repair, the landlord is limited to the amount by which his or her reversion is diminished. The remedy of damages is not available for non-payment of rent.

- The remedies of injunction and specific performance are discretionary and subject to the normal rules of equity. It used to be the case that landlords could not make use of specific performance; however, the case of **Rainbow Estates Ltd v Tokenhold Ltd** [1999] Ch 64 now appears to indicate that the remedy will be available in certain circumstances.

- Landlords may also levy distress – that is, enter the premises and seize the tenant's goods. The remedy is an ancient one and somewhat anachronistic today. There are significant human rights issues but, whilst there have been calls for its abolition, it is still available in both residential and commercial leases. In the latter, the Tribunals, Courts and Enforcement Act has made provision for the reform of the law on distress through CRAR, though this has still to be implemented.

Tenant's remedies

- As with landlords, tenants may obtain damages based on putting them in the same position as if the breach had not occurred. Tenants may obtain damages for discomfort and inconvenience from the landlord's breach if he or she remains in possession: **Calabar Properties Ltd v Stitcher** [1984] 1 WLR 287. Damages are calculated by reference to the rent payable for the period of the landlord's breach: **Wallace v Manchester City Council** [1998] EWCA Civ 1166.

- Tenants should not go on 'rent strike' as there is a risk of the lease being forfeited. A tenant may undertake the repairs themselves but deduct the cost from future payments of rent: **Lee-Parker v Izzet** [1971] 1 WLR 1688.

- A tenant may restrain a landlord from breaching or threatening to breach a covenant. Tenants may also claim specific performance to compel a landlord to carry out his or her obligations. This may be done under the auspices of the Landlord and Tenant Act 1985 s.17(1) or by way of the general supervisory jurisdiction of the courts: **Jeune v Queens Cross Properties Ltd** [1974] Ch 97. Historically, tenants have had greater access to this remedy than landlords, though this must be viewed guardedly as the courts are reluctant to grant specific performance: **Newman v Framewood Manor Management Co. Ltd** [2012] EWCA Civ 159; **Ruxley Electronics and Construction Ltd v Forsyth** [1996] AC 344.

Further reading

Cowan, 'Harassment and Unlawful Eviction in the Private Rented Sector – A Study of Law In (-) Action' [2001] 65 *The Conveyancer and Property Lawyer* 249

Elliott, 'Non-Derogation from Grant' (1964) 80 *Law Quarterly Review* 244

Gravells, 'Forfeiture of Leases for Breach of Covenant: Pre-Action Notices and Remediability' (2006) *Journal of Business Law* 830

Hatfield, 'Is Specific Performance an Option for Landlords?' (2012) *Solicitors Journal* Vol. 146 No. 42

Humphreys, 'Has CRAR Been Lost Forever?' (2009) *Estates Gazette* No. 0915 96

Law Commission, *Landlord and Tenant: Distress for Rent* Law Com No. 194 (2001)

Law Commission, *Renting Homes* Law Com No. 284 (2003)

Law Commission, *Termination of Tenancies for Tenant Default* Law Com No. 303 (2006)

Lord Chancellor's Department Consultation Papers: *Enforcement Review Consultation Paper No. 5: Distress for Rent*, May 2001

Lower, 'The Bruton Tenancy' 74 [2010] *The Conveyancer and Property Lawyer* 38

Roberts, 'The Bruton Tenancy: A Matter of Relativity' 76 [2012] *The Conveyancer and Property Lawyer* 87

Smith, 'The Clipping of a Dubious and Dangerous Method' [1992] 56 *The Conveyancer and Property Lawyer* 273

Smith, 'Disrepair and Unfitness Revisited' [2003] 66 *The Conveyancer and Property Lawyer* 112

Sparkes, 'Prudential Assurance Co. Ltd v London Residuary Body' (1993) 108 *Law Quarterly Review* 93

Tettenborn, 'Absolving the Undeserving: Shopping Centres, Specific Performance and the Law of Contract' [1998] 62 *The Conveyancer and Property Lawyer* 23

Tromans, 'Forfeiture of Leases: Relief for Underlessees and Holders of Other Derivative Interests' [1986] 49 *The Conveyancer and Property Lawyer* 187

Walton, 'Landlord's Distress – Past Its Sell By Date?' [2000] 64 *The Conveyancer and Property Lawyer* 508

Commonhold

Aims and objectives

After reading this chapter you should be able to:

- Understand the nature of commonhold as a form of land-holding.
- Know how a commonhold estate is created.
- Understand how commonhold operates.
- Know how a commonhold is terminated.

Introduction

Commonhold is a system of land-holding that was introduced by the Commonhold and Leasehold Reform Act ('CLRA') 2002, coming into force on 27 September 2004. It is an entirely new concept that essentially makes use of both freehold and leasehold estates and turns them into a form of common ownership. Commonhold applies where an area of land, usually a building, is split into a number of separate units and thus it can be quickly seen that commonhold is intended to operate in blocks of flats; however, it can apply to commercial premises or combinations of both residential and commercial premises. In order for a commonhold to exist, it must consist of both common parts of a building and at least two units. Thus, for example, in an apartment block there are hallways, stairs and possibly gardens that are all used by the individual flat or apartment owners. Whilst commonhold can apply to two pieces of land, there must be mutual obligations or shared facilities between the two pieces of land. Normally, therefore, a commonhold operates where the units are organised in a vertical structure, as in an apartment block.

Why commonhold?

Normally, in an apartment block (it is easier to use this as an example), the owner of a unit has a lease. There are sound reasons for this. As we have already seen, a freehold is the nearest one can get to absolute ownership of land. Theoretically, at least, if one holds the freehold of a fifth-floor flat then one possesses a 'flying freehold'. If the block of flats then has a major fire so that the building is badly damaged and has to be demolished,

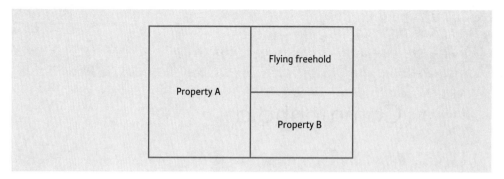

Figure 7.1

then technically the fifth-floor apartment owner has the freehold of a block of air above the ground. Clearly, this poses a problem where the owners of the land or apartments below are not inclined to re-build the apartment block. Commonly, however, flying freeholds arise in situations where the upper floors of a house overlap another house next door, as in Figure 7.1.

Here problems of support may arise if the owner of property B weakens the structure of the property below. Similarly, if the owner of property A fails to maintain their property – for example, repair a leaking roof – then this will adversely affect the owner of property B. Whilst these problems can be reconciled by the owners entering into covenants to maintain their respective properties, these 'positive' covenants do not 'run' with the land to bind successive owners in freehold land. The result of this can often be that mortgagees will not lend where a flying freehold exists.

Traditionally, then, in apartment blocks owners of apartments are only given leases since one of the quirks of land law is that positive covenants will run with the land. Leases, however, can have their own problems. Firstly, there is a perception that it is better to be an owner of one's property rather than being a tenant, despite the fact that one's lease may well be a long lease, say, 99 years, and therefore there is little difference.

Secondly, whilst a long lease may start off being all good and well, once the term is reduced to 70 years it becomes, essentially, a diminishing asset and it may equally be difficult to persuade a mortgagee to lend on the property as the mortgagee will not consider the lease to be good security for the loan. In order to avoid such a situation, the Leasehold Reform, Housing and Urban Development Act ('LRHUDA') 1993 provides that a 'qualifying tenant' has the right to surrender their existing lease and acquire a new lease that will be at a peppercorn rent and will be for a term expiring 90 years after the end date of the existing lease. It should be noted that the Act only applies to 'flats'.

Example

T has a lease of a flat which has 50 years unexpired at a ground rent of £240 per annum. If T exercises his right under the 1993 Act, he will then have a lease for 140 years and will not have to pay the £240 per annum.

In order to be a 'qualifying tenant', the tenant must have been the registered owner of the property with a long lease for at least two years immediately preceding their notice of claim: LRHUDA 1993 s.39(2)a (as amended by the CLRA 2002 s.130). In order to make use of this manner of enfranchisement, the lease has to be a 'long lease' – that is, a term of years certain which, when granted, was for a period in excess of 21 years: LRHUDA 1993 s.7(1).

In order to compensate a landlord for their loss of ground rent and the fact the landlord will not get possession when their original lease expires, the 'qualifying tenant' extending their lease has to pay a premium. Generally, the shorter the period unexpired, the greater the premium that has to be paid.

Thirdly, leaseholders in multiple-unit developments often have difficulty with their landlords, particularly with regard to the willingness of landlords to maintain the building properly and carry out repairs.

Fourthly, leaseholders are always subject to the possibility of having their leases forfeited because of what may be relatively minor breaches of covenant.

It is out of the above difficulties, perceived or otherwise, that the concept of commonhold developed. In a commonhold structure, each owner of a unit – a flat – has a freehold estate and, at the same time, becomes a member of a 'commonhold association' which owns and is responsible for the common areas of the building and its grounds. In this way, those holding under a commonhold estate effectively manage and control the common areas and are able to apply positive obligations against each and every commonholder. The commonhold association owns the freehold of the common areas.

Commonhold is very closely based on concepts that are found in other common law jurisdictions – 'condominiums' in the USA and 'strata titles' in Australia. Despite the fact that the Law Commission in its report, *Making Land Work: Easements, Covenants and Profits à Prendre* (Law Com 327 (2011)) considers commonhold to be an important addition, particularly with regard to the running of positive covenants in freehold land, it has been something of an abject failure. Its complexity and cost, the fact that all unit holders are required to consent for a commonhold application to be made and resistance from developers in new multi-unit developments have meant that very few commonhold developments have been created – as at 20 February 2008 HM Land Registry reported that there were only 14 commonhold schemes registered. For this reason, only an outline of the processes involved with creating a commonhold scheme will be discussed here and, in any event, the overall complexity puts it outside of the remit of this book.

Creation

There are limitations on the type of land that may be subject to commonhold; thus commonhold can only be created in respect of freehold land that has already been registered at the Land Registry; furthermore, the freehold title must have a title absolute: CLRA 2002 s.2. Even in such circumstances, commonhold cannot be created in respect of land that wholly comprises flying freeholds (that is, where any property between the land and the freehold is not comprised freehold title), (CLRA 2002 Sched. 2 para 1); agricultural land (CLRA 2002 Sched. 2 para 2); and land held with a contingent title (that is, the land may revert to a person other than the current registered proprietor) (CLRA 2002 Sched. 2 para 3).

In order for commonhold land to be created, an application is made to the Chief Land Registrar where the land is registered as a 'freehold estate in commonhold land'. The application must be accompanied by the consents of all the persons specified in the CLRA s.3 (i.e. the registered proprietor of the freehold estate and all the persons owning leasehold estates granted for 21 years or more), together with anyone having a charge over the whole or part of the land (i.e. mortgagees). Clearly, therefore, in relation to an existing development, the number of consents could be quite large. This contrasts with the case of a developer who wishes to create a commonhold out of a new development since only the developer's consent is usually required here.

It should be stated that few developers have shown any interest in creating a commonhold estate. In addition to the above, the land can only be registered with a commonhold title if a commonhold association exists.

The commonhold association and management

The commonhold association is registered as the proprietor of the common parts and the individual unit holders are registered as proprietors of their own individual units. Both the commonhold association and individuals have their own distinct freehold titles and thus the original leases held by the individual unit holders are closed.

The commonhold association is a company limited by guarantee: CLRA 2002 s.34(1) and therefore has to comply with the normal requirements of the Companies Acts with regard to filing accounts, etc. Whilst, as with any company, the commonhold association company has a Memorandum of Articles and Association that sets out its powers and obligations, in fact such powers and obligations are set out in the Commonhold Regulations Act 2004 Sched. 1 and 2 and cannot be changed. Clearly, the principal objective of the commonhold association is to act for the benefit of the unit holders (i.e. the flat owners), and, to that extent, the directors have a duty under the regulations to use their powers with the rights and employment of the individual unit holders in mind.

At the core of the commonhold association is the 'commonhold community statement'. Essentially, this is the constitutional framework that binds the whole commonhold community. This statement must be in a prescribed form and will identify the individual units and their location. The statement also identifies the common parts – typically stairs, lifts, gardens, utilities, ducting and such like. The statement does not only make provision for the use of the common parts but also sets out the rights and obligations of the unit holders. In particular, the statement regulates the financial obligations of the unit holders with respect to the maintenance of the common parts and the overall costs of the commonhold development. The directors of the commonhold association have a statutory responsibility to establish and maintain a 'reserve' fund for the repair and maintenance of the development. Unit holders are generally required to contribute to this fund by way of a levy or service charge. Rules are set out with regards to insurance, maintenance and repair. The statement also sets out a scheme for dispute resolution, but only between unit holders and the commonhold association, *not* between unit holders themselves.

It is clear from the above that the commonhold community statement is a significant – and indeed a substantial – document that attaches automatically to each unit, irrespective of any charges in ownership of an individual unit. This is important since, as alluded to earlier, one of the great difficulties in terms of freehold land is the transmission of the burden of covenants, particularly with regard to positive covenants. The automatic transmission of the rights and duties of the commonhold community statement is given statutory force under the CLRA 2002 s.16(1).

Termination of a commonhold scheme

Termination of a commonhold scheme, because the association is a company limited by guarantee, follows procedures similar to a company winding-up under the Companies Act but with additional processes involved to protect unit holders where appropriate.

There are three means by which a commonhold scheme can be brought to an end – one procedural and two substantive.

Firstly, the procedural process for terminating a scheme is found in the CLRA 2002 s.55. Here a court may order the cessation of a commonhold. This would normally be used if there is some defect in the legal structure of the commonhold association or where the registration process is otherwise flawed.

Secondly, the unit holders may pass a winding-up resolution – this is essentially a voluntary winding-up. This may arise because the unit holders may wish to collectively realise the value of the development or because they wish to return to a more conventional land-holding structure. In order to do this, 100 per cent of the unit holders must pass a resolution to this effect and appoint a liquidator. The liquidator then applies to the Land Registry for a termination and provides a 'termination statement'. Essentially, the termination statement is drawn up by the association; however, the liquidator is required to declare his or her approval of it. The statement sets out how the assets of the association and the interests of the unit holders are to be dealt with. Once the registrar gives effect to the statement, the freehold of the entire development, including the freehold estate of each unit holder, is vested in the commonhold association as the registered proprietor so that the whole development can then be sold and the proceeds distributed to each unit holder in accordance with the terms of the termination statements.

It is possible for the commonhold to be dissolved without the consent of 100% of the unit holders. Thus, where at least 80% of the unit holders vote in favour of a winding-up resolution and a 'termination statement resolution', the liquidator may apply to the court for an order in which the terms of a termination application for the registrar are set out. Clearly, the buyout of uncooperative unit holders raises issues of minority protection. Immediately, there may be a violation of the European Convention on Human Rights Article 1 of the First Protocol – a right to peaceful enjoyment of possessions, but this largely depends on the circumstances applicable to each case, such as the levels of compensation both to unit holders and mortgagees and the reasons for the termination.

Thirdly, it is possible for a court to make a winding-up order compulsorily on the grounds of insolvency: CLRA 2002 ss.50–54. The normal process here is for the court to make a succession order and substitute a new commonhold association in place of the old. The new association will then be registered as the registered proprietor of the freehold of the common parts. If the court finds it is not possible to make such a substitution then it may order the cessation of the commonhold and the assets will then be dealt with according to a termination statement.

Summary

- Commonhold was introduced by the Commonhold and Leasehold Reform Act 2002 so that developments – whether residential or commercial – can have a form of common ownership.

- Unit (or flat) owners will have the freehold of their individual units but a 'commonhold association' will be the registered proprietor of the common parts.

- The use of commonhold avoids the difficulties of the enforcement of positive covenants in freehold land between successors in title of the original parties.

- Commonholds can only be created in respect of freehold land but there must be no 'flying freehold', or agricultural land or land held with a contingent interest over the development in question.

- For a commonhold there must be a commonhold association which is the registered proprietor of the freehold of the common parts. The association is governed by the 'commonhold community statement' that sets out the rights and obligations of the association and the individual unit holders.
- Commonholds may be terminated:
  - by the court where there are procedural defects in the application for commonhold;
  - by a voluntary winding-up of the commonhold association by the unit holders;
  - by a compulsory winding-up by the court in the case of the commonhold association becoming insolvent.

Further reading

Clarke, 'The Enactment of Commonhold: Problems, Principles and Perspectives' [2002] *The Conveyancer and Property Lawyer* 349

Grove, 'A Developer's Guide to Commonhold' (2005) 155 *New Law Journal* 208

Roberts, 'Commonhold: A New Property Term – But No Property in a Term' [2002] *The Conveyancer and Property Lawyer* 341

Smith, 'The Purity of Commonholds' [2004] *The Conveyancer and Property Lawyer* 194

Wong, 'Potential Pitfalls in the Commonhold Community Statement and the Corporate Mechanisms of the Commonhold Association' [2006] *The Conveyancer and Property Lawyer* 14

8

Licences and proprietary estoppel

Aims and objectives

After reading this chapter you should be able to:

- Understand the nature of licences and proprietary estoppel.
- Recognise the various types of licence and understand their nature.
- Understand the relationship of contractual licences and constructive trusts.
- Recognise and understand the elements required for the operation of proprietary estoppel.
- Understand how the estoppel equity is satisfied.
- Understand the nature of proprietary estoppel in relation to third parties.
- Understand and distinguish constructive trusts and proprietary estoppel.

Introduction

Apart from certain statutory rights, there is no general right to enter land belonging to someone else and indeed it was stated in **Entick v Carrington** (1765) 2 Wils KB 275 that 'our law holds the property of every man so sacred, that no man can set foot upon his neighbour's close without his leave'. It has already been seen that an owner of land will have either a freehold or leasehold estate in land by which the owner can prevent third parties from entering the land. Those third parties that do enter the land will do so either by way of a trespass, an interest in land, or a licence. Trespass arises where the latter two incidents of entry are not present and such an entry is actionable in tort. Interests in land, on the other hand, are proprietary interests in land and arise by way of easements or restrictive covenants that benefit a dominant tenement and impose a burden or restraint on the way the owner of the servient land enjoys their land. These types of interest are not personal rights but rights which attach to the land itself. Between the pole positions of trespass and an interest in land there are a myriad of situations where a third party can lawfully enter the property belonging to someone else. Sometimes a licence may mirror a legal interest in land, thus a licence or permission to use a footpath may be indistinguishable from a right of way by way of an easement. The fundamental principle, though, is that a licence does not amount to a proprietary interest in land, as stated by Vaughan CJ in **Thomas v Sornell** (1673) Vaugh 330:

> A dispensation or licence properly passeth no interest nor alters or transfers property in anything, but only makes an action lawful, which without it had been unlawful.

The concept of the licence is extremely wide. On the one hand, it will encompass the occasional entry of the land, such as a licence to fish, park a car or attend a cinema or an implied licence permitting a milkman or a postman to enter one's land. On the other hand, a licence may permit long-term use or occupation of the land to the extent that the licence may be indistinct from a lease. It is, however, in this latter example vital to make the distinction since a lease gives the lessee exclusive possession of the land to the extent the lessee may exclude persons, including the lessor, from entering the property. This is not the case with a licence so, for instance, an occupier of a hotel room is unable to exclude the management of the hotel from entering the room. In that respect, a lease falls within the realms of real property, whereas a licence falls within the realms of personal property.

Licences can be created by writing or orally. Unlike estates and interests in land, there are no formal requirements needed to create a licence – other than that in contractual licences the requirements of the law of contract have to be adhered to. Licences, however, may be incidental to the creation of an estate or interest in land and, to that extent, they may form part of a deed or registered disposition with regards to the estate or interest being created. Thus the purchase of a house may give the owner a licence to make use of a tennis court in the vicinity of the house. The danger in such circumstances is that the nature of the licence becomes blurred within the formal documents. It is, however, important to recognise that some licences by their very nature cannot be a proprietary right, such as a licence to fish. Other licences may arise where the formal requirements to create a proprietary interest are not met. Similarly a licence may arise because there are elements lacking for the creation of a proprietary interest, such as a lease. Thus in **Street v Mountford** [1985] AC 809 (HL) Lord Templeman stated at 816:

> The traditional view that the grant of exclusive possession for a term at a rent creates a tenancy is consistent with the elevation of a tenancy into an estate in land. The tenant possessing exclusive possession is able to exercise the rights of an owner in land, which is in the real sense his land albeit temporarily and subject to certain restrictions. A tenant armed with exclusive possession can keep out strangers and keep out the landlord unless the landlord is exercising limited rights reserved to him by the tenancy agreement to enter and view and repair. A licensee lacking exclusive possession can in no sense call the land his own and cannot be said to own any estate in land. The licence does not create an estate in land to which it relates but only makes an act lawful which would otherwise be unlawful.

Thus if no exclusive possession is granted in the case of a purported lease, or if the relevant formalities for a deed or writing are not complied with, a licence must ensue. It also follows that the creation of such a licence can arise either deliberately or accidently so as to create a right *over* land as opposed to a right *in* the land.

The relationship between a licensor and licensee is essentially a contractual relationship based on offer, acceptance and intention to create legal relations, capacity and the exchange of consideration, though bare licences are based on a purely gratuitous arrangement. It is, however, possible for the relationship between the parties to arise not by way of a contractual relationship but by way of the equitable principles of proprietary estoppel. Proprietary estoppel gives rise to a separate and independent means of framing a relationship between the parties. Licences and proprietary estoppel are not necessarily mutually exclusive and indeed the facts of individual cases provide an alternative view of the relationship. The distinction between the two is important, though, since proprietary estoppel has now been held to create a proprietary interest in the land. This concept will be considered later in this chapter.

Types of licence

There are various types of licence that provide for lawful entry or occupation of land. To a degree the classification arises out of the particular context in which the licence arises. The nature of a particular type of licence gives rise to issues as to the nature of the licence and its mode of creation, the relationship between the licensor and licensee, the revocability of the licence, the effect on third parties and its relationship to an interest in land.

Bare licence

This is the simplest form of licence in which permission is given to someone to enter on the land where no consideration is provided by the licensee. Such licences can arise expressly – for example, inviting friends around for dinner, or by implication. In *Robson v Hallett* [1967] 2 QB 939 the Court of Appeal stated that occupiers of dwelling houses gave implied licences to any member of the public to come on to the licensor's land and ask permission to conduct business with the owner – for example, a milkman. No formalities are required and whether or not a licence is created arises from the facts of the particular case.

Bare licences are revocable at will, provided the licensee is given a reasonable time to leave the premises. Whilst such a licence may be given for a particular duration of time, the licensor does not have to abide by this and can withdraw the licence at any time. The licensee has no redress in damages or specific performance should this occur. Once the licence is withdrawn, the licensee becomes a trespasser.

Since a bare licence can be withdrawn at will, it follows that it is incapable of binding a third party. No interest in land arises from a bare licence.

Licences coupled with an interest

It is possible for a landowner to grant a profit à prendre, a right to take something from the land such as fish or wood, to another (see Chapter 13). Clearly, in order to exercise this right, the owner of the profit has to be able to access the land. Thus a right to take fish from a river would be rendered defunct if one were not able to access the river. The licence therefore is ancillary to the profit à prendre so that it facilitates the profit. On the face of things, the licence appears to be a proprietary interest, since its existence is attached to that of the interest. Should the licence be revoked, this will give rise to an action by the owner of the interest since, essentially, the revocation is removing the interest as well. Since the licence is coupled with the interest, this means that third parties who are bound by the interest also take subject to the licence: *Wood v Leadbitter* (1845) 13 M & W 838. Such licences are, of course, not proprietary interests, despite their 'coupling' with the interest.

Contractual licences

Nature and creation

A contractual licence is a permission to enter land based on a contract and, in this respect, it is to be distinguished from a bare licence. An example may be a contract for a hotel room or a theatre ticket. Such licences may be created orally or in writing. They do not have to comply with the requirement of the Law of Property (Miscellaneous Provisions) Act 1989 s.2 since they are not contracts for the disposition of an interest in land in that they are not proprietary in nature.

Contractual licences are capable of providing for long-term occupation of the land, though crucially the licensee does not enjoy exclusive occupation of the land and therefore, as we have seen in Chapter 6, such licences are incapable of being leases by virtue of this requirement in leases.

Revocability of contractual licences

Whilst we have seen that bare licences can be revoked at will with no redress for the licensee, revocation of a contractual licence may give rise to an action for breach of contract. The result is that either party may sue for damages for any losses arising from the breach.

Wood v *Leadbitter* (1845) 13 M & W 838

The plaintiff purchased a four-day pass to see a race meeting at Doncaster racecourse. He was asked to leave and, when he refused to do so, he was forcibly ejected from the course. He claimed that, because he had a contractual licence, this was irrevocable, so that his removal amounted to an assault. It was held that, since he did not have a licence coupled with an interest, his licence was revocable, although he could sue for damages for breach of contract since there was no good reason for the contract to be revoked by the defendant. With regard to the assault, because the contract was revocable, the plaintiff became a trespasser, which entitled the defendant to eject him using reasonable force. His action therefore failed.

One issue that arises out of cases such as *Wood* v *Leadbitter* above is whether a court can grant specific performance of the contract. If a court granted specific performance, however, this would invariably mean that the licence would be irrevocable. Thus, in circumstances such as *Wood* v *Leadbitter*, the actions of the defendant would be to render his removal an assault. The role of equity to restrain a breach of a contractual licence was considered by the House of Lords in *Millennium Productions Ltd* v *Winter Garden Theatre (London) Ltd* [1946] 1 All ER 678.

Millennium Productions Ltd v *Winter Garden Theatre (London) Ltd* [1946] 1 All ER 678

The plaintiff was granted a licence to use the defendant's theatre for six months, with an option to renew after that time. The option was renewed on a number of occasions. The defendant then revoked the licence, despite the fact that the plaintiff was not in breach of the contract. The Court of Appeal held that, since there was no power to revoke the licence under the terms of the contract, it was irrevocable.

The House of Lords held that the power of a court to grant an injunction to prevent a breach of contract depended on the contract containing either an express or an implied negative clause. The court considered that the grant of the option was irrevocable and therefore the contract contained by implication a clause by the licensor not to revoke it (i.e. a negative clause).

The situation becomes therefore that, if a contract contains either an express or implied term that it is not to be revoked by the licensor, an injunction may be awarded to prevent the contract being revoked, so that it becomes irrevocable. At the end of the day, the House of Lords found that the contract in this particular case could not be constrained as irrevocable and refused the injunction; nevertheless, the wider principle provides for that possibility in an appropriate case.

The House of Lords considered that the decision in **Wood v Leadbitter** (1845) 13 M & W 838 could no longer be regarded as good authority and approved of the decision in **Hurst v Picture Theatres Ltd** [1915] 1 KB 1 where Buckley LJ stated at 10 that:

> If there be a licence with an agreement not to revoke the licence, that, if given for value, is an enforceable right. If the facts . . . are . . . that the licence was a licence to enter the building and see the spectacle from its commencement until its termination then there was included in that contract a contract not to revoke the licence until the play had run to its termination.

On this basis, the contract to see the play was an irrevocable licence, a breach of which could be restrained in equity.

The same effect arising from injunctions can also be applied to actions for specific performance where a breach arises before the licensee actually enters the premises. Thus in **Verrall v Great Yarmouth Borough Council** [1981] QB 202 a council repudiated a contract to allow the National Front to use a hall for an annual conference. Here the Court of Appeal applied the principle set out in **Millennium Productions** and granted specific performance of the contract.

So far, we have seen cases where the irrevocable contract to enter and occupy the premises is for a relatively short period and for a particular purpose. The question therefore arises as to whether a contract for a long period can be irrevocable since it is not hard to see that such an arrangement could give rise to an occupational licence that is similar to a tenancy. In **Millennium Productions** there was no time limit set for the duration of the contractual licence, but it was clearly not intended that it should be perpetual. The decision therefore is confined to the fact that the parties are not able to revoke the contract without a reasonable period of notice and a term was implied to this effect.

There is, however, no reason why contracts that envisage longer periods of occupation cannot be brought within the same criteria. This therefore raises a particular issue as to whether the principle of irrevocability can be applied to residential licences, as opposed to the commercial agreements in the cases seen above. Such an application of the principle can be seen in the case of **Tanner v Tanner** [1975] 1 WLR 1347.

Tanner v Tanner [1975] 1 WLR 1347

Here the plaintiff, a milkman, was a married man who entered into a relationship with the defendant, who took the plaintiff's name. 'Mrs Tanner' then became pregnant with twin girls and after their birth the couple decided to purchase a home. The house was put in Mr Tanner's name and Mrs Tanner moved out of her rent-controlled flat into the house with her two daughters. In fact, the plaintiff never lived in the house and three years later he demanded that the defendant move out and obtained an order for possession. Although the defendant was re-housed by her local council, she nevertheless appealed against the possession order.

Whilst the case can be argued on the basis of proprietary estoppel, Lord Denning in the Court of Appeal implied a contract into the arrangement, even though it is clear the parties had no intention of creating a contractual relationship between themselves. Thus Lord Denning stated at 1350:

> It seems to me . . . an inference [is] to be drawn, namely that in all the circumstances it is to be implied that she had a licence – a contractual licence – to have accommodation in the house for herself and the children so long as they were of school age and the accommodation was reasonably required for her and the children. There was, it is true, no express contract to that effect, but the circumstances are such that the court should imply a contract by the

plaintiff . . . It was a contractual licence of the kind which is specifically enforceable on her behalf; and which the plaintiff can be restrained from breaking; and he could not sell the house over her head so as to get her out of the way.

In fact, since the defendant had already moved out, she was awarded compensation; nevertheless, the fact remains that equity may step in to render such a contract irrevocable and capable of being enforced by specific performance.

The finding of such an implied contract was also followed in *Hardwick v Johnson* [1978] 1 WLR 683 and in *Chandler v Kerly* [1978] 1 WLR 693. However, in *Horrocks v Forray* [1976] 1 WLR 230 and *Coombes v Smith* [1986] 1 WLR 808 no such implied contract was found in similar circumstances to those in *Tanner v Tanner* on the basis that there was, firstly, no intention to create legal relations and, secondly, no sufficient consideration between the parties. Clearly, the finding for an implied *contract* is a significant step – certainly one that goes beyond implying a *term* that a contract is itself irrevocable. The principle remains, however, that if a contract can be found in domestic circumstances, there seems to be no reason why it cannot be made irrevocable and the duration of occupation is capable of being extensive.

Contractual licences and third parties

So far we have seen that contractual licences are a purely personal interest between the licensor and licensee and confer no proprietary interest. The effect of this is that a contractual licence is incapable of binding a third party who takes the land from the licensor, unless the Contracts (Rights of Third Parties) Act 1999 applies. Of course, if the licensor transfers the land to a third party, he or she will still be liable to the licensee but here the remedy is limited to damages only, since the acquisition of the land by the third party will prevent an equitable remedy from being granted to enforce the contract between the licensor and licensee.

The question that arises, though, is whether contractual licences are capable of being elevated to the status of a proprietary interest in land so that a third party is capable of being bound by the contractual licence.

It was shown in *Thomas v Sorrell* (1673) Vaugh 330 that a licence does not amount to a proprietary interest in land, so a third party cannot be bound by a licence. This position has been confirmed by the House of Lords in *King v David Allen and Sons (Bill Posting) Ltd* [1916] 2 AC 54 and by the Court of Appeal in *Clore v Theatrical Properties Ltd* [1936] 3 All ER 483. Despite this principle, there have been attempts to challenge this orthodox position and elevate contractual licences to the status of a proprietary interest in land in much the same way as was achieved with restrictive covenants through *Tulk v Moxhay* (1848) 2 Ph 774.

Much of the focus surrounding the developments here has arisen out of occupational residential licences that resemble tenancies. The breeding ground for this development was the state of the rental housing market in the 1970s. During this period, the statutory protection afforded to tenants by the Rent Acts meant that landlords became wary of providing a tenancy whereby it was extremely difficult, if not well-nigh impossible, to regain possession of their properties. Many landlords left the rental housing market altogether, creating a grave shortage of rental property. Naturally, others however moved towards giving their 'tenants' a licence rather than a lease, since licensees held no security of tenure and were placed outside of protection afforded by the Rent Acts. The result of this was that, if the property was sold to a third party, the contractual licence stood to be defeated by that sale since the third party would not be bound by the licence and, as we have already seen, equity would not intervene to enforce the licence in such circumstances. This is the scenario under discussion here since, as we examined in Chapter 6 in *Street* v *Mountford* [1985] AC 809, the courts would treat such sham licences as tenancies and, of course, they then became proprietary interests which would bind third parties.

The commencement of the challenge towards licences and their enforceability began with the dicta of the indomitable Lord Denning in *Errington* v *Errington and Woods* [1952] 1 KB 290.

Errington v Errington and Woods [1952] 1 KB 290

A father purchased a house, with the aid of a mortgage, to provide a home for his son. The father promised his son and daughter-in-law that, if they paid the mortgage instalments, he would transfer the house to them when the mortgage was discharged. Subsequently, the father died and left all his property to his widow. The son and his wife then split up and the son returned to live with his mother, who then took proceedings for possession of the house so that she could evict her daughter-in-law.

The Court of Appeal held that the daughter-in-law was entitled to remain in possession of the house whilst she continued to pay the mortgage instalments. Lord Denning considered that the irrevocable nature of the contract meant that equity was capable of enforcing a licence and rendering it binding on a third party transferee of the land. He stated at 208, 209:

> Law and equity have been fused for nearly 80 years, and since 1948 it has been clear that, as a result of the fusion, a licensor will not be permitted to eject a licensee in breach of a contract to allow him to remain . . . This infusion of equity means that contractual licences now have force and validity of their own and cannot be revoked in breach of contract. Neither the licensor nor anyone who claims through him can disregard the contract except a purchaser for value without notice.

The decision can be criticised on a number of fronts. Firstly, and most obviously, it contradicts the principled position set out in the *King* and *Clore* cases above. Secondly, the mother was not a third party in any event since she was suing as executrix of her husband's estate and, as such, should be bound in any event in the same way as the father would have been. Thirdly, Lord Denning recognised that the daughter-in-law had no right to remain at law 'but only in equity, and equitable rights now prevail'. Thus the ability of the licensee, the daughter-in-law, to remain is dependent on an equity arising. So if there are circumstances in which equity is either unwilling or unable to grant discretionary relief then a contractual licence cannot exist as an interest in and per se that is capable of binding a third party.

Despite these matters, the decision in *Errington* was followed in a number of cases that appeared to be establishing a recognition that a contractual licence had the force of a proprietary interest in land.

Binions v Evans [1972] Ch 359

In this case the defendant's husband had been employed by the Tredegar Estate and lived rent-free in a cottage owned by the estate. When her husband died, the defendant was allowed to remain in the cottage as a tenant in will rent-free for the rest of her life. In return for this arrangement, the defendant was required to keep the cottage in a good state of repair. The cottage was then sold to the plaintiffs at a reduced price because of a term in the contract that the plaintiffs were to take the property subject to the defendant's interest in the cottage. The plaintiffs then gave her notice to quit the cottage.

The Court of Appeal held that she was entitled to remain in the cottage for the rest of her life. The reasons for the decision, however, were not unanimous since Megaw LJ and Stephenson LJ considered that the defendant had a life interest under the Settled Land Act 1925. Lord Denning, however, stated that the contractual licence gave rise to an equitable interest in the cottage that bound a third party who had expressly bought the cottage with notice of and subject to the contractual licence – and, indeed, obtained it at a reduced price because of the interest.

Whilst the reasoning in the *Errington* and *Binion* cases has been applied in subsequent cases, there was a persistent disquiet about the elevation of contractual licences to the status of a proprietary interest and inevitably it was only a matter of time before it would come under close scrutiny. This occurred in the case of *Ashburn Anstalt* v *Arnold* [1989] Ch 1 in which orthodoxy was re-asserted by the Court of Appeal, which categorically rejected the proposition that a contractual licence could amount to a proprietary interest in land that bound successors in title to the licensor. The Court of Appeal, having reviewed all the decisions prior to *Errington*, considered that the decision in that case could not be reconciled with the earlier decisions such as *King* and *Clore*, amongst others. The Court of Appeal considered that the cases before *Errington* set out a clear and well-understood principle that contractual obligations gave rise to no estate or interest in land as understood within the definition of proprietary rights. The Court of Appeal considered that *Errington*, having made no reference to the *King* case, was decided per incuriam.

The analysis of the Court of Appeal as regards the status of contractual licences was dealt with as obiter; however, its conclusions have now been confirmed on a number of occasions. Thus in *Camden London Borough Council* v *Shortlife Community Housing* (1992) 90 LGR 358 it was stated by Millett J that the Court of Appeal had 'finally repudiated the heretical view that a contractual licence creates an interest in land capable of binding third parties'. Similarly, in *Lloyd* v *Dugdale* [2002] 2 P & CR 13 it was stated by Sir Christopher Slade that, 'Notwithstanding some previous authority suggesting the contrary, a contractual licence is not to be treated as creating a proprietary interest in land so as to bind third parties who acquire the land with notice of it on this account alone.'

Contractual licences and constructive trusts

In *Binions* v *Evans* [1972] Ch 359 Lord Denning proposed a second method by which a contractual licence might bind a third party – the presence of a constructive trust. He stated that the third party purchasers of the cottage would have a constructive trust imposed on them because they had purchased the property subject to the defendant's interest in the cottage, for which they had paid a reduced price, so it would be inequitable for them to turn her out of the cottage.

This proposition was considered by the Court of Appeal in *Ashburn Anstalt*. The Court of Appeal accepted that there could be circumstances in which a third party might be bound by a contractual licence and that this could arise if the circumstances were such as to give rise to a constructive trust. The Court of Appeal, however, emphasised that, whilst a contractual licence could bind a third party, the third party was bound not by the contractual licence per se but by the constructive trust.

Some care has to be exercised here. The fact that a person sells land 'subject to' a contractual licence will not, per se, give rise to a constructive trust that will bind a purchaser. The court considered that the words 'subject to' will put the purchaser on notice of the contractual licence but that notice alone is not enough. In order to impose a constructive trust it is necessary to demonstrate that the conscience of that particular purchaser is affected in order to render the constructive trust and hence the contractual licence binding on a purchaser.

The Court of Appeal in *Ashburn Anstalt* considered that the fact that the purchaser in *Errington* had acquired the cottage at a reduced price in consequence of the purchaser taking the cottage 'subject to' the contractual licence did give rise to such a constructive trust. In this respect, the Court of Appeal considered that Lord Denning was correct in his assertion that the purchaser took subject to the defendant's right to be entitled to remain in the cottage. Again, it needs emphasising that it is not the contractual licence that is binding on the purchaser but the fact that the constructive trust imposed on the purchaser requires them to comply with their agreement to allow the licensee to remain in occupation of the land. In *Ashburn Anstalt* itself, the absence of a reduced price precluded a constructive trust from arising, since here the conscience of the estate owner, the purchaser, was not affected to give rise to the equity forming the basis of the constructive trust.

In *Lloyd* v *Dugdale* [2002] 2 P & CR 13 Sir Christopher Slade set out the relevant principles for the establishment of the intervention of equity in establishing a constructive trust so as to protect a contractual licence. These are:

(i) There is no general rule that the court will impose a constructive trust on the purchaser to give effect to the prior interests or encumbrances which the vendor has stated the sale will be subject to. In order to establish a personal constructive trust, a standard form contract expressing that the sale is subject to encumbrances will not suffice. The contract will have to make specific reference to the prior interest or encumbrance as regards the contractual licence to establish the personal constructive trust.

(ii) A court will not impose a constructive trust unless it is satisfied that the purchaser's conscience is so affected that it would be inequitable to allow them to deny the claimant an interest in the property.

(iii) In deciding whether the purchaser's conscience is affected, the crucially important question is whether the purchaser has undertaken a new obligation to give effect to the relevant encumbrance. Without such an undertaking to give effect to such a new obligation, will a constructive trust be imposed?

(iv) A contractual licence is not to be treated as creating a proprietary interest in land so as to bind third parties who acquire the land with notice of it on this account alone.

(v) Proof that the purchase price has been reduced on the footing that the purchaser would give effect to the prior encumbrance/contractual licence may provide some evidence that the purchaser has undertaken a new obligation so as to create a constructive trust. It should be noted, however, that because certainty is of 'prime importance' in relation to title to land, it is 'not desirable' that a constructive trust should be imposed on inferences from 'slender materials'.

The five principles set out above apply rigour to the finding of a constructive trust to give effect to a contractual licence against a third party. It is clear that the courts are no longer prepared to use the process in order to avoid accepted principles applying to proprietary interests in land.

Estoppel licences

Nature

An estoppel licence to occupy land may arise where a person is able to show that they have an interest in land or a right to use land that emanates from a promise or an assurance that has been made to that person which he or she has relied upon. The principles associated with so-called proprietary estoppel will be considered shortly but it is useful to mention the three elements required to raise the 'equity' based on unconscionability in this context.

(i) Assurance – the owner of the land must have given an assurance to the person claiming the 'equity' that that person will be entitled to some interest or right in relation to the land.

(ii) Reliance – the claimant can only establish their equity by demonstrating that they relied on the assurance made to them by the owner.

(iii) Detriment – the equity will only arise in favour of a claimant who has acted to their detriment in reliance on the assurance. Unconscionability is derived from this element of detrimental reliance so as to prevent the landowner from relying on their strict legal rights. In *Grant* v *Edwards* [1986] Ch 638 it was stated that a detriment may arise where a claimant has merely changed their position in reliance on the assurance made to the claimant.

Where a claimant has established an equity, this does not, per se, provide an indication of the type of interest that may derive from the equity. The court has a wide discretion to apply an appropriate remedy that 'satisfies' the equity. This may range from an award of damages to transferring the freehold to the claimant, as in *Pascoe* v *Turner* [1979] 1 WLR 431, or giving the claimant a lease in the property, as in *Griffiths* v *Williams* (1977) 248 EG 947. On the other hand, a court may simply award the claimant a licence to remain on the land in question. Thus in *Greasely* v *Cooke* [1980] 1 WLR 1306, a former maid continued to live in a house as the cohabitee of the owner's son and looked after the members of his family. She could have left and got a job elsewhere but was encouraged to stay on the promise that she was to regard the house as her home for the rest of her life. The court held that she was entitled to remain there for as long as she wished.

Similarly in *Re Sharpe (A Bankrupt)* [1980] 1 WLR 219 it was held that, where a nephew borrowed money from his aunt on the strength of a promise that the aunt could live with the nephew and his wife for life, this gave rise to an irrevocable licence to occupy the home until the loan was repaid.

It should be noted that the revocability/irrevocability of an estoppel licence is dependent on the terms of the licence imposed by the court.

Estoppel licences and third parties

The problem as to whether a successor in title to the licensor is bound by the interest depends on whether the interest arises at the time of the events giving rise to the estoppel or when the court actually provides a remedy to 'satisfy' the equity. Whilst it seems to be the case that the interest arises before the court makes an award, this poses little in the way of a problem as regards the parties themselves. Whether or not the incipient interest binds a successor in title is more elusive. In truth, different considerations apply in cases relating to an incipient, inchoate interest than those applying to estoppel licences awarded by a court.

As regards the binding nature of incipient interests, the Land Registration Act 2002 s.116 provides 'for the avoidance of doubt that in relation to registered land an equity by estoppel . . . has effect from the time the equity arises as an interest capable of binding successors in title'. An equity by estoppel will gain priority over a subsequent registered disposition for valuable consideration if it is protected by a notice under the Land Registration Act 2002 s.32 or if it falls within Schedule 3 para 2 as an interest that is overriding by virtue of the actual occupation of the owner of the interest: Land Registration Act 2002 s.29(1) and s.29(2).

With regard to the binding nature of incipient interests in unregistered land, we have seen in Chapter 3 that an equity arising by proprietary estoppel gives rise to an equitable interest that is determined by the doctrine of notice and that such an interest is incapable of being registered as a land charge under the Land Charges Act 1972: *E R Ives Investments Ltd v High* [1967] 2 QB 379.

Whether or not an estoppel licence awarded by a court is capable of binding a successor in title to the licensor has in the past been subject to some debate. In *Re Sharpe (A Bankrupt)* [1980] 1 WLR 219 the estoppel licence granted to the aunt bound the nephew's trustee in bankruptcy. In *Ashburn Anstalt v Arnold* [1989] Ch 1 the Court of Appeal held that, in the absence of a constructive trust, an estoppel licence was not capable of binding a successor in title. Technically, however, if a constructive trust does exist so that the court makes an award that amounts to an interest that is capable of protection, such as a lease, then the normal rules of priority within the Land Registration Act 2002 and the unregistered land regime should apply.

Proprietary estoppel

Introduction

Proprietary estoppel provides a means by which interests in land may be acquired informally alongside the operation of constructive trusts. We have seen previously that land law tends to be hidebound by formality, requiring either a deed or writing to formalise a particular arrangement. Proprietary estoppel, though, provides a means of modifying – or, indeed, counteracting – the effect of some of these formalities. Thus, as we noted in Chapter 4 in *Yaxley v Gotts* [2000] Ch 162 Robert Walker LJ stated at 174, in relation to the Law of Property (Miscellaneous Provisions) Act, that he had:

> . . . no hesitation in agreeing . . . that the doctrine of proprietary estoppel may operate to modify (and sometimes perhaps even counteract) the effect of s.2 of the Act 1989. The circumstances in which s.2 has to be complied with are so various and the scope of the doctrine of estoppel is so flexible, that any general assertion of s.2 as a 'no go area' for estoppel would be unsustainable.

The flexibility of the doctrine however also conjures up certain dangers if land law is not to descend into the 'ungodly jumble' described by Cromwell. Thus, as declared by Walker LJ in *Cobbe v Yeoman's Row Management Ltd* [2008] 1 WLR 1752 at para 46, proprietary estoppel

> . . . is not a sort of joker or wild card to be used whenever the court disapproves of the conduct of a litigant who seems to have the law on his side . . .

It is therefore vital that the operation of a proprietary estoppel is confined within certain principles. Nevertheless, the doctrine does have a part to play in modern land law since the strict formalities required in modern land law, particularly since the passing of the Land Registration Act 2002, invariably throw up situations where the strict application of the law may create unfair consequences that need to be mitigated. As Lord Denning stated in *Crabb v Arun District Council* [1976] 1 Ch 179 at 187:

> Equity comes in . . . to mitigate the rigours of strict law . . . It will prevent a person from insisting on his strict legal rights . . . when it would be inequitable for him to do so having regard to the dealings which have taken place between the parties.

The role of the doctrine therefore is an important one and recognised within the statutory formalities that now delineate modern land law. Evidence of this can be seen in the Land Registration Act 2002 s.116, which we referred to above. The Law of Property (Miscellaneous Provisions) Act 1989 s.2(5), whilst expressly preserving the operation of constructive trusts, made no reference to proprietary estoppel; nevertheless, in cases such as *Yaxley* v *Gotts* and *Cobbe* v *Yeoman's Row Management Ltd,* the courts considered that proprietary estoppel may provide an exception so long as 'the ingredients for a proprietary estoppel are present'.

Proprietary estoppel arises where a property owner makes a representation to another that they will have or do have some right on the owner's land. Thus, if the representee acts on the promise of the landowner, the representor, to their detriment so that it would be unconscionable, unfair or inequitable for the representor to break their promise and seek to enforce their strict legal rights then they will be stopped from asserting their strict legal rights.

From this it is important to distinguish between proprietary estoppel and the operation of constructive trusts. As we have seen above, proprietary estoppel is framed within representations made by one person to another, whilst constructive trusts rely upon the common intentions of the parties. The lines between the two often become blurred and in any event it is possible for a constructive trust to arise independently of a claim based on proprietary estoppel. We will look at the distinctions between the two later.

The elements required for the operation of proprietary estoppel

Proprietary estoppel has existed in English law for many years but in *Willmott* v *Barber* (1880) 15 ChD 96 Fry LJ set out the criteria needed to establish proprietary estoppel, often referred to as the 'five probanda'. These were:

(i)   The claimant must have made a mistake about his or her legal rights over land belonging to another.

(ii) The claimant must have spent money or carried out some action on the faith of that mistaken belief.

(iii) The defendant must know of the claimant's mistaken belief.

(iv) The defendant must know of the existence of his or her own legal rights and that these are inconsistent with the right claimed by the claimant.

(v)   The defendant must have encouraged the claimant to incur expenditure, either directly or indirectly, or by abstaining from enforcing his or her strict legal rights.

The five probanda imposed highly onerous conditions – not least of which is that the criteria only applied where a claimant acted in the belief that they had an existing right in the defendant's land. In many respects it is not that surprising that the criteria were strict since, after all, the claimant is attempting to assume an interest over the owner's land that would bind not only the owner but their successor in title.

Over the years, however, there was an almost inevitable tightening of the formalities required to create and acquire interests in land so that proprietary estoppel took on a more important role as the scope for a finding of unconscionable behaviour by a defendant became greater. The five probanda became increasingly unable to cope with these changes so that a more flexible and simpler approach became necessary. The modern criteria emerged from the case of *Taylor Fashions Ltd* v *Liverpool Victoria Trustees Co. Ltd* [1982] QB 133 where Oliver J stated at 151:

> . . . more recent cases indicate . . . that proprietary estoppel . . . requires a very much broader approach which is directed rather at ascertaining whether, in particular individual

circumstances, it would be unconscionable for a party to be permitted to deny that which, knowingly or unknowingly, he has allowed or encouraged another to assume to his detriment than to inquiring whether the circumstances can be fitted within the confines of some pre-conceived formula serving as a universal yardstick for every form of unconscionable behaviour.

Following from the re-instatement in Taylor Fashions Ltd three principles have to be established by the claimant to establish a proprietary estoppel equity:

(i)   The claimant must show that the landowner provided an *assurance which gave rise to an expectation* in the claimant that he or she was entitled to an interest in land.

(ii) The claimant must have placed *reliance* on the assurance of the landowner.

(iii) The claimant must have acted to his or her *detriment* as a consequence of the assurance so that it would be *unconscionable* to deny the claimant a remedy.

The three criteria for the establishment of an estoppel equity should not be seen as individual watertight components and they need to be considered 'in the round', thus in **Gillett v Holt** [2000] 2 All ER 289 Walker LJ stated:

> . . . it is important to note at the outset that the doctrine of proprietary estoppel cannot be treated as subdivided into three or four watertight compartments. In the course of oral argument in this court it repeatedly became apparent that because the quality of the relevant assurances may influence the issue of reliance, that reliance and detriment are often inter-twined, and that whether there is a distinct need for a 'mutual understanding' may depend on how the other elements are formulated and understood. Moreover, the fundamental principle that equity is concerned to prevent unconscionable conduct permeates all the elements of the doctrine. In the end the court must look at the matter in the round.

Further, in **Thorner v Major** [2009] UKHL 18 the House of Lords stated that, as well as looking at the case contextually, the proper approach is to examine the criteria holistically in deciding whether the landowner may retract his or her assurance to the claimant. Before examining each of the criteria in turn, it is as well to bear in mind in adopting this approach that the fact of unconscionable behaviour stands in the centre of the doctrine and that this must result from the consideration of the other criteria so as to excuse any formal requirements.

Assurances giving rise to an expectation

It is clear that in order to establish an estoppel equity the landowner must have made an assurance (or representation) to the claimant to the effect that the landowner will either give the claimant some present or future right or use over the land, or, refrain from seeking to enforce their strict legal rights.

One case that provides an illustration of an assurance giving rise to an expectation is that of **Crabbe v Arun District Council** [1976] Ch 179.

Crabbe v Arun District Council [1976] Ch 179

The plaintiff owned a plot of land that had access on to a road owned by the council. He wanted to sell part of his land and this part enjoyed the rights of access; however, he required another right of access on to the road for the land he was to retain. The council informally agreed to give him the right of access he needed. The plaintiff then proceeded to sell his land but did not reserve a right of way across it, relying on the informal agreement of the council to allow him the secondary right of access. In fact, the council did not grant him the right of access, so his retained land became landlocked.

Lord Scarman in the Court of Appeal referred to Lord Kingsdown's speech in *Ramsden v Dyson* (1866) LR 1 HL 129:

> The rule of law applicable to the case appears to be this: If a man, under a verbal agreement with a landlord for a certain interest in land, or, what amounts to the same thing, under an expectation, created or encouraged by the landlord that he shall have a certain interest, takes possession of such land, with the consent of the landlord, and upon the faith of such promise or expectation, with the knowledge of the landlord, and without objection by him, lays out money upon the land, a court of equity will compel the landlord to give effect to such promise or expectation.

The Court of Appeal therefore found that the council had led the plaintiff to believe that he would be granted the necessary access and had encouraged him, by not warning him that the decision to allow the right of access lay with the council rather than the council officers, so that the plaintiff acted to his detriment in selling his land without reserving a right of way over it. There thus arose an equity which was filled by the court requiring the council to provide the necessary access to the plaintiff's land.

Cases involving an assurance giving rise to an expectation have also arisen where a representor makes representations as to what will happen to their property on their death. Of course, these types of discussions or conversations are quite common in families. The representation may amount to a conversation as to the share a person will receive on the death of the representor, or it may be an assurance to a child or a mistress that they can continue to live in the property. On the death of the representor it might be the case that they do something very different. In such circumstances, in the absence of a common intention setting up a constructive trust, proprietary estoppel provides a means of holding the estate of the representor to their promise.

Gillett v Holt [2001] Ch 210

The plaintiff (Gillett) worked for the defendant (Holt) for 40 years as his farm manager and later as his business partner. Over the years, Holt made several assurances that Gillett would be the principal beneficiary under his will and indeed made a number of wills in which these assurances were reflected. In 1992, however, Holt formed a friendship with another person and the relationship between himself and Gillett deteriorated. Gillett was then dismissed in 1995 and Holt altered his will, making no provision for Gillett. Gillett brought an action in proprietary estoppel and succeeded.

The Court of Appeal held that the repeated assurances over a long period of time entitled Gillett to inherit the property. The court stated that the inherent revocability of testamentary dispositions is irrelevant to a promise or assurance as to a representor's statement of intentions. Walker LJ stated at 228:

> In the generality of cases that is no doubt correct, and it is notorious that some elderly persons of means derive enjoyment from the possession of testamentary power, and from dropping hints as to their intentions, without any question of an estoppel arising. But in this case Mr Holt's assurances were repeated over a long period, usually before the assembled company on family occasions, and some of them were . . . completely unambiguous.

In this case, therefore, there was more than just a single statement but repeated assurances over a long period of time that clearly indicated that Holt intended to carry out his assurance. The court considered that it was necessary to examine the context and surrounding circumstances in order to ascertain the assurance of future expectation made by the landowner.

Thorner v Major [2009] 1 WLR 776

David Thorner ('David') worked without payment for 30 years on a farm owned by his cousin Peter Thorner ('Peter'). Peter had no children but, being a somewhat unforthcoming individual, never discussed with David what would happen to the farm should he die, though David formed the impression from occasional remarks by Peter that he wanted David to inherit the farm. At one point, Peter did in fact make a will leaving the farm to David, but later revoked it for a reason not connected with David and failed to make a new will. Peter subsequently died intestate and his personal representatives intended to deal with the farm in accordance with the rules relating to intestacy. David claimed that he had the right to take ownership of the farm, basing his claim on proprietary estoppel. He claimed that he had relied on the assurances of Peter that he would inherit and that he had not pursued other opportunities of employment and thereby had acted to his detriment.

At first instance, the judge held that all the criteria required for the establishment of an estoppel equity had been established and ordered that David should take the farm. In the Court of Appeal, however, it was held that the assurances provided by Peter lacked clarity and that there was nothing to suggest that Peter intended that David should rely on the assurances that he had tentatively provided.

In the House of Lords, the decision of the Court of Appeal was reversed. In terms of discovering the clarity of the assurance given, the House of Lords found that it was clear and equivocal. The property David was to receive was certain and it was manifest that the assurances were intended to be taken seriously by David. The House of Lords considered that the relevant assurance to David was 'clear enough' and that what amounts to sufficient clarity is 'hugely dependent on context'. Further, what is 'clear enough' had to be considered in the context of what David understood the assurance to be, since he was the one who had dealt with Peter's unforthcoming character. Peter was providing him with an assurance that he would inherit the farm and David relied on this.

In arriving at a decision, a court must take an objective view as to whether a defendant had intended that the claimant should rely on their assurance. The Court of Appeal in *Thorner* had adopted a subjective approach: had Peter intended that David would rely on his assurance about the farm so as to influence him to forgo the other opportunities available to him? The House of Lords stated that an objective approach should be adopted: a man must be taken to intend what a reasonable person would understand him to intend. Thus Lord Hoffman stated at 779, para 5:

> In my opinion it did not matter whether Peter knew any of the specific alternatives which David might be contemplating. It was enough that the meaning he conveyed would reasonably have been understood as intended to be taken seriously as an assurance that can be relied upon.

Central to the establishment of a proprietary estoppel claim is that the representor has, by their words or actions, led the representee to believe that they will acquire rights in their, the representor's property. In *Cobbe v Yeoman's Row Management Ltd* [2008] 1 WLR 1752, the facts of which have already been set out in Chapter 4, there was no question of the claimant having an expectation that he would receive an interest in the company. His expectation was that in the future there would be some negotiations that would lead to a contract whereby such an interest might materialise. Lord Scott in that case made it clear that an expectation of a 'certain interest in land' was a central feature of the criteria set out in Taylor Fashions. The expectation in *Cobbe* was vague in that it was merely an expectation of further negotiations. In a commercial context the parties and businessmen entered into a relationship at arm's length and therefore should have been aware of the legal niceties required to render a legally binding relationship – a gentleman's agreement is not capable of giving rise to an estoppel.

In family and domestic relationships, the context of the assurance is entirely different. Lord Walker in *Thorner* stated that in such a domestic context the expectation does not necessarily need to be specific or precise, though the relevant assurance must be clear and equivocal before it can be relied upon to found an estoppel. This is dependent on the context, though, since in domestic cases it is rare to find the expectation defined in legal terms. Provided, however, that the assurance is 'clear enough' this will be sufficient to find the necessary assurance to set up an estoppel. Thus Lord Neuberger in *Thorner* stated at 801, para 84:

> as Lord Scott pointed out there must be some sort of an assurance which is clear and unequivocal before it can be relied upon to found an estoppel. However, that proposition must be read as subject to three qualifications. First, it does not detract from the normal principle . . . that the effect of words or actions must be assessed in their context.

As regards the need for the physical extent of the land to be defined, we have already seen in *Cobbe* that, whilst there was certainty as to the identity of the property, the nature of the interest was vague and imprecise. As Lord Neuberger pointed out in *Cobbe*:

> The parties had intentionally not entered into any legally binding arrangement . . . they had left matters on a speculative basis, each knowing full well that neither was legally bound – see para 27. There was not even an agreement to agree (which would have been unenforceable), but, . . . merely an expectation that there would be negotiation. And as he pointed out (para 18), an 'expectation dependent upon the successful negotiation is not an expectation of an interest having [sufficient] certainty'.

In *Thorner* it had been argued that the extent of the farm was not sufficiently certain and over the years various parts of the farm had been sold or bought. The House of Lords had little difficulty in dispensing with this argument. Their Lordships stated that there was no doubt as to what was the subject of the assurance, namely the farm as it existed from time to time, and that the interest to be recovered by David was clear in that it was the farm as it existed at the time of Peter's death. Thus the subject of the equity could be identified conceptually the moment the equity came into existence but its precise extent crystallised on Peter's death.

Summing up, it is important that commercial and domestic disputes involving proprietary estoppel do not have to be dealt with in the same way and that the finding of an estoppel equity is discovered by an holistic analysis of the facts. Whilst the strict approach adopted in *Cobbe* might have its place in a commercial context where the parties are businessmen capable of seeking legal representation, such an approach is unrealistic in a domestic situation where a 'clear enough' approach is sufficient to find for an assurance. Context therefore is everything, so if the assurance is clear enough in context and relates to property that is identifiable at the time, the equity crystallises.

Reliance

The assurance of an expectation must give way to the representee claimant relying on the assurance in such a way that they have acted differently on the strength of the reliance. It was held in *Thorner* that, if it is reasonable for a claimant to rely on the assurance made to them, then it is not open for the defendant to claim that they did not intend the assurances to be relied upon.

In *Taylor Fashions* it was clear that it is reasonable for the claimant to have relied on the assurance provided; however; in *Greasely* v *Cook* [1980] 1 WLR 1306 it was stated that reliance may be inferred, with the effect that the burden of proof is reversed, requiring the defendant to prove that the claimant had, in fact, not relied on the defendant's assurance.

Reliance and detriment are intertwined and indeed reliance provides the causal link between the assurance and the detriment suffered by the claimant in changing his or her position. To that extent there is considerable overlap between reliance and detriment. Thus in *Amalgamated Investment and Property Co. Ltd* v *Texas Commerce International Bank Ltd* [1982] QB 84 Lord Goff stated at 104:

> . . . the question is not whether the representee acted, or desisted from acting, solely on reliance on the encouragement or representation of the other party: the question is rather whether his conduct was so influenced by the encouragement or representation . . . that it would be unconscionable to enforce his strict legal rights.

The change in position may be demonstrated by the expenditure of money or undertaking improvements to property.

Inwards v Baker [1965] 1 All ER 446

Baker's son wished to build himself a house and Baker suggested that he build the house on his land as this would enable the son to build a larger house. In reliance on his father's suggestion, the son then spent a considerable amount of money building the house and afterwards continued to live there in the belief that he would be able to remain there for the rest of his life. When his father later died, it transpired that the father had left the property to other people, one of whom, Inwards, then started proceedings to recover the property. The son argued that Inwards was stopped from seeking possession.

The Court of Appeal held that the son had a licence that enabled him to remain in the property for so long as he wished. Clearly, the son had altered his position to his detriment based on his reliance on the assurance of an expectation from his father.

Where, however, a claimant incurs a detriment irrespective of the defendant's conduct then no reliance will arise. Thus in *Stillwell* v *Simpson* (1983) 133 NLJ 894 the claimant carried out repairs on the house of which he was a tenant. He could not establish reliance since his actions were not based on the promise by his landlady that he could have the property on her death, but on the fact that he knew she could not afford to do the repairs herself and that the repairs were for his own benefit anyway.

The issue of mixed motives in terms of detrimental reliance can throw up some questions regarding the issue of reliance. For instance, there can be many reasons why a person acts in the way he or she does and not all of these reasons are necessarily founded on the assurance that has been made to the claimant. A case which dealt with such an issue is that of *Campbell* v *Griffin* [2001] EWCA Civ 990.

Campbell v Griffin [2001] EWCA Civ 990

Campbell answered an advertisement offering lodging and, as a result, lived with an elderly couple, Mr and Mrs Ascough, for a number of years, paying rent to them. Over the years, he became like a son to them, acting as an unpaid carer as the couple became more frail. Over those years, the couple made a variety of assurances to him that he would have a home for life. Mr Ascough changed his will to give effect to his assurance but Mrs Ascough was unable to do this because of her senility. Mr Ascough then died and his wife took the property by right of survivorship. When Mrs Ascough died, the property passed to the beneficiaries under her will, who sought possession of the property. Mr Campbell raised the proprietary estoppel in a response to the claim of the beneficiaries under the will.

At the hearing, the claimant stated that he would have helped Mr and Mrs Ascough regardless of any assurances they had given to him as regards the property. They had treated him as a son and he felt affectionately and compassionately towards them.

At first instance, the judge considered that he had not acted in reliance on the assurance given to him – that is, his actions were not motivated by the assurances, and therefore declined his claim to proprietary estoppel.

The Court of Appeal considered that the fact that a claimant had several reasons for acting to his detriment did not prevent an estoppel from arising. On the other hand, no reliance will arise where a claimant has incurred a detriment independently of the assurances provided by the defendant. Thus if a claimant spends money or incurs expenses irrespective of an assurance, this would not be sufficient to set up a reliance within the requirements of *Taylor Fashions Ltd*; *Orgee* v *Orgee* [1997] EGCS 152.

Detriment

It has been seen already that reliance can be inferred from conduct: *Greasely* v *Cook* [1980] 1 WLR 1306; however, it is essential that the claimant demonstrates that a detriment has actually arisen in reliance on an assurance of an expectation. The detriment may amount to the incurrence of expenditure, but could equally be improvements to property or advancing money to a landowner in return for an assurance. It should be noted that the detriment does not have to be property- or money-based. The provision of care is sufficient as seen in *Campbell* v *Griffin* above and also in *Re Basham* [1986] 1 WLR 1498.

Clearly, the categories of detrimental reliance are not closed so that in addition to care, the detriment may take the form of services based in the family home: *Greasely* v *Cook* [1980] 1 WLR 1306; working the farm: *Gillett* v *Holt* [2001] Ch 210; *Thorner* v *Major* [2009] 1 WLR 776; or giving up work and a home in order to live with the representor: *Jones* v *Jones* [1977] 1 WLR 438.

It should be noted that the detriment must be incurred by the claimant to whom the assurance of the expectation is made. Thus in *Lloyd* v *Dugdale* the claimant could not claim proprietary estoppel in order to remain in possession of some property since the detriment that arose had been undertaken by his company, not himself. The court rejected the argument that a derivative detriment was possible.

Unconscionability

Unconscionability is key to the criteria set out by Oliver J in *Taylor Fashions Ltd* so the requirements for proprietary estoppel are only established if the claimant is left inequitably disadvantaged by their reliance on an assurance of an expectation made by the defendant. Ultimately, therefore, it is a finding of unfairness from a total analysis of the facts in the context of the three criteria previously examined that allows a departure from the normal principles of property law, whether based on common law or in statute. Thus in *Cobbe* v *Yeoman's Row Management Ltd* [2008] 1 WLR 1752 Lord Walker stated that even if the other elements of estoppel 'appear to be present but the result does not shock the conscience of the court, the analysis needs to be looked at again'.

Satisfying the estoppel equity

Once a claimant has demonstrated the requirements of assurance, reliance, detriment and the ensuing unconscionability then they are said to have generated an estoppel equity that provides the right to prevent the defendant from insisting on their strict legal rights to defeat the estoppel equity. At this point, the court has to decide how the equity is to be satisfied – that is, determine what interest should be awarded to the claimant in order to satisfy the incipient or inchoate equity that they now possess. The courts have a wider discretion here, ranging from interests in land to occupational licences, to straightforward monetary compensation. The base line, however, for deciding these matters was set out by Lord Scarman in *Crabb v Arun District Council* [1976] Ch 179 in which he stated that the duty of the court was to provide the 'minimum equity to do justice to the plaintiff'.

In some cases, the courts have ordered that the landowner transfer to the claimant the legal fee simple estate such as in *Dillwyn v Llewelyn* (1862) 4 De GF & J 517 and *Pascoe v Turner* [1979] 1 WLR 431 where this estate was transferred to the landowner's mistress.

Dillwyn v Llewelyn (1862) 4 De GF & J 517

A father, the defendant, signed a memorandum that he would give part of his land to his son, the plaintiff, to enable the son to build a house on it. The son built the house at a cost of £14,000. The father then died without having made any alteration to his will to take into account the memorandum. The son then sought an order requiring the fee simple to be conveyed to him.

The court held that, whilst the equitable principle held that a voluntary agreement will not be completed or assisted by a court of equity, it considered the ownership of the house and the ownership of the estate should be regarded as co-extensive and co-equal. The court ordered the conveyance of the land to the son on the basis that the son, relying on his father's memorandum, had expended money building the house.

Pascoe v Turner [1979] 1 WLR 431

The plaintiff and the defendant lived together in a house that had been purchased by the plaintiff. After nine years, the relationship ended and the plaintiff moved out of the house. On several occasions, the plaintiff told the defendant that the house and the contents were hers but made no attempt to convey the property to her. On the basis of the representations made to her, the defendant spent money redecorating the house, improving it and carrying out repairs. She also bought furniture and furnishings for the house. The plaintiff then attempted to state that the defendant only had an occupational licence and sought possession of the property.

It was held that the circumstances gave rise to an estoppel equity. Cumming-Bruce LJ stated at 436:

> For this is a case of estoppel arising from the encouragement and acquiescence of the plaintiff . . . when in reliance upon his declaration that he was giving and, later that he had given the house to her, she spent a substantial part of her small capital upon repairs and improvements to the house.

The court then considered how her equity was to be satisfied. The court stated that it had to consider all the circumstances and decide how equity would do justice to her, having regard to the way in which she changed her position for the worse by reason of the encouragement of the plaintiff. The court could satisfy the equity either by way of a licence to occupy the house for her lifetime or by transferring the legal fee simple to her. The court considered that the conduct of the plaintiff drew the inference that he would be determined to pursue his purpose of evicting her with any legal means at his disposal 'with ruthless disregard of the obligations binding upon [his] conscience'. If the court granted her licence, she had no interest that could be registered as a land charge and she could find herself ousted by a purchaser for value without notice. Weighing up these considerations and the need to provide the defendant with security of tenure, quiet enjoyment and freedom of action in respect of repairs and improvements without interference from the plaintiff, it was appropriate to order the plaintiff to transfer to the defendant the fee simple.

In other cases, the court has ordered that the claimant be given a lease as in *Yaxley v Gotts* [2000] Ch 162 where the claimant obtained a 99-year lease of the ground floor of a house which had been orally agreed with the defendant owner. Clearly, a court must take into account all the circumstances of the case in assessing how the equity might be satisfied. The discussions in *Pascoe v Turner* [1979] 1 WLR 431 give some direction as to the considerations in that particular case, but it is not always appropriate to award a claimant a full legal estate in the land. For instance, in *Campbell v Griffin* [2001] EWCA Civ 990 Campbell entered the property originally as a lodger and it would not be appropriate to transfer a life interest in the property to him so instead the court awarded him £35,000. In making such an award, the court considered it avoided the complications that might ensue in the award of a life interest under a trust and the difficulties that may follow vis à vis such matters as maintenance of the property.

Between the two positions of transferring a legal estate to the claimant and awarding compensation the courts have to strike a balance between basing an outcome on the loss arising from the reliance on the assurance by the claimant and satisfying the expectations of the claimant from the assurances given to them. Compensation by means of fulfilling the 'loss' arising from the reliance is clearly evidenced in *Campbell v Griffin*. The award here would not have been enough to enable the claimant to purchase another house, but it would have gone a long way towards allowing him to do so. In *Pascoe v Turner* there was a clear expectation that the defendant was to own the house but here the court took a realistic view of what was likely to occur in the future, given the character of the plaintiff. The overall aim, however, is not to make an award that provides a greater remedy than the expectation. Thus in *Gillett v Holt* [2001] Ch 210 it was stated by Walker LJ at 237 that the court has to make an assessment of:

> ... the maximum extent of the equity. The court's aim is, having indentified the maximum, to form a view as to what is the minimum required to satisfy it and do justice between the parties. The court must look at all the circumstances, including the need to achieve a 'clean break' so far as possible and avoid or minimise future friction.

In *Gillett v Holt*, Gillett was awarded £100,000 together with the freehold of one of the farms in compensation for his loss of being excluded from the farming business. The court acknowledged, though, the unusual difficulties in arriving at a way of satisfying his equity. Clearly, his expectations could not be fully realised, not least because Holt was still alive. The business was arranged over several farms, some of which were owned by a separate company, and the process of unpicking the business structure would have created intractable problems. In arriving at a remedy, the court was therefore driven to achieve a 'clean break' result.

In some cases, however, a court may not grant relief at all, despite the considerations of reliance and expectation. Central to the doctrine of proprietary estoppel is the requirement to do what is necessary to avoid an unconscionable result and therefore to produce a remedy that is disproportionate is clearly inappropriate. In *Sledmore v Dalby* [1996] 72 P & CR 196 Hobhouse LJ, after referring to an Australian authority, *Commonwealth of Australia v Vermayen* (1990) 170 CLR 394, observed the need to recognise proportionality between remedy and detriment and stated:

> ... the end result must be a just one having regard to the assumption made by the party asserting the estoppel and the detriment which he has experienced.

In *Sledmore* v *Dalby* (1996) 72 P & CR 196 Mr and Mrs Sledmore jointly purchased a house in 1962. In 1965 their daughter married Mr Dalby and they both moved into the house as tenants and paid rent until Mr Dalby became unemployed in 1976, though they continued to pay the outgoings. Mr Dalby made substantial improvements to the property between 1976 and 1979 and was encouraged to do so by his father-in-law, Mr Sledmore, who had also formed an intention to give the couple the house. In 1979 Mr Sledmore conveyed his freehold interest in the house to his wife, who then changed her will so that only their daughter would inherit the property. In 1980 Mr Sledmore died, followed by his daughter in 1983. Mr Dalby continued to live in the house, but refused to pay rent.

In 1990 Mrs Sledmore brought an action for possession against Mr Dalby, who by this time was employed, though he did not live in the house full-time. The house was occupied by one of Mr Dalby's daughters, who was 27 and in full-time employment. By this time, Mrs Sledmore's finances were in a poor state and she was on income support and in arrears with her mortgage.

The Court of Appeal, despite recognising that Mr Dalby had an estoppel equity, granted Mrs Sledmore possession of the property. The court took into account the circumstances of the parties and considered that Mrs Sledmore had more pressing needs, whilst Mr Dalby was in full employment and, in any event, did not live in the house most of the time. Whilst it was true his daughter lived in the house, the court considered that, since she was 27, in full-time employment and independent, she could maintain herself. The court considered that Mr Dalby had lived in the house rent-free for 18 years but the insurance had been paid for by Mr and Mrs Sledmore, who had also paid for the house to be re-roofed. The court considered that Mr Dalby was capable of paying for his own accommodation. Balanced against these facts, Mrs Sledmore was in a vulnerable position, likely to lose her own accommodation and had a pressing need for the house that in fact belonged to her. The court considered that the minimum equity to do justice to Mr Dalby was an equity which had expired.

The approach of the courts in searching for a remedy to satisfy an estoppel equity is not founded on one correct formula. The matter is entirely discretionary, balanced against the particular circumstances of the case. This wide approach was adopted in *Jennings* v *Rice* (2003) 1 P & CR 8 where the Court of Appeal made an award of £200,000 to Jennings, who, having worked for an elderly widow for many years, acted to his detriment by becoming her carer in reliance on her assurance that she would 'see to it' that he would benefit from her will when she died. In the event, when she did die, she left no will, but an estate that was worth £1.28 million.

At first instance, it was accepted that an estoppel equity arose based on the fact of Jennings acting to his detriment in reliance on her assurances and the finding it was unconscionable for her to renege on those assurances. Jennings' claim to be entitled to the whole of the estate was rejected since he clearly did not know the full extent of her estate and could not have expected such an amount. Equally, his claim to what was a sizeable house and the contents was also rejected as it was clear it was not suitable for a single person and anyway the value of £435,000 was considered excessive. The trial judge considered that the proper amount to be awarded was the estimated cost of the nursing care (i.e. £200,000) which would have enabled Jennings to purchase an appropriate house for his needs. Jennings then appealed to the Court of Appeal for a greater amount but this was rejected.

The Court of Appeal emphasised the principle that the amount to be awarded was the 'minimum equity required to do justice'. The court reviewed various means by which this could be achieved once this basic principle had been established, and re-stated that the aim was either to fulfil the claimant's expectations or to compensate him for his detrimental reliance. It was stated that the court must take a principled approach and could not exercise an unfettered discretion based on an individual judge's idea of what is fair. It was for the court to 'satisfy the equity', not to satisfy the claimant's expectations. Thus Walker LJ stated:

> The equity does not arise from the claimant's expectations alone, but from a combination of expectations, detrimental reliance and the unconscionabless of allowing the benefactor to go back on assurances . . .

A court therefore has a wide judgmental discretion and as Walker LJ continued:

> It would be unwise to attempt any comprehensive enumeration of the factors relevant to the exercise of the court's discretion, or to suggest any hierarchy of factors . . . To these can safely be added the court's recognition that it cannot compel people who have fallen out to live peaceably together, so that there may be a need for a clean break; alterations in the benefactor's assets and circumstances, especially where the benefactor's assurances have been given, and the claimant's detriment has been suffered, over a long period of years; the likely effect of taxation; and (to a limited degree) the other claims (legal or moral) on the benefactor or his or her estate. No doubt there are many other factors which it may be right for the court to take into account in particular factual situations.

Whilst Lord Scarman's base line in *Crabbe* is the starting point, the discretion exercised by the court along the lines stated above is nevertheless challenged where the expectation is vague. In these circumstances, Walker LJ considered that the satisfaction of the equity may well be more limited and here a court has to take a proportionate view of any assessment. Thus a court may simply award a mere right of occupancy and no more, as in *Greasely* v *Cook* [1980] 1 WLR 1306 and similarly in *Inwards* v *Baker* [1965] 2 QB 29.

The nature of proprietary estoppel and third parties

The establishment of proprietary estoppel provides the claimant with an entitlement to relief in equity, but the question arises as to whether the estoppel equity generated is a personal interest or a proprietary interest in the land. If the equity is satisfied by a court granting an estate an interest in land, such as a fee simple or a lease, then issues of priority are determined by the normal processes for protecting that interest. As we have seen, however, there is more of a problem if the court merely awards an occupational licence. Such a licence does not generate a proprietary interest, even if that is irrevocable, and as such is capable of being destroyed by the defendant representor selling the property to a purchaser for value who has no notice of the occupational licence. It was this problem that was in the mind of the court in *Pascoe* v *Turner* [1979] 1 WLR 431. Of course, if the equity is satisfied by the payment of compensation, there is no question of priorities other than that the land would be charged with the award that has been made.

Prior to the Land Registration Act 2002, there were mixed opinions and much debate as to whether an estoppel equity did or did not form the basis of a proprietary interest in land. Certainly, the view was that an inchoate/incipient estoppel equity was historically not recognised as a proprietary interest in land. However, in *E R Investments Ltd* v *High* [1967] QB 379 and in *Re Sharpe (A Bankrupt)* [1980] 1 WLR 219 an estoppel equity (a licence) was capable of existing as an equitable interest in land and thus capable of binding a third party, subject to the doctrine of notice, since in unregistered land there was no question of the equity being registrable as a land charge within the Land Charges Act 1972. In registered land, however, it was considered in *Lloyd* v *Dugdale* [2002] P & CR 13 that an estoppel equity was capable of taking effect as an overriding interest under the Land Registration Act 1925 s.70(1)g as a right of a person in actual occupation.

Whatever the debates about the standing of estoppel equities in the past, the passing of the Land Registration Act 2002 has put any debate to bed in that s.116 has now declared 'for the avoidance of doubt that an equity by estoppel and a mere equity has effect from the time the equity arises as an interest capable of binding successors in title'. Thus an estoppel equity will bind a purchaser for valuable consideration if it is protected by a notice under the Land Registration Act 2002 s.32 or if it falls within Schedule 3 para 2 as an interest that is overriding by virtue of the actual occupation of the owner of the interest.

Constructive trusts and proprietary estoppel

In examining proprietary estoppel it has no doubt come to mind that there are striking similarities between proprietary estoppel and constructive trusts. In proprietary estoppel there is a requirement for a detrimental reliance based upon the assurance of an expectation from the representor so that it is unconscionable for the representor to renege or retract his or her promise. So, too, in constructive trusts there is a requirement for a detrimental reliance – though here it is based upon a common intention of an assurance as regards the ownership of the property. The two concepts achieve the same thing in that they provide an informal means by which a person may acquire from the landowner an interest in land.

The commonality between the two concepts has, from time to time, raised the spectre of whether they should be assimilated. It will be remembered that we started our examination of proprietary estoppel by referring to Walker LJ in **Yaxley v Gotts** [2000] Ch 162, where he considered that the exception to the requirement of writing in the Law of Property (Miscellaneous Provision) Act 1989 s.2(5) that refers to 'resulting, implied or constructive trusts' should be extended to proprietary estoppel and not to do so would be 'unsustainable'. Similar views were also expressed in **Cobbe v Yeoman's Row Management Ltd** [2008] 1 WLR 1752. In **Stokes v Anderson** [1991] 1 FLR 391 Nourse LJ stated:

> It is possible that the House of Lords will one day decide to solve the problem either by assimilating the principles of Gissing v Gissing and those of proprietary estoppel, or even by following the recent trend in other commonwealth jurisdictions towards more generalised principles of unconscionability and unjust enrichment.

There are, however, differences of principle between the two concepts. Constructive trusts arise from a common intention, whilst proprietary estoppel arises from a unilateral assurance provided by the representor, with the representee often taking a passive role. Constructive trusts provide a distinct share in the beneficial ownership of the property, whilst proprietary estoppel is discretionary and may produce anything from a full fee simple being transferred to the representee, through various shades of interest, down to compensation only, and sometimes nothing at all. In this sense, proprietary estoppel is more flexible. It is perhaps these differences that led Walker LJ to come the full circle and declare in **Stack v Dowden** [2007] AC 432 at para 37:

> I have to say that I am now rather less enthusiastic about the notion that proprietary estoppel and 'common interest' constructive trusts can or should be completely assimilated. Proprietary estoppel typically consists of asserting an equitable claim against the conscience of the 'true' owner. The claim is a 'mere equity'. It is to be satisfied by the minimum award necessary to do justice . . . which may sometimes lead to no more than a monetary award. A 'common intention' constructive trust, by contrast, is identifying the true beneficial owner or owners, and the size of their beneficial interests.

For now, at least, it seems the appetite for assimilation of proprietary estoppel and constructive trusts has gone away, enabling the judiciary to have more 'tools in the box' for dealing with informal arrangements as regards ownership of interests in land.

Summary

Licences

- A licence confers no interest in land; essentially it is a personal right given by a licensor to a licensee that prevents what would otherwise be regarded as a trespass.
- The concept of a licence covers a myriad of different situations, ranging from parking a car through to a long-term permit to occupy land.
- One vital distinction between a lease and a licence is that the former gives a tenant exclusive possession of the land, even as regards landlords. A licence confers no such right and a landowner is free to enter the land at will.
- There are no formal requirements for the creation of a lease, though sometimes they may be conferred in a deed, particularly if the licence is attached or incidental to creation of an estate or interest in land.
- The relationship between the licensor and the licensee is essentially a contractual one.

Types of licence

Bare licence

- Essentially, this is a mere permission to enter the land belonging to another. A bare licence may be express or implied: *Robson v Hallett* [1967] 2 QB 939.
- Bare licences are revocable at will, provided the licensee is given reasonable time to leave the premises. Afterwards, he or she becomes a trespasser.
- Bare licences are not binding on third parties and no interest in land arises from such a licence.

Licences coupled with an interest

- This is a licence that enables the owner of an interest, such as a profit à prendre, to exercise the rights attached to the interest.
- If the licence is revoked, this will give rise to an action by the owner of the interest since essentially the revocation is removing the interest as well.
- Third parties taking subject to the interest also take subject to the licence.

Contractual licences

- Essentially this is a permission to enter land by way of a contract and in this respect it is distinguishable from a bare licence.
- No formalities are required.
- Revocation of a licence may give rise to an action for breach of contract.
- It is possible for the contract to be enforced by specific performance, in which case the licence may become irrevocable: *Millennium Productions Ltd v Winter Gardens Theatre (London) Ltd* [1946] 1 All ER 678.

- Contractual licences (in the absence of the application of the Contracts (Rights of Third Parties) Act 1999) are incapable of binding a third party, though a licensor may remain liable to the licensee for breach of contract: *King v David Allen and Sons (Bill Posting) Ltd* [1916] 2 AC 54.

- In *Errington v Woods* [1952] 1 KB 290 it was considered that an irrevocable contractual licence was capable of binding third parties, *but* see now *Ashburn Anstalt v Arnold* [1989] Ch 1 where Errington was declared to be per incuriam.

- Note that third party purchasers can only be bound by a contractual licence if it is possible to attach a constructive trust to the conscience of the purchaser: *Lloyd v Dugdale* [2002] 2 P & CR 13.

Estoppel licences

- An estoppel licence to occupy land may arise where a person is able to show that they have an interest in land or a right to use land that emanates from a promise or assurance that has been made to that person which he or she has relied upon.

- Three elements are required to raise the estoppel equity: assurance, reliance and detriment.

- The question as to whether third parties are bound by an estoppel licence depends on the remedy provided by the court to satisfy the equity.

- The Land Registration Act 2002 s.116 now provides that an equity by estoppel has effect from the time the equity arises as an interest capable of binding successors in title.

Proprietary estoppel

Nature

- Proprietary estoppel arises where a proprietary owner makes a representation to another that they will have or currently have some right on the owner's land. If the representee acts on the promise to the landowner, the representor, to their detriment so that it would be unconscionable for the representor to break their promise and seek to enforce their strict legal rights then they will be stopped from breaking their promise.

- It is important to distinguish between proprietary estoppel, which is framed within representations made by one person to another, and constructive trusts, which rely on the common intentions of the parties.

Elements required for the operation of proprietary estoppel

- Originally, these were framed within the 'five probanda' set out in *Willmott v Barber* (1880) 15 ChD 96 but have now been restated in *Taylor Fashions Ltd v Liverpool Victoria Trustees Co. Ltd* [1982] QB 133 as:
  (i)   an *assurance* by the landowner giving rise to an expectation;
  (ii) the claimant must have *relied* on the assurance of the landowner; and
  (iii) the claimant must have acted to their *detriment* as a consequence of the assurance so that it is *unconscionable* to deny the claimant a remedy.

Satisfying the equity

- Once the above elements have been established, the court has to decide how the equity is to be satisfied.

- The base line for deciding how the equity is to be satisfied was set out in *Crabb v Arun District Council* [1976] Ch 179 as the 'minimum equity required to do justice to the plaintiff'.

- The court has a wide discretion to provide the minimum equity to do justice to the party:
  - Convey the full fee simple: *Dillwyn* v *Llewelyn* (1862) 4 De GF & J 517; *Pascoe* v *Turner* [1979] 1 WLR 431.
  - Convey a lease: *Griffiths* v *Williams* (1977) 248 EG 947.
  - Award compensation: *Gillett* v *Holt* [2001] Ch 210; *Jennings* v *Rice* (2003) 1 P & CR 8.
  - Award a right of occupancy: *Greasely* v *Cook* [1980] 1 WLR 1306; *Inwards* v *Baker* [1965] 2 QB 29.
- The basic principle in finding the 'maximum equity' is either to fulfil the claimant's expectations or to compensate him/her for their detrimental reliance but the result must be proportionate: *Jennings* v *Rice* (2003) 1 P & CR 8.

Proprietary estoppel and third parties

- If the equity is satisfied by a court granting an estate or interest in land then issues of priority are determined by the normal processes for protecting the particular interest.
- If the court decides to award an occupational licence, this is capable of being destroyed by a conveyance to a third party purchaser for value without notice of the licence; however, see now the Land Registration Act 2002 s.116.

Further reading

Licences

Battersby, 'Contractual and Estoppel Licences as Proprietary Interests in Land' [1991] 55 *The Conveyancer and Property Lawyer* 36

Battersby, 'Informal Transactions in Land, Estoppel and Registration' (1995) 58 *Modern Law Review* 637

Bridge, 'Tenancies at Will in the Court of Appeal [1991] *Cambridge Law Journal* 232

Bright, 'Leases, Exclusive Possession and Estates' (2000) 116 *Law Quarterly Review* 7

Dixon, 'The Non-Proprietary Lease: The Rise of the Feudal Phoenix' [2000] *Cambridge Law Journal* 25

Dixon, 'An Everyday Story of Country Folk: Proprietary Estoppel and Licences' (2004) 41 *Student Law Review* 52

Hill, 'The Termination of Bare Licences' [2001] *Cambridge Law Journal* 89

Kerbel, 'Unreasonable Revocation of a Licence' [1996] 60 *The Conveyancer and Property Lawyer* 63

Moriarty, 'Licences and Land Law: Legal Principles and Public Policies' (1984) 100 *Law Quarterly Review* 376

Routley, 'Tenancies and Estoppel – After Bruton v London and Quadrant HT' [2000] *Modern Law Review* 424

Street, 'Coach and Horses Trip Cancelled? Rent Act Avoidance after Street v Mountford' [1985] 49 *The Conveyancer and Property Lawyer* 328

Proprietary Estoppel

Cooke, 'Estoppel and the Protection of Expectations' (1997) 17 *Legal Studies* 258

Dixon, 'Proprietary Estoppel: A Return to Principle?' [2009] 73 *The Conveyancer and Property Lawyer* 260

Dixon, 'Defining and Confining Estoppel' (2010) 30 *Legal Studies*

Etherton, 'Constructive Trusts and Proprietary Estoppel: The Search for Clarity and Principle' [2009] 73 *The Conveyancer and Property Lawyer* 104

Gardner, 'The Remedial Discretion in Proprietary Estoppel' (1999) 115 *Law Quarterly Review* 438

Griffiths, 'Proprietary Estoppel – The Pendulum Swings Again?' [2009] 73 *The Conveyancer and Property Lawyer* 41

Milne, 'Proprietary Estoppel in a Procrustean Bed' (2011) MLR 412

Thompson, 'Estoppel: A Return to Principle' [2001] 65 *The Conveyancer and Property Lawyer* 13

Thompson, 'Estoppel, Reliance, Remedy and Priority' [2003] 67 *The Conveyancer and Property Lawyer* 157

Thompson, 'The Flexibility of Estoppel' [2003] 67 *The Conveyancer and Property Lawyer* 225

Thompson, 'Constructive Trusts, Estoppel and the Family Home' [2004] 68 *The Conveyancer and Property Lawyer* 496

Wells, 'The Element of Detriment in Proprietary Estoppel' [2001] *The Conveyancer and Property Lawyer* 65 13

9

Adverse possession

Aims and objectives

After reading this chapter you should be able to:

- Understand the nature of adverse possession.

- Know and understand how a claim to adverse possession is established.

- Understand how the limitation period arises in unregistered and registered land.

- Know how the limitation period is stopped from running.

- Understand the effects of adverse possession in unregistered land and under the Land Registration Act 1925.

- Understand how adverse possession arises under the Land Registration Act 2002.

- Explain the human rights dimension in adverse possession.

Introduction

The law relating to adverse possession, often referred to quite wrongly as 'squatter's rights', is based on the concept of the limitation of actions. The principle is that, where a cause of action arises, the litigation must be commenced within a certain time period and, if not, the claimant loses the right to pursue the legal claim. It seems astonishing therefore that, despite the requirements for establishing a title to land, particularly under the Land Registration Act 2002, a trespasser can acquire a better title to land than a legitimate owner to whom the title has been conveyed. The explanation for acquisition of land in this way lies in the fact that English land law is not founded on owners of land acquiring absolute titles to their property. As we have seen, the nearest one gets to absolute ownership is through the doctrine of estates, with the result that one's title is only relative to another competing claim. In other words, where there are two competing claims, a court is not seeking to discover who the 'owner' of the property is, but to decide who has a better claim vis à vis the other party. A court therefore is not concerned with attempting to discover some abstract right but to judge the strength of one claim against another and, once it has reached a decision, applying an appropriate remedy.

The arguments for allowing adverse possession are founded, at least partly, on the principle that land is a finite resource. Therefore, if an owner of land has 'lost sight' of the land, forgotten about it or abandoned it and someone else has taken over occupation of it, then it makes sense for ownership to be passed over to the interloper. Adverse possession provides a means by which land can be brought back into social or economic use and is framed between the principle that 'possession is nine-tenths of the law' and that of 'use it or lose it'. Sometimes adverse possession can provide truly astonishing results where significant areas of land or a house worth many millions of pounds is acquired by this process. The truth, however, is that the vast majority of claims concern relatively small parts of a garden where there has been boundary 'creep'. That is not surprising since boundaries can often be vague – particularly where the history of the boundary may be 'lost' as the adjoining properties have passed from one owner to another.

It should be stated that issues relating to relativity of title are more likely to arise out of unregistered land rather than registered land. As we have seen previously, in unregistered land title and ownership are determined by establishing a good root of title going back at least 15 years. Adverse possession has a legitimate role to play if any of the title deeds are lost or a good root of title cannot be established. In these circumstances, it is often mere possession that provides a solution to determining ownership of land in relative terms. In the case of registered land, the position does not tend to be so fluid. With registration of title there is a state-guaranteed title to the land with the avowed aim of the Land Registration Act 2002 being to bring all matters relating to the land on to the registered title, subject to a power to rectify the title. The position is now becoming a great deal more focused as we move towards a system of e-conveyancing. The fact remains, however, that some 30% of the land area in England and Wales is still unregistered land (despite the fact that 85% of properties are now within the registered land regime), and therefore claims to adverse possession are not something about to be consigned to the annals of English land law history. In any event, since registration of title on first registration is still based on the need to prove title based on unregistered land principles, registration of title per se is not a panacea that is likely to rid us of adverse possession claims at the moment, though they will become increasingly rare and improbable.

The existence of a comprehensive system of land registration under the Land Registration Act 2002 alongside unregistered land provides two distinct mechanisms for handling adverse possession; however, the means of establishing a right by adverse possession remains factually the same and we will examine this aspect first of all.

Establishing adverse possession

The principles for establishing adverse possession are to be found in a wealth of case law and not in statute. Some of the cases are conflicting and others complementary to each other. Judicial decisions, whilst providing flexibility in determining the existence of adverse possession, can also make it difficult to predict. In *J A Pye (Oxford) Ltd* v *Graham* [2003] 1 AC 419, the House of Lords provided a statement of the fundamental requirements needed to prove a claim to adverse possession. It must be emphasised that the fundamental requirements set out in this case only provide guidelines so as to allow for flexibility, depending on the circumstances of a particular case.

J A Pye (Oxford) Ltd v Graham [2003] 1 AC 419

The claimant (J A Pye Ltd) had the registered title to some agricultural land, with Graham, a local farmer, controlling the vehicular access to it. Until 31 August 1984, the defendant had used the land for grazing his cattle with the consent of the claimant – i.e. the defendant had a licence to use the land. When the licence expired, Graham, who was willing to pay for the grazing rights, made several requests to have the licence renewed. He received no response to these requests but nevertheless continued to farm the land for some 14 years, from 1986 to 1999, treating the land as his own. The claimant did nothing on the land for the 14-year period. In 1997, Graham registered a caution against the claimant's registered title, claiming title by adverse possession. The claimant attempted to warn off the caution entered by Graham and, in April 1998, commenced an action for possession.

In order to establish a claim for adverse possession, Graham had to show that he had *dispossessed* Pye for more than 12 years so that Pye's action fell within the Limitation Act 1980 s.15(1), which provides:

> No action shall be brought by any person to recover any land after the expiration of 12 years from the date on which the right of action accrued to him, or if it first accrued to some person through whom he claims, to that person.

The date for determining the accrual of the right of action is set out in Schedule 1 para 1:

> where the person bringing an action to recover land, or some person through whom he claims, has been in possession of the land, and has while entitled to the land been dispossessed or discontinued his possession, the right of action shall be treated as having accrued on the date of the dispossession or discontinuance.

Thus in order to establish adverse possession it needs to be established when the dispossession took place. The House of Lords held that dispossession arises when one person takes possession from another, without consent, bearing in mind there can only be one possessor at a time. But how is possession proven? The House of Lords held, concurring with the judgment of Slade J in ***Powell v McFarlane*** (1977) 38 P & CR 452, that possession comprises two elements:

(i) a sufficient degree of physical custody and control ('factual possession');

(ii) an intention to exercise such custody and control on one's own behalf for one's own benefit ('intention to possess' or 'animus possidendi').

It is these two elements that will frame the consideration of how adverse possession is established.

The fact of possession

The fact of possession was set out in ***Powell v MacFarlane*** (1970) 38 P & CR 452 by Slade J as follows:

> Factual possession signifies an appropriate degree of physical control. It must be a single and [exclusive] possession, though there can be a single possession exercised by or on behalf of several persons jointly. Thus an owner of land and a person intruding on that land without his consent cannot both be in possession of the land at the same time. The question what acts constitute a sufficient degree of exclusive physical control must depend on the circumstances, in particular the nature of the land and the manner in which land of that nature is commonly used or enjoyed . . . Everything must depend on the particular circumstances, but

broadly, I think what must be shown as constituting factual possession is that the alleged possessor has been dealing with the land in question as an occupying owner might have been expected to deal with it and that no-one else has done so.

One must therefore look at the circumstances of the particular case to establish whether factual possession has arisen so that the squatter is occupying the land as an owner might be expected to do so. This may be demonstrated by living in the house or cultivating the land to the exclusion of others, including the owner himself: *Littledale* v *Liverpool College* [1900] n1 Ch 19. Thus in *Pye* v *Graham* the defendants were in occupation of the land which was within their physical control to the physical exclusion of the claimant by way of the hedges and the key to the gate that barred the access route.

The matter of factual possession is clearly one of degree, so that acts that are temporary in nature, such as planting vegetables every summer, would probably not be enough in relation to a garden. On the other hand, some pieces of land have very limited uses and here the degree of physical control may be more limited than, for instance, in the case of a house. Thus in *Red House Farms (Thornden) Ltd* v *Catchpole* [1977] 2 EGLR 125, shooting game over a piece of moorland was a sufficient act of possession since the land itself had very limited uses. Similarly, trivial acts of trespass, such as allowing children to play on the land, were held to be insufficient: *Techuild Ltd* v *Chamberlain* (1969) 20 P & CR 633.

It is the overriding effect of possession that is important, so delineating the land by erecting fences or planting hedges is a good indicator of an exertion of control over the land, thereby establishing factual possession. Changing locks or erecting buildings on the land achieves the same purpose. The fact that the act of possession is referable to some other objective that has the effect of demonstrating factual possession is not necessarily fatal to a claim. Thus in *Hounslow London Borough Council* v *Minichinton* (1997) 74 P & CR 221 the squatters used a piece of land as part of their garden. They enclosed the disputed land so as to keep their dogs from roaming. It was argued that the enclosure was to keep the dogs in rather than to keep others out. Millett LJ rejected that argument, stating:

> Their motive is irrelevant. The important thing is that they were intending to allow their dogs to make full use of what they plainly regarded as their land, and which they used as their land.

But the facts of a particular case are all-important and there are instances where motive has played a part in determining whether possession has arisen factually. In *Inglewood* v *Baker* [2002] EWCA Civ 1733, a squatter claimed he had been in possession of a piece of woodland. He had erected a fence in 1984; however, the Court of Appeal held he had erected the fence to keep his sheep in, not the owner out. Unlike the *Minchinton* case, where the land was incorporated into the garden, here the land was adjacent to the squatter's and was used for feeding sheep, dumping rubbish, shooting and motorbike riding. The only manifestation of possession was the fence and the motive behind this was to keep livestock in. *Minchinton* was not referred to in *Inglewood* and the two cases are difficult to reconcile. It is suggested, though, that the decision in *Minchinton* is to be preferred since it provides a clear statement that, if one can demonstrate exclusive control, any other adjunctive reason for that control does not preclude the establishment of rights by adverse possession.

Another significant indicator of factual possession is the voluntary payment of council tax or water rates, though it should be noted that this is an evidential feature of the fact of possession: *Cooke* v *Dunn* (1998) 9 BPR 16489.

The intention to possess – animus possidendi

Factual possession is not enough since there must also be an *intention* to possess. Thus, if a person is in possession of a house, their presence could be explained by them being a squatter; a friend of the owner, looking after the house; or a trespasser. The fact of the person being in possession does not per se point to legal possession. If the person is a squatter attempting to claim adverse possession, their intention is to remain in the premises for as long as they can, while in the case of the friend or trespasser that is clearly not their intention. The determining feature, therefore, is the matter of intention to possess and put the land to their own use, whether or not they were aware that some other person, including the owner, might have a claim in the land. In *Pye v Graham*, the House of Lords held that Graham was in control of the land without the consent of the owner prior to 30 April 1986 and was managing the land as an owner might manage it. Graham had therefore manifestly intended to assert possession over the owner and had done so for 14 years, so that the owner was barred from bringing the claim, and thus Graham established title to the land.

Another point that needs to be made here is that it is the intention to possess and not to own the land that prevails. Thus in *Buckinghamshire County Council v Moran* [1990] Ch 623 Hoffman J stated that what is required is 'not an intention to own or even an intention to acquire ownership but an intention to possess'. In that case, the defendant incorporated a parcel of land into his garden that the local authority acquired as part of a road widening plan. The defendant cultivated the garden and maintained the boundary fences. The Court of Appeal held that the degree of physical control he had exercised over the land was sufficient to give rise to possession of the land. In particular, the defendant had acquired the land from his predecessor in title with the rights they had acquired over the land. In 1976, the local authority stated that he had no right to use the land but nothing was done until 1985, when it began possession proceedings. The Court of Appeal held that this was too late and the defendant had established rights by adverse possession. The focus is therefore on the mind of the squatter so that the knowledge on the part of the squatter that the owner wants to make use of the land in the future, as in the Graham case itself, is irrelevant. One must bear in mind here that claimants in adverse possession may believe that the land belongs to them already, whilst others may be fully aware that the land does not belong to them. Both these aspects are also irrelevant, subject to one proviso, in that if a squatter believes their own presence on the property is because of the consent of the owner then a claim will fail since ultimately the squatter does not have control of the land: *Clowes Developments (UK) Ltd v Walter* [2005] EWHC 669 (Ch).

It follows that a tenant cannot acquire rights of adverse possession since to do so would be to deny their landlord's title, which, as we have seen in Chapter 6, a tenant cannot do until such time as the lease has ended. In the case of implied periodic tenancies, such as leases that run from year to year or month to month, the Limitation Act 1980 Schedule 1 para 5(1) and (2) provides that time runs from the end of the first year (or other period) or if rent is paid, from the date of the last payment of rent received by the landlord.

Similarly, if a person occupies land under a licence from the paper owner, adverse possession cannot be established. This is clearly the case with regards to an express licence, though even with these the informal nature of licences actually comes to an end. The case of *Pye v Graham* itself is an example of the position regarding licences since here Graham held the land initially under a series of 11-month licences and it was fairly easy to discern when the last licence had come to an end, prompting the start of the limitation period. The same is not necessarily the case with open-ended licences where the licence operates on a continuing basis, as held in *Trustees of Grantham Christian Fellowship* v *Scouts Association* [2005] EWHC 209 CL.

Express licences, however, can have a particularly important use in preventing a licensee from acquiring ownership by adverse possession.

BP Properties Ltd v Buckler [1988] 55 P & CR 337

Following attempts to evict a disabled woman at the end of her lease and the ensuing bad publicity, BP wrote to the woman, giving her the right to live in the property rent-free for the rest of her life. The woman did not respond to the letter but on her death her son attempted to establish that his mother had acquired the title by adverse possession.

The Court of Appeal held that, despite not accepting the licence, Mrs Buckley in fact held on that basis. No doubt, if she had rejected the offer, BP would have given her notice to quit. Since she did not indicate the refusal, BP was entitled to treat her as a licensee and as such her possession was not 'adverse'.

The doctrine of implied licences at one time provided particular difficulties with regard to the establishment of rights to land by adverse possession. The doctrine arises where a person occupies land in a manner that is consistent with the future intentions of the paper owner to make use of the land. In such a situation, the act of occupation by the squatter is not considered to be an act of dispossession since there is no evidence of the paper owner discontinuing their possession of the land. The doctrine appears to have emanated from the case of *Leigh* v *Jack* (1879) 5 Ex D 264.

Leigh v Jack (1879) 5 Ex D 264

The owner of the land intended to build a road upon it, but had taken no steps to actually construct the road. From 1854 the owner of neighbouring land started to store materials on the land and in 1865 and 1872 erected fences on the land.

The Court of Appeal held that the actions of the neighbour could not amount to adverse possession since the actions were consistent with the use of the owner of the paper owner not to cultivate or develop the land. The neighbour therefore had an implied licence which prevented adverse possession from being set up on the land.

The principle was applied in the case of *Wallis's Cayton Bay Holiday Camp Ltd* v *Shell-Max and BP Ltd* [1975] QB 94, CA.

Wallis's Cayton Bay Holiday Camp Ltd v Shell-Max and BP Ltd [1975] QB 94, CA

In this case, Shell-Mex acquired land that was to be on the side of a new road that the local authority proposed building. The local authority abandoned its plans and so Shell-Mex offered to sell the land to the holiday camp, which had been using the land as a farm and an entrance to the camp. The owners of the holiday camp did not respond to the offer but continued to use the land for 12 years and then claimed ownership by adverse possession.

The Court of Appeal held that a claimant does not establish adverse possession by entering on to the land but by performing no acts that are inconsistent with the use of the paper owner. The use by the squatter in such circumstances is said to be ascribed to a licence being given to them by the paper owner.

The doctrine of implied licence was always considered to be of a dubious nature since it is based on the intentions of the paper owner and not the intentions of the squatter. Thus in *Pye* v *Graham* Lord Browne-Wilkinson stated that 'the suggestion that the sufficiency of the possession can depend on the intention not of the squatter but of the true owner is heretical and wrong'. The Limitation Act 1980 Schedule 1 para 8(4) now specifically over-rules the establishment of an implied licence in this way, though of course there is still room for a licence to be implied from the facts of a particular case.

One final point should be noted in that a squatter is under no obligation to inform the owner that they, the squatter, are in possession: *Topplan Estates Ltd* v *Townley* [2005] 1 EGLR 90.

The limitation period

So far, we have been considering how adverse possession is established factually and we now need to consider the mechanisms for handling claims in adverse possession. It is important to emphasise that the prescribed times for establishing adverse possession are different for unregistered land and registered land under the Land Registration Act 1925, as opposed to registered land under the Land Registration Act 2002. We will commence by looking at the time periods for unregistered land and registered land under the Land Registration Act 1925 and considering the effects adverse possession has in each of these forms. We will then look at the new system for adverse possession brought in by the Land Registration Act 2002.

Establishing the prescribed period in unregistered and registered land under the Land Registration Act 1925

The Limitation Act 1980 applies to unregistered land and registered land, providing the required period of time is established prior to 13 October 2003 when the Land Registration Act 2002 came into operation.

We have seen that adverse possession is not so much a matter of a squatter establishing rights as barring the owner from recovering land because his or her claim is outside of the limitation period.

As seen earlier, for most land, the limitation period is set out by the Limitation Act 1980 s.15 as 12 years from the moment the squatter begins their adverse possession of the land: Schedule 1 para 1. Where the land is owned by the Crown, the period of limitation is 30 years from the moment the adverse possession commences: Schedule 1 para 11, as is the period of limitation where the land is owned by a spiritual or charitable corporation sole, for instance, a bishop: Schedule 1 para 10.

It is important that the period of adverse possession is continuous; if there is any break in the adverse possession the time re-starts and a full period of limitation will then be required. The time does not, however, stop running if the squatter transfers the land to someone else. Thus if a person owns a house and is establishing adverse possession over an adjoining piece of land then, on the sale of the house to a purchaser, the period of time continues to run for the new owner of the house, as set out in Schedule 1 para 8(1).

> No right of action to recover land shall be treated as accruing unless the land is in the posses-sion of some person in whose favour the period of limitation can run (referred to below in this paragraph as 'adverse possession'); and where under the preceding provisions of this Schedule any such right of action is treated as accruing on a certain date and no person is in adverse possession on that date, the right action shall not be treated as accruing unless and until adverse possession is taken of the land.

In the case where the owner has a lease, the period of limitation is again 12 years: *Chung Ping Kwang v Lam Island Co. Ltd* [1997] AC 38. The limitation period has no effect on the landlord of the leaseholder since they have no right to possession at all until the end of the tenant's lease. The adverse possession therefore is against the tenant, not the landlord. Once the lease comes to an end, in order to establish adverse possession against the landlord, another period of 12 years must be established against them before they are barred from recovering possession: s.15 and Schedule 1 para 4. One complication that can arise here is if the lease provides the tenant with an option to renew their lease on its expiry. In such a situation, the landlord cannot then go into possession since the squatter may rely on the tenant's option to renew to prevent the landlord from taking possession. The logic is sound since the landlord would not, in any event, have been able to evict their own tenant because of the option and therefore they should not be able to displace the squatter.

It is possible for the operation of the period of limitation to be postponed. Thus s.32(1) provides that, if the claim for adverse possession is based on the fraud of the squatter, or the squatter has deliberately concealed any fact relevant to the owner's right of action, or the claim is for relief from the consequences of a mistake, the limitation period does not begin to run until the owner/claimant has discovered the fraud, concealment or mistake, or could, with reasonable diligence, have discovered it. In *Beaulane Properties Ltd v Palmer* [2006] Ch 79 the squatter misled an agent of the owner that he had an arrangement as regards the land with the previous owner. As a result, the commencement of the period of limitation was delayed until the withheld fact had become known.

Stopping the time running

The limitation period can be stopped from running in the following ways:

Successful action for possession

If the owner brings possession proceedings before the expiry of the limitation period and is successful in their action then time, for limitation purposes, ceases to run. As we have seen, the normal period is 12 years, but, where the Land Registration Act 2002 applies, the owner must bring his successful action for possession within 10 years of the squatter applying for registration of his title: Land Registration Act 2002 Schedule 6 para 1.

Written acknowledgement

By the Limitation Act 1980 s.29 if the squatter acknowledges the title of the owner then the time period commences from the date of the acknowledgement. By s.30, to be effective, the acknowledgement must be in writing and signed by the person making it, the squatter. Whilst oral acknowledgement is not sufficient, it should be borne in mind that implicit acknowledgement may arise if the squatter offers to buy the property from the owner or pay rent to the owner: *Colchester Borough Council v Smith* [1992] Ch 421.

Cessation of possession

Clearly, if the squatter goes out of possession before the expiry of the limitation period, that extinguishes their claim. It should be borne in mind, however, that another possessor taking from the squatter takes over the period that has already accrued and may then go on to accumulate the requisite amount of time so that they can set up a claim to adverse possession in their own right: *Allen v Matthews* [2007] P & CR 441.

If the paper owner retakes physical possession of the land in the sense of retaking custody and control, this would normally operate to stop the clock. Therefore mere possession does not per se cause the clock to stop as there must be a degree of control exercised. This prevents mere symbolic acts of possession operating to prevent adverse possession from being established: *Smith* v *Waterman* [2003] All ER (D) 72. Possession is therefore more than mere occupancy, as indicated in *J A Pye (Oxford) Ltd* v *Graham* [2003] 1 AC 419 and this is true even for a paper owner retaking possession to prevent the limitation period from continuing.

Adverse possession and unregistered land

The effect of the application of the Limitation Act 1980 is to extinguish the title of the owner: s.17 so that the squatter now becomes the fee simple owner. The squatter, however, takes subject to all interests that might affect the land, such as easements or restrictive covenants, since he is not a purchaser of the land. Therefore the fact that they have no notice of such interests or whether or not the interests are registered under the Land Charges Act 1972 is irrelevant: *Re Nisbet and Potts' Contract* (1906) 1 Ch 386.

Since the adverse possession has arisen under the Limitation Act 1980, there is no question of a conveyance being made to the squatter. If they intend to sell the land, they would normally be required to make a declaration as to their title and a purchaser would invariably require an indemnity from them, usually by way of title insurance. In such circumstances, the squatter would be wise to register their title at the Land Registry with a possessory freehold title, which, by the Land Registration Act 2002 s.62(4), may be upgraded to an absolute title after 12 years.

As we have noted earlier, a claim to adverse possession against a lease will, following the requisite limitation period, extinguish the lease but not the landlord's title. Once the lease expires, a landlord is able to go into possession against the squatter, unless a further 12-year period accrues against the landlord themselves. Note the matters regarding options to renew, though.

The squatter's rights to adverse possession could, however, be extinguished by the actions of the tenant they have derived their rights from since that tenant remains the tenant of the landlord. Thus, if the tenant surrenders their lease to the landlord, the landlord would have an immediate right of entry on to the premises and could then evict the squatter: *Fairweather* v *St Marylebone Property Co. Ltd* [1963] AC 510. Furthermore, if the tenant acquires the landlord's reversion, their lease will merge into that reversion so that the tenant will acquire a fresh right of action in the same way the landlord would have done on a surrender of the lease: *Taylor* v *Twinberrow* [1930] 2 KB 16.

Adverse possession under the Land Registration Act 1925

Here we are examining the effect of adverse possession on registered land where the 12-year limitation period is completed prior to 13 October 2003 when the Land Registration Act 2002 came into force.

The problem with registered land is that it is simply not possible to remove the registered proprietor from the title even though they were disbarred from taking action against the squatter by virtue of the Limitation Act 1980 s.15. In order to deal with this issue the Limitation Act 1980 s.75 provides:

(1) The Limitation Acts shall apply to registered land in the same manner and to the same extent as those Acts apply to land not registered, except that where, if the land were not registered, the estate of the person registered as proprietor would be extinguished, such estate shall not be extinguished but shall be deemed to be held by the proprietor for the time being on trust for the person who, by virtue of the said Acts, has acquired title against any proprietor, but without prejudice to the estates and interests of any other person interested in the land whose estate or interest is not extinguished by those Acts.

(2) Any person claiming to have acquired a title under the Limitation Acts may apply to be registered as proprietor thereof.

The effect of this provision is that, since the squatter is entitled to be entered as the registered proprietor, the registered proprietor, who is the paper owner out of whom the adverse possession arises, holds the squatter's title on trust. The registered proprietor/paper owner therefore holds the legal title and the squatter has a beneficial title to the property. This equitable interest originally took effect as an overriding interest under the Land Registration Act 1925 s.70(1)f but is now protected as an interest that is overriding under the Land Registration Act 2002 Schedule 3 para 2. The effect therefore is that if the registered proprietor sells their land, any purchaser would take subject to the squatter's overriding interest by virtue of the Land Registration Act 2002 s.29 and s.30. If the transfer by the registered proprietor is to someone other than a purchaser, the squatter's right to be entered as the registered proprietor binds the transferee under the 'basic rule' for priority found in the Land Registration Act 2002 s.28. Once the squatter is entered in the register as the registered proprietor, the trust established under s.75 then comes to an end.

The cutoff date of 13 October 2003 for the entry into force of the Land Registration Act can pose a problem for a squatter since the new Act introduces a completely new set of rules for dealing with the issue of adverse possession. The Land Registration Act 2002 provides transitional arrangements for dealing with adverse possession under Schedule 12 para 18 so that if the squatter established 12 years' adverse possession so that their registered estate is held in trust for them by virtue of the Limitation Act 1980 s.75 immediately before the coming into force of the Land Registration Act 2002, they are entitled to be registered as the proprietor of the estate.

On the other hand, if the squatter had *not* established their 12 years' adverse possession prior to the coming into force of the Land Registration Act 2002 then their position falls to be considered within that regime, which is a good deal more hostile towards the concept of adverse possession. The period of adverse possession will still accrue towards the lesser 10-year period under the Land Registration Act 2002. The general scheme within that Act provides significant limitations on the concept, aimed at reducing all estates and interests on to the register, as discussed at the start of this chapter.

Adverse possession under the Land Registration Act 2002

The Land Registration Act 2002 has brought about a significant and fundamental change in regulating the effects of adverse possession in the context of registered land. It has been seen in other parts of this book that the objective of the Land Registration Act 2002 is to develop and put in place a scheme whereby the register reflects accurately what is taking place on the land. In this way, the state-guaranteed title provides a readily provable means of establishing title and interests that benefit and burden the land and, of course, provides the means by which the objective of e-conveyancing is achieved. It can be seen that adverse possession threatens all these objectives and thus the Land Registration Act 2002 has attempted to curtail the effects of adverse possession.

The process of how a claim in adverse possession can be claimed in terms of possession and intention remains the same; however, the Act provides a procedure whereby such claims can be brought onto the register of title. The new scheme in relation to adverse possession in registered land is found in Land Registration Act 2002 ss.96–98 and Schedule 6. The new scheme applies to all claims for adverse possession for which the limitation period under the Limitation Act 1980 was not completed prior to 13 October 2003. The first and most fundamental change is that by s.96 no period of possession under the Limitation Act 1980 can operate to deprive a registered proprietor of his title. There is therefore no period of limitation under the Land Registration 2002. In addition, the statutory trust which we saw operating in the content of the Land Registration Act 1925 is abolished. Instead, the Land Registration Act 2002 provides a procedure whereby the squatter has to apply to the Registrar to be registered as the proprietor of the title. Once an application is made, the process under Schedule 6 is triggered so that the paper owner is given the opportunity of challenging the application by the squatter. The Land Registration Act 2002 therefore provides a reversal of roles. Under the previous law, it was the paper owner who had to be alert to the challenge to their title by the squatter, who could largely remain passive on the property. Now it is the squatter who must take action and the paper owner, the registered proprietor, can remain passive until they are alerted by the new process to a claim for adverse possession by the squatter.

The Land Registration Act 2002 scheme

Under the new scheme a squatter who wishes to be entered on the register as the registered proprietor can do so in two ways – by application and by court order.

The basic principles

Under Schedule 6(1) a person may apply to be entered as the registered proprietor if they have been in adverse possession of the estate for a period of 10 years ending on the date of the application. Two matters flow from this. Firstly, a squatter must establish their adverse possession substantively by reference to the principles set out in *Pye* v *Graham* – i.e. the fact of possession and animus possidendi. Secondly, the 10-year period is not a limitation period but a threshold period before which a claim cannot be made. In calculating the 10-year threshold period, Schedule 6 para 11(2) provides that a period of less than 10 years commenced by one person may be completed by another taking over possession of the land.

Once the registrar receives an application and is satisfied that there is an arguable case for substantive adverse possession, a notice is sent to the current registered proprietor, together with a notice to any legal mortgagees, to the proprietor of any superior registered estate – i.e. a landlord where the adverse possession is against a lease, the freeholder or any intervening landlord, and certain other persons: Schedule 6 para 2.

If the current registered proprietor does not respond to the notice, it will result in the adverse possessor being entered as the registered proprietor: Schedule 6 para 4. It is still possible, however, for the current registered proprietor to apply to have the register rectified back in their favour if the claim proves to be incorrect.

Baxter v *Mannion* [2011] 1 WLR 1594

In this case, Baxter ('B') applied to the Land Registry to be entered as the registered proprietor of a field by way of adverse possession. The registrar gave notice of the application to Mannion ('M'), who failed to respond to the notice within the prescribed period of 65 days (Schedule 6 para 3(2) and the Land Registration Rules 2003 r.189). B was therefore entered as the registered proprietor of the field. M then applied for rectification of the register on the basis that B had not been in adverse possession of the land and therefore the registration of B as the registered proprietor was a mistake under Schedule 4 para 5. M's application was upheld by the adjudicator and the High Court on the basis that B had not satisfied the substantive requirements of proving adverse possession.

B argued that Schedule 4 para 5 only allowed for a challenge on procedural grounds. This was rejected by the Court of Appeal since there was no indication that 'mistake' was confined in this way. Further, the Court of Appeal considered that Schedule 4 para 6(1) would not apply to prevent rectification in that there was no evidence of fraud. It was, however, considered that under Schedule 4 para 6(2) it would be unjust not to order for rectification since otherwise M would lose his land for the sake of a bureaucratic process, whilst B would gain land when he had never been in adverse possession.

If the current registered proprietor responds, various options are open to them, not least of which is simply consenting to the registration of the squatter, though such a response would be unlikely. The current registered proprietor is entitled to object to the application by way of the Land Registration Act 2002 s.73(1), stating the reasons for the objection. Clearly, the main reason here will be the fact that there is no substantive adverse possession. If the parties cannot negotiate a settlement then the matter will be referred to the adjudicator for resolution.

Finally, the current registered proprietor may serve a counter-notice on the Registry under the terms of Schedule 6 para 5. Essentially, this amounts to a peremptory challenge which will, unless exceptional circumstances apply, result in the squatter's application being defeated. It can be seen immediately that this process achieves two objectives. Firstly, it affirms the principle that the register is a definitive statement as to the state of the title, providing protection to those who are the registered proprietors. Secondly, it seeks to drive out the unruly nature of adverse possession as a means of de-stabilising the principle of state-guaranteed title to the land. The effect of a counter-notice therefore is that the registrar must reject the squatter's application unless the squatter can demonstrate that the three exceptional circumstances set out in Schedule 6 para 5 apply to them (see below).

Despite the effect of the counter-notice, a squatter who cannot bring themselves within the three exceptional circumstances has a further chance of becoming the registered proprietor. Thus Schedule 6 para 6(1) provides that the squatter can re-apply if they remain in adverse possession of the estate throughout the period of two years from the date of the rejection of their initial application. If the squatter can demonstrate this, then they are entitled to be entered as the registered proprietor, irrespective of any objections of the registered proprietor. Essentially, therefore, the registered proprietor must ensure that, following the rejection of the application by the registrar under Schedule 6 para 5, they take steps to bring the adverse possession to an end by either evicting the squatter or regularising the squatter's possession by way of a licence or a tenancy, which will cause the substantive adverse possession to be terminated.

The three exceptions

As we have already noted, a squatter can establish their right to be the registered proprietor despite the objections of the current registered proprietor in three exceptional cases set out within Schedule 6 para 5.

Schedule 6 para 5(2) – Estoppel

This provides:

> The first condition is that –
>
> (a) it would be unconscionable because of an equity by estoppel for the registered proprietor to seek to dispossess the applicant, and
> (b) the circumstances are such that the applicant ought to be registered as the proprietor.

An estoppel may arise where the registered proprietor has made some assurances to the adverse possessor, who has relied on those assurances to their detriment. From one point of view it may be suggested that a person who is in possession of land by way of proprietary estoppel is unlikely to be in adverse possession. In any event, one would have thought the claimant would establish their rights by proprietary estoppel without recourse to adverse possession. The Law Commission and the Land Registry has provided examples of how this may occur. For instance, the adverse possessor may build on the registered proprietor's land in the mistaken belief that the land belongs to them and the registered proprietor may acquiesce in this mistake. Alternatively, it may arise where there is an informal arrangement for the sale and purchase of the land for valuable consideration and the adverse possessor then goes into possession believing they are now the owner of the land.

Para 5(2)b needs to be examined carefully since it states that the 'applicant *ought* to be registered'. There is thus a discretion here so that, even if an applicant can establish both adverse possession and proprietary estoppel, there is still room for a refusal to register him or her as the registered proprietor. There is no guidance within the Land Registration Act 2002 as to the potential grounds for refusal and therefore judicial impression is required to throw further light on this.

Schedule 6 para 5(3) – Some other reason for the squatter to be registered as the proprietor

This provides:

> The second condition is that the applicant is for some other reason entitled to be registered as the proprietor of the estate.

Clearly, this is a 'catch all' and open ground for the basis of a challenge by an adverse possessor. Again the Law Commission and Land Registry have provided some examples of when it might apply. It is suggested it may be used if the squatter is entitled to the land under a will or intestacy, or where a purchaser has gone into possession following the payment of the purchase price, but the land has not been transferred to him or her. These examples seem peculiar since, as with proprietary estoppels, one would have considered that the squatter would have a claim independently of adverse possession in any event. The scope of the provision remains elusive and again judicial impression is called for to establish clarification.

Schedule 6 para 5(4) – Boundary disputes

This provides:

The third condition is that –

(a) the land to which the application relates is adjacent to land belonging to the applicant,
(b) the exact line of the boundary between the two has not been determined under rules under section 60,
(c) for at least ten years of the period of adverse possession ending on the date of the application, the applicant (or any predecessor in title) reasonably believed that the land to which the application relates belonged to him, and
(d) the estate to which the application relates was registered more than one year prior to the date of the application.

Boundary disputes are a common cause of discontent between neighbours. Sometimes the exact boundary lines have never been certain so that neighbours proceed to delineate their boundaries as they believe them to be. In other cases, the boundary lines may have altered by way of informal arrangements. In either case, the boundary lines on the ground do not reflect the boundaries as they appear on the title plan. This exception therefore provides an opportunity to reconcile the various situations which might arise. Thus, if the squatter has been in adverse possession of land that they 'reasonably believed' belonged to them for a period of 10 years immediately preceding their application, the Land Registration Act 2002 provides a mechanism by which they can be made the registered proprietor of the disputed land.

The effect of the registration of the adverse possessor

Where an adverse possessor becomes the registered proprietor, the person from whom they take the estate has their estate extinguished. The adverse possessor becomes the registered proprietor of that estate, whether it be freehold or leasehold – whichever is the case: Schedule 6 para 9(1).

The adverse possessor takes the estate subject to any interests affecting the estate, whether legal or equitable. They therefore take subject to any easements, profits à prendre or restrictive covenants: Schedule 6 para 9(2). The one exception of this is that the adverse possessor takes free of any registered charge affecting the estate immediately before their registration as the proprietor. The logic behind this is that when the adverse possessor made their application, the owner of the registered charge (the legal mortgagee) would have been notified of the application and would have had the opportunity to object. If the owner of the registered charge has not taken that opportunity then they have only themselves to blame. This exception does not, however, apply if the adverse possessor has gained their registration as proprietor under one of three exceptions in Schedule 6 para 5.

Adverse possession and human rights

Inevitably, perhaps, adverse possession raises issues as regards the contravention of human rights – after all, an estate owner is losing their land. The focus here lies in the European Convention on Human Rights Article 1 Protocol 1 as embedded in the Human Rights Act 1998 Article 1 Protocol 1 which provides:

Every natural or legal person is entitled to the peaceful enjoyment of his possessions in the public interest and subject to the conditions provided for by law and by the general principles of international law.

The preceding provisions shall not, however, in any way impair the right of a State to enforce such laws as it deems necessary to control the use of property in accordance with the general interest or to secure the payment of taxes of other contributions or penalties.

In both unregistered land and registered land, under the Land Registration Act 1925, owners subject to adverse possession are deprived of their title without compensation and thus there appears to be a breach of the convention. Having said this, the convention is clear that interference in private rights in this way may be justified as being in the public interest. Nevertheless, in *J A Pye (Oxford) Ltd* v *Graham* [2003] 1 AC 419 the fact that the Land Registration Act 1925 imposed a trust on the registered title, promoting the squatter to a beneficiary under the trust from which he could then apply to be the registered proprietor in place of the paper owner, gave rise to some foreboding about the implications of the human rights perspective on the paper owner. A particular concern was the fact that the loss of ownership was uncompensatable. In that case, at first instance, Neuberger J was particularly apprehensive about the impact of the convention on adverse possession, but nevertheless provided a robust defence of the principle. He stated [2000] (Ch 710):

> A frequent justification for limitation periods generally is that people should not be able to sit on their rights indefinitely . . . However, if as in the present case the owner of land has no immediate use for it and is content to let another person trespass on the land for the time being, it is hard to see what principle of justice entitles the trespasser to acquire the land for nothing from the owner simply because he has been permitted to remain there for 12 years. To say that in such circumstances the owner who has sat on his rights should therefore be deprived of his land appears to me to be illogical and disproportionate. Illogical because the only reason that the owner can be said to have sat on his rights is because of the existence of the 12 year limitation period in the first place; if no limitation periods existed he would be entitled to claim possession whenever he actually wanted the land . . . disproportionate because, particularly in a climate of increasing awareness of human rights including the right to enjoy one's own property, it does seem draconian to the owner and a windfall to the squatter that, just because the owner has taken no steps to evict a squatter for 12 years, the owner should lose . . . land to the squatter with no compensation whatsoever.

The matter was not considered in the Court of Appeal, but in the House of Lords the unfairness of the result was clearly of some concern. Thus Lord Bingham stated (para 2):

> The Grahams have acted honourably throughout. They sought rights to graze or cut grass on the land after the summer of 1984, and were quite prepared to pay. When Pye failed to respond they did what any other farmer in their position would have done: they continued to farm the land. They were not at fault. But the result of Pye's inaction was that they enjoyed the full use of the land without payment for 12 years. As if that were not gain enough, they are then rewarded by obtaining title to this considerable area of valuable land without any obligation to compensate the former owner in any way at all. In the case of unregistered land, and in the days before registration became the norm, such a result could no doubt be justified as avoiding protracted uncertainty where the title to land lay. But where land is registered it is difficult to see any justification for a legal rule which compels such an apparently unjust result, and even harder to see why the party gaining title should not be required to pay some compensation at least to the party losing it.

Similarly, Lord Hope referred to the concept of adverse possession and the 'apparent injustice of it'. These comments are not very surprising when one considers that the land in question was worth £10 million when the case came to trial and thus the uncompensatable loss to J A Pye Ltd was considerable. The House of Lords did not, however, consider the impact of the Human Rights Act 1998 since this was not in force at the time of the leaving, coming into force on 2 October 2000. J A Pye Ltd nevertheless took the case to the European Court of Human Rights ('ECHR') but in this action it sought to obtain compensation, not from the Grahams but from the UK government. J A Pye Ltd argued that, as a result of the operation of the Land Registration Act 1925 and the Limitation Act 1980, they had been deprived of their ownership of the land. Furthermore, the company contended that their loss was so great and the windfall gained by the Grahams so significant that fair balance was upset.

In *J A Pye (Oxford) Ltd* v *United Kingdom* [2005] 3 EGLR 1 the ECHR found that the Land Registration Act 1925 and the Limitation Act 1980 amounted to a deprivation of the company's title and upset the fair balance between the demands of the public interest on the one hand and the company's right to their peaceful enjoyment of their property. The ECHR considered the company was entitled to compensation from the government as its rights under the convention had been violated. The UK government then appealed to the Grand Chamber of the ECHR and won by a majority of 17 to 10. Before considering the judgment of the Grand Chamber it is worth considering another case on adverse possession that had come before the English courts in the meantime, *Beaulane Properties Ltd* v *Palmer* [2006] Ch 79.

Beaulane Properties Ltd v Palmer [2006] Ch 79

The facts of this case are remarkably similar to *J A Pye (Oxford) Ltd* v *Graham*. Again, the land in the centre of the action was agricultural land held by Beaulane Properties Ltd ('B'). The company intended to develop the land at a future date. Palmer owned adjoining land under a licence from the predecessors in title to B but, following the sale, continued to use the land from October 1986. The defendant subsequently applied to the Land Registry for first registration of title by way of adverse possession. It was held that the 12-year limitation period ended in June 2003. This date was crucial as it was after the date when the Human Rights Act 1998 came into force, though before the coming into force of the Land Registration Act 2002. This meant B could take advantage of the 1998 Act.

The claimant contended that the effect of the Land Registration Act 1925 when read together with the Limitation Act 1980 was to deprive them of their title without compensation. The company claimed that this was contrary to the Human Rights Act 1998 Schedule 1 Part II Article 1 so that the court was obliged to give effect to the provisions so as to render them compatible with the European Convention on Human Rights. The court held that the effect of the Land Registration Act 1925 and the Limitation Act 1980 was to deprive the landowner of their rights to the land and that this amounted to deprivation of possession within the 1998 Act. The court held there was no public or general interest justifying that deprivation, thus bringing the legislation within the Human Rights Act 1998, so that by s.3 of the Act the court had to give effect to the provisions so as to render them compatible with the European Convention on Human Rights.

Controversially, however, Strauss QC considered that the Land Registration Act 1925 s.75 could be interpreted in such a way that Palmer's action was not inconsistent with any use or intended use of the land by B, so that his possession of the land was not adverse and thus his claim failed. Essentially, therefore, what Strauss QC was doing here was to resurrect the doctrine of implied licences under *Leigh* v *Jack* (1879) 5 Ex D 264, which was specifically overruled by the Limitation Act 1980 Schedule 1 para 8(4). The judgment was controversial not only from that point of view but also because he should have made a declaration of incompatibility under the Human Rights Act 1998 and followed the decision of the House of Lords in *J A Pye (Oxford) Ltd* v *Graham*. The decision of Strauss QC, however, was clearly in line with the first instance decision in the European Court of Human Rights which the UK government had referred to the Grand Chamber.

The Grand Chamber of the European Court of Human Rights considered that the Land Registration Act 1925 and the Limitation Act 1980 did not upset the fair balance between a landowner's right to peaceful enjoyment and the demands of the public interest. The court considered that the matter of limitation did not amount to a deprivation of possession but was a means of controlling land use which did not require compensating. The Grand Chamber considered that the use of limitation gave rise to a legitimate objective in the public interest. The court considered that J A Pye should have been aware of the limitation period and could have taken steps to stop the time from running. The substantial minority of the court, however, were vociferous in putting forward the view that, because of the absence of compensation, more robust measures were needed to protect the landowner's rights to the land. Since there were no notification processes within the Land Registration Act 1925 so as to alert the landowner, there were no effective safeguards and thus no fair balance was achieved.

The effect of the Land Registration Act 2002 has, as we have seen, placed severe limitations on the ability of a trespasser to set up adverse possession in respect of registered land. The doctrine of relativity of title based on possession now has only very limited influence of ownership following the passing of this Act. The position of registered proprietors is now very much more robust. Remember again the objectives behind the Land Registration Act 2002; the overall effect is, as stated by Lord Hope in *J A Pye (Oxford) Ltd v Graham* (para 73):

> . . . a much more rigorous regime has now been enacted in Schedule 6 to the Land Registration Act 2002. Its effect will be to make it much harder for a squatter who is in possession of registered land to obtain a title to it against the wishes of the proprietor. The unfairness in the old regime which this case has demonstrated lies not in the absence of compensation, although that is an important factor, but in the lack of safeguards against oversight or inadvertence on the part of the registered proprietor.

Adverse possession is thus very much more limited and if it is to occur anywhere it is in relation to unregistered land.

Summary

Introduction

- Adverse possession arises where a 'squatter' acquires a right to the title in land over the paper owner. It arises in the context of the paper owner becoming statute-barred in an action to recover land from the squatter. It operates not so much to give the squatter the title to the land as to prevent the paper owner from taking action to enforce their title in the face of a trespass by the squatter. The paper owner must take action within the limitation period set out in the Limitation Act 1980 s.15 – that is, 12 years from the moment the adverse possession commences by the squatter.

- These principles apply in relation to unregistered land and registered land where the period of adverse possession is completed before 13 October 2003, which is the date the Land Registration Act 2002 came into force.

- In the case of leasehold land, the period of limitation is also 12 years: *Chung Ping Kwang v Lam Island Co. Ltd* [1997] AC 38. The period of limitation has no effect on the landlord of the leaseholder against whom the adverse possession is being claimed since the landlord has no right to possession. Once the lease has come to an end, a 12-year period must be established against the landlord to set up adverse possession against their estate: Limitation Act 1980 Schedule 1 para 4.

● Under the Land Registration Act 2002 there is no period of limitation. Once the squatter has been in adverse possession for 10 years they may apply for registration of title, which will trigger a notice to be sent to the registered proprietor. Subject to the three exceptions in the Land Registration Act 2002 Schedule 6 para 5, the registered proprietor then has a further two years to challenge the claim of the squatter or lose their title.

Establishing adverse possession

● In *J A Pye (Oxford) Ltd* v *Graham* [2003] 1 AC 419 the House of Lords provided a statement of fundamental requirements needed to prove the substantive existence of adverse possession – though these are guidelines only. The House of Lords held that, to establish a claim for adverse possession, a claimant squatter had to demonstrate that the paper owner had been dispossessed. Dispossession arises when one person takes possession from another without consent. The House of Lords held, concurring with the judgement in *Powell* v *McFarlane* (1977) 38 P & CR 452, that possession comprises two elements:
(i)   a sufficient degree of physical custody and control ('factual possession'); and
(ii) an intention to possess – animus possidendi.

Stopping the time running

● The limitation period will be stopped from running if the paper owner brings a successful action for possession within the limitation period. Equally, if the squatter acknowledges the title of the owner in signed writing then the period will commence from the date of the acknowledgement: Limitation Act 1980 s.29 and s.30. Clearly, if the squatter goes out of possession before the expiry of the limitation period then their claim will be extinguished. Remember if another person takes from the squatter then they also take over the period that has already accrued.

The effects of adverse possession

Unregistered land

● Here the effect is to extinguish the title of the owner: Limitation Act 1980 s.17 so that the squatter becomes the fee simple owner. Since there is no conveyance as such, a squatter should register a possessory freehold title at the Land Registry, which might be upgraded to an absolute title after 12 years: Land Registration Act 2002 s.62(4).

Registered land under the Land Registration Act 1925

● Here the 12-year limitation period must have been completed prior to 13 October 2003.

● The paper owner retains their registered title but is deemed by the Land Registration Act 1925 s.75 to hold it on trust for the squatter who holds a beneficial interest in the property which originally took effect as an overriding interest under s.70(1)f of the Land Registration Act 1925.

● If the registered proprietor sells the land to a purchaser, that purchaser takes subject to the squatter's overriding interest: Land Registration Act 2002 s.29 and s.30.

● If the registered proprietor transfers the land to a person other than a purchaser then the squatter's right to be entered as registered proprietor binds the transferee: Land Registration Act s.28.

Registered land under the Land Registration Act 2002

- There is no longer any limitation period here and a new scheme set out in ss.96–98 and Schedule 6 is applied.

- The onus is now on the part of the squatter to establish substantive adverse possession and 10 years of adverse possession. However, this is *not* a limitation period but a threshold period: Schedule 6 para 11(2) by which the squatter applies to be entered as the registered proprietor.

- On receipt of the application, the registrar sends a notice to the present registered proprietor who then has two years to defeat the claim, subject to three exceptions.

Further reading

Dixon, 'Adverse Possession, Human Rights and Land Registration: And They All Lived Happily Ever After?' [2007] 71 *The Conveyancer and Property Lawyer* 552

Dixon, 'Human Rights and Adverse Possession: The Final Nail?' [2008] 72 *The Conveyancer and Property Lawyer* 160

Dixon, 'Adverse Possession and the Land Registration Act 2002' [2009] 73 *The Conveyancer and Property Lawyer* 169

Dixon, 'At the Sharper End' [2011] 75 *The Conveyancer and Property Lawyer* 335

Dockray, 'Why Do We Need Adverse Possession?' [1985] 49 *The Conveyancer and Property Lawyer* 273

Griffiths, 'An Important Question of Principle – Reality and Rectification in Registered Land' [2011] 75 *The Conveyancer and Property Lawyer* 331

Halstead, 'Human Property Rights' [2002] 66 *The Conveyancer and Property Lawyer* 153

Harplum and Radley-Gardner, 'Adverse Possession and the Intention to Possess: A Reply' [2001] 65 *The Conveyancer and Property Lawyer* 155

Radley-Gardner and Small, 'Shut out of Europe' (2007) *Estates Gazette* 228

Tee, 'Adverse Possession and Estoppel' [2004] 68 *The Conveyancer and Property Lawyer* 137

Part 3

The ownership of land

10

Successive interests in land

Aims and objectives

After reading this chapter you should be able to:

- Identify what is meant by successive and concurrent interests.
- Understand the nature of strict settlements.
- Understand the nature of trusts for sale and how they operate under the Trusts of Land and Appointment of Trustees Act 1996.
- Understand the rights, duties and powers of trustees and beneficiaries under a trust of land.

Introduction

In Chapter 2 we saw how equity developed the notion of a trust where the legal and equitable titles may be split between the trustees and the beneficiaries, as shown in Figure 10.1.

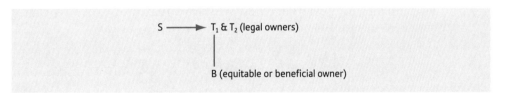

Figure 10.1

This type of trust is known as a 'bare' trust if B is of full age and he or she will hold an equitable fee simple. The trustees, T_1 and T_2 simply have the obligation to hold the legal estate on trust for B.

We also saw that it was possible by use of the trust to create a succession of interests, as in Figure 10.2.

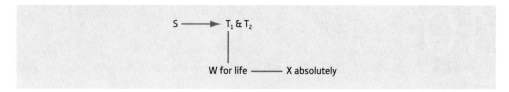

Figure 10.2

In the above example, W is entitled to enjoy the benefit of the estate for her lifetime and on W's death the land would then pass to X absolutely. We know that a trust must arise here since from the Law of Property Act 1925 s.1(1) a life interest cannot exist as a legal estate but only as an equitable interest, thus the land must be held behind a trust. The interest of X would be an equitable fee simple since there are no words of limitation that cut down the estate into something less. Whilst this could exist as a legal estate, in fact S (the settlor) has intended that X's interest is to exist in equity (at least initially).

By the settlor constructing the trust in the above way, it is possible for him to create a succession of interests that could cover many years. There may be all sorts of reasons for a settlor wishing to create such a trust. In the case of the trust in Figure 10.2 the settlor only wishes his wife to enjoy the property for her lifetime since he may be concerned that if he gave her the property absolutely she could sell it or leave it to some other person and in this way his son might not receive any benefit from X's labours to acquire the property in the first place. S, therefore, in creating the trust, has limited W's ability to deal with the property to the detriment of X. Since X is only entitled to his property after W's interest has expired on her death, he is said to have a 'remainder'.

It can quickly be seen that S could create a succession of interests that reaches far into the future. In the past (and to some extent now) land was regarded as the ultimate indicator of wealth and therefore landowners were keen on preventing the land being sold or dissipated in the future, so that the land could be retained within the family. There were many ways in which the land could be 'lost'. For instance, if S (or a successor) only had daughters, the land could be lost through marriage. Equally, S (or a successor) could have a son who turns out to be a wastrel and so might sell or gamble the family estate away. By creating a succession of interests, S could attempt to guard against these future threats. Thus, for instance, he could create a trust as in Figure 10.3.

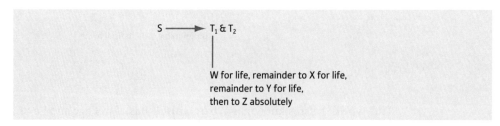

Figure 10.3

Each of the above individuals, W, X, Y and Z, are termed 'tenants for life' (nothing to do with leases) as and when their own interest 'falls in' on the death of the predecessor and their individual interest comes into their possession. The arrangement of a succession of interests in the form of Figure 10.3 is known as a 'settlement'.

At this point, it is useful to distinguish between successive interests of the type seen above and 'concurrent' interests. Concurrent interests exist where two or more people own a piece of land at the same time.

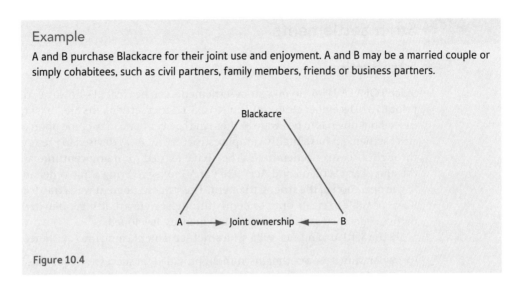

Example

A and B purchase Blackacre for their joint use and enjoyment. A and B may be a married couple or simply cohabitees, such as civil partners, family members, friends or business partners.

Blackacre

A ⟶ Joint ownership ⟵ B

Figure 10.4

Where interests are held concurrently, a trust must also exist since the Law of Property Act 1925 ss.34(2), 35 and 36(i) provides that most co-owners hold the legal estate on trusts for themselves as beneficiaries. A great deal more will be said about this in Chapter 11; however, for the moment, the position can be represented as in Figure 10.5.

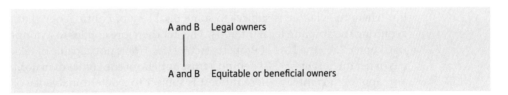

A and B   Legal owners

A and B   Equitable or beneficial owners

Figure 10.5

Thus A and B hold the legal title on trust for themselves as beneficiaries or equitable owners.

Until the passing of the Trusts of Land and Appointment of Trustees Act 1996 ('TOLATA') successive interests could be created by way of either a 'strict settlement' or a trust for sale (which also dealt with concurrent interests). Strict settlements were regulated by the Settled Land Act 1925 and trusts for sale by the Law of Property Act 1925. Both of these methods have been eclipsed by the introduction of trusts of land under TOLATA, which introduced a much simpler regime for dealing with successive and concurrent interests. Both strict settlements and trusts for sale still exist, although they are of far less importance than they were, and for that reason we will look at these before examining the new regime of the trust of land under TOLATA. One further point that should also be made at this juncture is that under TOLATA 1996 Sched. 1 para 5 entailed interests can no longer be created. Where a person purports to grant an entailed interest (see Chapter 2), the instrument creating the interest is not effective to grant an entailed interest and instead operates as a declaration that the property is held in trust absolutely for the grantor. If a grantor instead purports to declare him/herself as having an entailed interest, this is ineffective.

Strict settlements

Introduction

Since TOLATA 1996, no new strict settlements can be created – however, those that existed prior to 31 December 1996 continue to exist. Strict settlements are, in fact, very rare beasts indeed but one has to be aware of them in the event one may come upon one of them. The strict settlement has a highly complex structure that was devised to preserve a family estate through successive generations. They have existed for many centuries and indeed it was the aim of the Settled Land Act 1926 ('SLA') to try to bring some order and simplification to the operation of the strict settlement. The strict settlement was a trap for the unwary and it was possible to create one accidentally through careless drafting, often to the dismay of the parties concerned as severe fiscal consequences developed.

By the Settled Land Act 1925 s.1 a strict settlement came into existence:

(i) where any deed or other instrument provided for successive equitable interests limited in trust, or

(ii) where an interest in land was conferred on a grantee in possession subject to some contingency or disability that qualified his or her entitlement or capacity to hold the interest and this conferment was limited in trust.

We have already seen an example of (i) above – i.e. a gift to W for life, remainder to X absolutely. Clearly, this example demonstrates a succession of equitable interests.

With regards to (ii) above – this refers to conferments of absolute beneficial interests but where the grantee is subject to some disability or contingency that prevented them acquiring the absolute legal interests. The Act therefore applies to a minor who, as we saw in Chapter 2, by the Law of Property Act 1925 s.1(6) is not capable of taking a legal estate. His or her interest *must* exist behind a trust until he or she comes of majority. The provision also applies to grantees whose interest is subject to a determinable fee or where the land in question, either a legal freehold or leasehold, was contingent on the happening of any event. The provision also caught any land that was charged via a family arrangement with the payment of any sums either by way of a rentcharge, payment of capital money or any other periodic sums for the benefit of any person.

The above principles are undoubtedly complex but essentially the circumstances in which a strict settlement arises are: where a person's interest is limited in succession (i.e. he or she has a life interest); where the interest is contingent on the happening of some event, or where the land is charged by the payment of some money under a family arrangement – as found, for instance, under a marriage settlement. Apart from the latter, the land in question had to be 'limited in trust' – thus if there was no trust there could not be settled land. Where the property is given in a will then, of necessity, a trust is created since the legal estate is vested in the personal representatives of the testator. Where a disposition was made inter vivos it could be made in two ways: by a single document in which the legal estate remained with the settlor and the equitable interest would be transferred to the beneficiaries; or by way of a vesting deed together with a trust instrument in which the legal estate was vested in the tenant for life.

If the land was held on an 'immediate trust for sale' the land could not be settled land. The two were mutually exclusive.

The characteristics of a strict settlement

As we have seen, a strict settlement or settled land lies behind a trust and therefore there must be trustees of the settlement and beneficiaries, as with any conventional trust. Beneficiaries could be the person who has the interest in possession, the life tenant, and those who held interests in the remainder. By the Settled Land Act 1925 the person who is of full age and entitled to immediate possession is referred to as the 'tenant for life'.

One of the problems facing a settlor under a settlement is who is going to manage the land over the period of the settlement. Clearly, a settlement with a succession of interests could go on for many years and thus to appoint trustees to this role encounters difficulties in terms of the longevity of the trustees and providing for successors as each trustee passes away. The strict settlement avoided this difficulty by providing that the holder of the legal estate is not the trustee of the settlement but the tenant for life. The tenant for life therefore not only has the beneficial interest but also the legal estate, provided he or she is of full age. If the tenant for life is a minor then the legal estate is held by the statutory owners. These are his or her personal representatives and the land is vested in them – for instance, where the testator created a settlement in a will and then died. If there are no such personal representatives then the legal estate is held by the trustees of the settlement as statutory owners.

There were evident advantages in having the tenant for life holding the legal estate since, as the person holding the land, they were in the best position to manage the land; however, settlements created before 1925 often put severe restrictions on how the tenant for life might deal with the land. The Settled Land Act 1925 resolved this position by providing the tenant for life with statutory powers to deal with the land. We will consider these statutory powers in more detail later but, broadly speaking, the Settled Land Act 1925 gave the tenant for life the power to sell the land, grant leases over it, mortgage it, or grant options over it. The problem here is that there is always the possibility that the tenant for life could abuse their position and therefore the settlement also provided for the appointments of 'trustees of the settlement'. These trustees have responsibility to supervise the tenant for life in case they should abuse their position, and to ensure that the interests of the other beneficiaries entitled under the settlement are protected. The Settled Land Act 1925 s.30 sets out who the trustees of the settlement may be. The effect of the above is that a settlement has three heirs, unlike a conventional trust: see Figure 10.6.

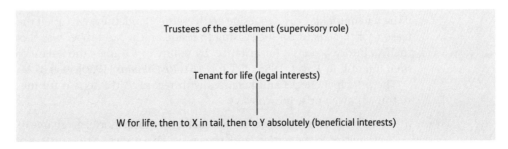

Figure 10.6

The creation of Settled Land Act settlements

Settlements under the Settled Land Act 1925 can be created in two ways. Firstly, under the Settled Land Act 1925 s.6 a settlement can be created in a will and the will itself then becomes the trust instrument. Once the testator dies, the personal representatives hold the settled land on trust and, if and when required to do so, convey the land to the tenant for life (or statutory owner) – if there are more than one, as joint tenants.

Secondly, if the settlement is created inter vivos then under the Settled Land Act 1925 ss.4 and 5 two deeds are required: a vesting deed and a trust instrument. The purpose of the vesting deed is simply to describe the land subject to the settlement, the names of the trustees of the settlement, any additional or larger powers conferred by the trust instrument on the tenant for life relating to the settled land, and a statement that the settled land is vested in the tenant for life (i.e. the person to whom the settled land is to be conveyed on the terms of the settlement).

The trust instrument declares the trusts affecting the settled land, appoints the trustees of the settlement and provides for the appointment of new trustees when appropriate. Importantly, it also sets out any additional powers to those included in the Settled Land Act 1925.

The statutory powers of the tenant for life

As we have mentioned previously, settlements often placed severe restrictions on the tenant for life's dealings with the land, to the extent that the hands of the tenant were effectively tied. In order to relieve the tenant for life from these restrictions the Settled Land Act 1925 provided the tenant for life with statutory powers to manage the settled land, though these contain some checks and balances to prevent the tenant for life from pursuing their dominant position. In particular, the exercise of the statutory powers is supervised by the trustees of the settlement. Furthermore, by the Settled Land Act 1925 s.107, the tenant for life is trustee of their powers in the sense that they have a duty to exercise their powers in the interest of all parties (i.e. the beneficiaries) entitled under the settlement.

The checks and balances within the Settled Land Act 1925 not only strike at the tenant for life but also at the settlor. As stated above, prior to the Settled Land Act 1925, the settlor could place significant limitations on the tenant for life to manage the settled land and in this way a deceased settlor could effectively fetter the management of the land for many years. One of the aims of the Settled Land Act 1925 was to free this 'dead man's grip' on the management of the land. To this end, the Settled Land Act 1925 s.106 provides that any provision in a settlement that purports or attempts to prohibit or prevent a tenant for life from exercising their statutory powers, or which attempts or is intended to induce a tenant for life from exercising their statutory powers is void. An example of this can be seen where a settlor attempts to place a condition of occupation within the settlement so that, if the tenant for life ceases to reside on the settled land, they will forfeit their interest. If the reason for the tenant for life ceasing to reside on the land is because they have exercised their statutory powers – for instance, by selling or leasing – the tenant for life will retain their interest. **Re Paget** (1885) 30 Ch D 161; **Re Gibbons** [1920] 1 Ch 372.

The principal checks and balances with regard to the tenant for life exercising their statutory powers arise in two ways:

(i) If the tenant for life wishes to sell, exchange, lease, mortgage/charge or grant an option with regard to the settled land, they must give notice to the trustees of the settlement: Settled Land Act 1925 s.101(1).

(ii) If the tenant for life wishes to exercise certain other powers – to dispose of the principal mansion house (including any of the grounds), cut and sell timber, compromise and settle disputes relating to any part of the settled land, or sell chattels – they may not do so without the consent of the trustees of the settlement or of the court. The reason for the extra protection afforded here is that such actions are likely to have a long-term effect and compromise the settled land for the tenant for life's successors: Settled Land Act 1925 ss.65–67.

The role and duties of the trustees of the settlement

As already stated, the role of the trustees of the settlement is principally of a supervisory nature. Central to this is the requirement under s.101 above that the tenant for life must give one month's notice of their intention to exercise their statutory powers. It is possible for the trustees to waive the one month's notice and accept notice of less than a month. The provision is weakened somewhat, however, in that a tenant for life does not have to give notice of their specific intentions since s.101(2) provides that the notice may be of a general intention to exercise their powers, though by s.101(3) a tenant for life must furnish a trustee with such particulars or information as may reasonably be required by the trustee from time to time. It should be noted that the ability to give notice of a general intention does not apply with regards to the intention of the tenant for life to mortgage the settled land; this must be specific. Whilst the tenant for life must give notice of the exercise of their statutory powers there is no obligation on the trustees of the settlement to intervene in any dealing proposed by the tenant for life.

There are two other important aspects to the requirement of notice. Firstly, the notice is not valid unless, at the date of the notice, the trustee is a trust corporation or the number of trustees is not less than two. Clearly, this is needed to ensure that the equitable interests are overreached. It will be recalled from Chapter 3 that, if a purchaser pays their purchase monies to a trust corporation or two trustees, the purchaser acquires the legal title free from all the equitable/beneficial interests existing in the land. Thus s.101(1) is designed to ensure that the requirements for overreaching are present. It will be noted that the purchaser must pay the purchase price to the trustees of the settlement rather than the tenant for life so as to ensure that it is not possible for the tenant for life to make off with the proceeds to the detriment of the other beneficiaries.

A second important aspect as far as a purchaser of the settled land is concerned is that s.101(5) provides that a person dealing in good faith with the tenant for life is not concerned as to whether the tenant for life has complied with the procedural requirements for the giving of notice.

Protecting the beneficiaries

Beneficiaries are protected in a number of ways since, as we have seen, the role of the trustees of the settlement is to police the settlement and the conduct of the tenant for life. This is done by way of the notice and consent requirements considered above. Additionally, the overreaching provisions and the requirement that a purchaser of settled land must pay the capital monies to two trustees of the settlement ensure that capital monies are secure.

The Settled Land Act 1925 also provides two other mechanisms in s.13 and s.18 that give a degree of protection. On the face of things, these mechanisms appear quite powerful, but in practice they are limited.

Firstly, in relation to s.13 we have seen that, to create a settlement inter vivos, two documents are required: a vesting deed and a trust instrument. It will be recalled that the purpose of the former is to vest the settled land in the tenant for life. Section 13 provides that until a vesting deed is executed by a tenant for life (or other statutory owner) no disposition of a legal estate shall take effect to transfer the legal title to a prospective purchaser. In such a case, the disposition by the tenant for life will only take effect as a contract to carry out the transaction for valuable consideration. Section 13 is thus a 'paralysing section' preventing the disposal of the legal estate until a vesting deed has been executed. This is all well and good; however, s.13 is subject to four exceptions, the most important of which is that it does not apply where a disposition is made to a purchaser of a legal estate without notice of the lack of a vesting deed. Since the innocent purchaser will still acquire the legal estate, it can quickly be seen that the protection afforded by s.13 as far as the beneficiaries are concerned is limited at best.

Secondly, once the vesting deed has been executed, then the tenant for life or statutory owner has the legal estate. Even so, they are clearly not able to deal with it freely since they can only exercise the statutory powers conferred by the Settled Land Act 1925, together with any additional powers conferred on them by the trust instrument. By s.18, if the tenant for life attempts to dispose of the property in contravention of the Settled Land Act 1925, their disposition is void except to the extent that the tenant for life's own beneficial interest is bound by the disposition. Thus the disposition will only operate to give a purchaser the tenant for life's own beneficial/equitable interests.

Weston v Henshaw [1950] Ch 510

In this case, a father sold his land to his son but later re-purchased it. In his will, the father created a settlement so that the land went to his son for life, with remainder to his grandson. When the father died, the son became the tenant for life and, once the executors had made a vesting deed, held the legal title. The son then took out a mortgage for his own personal needs. This was outside of the powers of the Settled Land Act 1925 s.71, which provides that the power to mortgage must be with a view to paying for any improvements authorised by the Act. The son obtained the mortgage by only showing to the mortgagee the original title he held when he purchased the property from his father.

It was held that the improper mortgage was void so that the grandson was not bound by the mortgage and the mortgagee lost their security on the mortgage.

In the above case, there was clearly a fraud exercised by the son. However, under normal circumstances a purchaser would inspect the vesting deed and this would alert them to the need to ensure that the tenant for life was acting in a manner authorised by the Act or the additional powers conferred on them. Nevertheless, the facts of **Weston v Henshaw** demonstrate that a concerted effort by a tenant for life can pose a risk to a purchaser.

Protecting the purchaser

Apart from the overreaching arrangements, which we have already examined, the Settled Land Act 1925 s.110 provides purchasers with another protection measure. Section 110 provides that, where a purchaser deals with the tenant for life or statutory owner in good faith then against everyone entitled under the settlement (i.e. the tenant for life and persons entitled in remainder), the purchaser is conclusively taken as having given the best consideration reasonably obtainable and as having complied with all the provisions of the Settled Land Act 1925. Section 110 only provides protection where the transaction is authorised by the Act or where there is some minor procedural defect. The provision will not protect a purchaser if the transaction is wholly outside the powers of the tenant – hence the mortgagee in **Weston v Henshaw** could not rely on s.110 to protect them.

Trusts for sale

Introduction

Trusts for sale were the second method of regulating successive interests in land prior to TOLATA 1996 but, unlike strict settlements, they were allowed to continue following the passing of TOLATA. Trusts for sale stood outside the Settled Land Act 1925, which governs strict settlements, as the Act specifically excluded 'immediate binding trusts for sale' from the definition of a strict settlement.

For a trust for sale to exist there had to be a 'trust for sale', that is the trustees were under a duty to sell the land, though under the Law of Property Act 1925, the trustees had a power to postpone the sale. If no duty to sell was imposed then a strict settlement was created instead. Similarly, it was important that there was an 'immediate' trust for sale and thus a trust for sale to take effect in the future could not be a trust for sale and, again, a strict settlement arose since there was no such limitation on these settlements. The trust for sale had to be 'binding' in the sense that it had to be capable of binding the whole of the legal estate.

It is important to note that *express* trusts for sale are now regulated by TOLATA 1996, which introduced a new 'trust of land' regime. TOLATA 1996 therefore governs both trusts for sale and trusts of land. It must be emphasised that a new trust for sale can only arise if it is created expressly, otherwise a successive interest must exist as a trust of land. The position can be seen in Figures 10.7 and 10.8.

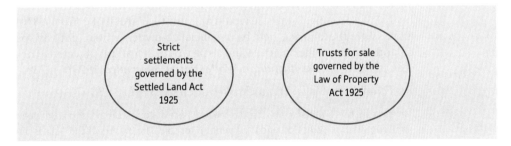

Figure 10.7 Successive interests pre-1996 position

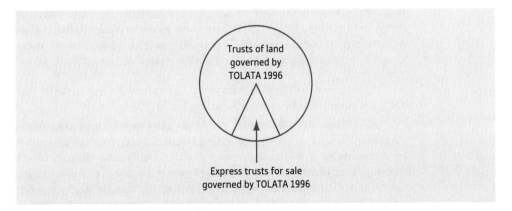

Figure 10.8 Successive interests post-1996 position

The differences between trusts of land and trusts for sale are negligible, though the dominant regime is one of trusts of land. However, before embarking on an examination of trusts of land, it is worth looking at some of the differences that do exist between trusts for sale and trusts of land.

The trustees for sale

As we stated earlier, the central feature of a trust for sale is that the trustees are under a *duty* to sell the land. Usually, the deed creating the trust provided the trustees with a *power* to postpone a sale. However, in the absence of such a power, the Law of Property Act 1925 s.25 implied a power to postpone a sale in any event. TOLATA 1996 also implies such a power in s.4(1) though the power exists here even if there is an express provision to the contrary. The result of this is that trustees for sale cannot be liable in any way, even if they decide to exercise their power to postpone sale indefinitely – TOLATA 1996 s.4(1).

There is a difference between the concept of a trust for sale pre-TOLATA and the new trust of land regime now in force. Under a trust for sale, the duty is imposed on all the trustees and so, if the majority of trustees wish to postpone the sale but a minority do not, the land *must* be sold. The position therefore is that, if the trustees wish to exercise their discretionary power to postpone sale, they must act with unanimity. In a trust for land, however, there is no duty to sell, assuming there is no express trust for sale. Consequently, if the trustees wish to sell, this amounts to an exercise of their discretionary power and they must act unanimously.

Clearly, then, prior to TOLATA 1996, it was possible for a minority of trustees to enforce a sale of the land, though this was subject to two provisos. The minority could not compel a sale if this was, firstly, contrary to the spirit or object for which the land was purchased or held; and, secondly, if the sale would amount to a breach of contract. The positions often arose where the land was held by beneficial co-owners who might have purchased a piece of land with a specific objective and a sale would defeat this objective. The principle can be seen in the case of *Re Buchanan-Wollaston's Conveyance* [1929] Ch 738.

Re Buchanan-Wollaston's Conveyance [1939] Ch 738

In this case there were four houses on the seashore at Lowestoft in Suffolk. Between the four houses and the sea was a piece of land that went up for sale. The owners of the houses became concerned that, if the land was sold to a developer, any new development would take away their view, with the consequence that the value of their respective properties would be devalued. The four owners came together and bought the piece of land jointly as tenants in common. All was well and they preserved their view of the sea until one of the owners subsequently sold his house and moved away. Since he no longer had any use for the land in front of the house, he requested that the land be sold so that he could realise his share. The other co-owners resisted this but of course, under a trust for sale, their duty was to sell and they could only postpone sale if all four acted unanimously.

Sir Wilfred Greene in In the Court of Appeal upheld the first instance decision of Farwell J that a sale should not be enforced, stating (at 747):

In the present case, Farwell J . . . gave a perfectly definite and unhesitating answer to [the question], with which I entirely agree. He said in effect 'Here is a person who has contracted with others for a particular purpose, and the effect of the contract is to impose upon the power of the trustees to sell this land, certain restrictions . . . It is not right that the court of equity should in those circumstances, on the invitation of a person who has not acted in accordance with the contract, and is opposed by other persons interested, exercise the power of the Court and make an order for sale.'

Thus a sale would not be ordered where the underlying purpose for the original purchase continued.

A trust of land, however, is not a trust for sale and is a great deal more neutral in its approach to the enforcement of such since there is no duty to sell. Under TOLATA 1996 s.14(1) the court may order a postponement of sale against the wishes of either the majority or minority of the trustees on any application of a person who is a trustee of land or has an interest in the land subject to the trust. In s.15(1) the Act sets out the matters which the court can take into account in deciding whether or not to order a sale: the intention of the person(s) who created the trust; the purposes for which the property subject to the trust is held; the welfare of any minor who occupies or who may reasonably be expected to occupy any land subject to the trust; and the interests of any secured creditor of any beneficiary.

The doctrine of conversion

The maxim of equity is that 'equity looks on that as done that ought to be done'. The effect of this maxim on a trust for sale pre-1997 was that, since there was a duty to sell, this had already been done as it 'ought to be done'. The result of this was that the interests of the beneficiaries lay not in the land but in the proceeds of sale and thus their interest lay in personalty, not realty. It did not matter whether the land was sold or not; that is where the interests of the beneficiaries lay. Over the years, this position became unsustainable, particularly with regard to such areas as the family home. The idea that a couple who bought a house together and therefore, as co-owners, held the legal title on trust for themselves under an implied trust for sale, had an interest in the proceeds of sale rather than in the land itself, was clearly an aberration, since they had purchased the house to live in, not to sell it. This position was rectified by TOLATA 1996 s.3(1) which abolished the doctrine with respect to express trusts for sale so that the land was not regarded as personalty in the proceeds of sale.

Trusts of land

Introduction

Trusts of land were introduced as a completely new trust by TOLATA 1996. Trusts of land are defined in s.1(1)a as follows:

> 'trust of land' means any trust of property which consists of or includes land.

Section 1(2)a provides that a trust in s.1(1)a refers to any description of a trust, whether express, implied, resulting or constructive, including trusts for sale and bare trusts.

As we have already seen, TOLATA 1996 s.2(1) provided that no new settlements could be created and any attempt to create a settlement would take effect as a trust of land. Similarly, a trust of land encompasses trusts for sale within its definition so, while it is still possible to create an express trust for sale, this falls within the ambit of TOLATA 1996.

The result, therefore, is that a trust of land will apply where there is a trust of successive interests, as in a settlement (i.e. to W for life, remainder to B), or where there is a trust of concurrent interests, as where two or more persons buy a house together, provided the trust 'consists of or includes land'. All are subject to the legal regime set out in TOLATA 1996.

Creation of a trust of land

By the Law of Property Act 1925 s.53(1)b a 'declaration of a trust respecting land or any interest therein must be manifested and proved by some writing signed by some person who is able to declare such trust or by his will'. Thus the creation of the trust must be evidenced in writing; however, the declaration itself need not be in writing and indeed can be made orally, provided it is supported by some written acknowledgement – for instance, a letter. The writing and the declaration of trust do not have to be contemporaneous with each other: *Rochefoucauld v Bowstead* [1897] 1 Ch 196. Failure to comply with the requirements of s.53(1)b renders the declaration unenforceable, not void.

Not all trusts of land have to comply with s.53(1)b as s.53(1)c provides that resulting, implied and constructive trusts are exempt as these arise by operation of law.

Trusts created by will must comply with the Wills Act 1837 – that is, they must be in writing, signed by the testator or by someone in his presence and by his direction. The signature must be made or acknowledged in the presence of two witnesses who must then sign in the presence of the testator.

Powers and duties of trustees under TOLATA

General powers

The main power of trustees is found in s.6(1) which provides that trustees of land have authority to exercise 'all the powers of an absolute owner'. The effect is that the trustees can deal with the property as if it were their own, subject to any express provision made in the disposition (s.8(1)). Thus under TOLATA 1996 trustees are free of the restrictions that we saw under strict settlements and the old trusts for sale.

Specific powers

In addition to the trustees having the power of an absolute owner, TOLATA also provides the trustees with specific powers.

The power to buy, lease and mortgage land

By s.6(3), as amended by the Trustee Act 2000 s.8, a trustee may acquire freehold or leasehold land in the United Kingdom, whether as an investment, for occupation by a beneficiary, or for any other reason. Importantly, trustees are able to raise a mortgage for the purchase of land. This contrasts sharply with the position before TOLATA; in particular, under the Settled Land Act 1925, the power to raise money by mortgage was, inter alia, confined to the carrying out of repairs.

Under the pre-1997 law, the power of trustees to acquire land was very limited, unless expressly allowed in the trust instrument. In particular, trustees could not purchase land for occupation by a beneficiary. This made it difficult, for instance, if a beneficiary was a widow and left in a large house which was clearly too big for her – both as a place of residence and to maintain. Trustees in this situation could sell the house but they were not empowered to purchase another property for occupation by the widow. Similarly, trustees were not able to take leases of property for more than 50 years, the reason being that a long lease could bind the trust far into the future and affect those entitled in remainder where there was settlement. TOLATA therefore stands in freeing up the powers of trustees.

In buying, leasing or mortgaging land, trustees are required, unless exempt by the trust instrument, to comply with the duty of care set out in the Trustee Act 2000 s.1(1) which provides:

Whenever the duty . . . applies to a trustee, he must exercise such care and skill as is reasonable in the circumstances, having regard in particular –

(a) to any special knowledge or experience that he has or holds himself out as having, and
(b) if he acts as a trustee in the course of a business or profession, to any special knowledge or experience that it is reasonable to expect of a person acting in the course of that kind of business or profession.

The power to partition

Section 7 provides:

The trustees of land may, where the beneficiaries of full age are absolutely entitled in individual shares to land subject to the trust, partition the land, or any part of it . . .

The effect of this provision is that trustees have the power to divide up the land and convey to each beneficiary their own separate, physical portion of the land, thus destroying the co-ownership relationship between the beneficiaries. The conditions required for partition should be noted; furthermore, before the trustees can partition, s.7(3) provides that the trustees must obtain the consent of the beneficiaries.

As can be seen from s.7(1), this power can be expressly excluded by the trust instrument.

Compulsory conveyance to the beneficiaries

By s.6(2), the trustees have the right to demand that the beneficiaries should have the legal estate conveyed to them and thereby terminate the trust, even if the beneficiaries have not required the trustees to do so. The beneficiaries must be of full age and capacity and be absolutely entitled to the land. The beneficiaries are required to do whatever is necessary to ensure that the legal title vests in them, thus preventing the beneficiaries obstructing the trustees from this action. If the beneficiaries fail to ensure that the legal title vests in them, then the court can compel them to do so by court order. If the conveyance is to two or more beneficiaries then, as per co-ownership of land, they will hold the legal title on trust for themselves. If the conveyance is to one beneficiary then that person will become absolutely entitled to the land in question.

The power to delegate

The general rule as regards the office of trustee is that it cannot be delegated – delegatus non potest delegare – however, TOLATA 1996 and the Trustee Delegation Act 1999 provide an exception to this principle. Delegation may arise by way of individual delegation by a trustee or by way of collective delegation. It should be noted that the duty of care in the Trustee Act 2000 applies to trustees in deciding to delegate their functions.

Individual delegation

The Trustee Delegation Act 1999 provides that, unless there is intention expressed in the instrument, a trustee who is also a beneficial owner may individually, by way of power of attorney, delegate any or all of his or her functions as a trustee. This power to delegate is confined to trustees of land and may apply to the land itself, the proceeds of sale of land or the income from land.

As indicated earlier, delegation can only be used if the trustee (i.e. the donor of the power) has a beneficial interest in the property. An example of the power therefore could arise in the case of a husband and wife who own their own home and hold the legal estate on trust for themselves. It is possible that the husband might wish to make a power of attorney in favour of his wife, so that if he became mentally incapable, his wife could deal with the co-owned land. Prior to the Trustee Delegation Act 1999 this would not have been possible, because the trustee was not able to delegate his functions to another trustee, the wife. The husband would have had to give the power to a third party. Section 1 of the 1999 Act now permits the husband to delegate any of his functions as a trustee to any person of his choosing.

A person, such as a purchaser, dealing with a donee of a power of attorney under s.1 (i.e. the wife above) needs to know that the donor of the power has a beneficial interest in the land, but investigating the title to a beneficial interest can be difficult. To overcome this problem, s.2(1)–(3) of the Act provides that, in favour of a purchaser, a signed statement by the donee made at the time of the exercise of the function, or within three months thereafter, that the donor had the beneficial interest is conclusive evidence of that fact.

Before moving on to look at collective delegation, it is worthwhile noting that, on a sale of land, for overreaching to apply a purchaser must obtain a valid receipt, signed by two trustees, for the capital monies. Where a trustee has delegated his powers to a co-trustee under a power of attorney, that single co-trustee acting in two capacities cannot give such a valid receipt.

Collective delegation

By TOLATA 1996 s.9, trustees of land have the power to collectively delegate 'to any beneficiary or beneficiaries of full age and beneficially entitled to an interest in possession . . . any of their functions as trustees which relate to the land'. The power is subject to the trust and may be prohibited by the trust instrument. The power must be given by all the trustees; however, it can be revoked by any one or more of them, unless the power of attorney through which the delegation is made is expressed to be irrevocable. The delegation may be for a definite or for an indefinite period of time.

Whilst a beneficiary, as donee of the power, stands 'in the same position as trustees' and is thus subject to the same duties and liabilities, by s.9(7) such a beneficiary is not regarded as a trustee for any other purposes, particularly with regard to requirements relating to the payment of capital money.

When the trustees have collectively delegated any or all of their functions, they are required to review the delegation: s.9A(3)a and, in carrying out their review, again, the statutory duty of care under the Trustee Act 2000 s.1 applies. Provided the trustees comply with this duty, they will not be liable for the acts or defaults of the beneficiary or beneficiaries.

Duties of trustees

Apart from having general and specific powers, TOLATA 1996 imposes certain duties on trustees.

The duty to obtain consents

A settlor may impose on trustees a duty to obtain the consent of a named person or persons before the trustees exercise any specified acts – for instance, a sale of the land. If the trust instrument requires the consent of more than two persons, then the consent of any two of them for the exercise of the function is sufficient in favour of the purchaser. It should be noted, though, that whilst this protects a purchaser of the land, trustees are still liable for breach of trust for failing to obtain the requisite consents. Consents can be a useful way of ensuring that a beneficiary is able to retain occupation so long as he or she is required to give consent to a sale by the trustees.

The duty to consult the beneficiaries

Section 11(1) provides:

> The trustees of land shall in the exercise of any function relating to land subject to the trust –
>
> (a) so far as practicable, consult the beneficiaries of full age and beneficially entitled to an interest in possession in the land, and
> (b) so far as consistent with the general interest of the trust, give effect to the wishes of those beneficiaries, or (in case of dispute) of the majority (according to the value of their combined interests).

The duty is clearly not an absolute one since the trustees are only required to consult 'so far as practicable' and only then with beneficiaries who are of full age and who are beneficially entitled to an interest in possession in the land. Having consulted the beneficiaries, the trustees do not necessarily have to apply any recommendations or comments made by the beneficiaries in response to the consultation unless they are 'consistent with the general interest of the trust'. Where the wishes of the beneficiaries are so consistent but the beneficiaries are in disagreement, then the trustees should apply the wishes of the majority, according to the value of their combined interests. The majority therefore is not assessed by a poll or on a 'show of hands'. There is no duty to consult a beneficiary who is also a trustee, apparently: ***Notting Hill Housing Association v Brackley*** [2002] HLR 10. The duty to consult may be limited or excluded by an express provision in the instrument creating the trust.

With regard to trusts arising prior to the 1996 Act, in the case of implied, resulting and constructive trusts the duty to consult is imposed by TOLATA; however, with regard to trusts created by will, no duty to consult is imposed. In the case of express trusts created inter vivos, no duty to consult is imposed unless the settlor executes a deed declaring that the duty to consult will apply.

Rights of beneficiaries

We saw earlier that the view of land as a commercial/financial entity based on the proceeds of sale began to evolve into that of an entity based on enjoyment or use of the land. This 'emancipation' evolved over many years and, as it evolved, the rights of the beneficiaries also developed. The result of this was the wresting of control and management of the land from the trustees. Eventually, this evolution culminated in the passing of TOLATA 1996, where the rights of beneficiaries were given formal statutory recognition, while ensuring that a balance was maintained with the trustees who moved more towards a supervisory role in which they had to have regard to the rights of the beneficiaries.

It should be noted that the rights of the beneficiaries are concomitant with the duties of trustees and these are in addition to the rights of the beneficiaries below.

The right to occupy trust land

Prior to TOLATA 1996 the doctrine of conversion meant that the rights of the beneficiaries lay in personalty – the proceeds of sale – and not in realty, the land itself. The effect of this was that beneficiaries had no rights of occupation and, until the land itself was sold, they were only entitled to the rents and profits from the land. As we saw earlier, this approach became increasingly unsustainable as the social view of occupation changed so that the courts moved away from archaic doctrine that existed under the trust for sale. The principles developed by the courts were ad hoc and can be seen, for example, in the case of ***Bull v Bull*** [1955] 1 QB 234 where Lord Denning considered that a beneficiary had a right of occupation over and above the duty to sell if the purpose of residential use was the 'prime object of the trust'. In this way the courts evaded the principles of the trust for sale; however, the position was never really satisfactory and TOLATA 1996 provides a coherent approach to this issue. Before embarking on an examination of s.12, it should be noted that a right of occupation of a person holding an equitable interest in the land can have important connotations since it will be binding against third party purchasers as an interest that is overriding under the Land Registration Act 1996 Schedule 1 and 3 para 3.

Section 12 provides:

(1) A beneficiary who is beneficially entitled to an interest in possession in land subject to a trust of land is entitled by reason of his interest to occupy the land at any time if at that time –
  (a) the purposes of the trust include making the land available for his occupation (or for the occupation of beneficiaries of a class of which he is a member or of beneficiaries in general), or
  (b) the land is held by the trustees so as to be so available.

(2) Subsection (1) does not confer on a beneficiary a right to occupy land if it is either unavailable or unsuitable for occupation by him.

(3) This section is subject to section 13.

Thus a beneficiary who is entitled to an interest in possession has a general right of occupation. The right of occupation, however, is subject to certain limitations in that the entitlement to occupy is only available if the purpose of the trust is to 'include making the land available for his occupation'. From this one can see that the provision appears to embody the 'prime object of the trust' approach, as seen in *Bull v Bull* [1955] 1 QB. Thus, if the trust is formed in such a way that it envisages one or more of the beneficiaries would remain in residential occupation, such as a widow, then the trustees would have to accede to the entitlement of the beneficiary. On the other hand, if the prime object is to realise the capital, then the trustees would dispose of the land and distribute the proceeds, like personal representatives winding up an estate on the death of a testator. The case of *Barclay v Barclay* [1970] 2 QB 677 serves as an example of the type of situation in which the trustees might deny a right of occupation to a beneficiary.

Barclay v *Barclay* [1970] 2 QB 677

A testator left his bungalow to five beneficiaries under his will. The property was left with an instruction that, on his death, the property was to be sold and divided amongst the beneficiaries. One of the beneficiaries had been living in the bungalow at the time of the testator's death and continued in occupation afterwards. The beneficiary brought an action with a view to remaining in the property, thus postponing the sale.

The Court of Appeal held that the property should be sold and distinguished the case from *Bull v Bull*. Here it was made quite clear by the testator that the prime purpose of the trust was for the bungalow to be sold. As the purpose was not to provide a home for the beneficiaries, the beneficiary could not establish a right to remain in the property.

In addition to the above limitation, the trustees only need to accede to the right of occupation by a beneficiary if the property is available for occupation. Thus, for example, if the property has a tenant in it, the property is clearly not available for occupation. Similarly, a beneficiary has no right of occupation if the property is unsuitable – if, for instance, as we saw earlier, the house is large and rambling, it would be unsuitable for occupation by an elderly widow on her own. In deciding whether the property is unsuitable it was held in **Chan v Leung** [2003] 1 FLR 23 that regard should be had to the general physical characteristics of the property and the personal circumstances of the beneficiary. Another consideration might be the personalities of the different beneficiaries occupying the premises. If the personalities are such that the occupiers would be in conflict, occupation by one or all of the beneficiaries may be inappropriate.

Apart from the limitations set out above, s.13 allows the trustees to exclude or restrict the right of occupation. Section 13 provides:

(1) Where two or more beneficiaries are (or apart from this subsection would be) entitled under section 12 to occupy land, the trustees of land may exclude or restrict the entitlement of any one or more (but not all) of them.

(2) Trustees may not under subsection (1) –
    (a) unreasonably exclude any beneficiary's entitlement to occupy land, or
    (b) restrict any such entitlement to an unreasonable extent.

(3) The trustees of land may from time to time impose reasonable conditions on any beneficiary in relation to his occupation of land by reason of his entitlement under section 12.

As can be seen, if there are two or more beneficiaries with a right of occupation then the trustees may exclude one or more but not ALL of them. In any event, the decision to exclude must not be exercised unreasonably and in particular, by s.13(7)a, trustees may not exclude a person who is already in occupation, either by way of the right of occupation under s.12 or for any other reason – i.e. if a person is in occupation because the property is the family home and the occupier, for example a wife, has an entitlement under the Family Law Act 1996. Furthermore, the trustees must not exercise their discretion in a manner that is likely to result in a person in occupation ceasing to occupy the land, unless that person consents or the court approves of the trustees' actions: s.13(7)b. The court must have regard to the factors in s.13(4) – see below – in giving its approval or not to the exercise of the trustees' discretion.

It can also be seen that trustees may impose reasonable conditions on a person occupying the premises. Section 13(5) provides that trustees may require a beneficiary to pay any outgoings or expenses, or assume any obligations in relation to the land or any other activity that might take place there.

Of course, if one beneficiary is allowed to occupy and another is excluded, this might result in a detriment being incurred by the excluded beneficiary. With regard to this, s.13(6) allows the trustees to impose conditions on the occupier that require him or her to pay compensation to the excluded beneficiary. For instance, the trustees could require the occupier to pay rent to the excluded beneficiary. Alternatively, the trustees may impose a condition that an occupier is required to forgo any payment or other benefit that he or she would otherwise be entitled to.

Section 13(4) provides guidance to the trustees in exercising their powers under this provision. Thus the trustees must take into account:

(a) the intention of the person or persons who created the trust;

(b) the purposes for which the land is held; and

(c) the circumstances and wishes of each of the beneficiaries who is entitled to occupy the land under section 12.

The right to appoint and remove trustees

Generally speaking beneficiaries do not have the power to appoint or remove trustees under the law of trusts unless such a power is expressly conferred upon them. Under TOLATA

1996 s.19 beneficiaries under a trust of land who act unanimously and who are of full age and capacity and absolutely entitled to the property subject to the trust may give directions:

(a) to a trustee or trustees to retire from the trust, and

(b) to the trustees or trustee for the time being (if none to the personal representative of the last person who was a trustee) to appoint by writing to the person or persons nominated in their direction to be appointed as a trustee or trustees.

The direction or directions given by the beneficiaries must be in writing. The rights of the beneficiaries to remove or appoint are only exercisable if there is no other person nominated under the trust instrument (if any) for the purpose of appointing a new trustee. It should be noted that the trust instrument may exclude this statutory right of the beneficiaries.

The rights of beneficiaries under s.19 are in addition to the rights of beneficiaries under the rule in *Saunders* v *Vautier* which we examined in Chapter 2.

The right to the proceeds of sale

It will be recalled that, when the land is sold and the beneficial interests are overreached, the interests of the beneficiaries are deflected into the proceeds of sale. The beneficiaries are therefore entitled to the proceeds of sale; however, this can amount to different things, depending on the classification of the beneficiaries. Thus, if the trust of land arises out of co-ownership the beneficiaries will be entitled to their appropriate share, depending on whether they hold as joint tenants or tenants in common. On the other hand, where there are successive interests, the tenant for life is not entitled to the capital monies, but only to the income generated from the capital monies. The tenant for life is therefore an 'income beneficiary'. The beneficiary entitled in remainder, the 'capital beneficiary', may take the capital monies, but only on the death of the tenant for life. Trustees have a duty when investing to take into account the different interests of the life tenant and the remainderman and have regard to the standard investment criteria contained in the Trustee Act 2000 s.4.

Dispute resolution by the courts in relation to trusts of land
Under TOLATA 1996

Whilst the courts have always had the ability to carry out their inherent jurisdiction to resolve disputes, the Law of Property Act 1925 s.30 provided a statutory jurisdiction to resolve disputes in relation to trusts of land. The machinery for dispute resolution in relation to trusts of land is now contained in TOLATA 1996 s.14 and s.15. In the past, many of the disputes arose out of the duty to sell and the discretion to postpone sale under trusts for sale; however, under TOLATA, as we have seen, the position of the trustees is a great deal more neutral as they have no duty to sell. The result of this is that the position of trustees under a trust of land is more uncertain and therefore there is more potential for matters to be brought before the courts. Whilst the dispute resolution machinery is applied in relation to disputes between the legal owners and equitable owners, generally, in relation to trusts of land, many of the disputes arise out of co-ownership situations, particularly with regard to cohabitees. The machinery casts its net wider, though, and to that extent the machinery may be utilised by creditors or trustees in bankruptcy.

The machinery for dispute resolution in relation to trusts of land is now contained within TOLATA 1996 s.14 and s.15. Section 14 provides details as to who can make an application to the court and the types of order a court may wish to apply. Section 15, on the other hand, contains the matters to which a court must have regard in relation to applications under s.14. We will consider each of these provisions in turn.

Section 14 provides:

(1) Any person who is a trustee of land or has an interest in property subject to a trust of land may make an application to the court for an order under this section.

(2) On an application for an order under this section the court may make any such order –
 (a) relating to the exercise by the trustees of any of their functions (including an order relieving them of any obligation to obtain the consent of, or to consult, any person in connection with the exercise of any of their functions), or
 (b) declaring the nature or extent of a person's interest in property subject to the trust, as the court thinks fit.

(3) The court may not under this section make any order as to the appointment or removal of trustees.

(4) The powers conferred on the court by this section are exercisable on an application whether it is made before or after the commencement of this Act.

It can be seen immediately from s.14(1) that the class of persons who can apply to the court is very wide indeed and is not confined to the trustees under the trust of land since the provision refers to any person who 'has an interest in the property subject to a trust of land'.

The provision therefore relates to:

- trustees of a trust of land;
- beneficiaries with interests in possession;
- mortgagees of land subject to a trust of land;
- creditors with a charge over the property;
- a trustee in bankruptcy of a beneficiary whether in possession or in remainder.

On the face of things, the provision relates to property which is subject to a trust of land and one may be forgiven for thinking this relates to land. In fact, it is far wider than this, since s.17(2) states that s.14 applies in relation to a trust of the proceeds of sale of land. Section 17(3) then provides that 'trust of the proceeds of sale of land' means any trust of property which consists of or includes any proceeds of a disposition of land held in trust or any property representing any such proceeds. Thus s.14 applies not just in relation to real property but also personal property, despite the fact that we are in the realms of trusts of land.

S.14(2) provides the court with discretion to make any order it thinks fit relating either to the trustees exercising their functions or to the nature or extent of a person's interest in property subject to the trust. This includes relieving the trustees of their duty to consult with or obtain the consent of any person connected with the property. Thus, the court is able to remove the need for trustees to obtain the consent of a beneficiary where that beneficiary refuses to provide consent or where the whereabouts of the beneficiary are unknown. The court also has the power to declare the nature or extent of a person's interest in the property subject to the trust. The court therefore has the power to settle disputes as to the relative shares belonging to each beneficiary subject to the trust.

In exercising its discretionary powers the court must have regard to the matters set out in s.15 which provides:

(1) The matters to which the court is to have regard in determining an application for an order under section 14 include –
 (a) the intentions of the person or persons (if any) who created the trust,
 (b) the purposes for which the property subject to the trust is held,
 (c) the welfare of any minor who occupies or might reasonably be expected to occupy any land subject to the trust as his home, and
 (d) the interests of any secured creditor of any beneficiary.

(2) In the case of an application relating to the exercise in relation to any land of the powers conferred on the trustees by section 13, the matters to which the court is to have regard also include the circumstances and wishes of each of the beneficiaries who is (or apart from any previous exercise by the trustees of those powers would be) entitled to occupy the land under section 12.

(3) In the case of any other application, other than one relating to the exercise of the power mentioned in section 6(2), the matters to which the court is to have regard also include the circumstances and wishes of any beneficiaries of full age and entitled to an interest in possession in property subject to the trust or (in case of dispute) of the majority (according to the value of their combined interests).

(4) This section does not apply to an application if section 335A of the Insolvency Act 1986 . . . applies to it.

It is clear that there will be situations in which the criteria in s.14(1) will conflict with one another, particularly with regard to (a) and (b) and, in those circumstances, the court will have to exercise its judgment as to which will prevail. This, however, applies in the wider sense as well; thus in **Mortgage Corporation v Shaire** [2001] Ch 743 Neuberger J considered that, once the relevant factors are taken into account – both those under s.15(1) and other factors that might impinge in a particular case – the court was free to give whatever emphasis it liked to each factor in reaching a decision. In making this decision, the courts have, by s.15(2), to take into account the circumstances and wishes of any beneficiaries who are entitled to occupy the land under s.12 (i.e. they have the right of occupation). In relation to any other application outside of s.12, the court must take into account the circumstances and wishes of any beneficiaries of full age and entitled in possession, or, in the case of a dispute, the circumstances and wishes of the majority according to the value of their combined interests. The decision by the court is, of course, not confined to whether to sell or not sell as the court can make any order it 'thinks fit'. Thus s.15 provides for wider discretion than the pre-TOLATA law contained in the Law of Property Act 1925 s.30 which was predisposed towards the sale of the property.

This was epitomised in the case of **Re Mayo** [1943] Ch 302.

Re Mayo [1943] Ch 302

Three trustees were in disagreement over whether or not to sell the land subject to a trust for sale. One trustee wanted to sell but was resisted by the remaining two, who wished to retain the land.

Held: The Court ordered that the land be sold, despite the wishes of the majority of the trustees. Under a trust for sale there was a duty to sell the property – this, after all, was the main purpose of a trust for sale. The power to postpone a sale could only be exercised if the trustees acted with unanimity.

The court under s.15 can order a sale but equally it might not, or it might order a sale but postpone it until some future date or the occurrence of some event – for example, any children gaining majority, in order to ensure that, until that point, the children have a roof over their heads. Equally, the court could order the land to be partitioned if the court considered this was a credible and viable option. The movement therefore from a trust for sale under the Law of Property Act 1925 to a trust of land under TOLATA 1996 has been profound. Certainly, the Law Commission in *Transfer of Land: Trusts of Land* (Law Com No. 181) 1989 stated that, 'a restructuring of the trust powers, and in particular the elimination of the duty to sell, should clear the way for a genuinely broad and flexible approach.

The courts will not be required to give preference to sale, and, in making orders, will not be restricted to making ones which are simply ancillary to sale.' That said, the Law Commission considered that the criteria that would eventually find their way into TOLATA 1996 and which the courts had 'evolved for settling disputes over trusts for sale are ones which will continue to have validity in the context of the new system'. Thus much of the case law that arose before the passing of TOLATA 1996 still has validity as exhibits of how the courts may exercise their discretion in the future. As Neuberger J stated in *Mortgage Corporation* v *Shaire* [2001] Ch 743 at 761:

> . . . to throw over all the wealth of learning and thought given by so many eminent judges to the problem which is raised on an application for sale of a house where competing interests exist seems somewhat arrogant and possibly rash. On the other hand, where one has concluded that the law has changed in a significant respect so that the court's discretion is significantly less fettered than it was, there are obvious dangers in relying on authorities which proceeded on the basis that the court's discretion was more fettered than it now is. I think it would be wrong to throw over all the earlier cases without paying them any regard. However, they have to be treated with caution, in the light of the change in the law, and in many cases they are unlikely to be of great, let alone decisive, assistance.

It is useful to examine the criteria set out in s.15(1) in order to see how they may be applied, though it must be stressed, as stated earlier, that the criteria should not place a straitjacket on the discretion of the courts and the criteria may be applied singly, together or in the context of other relevant circumstances that may arise in individual cases.

'The intentions of the person . . . who created the trust' – s.15(1)a

A prime example of the application of this criterion can be seen in the case of *Barclay* v *Barclay* [1970] 2 QB 677 where the testator made it clear that on his death the property was to be sold and divided amongst the beneficiaries. Thus, despite the fact that one of the beneficiaries had occupied the property during the lifetime of the testator and wished to continue to live in the property, the Court of Appeal considered that the intentions of the testator were decisive and ordered that the property be sold.

'The purposes for which the property subject to the trust is held' – s.15(b)

This has always been an important consideration for the court to take into account. It should be noted that the purposes can arise expressly between the parties, as in *Re Buchanan-Wollaston's Conveyance* [1939] Ch 738, which we have already considered, or informally. In a way the provision is a type of statutory estoppel where the parties, having bought property with a particular purpose in mind, may be prevented from substituting that purpose with something else so that the property is either sold or not. Of course, circumstances change and what may be a perfectly sound and reasonable objective for the setting up of the trust of land in the first instance may be overturned by subsequent events. Many cases in this area arise in the context of the family home and the breakdown of relationships. A word of warning is required here as cases involving the matrimonial home today are largely governed by family divorce law and the rights of the parties have changed in line with changes to family law, where the courts have extensive powers to make property adjustment orders. Some of the cases pre-date TOLATA 1996, where married couples were treated much as cohabitees. Thus many of the cases arising today are concerned with cohabitation (which is more prevalent today anyway) than with married couples – but, of course, not exclusively so, since trusts of land arise in a myriad of different situations.

Jones v Challenger [1961] 1 QB

In this case a married couple purchased a house together but later they split up and the wife went to live with another man. Her husband remained in the house. The wife applied for an order of sale which was resisted by the husband as he wished to continue to live in the property.

The Court of Appeal held that the house was acquired as the matrimonial home but, unlike in **Re Buchanan-Wollaston's Conveyance**, with the end of the marriage the purpose for purchasing the house was dissolved and thus the primacy of the duty to sell under the Law of Property Act 1925 s.30 as a trust for sale was restored and the house should be sold.

Re Evers' Trust [1980] 1 WLR 1327

A couple cohabiting together bought a house as joint tenants for themselves and three children. The relationship broke down and the father left. The rest of the family continued to live in the house. The father then applied for an order of sale under the Law of Property Act 1925 s.30.

The Court of Appeal refused to give an order for sale. The couple had purchased the property as a family home for themselves and the three children. The father's contribution was less than the mother's contribution and amounted to less than one-fifth of the purchase price, whilst the mother had invested virtually all her capital in the property. The court found that the underlying purpose of the trust for sale was to provide a home for the whole family for an indefinite period. The mother was prepared to meet the mortgage repayments but would have found it difficult to raise the money to buy out the father or meet the costs of purchasing another property. There was no evidence that the father needed to realise his investment in the property. The court held that, whilst it would be wrong to order a sale at the time, the circumstances might change, so that when the youngest child reaches the age of 16 or the mother re-marries, or becomes able to buy out the father, then at that time an order of sale might be appropriate.

Stott v Ratcliffe (1982) 126 Sol Jo 310

In this case a son was persuaded by his father to give up his job and then contribute towards the purchase of the father's house. The expectation was that, by making this contribution, the son would be able to live in the house for the rest of his life. The father then died and his widow succeeded to the father's share in the property. The widow applied for an order of sale. The court refused the order on the basis that it would be inequitable to defeat the object of the original agreement, which was to provide the son with a place to live in the long term.

'The welfare of any minor who occupies or might reasonably be expected to occupy any land subject to the trust on his home' – s.15(1)c

If there are any children occupying the property (or they might reasonably be expected to do so) then TOLATA 1996 clearly provides that their interests should be afforded special protection. Previously, the presence of children was regarded as merely being incidental to the decision as to whether to order a sale or not. As seen already in **Re Evers' Trust**, the welfare of children is regarded as important, though only to the extent of postponing the inevitable sale once they become 18. Again, however, this very much depends on the individual circumstances of the case. In **Bank of Ireland Home Mortgages v Bell** [2001] 2 FLR 809 it was held that the interests of a child who was almost 18 would be given relatively little consideration by the court in considering whether or not to order a sale.

The position of children can be seen clearly in **Rawlings v Rawlings** [1964] P 398 in which Salmon LJ stated:

If there were young children, the position would be different. One of the purposes of the trust would no doubt have been to provide a home for them, and whilst that purpose still existed a sale would generally not be ordered. But when those children are grown up and the marriage is dead, the purposes of the trust have failed.

The overriding factor is the need to provide a home for children and thus the same principles would apply if grandparents looked after their grandchildren: *First National Bank* v *Achampong* [2003] EWCA Civ 487.

'The interests of any secured creditor of any beneficiary' – s.15(1)d

So far the criteria the courts consider in s.15 with regards to the determination of an order under s.14 have been very much concerned with the relationship between the parties themselves, their circumstances and the presence of children. However, s.15(1)d introduces consideration of the needs of secured creditors who might wish the property to be sold in order to recover their security.

Prior to TOLATA, the cases indicate that in exercising their discretion under the Law of Property Act 1925 s.30 courts would always prioritise the interests of a secured creditor over the interest of the beneficiaries, including their children, unless there were exceptional circumstances: *Lloyds Bank plc* v *Byrne & Byrne* [1991] 23 HLR 472; *Abbey National plc* v *Moss* [1994] 26 HLR 249. Following TOLATA 1996, the position with regards to secured creditors became very much more neutral and the primacy previously given to secured creditors was removed.

Mortgage Corporation v *Shaire* [2001] Ch 743

In this case, Mrs Shaire and her partner Mr Fox purchased a house together as cohabitees to provide a home for themselves and Mrs Shaire's son from her previous marriage. Mrs Shaire had a 75% share of the equitable interest and Mr Fox the remaining 25%. On the death of Mr Fox, it transpired that he had secretly mortgaged his 25% share by forging Mrs Shaire's signature on the mortgage documents. The mortgage company then sought an order of sale under s.14 in order to recover its security under the mortgage, which was in arrears.

The court held that, since Mrs Shaire was not responsible for the actions of Mr Fox, her share would not be the subject of the mortgage. On the other hand, Mr Fox's share could be recovered by the mortgagee if the property was sold.

Neuberger J considered that s.15(1) had changed the law that existed before TOLATA 1996 in that, under the previous legal regime, a sale would always be ordered where there was an application for sale either by a trustee in bankruptcy (*Re Citro* [1991] Ch 142) or by a mortgagee, unless there were 'exceptional circumstances'. As we shall see later, applications by trustees in bankruptcy are not dealt with by the Insolvency Act 1986 s.335A; however, in the case of applications by mortgagees/chargees, the 'interests of any secured creditors' were just one of the other four factors to be taken into account under TOLATA 1996. Neuberger J considered that the interests of any secured creditors were not to be given any primacy over the other three factors. He considered that s.15 provided the court with greater flexibility in determining whether or not to order a sale or, indeed, making other arrangements to safeguard the parties concerned.

Neuberger J considered that to require Mrs Shaire to leave the property that had been her home for nearly 25 years would cause her hardship, though she would have a substantial sum to put towards another house. Neuberger J on the other hand recognised the significant disadvantages for the mortgagee, which, as a consequence of Mrs Shaire's continued occupation, would be locked into a 25 per cent share with no proper return on its loan or proper protection as far as insurance and repair of the property were concerned. Neuberger J therefore attempted to reconcile the different needs of the parties. He did this by turning the 25 per cent equity share into a mortgage on which Mrs Shaire had to pay interest. In this way, Mrs Shaire retained possession and the mortgagee, as a lender of money, would receive a proper return on its investment.

The case of *Mortgage Corporation v Shaire* demonstrated the new flexibility that s.15 now provided. Certainly, the court had to take account of the four factors contained in s.15(1) as a whole but it concerned could also take into account the 'circumstances and wishes of any beneficiaries of full age and entitled to an interest in possession, subject to the trust or the majority of beneficiaries according to the value of their combined interests' under s.15(3). Clearly, then, there was a profound change of approach from the trust for sale under the Law of Property Act 1925 s.30 and trust of land under TOLATA 1996 s.14 and s.15. As Neuberger J stated himself at 758:

> . . . the very name 'trust for sale' and the law as it has been developed by the courts suggests that under this old law, in the absence of a strong reason to the contrary, the court should order a sale. Nothing in the language of the new code as found in the 1996 Act supports that approach.

Neuberger J's radical new approach signalled a new era for partners, either in marriage or in cohabitation, and children, but created uncertainty for the rights of secured creditors, on the face of things. However, this new order, whilst accepted de jure, was not necessarily applied de facto, as can be seen in the case of *Bank of Ireland Home Mortgages Ltd v Bell* [2001] 2 FLR 809.

Bank of Ireland Home Mortgages Ltd v Bell [2001] 2 FLR 809

In this case, a house was purchased to provide a home for a married couple and their son. The husband obtained a mortgage on the property by forging his wife's signature. The respective share of the parties at that time was 90% for the husband and 10% for the wife. The marriage subsequently broke down and the husband left, leaving his wife in occupation with the son, who was nearly 18. The mortgage was in arrears and the mortgagee sought possession and an order of sale of the property under s.14.

At first instance, the judge refused to order a sale, considering s.15(1)a and s.15(1)b – that is, the house was bought as a family home and that purpose was still current. He also took into account s.15(1)c, recognising the need for the welfare of the son to be addressed as he was still a minor. The wife was also in poor health.

The Court of Appeal, whilst approving of the decision in Shaire, reversed the decision of the judge at first instance and ordered a sale. It considered that the interests of secured creditors in terms of being inadequately protected should be a 'powerful consideration' when a court was exercising its discretion. Does this decision represent a return to the old convention? Possibly not. In arriving at its decision, the Court of Appeal stated that the factors contained in s.15(1)a and s.15(1)b had ceased to be relevant when the husband left. Furthermore, since the son was nearly 18 and soon to be out of his minority, his welfare under s.15(1)c was of relative unimportance. On the other hand, the debt to the mortgagee was a significant amount, £300,000, and was increasing daily with interest. No capital had been paid for eight years and there was little prospect of the money being repaid or the mortgagee receiving a proper return on its 'investment'. What is more, unlike in Shaire, the mortgagee would have a 90% interest in the property. The Court of Appeal considered that it would be unfair on the mortgagee to be kept out of the property and have to wait for the money when there was no or little prospect of recovering the debt, which exceeded the value of the property and was increasing on a daily basis. The Court of Appeal considered that the ill health enjoyed by the wife could only be a factor influencing a postponement of the order of sale rather than refusing.

The difference between the two cases of **Shaire** and **Bell** lies in the importance given to the interests of the secured creditors. In **Bell** Gibson LJ stated:

> The 1996 Act, by requiring the court to have regard to the particular matters specified in section 15, appears to me to have given scope for some change in the court's practice. Nevertheless, a powerful consideration is and ought to be whether the creditor is receiving proper recompense for being kept out of his money, repayment of which is overdue.

This statement therefore leans away from the radical approach of Neuberger J, in which all the factors contained in s.15 are to be given equal weighting, towards that of 'scope for some change in the court's practice' set out by Gibson LJ. In **Bell**, therefore, the interests of secured creditors are given more weight – in effect, primus inter pares – in determining the discretion of the court. The real difference between the two cases lies in the relative positions of the mortgagees. In **Shaire** the interests of the mortgagee could be secured, particularly since it would have a 25% share. In the **Bell** case, the interest of the mortgagee was at considerable risk and it would only receive a 10% share in the property. It has to be questioned whether Neuberger J would have come to a very different decision if he had not been able to secure the interests of the mortgagee in that case. Such a situation can be seen in the case of **Edwards v Lloyds TSB Bank plc** [2004] EWHC 1745 where the facts were similar to the **Bell** case.

Edwards v Lloyds TSB Bank plc [2004] EWHC 1745

Mr and Mrs Edwards were joint owners of their home in which they each had a 50% share. The marriage broke down and Mr Edwards left, leaving his wife in occupation with their two children, who were aged 15 and 13 when the case came to court. The husband then took out a mortgage, forging his wife's signature in the process. The effect of this was that only the husband's 50% share was charged with the mortgage. Mr Edwards then disappeared and could not be traced and no interest was being paid on the mortgage. The bank therefore made an application for the sale of the property.

Park J refused the application for sale as he considered that to make an immediate order of sale would have 'unacceptably severe' consequences for Mrs Edwards and the children. He stated that, in arriving at this decision, he had to 'weigh up the various factors which are relevant and do the best I can to reach a balanced conclusion'. He considered that Mrs Edwards had a rather better case than Mrs Shaire to remain in the property in that, if it was sold, it was highly unlikely that her share would provide her with enough equity to purchase another home for herself and her two children.

Park J also identified the fact that in **Shaire** and **Bell** the debt owed to the bank exceeded the value of the interest that the bank held. In **Edwards**, however, the value of the bank's security amounted to £70,000, whereas the husband's debt to the bank was unlikely to be more than £40,000. Whilst no interest was being paid on the debt and this was continuing to accrue, it would be some time before the security would be insufficient to meet the debt.

The position therefore appears to be that, where the interests of the creditor are secure, a sale is unlikely to be ordered, though the application will invariably be balanced against the other factors in s.15(1) and, indeed, the wider circumstances that might arise in individual cases.

Clearly, s.15 provides the courts with wider discretion as regards applications for orders of sale, though the interest of creditors does appear to continue to have a significant influence on how the courts exercise that discretion. The problem for the creditor is there is at least an element of doubt as to whether they can recover their money. It appears, however, that this difficulty can be sidestepped by the creditors relying on the more favourable provisions contained in the Insolvency Act 1986 s.335A where the creditor declares the defaulting beneficiary bankrupt.

Under the Insolvency Act 1986 s.335A

Where a beneficiary under a trust of land is declared bankrupt then an application for sale under s.14 by the trustee in bankruptcy will be considered under the criteria set out in s.335A where the factors contained in s.15(1)a and (b) cease to be relevant – s.15(4).

Section 335A provides:

(1) Any application by a trustee of a bankrupt's estate under section 14 of the Trusts of Land and Appointment of Trustees Act 1996 (powers of court in relation to trusts of land) for an order under that section for the sale of land shall be made to the court having jurisdiction in relation to the bankruptcy.

(2) On such an application the court shall make such order as it thinks just and reasonable having regard to –
  (a) the interests of the bankrupt's creditors;
  (b) where the application is made in respect of land which includes a dwelling house which is or has been the home of the [bankrupt or the bankrupt's spouse or civil partner or former spouse or former civil partner] –
    (i) the conduct of the [spouse, civil partner, former spouse or former civil partner], so far as contributing to the bankruptcy,
    (ii) the needs and financial resources of the [spouse, civil partner, former spouse or former civil partner], and
    (iii) the needs of any children; and
  (c) all the circumstances of the case other than the needs of the bankrupt.

(3) Where such an application is made after the end of the period of one year beginning with the first vesting under Chapter IV of this part of the bankrupt's estate in a trustee, the court shall assume, unless the circumstances of the case are exceptional, that the interests of the bankrupt's creditors outweigh all other considerations.

(4) The powers conferred on the court by this section are exercisable on an application whether it is made before or after the commencement of this section.

The role of a trustee in bankruptcy is to realise and distribute the assets of the bankrupt in order to satisfy the claims of the bankrupt's creditors. If a bankrupt is a beneficiary under a trust of land, then the trustee in bankruptcy is under s.14(1) a person who has 'an interest in property subject to a trust of land' and as such may make an application for an order of sale. It should be noted, however, that there are certain protections available to prevent orders for sale of the property being made pointlessly where no or little net gain will be received by the creditors. S.313A(2), as inserted by the Enterprise Act 2002 s.261, provides that an application for sale must be dismissed if net value of the interest of the bankrupt is below a prescribed amount, currently £1000. That said, under s.335A(2) a court may make any order 'as it thinks just and reasonable having regard to the interests of the bankrupt's creditors' and 'all the circumstances of the case other than the needs of the bankrupt'.

It will be noticed that s.335A provides that different considerations may be taken into account, depending on whether the application for sale is less than one year after the bankrupt's estate becomes vested in the trustee in bankruptcy or whether the application is made more than one year after the bankrupt's estate becomes vested in the trustee in bankruptcy. Where the application is made more than one year after the estate becomes vested the trustee, then the court's discretion is controlled by a statutory presumption that the 'interests of the creditors outweigh all other considerations' unless 'the circumstances of the case are exceptional'. The interests of the bankrupt's creditors therefore take priority over everything else.

The principle behind the time constraints is that the bankrupt should be given a one-year period of grace to adjust to his or her new financial position and to alleviate hardship and to prevent the bankrupt, and possibly his or her family, being suddenly thrown out on to the street. The intention is therefore to postpone a sale for a period of one year to allow the family to make new arrangements, but not for any longer unless there are exceptional circumstances present.

After one year only the presence of 'exceptional circumstances' will displace the presumption that the interests of creditors outweigh all other considerations. However, the finding of exceptional circumstances is not one the courts accede to readily and, in truth, there are few cases that demonstrate such a finding, so an order for sale is almost inevitable.

In *Re Holliday* [1981] Ch 405 the court indeed found for exceptional circumstances when it considered that to order an immediate sale would cause significant hardship to the bankrupt's ex-wife and three young children, who were still living in the property. The court considered that the interests of the creditors would not be prejudiced by deferring the sale for five years, by which time the eldest child would be 17 years of age.

It was undoubtedly the fact that the creditors would not suffer any great hardship that lay at the nub of the court's decision and one should not read into the law following this case that domestic hardship will provide relief on grounds of exceptional circumstance. The case, in any event, pre-dated the Insolvency Act 1986 and therefore reliance on it is, at best, tenuous. Of greater significance is the case of *Re Citro (A Bankrupt)* [1991] Ch 142, which was decided under the Insolvency Act 1986. It demonstrated that domestic hardship would not be regarded as an exceptional circumstance and illustrated the strict approach that the courts would henceforth adopt.

The case of *Re Citro* concerned a family home where the beneficial interest was shared between the bankrupt and his wife. The court postponed the order of sale until their youngest child was 16 years of age. The Court of Appeal reversed the decision of the court of first instance and considered that the domestic hardship and distress was not exceptional. Nourse LJ stated at 157:

> Where a spouse who has a beneficial interest in the matrimonial home has become bankrupt under debts which cannot be paid without the realisation of that interest, the voice of the creditors will usually prevail over the voice of the other spouse and a sale of the property ordered within a short period. The voice of the other spouse will only prevail in exceptional circumstances . . . What then are exceptional circumstances? As the cases show, it is not uncommon for a wife with young children to be faced with eviction in circumstances where the realisation of her beneficial interest will not produce enough to buy a comparable home in the same neighbourhood, or indeed elsewhere. And, if she has to move elsewhere, there may be problems over schooling and so forth. Such circumstances, while engendering a natural sympathy in all who hear of them, cannot be described as exceptional. They are the melancholy consequences of debt and improvidence with which every civilised society has been familiar.

'Melancholy consequences' indeed and one may be forgiven for thinking one had been plunged into some work by Dickens. Certainly the Cork Report (1982) which led to the passing of the Insolvency Act 1986 envisaged a somewhat less harsh regime. It stated:

> It would clearly be wrong to allow a debtor or his family to continue to live in lavish style at the expense of the debtor's creditors for an extended period. Nevertheless considerable personal hardship can be caused to the debtor's family by a sudden or premature eviction, and we believe it to be consonant with present social attitudes to alleviate the personal hardships of those who are dependent on the debtor but not responsible for his insolvency, if this can be achieved by delaying for an acceptable time the sale of the family home. We propose therefore to delay, but not to cancel, enforcement of the creditors' rights . . .
>
> Nevertheless we consider that any new Insolvency Act should confer on the Court a specific power to postpone a trustee's rights of possession and sale of the family home. In exercising this power the Court should have particular regard to the welfare of any children of the family and of any adult members of the family who are ailing or elderly [. . .] Giving this power to the court will, we hope and expect, serve to support the natural inclination of the usually sympathetic [trustee in bankruptcy], and to protect the debtor's family in those cases where lack of sympathy with, or anger at, the debtor produces unfortunate and undeserved consequences for his family.

Certainly, the interpretation given to 'exceptional circumstances' does not appear to reflect the stance in the Cork Report and therefore the question remains as to what exactly the courts consider to be circumstances that are exceptional. In *Hosking* v *Michaelides* [2004] All ER (D) 147 Morgan J considered 'exceptional' to be something 'out of the ordinary course, or usual, or special or uncommon'. From this it may be discerned that cases that give rise to a postponement of sale because of exceptional circumstances are rare. The cases tend to point towards severe or chronic ill health or mental illness. In *Re Bremner* [1999] 1 FLR 912, the bankrupt was elderly and terminally ill with cancer, but it is noticeable that the sale was postponed for three months until after the death of the bankrupt so as to provide for the needs of his wife who was his carer. The logic is correct since s.33A(2)c specifically excludes the needs of the bankrupt when the court considers all the circumstances of the case. It should also be noted here that the postponement of sale in this case was so short as to not affect the interests of the creditors.

In *Claughton* v *Charalambous* [1999] 1 FLR 740 the bankrupt and his wife were beneficial co-owners of the family home; however, the wife, Mrs Charalambous was in chronically poor health and had a reduced life expectancy. In addition, Mrs Charalambous was disabled and had mobility issues, so the family home had been altered to allow her to cope with her disability. Clearly, it would have been difficult for her to find somewhere to live that had the same adjustments to the property. The judge considered these circumstances to be exceptional and postponed the sale while she continued to live in the home.

In many of the cases where exceptional circumstances result in a postponement of sale, the interests of the creditors are not prejudiced or the effects are minimised. It is rare to find otherwise but in *Nicholls* v *Lan* [2007] 1 FLR 744, the sale was postponed despite the adverse effect on the creditors in that the eventual proceeds of sale would not be sufficient to pay the outstanding debts. In this case, the sale was postponed for 18 months because the bankrupt's wife suffered from severe schizophrenia and an enforced sale would have given rise to specific psychiatric issues. What is unusual in this case was that the 18-month postponement was to enable her to raise funds to buy out the bankrupt's share of the property.

It remains the case that there is great uncertainty as to what circumstances are exceptional so as to postpone sale after the one-year period. In each case, the court has to make a value judgment based on the facts of the case in question. However, it was suggested in *Barca* v *Mears* [2004] EWHC 2170 that, where a court simply presumes a sale after the one-year period, without considering whether exceptional circumstances exist or not, this might well operate in contravention of Article 8 of the European Convention of Human Rights: the right to respect family life and home. The point that arises here is that the convention requires the court to make a proper assessment of any exceptional circumstances that might arise and not simply apply an automatic order of sale in favour of the trustee in bankruptcy or the creditors. It should be borne in mind that it is not the order of sale per se that is in contravention of the Convention. The difficulty is that the right to family life and home receives little in the way of consideration unless the exceptional circumstances are 'out of the ordinary course, or unusual, or special or uncommon'. In *Barca* v *Mears* Strauss QC considered that in order to comply with Article 8 a rather more sympathetic view of exceptional circumstances along the lines of *Re Holliday* might be required. The effect would be that, whilst the interests of the creditors will continue to outweigh the interests of the other parties, it would be open for the court 'to find that, on a proper consideration of the facts of a particular case, it is one of the exceptional circumstances'.

Whilst the current issues concerning the compatibility of s.335A with Article 8 are procedural, the proposal in *Barca* v *Mears* appears to suggest that a substantive change is required to the definition of exceptional circumstances. One difficulty, however, arises if there are no exceptional circumstances for a court to consider. Would the presumption in favour of the creditors breach Article 8? Two aspects would suggest not. Firstly, it should be remembered that the courts are not bound to order a sale under s.335A; and, secondly, the fact that s.335A allows for a one-year adjustment period might ensure compatibility with Article 8.

The proposals suggested by Strauss QC have not been developed any further. In *Donohue* v *Ingram* [2006] EWHC 282 it was stated that the present narrow view of exceptional circumstances was not consonant with Article 8, which required that greater weight should be given to the needs of the bankrupt's partner and children; however, in that case it was stated that, even on a wider interpretation of s.335A, there were still no exceptional circumstances and a sale would be ordered anyway.

In *Nicholls* v *Lan* [2007] 1 FLR 744 the court considered there was no conflict between s.335A and Article 8 and that the requirement to balance the various interests encapsulated the requirements of Article 8 'precisely'.

Protecting purchasers

Overreaching

We have seen already in Chapter 3 the dangers involved in a purchaser acquiring property in which equitable rights of third parties exist. You will recall that, unless the purchaser is a bona fide purchaser for value of the legal estate without notice of the equitable interests under a trust, they take from the land subject to the rights of the owners of the equitable interests, the beneficiaries. We saw also that the statutory overreaching provisions contained in the Law of Property Act 1925 s.2(1) and s.27 (as amended by TOLATA 1996 Sched. 3 para 4(1)) continue to apply to trusts of land, whether unregistered or registered land. These provisions provide that, if a purchaser pays their money to two trustees or a trust corporation and obtains a valid receipt from them, they take free of the equitable interests even if they are aware of them. The equitable interests are therefore overreached so that they are swept off the land and into the proceeds of sale, which are then held in trust.

Two points follow from the above. Firstly, a purchaser should always ensure that they pay the purchase money to the trustees, never the beneficiaries. The exception to this might be if a beneficiary is also a trustee, but here the purchaser should ensure that they pay the money to that person acting in their capacity as trustee, not beneficiary. Secondly, in order to get the protection of the above provisions, they should ensure that they pay the purchase money to at least two trustees and if there are fewer than two they should insist that another trustee is appointed. For this reason the Trustee Act 1925 s.36 (as amended by TOLATA 1996) provides extensive powers for the appointment of new trustees.

We saw how the above process worked in Chapter 5 when we examined the cases of *Williams & Glyn's Bank plc* v *Boland* [1981] AC 487 and *City of London Building Society* v *Flegg* [1988] AC 54. In *Boland* it will be recalled that Mr Boland held the legal title on trust for himself and his wife. He took out a mortgage without consulting with his wife. When he defaulted on his repayments, the bank, as mortgagee, sought possession of the property. The wife was able to successfully claim that, as the bank had only paid the purchase money, i.e. the loan, to one trustee, her beneficial interest was not overreached. The bank therefore took the property subject to her beneficial interest. This position was sharply contrasted in *Flegg* where the building society did pay the loan money to two trustees, with the effect that the beneficial interests of Mr and Mrs Flegg were overreached and thus moved into the proceeds of sale, which were represented by the difference between the price the property was sold for and the money owed to the bank. This money was then held by Mr and Mrs Maxwell-Brown on trust for themselves and the Fleggs. In order to recover their share of the money, the Fleggs would then be forced to sue the Maxwell-Browns. Of course, such an action would be worthless if there was no equity left when the house was sold or the trustees had absconded with the money.

Clearly, there are great dangers for a purchaser or mortgagee where there is only one trustee – and it is not as if this matter is uncommon. In an age where cohabitation has become an accepted part of domestic life, it is, in fact, quite common for one of the partners ('M') to have purchased a house into which a partner ('W') subsequently moves. As we will see later, it is possible for W to subsequently acquire an equitable interest in the property that was formerly in the sole ownership of M. In such a situation, the legal ownership remains in M's name only and therefore overreaching cannot be triggered if the property is subsequently sold, or the parties fall out, or if the property is mortgaged by M and the mortgagee subsequently seeks an order for possession under TOLATA 1996 s.14. Usually in such a situation, W is in occupation and therefore can claim protection under the Land Registration Act 2000 Schedule 3 para 2 by way of an interest that is overriding. If, however, W has moved out then it is possible that the protection afforded by Schedule 3 para 2 would not be available to W and the purchaser/mortgagee will take free of W's equitable interest by virtue of the Land Registration Act 2000 s.29.

If the property is unregistered land then the interest of W is a 'family interest' and is governed by the doctrine of notice. Thus, if the purchaser is a bona fide purchaser for value of the legal estate without actual constructive notice of W's interest, the purchaser will take free of W's interest.

Protection for purchasers where the trustees are in breach of their duties

In considering trusts of land, we have seen that TOLATA 1996 imposes a number of duties on trustees and further under s.8 the settlor may seek to exclude or restrict the powers of trustees. Obviously, if the trustees fail to comply with their duties or limitations then they will be in breach of trust and be liable to the beneficiaries for such a breach, but what about the purchaser? What protections are offered to the purchaser since it will be nigh on impossible to discover if such a breach has arisen?

Pre-eminent amongst these duties is that of consent under TOLATA 1996 s.10. Section 10 allows a settlor to impose on trustees a duty to obtain the consent of a named person or persons before the trustees exercise any specified acts, such as selling or mortgaging the property. Often the named person or persons will be the beneficiaries. But what if the trustees do not obtain the relevant consents? Firstly, it must be remembered that, if the exercise of any functions of the trustees is subject to the consent of more than two persons, the consent of any two such persons is deemed sufficient in favour of the purchaser: s.10(1). But what if no consents are obtained at all? Similarly, what happens if the trustees do not comply with their duty to consult with the beneficiaries under TOLATA 1996 s.11? The position here differs, depending on whether the land is unregistered or registered land.

In unregistered land, TOLATA 1996 s.16 (which *only* applies to unregistered land) provides that a purchaser need not be concerned to see that the trustees have complied with their obligations to have regard to the rights of the beneficiaries, or to consult with them or give effect to their wishes, provided that the purchaser has no actual notice of the limitation. Whilst there is no mechanism for any such limitation to be registered under the Land Charges Act 1972, the trustees must take all reasonable steps to bring the limitation to the notice of the purchaser. The limitations will be expressly contained in the disposition creating the trust; however, it is suggested that in a family co-ownership situation such a limitation would be rare, as indeed would a new trust in unregistered land.

In registered land, since the requirement for consent will be included in the disposition creating the trust – i.e. the conveyance – then the requirement will be entered as a restriction on the register of title. The restriction will inform a purchaser of the need to ensure that the relevant consents are obtained and provides that no registration of a registered disposition can take place until the terms of the restriction are complied with. The effect is that any disposition made by trustees must be in accordance with the restrictions. A purchaser is not concerned with any limitations on the powers of trustees that are not protected on the register: Land Registration Act 2002 s.26.

Protection for purchasers where overreaching has failed
Beneficiaries' consent to a disposition

Where the purchaser has failed to pay their purchase money to two trustees, as in Boland, the purchaser will take subject to the beneficial interests that exist in the property, subject to the provisions already set out above. However, it is still possible for purchasers to take priority over the interest of the beneficiary if the beneficiary has either impliedly or expressly consented to the surrender of their interest in favour of the purchaser. Following **Boland**, it became common for mortgagees to specifically enquire of trustees as to who lived in the property (because of s.70(1)g overriding interests, now Schedule 3 para 2) and then require those persons to consent to the transaction and surrender their priority to the purchaser/mortgagee prior to any money being advanced. Mere knowledge of the transaction by the beneficiary is insufficient to provide this relief for the purchaser and a court must be satisfied that consent has expressly or impliedly been given: *Skipton Building Society* v *Clayton* (1993) 66 P & CR 223.

Usually, a mortgagee will insist on the beneficiary signing a consent form so that the release of the priority to the mortgagee arises expressly; however, this release may arise impliedly if the beneficiary, for instance, attended the bank with the trustee – as a wife may do with her husband if the house is in the husband's name alone. Here the wife impliedly consents to the granting of the mortgage, so she cannot later claim that her beneficial interest takes in priority to the interest of the mortgagee. Essentially, the same principle arises if a couple decide to raise a mortgage for the purpose of purchasing a property, which is subsequently conveyed into one party's name. Here the beneficial owner knew from the start that the property could not be purchased without a mortgage and therefore impliedly provides consent. The principle can be seen in the case of ***Bristol and West Building Society v Henning*** [1985] 1 WLR in which two people purchased a house together but both were aware that a mortgage was needed to complete the purchase. The mortgage was taken by the man and the conveyance transferred the property into his name also. It was held that his partner could not claim priority to the mortgagee. The Court of Appeal considered that it was clear that she authorised her partner to raise the purchase price by way of the mortgage, thereby consenting to her own beneficial interest also being charged.

The property in ***Henning*** consisted of unregistered land, but shortly afterwards the same principles were applied to registered land in the case of ***Paddington Building Society v Mendelsohn*** (1985) 50 P & CR 244. These principles were also extended in the case of ***Abbey National Building Society v Cann*** [1991] 1 AC 56. In this case, a mother and son were purchasing a house together and Mrs Cann was fully aware that a mortgage would need to be raised for the purchase, even though part of the purchase price was to be raised by the sale of her own property. The son took his mother's money, but instead of putting all of it towards the purchase, he in fact took out a bigger mortgage than was intended in the agreement between them. It was held that Mrs Cann had changed her beneficial interest to the full extent of the larger sum borrowed and not just to the extent of her more limited authorisation. It should be noted that the mortgagee here did not rely on Mrs Cann's authorisation as it was not even aware of her existence.

A word of warning is needed here. The principle does not apply if the single legal owner is borrowing money for their own purpose, as seen in ***Boland***. The whole point is that the beneficiary is impliedly acquiescing in the raising of a loan by way of a mortgage for the purchase of property for joint beneficial ownership, although such situations would normally arise where the parties already own the property but are borrowing for improvements, such as an extension.

It should be remembered that, generally speaking, a mortgagee would not have to rely on implied consent today since the mortgagee will invariably require an express consent form to be signed by the beneficial owner.

Failure to comply with the overreaching requirements

We have seen that, for overreaching to apply, the purchaser or mortgagee must pay the purchase money to two trustees or a trust corporation. Thus overreaching relies on the payment of capital money to the trustees but what if no capital money is paid so that the transaction is outside of the Law of Property Act 1925 s.27? This is a very unusual situation but nevertheless it arose in the case of ***State Bank of India v Sood*** [1997] Ch 276.

State Bank of India v *Sood* [1997] Ch 276

The case involved seven defendants, of whom only two were the legal owners and trustees of the property. All the defendants occupied the premises and, to that extent, they had an overriding interest under the Land Registration Act 1925 s.70(1)g (now Schedule 3 para 2). The two trustees took out a mortgage, but rather than raise the mortgage for the release of capital money, they used the mortgage to guarantee their existing debts and any future indebtedness. Thus no capital money was advanced by the bank at all. One of the trustees was then made bankrupt and the bank sought possession of the house, relying on the overreaching provisions under the Law of Property Act 1925 s.27 and ***Flegg*** to avoid the claims of the other beneficial owners. The problem was, of course, that the bank did not fall within s.27(2) because no capital money had been paid over to the two trustees as per the Law of Property Act 1925 s.2(1)(ii).

The Court of Appeal held that the beneficial interests had nevertheless been overreached. Gibson LJ considered that the absence of capital money did not prevent overreaching from arising. In effect, he stated that the Law of Property Act 1925 s.27 only became relevant where capital money actually arose. Thus if no capital money was paid at the time the mortgage was executed overreaching still occurred; however, once capital money was paid then s.27(2) had to be complied with for the mortgagee to obtain a good receipt. The point is that overreaching still applies even if no capital monies are paid to the two trustees.

Protecting the purchaser when the trust of land comes to an end

We started our discussion by referring to TOLATA 1996 s.1(1) which defined a trust of land as 'any trust of property which consists of or includes land'. The question here is: what protection is offered to the purchaser if the trust comes to an end? This may arise in two ways, by discharge of trust or the right of survivorship under a joint tenancy.

Discharge

Once all the beneficiaries become of full age and capacity and are absolutely entitled to the property, the trustees may discharge themselves from the trust, bringing the trust to an end since there is little point in the trustees holding the legal title when they no longer have any functions to perform under the trust. This might arise where a testator has left his property to his wife for life and then to his children absolutely. When the testator dies, his trustees will hold the legal title on the trust, as set out in the will. Once the wife dies, if the children are of full age and capacity and absolutely entitled to the property – that is, the trustees have no duties to perform or there are no conditions attached to the gift to the children – the job of the trustees is done. The trustees should then convey the legal title to the beneficiaries and at this point by s.16(4) they should also execute a deed of discharge, declaring that they are discharged from the trust in relation to that land. Once this is done, by s.16(5) any subsequent purchaser of the land to which the discharge relates is entitled to assume from that date that the land is not subject to the trust, unless the purchaser or registrar has actual notice that the trustees were mistaken in their belief that the land was conveyed to beneficiaries of full age and capacity who were absolutely entitled to the land subject to the trust.

It should be noted carefully that the above provision only applies to unregistered land and therefore it will be of importance to registrars as regards first registration rather than subsequent purchases of the land. The reason for this is that, when the trustees convey the unregistered land to the beneficiaries, this is a 'trigger' for the purposes of registration, and thus the termination of the trust by the conveyance to those absolutely entitled must be completed by registration.

Survivorship under a joint tenancy

Where land is held by co-owners then they will hold the legal title on trust for themselves, as shown in Figure 10.9.

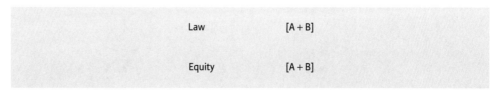

| Law | [A + B] |
| Equity | [A + B] |

Figure 10.9

Where both the legal title and equitable title are held as joint tenants (as we will see in Chapter 11) the legal title *must* be held as a joint tenancy and the rights of survivorship (jus accrescendi) applies. (Note: A joint tenancy is indicated by square brackets – '[A + B]'). This means that on the death of the joint tenant, for instance B above, his or her share passes to the survivor automatically. At this point, the trust of land comes to an end, as the remaining joint tenant is now solely and absolutely entitled to the land. See Figure 10.10.

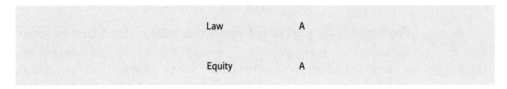

Figure 10.10

In unregistered land in this situation there is now a problem for the purchaser since clearly the title deeds would still indicate the presence of a joint tenant who would have held the land for themselves under a trust of land. Is it safe for the purchaser now to enter into a transaction with only one person? Normally, of course they should ask for the appointment of a second trustee in order to ensure that the overreaching provisions under the Law of Property Act 1925 s.27(2) are complied with. Their concerns are very real since one of the parties might have severed their joint tenancy in equity. (Note: it is never possible to sever a joint tenancy at law.) The severance would have created a tenancy in common in equity so that they would then have had a separate distinct share which could be passed to anyone entitled under their will or under the rules governing intestacy. See Figure 10.11.

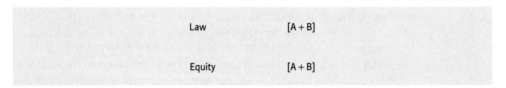

Figure 10.11

B severs their joint tenancy in equity so that the position is now as shown in Figure 10.12.

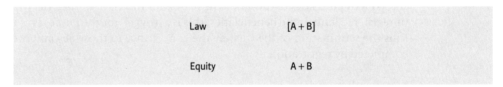

Figure 10.12

On B's death his share passes to X so the position is now as shown in Figure 10.13.

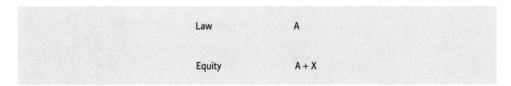

Figure 10.13

If A, as trustee, now sells the land to the purchaser (P), P would need to pay their purchase money to two trustees in order to overreach the beneficial interests of A and X. Clearly, this is not the case and therefore P will be bound by the beneficial interests.

Usually when a joint tenant severs the joint tenancy, a rule or memorandum of severance is endorsed on the title deeds and this will give P notice that the severance has taken place and they can rely on the sale by A alone. The trouble is, if such a memorandum is not endorsed, this does not preclude the possibility of the severance of the joint tenancy having occurred. Thus the absence of the memorandum is no guarantee that there has been no severance at some point up to the death of B and that A, rather than holding both the legal and equitable titles in his or her sole name, is actually holding the legal title on trust for himself or herself and another person, X. In such a situation, it is vital that the purchaser asks for a second trustee to be appointed so that the conditions required for overreaching are complied with.

The above position is highly inconvenient and to resolve this inconvenience the Law of Property (Joint Tenants) Act 1964 was passed. Section 1(1) of the 1964 Act provides that, in favour of the purchaser of a legal estate, if the sole survivor of two or more joint tenants sells the property they are deemed to be solely and beneficially entitled to the property. The purchaser will therefore take free of any other beneficial interests that might subsequently appear. In order to take advantage of this provision, a memorandum of severance signed by the joint tenants – or one of them – recording the fact that the joint tenancy was severed in equity and giving the date of the severance must be endorsed on or annexed to the conveyance which originally vested the legal estate in the joint tenants.

It should be noted that the above provision does not apply to registered land. The position here is that, where the co-owners are joint tenants at both law and equity, they will be entered on the register of title as the registered proprietors. In such an instance, there will be no restriction entered on the register requiring any purchase money to be paid to two trustees. When a joint tenant dies, all the survivor needs to do is to supply the HM Land Registry with evidence of the death – a death certificate will do – and the registrar will then amend the entry to show that the survivor is the sole registered proprietor of the property. The purchaser can now purchase the property from the survivor, confident that they can rely on the register.

Summary

Definition: A successive interest arises where the beneficial interest is held on trust for a succession of interests in equity – for example, to A for life, remainder to B.

Definition: A concurrent interest arises where two or more people own a piece of land – for example, the beneficial interest is held on trust for two or more people who are presently entitled to the property, with A and B holding the legal estate on trusts for themselves as beneficial owners.

Strict settlements

- Such arrangements were formerly governed by the Settled Land Act 1925; however, they were abolished by TOLATA 1996.
- Trustees of the settlement have no active duties to perform on a day-to-day basis and act in a supervisory role.
- The tenant for life has the day-to-day responsibility for the administration of the strict settlement.

Trusts for sale

- These were originally governed by the Law of Property Act 1925, unlike strict settlements, which were governed by the Settled Land Act 1925. Trusts for sale are now governed by TOLATA 1996 if an *express* trust for sale has been created, otherwise a successive interest must exist as a trust of land.
- Trustees have a *duty* to sell the land under a trust for sale, although they have an implied power, in the absence of an express provision, in TOLATA 1996 s.4(1). Trustees may postpone a sale indefinitely if they so wish.
- Pre-TOLATA 1996 – If some trustees wanted to sell but others did not then the property *had* to be sold as there was a duty to sell. The trustees had to act with unanimity to *postpone* sale.
- Post TOLATA 1996 – There is now no duty to sell (provided there is no express trust for sale). If the trustees wish to *sell*, they must act unanimously.
- *Re Buchanan-Wollaston's Conveyance* [1939] Ch 738.

Doctrine of conversion

- Pre-TOLATA 1996 beneficiaries under a trust for sale did not have an interest in land because of the duty to sell – 'equity looks on that as done which ought to be done' – thus their interest always lay in the proceeds of sale.
- Post-TOLATA 1996 by s.3(1) the doctrine of conversion was abolished so that the interests of the beneficiaries now lie in the land, not in the proceeds of sale.

Trusts of land

- These were introduced by TOLATA 1996 and defined in s.1(1) as 'any trust of property which consists of or includes land'.
- The expression 'trust' refers to any description of a trust, whether express, implied, resulting or constructive trusts. It includes trusts for sale and bare trusts.
- Trusts of land apply to successive interest trusts, as in a settlement, or where there is a trust of concurrent interests, as in co-ownership.

Creation of trusts

- Express inter vivos trusts must comply with the requirements of the Law of Property Act 1925 s.53(1)b – there must be a declaration evidenced in writing and signed by the person able to declare the trust. Trusts created by will must comply with the Wills Act 1837.
- Resulting, implied and constructive trusts do not have to comply with s.53(1)b: s.53(1)c.

Powers and duties of trustees

General powers

By s.6(1) trustees have authority to exercise 'all the powers of an absolute owner'. Trustees can therefore deal with the property as if it were their own, subject to any express provisions in the disposition: s.8(1).

Specific powers

(a) The power to buy, lease and mortgage land – Trustees may acquire freehold or leasehold land for investment, occupation or any other purpose: s.6(3). Note the statutory duty of care in the Trustee Act 2000 s.1(1).

(b) The power to partition – By s.7 trustees may divide up the land and convey it to each beneficiary.

(c) Compulsory conveyance to the beneficiaries – By s.6(2) trustees have the right to demand that the beneficiaries have the legal estate conveyed to them if they are of full age and capacity and absolutely entitled to the property.

(d) The power to delegate – Whilst the general rule is that a trustee cannot delegate their office, TOLATA 1996 and the Trustee Delegation Act 1999 allow for this. Delegation may be made to an individual or, under TOLATA 1996 s.9, there may be collective delegation.

Duties of trustees

- The duty to obtain consents: s.10 A settlor may require trustees to obtain the consent of any named person or persons before exercising any of their powers.

- The duty to consult: s.11 Trustees carrying out their functions are required to consult with beneficiaries who are of full age and beneficially entitled to an interest in possession, but only so far as this is practicable.

Rights of beneficiaries

The right to occupy trust land: s.12

- Originally, beneficiaries had no such right of occupation because of the duty to sell under a trust for land. Note, however, **Bull v Bull** [1955] 1 QB 234, where Denning LJ considered that if residential use was the 'prime object of the trust', this overrode the duty to sell.

- Under TOLATA 1996 s.12, beneficiaries now have a general right of occupation, but only if the purpose of the trust is to make the land available for occupation.

- **Barclay v Barclay** [1970] 2 QB 677

- By s.13 trustees may exclude or restrict the right of occupation so that the trustees may exclude one or more beneficiaries but not all of them. Trustees may also impose conditions on the persons in occupation of the premises.

The right to appoint and remove trustees: s.19

If beneficiaries act unanimously and are of full age and capacity and absolutely entitled to the property, they may direct trustees to retire from the trust and direct trustees to appoint by writing the person(s) nominated.

The right to the proceeds of sale

When land is sold, the beneficiaries are entitled to the proceeds of sale; however; life tenants are only entitled to income, whilst remaindermen are entitled to the capital but only on the death of the life tenant.

Dispute resolution

Under TOLATA 1996

Prior to TOLATA 1996, the courts had statutory jurisdiction to resolve disputes under the Law of Property Act 1925 s.30. This machinery is now contained in s.14 and s.15 of TOLATA 1996. Section 14 sets out who can make an application to the court and the types of order available to the court. Section 15 contains the matters to which the court must have regard in relation to applications made under s.14.

Under the Insolvency Act 1986 s.335A

Where a beneficiary under a trust of land is declared bankrupt, an application for an order of sale under s.14 by the trustee in bankruptcy will be considered under the criteria set out in s.335A rather than TOLATA 1996 s.15.

Under s.335A a court can make any order it thinks just and reasonable having regard to:

(a) the interests of the creditors;

(b) in respect of a dwelling house – the conduct of the spouse, civil partner, etc. of the bankrupt; the needs of the spouse, civil partner etc.; and, the needs of any children;

(c) all the circumstances of the case other than the needs of the bankrupt.

After a period of one year, the court assumes – unless the circumstances of the case are exceptional – that the interests of the bankrupt outweigh all other considerations.

'Exceptional circumstances'

Consider:

> *Re Holliday* [1981] Ch 40
>
> *Re Citro (A Bankrupt)* [1991] Ch 142
>
> *Hosking* v *Michaelides* [2004] All ER D147
>
> *Re Bremner* [1999] 1 FLR 912
>
> *Claughton* v *Charalambous* [1999] 1 FLR 740
>
> *Barca* v *Mears* [2004] EWHC

Protecting purchasers

Overreaching

Governed by the Law of Property Act 1925 s.27 s, amended by TOLATA 1996.

In order to overreach the beneficial interests under a trust of land, a purchaser must ensure that they pay their money to two trustees or a trust corporation and obtain a valid receipt from them.

> *Williams & Glyn's Bank plc* v *Boland* [1981] AC 487
>
> *City of London Building Society* v *Flegg* [1988] AC 54

Protecting purchasers when the trust of land comes to an end

- Discharge – s.16
- Survivorship under a joint tenancy
- Law of Property (Joint Tenants) Act 1964

Further reading

Strict settlements

Baker, *An Introduction to English Legal History*, Oxford University Press (2007)

Trusts for sale

Harwood, 'Gathering Moss – Trusts for Sale' [1996] *Family Law* 293

Trusts of land

Baker, 'The Judicial Approach to "Exceptional Circumstances" in Bankruptcy: The Impact of the Human Rights Act' [2010] 74 *The Conveyancer and Property Lawyer* 352

Dixon, 'Trusts of Land, Bankruptcy and Human Rights' [2005] 69 *The Conveyancer and Property Lawyer* 61

Insolvency Law and Practice: Report of the Review Committee (The Cork Report) Cmnd 8558 (1982)

Law Commission Report, *Transfer of Land, Overreaching: Beneficiaries in Occupation*, Law Com No. 188 (1989)

Oldham, 'Overreaching Where No Capital Monies Arise' [1997] *Cambridge Law Journal* 494

Pascoe, 'Section 15 of the Trusts of Land and Appointment of Trustees Act 1996: A Change in the Law' [2000] *The Conveyancer and Property Lawyer* 315

Pascoe, 'Right to Occupy under a Trust of Land: Muddled Legislative Logic?' [2006] 70 *The Conveyancer and Property Lawyer* 54

Pawlowski, 'Ordering the Sale of the Family Home' [2007] 71 *The Conveyancer and Property Lawyer* 78

Probert, 'Creditors and Section 15 of the Trusts of Land and Appointment of Trustees Act 1996 – A Change in the Law' [2002] 66 *The Conveyancer and Property Lawyer* 315

11

Co-ownership I – the structure

Aims and objectives

After reading this chapter you should be able to:

- Understand the nature of co-ownership.
- Understand the requirements for a joint tenancy.
- Understand the requirements for a tenancy in common.
- Know the differences between a tenancy in common and a joint tenancy and be able to distinguish between them.
- Understand the impact of *Stack* v *Dowden* and *Jones* v *Kernott*.
- Understand and apply the doctrine of severance.
- Know the means by which the co-ownership relationship terminates.

Introduction

In the previous chapter we looked at situations where there were successive interests in land, where property is given to one person for their lifetime (the life tenant) after which the property passed to another person (the remainderman). Having said this, it must be remembered that trusts of land arise in any situation where land is held on trust and therefore trusts of land apply equally to co-ownership as where there is a trust comprising successive interests.

An understanding of the way land is divided into legal and equitable titles is essential to the understanding of co-ownership and you should be aware that co-ownership can arise in relation to both legal and equitable interests or either of them.

Example

Harvey and June buy Blackacre together, but only the legal title is put into Harvey's name, as shown in Figure 11.1.

Legal	H
Equitable	H + J

Figure 11.1

Example

Peter and Barbara buy Redacre together, but the legal title is put into both names, as shown in Figure 11.2.

Legal	P + B
Equitable	P + B

Figure 11.2

Example

Paula dies, leaving Greenacre to her son, William, who is only 12 years of age. Paula's executors and trustees under the will are Amy and John. Since William is a minor, he cannot own the legal estate in land by virtue of the Law of Property Act 1925 s.1(6). Amy and John are required to look after Greenacre until William comes of age. The position is as shown in Figure 11.3.

Legal	A + J
Equitable	W

Figure 11.3

The circumstances in which a person can have an equitable interest or beneficial title in the land can vary. There can be an express trust set up or there may be a trust implied by law, as in the case of William in the example above, whose interest must exist behind a trust given that he is a minor. Of course, Paula may have also set up an express trust to this effect under her will. For instance, she may decide that William should not get Greenacre until he is 25 years of age, in which case William's interest is subject to this express trust. An equitable interest may also arise by way of either a resulting or constructive trust in which equity provides a person with a beneficial interest in the property. This often occurs in a marriage situation where a husband and wife buy a house together and the house is placed in the husband's name alone. The husband, if the couple split up, might allege that, because he paid all the mortgage instalments, he should be entitled to the house absolutely in both law and equity. The wife, on the other hand, might argue that she had made a contribution to the purchase by contributing to the initial deposit. In such circumstances, the court may declare that the wife has a beneficial interest in the house so that the husband holds the legal title on trust for himself and his wife, as shown in Figure 11.4.

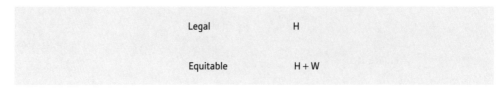

| Legal | H |
| Equitable | H + W |

Figure 11.4

In this chapter we will not be concerned at how wives or partners acquire their beneficial interests; this will be considered in the next chapter. For the moment, we will be looking at how the mechanisms relating to co-ownership work generally.

In modern land law there are two forms of co-ownership: joint tenants and tenants in common. We will look at each of these in turn, but before we do so, please note that in the diagrams that appear we will identify a joint tenancy by square brackets, thus '[A + B]'. A tenancy in common will be identified without the brackets, thus 'A + B'.

Joint tenancy

Single composite ownership

In a joint tenancy, the co-owners hold the land as one and they are not regarded as having shares in the land. Whilst they hold the land together, each cannot point at a part of the land and say 'That belongs to me'. The co-owners therefore are treated as being a single composite entity, i.e. [A + B].

In order for a joint tenancy to exist, four criteria must be met; these are known as the 'four unities'.

The four unities are:

(i) unity of title;

(ii) unity of possession;

(iii) unity of time;

(iv) unity of interest.

Unity of title

This means that all the co-owners must have acquired their title by the same means, i.e. the same document. Thus, if A and B purchase a house together, they will both acquire the land by way of the same transfer document, which, when registered, will vest them both with the legal title. It should be noted that unity of title is a matter of substance. It is true that parties usually acquire their title through the same document, but this is not necessarily the case in order to establish unity of title. Thus the two parties might sign different leases with a landlord but the circumstances are such that they are clearly leasing the property jointly, as in the case of ***Antoniades v Villiers*** [1990] 1 AC 417 where a couple took a one-bedroomed flat but signed separate leases.

Unity of possession

This means that both the co-owners must be equally entitled to take possession of the whole land. Thus if A and B acquire Blackacre and A states that the paddock belongs to him alone there can be no unity of possession and therefore there cannot be a joint tenancy.

Unity of time

This means that the co-owners must have acquired their title at the same time. Thus, in the example above, if A and B purchased Blackacre together and had it transferred to them at the same time, this unity would be satisfied.

Unity of interest

This means that the co-owners' interests must be identical. Thus if A has a life interest and B has a fee simple absolute in possession they cannot hold as joint tenants as they have different interests. Thus, for a joint tenancy to exist, the interests of each co-owner must be for the same extent and duration, and must be of the same nature.

The right of survivorship ('jus accrescendi')

An extremely important characteristic of a joint tenancy is the right of survivorship or jus accrescendi. As we saw earlier, since a joint tenancy is regarded as a single composite owner-ship of the land, unless there is severance of joint tenancy (which we will discuss later) the parties are not free to dispose of a share of the property since they do not own a distinct share. Thus, if one of the co-owners dies, that person cannot dispose of his or her share freely and the remaining joint tenants acquire that person's interest. As each joint tenant dies, so the remaining joint tenants acquire the interest of the deceased person until there is only one joint tenant remaining, who would then have sole ownership of the entire property to do with as he or she pleases.

Example

Antonia and Bill purchase Blackacre together as joint tenants in law and equity, as shown in Figure 11.5.

Legal	[A + B]
Equitable	[A + B]

Figure 11.5

Bill dies and in his will he leaves all his property to his cousin, Kathleen. Kathleen considers that she will inherit Bill's share of Blackacre; however, she is wrong. Since Antonia and Bill own Blackacre as joint tenants, on Bill's death his own share will pass to Antonia by way of survivorship so that she now becomes the sole owner of Blackacre (see Figure 11.6).

Legal   A

Equitable   A

Figure 11.6

It can be seen then that the right of survivorship takes precedence over a joint tenant's will or if he or she dies intestate. This is particularly convenient in a marriage situation since, if the husband dies, his share will pass automatically to his wife.

Joint tenancy of the legal title

Prior to the passing of the Law of Property Act 1925, it was possible for the legal title to be held as either a joint tenancy or a tenancy in common. Following the passing of the Law of Property Act 1925, by virtue of s.1(6) and s.34(2) it was no longer possible to create a *legal* tenancy in common. It is therefore vitally important that in co-ownership the legal title *must* be held on a joint tenancy and *never* a tenancy in common. The reason for this change lies in the fact that one of the aims of the 1925 legislation was to facilitate the transfer of land, and preventing individual owners from transferring their shares by way of imposing a joint tenancy made the transfer of property simpler. Further, because of the right of survivorship, the number of joint tenants would eventually decrease to one, making it far simpler for the purchaser who would have to investigate the legal title.

The aim of the 1925 legislation in facilitating the transfer of property can also be seen by the fact that s.34(2) also restricted the number of legal owners to four. If there are more than four owners, the first four will appear on the title but they will hold this on trust for themselves and the other co-owners.

Example

Antonia, Bill, Charles, David and Enid purchase Redacre together as joint tenants. The first four names will appear on the register of title but this will be held on trust for all five of them, as shown in Figure 11.7.

Legal   [A + B + C + D]

Equitable   [A + B + C + D + E]

Figure 11.7

Severance of joint tenancy in equity

Whilst there must be a joint tenancy with regards to a legal estate, it is possible to convert a joint tenancy in equity by way of severance. It is important to remember the rule: *severance only in equity*. Before considering severance in detail, however, it is convenient to examine the nature of a tenancy in common first.

Tenancy in common

Undivided shares in land

Tenancies in common can only arise as equitable interests. Tenants in common are entitled to a share of the property, which they can freely dispose of during their lifetime by selling it or giving it away, or by will or by intestacy. See the example below and contrast it with the example above.

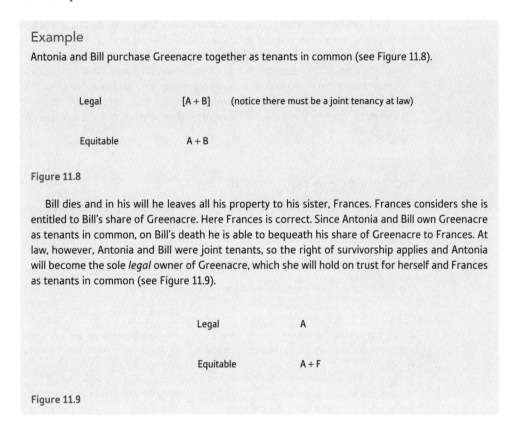

> **Example**
>
> Antonia and Bill purchase Greenacre together as tenants in common (see Figure 11.8).
>
> Legal   [A + B]   (notice there must be a joint tenancy at law)
>
> Equitable   A + B
>
> **Figure 11.8**
>
> Bill dies and in his will he leaves all his property to his sister, Frances. Frances considers she is entitled to Bill's share of Greenacre. Here Frances is correct. Since Antonia and Bill own Greenacre as tenants in common, on Bill's death he is able to bequeath his share of Greenacre to Frances. At law, however, Antonia and Bill were joint tenants, so the right of survivorship applies and Antonia will become the sole *legal* owner of Greenacre, which she will hold on trust for herself and Frances as tenants in common (see Figure 11.9).
>
> Legal   A
>
> Equitable   A + F
>
> **Figure 11.9**

Rather confusingly, the Law of Property Act refers to a tenancy in common as being an 'undivided share' in land, but remember, this is referring to the land itself being undivided rather than the proportionate parts of their share. The land itself is co-owned and so, whilst the parties may have a half, quarter or one-eighth share, etc., an individual cannot point to part of the land and say 'that part belongs to me'.

Only unity of possession

Whilst the four unities may be present in a tenancy in common, only unity of possession is actually required. This is fairly obvious since, if there was no unity of possession, there would be no co-ownership anyway, as each party would be claiming a specific part of the land in question.

One unity that is particularly absent in a tenancy in common is the unity of interest, since the proportions in which the tenants hold the land may be, and often are, very different in that one party may hold a half share whilst three others may hold a one-sixth share each. Each of these shares can be disposed of during the lifetime of the tenant, or on his or her death, since there is no right of survivorship in a tenancy in common. This is an important consideration in some relationships – whether private or commercial – where the parties may not want their share to devolve automatically to their co-owner on their death.

Example

Richard and Denise decide to set up home together and jointly purchase Blackacre. Both Richard and Denise have been married before and have children from their previous relationships. They both wish their children to inherit their share of Blackacre when they die. Clearly, they will hold the legal title as joint tenants, but it would be inappropriate for them to hold as joint tenants in equity since here the right of survivorship will mean that the share of each will automatically pass to their partner. They should ensure that the equitable interest is conveyed to them as tenants in common since they can now draft their wills so that their respective children inherit their share.

No tenancy in common at law

As we have noted already, it is not possible to create a tenancy in common at law. Any attempt to convey a legal title to co-owners as tenants in common will simply mean that they will have a joint tenancy at law, provided the four unities are present, and a tenancy in common in equity.

The difference between joint tenancies and tenancies in common

Joint tenancy	Tenancy in common
The right of survivorship applies once co-owner's shares devolve automatically to the other co-owners on death.	No right of survivorship – a co-owner may devolve their share to anyone during their lifetime or on their death.
Can exist as a legal estate or an equitable interest.	Cannot exist as a legal interest.
The 'four unities' must be present.	Only unity of possession *must* exist.
A joint tenancy operates as a single composite ownership, so that all the co-owners own the whole.	The tenants in common own a proportionate undivided share of the property.

Distinguishing between joint tenancies and tenancies in common in equity

Having examined the differences between joint tenancies and tenancies in common, we now need to examine how each type is created in practice in equity. We do not need to consider the legal estate here as we have been at pains to point out this can only exist as a joint tenancy.

A joint tenancy or a tenancy in common can arise by way of an express declaration or by the application of certain equitable presumptions. It should, however, be borne in mind that these processes may be upset by the application of the general law.

Express declaration

It is possible for the parties to make an express provision in the conveyance or transfer as to how they are to hold their beneficial interests. So, for example, if the property is still unregistered, the conveyance may declare that the parties are to hold the land as joint tenants or tenants in common of the beneficial interest. Often, however, the conveyance may not be so explicit and may describe the parties as having an 'undivided share' which, as we have already seen, connotes a tenancy in common. In some cases, though, the conveyance does not use such terms but uses expressions that amount to 'words of severance'. Words of severance are any words that indicate that the co-owners are to have distinct shares. Thus, words such as 'equally', 'in equal shares' or 'to be divided between' indicate that a tenancy in common is being created. Similarly, if the conveyance measures the shares the parties are to receive, it will also indicate that a tenancy in common is being created – for example, A is to have a two-thirds share and B a one-third share.

In registered land, the transfer form enables the parties to determine how the parties are to hold the beneficial interest. The transfer form, known as Form TR1 (see Figure 11.10), was introduced under the Land Registration Rules 1997 to enable the parties to state if they hold the property as joint tenants on trust for themselves, or as tenants in common in equal shares, or whether they are to hold the property on trust – which would apply if the parties were to hold the beneficial interests in unequal shares. Once the Land Registry has received this form, it makes the appropriate entry in the register to reflect the responses in Form TR1. It is, however, not obligatory for the parties to complete this part of the form and declare the nature of their beneficial interests. In **Stack v Dowden** [2007] UKHL 17, the size or type of each owner's share was not declared, with the result that Ms Dowden was able to claim a larger share of the beneficial interest. In that case, Baroness Hale considered it was unfortunate that this part of Form TR1 was not mandatory as the type of problem that arose in **Stack v Dowden** would not have materialised since the equitable interests of the parties would have been decided and declared at the outset, but more on this case later.

By virtue of the Land Registration Act 2002 s.44(1) the registrar is obliged to enter a restriction on the land register when presented with co-ownership of land and thus a trust of land. The Land Registration Act 2002 s.44(1) provides:

> If the registrar enters two or more persons in the register as the proprietor of a registered estate in land, he must also enter in the register such restrictions as rules may provide for the purpose of securing that interests which are capable of being overreached on a disposition of the estate are overreached.

The restriction entered on the register is usually framed in the following terms:

> No disposition by a sole proprietor of the registered estate . . . under which capital money arises is to be registered unless authorised by an order of the court.

Two matters arise from this restriction. Firstly, a purchaser is not able to look behind the trusts to see what the terms of the trust are. This is because of the 'curtain' principle that we referred to in Chapter 5. The purchaser therefore only has knowledge of the fact of the trust. Secondly, the restriction alerts the purchaser that they must pay their purchase monies to two trustees and obtain a valid receipt from them. As we saw in the previous chapter, if the purchaser does this, then the overreaching provisions in the Law of Property Act 1925 s.27(2) apply (as amended by TOLATA 1996) so that they can disregard the beneficial interests which are swept off the land.

Land Registry
Transfer of whole of registered title(s)

If you need more room than is provided for in a panel, and your software allows, you can expand any panel in the form. Alternatively use continuation sheet CS and attach it to this form.

Leave blank if not yet registered.	**1** Title number(s) of the property:
Insert address including postcode (if any) or other description of the property, for example 'land adjoining 2 Acacia Avenue'.	**2** Property:
	3 Date:
Give full name(s).	**4** Transferor:
Complete as appropriate where the transferor is a company.	**For UK incorporated companies/LLPs** Registered number of company or limited liability partnership including any prefix: **For overseas companies** (a) Territory of incorporation: (b) Registered number in the United Kingdom including any prefix:
Give full name(s).	**5** Transferee for entry in the register:
Complete as appropriate where the transferee is a company. Also, for an overseas company, unless an arrangement with Land Registry exists, lodge either a certificate in Form 7 in Schedule 3 to the Land Registration Rules 2003 or a certified copy of the constitution in English or Welsh, or other evidence permitted by rule 183 of the Land Registration Rules 2003.	**For UK incorporated companies/LLPs** Registered number of company or limited liability partnership including any prefix: **For overseas companies** (a) Territory of incorporation: (b) Registered number in the United Kingdom including any prefix:
Each transferee may give up to three addresses for service, one of which must be a postal address whether or not in the UK (including the postcode, if any). The others can be any combination of a postal address, a UK DX box number or an electronic address.	**6** Transferee's intended address(es) for service for entry in the register:
	7 The transferor transfers the property to the transferee
Place 'X' in the appropriate box. State the currency unit if other than sterling. If none of the boxes apply, insert an appropriate memorandum in panel 11.	**8** Consideration ☐ The transferor has received from the transferee for the property the following sum (in words and figures): ☐ The transfer is not for money or anything that has a monetary value ☐ Insert other receipt as appropriate:

Figure 11.10 Reproduced with kind permission of Land Registry – Transfer of whole of registered title(s) http://www.landregistry.gov.uk/_media/downloads/forms/TR1.pdf. © Crown copyright 2012 Land Registry.

Place 'X' in any box that applies.	9	The transferor transfers with

Add any modifications.

9 The transferor transfers with

☐ full title guarantee

☐ limited title guarantee

Where the transferee is more than one person, place 'X' in the appropriate box.

10 Declaration of trust. The transferee is more than one person and

☐ they are to hold the property on trust for themselves as joint tenants

☐ they are to hold the property on trust for themselves as tenants in common in equal shares

Complete as necessary.

☐ they are to hold the property on trust:

The registrar will enter a Form A restriction in the register *unless*:

☒ an 'X' is placed:
  ☒ in the first box, or
  ☒ in the third box and the details of the trust or of the trust instrument show that the transferees are to hold the property on trust for themselves alone as joint tenants, *or*
☒ it is clear from completion of a form JO lodged with this application that the transferees are to hold the property on trust for themselves alone as joint tenants.

Please refer to Land Registry's Public Guide *18 – Joint property ownership* and Practice Guide *24 – Private trusts of land* for further guidance. These guides are available on our website www.landregistry.gov.uk

Insert here any required or permitted statement, certificate or application and any agreed covenants, declarations and so on.

11 Additional provisions

The transferor must execute this transfer as a deed using the space opposite. If there is more than one transferor, all must execute. Forms of execution are given in Schedule 9 to the Land Registration Rules 2003. If the transfer contains transferee's covenants or declarations or contains an application by the transferee (such as for a restriction), it must also be executed by the transferee.

12 Execution

If there is more than one transferee and panel 10 has been completed, each transferee may also execute this transfer to comply with the requirements in section 53(1)(b) of the Law of Property Act 1925 relating to the declaration of a trust of land. Please refer to Land Registry's Public Guide *18 – Joint property ownership* and Practice Guide *24 – Private trusts of land* for further guidance.

WARNING
If you dishonestly enter information or make a statement that you know is, or might be, untrue or misleading, and intend by doing so to make a gain for yourself or another person, or to cause loss or the risk of loss to another person, you may commit the offence of fraud under section 1 of the Fraud Act 2006, the maximum penalty for which is 10 years' imprisonment or an unlimited fine, or both.

Failure to complete this form with proper care may result in a loss of protection under the Land Registration Act 2002 if, as a result, a mistake is made in the register.

Under section 66 of the Land Registration Act 2002 most documents (including this form) kept by the registrar relating to an application to the registrar or referred to in the register are open to public inspection and copying. If you believe a document contains prejudicial information, you may apply for that part of the document to be made exempt using Form EX1, under rule 136 of the Land Registration Rules 2003.

© Crown copyright (ref: LR/HO) 10/12

Figure 11.10 *(cont'd)*

Example

Antonia and Bill are the registered proprietors of Blackacre, which has been transferred to them as tenants in common. When Blackacre was transferred to them, the Land Registry would have entered a restriction on the title. This is important since the purchaser would now know that they have to pay their purchase monies to two trustees, Antonia and Bill, to overreach the beneficial interests. The position is shown in Figure 11.11.

Legal   [A + B]

Equitable   A + B

Figure 11.11

However, because Antonia and Bill hold as tenants in common, it is possible for, say, Bill to have sold his share to Charles. The position is now as shown in Figure 11.12.

Legal   [A + B]

Equitable   A + C

Figure 11.12

You will notice that the ownership to the legal title does not change – remember, there is no severance allowed of a joint tenancy at law, so Antonia and Bill will continue to hold the legal title in their names but on trust for Antonia and Charles. Since there has been no change in the legal title, there is no way that a purchaser will be aware of the change in the equitable title as the curtain principle prevents them from seeing this information. That, in itself, is of no concern to the purchaser providing they pay their purchase money to the two trustees, Antonia and Bill, since the overreaching process means that the beneficial interests of Antonia and Charles are swept off the land into the proceeds of sale. If Charles needs to recover his share of the property, he will need to pursue Antonia and Bill.

Where the property is conveyed to the co-owners as joint tenants in law and in equity, the entering of the restriction is unnecessary since, unless the joint tenancy in equity is severed, a purchaser will know there will be no other undisclosed beneficial interests. If, in the future, severance does take place, a purchaser will know that there are two trustees and the overreaching provisions will apply. As we have seen, with a joint tenancy comes the right of survivorship, and eventually, as the joint owners die, the property will be held by a sole owner. As we saw in the last chapter, the purchaser is protected here by the operation of the Law of Property (Joint Tenants) Act 1964 s.1.

Where there is no express declaration

Where there is no express declaration or words of severance then, providing the four unities were present, a presumption of a joint tenancy arises, based on the principle that 'equity follows the law'. The effect therefore is that, if the land is conveyed to the co-owners as joint tenants, then, in the absence of other evidence, they hold as joint tenants in both equity and law. This position was confirmed in the case of **Stack v Dowden** [2007] UKHL 17 in which Baroness Hale confirmed that this was always the starting point in deciding the interests of the parties.

Equity, however, does not favour joint tenancies since it considered the lottery effect of the right of survivorship to be unfair; indeed, the position was summed up in the maxim 'survivorship is odious in equity'. There are therefore circumstances in which equity does not follow the law and imposes its own counter-presumptions so that the parties are presumed to have intended to create a tenancy in common. There are four sets of circumstances that we need to consider here.

Land held by business partnerships

Where co-ownership is of a commercial nature, equity considers the right of survivorship to be inappropriate and that the co-owners hold that beneficial interest as tenants in common: **Lake v Craddock** (1732) 3 PWMS 158. The presumption is based on the reasoning that business co-owners would always wish their interest to fall into their estate and pass under the terms of their will or intestacy. This principle also applies where there is a tenancy of business premises granted to the parties as joint tenants who each occupy separate areas – for instance, if two businesses share business premises: **Malayan Credit Ltd v Jack Chia-MPH Ltd** [1986] AC 549.

Money lent on a mortgage

If two people, A and B, lend money to an owner of property, M, and as security for the loan M mortgages the property to A and B, then in those circumstances A and B hold their interest in the property as tenants in common. The reason behind this presumption is that equity presumes that if a person lends their own money then they intend to take back their own money from the transaction: **Morley v Bird** (1798) 3 Ves 628. It should be noted that this presumption applies whether or not the parties lend money in equal shares.

The purchase of land in unequal shares

Where co-owners contribute to the purchase price in unequal shares – for example, A pays £150,000 and B pays £50,000, then equity considers it unfair to impose a joint tenancy on the parties so that the right of survivorship will deprive a party of their interest on their death. The effect therefore is that each party will hold an equitable interest in proportion to their own contribution. Essentially, the parties hold the legal title as joint tenants on a resulting trust for themselves as tenants in common in equity: **Bull v Bull** [1955] 1 QB 234.

It should be noted that the converse is also true in that, if the parties contribute in *equal* shares, they may be regarded as being presumed to hold as joint tenants as in either case the presumption can be rebutted by evidence to the contrary.

Inference of a common intention to create a tenancy in common

Overruling the presumption that 'Equity follows the law'

This exception to the principle that equity follows the law emerged out of the cases of **Stack v Dowden** [2007] UKHL 17 and **Jones v Kernott** [2011] UKSC 53. These two cases are very important and raise issues relating to whether there is a joint tenancy or tenancy in common and the proportions of the respective beneficial shares. For the moment, we will confine ourselves to the former matter. In these cases, the House of Lords and the Supreme Court recognised that, in the absence of any evidence to the contrary, where a couple purchase a family home in their joint names, the presumption is that they intend to own the property jointly in equity also. The courts, however, decided that, if a party can demonstrate a common intention that the equitable interest was to be held as a tenancy in common, the courts will apply that intention. Importantly, though, the common intentions of the parties may change over the course of the relationship so that, whilst the parties may start off having a common intention to hold the equitable interest as joint tenants (which would, in any event, be presumed in the absence of contrary agreement), circumstances may arise during the course of the relationship so that a tenancy in common is inferred. The courts considered that a constructive trust may arise during the relationship that effectively changes the shares of the parties, thus producing a revised position. So, whilst parties start off with a joint tenancy, the fact that exceptional circumstances cause a shift to unequal shares produces the tenancy in common.

Stack v Dowden [2007] UKHL 17

The parties were an unmarried couple who, while living together for several years, had purchased a house for themselves and their children as the family home. The house had been registered in their names as joint tenants. At that time, Form TR1 did not provide the transferees with the opportunity to state that they were holding the property in trust for themselves, or how they wished to hold their beneficial interests. Eventually, the relationship broke down and Mrs D ('D') served a notice on her former partner, Mr Stack ('S'), that she was severing her joint tenancy, which would have the effect of converting her interest into a tenancy in common.

S then applied for and obtained from the court an order under TOLATA 1996 s.14 that the property should be sold and the proceeds divided on a 50:50 basis between himself and D. D considered this to be unfair as she had made a greater contribution towards the cost of purchasing the property and appealed to the Court of Appeal, which held that she was entitled to a 65% share in the property.

S appealed to the House of Lords, stating that the decision in *Goodman v Gallant* [1986] Fam 106 stated that, where a joint tenancy was severed, this produced a tenancy in common based on a 50:50 share. In the House of Lords, Baroness Hale provided the leading judgment, which Lords Hoffman, Hope and Walker all concurred with.

Baroness Hale's starting point was not controversial and provided a reinstatement of established principles: that is, in the absence of agreement to the contrary, the presumption is that equity follows the law and that the beneficial interests should reflect the legal interests in the property so that these interests would also be held as joint tenants. She stated that the onus is on the party seeking to show that the beneficial interest is different from the legal ownership – i.e. a joint tenancy. Lord Neuberger, however, dissented from this proposition, stating in *Stack v Dowden* at para 69:

> Where the only additional relevant evidence to the fact that the property has been acquired in joint names is the extent of each party's contribution to the purchase price, the beneficial ownership at the time of acquisition will be held, in my view, in the same proportions as the contributions to the purchase price. That is the resulting trust solution.

Lord Neuberger considered that equity has always favoured the solution of the resulting trust. In arriving at this opinion, he relied on a series of cases: *Dyer v Dyer* (1788) 2 Cox EqCas 92; *Pettitt v Pettitt* [1970] AC 777; *Gissing v Gissing* [1971] AC 886; and *Malayan Credit Ltd v Jack Chia-MPH Ltd* [1986] 1 AC 549 in which Lord Brightman approved the view that a joint tenancy in equity is rebutted where the legal owners 'have provided the purchase money in unequal shares'. He also referred to the decision in *Westdeutsche Landesbank Girozentrale v Islington Borough Council* [1996] AC 669 where Lord Browne-Wilkinson stated that a resulting trust arises:

> where A . . . pays (wholly or partly) for the purchase of property which is vested . . . in the joint names of A and B, there is a presumption that A did not intend to make a gift to B . . . the property is held . . . in shares proportionate to their contributions.

The rest of the House of Lords did not concur with this view and considered that, in the absence of the parties' agreement, the proportion in which the parties contribute to the purchase of their property should not determine their entitlement as to their shares in the property. Baroness Hale considered that the law had moved on 'in response to changing social and economic conditions'. She considered that the search now 'is to ascertain the parties' shared intentions, actual, inferred or imputed, with respect to the property in the light of their whole course of conduct in relation to it'. The result of this was that the House of Lords rejected the presumption of a resulting trust and the notion that a tenancy in common would arise from the parties making unequal contributions to the purchase price.

The position is clear then that, in a domestic situation, the basic presumption holds good that equity follows the law and that if the transfer is into joint names then unequal contributions do not displace the principle that the parties will hold the legal and beneficial titles on the basis of a joint tenancy. This position is confirmed in the case of *Jones* v *Kernott* [2011] UKSC 53 where Baroness Hale and Lord Walker stated at para 15:

> At its simplest the principle in Stack v Dowden is that a 'common interest' trust for the cohabitants' home to belong to them jointly in equity as well as on the proprietorship register, is the default option in joint name cases. The trust can be classified as a constructive trust, but it is not at odds with the parties' legal ownership. Beneficial ownership mirrors legal ownership. What it is at odds with is the presumption of a resulting trust.

Having said all this, the presumption of a beneficial joint tenancy is capable of being displaced, either at the time of the transfer or, indeed, later on in the relationship. As indicated earlier, the onus of seeking to prove this displacement lies on the party seeking it; however, their lordships stated that this burden is not easy to establish. Baroness Hale considered that the task was not something 'to be lightly embarked upon'. She considered that there were many factors that might be relevant to divining the parties' true intentions and that even the parties' individual characters and personalities may be a factor. She emphasised the difficulty by stating in *Stack* v *Dowden* at para 69:

> At the end of the day, having taken all this into account, cases in which joint legal owners are to be taken to have intended that their beneficial interests should be different from their legal interests will be very unusual.

Baroness Hale set out the types of factor that might be relevant as displacing the presumption, such as:

- advice or discussions at the time of the transfer that might shine light on the intentions of the parties;
- the reasons why the home was acquired in their joint names;
- the purpose for which the home was acquired;
- the nature of the parties' relationship;
- how the purchase of the home was financed, both initially and subsequently;
- how the parties arranged their finances, whether separately or together or 'a bit of both';
- how they paid for the outgoings on the property and their other household bills.

This was not, however, to be considered as an exhaustive list.

At the end of the day, the House of Lords decided that the case before them fell into one of the 'unusual' cases Baroness Hale referred to. Significantly, D had made a far greater contribution to the purchase of the property than S. Further, the couple had organised their finances so that they were almost entirely separate and they had separate bank accounts. Most of S's mail and bank statements were sent to his father's postal address. In short, their relationship could only be described as 'semi-detached'. On this basis, the House of Lords decided that there should be a 65:35 division of the property in favour of D since the conduct of the parties adduced the fact that the parties did not intend that a joint tenancy along with the right of survivorship should arise. The parties were never operating on the basis of a common purse.

In **Stack v Dowden** Baroness Hale considered that, whilst the parties might have set out with a common intention that their beneficial interests would be held jointly, it was possible for this position to change over the course of their relationship and, indeed, it was possible for their position to change following the end of the relationship. Such a situation occurred in the case of **Jones v Kernott** [2011] UKSC 53.

Jones v Kernott [2011] UKSC 53

The case concerned a couple who purchased a house together in 1985 for £245,000. Ms Jones ('J') contributed £6000 to the purchase price, with the remainder being funded by way of a mortgage. J paid the outgoings on the property, including the mortgage and the bills. Mr Kernott ('K') paid for the improvements to the property. In 1993 the couple split up; K moved out and made no further financial contributions to the property. The couple then cashed in a joint life insurance policy and divided the proceeds, with K using his share to purchase a property for his own use in 1996.

In 2006 K decided to seek his share of the original family home from J, who then sought a declaration to the effect that she was the sole beneficial owner. Whilst J acknowledged that they had initially purchased the property as joint owners, J argued that K had a reduced beneficial interest by having not made any contribution since moving out of the property 13 years earlier. K argued that, on the basis that equity follows the law, the property was held jointly both in law and in equity and, as such, it should be divided on a 50:50 basis.

In the County Court and High Court it was held that K was entitled to a mere 10% of the value of the property, based on the fact that J had made significant contribution towards the property both before and during the 13-year separation period. The judge also considered that K had shown no interest in the property during the separation period and, in addition, he had received a share of the insurance policy, which enabled him to purchase another property. However, he was only able to pay the mortgage instalments because he was not contributing to the purchase of the former family home, not contributing towards the support of his children. The judge considered the decision in **Stack v Dowden** in that, whilst equity followed the law, it was possible for the intentions of the parties to change. Furthermore, the judge found that following the case of **Oxley v Hiscock** [2005] Fam 211 he was obliged to arrive at a decision that was fair and just for both parties, given the background of the circumstances.

K appealed and the Court of Appeal overturned the decision at first instance. The Court of Appeal also had regard to **Stack v Dowden** and found that, since the parties had never discussed how they held their property or drawn up a document indicating this, the presumption was that where two people buy a property in joint names then they held the equitable interest jointly. The Court of Appeal considered there was no evidence to prove that the intentions of the parties had changed following their separation and, as such, the presumption of joint entitlement had not been overturned. It should be noted that, at the time of the transfer, there was no facility on Form TR1 enabling the transferees to clarify the beneficial ownership of the property. The Court of Appeal therefore held that J and K had a 50:50 share in the family home.

J appealed to the Supreme Court, which unanimously reversed the decision of the Court of Appeal and reinstated the decision from first instance that J and K were to hold the beneficial interest on a 90:10 proportion respectively. The Supreme Court affirmed the decision in **Stack v Dowden** that the intentions of the parties under the common intention trust is capable of changing the proportionate shares of the parties and overturned the presumption that a transfer into joint names at law also carries with it a jointly held beneficial interest. The Supreme Court applied the following principles where a family home is bought in the joint names of a cohabiting couple who are both responsible for any mortgage without declaration of their beneficial interests:

1 The starting point is that equity follows the law and they are joint tenants in both law and equity.

2 This presumption can be displaced by showing:

   (a) that the parties had a different common intention at the time they acquired the home; or

   (b) that they later formed the common intention that their respective shares would change.

3 Their common intention is to be deduced objectively from their conduct.

4 Where it is clear that the parties did not intend a joint tenancy at the outset, or had changed their original intention, but it is not possible to ascertain by direct evidence or by inference what their actual intention was as to the shares in which they would own the property then the principle set out by Chadwick LJ in **Oxley v Hiscock** [2005] Fam 211 para 69 would be applied – that is: 'each is entitled to that share which the court considered fair having regard to the whole course of dealing between them in relation to the property'. The Supreme Court considers that the 'whole course of dealing' should be given a broad meaning, enabling a range of factors to be taken into account 'as may be relevant to ascertaining the parties' actual intentions'.

5 Each case will turn on its own facts. Financial contributions are relevant but there may be other factors that might enable a court to decide that shares were either intended, as in 3 above, or fair, as in 4 above.

The Supreme Court demonstrated that whilst its primary aim is to ascertain the actual intentions of the parties, whether expressed or inferred, if it is not possible to do so then the court may 'impose an intention which the parties may never have had'. This paves the way for a court to make a decision based on what it believes to be fair in cases where the intentions of the parties are not known. It is on the last point that the members of the Supreme Court had different opinions. Should the new intentions of the parties be *imputed* to them by the court, or should the new intentions be *inferred* by the court having regard to the conduct of the parties? The difference between the two is important, as Neuberger LJ stated in **Stack v Dowden** at para 136:

> An inferred intention is one which is objectively deduced to be the subjective actual intention of the parties, in the light of their actions and statements. An imputed intention is one which is attributed to the parties, even though no such actual intention can be deduced from their actions or statements, and even though they had no such intention. Imputation involves concluding what the parties would have intended, whereas inference involves concluding what they did intend.

Clearly, there are conceptual differences between the two mechanisms of determining the positions of the parties. Lord Neuberger considered that, whilst the intentions of the parties may be inferred from their actions, these intentions may not be imputed. Baroness Hale and Lord Walker considered that, in practice, the difference between the two was marginal and indicated that imputing intentions to the parties was a last resort if it was impossible 'to divine a common intention as to the proportions' in which the beneficial interests were to be shared. They stated that the courts had a duty to reach a decision even in the most difficult cases where there is sparse and conflicting evidence. Obviously, there are dangers in ascribing intentions to the parties that they may never have had. However, in the absence of subjective intentions, the courts need to arrive at a decision as to the proportions of the beneficial interests on an objective assessment as to what was fair; fairness being based on what the parties, as reasonable people, would have thought at the relevant time, regard being had to their whole course of dealing in relation to the property. They stated:

> . . . where the parties already share the beneficial interest, and the question is what their interests are and whether their interests have changed, the court will try to deduce what their actual intentions were at the relevant time. It cannot impose a solution upon them which is contrary to what the evidence shows that they actually intended. But if it cannot deduce exactly what shares were intended, it may have no alternative but to ask what their intentions as reasonable and just people would have been had they thought about it at the time. This is the fallback position which some courts may not welcome, but the court has a duty to come to a conclusion on the dispute put before it.

Lord Collins did not express any strong views on the matter and considered that the difference between inference and imputation would hardly ever matter and 'that what is one person's inference will be another person's imputation'. Lord Kerr, however, considered that there was a strong demarcation line between the two concepts. He questioned the appropriateness of imputing an intention that is 'in the final analysis . . . wholly unrelated to the ascertainment of the parties' views'. He considered that, once it is not possible to infer an intention, the court should simply base its decision on what is fair, which is a different exercise than deciding what the parties actually intended. Lord Wilson also considered that the intentions of the parties could be imputed, though he considered that this related to the size or proportions of the parties' interests. He considered this was necessary since, whilst it was possible to infer from the matrix of facts surrounding the relationship of the parties and to depart from the presumption that they held the beneficial interest jointly, it would be rare for this to determine the actual proportions. This could only be decided on what is fair against the matrix of facts and that the proportions arrived at would be imputed to the parties.

Other matters arising out of *Stack v Dowden*

The burden of proof in displacing the joint tenancy presumption

It was stated earlier that the onus of seeking to displace the presumption of a joint tenancy is not easy and that Baroness Hale considered that it was not something 'to be lightly embarked upon'. Indeed, Baroness Hale considered that the cases where joint legal owners are to be taken as having intended that their beneficial interests would be held differently will be 'very unusual'. The question that emerges from this is: just how easy or difficult is it to establish the displacement? A number of cases have emerged that have dealt with this point.

Adekunle v *Ritchie* [2007] BPIR 1177

In this case, a son and his mother owned a property in joint names. Initially, the son lived with his mother, but they later quarrelled so he moved out. Originally, the mother had purchased the property under the Right to Buy scheme, which allowed council house tenants to purchase their houses; however, since she could not get a mortgage in her own right, her son had agreed to be a party to the mortgage. Mother and son were registered as joint legal owners; however, there was no declaration made as to the decision of the beneficial interests on Form TR1. The mother died and the executors applied for an order of sale under TOLATA 1996 s.14 so that the proceeds could be divided among the mother's 10 children. Her son opposed the application and claimed that, as they held the property as joint tenants, the right of survivorship applied and he was entitled to sole ownership of the property.

The court applied **Stack v Dowden** and decided the circumstances were such that there was a common intention that the beneficial interest would not be held as a joint tenancy but as beneficial tenants in common. The judge considered there was evidence that the parties had not intended to hold equal equitable shares. The mother had obtained a substantial discount on the property by virtue of the Right to Buy scheme and her occupation of the property, and although mother and son had taken out a joint mortgage to which both contributed, in fact the mother had made all the repayments on her own following her son's departure from the property. The judge also took into account the fact that the principal purpose for the purchase was to provide a home for the mother and that the mother would never have intended to deprive her other nine children of a share from the sale of her house, which was her principal asset. It was noted that the financial affairs of mother and son were kept entirely separate. The judge found that the shares of mother and son would be calculated on a 70:30 respective share basis.

The judge in the case considered the burden of proving a displacement of the joint tenancy presumption and finding a common intention that they held the beneficial interest in unequal shares to be lighter in circumstances where the co-owners are not living together.

Fowler v *Barron* [2008] EWCA Civ 377

Here the couple lived together for some 17 years in a house that was registered in their joint names. There was no declaration as to how the beneficial interest was to be shared. Mr Barron paid all the mortgage repayments and other outgoings on the property. The couple then split up and Mr Barron claimed the whole of the beneficial interest, despite the fact that the house was in joint names.

At first instance, the judge agreed with Mr Barron's claim and awarded him the entire beneficial interest, finding that there was no common intention that the beneficial interest should be shared equally. At the time of the judgment the judge did not have the benefit of the House of Lords decision in **Stack v Dowden**, only the Court of Appeal decision. Mrs Fowler appealed.

In the Court of Appeal, reference was made to the judgment of Baroness Hale in **Stack v Dowden** in the House of Lords. Arden LJ considered that the judge at first instance had put too much emphasis on the financial contributions made by Mr Barron. Arden LJ, following Baroness Hale's judgment, stated that, in arriving at a decision about the beneficial interest, it was necessary to look at the totality of the parties' conduct in arriving at the common intentions of the parties. Arden LJ stated that, since the property had been bought in joint names and given there was no express declaration of the beneficial interest on the transfer form, the presumption that 'equity follows the law' applied and thus a presumption of a joint beneficial interest arose.

In the case, Mr Barron had argued that he only intended that Ms Fowler would benefit on his death and that he did not understand the effects of putting the house into their joint names at law. Arden LJ considered that, to rebut the presumption, there had to be a *shared* common intention that the beneficial interest would be held otherwise than in joint names. Since Mr Barron had not made his intentions known to Ms Fowler, there was no shared common intention. Arden LJ also considered that, whilst Mr Barron had made all the financial contributions to the costs of the mortgage and the other outgoings, both direct and indirect, Ms Fowler had gone out to work and used her income to purchase family holidays and clothes for the children. Arden LJ found that the parties were not concerned as to who paid for what during the currency of their relationship and indeed the existence of mutual wills provided additional evidence that they held the beneficial interest together. The existence of the mutual wills provided an indication that each party had a beneficial interest to convey, since otherwise there was no need for such a will.

The Court of Appeal, looking at the totality of the relationship and not just the financial contributions, did not consider that the presumption of equal beneficial interests had been successfully rebutted and declared that Ms Fowler was entitled to a half share in the property and that an order for sale should be ordered. It should be noted that this finding of a joint beneficial ownership implies a joint tenancy in equity; however, the point is academic, since if it was a joint tenancy, Ms Fowler would have severed it, giving her a tenancy in common but with a 50% interest in the property. Toulson LJ stated that the burden of overturning the presumption is a heavy one and reiterated the point emphasised by Lord Walker and Baroness Hale that it is unusual for joint legal owners to have beneficial interests that are different from their legal interests. He stated that in ***Stack v Dowden*** the House of Lords considered the facts to be very unusual, but there was nothing unusual in the case before him. He concurred with Arden LJ that a common intention could not be inferred from the parties' conduct so as to deprive Ms Fowler of her original half-share.

Stack v Dowden and the family home

The basis behind ***Stack v Dowden*** lies in the arena of constructive trusts, which we will discuss in the next chapter. However, many of the cases in the House of Lords referred to cohabitees or (in the earlier cases) married couples – remember here the earlier proviso that, following the Matrimonial Causes Act 1973, the courts had wide powers, on divorce, to make property adjustment orders as regards married couples. To what extent does the ***Stack v Dowden*** decision cast its net wider to encompass other relationships within a family?

Stack v Dowden is vague on this point, though Baroness Hale stated that, in quantifying the beneficial interest and the common intentions of the parties, 'context is everything and the domestic context is very different from the commercial world'. She seemed, therefore, to be pitching the principles in the case towards the domestic situation. In setting the context for her judgment, she referred to the 8th Programme of Law Reform of the Law Commission (Law Com No. 274) where, under Item 1, the Law Commission set out to review the law as it relates to the property rights of those who share a home. This covered 'a broad range of people, including friends and relatives who share a home as well as unmarried couples and married couples (other than on the breakdown of marriage)'.

Clearly, ***Stack v Dowden*** seems to apply in this wider context and, of course, an example of this can be seen in ***Adekunle v Ritchie*** [2007] BPIR 1177. In that case it was proposed that ***Stack v Dowden*** only applied to relationships that involved a sexual relationship, which was rejected by the court. Indeed, in ***Laskar v Laskar*** [2008] EWCA Civ 347, which involved a house purchased by a mother and daughter, Lord Neuberger concurred with the stance taken in *Adekunle v Ritchie*. As we have seen, Lord Neuberger provided the dissenting judgment in *Stack v Dowden*, preferring a resulting trust solution to a situation where the property was jointly purchased with each party making different contributions to the purchase price. The resulting trust solution provides that, where property is acquired in joint names, then the beneficial interest will be held in the same proportions as the purchase price. One reason behind his stance is that the same principles should apply in assessing the appointment of the beneficial interests as between the legal owners, whether 'in a sexual, platonic, familial, amicable or commercial relationship'. In *Laskar v Laskar*, however, Lord Neuberger accepted there was a difference between familial/amicable relationships, etc. and commercial relationships. In that case, which involved a mother and daughter purchasing a house together for investment purposes, the house was never occupied by the mother or daughter but was let out to tenants. Lord Neuberger had no problem in deciding that the principles had no application to such a situation and decided the case on resulting trust principles.

Sole legal ownership

Cases where the legal interest is held in single ownership are very different from where the legal interest is held in joint names. As we have seen, in the latter there is a presumption that the beneficial interest is also held jointly. In sole legal ownership the presumption is that of sole beneficial ownership. Where a person wishes to establish that he has a beneficial interest 'the onus is on the party who wishes to show that he has any beneficial interest at all, and if so what that interest is' per Lord Hope in *Stack v Dowden*. The problem of establishing beneficial interest in such a context falls back on the processes found in resulting trusts and constructive trusts, which we will discuss in the next chapter.

Severance

We have already seen, and emphasised the importance of, the rule that at law it is only possible to have a joint tenancy – Law of Property Act 1925 s.1(6) and s.34(2). In equity, we may have a joint tenancy or a tenancy in common, or indeed both in certain situations. We have noted that *in equity* it is possible to sever the joint tenancy and convert it into a tenancy in common where the beneficial owners have a distinct share in the property.

We now need to consider the various ways in which the holder of a beneficial joint tenancy can sever his or her interest. Always remember that it is not possible to sever the joint tenancy at law since the Law of Property Act 1925 s.36(2) provides:

> no severance of a joint tenancy of a legal estate, so as to create a tenancy in common, shall be permissible, whether by law or otherwise, but this subsection does not affect the right of a joint tenant to release his interest to the other joint tenants, or the right to sever a joint tenancy in an equitable interest whether or not the legal estate is vested in the joint tenants . . .

There can be many reasons why a joint tenant may wish to sever his or her joint tenancy. Often it will be because the joint tenant wishes to avoid the right of survivorship enjoyed by his or her co-joint tenants since there is a desire for the severing joint tenant to pass his or her interest on to a beneficiary under his or her will. On the other hand, a joint tenant may wish to sell his or her share of the property in order to realise the capital value of his or her interest.

Where a person severs his or her joint tenancy he or she will be entitled to a tenancy in common based on an equal division. Thus if three people purchase a property together as joint tenants, in both law and equity when one severs he or she will be entitled to a one-third share of the beneficial interest, irrespective of the proportion contributed to the purchase price: *Goodman v Gallant* [1986] Fam 106, subject to the decision in *Stack v Dowden* [2007] UKHL 17.

Severance may arise in the following ways.

Statutory written notice

This form of severance is found within the Law of Property Act 1925 s.36(2) and is the simplest and most convenient means by which severance can take place. Section 36(2) provides:

> . . . where a legal estate (not being settled land) is vested in joint tenants beneficially, and any tenant desires to sever the joint tenancy in equity, he shall give to the other joint tenants a notice in writing of such desire or do such other acts or things as would, in the case of personal estate, have been effectual to sever the tenancy in equity, and thereupon the land shall be held in trust on terms which would have been requisite for giving effect to the beneficial interests if there had been an actual severance.

It will be noticed that severance under s.36(2) can be carried out entirely unilaterally and there is no requirement for the severing joint tenant to obtain the consent of his or her co-owners. Equally, there is no prescribed form required, although the notice must clearly express an intention to sever the joint tenancy immediately. It is therefore not possible to draft the notice in such a way that it is to take place in the future: *Harris v Goddard* [1982] 1 WLR 1203.

It is not necessary to show that the notice has been received or read by the other joint tenants, though there must be evidence that the notice has been delivered to them. The Law of Property Act 1925 s.196(3) provides that the notice will 'be sufficiently served if it is left at the last-known place of abode or business in the United Kingdom of the . . . person to be served'. Further, the Law of Property Act 1925 s.196(4) provides that a notice 'shall be sufficiently served, if it is sent by post in a registered letter addressed to the . . . person to be served'. Providing these formalities are carried out, it does not matter if the notice has not actually been received by the other joint tenants; thus if the notice is lost in the post it will still be deemed to have been effective: *Re 88 Berkeley Road NW9* [1971] Ch 648. Equally, however, if a person sends the notice by registered post but then decides to change their mind, the notice in any event will still be effective: *Kinch v Bullard* [1999] 1 WLR 423.

One further note that should be made about s.36(2) is the reference to 'in the case of personal estate'. This refers to the doctrine of conversion under a trust for sale. It will be recalled that, under a trust for sale, there was a presumption that the property should be sold. By virtue of the equitable maxim 'equity looks on that as done which ought to be done' the presumption was that the sale had already taken place, so that the interests of the beneficiaries were not interests in land but interests in personalty (i.e. the proceeds of sale), under the doctrine of conversion. The doctrine of conversion was abolished in TOLATA 1996 s.3 and thus the reference to 'personal estate' here is no longer of any relevance although it remains within the provision.

The modes of severance contained within *Williams v Hensman*

In *Williams v Hensman* (1861) 1 John + H 546 Sir William Page Wood V-C stated:

A joint tenancy may be severed in three ways: in the first place, an act of any one of the persons interested in operating upon his own share may create a severance as to that share ... Each one is at liberty to dispose of his own interest in such a manner as to sever it from the joint fund – losing, of course, at the same time, his own right of survivorship. Secondly, a joint tenancy may be severed by mutual agreement. And, in the third place, there may be severance by any course of dealing sufficient to intimate that the interests of all were mutually treated as constituting a tenancy in common.

It is necessary to look at these three methods in more detail.

'An act of any one of the persons interested in operating upon his own share'

Of course joint tenants do not own a 'share' as such, since a joint tenancy is one of single composite ownership; however, if a person acts in a way that evinces a desire to hold an individual share in the beneficial interest then this will operate as a severance of the beneficial joint tenancy. This can arise in a variety of ways. If one disposes of his or her interest, this will amount to an act of severance as unity of title will be destroyed and, since the four unities are required for the existence of a joint tenancy, the result must be that this amounts to severance. Typically, therefore, if one sells one's share to a purchaser, this will amount to severance. Two things should be noted here. Firstly, it is not possible to sell/transfer the legal title to the purchaser, since this would amount to a severance of the legal joint tenancy, which, as we have already seen, is not possible. Secondly, the act of severance arises on the exchange of contracts since, again, as we have already seen, the purchaser at this point acquires a beneficial interest in the property.

If a joint tenant acting alone mortgages his or her interest in the property (it is only possible for the joint tenant to mortgage his or her 'share' since a joint tenant acting alone clearly cannot charge the interests of his or her fellow beneficial owners) such an act must amount to an act of severance. The same is not true if the joint tenants acting collectively mortgage the whole beneficial interest, since this represents a mortgage on the single composite beneficial interest under the joint tenancy. The same is also true if a joint tenant fraudulently attempts to create a charge over a fellow joint tenant's share. Thus in *First National Securities v Hegarty* [1984] 1 All ER 139 a husband forged his wife's signature in order to mortgage the legal estate. It was held that this amounted to an act of severance by the husband so that the mortgage only attached to his own beneficial interest.

An act of bankruptcy will also amount to an act of severance – albeit one that is involuntary. In a bankruptcy, the bankrupt joint tenant's share is transferred to his or her trustee in bankruptcy by the court so that the joint tenant's share is available to satisfy his creditors.

A word of warning: it is not possible for severance to operate by will. The reason for this is that the right of survivorship operates immediately on the death of the joint tenant and thus it is too late for the will to operate as an act of severance. Having said this, in some circumstances the making of wills in collaboration with other joint tenants may operate as severance, as held in *Re Woolnough* [2002] WTLR 595, but this is severance by mutual agreement, which we discuss next.

Mutual agreement

Severance can arise if all the joint tenants are in agreement. The agreement need not be in writing and can arise either expressly or impliedly.

Burgess v Rawnsley [1975] Ch 429

In this case a couple, Mr Honick and Mrs Rawnsley, purchased a house together as joint tenants in law and in equity. Their relationship broke down and the couple began negotiations to enable Mr Honick to purchase Mrs Rawnsley's share of the property. Initially, a price was agreed at £750 but Mrs Rawnsley went back on her word and demanded more money. Before an agreement could be reached, Mr Honick died. The question then arose as to whether the joint tenancy had been severed. If not, Mrs Rawnsley was entitled to Mr Honick's share by virtue of the right of survivorship.

It was held that the negotiations for the transfer of Mrs Rawnsley's share to Mr Honick and the initial agreement for the sale at £750 amounted to an act of severance. This was despite the fact the agreement was not evidenced in writing under the Law of Property Act 1925 s.40 (now the Law of Property (Miscellaneous Provisions) Act 1989 s.2). If there had been evidence in writing then, as we have already noted, this would have been sufficient to bring the transaction with the first head under **Williams v Hensman** above. The absence of a written agreement would normally have meant that the agreement was unenforceable; however, in the case Browne LJ stated that the requirement of writing only applies in relation to alienation by a joint tenant to a third party and 'does not apply to severance by agreement between the joint tenants' inter se. The difficulty with this, though, is that in the Law of Property (Miscellaneous Provisions) Act 1989 s.2 the provision requires that any contract for the 'sale or disposition of an interest in land' is required to be in writing. If the case of **Burgess v Rawnsley** took place under this provision it is clear that the agreement for the sale of Mrs Rawnsley's share would now be void. It appears, however, that, whilst the mutual agreement arises out of the 'contract', it is not subject to the formalities required for such a contract. Indeed, Lord Denning stated that, even if an agreement had not been reached, there was sufficient evidence to provide an indication of the parties' intention to sever, by way of their mutual conduct. It appears that severance by mutual agreement is not required to adhere to the formalities required for the sale of disposition of an interest in land and, in this respect, it amounts to a distinct category.

The position above arose again in the case of **Hunter v Babbage** [1994] EGCS 8. In this case, a divorcing couple entered into an agreement for the division of their property on their divorce. Applications were made for the sale of the former matrimonial home and an affidavit was sworn that indicated that the defendant intended to apply for ancillary relief including a property adjustment order. Whilst the affidavit was sufficient to sever under s.36 it was not a notice under s.36 since it related to *future* severance. The husband died before the agreements could be formalised. It was held that a mutual agreement to sever can include an agreement to deal with the property in a way which involves severance and that this operates independently of the agreement. The agreement, though unenforceable, would operate to sever the joint tenancy.

We stated earlier that, whilst a will will not operate as a severance, where joint tenants together make wills that indicate they wish their shares in the joint tenancy to devolve according to their respective wills, this will operate as a severance. Such a situation arose in the case of **Re Woolnough** [2002] WTLR 595.

Re Woolnough [2002] WTLR 595

In this case, a brother and sister were joint tenants of a property. They both went to a solicitor to make their wills, in which they desired to leave their respective interests to each other but with a remainder to their niece. Subsequently, following his sister's death, the brother decided to change his will. However, he could only do this if making the earlier wills had operated so as to sever the joint tenancy.

The court held that for each party to leave their share to each other with a remainder to their niece demonstrated an intention to sever the joint tenancy. A similar situation would also arise if joint tenants make mutual wills leaving their respective shares to other third party beneficiaries since this would amount to severance by mutual agreement: *Re Wilford's Estate* (1879) 11 Ch D 267.

'Any course of dealing [intimating] that the interests of all were mutually treated as constituting a tenancy in common'

Where there has been no agreement to sever a joint tenancy, the conduct of the parties may be examined to discover if there is a mutual intention to sever by the joint tenants. *Burgess* v *Rawnsley* appears to provide evidence of such an instance, though the Court of Appeal was clear that this case fell within Sir William Page Wood's second head of severance. It is clear from his judgment that there needs to be some evidence of mutual conduct, thus Sir John Pennywick stated at 447 that 'negotiations which, although not otherwise resulting in any agreement, indicate a common intention that the joint tenancy should be regarded as severed'. Clearly, many instances of this head fall within the facts of the particular case. Sometimes discussions between the parties may have commenced but not concluded and, in such circumstances, the courts will not find for a mutual intention to sever. Certainly, there has to be something more than a 'mere verbal notice', as pointed out by Sir John Pennywick. Note also that this head rests on the basis of mutual intention, though Lord Denning stated obiter at 439 that 'it is sufficient if there is a course of dealing in which one party makes it clear to the other that he desires that their shares should no longer be held jointly but in common'. However, on the face of things this appears to go too far in that it seems to suggest that a unilateral declaration is sufficient.

Forfeiture

The right of survivorship in a joint tenancy ensures that, when a joint tenant dies, his or her interest passes to the surviving joint tenant(s). It is contrary to public policy for a joint tenant to kill a fellow joint tenant and therefore benefit from the rights of survivorship in that no one may benefit in law from their crime: *In the Estate of Hall* [1914] P 1. The rule applies whether the killing amounts to murder, manslaughter or where the offence of aiding and abetting a suicide is committed.

The effect of such a killing on co-ownership is not, however, a settled one in English law. Two potential ways of dealing with such a situation have been identified. Firstly, the killing is an act of severance converting the joint tenancy into a tenancy in common. For example, A and B are the co-owners of Blackacre and hold the legal title on trust for themselves as joint tenants in equity. A murders B. A now holds the legal estate solely (because of the right of survivorship) on trust for himself and B's estate as tenants in common (see Figure 11.13).

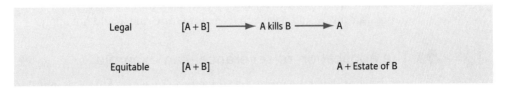

Figure 11.13

Where there are three (or more) co-owners, the automatic application of severance will have the effect of converting all the beneficial interests into tenants in common. For example, A, B and C own Blackacre and hold the legal estate on trust for themselves as joint tenants in equity. A murders B. A and C now hold the legal estate as joint tenants in common (see Figure 11.14).

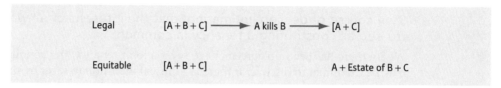

| Legal | [A + B + C] ⟶ A kills B ⟶ [A + C] |
| Equitable | [A + B + C]   A + Estate of B + C |

Figure 11.14

The second potential effect is not to have an automatic severance of the joint tenancy in equity but to have a constructive trust imposed. Where there are three or more co-owners, this has a slightly different effect, since here A and C will hold the legal estate on trust for A and C as joint tenants for two-thirds and C has one-third (see Figure 11.15).

Legal	[A + B + C] ⟶ A kills B ⟶ [A + C]
Equitable	[A + B + C] [A + C] + C
	2/3 1/3

Figure 11.15

The logic behind this approach is that a constructive trust is imposed to prevent a killer obtaining an unjust enrichment and thereby benefiting from their crime. Having said this, the killer is not prejudiced from the imposition of the trust in that they stand to forfeit their own interest in the land. Thus whilst they cannot acquire a share of the deceased's interest, which will pass to the other survivor (C), they will be entitled to retain their beneficial joint tenancy with C. In this way A is in no worse position but equally cannot benefit from his crime. This was the approach taken in the Australian case of **Rasmanis v Jurewitsch** (1969) 70 SR (NSW) 407.

It should be noted that under the Forfeiture Act 1882 the courts have a power to modify the application of the forfeiture rule. The court will have regard to the circumstances of the case and the conduct of the person committing the offence and do what is just and equitable as regards the rule. This would be of particular relevance in assisted suicide cases. Technically, in such cases the person is aiding and abetting a suicide and the forfeiture rule would apply. On 29 February 2010 the Director of Public Prosecutions announced that a difference should be made between malicious acts and those where a person acts out of compassion to assist the suicide of a person who has a terminal illness who is experiencing unbearable suffering. In the case of the latter, the Director of Public Prosecutions would not consider a prosecution to be appropriate. It would seem reasonable that, in such circumstances, a court would decide that the forfeiture rule would not apply.

The application of severance – an example

Having considered the means by which severance may arise, it is useful to see an example of how it operates.

A, B, C, D and E purchase Blackacre as joint tenants in law, as they must because of the operation of the Law of Property Act 1925 s.1(6) and s.34(2), and joint tenants in equity. Section 34(2) provides that the maximum number of legal owners is restricted to four. The position therefore is as shown in Figure 11.6.

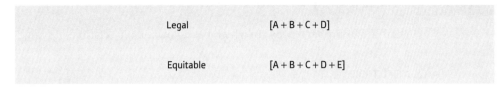

Figure 11.16

Note that each co-owner does not own a one-fifth share since they all own Blackacre as single composite owners.

E dies. Here the right of survivorship will apply in relation to her joint tenancy in equity and her share will pass to the other co-owners. Since E does not have a legal interest this is unaffected – see Figure 11.17.

Legal   [A + B + C + D]

Equitable   [A + B + C + D]

Figure 11.17

B decides that he wishes his share to pass to his wife on his death and serves notice to the other joint tenants under the Law of Property Act 1925 s.36(2). This will operate to convert his joint tenancy to a tenancy in common in equity. B will now own a one-quarter share whilst A, C and D will own three-quarters collectively. The structure of the co-ownership now appears as in Figure 11.18.

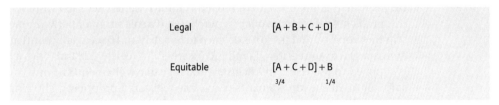

Figure 11.18

It can be seen that A, C and D remain as joint tenants.

D now decides to sell his interest to X. This operates as severance under *Williams* v *Hensman* [1861] 1 John + H 546 since there is no longer any unity of title. The position at law is unaffected by this, therefore the title appears as in Figure 11.19.

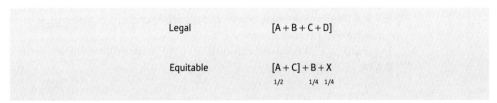

Figure 11.19

Thus A and C own one-half of the equitable interest as joint tenants, whilst B and X will own a one-quarter share each.

Terminating the co-ownership relationship

There are a number of ways in which the co-ownership relationship might end.

Partition

As we have already seen in the previous chapter, partition is the process whereby the land is physically divided up between the co-owners so that each co-owner becomes the sole owner of a distinct part of the land. Whilst all the co-owners can agree to organise their ownership in this way, it should be borne in mind that under TOLATA 1996 s.7(1) the trustees have a power to do this, although by s.7(3) the consent of the beneficiaries is required in order to give effect to it. If the land is unregistered, partition is a 'trigger' for compulsory first registration under the Land Registration Act 2002.

Union of the land in a sole tenant

Co-ownership ceases if the land becomes vested in a single beneficial owner. This arises where there is a joint tenancy in both law and equity because of the right of survivorship. This commonly arises where a husband and wife buy a property together, so when one of them dies the survivor becomes the sole owner of the property. It should be remembered from the previous chapter that this creates difficulties if a surviving co-owner decides to sell the property since there is no guarantee to a purchaser that the deceased co-owner had formerly severed their beneficial joint tenancy. As we saw, it is usual for a note or memorandum of any severance to be endorsed on to the title; however, the absence of such a note or memorandum is no guarantee that this has not occurred. We noted in the previous chapter that the Law of Property (Joint Tenants) Act 1964 s.1 provides a solution to this problem so that, in favour of a purchaser, if a sole survivor of two or more joint tenants sells the property, that person is deemed to be solely and beneficially entitled to the property, at least as far as unregistered land is concerned. In registered land, once a death certificate is supplied to the HM Land Registry, the registrar will amend the entry to show that the survivor of all the joint tenants is the sole registered proprietor, allowing a purchaser to purchase the property from the survivor confident that they can rely on the register.

It is also possible for one co-owner to 'buy out' the interests of all the other co-owners so he or she is now the sole owner of the property.

Sale

The co-owners may agree to sell the property, in which case, the overreaching provisions apply and their interests are converted into the proceeds of sale which they can then divide up into their respective shares.

It should be also borne in mind that a court may order a sale as per its discretion under TOLATA 1996 s.14.

Summary

Introduction

Co-ownership relates to a position where there are *concurrent* interests in the property. The law on co-ownership is really about assessing how the respective rights of the co-owners devolve as regards the legal and equitable/beneficial interests pertaining to the property.

There are two forms of co-ownership:

- joint tenants, and
- tenants in common.

Joint tenancy

Here the co-owners together own the whole property as a single composite owner – they do *not* own a share.

For a joint tenancy to exist the 'four unities' must be present:

- unity of title;
- unity of possession;
- unity of time;
- unity of interest.

Joint tenancies are subject to the right of survivorship (jus accrescendi) so that on the death of a joint tenant the interest passes to the remaining joint tenants automatically until the last remaining joint tenant (in the absence of severance) becomes the sole owner of the property.

The legal title can only be held as a joint tenancy and can never be severed into tenancy in common: Law of Property Act 1925 s.1(6) and s.34(2).

If there are more than four legal owners then only the names of the first four appear on the title: Law of Property Act 1925 s.34(2).

Severance of a joint tenancy is permissible in equity only.

Tenancy in common

Tenancies in common only arise in equity (see above).

Tenants in common have an 'undivided share' in the property, which they are free to dispose of either by sale, gift, will or by intestacy.

Only unity of possession is required for a tenancy in common.

Distinguishing between tenancies in common and joint tenancies

Joint tenancies and tenancies can arise:

- By way of an express declaration as to the type of tenancy (in equity), e.g. the use of the expression 'undivided share' or other words of severance for a tenancy in common.
- Where there is no express declaration where (providing the four unities are present) 'equity follows the law' so that a joint tenancy is implied in both law and equity. Equity does not favour a joint tenancy and presumes a tenancy in common in four situations:
  - where land is held by business partnerships;
  - where money is lent on a mortgage;
  - where land is purchased in unequal shares;

- where there is an inference of a tenancy in common:

> *Stack* v *Dowden* [2007] UKHL 17
>
> *Jones* v *Kernott* [2011] UKSC 53

Severance

Remember, severance is only possible in equity – only a joint tenancy is allowed at law: Law of Property Act 1925 s.36(2). Severance can arise by way of:

(a) Statutory written notice: Law of Property Act 1925 s.36(2).

(b) *Williams* v *Hensman* (1861) 1 John + H 546 in which three methods were set out:
  (i) an act of any one of the person interested in operating on his own share;
  (ii) mutual agreement;
  (iii) any cause of dealing indicating a tenancy in common.

(c) Forfeiture.

Terminating co-ownership

This can arise by way of:

(a) Partition – physically dividing the land between the co-owners so that they become sole owners of distinct parts of the land.

(b) Union of the land in a sole tenant – when land becomes vested in a single beneficial owner – for example, in a joint tenancy the right of survivorship leaves a sole owner.

(c) Sale – the co-owners may agree to sell the property and the overreaching provision means that their shares are converted into money which they then distribute to each other according to their respective shares.

Further reading

Severance

Conway, 'Joint Tenancies, Negotiations and Consensual Severance' [2009] 73 *The Conveyancer and Property Lawyer* 67

Crown, 'Severance of a Joint Tenancy of Land by Partial Alienation' (2001) 117 *Law Quarterly Review* 477

Hayton, 'Joint Tenancies – Severance' (1976) *Cambridge Law Journal* 20

Nield, 'To Sever or Not to Sever: The Effect of a Mortgage by One Joint Tenant' [2001] 65 *The Conveyancer and Property Lawyer* 462

Percival, 'Severance by Written Notice – A Matter of Delivery?' [1999] 63 *The Conveyancer and Property Lawyer* 61

Tee, 'Severance Revisited' (1995) 59 *The Conveyancer and Property Lawyer* 105

Stack v Dowden

Cloherty and Fox, 'Proving a Trust of a Shared Home' (2007) *Cambridge Law Journal* 317

Dixon, 'Case Note on Stack v Dowden' [2007] 71 *The Conveyancer and Property Lawyer*

Dixon, 'The Never-Ending Story – Co-ownership After Stack v Dowden' [2007] 71 *The Conveyancer and Property Lawyer* 456

Gardner and Davidson, 'The Future of Stack v Dowden' (2011) 127 *Law Quarterly Review* 13

Harding, 'Defending Stack v Dowden' [2009] 73 *The Conveyancer and Property Lawyer* 309

Piska, 'Distractions Without a Difference? Explaining Stack v Dowden' [2008] 72 *The Conveyancer and Property Lawyer* 451

Swadling, 'The Common Intention Trust in the House of Lords: An Opportunity Missed' (2007) 123 *Law Quarterly Review* 511

Jones v Kernott

Briggs, 'Co-ownership – An Equitable Non-Sequitur' (2012) 128 *Law Quarterly Review* 183

Dixon, 'The Still Not Ended, Never Ending Story' [2012] 76 *The Conveyancer and Property Lawyer* 83

Gardner and Davidson, 'The Supreme Court on Family Homes' (2012) 128 *Law Quarterly Review* 178

Mel, 'Jones v Kernott: Inferring and Imputing in Essex' [2012] 76 *The Conveyancer and Property Lawyer* 167

Pawlowski, 'Imputed Intention and Joint Ownership – A Return to Common Sense' [2012] 76 *The Conveyancer and Property Lawyer* 149

Roche, 'Kernott, Stack and Oxley Made Simple: A Practitioner's View' [2011] 75 *The Conveyancer and Property Lawyer* 123

Yip, 'The Riles Applying to Unmarried Cohabitants' Family Home' [2012] 76 *The Conveyancer and Property Lawyer* 159

General

Gray and Gray, *Elements of Land Law*, Oxford University Press

Law Commission, *Sharing Homes: A Discussion Paper* (2002, Law Com No. 278)

Law Commission, *The Cohabitation: The Financial Consequences of Relationship Breakdown* (2007, Law Com No. 307)

8th Programme of Law Reform of the Law Commission (2001, Law Com No. 274)

12

Co-ownership 2 – the acquisition of a beneficial interest

Aims and objectives

After reading this chapter you should be able to:

- Know and understand the principles behind the acquisition of a beneficial interest in co-ownership.
- Recognise the difference between resulting and constructive trusts.
- Understand how the beneficial interest is quantified in resulting and constructive trusts.
- Recognise and understand the consequences of sole and joint name ownership in constructive trusts.

Introduction

The topic in context

In the previous chapter we examined the structure of co-ownership in terms of how it operated with particular reference to joint tenancies and tenancies in common. Much of what was discussed related to the beneficial interests and how these were administered within the legal regime.

In this chapter, however, we are going to examine how a person acquires a beneficial interest in the property. Often no problems arise where the legal title passes to the co-owners since, as we have already seen, the beneficial interests flow automatically from the legal relationship, though even here there may be a dispute as to the respective shares the co-owners own in relation to their beneficial interests. The other side of the coin is that, in some situations, a property is bought in the name of one party only and a third party then claims a share of the beneficial interests.

Many of the cases that are discussed in this chapter involve cohabiting, unmarried couples who decide to live together. Sometimes they may live together in a house which was already owned by one of the parties or they may decide to buy a house together. In the latter situation, the transfer will often convey the house to them jointly, and the legal and beneficial interests will be decided in the transfer. This is not always the case, though, and the house may be transferred into the name of one party only. The parties may both contribute towards the purchase price, but their finances may also be organised so that one party pays the mortgage, whilst the other pays for all the other outgoings, such as utility bills, food, holidays, etc.

In a cohabitee-type of situation, however it is organised, the parties may at the start of the co-ownership discuss how the beneficial interest is to be divided up, but it is equally common for the parties not to have any such discussion at all; after all, 'love is often blind'. The problem then arises if the relationship breaks down and there are disagreements as to the ownership of the beneficial interest or a party's respective share. The issues that relate to the beneficial interest do not necessarily result out of a breakdown in the relationship but may also arise out of claims by a trustee in bankruptcy, where a party becomes bankrupt, or where the mortgage is not paid and the bank or building society seeks possession of the property in order to realise its security. In such circumstances, the other co-owner may wish to lay claim to a beneficial interest that takes in priority to the claims of the trustee in bankruptcy or the mortgagee. Some of the issues and the regulation of these areas we have already examined in Chapter 10 on trusts of land.

Much of what will be discussed in this chapter will relate to cohabitants and the family home but it is as well to bear in mind that the principles that will be discussed here can also apply to non-cohabitant situations where the ownership of the beneficial interest is open to question. Of particular help in solving the problem of the beneficial interest may be the application of TOLATA 1996 s.14, which allows for a trustee of land or a person who has an interest in land to apply to the court for the court to decide the nature or extent of a person's interest in the property subject to the trust as the court thinks fit. The court may then have regard to the factors set out in s.15. This regime, however, is of little use if a cohabitant is neither a trustee of land nor a person interested – i.e. a beneficiary under the trust of land. What that person needs to do is, of course, to establish a beneficial interest and this is the question we will be examining here.

This is not an essay question answer and to arrive at a solution we will have to delve into the law of trusts, where there is some uncertainty as to how this applies in particular cases. In particular, there is a tension as regards what a 'fair' situation might be and whilst cases such as *Stack* v *Dowden* [2007] UKHL 17 have provided some illumination, the position is far from straightforward.

Before embarking on an analysis of how beneficial interests and respective shares arise we need to consider briefly the situation where the cohabitees are married or in a civil partnership.

Marriage and civil partnerships

Where the cohabitees separate or a couple get married and get divorced or obtain a decree of nullity or judicial separation then, under the Matrimonial Causes Act 1973 s.24, the courts have extensive powers to make a property adjustment order. The effect of this is that the court may order one of the parties to transfer property to the other or give the other a beneficial interest in the property. Alternatively, the court may order that the property be sold and the proceeds divided amongst the individuals in the proportions decided by the court. In this way, reference to the law of trusts is avoided, but not necessarily entirely so. Thus if the parties merely separate, or one of them becomes bankrupt, or if a dispute arises as to the share of the beneficial interest on the death of one of the parties (assuming the right of survivorship under a joint tenancy does not apply), the reconciliation is again thrown back on to the law of trusts.

It should be noted that the Matrimonial Causes Act 1973 s.24 has no application to engaged couples since marriage is a pre-requisite for the Act to apply: *Mossop* v *Mossop* [1988] 2 All ER 202.

The Civil Partnership Act 2004 s.72 and Schedule 5 contain provisions very similar to the Matrimonial Causes Act 1973 s.24, so that, if the civil partnership is dissolved, the partners are treated in much the same way as married couples. Thus a court is able to make property adjustment orders and the application of the law of trusts is avoided, unless a property dispute arises as regards the beneficial interests on the death of one of the partners, again assuming there is not a joint tenancy with regard to the beneficial interests.

Before going on to look at the application of the law of trusts it is worthwhile noting the proviso given earlier that many of the cases relating to the law of trusts involve married couples. The reason we see these cases is that they date from a time before the Matrimonial Causes Act 1973, when the beneficial interests of married couples were also dealt with under the law of trusts.

The law of trusts in co-ownership

A typical scenario

It is useful at this stage to view a typical scenario that may develop as regards a dispute over the beneficial interest in a co-ownership/cohabitant situation.

Example

Peter Smith and Annie Hall, having been in a relationship for some years, decide to live together. A house, Whiteacre, is bought and conveyed into Peter's name alone. In order to purchase Whiteacre, Peter takes out a mortgage and pays the initial deposit. The couple agree that Peter will make the monthly mortgage repayments to the bank and the council tax. Annie agrees that she will pay the utility and food bills and that she will look after the house and bring up the children that they plan to have. Annie gives up her rented flat to move into Whiteacre with Peter. When their first child is born 12 months after the purchase of Whiteacre, she gives up her lucrative job and takes a low-paid, part-time post. Annie does not contribute directly to the purchase of the house but she does a great deal of the work attached to the house, including painting and helping with the renovation work, since the house was in need of substantial repairs when it was purchased. All the workmen and materials for the renovation work are paid for by Peter.

After five years living in Whiteacre, the couple decide to split up and Peter moves out.

Peter now seeks possession of the house since it is in his sole name. Annie claims that she has a beneficial interest in the house and that it was conveyed to Peter to hold it on a trust under which she is a co-beneficiary with Peter.

On the face of things, it appears that Annie has made a significant contribution to the family life and home and that, indirectly, she has contributed as much to the purchase of the house as Peter. She argues that it is only fair that she should have a beneficial interest so that, if the house is sold, she will have a sufficient share to purchase another home for herself and the child.

Unfortunately, as we shall see, it is very probable that Annie will have great difficulty in establishing her right to a share of the beneficial interest. Her best hope is that, by her conduct in giving up her secure flat and her lucrative job, she will persuade the court to infer a common intention that she was to receive a beneficial share.

The result of the above scenario is that the parties often become engaged in a protracted, expensive and often bitter round of litigation in order to establish or defend their interests in their property. But it does not have to be like this if the parties agree what their rights in the property will be prior to the purchase of the property. To reiterate, 'love is often blind' and, in many cases, couples do not contemplate the possibility of their relationship ending and the likely impact this will have later on. Often couples are poorly advised, as Lord Ward stated testily in **Carlton v Goodman** [2002] 2 FLR 259:

> Perhaps conveyancers do not read the law reports. I will try one more time: always try to agree on and then record how the beneficial interest is to be held. It is not very difficult to do.

Similar sentiments were expressed in the Court of Appeal in **Kernott v Jones** [2010] EWCA Civ 578 (the facts of which we have already examined) by Wall LJ who stated:

> I described this case as a cautionary tale. So, in my judgment, it is. The purchase of residential accommodation is perhaps the single most important financial transaction which any individual transacts in a lifetime. It is therefore of the utmost importance, as it seems to me, that those who engage in these transactions, and those who advise them should take the greatest of care over such transactions, and must – particularly if they are unmarried or if their clients are unmarried – address their minds to the size and fate of the respective beneficial interests on acquisition, separation and thereafter. It is simply impossible for a court to analyse personal transactions over years between cohabitants, and the costs of so doing are likely to be disproportionate in any event. Cohabiting partners must, it seems to me, contemplate and address the unthinkable, namely that their relationship will break down and that they will fall out over what they do and do not own.

The myth of the 'common law marriage' is still prevalent and widespread amongst the general population who believe that cohabitants have the same rights as married couples. As we can see nothing is further from the truth – with one possible exception: that is, where a partner dies, the surviving partner under the Inheritance (Provision for Family and Dependents) Act 1975 ('I(PFD)A') as amended by the Law Reform (Succession) Act 1995 ('LR(S)A') may make a claim against the deceased partner's estate on the basis that the distribution of the property is unreasonable. Originally, it had to be shown that the claimant was financially dependent on the deceased partner; however, the application is now based on whether the deceased, either by their will, intestacy or both, has made 'reasonable financial provision'. Thus financial 'dependence' is no longer required. The surviving cohabitant must demonstrate that, during the whole of a two-year period ending immediately before the death, the cohabitant was living in the same household as the deceased, either as husband or wife or as the civil partner of the deceased: LR(S)A 1995 s.2. It should be noted that the relationship need not be a sexual one: **Re Watson** [1999] 1 FLR 878. Further the provision requires more than de facto cohabitation prior to death and the court looks for a 'settled state of affairs during the relationship': **Gully v Dix** [2005] EWCA Civ 221. The legislation is interesting since, in deciding the matter and the extent of the financial support, the court can have regard to the contribution made by the cohabitant 'to the welfare of the family of the deceased, including any contribution made by looking after the home or caring for the family': I(PFD)A 1975 s.3[(2A)]. Paradoxically, these are factors which may not be used by a cohabitant like Annie attempting to claim against a *living* cohabitant such as Peter.

Acquiring and quantifying the beneficial interest

In analysing this area of co-ownership we will largely be referring to the typical example set out above; however, it must be borne in mind, as Baroness Hale pointed out in **Stack v Dowden**, 'cohabitation comes in many different shapes and sizes'. The principles we will be examining form part of the general law and, as such, it is normally flexible enough to deal with many of the different situations that can arise and this should be considered when examining the principles. Thus Lord Diplock in *Gissing* v *Gissing* [1970] 2 All ER 780 stated:

> The legal principles applicable to the claim are those of the English law of trusts and in particular, in the kind of dispute between spouses that comes before the courts, the law relating to the creation and operation of resulting, implied or constructive trusts.

The analysis of the law in trusts in co-ownership takes place on two levels – firstly, how a beneficial interest is acquired by a co-owner and, secondly, having established that the co-owner has a beneficial interest, how that interest is quantified. The principles applicable to these two requirements differ, depending on whether a claim is mounted by way of an express declaration of trust, a resulting trust or a constructive trust.

Express, resulting and constructive trusts

Express declarations of trust

It has already been seen that land may be transferred to two or more persons who then hold the legal title on trust for themselves as beneficial owners, either as joint tenants or tenants in common. This seems quite clear, though it is always possible for a third party to challenge this structure and allege that they too have a beneficial interest in the property. Equally, as we have seen in our example, it is possible for land to be transferred to one owner, Peter, who, as well as owning the legal title, also solely owns the beneficial interest. This also is open to challenge by a third party who may claim a share of the beneficial interest. The vehicles for mounting these challenges are resulting and constructive trusts. Before considering these vehicles it must also be remembered that the parties themselves may have concluded an agreement as regards the ownership of the equitable interests. If they have, then this will usually be conclusive. Thus, if land is conveyed to A and B on trust for themselves as tenants in common, the trust is clearly expressly declared. In the case of a transfer to two legal owners where they are also the beneficial owners, the principle is straightforward, but the same can also apply where land is transferred to A to hold it on trust for A. Again, a third party can lay claim to a beneficial interest, notwithstanding the declaration.

In order to create an express declaration of trust of land, the requirements of the Law of Property Act 1925 s.53(1)b must be complied with, which provides:

> a declaration of trust respecting any land or any interest therein must be manifested and proved by some writing signed by some person who is able to declare such trust or by his will.

It will be noticed that the provision does not require the declaration to be in writing but it must be 'manifested' or evidenced in writing. The declaration does not need to be in one document nor does the document need to be contemporaneous with the making of the declaration. All that is required is that, at some point, the declaration must be reduced into writing; an oral declaration is insufficient.

In a transfer or conveyance of land, the declaration of trust is normally contained within the transfer or conveyance. In *Stack* v *Dowden* it was stated that a statement declaring that a survivor of joint proprietors 'can give a valid receipt for capital money arising on a disposition of the land' did not amount to a declaration of trust, affirming the decisions to that effect in *Harwood* v *Harwood* [1991] 2 FLR 274; *Huntingford* v *Hobbs* [1993] 1 FLR 736; *Mortgage Corporation* v *Shaire* [2001] Ch 743. The reason for this is that the purpose behind this expression is not to declare a trust but to ensure that the survivor can give a valid receipt.

As we saw in the previous chapter, in *Stack* v *Dowden* Baroness Hale referred to Form TR1 and stated that, if cohabitants completed the relevant box, this would amount to an express declaration that they are to hold the property on trust for themselves, either as joint tenants or tenants in common, either in equal shares or on the trusts declared on the form. She stated that if that was 'invariably complied with, the problem . . . will eventually disappear'. Whilst completion of this form would reduce the uncertainty, it does not always do so. Firstly, the relevant box is not always completed; secondly, when a transfer is made to joint transferees, whilst the presumption is that the beneficial interests will be the same as the legal interests, this may not always be the case; thirdly, if the conveyance is made to one person only then the relevant box will invariably not be completed. This latter situation is particularly relevant where a person already owns the property and a new partner moves in so that they cohabit. In all these situations, an express declaration of trust is required and, if it is completed, this will be conclusive as to the beneficial ownership for the parties to the express declaration: *Goodman* v *Gallant* [1986] 1 All ER 311.

Where there is no express declaration of trust, the party claiming a beneficial interest or a revised share in the beneficial interest may nevertheless avoid the requirements of s.53(1) by relying on s.53(2). This provides:

> This section does not affect the creation or operation of resulting, implied or constructive trusts.

The position can be seen in *Stack* v *Dowden* and *Jones* v *Kernott* where the legal titles were held jointly but there was no express declaration as to the extent of the beneficial ownership so that the claimant could rely on a constructive trust to establish the extent of the beneficial interest. Similarly, in *McKenzie* v *McKenzie* [2003] 2 P & CR D15, where the title to a property was held jointly by a father and son but there was no express declaration as to the extent of the beneficial interest, the father was able to establish that he was the sole beneficial owner by way of a resulting trust. Thus in the absence of an express declaration of trust, resulting and constructive trusts may be used to establish – particularly where land is conveyed into one name alone – or vary the extent of a claimant's beneficial interest.

Resulting trusts

In *Dyer* v *Dyer* (1788) 2 Cox Eq Cas 92 it was stated that '. . . trust of a legal estate . . . results to a man who advances the purchase money'. It will be recalled that a resulting trust emanates from the Latin 'resultare': that is, 'springs back'. Thus if a house is purchased in the name of A, who may have provided part or none of the purchase price, a resulting trust arises in favour of the other party, B, who has provided part or all of the purchase price. A, in such a circumstance, is presumed to hold the legal title on a resulting trust for B.

The resulting trust arises from a presumed intention by B to own a share of the property, as evidenced by the contribution to the purchase price. It stands to reason that, if A, on the other hand, can demonstrate that the contribution was intended to be a loan or gift rather than an intention to own a share of the property, then the claimant, B, will not be able to establish – that is, acquire – a beneficial interest by way of a resulting trust.

If the claimant can establish a beneficial interest by way of a resulting trust, then that interest is in direct proportion to the contribution, so that the share of the beneficial interest reflects the contribution. It is an arithmetic calculation so that if a house is bought and transferred into the sole name of one partner (A) but the other (B) is able to demonstrate a contribution of 30% towards the purchase price, then the beneficial interest will be held in the ratio of 70:30.

Traditionally, the orthodox approach to resulting trusts is that they arise in instances of 'sole name' cases, as in the case of A and B above, where A's name goes on to the title but B's does not, so that A owns the legal interest on trust for himself/herself and B, usually as tenants in common based on the proportions contributed. Where the case is one of joint names – that is, the names of both parties go on to the title and both then hold the legal interest on trust for themselves – then this does not fall within the remit of a resulting trust but is instead dealt with by way of a constructive trust. As we saw in the previous chapter in **Stack v Dowden** and **Jones v Kernott**, in such a situation there is a presumption that the co-owners as joint tenants in law also hold the beneficial interests as joint tenants on the basis that 'equity follows the law'.

The difference between 'sole name' and 'joint name' cases is important since the means by which a beneficial interest is acquired and quantified is entirely different. In the early cases in this area there was often confusion between the two concepts of resulting trusts and constructive trusts and one should be aware of this when looking at these cases. For the moment, however, we will confine ourselves to examining resulting trusts.

In examining how a beneficial share is acquired under a resulting trust it was stated earlier that this was based on the contribution of the party not named on the title, i.e. B. However, we need to consider the nature of these contributions.

The contributions must be made towards the purchase of the property and thus expenditure on repairs will not count. The contributions to the purchase price may arise by way of a deposit and, indeed, in **Laskar v Laskar** [2008] EWCA 347 the Court of Appeal held that the entitlement to a discount on the price by way of an entitlement under the 'right to buy' provisions in the Housing Act 1985 would also amount to a contribution for the purpose of acquiring an interest by way of a resulting trust. Similarly in **Springette v Defoe** [1992] 2 FLR 388 a discount on the price because of the presence of a sitting tenant was also eligible as a contribution.

Whilst contributions towards mortgage payments have been held to amount to a contribution towards the purchase price, the courts have taken a narrow view of such payments. In *Cowcher v Cowcher* [1975] 1 WLR 425 it was held that where the parties have agreed from the outset to share the mortgage repayments, such repayments will amount to a contribution for resulting trust purposes. The same is not true, however, if one party makes a contribution to the mortgage once the house has been purchased – that is, transferred into the name of the sole owner. In such a situation, the contributions are not regarded as having been made towards the purchase price. The position was summed up by Gibson LJ in *Curley v Parkes* [2004] EWCA Civ 1515:

> The relevant principle is that the resulting trust of the property purchased in the name of another, in the absence of contrary intention, arises once and for all at the date on which the property is acquired. Because of the liability assumed by the mortgagor in a case where the monies are borrowed by the mortgagor to be used on the purchase, the mortgagor is treated as having provided the proportion of the purchase price attributable to the monies so borrowed. Subsequent payments of the mortgage instalments are not part of the purchase price already paid to the vendor, but are sums paid for discharging the mortgagor's obligations under the mortgage.

The reasoning seems distinctly strange and counterintuitive since surely all mortgage repayments from any party are essentially paying the mortgage loan. The logic is stranger still if the mortgagor, having taken out the mortgage, is unable to repay the mortgage and relies on his or her partner to make the repayments or otherwise default on the mortgage. Furthermore in *Laskar* v *Laskar* [2008] EWCA Civ 347 the Court of Appeal held that the mortgage of £43,000 was to be treated as a contribution of £21,500 by each of the joint owners as they were both severally and jointly liable for the repayments. The Court of Appeal, however, based its decision on the fact that the property was bought as an investment and that the mortgage repayments had been met out of the income from the property. Still further, in *Stack* v *Dowden*, Baroness Hale stated obiter that 'certainty, simplicity and first impression' seem to suggest that contributions to mortgage repayments should be regarded as a contribution to the purchase price for resulting trust purposes, 'particularly where a home is bought almost exclusively by means of a mortgage'. It would appear that the decision in *Curley* v *Parkes* should be viewed guardedly.

Since resulting trusts, at least according to orthodox theory, are based on direct financial contributions, the repayment of household expenses, looking after children and general housekeeping duties provide no contribution to the purchase of the property and as such do not count towards the acquisition of a beneficial interest. Whilst this may amount to a stereotype, it can be quickly seen that this would tend to prejudice the female partner. This position also ignores the often complex arrangements which take place between cohabitants, since these are often based on the fact of the male partner paying the mortgage repayments and the female partner paying the household expenses and looking after the home and children.

Such a position can be seen in *Burns* v *Burns* [1984] 1 All ER 244 where an unmarried couple had been living together for 19 years and where the man held the legal title to the family home. He had paid the deposit and all the mortgage repayments. Initially, the woman had given up work to look after the house and the children, but later she took up employment and used her income to pay for some of the domestic expenses, furniture and clothes for the children. She also undertook some maintenance work in the home, such as redecorating.

On the face of things, one might have considered that the contribution of the woman should have amounted to a contribution for the purposes of acquiring a beneficial interest. The Court of Appeal, however, held that, in the absence of a common intention inferred from some agreement, either express or itself inferred from the conduct of the partners, the contributions made by the woman were insufficient to provide her with a beneficial share of the family home. The decision in *Curley* v *Parkes*, whilst not dealing directly with this point, seems to militate against any change in the position. In *Laskar* v *Laskar*, though, it has to be stated that this case approaches the matter from a commercial direction.

The resulting trust is clearly an inflexible vehicle for acquiring a beneficial interest, being formed within the straitjacket of direct money contributions and the quantification question being answered by reference to a strict proportion of the amount contributed. Constructive trusts provide a much more flexible model for deciding both the acquisition and quantification issues. There have been attempts to narrow the ground between the two types of trust, hence the comment earlier as regards the confusion between the two concepts in earlier cases.

Prior to the passing of the Matrimonial Causes Act 1973, the courts, as we have previously stated, had to rely on the general law to resolve property disputes between spouses and cohabitants, though the latter were far less common at that time. There was an attempt at that time to move away from the distinction between the types of trust and in *Gissing* v *Gissing* [1971] AC 886.

Lord Diplock stated at 905:

> A resulting, implied or constructive trust – and it is unnecessary for present purposes to distinguish between these three classes of trust – is created by a transaction between the trustee and the [beneficiary] in connection with the acquisition by the trustee of a legal estate in land, whenever the trustee has so conducted himself that it would be inequitable to allow him to deny the [beneficiary] a beneficial interest in the land acquired. And he will be held so to have conducted himself if by his words or conduct he has induced the [beneficiary] to act to his own detriment in the reasonable belief that by so acting he was acquiring a beneficial interest in the land.

In order to escape the classical theory of the resulting trust, Lord Diplock propounded, in the context of the matrimonial home, a common intention trust based on an expressed or inferred agreement between the parties either at the time of the acquisition of the property, or later, that the party without the legal title is to have a beneficial interest in the property. In order to find an express agreement the courts had to find evidence of express discussions of 'any agreement, arrangement or understanding reached between [the parties] that the property is to be shared beneficially' (per Lord Bridge in *Lloyds Bank plc* v *Rosset* [1991] 1 AC 107 at 132). From such evidence, the courts would then conclude that there was an agreement as to a common intention as to the acquisition of a beneficial interest in the property by the beneficiary not on the legal title. The agreement or arrangement, however, could also be inferred from the conduct of the parties, either by direct contributions or by indirect contributions – for instance, the payment of household expenses provided that those payments were referable to the purchase of the property in the sense that they facilitated the owner of the legal estate paying the mortgage repayments.

By the adoption of such an approach, Lord Diplock freed the position of the parties from the straitjacket of the resulting trust. Lord Diplock, however, was faced with a secondary problem in relation to such an approach since, as we have seen, any express agreement or declaration would be caught by the requirements of the Law of Property Act 1925 s.53(1)b in that the agreement would have to be evidenced in writing. He therefore had to bring the agreement or transaction into the realms of equity in order to sidestep this provision. If he could do this, then he could bring the agreement or transaction within the ambit of the Law of Property Act 1925 s.53(2), which provides an exemption from the need for writing in the case of resulting, implied or constructive trusts. He achieved this by providing that the non-legal owner had to show some detrimental act in reliance on the agreement. In this way, the legal owner would be stopped from denying the agreement so that he or she would not be allowed to act inequitably. A trust could therefore be implied to prevent such conduct.

The approach of Lord Diplock provided a means by which co-ownership disputes, at least in the cohabitation context, could be moved away from the anachronistic concept of the resulting trust. The role of resulting trusts in this context was considered in the cases of *Stack* v *Dowden* and *Jones* v *Kernott*, although these cases are predominantly concerned with quantification, not acquisition. Such a review was necessary because resulting trusts have traditionally arisen in cases involving sole legal ownership, whilst constructive trusts have arisen in the case of joint legal ownership. In *Stack* v *Dowden* both Baroness Hale and Lord Walker considered that in the context of domestic disputes the tool of choice for settling the dispute should be the constructive trust, not the resulting trust. Thus Lord Walker stated:

> ... in a case about beneficial ownership of the matrimonial home or quasi-matrimonial home (whether registered in the names of one or two legal owners) the resulting trust should not in my opinion operate as a legal presumption, although it may (in an updated form which takes account of all significant contributions, direct or indirect, in cash or in kind) happen to be reflected in the parties' common intention.

Baroness Hale, in turn, stated that 'the presumption of a resulting trust is not a rule of law', seizing on Lord Diplock's assertion in *Pettitt* v *Pettitt* [1970] AC 777 at 823 that presumptions are:

> ... no more than a consensus of judicial opinion disclosed by reported cases as to the most likely inference of fact to be drawn in the absence of any evidence to the contrary.

Whilst Lord Diplock took the rebuttal of the presumption of a resulting trust results, in a sole name position, to the legal owner being absolutely entitled to it and a person making a contribution having no interest whatsoever, Baroness Hale was able to take the escape from the presumption in another manner. She stated that the law had moved on 'in response to changing social and economic conditions so that now the issue, whether in sole or joint name cases, is to ascertain the parties' shared intentions, actual, inferred or imputed, with respect to the property in the light of their whole course of conduct in relation to it'. She considered that 'who paid for what' in a domestic context is a very different issue today and that, in the context of co-ownership within intimate relationships, the appropriate way forward is by way of the constructive trust, not the resulting trust. But some care needs exercising here since the resulting trust is not a wholly defunct concept, as Baroness Hale stated:

> In law, 'context is everything' and the domestic context is very different from the commercial world. Each case will turn on its own facts.

Thus in cases such as *Laskar* v *Laskar* where the court considered this to be more akin to a commercial situation since the property had been purchased as an investment, the principles applicable to resulting trusts are still an appropriate means of deciding the acquisition and quantification questions.

Constructive trusts

Setting the context

The traditional view of the constructive trust in English law is that it is a substantive institution and, as such, only arises in certain situations. The American view, however, is that the constructive trust is a remedy to be imposed whenever a defendant's conduct is regarded as unconscionable. Following the seminal decision in *Gissing* v *Gissing* [1971] AC 886, Lord Denning seized on Lord Diplock's statement at 905 that a constructive trust would arise whenever a trustee 'has so conducted himself that it would be inequitable to allow him to deny to the [beneficiary] a beneficial interest in the land acquired' to forge an outcome based on fairness and justice. This highly flexible approach, which has since become known as the 'new model' constructive trust, arose where it was inequitable for the defendant to deny a claimant a beneficial interest in the property. Thus it was not considered necessary for the claimant to prove that he or she had made financial contributions but that the property had been purchased by way of their joint efforts.

In *Hussey* v *Palmer* [1972] 3 All ER 744 Lord Denning explained the new model in the following terms:

> . . . it is a trust imposed by law whenever justice and good conscience require it. It is a liberal process founded on large principles of equity, to be applied in cases where the defendant cannot conscientiously keep the property for himself alone, but ought to allow another to have the property or a share in it. The trust may arise at the outset when the property is acquired, or later on, as circumstances may require.

The principle set out by Lord Diplock was applied in a number of cases in the 1970s – *Binions* v *Evans* [1972] 2 All ER 70; *Cooke* v *Head* [1972] 2 All ER 38; and *Hussey* v *Palmer* [1972] 3 All ER 744. In *Cooke* v *Head* Lord Denning suggested that:

> . . . whenever two parties by their joint efforts acquire property to be used for their joint benefit, the court may impose or impute a constructive or resulting trust.

Later in the case of *Eves* v *Eves* [1975] 3 All ER 768 Lord Denning stated in relation to a woman claiming a beneficial share who had not made any financial contribution, though she had carried out heavy work in relation to the family home:

> and a few years ago even equity would not have helped her. But things are different now. Equity is not past the age of child bearing. One of her latest progeny is a constructive trust of a new model. Lord Diplock brought it into the world and we have nourished it . . .

In that case, Lord Denning stood out from the rest of the Court of Appeal and imposed a constructive trust on the basis of what was fair and in the interests of justice. The rest of the Court of Appeal resiled from this position and, whilst they found for a constructive trust, did so on the basis of an understanding between the couple.

The problem with Lord Denning's approach is that it was founded simply on what a judge would consider to be fair as between the parties and it was therefore highly subjective and contained no objective principles on which to found a constructive trust. Many considered that Lord Denning had been highly selective with regard to Lord Diplock's dicta and ignored the caveat in that dicta to the effect that a constructive trust would be imposed:

> if [the trustee] by his words or conduct . . . has induced the [beneficiary] to act to his own detriment in a reasonable belief that by so acting he was acquiring a beneficial interest in the land.

This statement reflected the orthodox view of the constructive trust and was adopted by Lord Bridge in the later seminal case of *Lloyds Bank plc* v *Rosset* [1991] 1 AC 107. The main criticism of Lord Denning's approach was that it was fluid and subjective and that it created uncertainty. This approach was roundly rejected in the case of *Burns* v *Burns* [1984] 1 All ER 244. In that case, the facts of which we have already examined, Fox LJ stated that, in order to acquire a beneficial interest, the claimant would have to demonstrate payments which were referable to the acquisition of the house. He considered that a payment could be so referable if the payer pays part of the purchase, contributes regularly to the mortgage instalments, pays off part of the mortgage, or makes a substantial contribution to the family expenses so that the mortgage instalments could be paid by the other party.

It is interesting to note here the flexible approach to quantifying the share of the beneficial interest – unlike resulting trusts, which we examined earlier. However, it must be borne in mind that Fox LJ emphasised that, to acquire a beneficial interest, there must be shown to be a common intention at the time the property was purchased that a claimant was to have a beneficial interest. It should be noted that it is not necessary to quantify the share of the beneficial interest at that point; that could arise later on, when the mortgage is repaid or the house sold. Then the share would be determined 'on the basis of what would be fair having regard to the total contributions, direct or indirect, which each spouse had made by that date' (per Lord Diplock in *Gissing* v *Gissing*).

It is perhaps interesting to at least note at this stage that in *Stack* v *Dowden*, in the later case of *Abbott* v *Abbott* [2008] 1 FLR 1451 and in *Jones* v *Kernott* it was possible to infer or impute a common intention as regards the beneficial ownership in order to find for a constructive trust, even though no such intention has arisen at the time of the acquisition. One objection to such an approach is that it appears to indicate a return to Denning's subjective test approach.

Before we move on to examine the 'common intention constructive trust' in terms of how one acquires a beneficial interest and, having done that, how one quantifies that interest in the modern era, it is worthwhile at this juncture reminding ourselves of some of the principles that we have covered so far:

(i) Where there is sole legal ownership, the presumption is one of sole beneficial ownership.

(ii) In sole legal ownership cases it is incumbent upon the non-owner to demonstrate that he or she has beneficial interest.

(iii) Where there is joint legal ownership, the presumption is one of joint beneficial ownership (a joint tenancy) – 'equity follows the law'.

(iv) In joint legal ownership cases it is incumbent upon the joint owner to demonstrate that the beneficial ownership is other than one of a joint tenancy so that the beneficial interest is one of unequal shares.

(v) Only in unusual cases are the above presumptions rebutted.

(vi) Whilst resulting trusts have been used in the past to rebut the presumptions in sole legal ownership cases, it is the constructive trust that is now the instrument of choice for both sole and joint legal ownership cases in the context of domestic disputes.

(vii) Under constructive trusts, the intentions of the parties are discovered by looking at their express or inferred common intention by looking at their whole conduct with regards to the property.

The modern era

Acquisition of the beneficial interest

In *Lloyds Bank plc* v *Rosset* [1991] AC 107 Lord Bridge provided the guidelines for the establishment of a common intention constructive trust.

Lloyds Bank plc v *Rosset* [1991] AC 107

A married couple decided to buy a rundown house to live in. The financing for the purchase came from a trust fund under which the husband was the beneficiary; however, the trustees of the fund insisted that the house had to be conveyed in the husband's name alone. The couple had the intention of renovating the house for use as the family home. In order to pay for the renovation work and without the wife's knowledge, the husband took out an overdraft with the bank, which was secured by way of a charge in favour of the bank. The wife believed all the money for the renovation work was being provided by the trust fund. The wife spent a great deal of time at the house, project managing the builders and planning the renovations. She also undertook some of the decorative work herself. Once the work was completed, the couple moved in, but the marriage ran into difficulties. The husband moved out, but left his wife and children in occupation of the house. He failed to keep up with the loan repayments and the bank then sought possession and sale of the house to recover its security.

> The wife claimed that she had a beneficial interest in the house by way of a constructive trust, which, coupled with the fact that she was in actual occupation, gave her an overriding interest by way of the Land Registration Act 1925 s.70(1)g and that the bank took possession subject to that overriding interest.

The House of Lords came to a unanimous decision that the wife had no beneficial interest and that she was not entitled to the protection of a constructive trust in that she failed to demonstrate that there existed a common intention between herself and her husband that she was to enjoy a shared ownership of the property.

Lord Bridge provided the leading judgment, with which the rest of their lordships concurred. Lord Bridge's judgment provided two distinct situations in which a common intention could be established: (i) where there was an express intention based on discussions between the parties that there was to be shared ownership; and (ii) where, in the absence of an express intention, such an intention could be inferred from their conduct.

Establishing an express common intention trust

The establishment of an express intention is largely a question of evidence of an express agreement, both at the time the property was acquired and afterwards. This evidence cannot be derived from the expectations of the parties arising from their relationship, or from their conduct alone. One difficulty here is the possible lack of evidence in writing to satisfy the Law of Property Act 1925 s.53(1)b since, unless the claim is underpinned by a detrimental reliance by the claimant, the agreement would be unenforceable. Lord Bridge stated at 132:

> The first and fundamental question which must always be resolved is whether, independently of any inference to be drawn from the conduct of the parties in the course of sharing the house as their home and managing their joint affairs, there has at any time prior to acquisition, or exceptionally at some later date, been any agreement, arrangement or understanding reached between them that the property is to be shared beneficially. The finding of an agreement or arrangement to share in this sense can only, I think, be based on evidence of express discussions between the partners, however imperfectly remembered and however imprecise their terms may have been. Once a finding to this effect is made, it will only be necessary for the partner asserting the claim to a beneficial interest against the partner entitled to the legal estate to show that he or she has acted to his or her detriment or significantly altered his or her position in reliance on the agreement in order to give rise to a constructive trust or proprietary estoppel.

Lord Bridge considered that the wife had not satisfied the evidential burden to demonstrate that there was an express common intention that she should have a beneficial share of the property. Lord Bridge, however, did provide two examples in cases where he thought such as express common intention had been established: *Eves v Eves* [1975] 1 All ER 768 and *Grant v Edwards* [1986] Ch 638. In both these cases, the man had made an excuse to his partner as to why the property was being conveyed into his name alone. In *Eves v Eves*, the man told his partner that he considered her to be too young to hold the legal title. In *Grant v Edwards* the woman was going through a divorce and her new partner told her that putting her name on the title would prejudice her divorce proceedings. In reality, in both these cases the man was merely protecting his interests if the relationship broke down and the reasoning provided was simply an excuse. Essentially, he was stating that he would like to put the house into joint names, and might do so in the future, but it was not appropriate to do so immediately for the reasons provided, although there was never any real intention to do so.

It can be seen at once that there is a striking resemblance here to proprietary estoppel, where a landowner deliberately misleads a person as to his or her rights in the property. This similarity can be clearly seen in the last sentence in the quotation above. It is, however, important to keep the concepts of constructive trusts and proprietary estoppel separate since the time at which the interest arises is different in each. Furthermore, the remedies available under constructive trusts and proprietary estoppel are also different. It should be noted, though, that the same facts can give rise to both a constructive trust and proprietary estoppel.

Detrimental reliance Evidence of an express common intention alone is insufficient to set up a constructive trust. As indicated earlier, to avoid the problems of the Law of Property Act 1925 s.53(1)b it is vital to establish a detrimental reliance as well, so that the court can bring the express agreement within the Law of Property Act 1925 s.53(2) exception, which we also noted in our examination of Lord Diplock's dicta in *Gissing v Gissing* [1971] AC 886 above. Thus the constructive trust is imposed because it is inequitable to allow the owner of the property to retain his or her absolute ownership against the background of the matrix of facts of the other party suffering a detriment by way of the express common intention.

The matter of detrimental reliance gives rise to the type of conduct required to establish such a detrimental reliance. Thus Lord Bridge stated at 132:

> Once a finding [of an express common intention] is made it will only be necessary for the partner asserting a claim to a beneficial interest against the partner entitled to the legal estate to show that he or she acted to his or her detriment or significantly altered his or her position in reliance on the agreement in order to give rise to a constructive trust . . .

Thus the type of action required does not necessarily have to be a direct contribution to the purchase price. Non-financial conduct is sufficient, as demonstrated in both *Eves v Eves* and *Grant v Edwards*. In the latter case, the view was taken that the contribution made by the female partner in paying the housekeeping expenses and looking after the children was referable to the ability of the male partner to make the mortgage repayments. The effect is that once an express common intention is established the type of activity required to establish the detrimental reliance may be relatively low, provided it is not de minimis, since there must be a 'substantial change of position'. Thus Browne-Wilkinson VC considered at 657 that, once a common intention had been established:

> In many cases of the present sort, it is impossible to say whether or not the claimant would have done the acts relied on as a detriment even if she thought she had no interest in the house. Setting up house together, having a baby, making payments to general housekeeping expenses (not strictly necessary to enable the mortgage to be repaid) may all be referable to the mutual love and affection of the parties and not specifically referable to the claimant's belief that she has an interest in the home . . . advised, once it has been shown that there was a common intention that the claimant should have an interest in the house, any act done by her to her detriment relating to the joint lives of the parties is, in my judgment, sufficient detriment to qualify. The acts do not have to be inherently referable to the house . . .

The point is that the claimant must have acted as she has in the belief that she expected, or understood herself to have, a beneficial interest in the property. Many types of act by the claimant will suffice, provided they are significant and demonstrate a change in position in reliance on the agreement.

In *Rosset* Lord Bridge considered that, whilst the wife had assisted in managing the renovation project and doing some redecoration work, this did not amount to a relevant change in position. It was considered that her actions were merely those of a wife providing personal assistance to the renovation of the home, the legal title of which was vested in her husband. Her actions did not comprise work 'upon which she could not reasonably have been expected to embark unless she was to have an interest in the house'. The House of Lords also considered that the value of the work done was minimal, given the overall value of the property.

Establishing an inferred common intention trust

In this second category of situations, Lord Bridge considered that a common intention could be established where there is no evidence to support an agreement to share. In this instance, the courts rely on the conduct of the parties that demonstrates a general common intention by both the parties that the claimant is to have a share of the beneficial interest. This conduct is taken to evince a constructive trust. Lord Bridge at 132 and 133 contrasted this category with the express agreement position in the following terms:

> In sharp contrast with this situation is the very different one where there is no evidence to support a finding of an agreement or arrangement to share, however reasonable it might have been for the parties to reach such an arrangement if they had applied their minds to the question, and where the court must rely entirely on the conduct of the parties both as the basis from which to infer a common intention to share the property beneficially and as the conduct relied on to give rise to a constructive trust. In this situation direct contributions to the purchase price by the partner who is not the legal owner, whether initially or by payment of mortgage instalments, will readily justify the inference necessary to the creation of a constructive trust. But, as I read the authorities, it is at least extremely doubtful whether anything less will do.

Clearly, *Rosset* adopts a very narrow view as to when an inferred common intention constructive trust may arise – that is, there must be 'direct contribution' to the purchase price by the partner who is not the legal owner. Until **Stack v Dowden** and **Jones v Kernott** the fact that family life revolved around a joint enterprise of one party paying the mortgage repayments and the other sharing in the household expenditure, maintenance of the property and upbringing of any children could not be used to infer the required common intention for a constructive trust.

Even where there are direct contributions to the purchase price, this does not necessarily evince a common intention to share the beneficial interest. For instance, in **Driver v Yorke** [2003] P & CR 210 a person was purchasing a flat by way of a mortgage; his two sons made occasional contributions to the mortgage repayments. It was held that these payments were not sufficiently connected with the notion of purchasing the property as to be regarded as a contribution to the purchase price for common intention purposes. A similar decision also arose in the case of **Lightfoot v Lightfoot-Brown** [2005] EWCA Civ 201.

This aspect of *Rosset* became subject to widespread criticism over the years as being too restrictive. To be fair, Lord Bridge did not completely rule out the possibility of finding for common intention by factors other than direct contributions, though he thought it 'doubtful whether anything less will do'. The result of this was that the courts began to adopt a more liberal approach. Thus in **Le Foe v Le Foe** [2001] 2 FLR 970 a more liberal approach was adopted so that, where the family finances were arranged so that the husband's finances paid the mortgage and the wife paid for day-to-day expenditure, the court found that the wife had made indirect contribution to the mortgage repayments. As it happened, the wife had also made some direct contributions from an inheritance so that she discharged the mortgage. The point is, however, the court was prepared to take a rather more open-minded approach to the issue, along the lines set out by Lord Diplock in *Gissing* v *Gissing*. In that case, it will be recalled that the wife was able to acquire a beneficial interest since, without her contribution, the husband could not have afforded to pay the mortgage.

An important case in the development of the inferred common intention trust is that of *Oxley* v *Hiscock* [2004] EWCA Civ 546. Here the Court of Appeal attempted to relax the criteria set by Lord Bridge in *Rosset* so that the 'change of position' necessary for the establishment of a constructive trust could be derived from a wider set of criteria than simply direct financial contributions.

Lord Bridge's dicta were also criticised as being too restrictive in *Stack* v *Dowden*. Thus Lord Walker stated:

> whether or not Lord Bridge's observation was justified in 1990, in my opinion the law has moved on, and your Lordships should move it a little more in the same direction.

Lord Walker evidently doubted whether Lord Bridge had taken full account of *Gissing* v *Gissing* in setting the criteria required for an inferred common intention constructive trust. Clearly, Baroness Hale was of the same mind and stated that Lord Bridge's dicta 'set that hurdle rather too high'. From this position it seems that, in sole name cases, the establishment of a beneficial interest by way of an inferred common intention constructive trust can be derived from a broader range of circumstances than that envisaged by Lord Bridge, though Lord Walker in *Stack* v *Dowden* was 'sceptical of the value of alleged improvements that are really insignificant, or elaborate arguments (suggestive of creative accounting) as to how the family finances were arranged'.

In joint name cases, the House of Lords stated that the fact that the legal title is vested in joint names raises a presumption in the absence of an express declaration that the beneficial title is also held jointly, though this presumption can be dislodged by evidence to the contrary. Thus the 'change of position' requirement for the establishment of a constructive trust in equal shares is implied, at least in domestic cases. Effectively, therefore, the burden of proof is reversed in joint name cases, in contrast with sole name cases, so that the onus is on the party to demonstrate that the beneficial title is not held jointly.

The quantification of the beneficial interest

Once a person has established that they have a share in the beneficial interest, it is then necessary to quantify that share, by way of either a resulting or constructive trust.

In the case of a resulting trust, as we have seen, the position is relatively straightforward since the beneficial interests are in direct proportions to the contribution made. It is a simple arithmetic calculation. In the case of constructive trusts, however, the position is not so straightforward. We have already, to a degree, touched on some of these issues above but it is now necessary to look at the matter in more depth. *Stack* v *Dowden* and *Jones* v *Kernott* are, of course, highly influential in this area since these two cases are really 'quantification' cases, as opposed to 'acquisition' cases. Before looking at the two cases in detail, it is useful to examine a number of Court of Appeal cases which led up to the decision in the House of Lords and the Supreme Court.

Before embarking on an analysis of quantification under a common intention constructive trust, it should be borne in mind that in co-ownership cases the courts do not have the discretion to make property adjustment orders of the type seen in the Matrimonial Causes Act 1973. The duty of the court is to award a share of the beneficial interests that is referable either to an express agreement or to direct/indirect contributions made under an inferred common intention based on the conduct of the parties. Any decision on quantification is not one to be based on what is 'fair'. The Law Commission in 'Sharing Homes' in July 2002 stated:

> If the question really is one of the parties' common intention, we believe that there is much to be said for adopting what has been called a 'holistic approach' to quantification, undertaking a survey of the whole course of dealing between the parties and taking account of all conduct which throws a light on the question what shares were intended.

Thus, as affirmed by Baroness Hale in *Stack* v *Dowden*, the result in terms of quantification must be what the parties intended in the light of their conduct and the courts cannot abandon the search for a result by resorting to what the 'court itself considers fair'. As Lord Neuberger stated in *Mortgage Corporation* v *Shaire* [2001] Ch 743, a judge does not possess 'some sort of roving commission' to fix the beneficial shares of the parties.

The starting point for assessing the size of a party's share is to search for an express agreement between the parties as to their respective shares. If such an express agreement is found, the courts will not depart from that agreement. This approach is reflected in Lord Diplock's dicta in *Gissing* v *Gissing* at 908, where he stated:

> In such a case the court must first do its best to discover from the conduct of the spouses whether any inference can reasonably be drawn as to the probable common understanding about the amount of the share of the contributory spouse upon which each must have acted in doing what each did, even though that understanding was never expressly stated by one spouse to the other or even consciously formulated in words by either of them independently. It is only if no such inference can be drawn that the court is driven to apply as a rule of law, and not as an inference of fact, the maxim 'equality is equity', and to hold that the beneficial interest belongs to the spouses in equal shares.

Thus in *Clough* v *Killey* (1996) 72 P & CR D 22 the agreement provided for the female partner (Killey) to receive a 50% share in the equity of the family home and that was awarded despite the fact that, on the evidence of her conduct, she should only have received a 25% share. Where there is no evidence of an express agreement, the courts have to arrive at a quantification based on the parties' whole course of dealing between them in relation to the property.

In examining the quantification issue it is useful to look at the question from the point of view of the sole name and joint name scenarios.

Sole name legal ownership

Where the legal title is in the name of one person only, the presumption is that any other cohabitant is entitled to no beneficial interest and the sole legal owner enjoys an absolute title. This presumption, however, began to be capable of being challenged, as in *Midland Bank plc* v *Cooke* [1995] 4 All ER 562, where Waite LJ stated that it was the duty of the court to undertake a survey of the whole course of conduct between the parties insofar *as this related to the parties*. He stated that this survey was not restricted to looking at direct contributions and that the court should look at any conduct that provides an insight as to how the shares in the beneficial interest were to be divided. Waite LJ considered that it was only if this search was inconclusive that a court should revert back to the maxim 'equity is equality'. He stated:

> Positive evidence that the parties neither discussed nor intended any agreement as to their beneficial interests does not preclude the court, on general equitable principles, from inferring one.

Midland Bank plc v *Cooke* [1995] 4 All ER 562

In this case a married couple purchased a house for £8,500, of which £6,540 was raised by way of a mortgage. A further £1,100 was provided by Mr Cooke's parents as a wedding present, with Mr Cooke providing the rest of the purchase price. The title to the house was placed in Mr Cooke's sole name. During the marriage, Mrs Cooke made no contribution to the mortgage repayments, though she did pay for the household expenses. The couple got into financial difficulties and the bank sought to repossess the home. Mrs Cooke claimed that she had an equitable interest in the home, despite the fact that she was not on the legal title.

At first instance the judge found that Mrs Cooke had acquired a 6.74% interest in the property, based on a straight arithmetic calculation. This reasoning was based on the fact that, in the absence of an agreement, on the basis of 'equity is equality', she was entitled to half the wedding gift, which amounted to a direct contribution of £550. Clearly, this decision is an application of resulting trust principles.

In the Court of Appeal, it was held that Mrs Cooke was entitled to a 50% share of the value of the home by way of an inferred common intention of the parties. Waite LJ considered that, once a direct financial contribution had been found, thus establishing an interest in the property, in the absence of any evidence of the parties' intentions as to their shares, the court was able to examine their 'whole course of dealings'. Thus, by looking at the whole dealings of the couple, he considered that Mrs Cooke was entitled to a 50% holding, though he reached this result 'without the need to rely on any equitable maxim as to equality'.

This decision therefore introduced a 'broad brush' approach in which the division of the beneficial interest was to be derived not just from any direct contributions but also indirect contributions in terms of the family life and how the day-to-day outgoings were broken down. As Waite LJ stated:

> One could hardly have a clearer example of a couple who had agreed to share everything equally: the profits of his business while it prospered, and the risks of indebtedness suffered through its failure, the upbringing of the children, the rewards of her own career as a teacher, and, most relevantly, a home into which he had put his own savings and to which she was to give over the years the benefit of the maintenance and improvement contribution . . . the conclusion becomes inescapable that their presumed intention was to share the beneficial interest in the property in equal shares.

Later cases such as ***Drake* v *Whipp*** [1996] 1 FLR 826 took Cooke further and considered that in such cases a 'court should approach the matter more broadly, looking at the parties' entire course of conduct together'. In ***Le Foe* v *Le Foe*** [2001] 2 FLR 970 it was stated that a 'holistic approach' should be taken, looking at the entire conduct of the parties and only if that is inconclusive should the court fall back on the 'equity is equality' maxim. A major breakthrough occurred in the case of ***Oxley* v *Hiscock*** [2004] EWCA Civ 546 where a new element was introduced into the equation – fairness.

Oxley v *Hiscock* [2004] EWCA Civ 546

In this case, the family home was registered in the name of Mr Hiscock ('H'), although the home had been purchased with the help of direct financial contributions by Mrs Oxley ('O'). H contributed £60,700 and O £36,300 to the purchase price of £127,000. The balance of £30,000 was raised by way of a mortgage, to which the court found that they had each contributed equally.

The relationship broke down and the house was sold. O claimed that H held the property on trust for them both in equal shares.

This case is clearly an example of a sole owner case in which a party (O) is attempting to establish a beneficial interest. As we have seen earlier, direct contributions were previously thought to create a resulting trust based on an arithmetic calculation. In this case, however, the Court of Appeal found that *any* financial contribution by the claimant towards the purchase of the family home satisfied the requirements for an 'implied bargain' constructive trust. The court stated that the beneficial shares can be quantified having regard to the 'whole course of dealing between them in relation to the property', at least in a domestic context. Chadwick LJ stated:

> . . . in many cases, the answer will be provided by evidence of what they said and did at the time of the acquisition. But in a case where there is no evidence of any discussion between them as to the amount of the share which each was to have – and even in the case where the evidence is that there was no discussion on that point – the question still requires an answer. It must now be accepted that . . . the answer is that each is entitled to that share which the court considers fair having regard to the whole course of dealing between them in relation to the property. And in that context, the whole course of dealing between them in relation to the property includes the arrangements which they make from time to time in order to meet the outgoings (for example, mortgage contributions, council tax and utilities, repairs, insurance and housekeeping) which have to be met if they are to live in the property as their home.

If the parties had come to an express agreement that they were to hold the property jointly that would have been the end of the matter and O would have held a beneficial interest with a 50% share. There was, however, no such express agreement. O could establish her beneficial interest by reason of her direct contributions by way of an inferred common intention based on her contributions. Chadwick LJ found that these contributions can be found from a wider source than merely direct contributions. In any event, the court found that, since they had made equal contributions, the beneficial interest was held on a 60:40 basis in favour of H. Chadwick LJ considered that to declare the parties were entitled to equal shares would be unfair to H in that insufficient weight would be given to the fact that his direct contributions were greater than O's.

Chadwick LJ therefore considered that, in the absence of an agreement, the court can apply judicial discretion in deciding the respective shares of the parties, having regard as to what it considers fair – 'having regard to the whole course of dealing between them *in relation to the property*' – and that the course of dealing will be examined holistically, taking into consideration the realities of domestic life, including how the various bills and outgoings are met. Thus non-financial conduct may also be taken into account, provided it is 'in relation to the property'. A broad brush approach is therefore adopted.

This approach was approved of in **Stack v Dowden** by Baroness Hale, though she expressed a preference for the Law Commission's statement in *Sharing Homes* as set out above, since it set out that the court is to search 'for the result which reflects what the parties must, in the light of their conduct, be taken to have intended'. The majority of the House of Lords did not approve of the expression 'fair' though, since the aim of the court is not to arrive at fairness between the parties but to discover the shared intentions of the parties, whether 'actual, inferred or imputed, with respect to the property in the light of their whole course of conduct in relation to it'.

Joint name legal ownership
So far the examination of quantification has centred on single name legal ownership and it is now necessary to examine this area in the context of joint name legal ownership.

In both *Stack* v *Dowden* and *Jones* v *Kernott* the House of Lords and the Supreme Court stated that, in the absence of any agreement to the contrary where they have declared in writing the nature and size of their respective shares, 'equity follows the law' so that joint legal owners are deemed to hold the beneficial title on a joint tenancy comprising a single composite ownership of the property. This position is, however, only a presumption, so if a party can demonstrate a common intention that the equitable interest was to be held as a tenancy in common then the courts will apply that intention. In the previous chapter we saw that if the parties decide to sever their joint tenancy then they will hold the equitable title on a 50:50 share.

In *Stack* v *Dowden* and *Jones* v *Kernott* it was recognised that the nature and size of the parties' respective shares may change over time. Thus the parties may start off owning the beneficial interest jointly, but this may change to a tenancy in common with the parties owning the beneficial title in unequal shares. Of course, it is also possible that the parties start their relationship with a tenancy in common with distinct shares and these also may change. In both situations, it all depends how their common intention evolves over the period of the relationship.

In domestic relationships, the party claiming the departure from the initial premise that joint legal ownership equals joint beneficial ownership has, in the absence of an express agreement, a heavy burden of proof. Indeed, in *Stack* v *Dowden* it was stated that such a departure from the basic premise will only occur in 'very unusual' cases and that it was a task that was not something 'to be lightly embarked upon'. In *Stack* v *Dowden* Baroness Hale set out the type of factors that a court might consider in divining the common intentions of the parties. These were set out in the previous chapter but it is important to bear in mind that the list is not intended to be exhaustive and it is merely illustrative. From these factors the courts can derive the common intentions of the parties. Furthermore, in *Jones* v *Kernott* it was stated that this common intention would be deduced objectively from their conduct. Where a court found that there was a common intention to depart from the presumption of joint beneficial ownership but it was not possible to determine the shares the parties held by direct evidence or by inference, then the court should apply the principle set out by Chadwick LJ in *Oxley* v *Hiscock*: that is, 'each is entitled to that share which the court considers fair having regard to the whole course of dealing between them in relation to the property'. The Supreme Court considered that the 'whole course of dealing' should be given a broad meaning, enabling a range of factors to be taken into account, 'as may be relevant to ascertaining the parties' actual intentions'. Thus in *Jones* v *Kernott* itself, *Fowler* v *Barron* [2008] EWCA Civ 377 and *Adelkunle* v *Ritchie* [2007] BPIR 1177 the courts held that the equitable shares of the parties differed from the basic premise of joint beneficial ownership.

Proprietary estoppel and co-ownership

It is possible for a cohabitant to establish an interest in the family home by way of the doctrine of proprietary estoppel. The boundary between proprietary estoppel and constructive trusts has now become very blurred. In order to invoke the doctrine, a woman, for instance, must establish that she has acted to her detriment on the faith of a belief, which was known and encouraged by her partner, that she has or will be given a right in or over the property. In such a situation, the court will not permit the other partner to insist on his strict legal rights if to do so would be inconsistent with the belief of the woman.

If the woman is able to satisfy the requirements set out above, the object of the court is to provide her with a remedy which will be the 'minimum equity to do justice to the plaintiff' – *Crabb* v *Arun District Council* [1976] Ch 179. It may be that an appropriate remedy would be to provide the woman with an interest in the property, but not necessarily so, even though this may be her expectation. The objective of the court is to remedy her detriment and thus a court may merely give her a licence to occupy the premises for a period of time, as opposed to a share in the beneficial interest. The court may be minded that, to correct the detriment, an award of damages may be appropriate. To that extent, proprietary estoppel is regarded as providing a 'mere equity' as opposed to a proprietary right per se.

The similarities between constructive trusts and proprietary estoppels can clearly be seen from the requirements of an assurance, a reliance and a detriment and, to that extent, it has been questioned whether the two concepts should be merged – at least in the domestic situation. Lord Walker in *Stack* v *Dowden* did not favour such an assimilation and saw the two concepts as operating in a different sphere; thus he stated:

> I have to say that I am now rather less enthusiastic about the notion that proprietary estoppels and 'common interest' constructive trusts can and should be completely assimilated. Proprietary estoppel typically consists of asserting an equitable claim against the conscience of the 'true' owner. The claim is a 'mere equity'. It is to be satisfied by the minimum award necessary to do justice . . . which may sometimes lead to no more than a monetary award. A 'common intention' constructive trust, by contrast, is identifying the true beneficial owner or owners, and the size of their beneficial interests.

Clearly, whilst the concepts may be similar in terms of certain key elements, the outcome in terms of remedies may be very different. A stark reminder of this can be seen in the case of *Matharu* v *Matharu* [1994] 2 FLR 597 where proprietary estoppel was used in the context of a family home ownership dispute. Here a father-in-law claimed possession of the former family home of his son and daughter-in-law, which the father-in-law owned, from the daughter-in-law, following the breakdown of their marriage and subsequent death of his son. The daughter-in-law claimed that she had an estoppel arising from a mistaken belief, known to her father-in-law, that her deceased husband owned the house and in which she had incurred a detriment by way of work she had undertaken. Whilst the court barred the father-in-law's action for possession, they did not award the daughter-in-law an interest in the property. The court held that the daughter-in-law had no more than a licence to remain in the house 'for her life or such shorter period as she may decide'. The licence given to her was subject to a condition that she took responsibility for the repairs and the financial outgoings, including the mortgage repayments. The decision is undoubtedly harsh and it is indeed puzzling why she should not get an interest if she had to continue to pay the mortgage repayments. There seems to be little incentive for her to remain in the property, given the conditions that she had to meet for a mere licence.

It is clear that common interest constructive trusts are the preferred vehicle for the establishment of an interest in property in a domestic situation. Plainly, *Stack* v *Dowden* and *Jones* v *Kernott* have now signalled the way forward in what appears to be 'closely [resembling] an act of judicial legislation' (Gray and Gray, *Elements of Land Law* (2009)).

Reform

Proposals for the reform of cohabitants' rights have been discussed for many years but with little progress. Indeed, the far-reaching decision in *Stack* v *Dowden* has often been referred to as judicial legislation in that it has gone a long way towards alleviating the apparent paralysis that besets governmental progress in dealing with the problems that abound in this area. Many European and Commonwealth countries have now passed legislation for the provision of the distribution of assets following the breakup of cohabiting couples. The attitude in England and Wales has been one of protecting the institution of marriage and a position that, if a couple wish to have such rights, then it is relatively easy to acquire them by marriage.

While some couples no doubt cohabit because they do not wish to formalise their relationship in this way, others do so, as Baroness Hale pointed out in **Stack v Dowden**, labouring under the myth of their rights in a 'common law' marriage and, in any event, few even consider the legal implications of either marriage or cohabitation. Certainly, cohabitation has been on the rise and in 2007 there were 2.3 million cohabiting couples in the UK (ONS, 2007), with this increase being seen against a background of rising levels of divorce. To this extent, cohabitation may now be seen as normative within the UK (Coast, *Currently Cohabiting: Relationship Attitudes, Expectations and Outcomes* (2009) LSE). It is interesting that, in this study, in 1998 16.6% of cohabitees considered the lack of legal status in cohabitation to be a disadvantage; whilst in 2003 this had doubled to 32.1%. In the same years, the perceived advantage of having no legal ties had decreased from 29.8% to 24.5%. The perceived financial advantages of cohabitation had also increased in these years, from 16.1% to 22.2%, whilst the perceived disadvantage of financial insecurity had decreased from 29% to 30.4%.

Clearly, the reasons for cohabitation are heterogeneous and therefore it has to be questioned whether statutory intervention is appropriate to regulate a relationship that is essentially amorphous. Other jurisdictions have done so and in October 2013 the Cohabitation Rights Bill was introduced into the House of Lords in response to the Law Commission in *Cohabitation: The Financial Consequences of Relationship Breakdown* (2006) (Consultation Paper No. 179) and the subsequently published report, *Cohabitation: The Financial Consequences of Relationship Breakdown* (2007) Law Com No. 307). The bill proposes a framework of rights, responsibilities and basic protections in the events of: cohabitants ceasing to live together; the death of a cohabitant; and, establishing an insurable interest for life insurance purposes. The porposal, broadly speaking, regulates cohabitation breakup only extending to those who had a child together or who have lived together for a continuous period of two years or more. In order to obtain a remedy, applicants would have to prove that they had made qualifying contributions to the parties' relationship which had given rise to certain enduring consequences at the point of separation. The scheme therefore would be very different from that which applies to married couples on divorce under the Matrimonial Causes Act 1973. Simply cohabiting, for however long, would not give rise to any presumed entitlement to share in any pool of property. In any event, it would be possible for eligible cohabitants to opt out of the scheme. The Law Commission recognised '. . . the strongly held view that it is wrong to force cohabitants who have chosen not to marry or form a civil partnership into a particular legal regime against their will. We agree that it is very important to respect the autonomy of couples who wish to determine for themselves the legal consequences of their personal relationships.'

One area where there has been a degree of progress relates to same-sex couples under the Civil Partnership Act 2004. Some of the consequences of this Act have already been discussed; however, the general thrust of the Act is to give same-sex couples a raft of rights and responsibilities if they register their partnership. Where a same-sex couple dissolves their partnership they are treated in the same way as a married couple when it comes to a court allocating partners their respective shares in the shared home. Where, however, the same-sex couple does not register their relationship, the principles relating to the acquisition and quantification of their respective shares in the beneficial interest are thrown back into the general principles set out in this chapter.

Summary

Marriage and civil partnerships

- The courts have wide powers to make property adjustments on divorce, nullity and judicial separation under the Matrimonial Causes Act 1973 s.24.
- Very similar provisions apply to partners in civil partnerships under the Civil Partnership Act 2004 s.72 and Schedule 5.

Express, resulting and constructive trusts

Express declarations of trust

In order to create an express declaration of trust the requirements of the Law of Property Act 1925 s.53(1)b have to be complied with:

> a declaration of trust respecting any land or interest therein must be manifested and proved by some writing signed by some person who is able to declare such trust or by his will.

Once a valid declaration of trust is completed this will be conclusive as to the beneficial ownership: *Goodman v Gallant* [1986] 1 All ER 311.

If there is no express declaration of trust within the requirements of the Law of Property Act 1925 s.53(1)b then it is possible for a resulting, implied, or constructive trust to arise within the Law of Property Act 1925 s.53(2) which excludes them from the requirements of s.53(1)b.

Resulting trusts

- Defined in *Dyer v Dyer* (1788) 2 Cox Eq Cas 92: '. . . The trust of a legal estate . . . results to a man who advances the purchase money.'

Example

If a house is purchased in the name of A, who may have provided part or none of the purchase price, a resulting trust arises in favour of the other party, B, who has provided part or all of the purchase price. A is presumed to hold the legal title on a resulting trust for B and him/herself, if he or she has provided some of the purchase price.

- The resulting trust arises from a presumed intention by B to own a share of the property, as evidenced by the contribution to the purchase price. BUT if A can demonstrate that B's contribution is intended to be a loan or a gift rather than intention to own a share of the property then no resulting trust arises.
- If a claimant can establish a beneficial interest by way of a resulting trust, then that interest is in direct proportion to the contribution. It is an arithmetic calculation based on *direct* contributions.

- Note: Resulting trusts arise in 'sole name' cases so that A owns the legal title on trust for him/herself and B as tenants in common. BUT if the case is a 'joint name' case, so that both names go on the legal title this is dealt with as a *constructive trust*. Here, following *Stack* v *Dowden*, the starting presumption is that the co-owners as joint tenants in law also hold the beneficial interests as joint tenants: 'equity follows the law'.

- The imposition of the presumption of a resulting trust is *not* a rule of law. The issue is 'to ascertain the parties' shared intentions, actual, inferred or imputed, with respect to the property in the light of their whole course of conduct in relation to it'.

Constructive trusts

Setting the context

- Lord Denning defined a constructive trust in *Hussey* v *Palmer* [1972] 3 All ER 744 in the following terms:

  . . . it is a trust imposed by law whenever justice and good conscience require it. It is a liberal process founded on large principles of equity to be applied in cases where the defendant cannot conscientiously keep the property for himself alone, but ought to allow another to have the property or a share in it. The trust may arise at the outset when the property is acquired, or later on, as circumstances may require.

- Denning's dictum arose out of Lord Diplock's statements in *Gissing* v *Gissing* [1971] AC 886; however, his formulation was very broad and fluid, emanating from what a judge considered fair as between the parties. It was thus very uncertain and not founded in firm principle. It was, though, more realistic and flexible than the resulting trust in that the division of the beneficial interest was not bounded by direct contributions but also included indirect contributions. The size of the beneficial interest was based on the actual, inferred or imputed common intentions of the parties, thus giving rise to the 'common intention' constructive trust.

The modern era

The acquisition of the beneficial interest

- The modern era of the common intention constructive trust is founded in the case of *Lloyds Bank plc* v *Rosset* [1991] AC 107. Lord Bridge identified two distinct situations by which a common intention could be established:
  (i) Where there was an *express* common intention trust. This cannot be framed from the expectations of the parties or by their conduct alone, unless underpinned by a detrimental reliance.
  (ii) In the absence of an express intention, where an intention is inferred from the conduct of the parties based on a general common intention that a claimant is to share the beneficial interest and that this conduct evinces a constructive trust.

- Lord Bridge based his inferred common intention trust around direct contributions and was 'doubtful whether anything less will do'. This approach was later criticised as too restrictive and Baroness Hale in *Stack* v *Dowden* considered he had 'set [the] hurdle rather too high'.

- In 'sole name' cases, *Stack* v *Dowden* considered that a beneficial interest could be derived from a broader range of circumstance.

- In 'joint name' cases, *Stack* v *Dowden* stated that the fact that the legal title is vested in joint names raises a presumption, in the absence of an express declaration, that the beneficial interest is also to be held jointly.

The quantification of the beneficial interest

Sole name cases

- The presumption here is that where the legal estate is vested in one person the claimant is entitled to no beneficial interest.

- This was challenged in *Midland Bank* v *Cooke* [1995] 4 All ER 562, where it was held that it was the duty of the court to survey the whole course of dealing between the parties insofar as the *dealing related to the parties*. If this search was inconclusive then the court should revert to the maxim 'equity is equality'. The case therefore introduced a 'broad brush' approach.

- See also:

  Drake v *Whipp* [1996] 1 FLR 826

  Le Foe v *Le Foe* [2001] 2 FLR 970

  Oxley v *Hiscock* [2004] EWCA Civ 546

- *Stack* v *Dowden* approved of Chadwick LJ's approach in *Oxley* v *Hiscock* in that, in the absence of an agreement, the court applies judicial discretion as regards the shares of the parties, 'having regards to the whole course of dealing between them *in relation to the property*'. The course of dealing is examined 'holistically' so that non-financial matters can be taken into account. The House of Lords did not, however, approve of the expression 'fair' – this is too uncertain and subjective.

Joint name cases

- The presumption here is that joint legal owners hold the beneficial title on a joint tenancy: 'equity follows the law'.

- If a party can demonstrate a common intention to hold the beneficial interest on a tenancy in common then the courts will apply that intention.

- Both *Stack* v *Dowden* and *Jones* v *Kernott* recognised that the parties' common intention can change over time, either rebutting the joint tenancy presumption or altering their respective shares. This common intention can be found from a wide variety of factors – i.e. a 'broad brush approach'.

Proprietary estoppel

- Whilst similar in many respects to constructive trusts, proprietary estoppel is different in that it abolishes a mere equity to remedy the detriment caused to one party rather than establishing a beneficial interest. It is no longer considered a way forward in deciding issues relating to co-ownership.

Further reading

Bridge, 'The Property Rights of Cohabitants – Where Do We Go From Here?' (2002) *Family Law* 743

Bridge, 'Cohabitation: Why Legislative Reform is Necessary' (2007) *Family Law* 911

Briggs, 'Co-ownership – An Equitable Non-Sequitur' (2012) 128 *Law Quarterly Review* 183

Cloherty and Fox, 'Proving a Trust of a Shared Home' (2007) *Cambridge Law Journal* 317

Da Costa, 'Stack v Dowden Revisited' (2007) 67 *Family Law Journal*

Dixon, 'The Never-Ending Story – Co-ownership After Stack v Dowden' [2007] 71 *The Conveyancer and Property Lawyer* 456

Dixon, 'The Still Not Ended, Never-Ending Story' [2012] 76 *The Conveyancer and Property Lawyer* 83

Etherton, 'Constructive Trusts and Proprietary Estoppel: The Search for Clarity and Principle' [2009] 73 *The Conveyancer and Property Lawyer* 104

Gardner, 'Family Property Today' (2008) 124 *Law Quarterly Review* 422

Gardner and Davidson, 'The Future of Stack v Dowden' (2011) 127 *Law Quarterly Review* 13

Gardner and Davidson, 'The Supreme Court on Family Homes' (2012) 128 *Law Quarterly Review* 178

Gray and Gray, *Elements of Land Law* (2009) Oxford University Press

Harding, 'Defending Stack v Dowden' [2009] 73 *The Conveyancer and Property Lawyer* 309

Law Commission, *Sharing Homes: A Discussion Paper* (2002) Law Com No. 278

Law Commission, *Cohabitation: The Financial Consequences of a Relationship Breakdown* (2007, Law Com No. 307)

Lee, 'Stack v Dowden: A Sequel' (2008) 124 *Law Quarterly Review* 209

Mee, 'Jones v Kernott: Inferring and Imputing in Essex' [2012] 76 *The Conveyancer and Property Lawyer* 167

Pawlowski, 'Imputed Intention and Joint Ownership – A Return to Common Sense' [2012] 76 *The Conveyancer and Property Lawyer* 149

Roche, 'Kernott, Stack and Oxley Made Simple: A Practitioner's View' (2011) 75 *The Conveyancer and Property Lawyer* 123

Yip, 'The Rules Applying to Unmarried Cohabitants' Family Home' [2012] 76 *The Conveyancer and Property Lawyer* 159

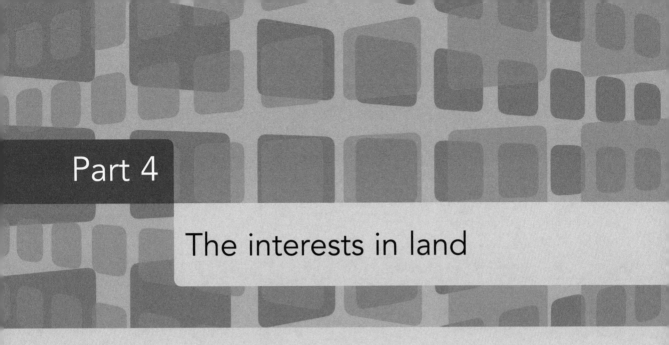

Part 4

The interests in land

13

Leasehold covenants

Aims and objectives

After reading this chapter you should be able to:

- Understand the principles regarding the enforcement of leasehold covenants between the landlord and tenant.
- Understand the principles relating to the running of covenants prior to the Landlord and Tenant (Covenants) Act 1995.
- Understand the principles relating to the running of covenants post the Landlord and Tenant (Covenants) Act 1995.
- Understand the position of sub-tenants in relation to leasehold covenants.

Introduction

The running of covenants

As we saw in Chapter 6, leases generally impose all sorts of rights and obligations contained in covenants on the parties to a lease. Often there will be express covenants but covenants may also be implied. In this chapter we are going to examine the degree to which the covenants bind the original parties to the lease and, more importantly, we are going to examine the degree to which the covenants are enforceable by and against assignees of the lease, whether by the landlord or the tenant. Additionally, we are going to consider whether a landlord, or their assignee, can enforce a covenant against a sub-tenant of a tenant and, indeed, the degree to which a sub-tenant can enforce the covenants against the original landlord, or their assignee. In legal parlance, then, we are going to examine how the benefit and burden of leasehold covenants 'run' with the land between the original parties and their successors in title. We alluded to some of the principles in Chapter 6 but now we need to examine the principles in a great deal more detail.

One should remember that the covenantor, whether the landlord or the tenant, is the person promising to carry out the covenant, whereas the covenantee, whether the landlord or the tenant, is the person seeking to enforce the covenant.

Covenants may arise in freehold or leasehold property and are generally used to retain the character and value of the property or to define the obligation of the parties in relation to it. Covenants can be positive or negative – i.e. restrictive covenants. Not surprisingly, a positive covenant requires the covenantor to perform some specified act in relation to the land, whilst a negative covenant restricts the covenantor from doing something on their own land. Whilst in this chapter we are focusing on leasehold covenants, one should note that in freehold land a positive covenant cannot bind anyone other than the original parties, unlike in leases. It is for this reason that flats are invariably leaseholds.

In examining the running of leasehold covenants we use the model shown in Figure 13.1.

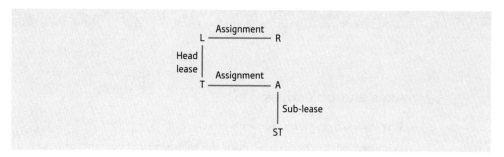

Figure 13.1

In this example, L has given T a lease, which we will refer to as the 'head lease'. L has then assigned his or her reversion to R, whilst T has assigned his or her lease to A so that, for example, if T has a 10-year lease then A will take this lease with the outstanding balance left on it. If T has occupied the premises for 2 years, A will have the 8 years outstanding. A has then granted a sub-lease to ST. The sub-lease cannot exceed the balance left on the lease.

Two sets of rules

The running of covenants in leases are to be found in two sets of rules: those that are contained in the pre-1996 common law and statutory rules and those that fall within the Landlord and Tenant (Covenants) Act 1995 ('LT(C)A') which brought about a radical overhaul of the principles relating to the transmission of leasehold covenants. The LT(C)A came out of the recommendations of the Law Commission in *Landlord and Tenant Law: Privity of Contract and Estate* (Law Com No. 174) and whilst it recommended that the Act should operate retrospectively, this was not enacted, with the exception of a limited number of provisions. The result of this is that leases created prior to 1 January 1996 are regulated by the old rules; those created after this date will be governed by the LT(C)A. Clearly, some leases can be created for very long periods of time, so the old rules will persist for many more years. It should also be noted that some leases, even though created after 1 January 1996, will be covered by the old rules because they were made under an agreement – for example, an option – made before that date. Further, some leases will be entered into because of an option to renew in a lease created prior to that date. The LT(C)A applies to both legal and equitable leases created after 1 January 1996.

In order to examine the running of covenants we will first consider the old rules and see how these apply to the various relationships that arise out of the example set out above.

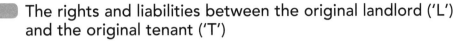

Leases created prior to 1 January 1996

The rights and liabilities between the original landlord ('L') and the original tenant ('T')

Figure 13.2

Between L and T (Figure 13.2) all covenants are enforceable by and against each other. Liability is based on the fact that, as well as creating a lease, the parties are bound by virtue of 'privity of contract'. Since the parties are entering into a contract, they are bound not only by the normal covenants that might be contained in the lease, but also by any personal covenants. For instance, if, as part of the contract, T has agreed to mow L's lawns every Sunday during the summer months, he or she will be bound by this personal covenant simply as a matter of the law of contract. The point is *all* covenants are enforceable by and against each other, irrespective of whether they are of a proprietary or personal nature.

The original tenant ('T')

Enduring liability

Since the liability of T is founded in contract, his or her liability on the covenants continues throughout the term of the lease, even if T has assigned his or her lease. T is therefore liable for breaches committed by his or her successors in title (assignees) and persons deriving title from him or her – i.e. A and ST. Normally, the lease will expressly state that he or she covenants for his or her successors in title or persons deriving title from him or her, but even if the lease does not expressly provide for this, such liability is, in any event, implied by virtue of the Law of Property Act 1925 s.79 –

> A covenant relating to any land of a covenantor . . . shall, unless contrary intention is expressed, be deemed to be made by the covenantor on behalf of himself his successors in title and the other persons deriving title under him or them, and shall have effect as if such successors and other persons were expressed.

Thus, if T has covenanted not to do or to perform a particular act, if a later assignee breaches the covenant then T remains liable to L, even though it may be many years after T has assigned his or her lease. For example, if T has assigned his or her lease to A and A has then assigned the lease to A_2 and A_2 fails to pay his or her rent, L can either take action against A_2 or T. This would be particularly useful to L if A_2 becomes insolvent or disappears and therefore the ability of L to recover his or her rent is limited or non-existent; he or she may sue T instead even if it is, for instance, 10 years since T had the lease: *Thursby v Plant* (1690) 1 Saund 230. T has no right to require L to exhaust his or her rights against A_2 before enforcing his or her remedies against T: *Allied London Investments Ltd v Hambro Life Assurance Ltd* (1984) 270 EG 948.

Clearly, L cannot proceed against T and A_2 with a view to recovering twice but he or she can take action against both at once so that, if either T or A_2 cannot individually pay for the loss, L can recover the amount of the loss from both jointly: ***Norwich Union Life Insurance Society*** v ***Low Profile Fashions Ltd*** (1992) 64 P & CR 187 (see Figure 13.3).

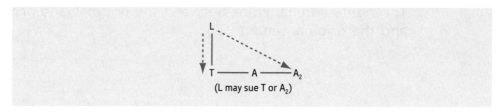

Figure 13.3

By this process, T remains liable throughout the term of the lease. This process can create real hardship for a tenant and this hardship was one of the factors that lay behind the passing of the LT(C)A 1995. Since the lease is based in contract, it is always possible for this continuing liability to be excluded and indeed s.79 allows for this. In reality, however, no landlord would grant a lease that would exclude a tenant's liability on his or her assignment of the lease to another, or if the tenant grants a sub-lease. There are, though, certain limitations on the liability of the tenant:

(i)   T is not liable if an assignee, A, surrenders his or her lease to L and L gives A a new lease. Here the original lease has ended and with it the liability of T.

(ii) The LT(C)A s.18 applies retrospectively so that T is not liable for any increase in the rent arising from the original lease being varied. It should be noted that T is only exempt from the *increase* in the rent that has resulted from the variation, so that if the rent is varied from £100 per week to £150 per week, T is only liable for the £100 per week. Thus privity of contract relates to the original contract, not to the varied contract. It should be noted here that many leases have rent review clauses included in them so that the rent can be increased to take account of inflation. Here T will be liable for the increase in the rent since the original contract envisaged such increases.

(iii) In ***City of London Corporation*** v ***Fell*** [1994] 1 AC 458 the House of Lords held that the continuing liability of an original tenant ceases upon the expiry of the agreed contractual term but the lease continues by virtue of the Landlord and Tenant Act 1954 since the liability of T arises in relation to the contractual term, not the term as extended by the Act.

(iv) The LT(C)A gives protection to former tenants who may become liable in respect of breaches of covenant following the assignment of the lease. Sections 17–20 apply to both pre- and post-1996 leases. The Act provides that T will no longer have to bear liability in respect to any 'fixed charges' that become payable under the lease except where, within six months of the fixed charge falling due under the covenant, L serves on T a notice informing T that the fixed charge is now due and that L intends to recover from T the amount of the fixed charge: LT(C)A s.17(2). Such a notice has two effects. Firstly, it warns T of his or her potential liability but it also limits the liability of T to the fixed charges incurred in the six months immediately preceding the service of the notice. Fixed charges are defined in s.17(6) and include rent, service charges or any liquidated damages in respect of a breach of covenant.

If L fails to serve an appropriate notice (often called a 'protective notice') T is automatically free from any liability to pay *any* amount in respect of a fixed charge.

If T makes a payment for the full amount demanded in L's protective notice, T is entitled to have L grant him or her an 'overriding lease' of the let premises. This overriding lease becomes interposed between L and the assignee in default: LT(C)A s.19. The effect of this is that T becomes the landlord in respect of the defaulting assignee and is thereby able to direct action against that assignee in the form of an action for damages or even forfeit the assignee's lease. In the case of the latter, T is then able to assign the lease to a third party as a means of offsetting his or her liability to L. T may request an overriding lease at the time of the making of the fixed charge payment or within 12 months of the date of the payments. The right to request an overriding lease is capable of being protected as a notice under the Land Registration Act 2002 or a C(iv) land charge in unregistered land. The new overriding lease contains the same covenants as the original lease, with the exception of personal covenants.

The tenant's right of indemnity

We have seen above that the LT(C)A has modified the extent of the liability of tenants for fixed charges; however, it will not go unnoticed that a tenant has enduring liability with respect to unliquidated damages that may be incurred by any of his or her subsequent assignees. This unquantified level of damages could, of course, be significant – for instance, if it relates to the repair of drains. In such circumstances, T, having paid damages, may then attempt to seek an indemnity from the assignee who has subsequently broken the covenant. This right is all well and good in theory, but in practice the right must be qualified by the fact that L is only usually taking action against T because his or her right against T's assignee is frail by virtue of that assignee being insolvent or untraceable. Thus T's right of indemnity is also subject to the same frailty. It is for this reason that a tenant should ensure that he or she has a right of re-entry against an assignee who is in breach of a covenant. These difficulties aside, a tenant has three means of obtaining an indemnity from a defaulting assignee:

Rule in Moule v Garrett (1872) LR 7 Ex 101

Under the rule in ***Moule* v *Garrett*** (1872) LR 7 Ex 101, a tenant may take direct action against the assignee who is in breach, thus, if A3 below is in breach, T can take direct action against him or her (see Figure 13.4).

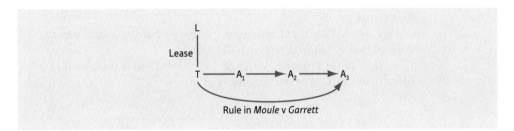

Figure 13.4

It can be seen that it does not matter if the assignee in breach has taken the lease from the tenant directly or from some intervening assignee. Essentially, the claim by the tenant here is based on quasi-contract under which 'the law implies an obligation between joint debtors to repay money paid by one of them for the exclusive benefit of the other, when both were legally liable to a common creditor' (Megarry and Wade, *The Law of Real Property* (2008)).

Express indemnity covenants

By this process, each assignee expressly covenants with their assignor to indemnify the assignor for a breach of covenant that arises following the assignment. The effect of this where there have been multiple assignments of the lease is to create a chain of indemnity covenants. In the example above, the process works as shown in Figure 13.5.

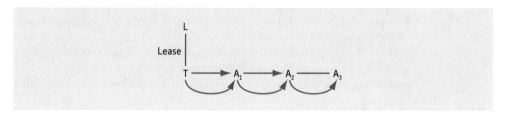

Figure 13.5

For T to recover the damages he or she has paid to L, he or she recovers from A_1, under the express indemnity clause in that assignment; A_1 recovers from A_2, who then recovers from A_3 – assuming A_3 is able to pay or has not disappeared! The only problem with this process is that, just like all chains, it is only as strong as the weakest link, so that if A_2, for instance, has died, disappeared or is insolvent, the chain stops there and can proceed no further.

Implied indemnity covenants

Where there is no express indemnity covenant as set out above, then such a covenant is implied by the Law of Property Act 1925 s.77 (unregistered land) and Land Registration Act 2002 s.134 and Schedule 12 para 20 (registered land). The covenant is implied subject to contrary intention and the provisions generally are excluded, otherwise it works in just the same way as an express indemnity covenant. It should be noted that, if there is no express indemnity covenant and implied covenants are excluded, it is still possible for the tenant to proceed under the rule in *Moule* v *Garret* above.

The original landlord ('L')

Just as T has enduring liability for the whole of the term of the lease, irrespective of the lease being assigned or a sub-lease created, so L is also liable throughout the term of the lease, irrespective of the fact that he or she may have assigned his or her reversion to, for example, R above.

One should note that L is liable not only to T but also to his or her assignees: *Celsteel Ltd* v *Alton House Holdings* [1985] 2 All ER 562.

By the Law of Property Act 1925 s.79, a landlord is presumed to have covenanted for him/herself and his or her successors in title.

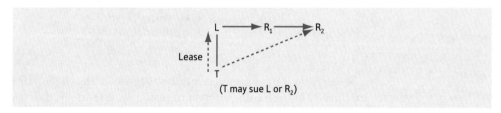

Figure 13.6

Market forces often dictate that L is in a stronger position than T and therefore L will often expressly exclude his or her liability following his or her assignment of the reversion.

So far, we have considered the continuing liability of the landlord for breaches of covenant – that is, the burdens of the covenants. With respect to the benefit of the covenants, whilst technically the landlord may have been able to sue for breaches of covenants throughout the duration of the lease, the Law of Property Act 1925 s.141(1) provides that the benefit of all proprietary leasehold covenants passes to his or her assignee (R) on the assignment of the reversion. Thus L loses his right to sue T (or his or her assignee) since this passes to his or her own assignee: *Re King* [1963] Ch 459. The effect of this is that L loses not only his or her future right to sue but also any existing rights to sue for breach of covenant at the time of the assignment. The assignment will therefore pass the right to sue to R, but also the accrued rights of L. Note that the same restriction does not apply to tenants who retain the right to sue for breaches that occur before their assignment of the lease to an assignee.

The rights and liabilities between assignees

So far, in considering the rights and liabilities of L and T, we have seen that these are based on privity of contract. In the case of the *assignees* of either L or T there can clearly be no privity of contract since they are not party to the contract. This is a fundamental principle of the law of contract since a stranger cannot have a right to enforce a contract conferred upon him or her – 'our law knows nothing of a jus quaesitum tertio arising by way of contract': per Viscount Haldane LC in *Dunlop Pneumatic Tyre Co. Ltd v Selfridge & Co. Ltd* [1915] AC 847 at 853. Leasehold covenants provide a notable exception to this principle since here the enforceability of covenants between assignees is based on privity of estate. The principle here is set out in *Spencer's Case* (1583) 5 Co Rep 16a, which provided that the benefit and burden of covenants extends beyond the original parties if the lease is a legal lease and the covenants could be said to 'touch and concern' the land. By this doctrinal shift in *Spencer's Case*, the benefit and burden of positive and restrictive covenants run with the lease of the tenant and the landlord's reversion and become imprinted on all assignees who are 'privy' to the leasehold estate (see Figure 13.7).

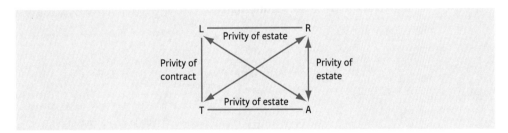

Figure 13.7

We now need to see how this doctrine is applied to assignees of the tenant and assignees of the reversion. However, it should be borne in mind that the issue of enforceability of the covenants lies in two questions: Has the burden of the covenants passed, and, has the benefit of the covenants passed? In answering these questions it is convenient to look at the issue of where the tenant has assigned his or her lease first and then look at the matter where the landlord has assigned his or her reversion.

Where the tenant has assigned his lease

The principle laid down in *Spencer's Case* provides that the assignee (A) is entitled to the benefit and is subject to the burden of all covenants that 'touch and concern' the land, whether the covenants are positive or restrictive, since there is privity of estate between A and L. It is now necessary to look at the components that give rise to privity of estate.

There must be a legal lease

Privity of estate and the running of the benefit and burdens of the covenants can only exist in relation to a legal lease – that is, the lease must be contained in a deed to satisfy the requirements of the Law of Property Act 1925 s.52. It was held in *Boyer* v *Warbey* [1953] 1 QB 234 that legal leases falling within the Law of Property Act 1925 s.54(2) exception – i.e. leases for three years or less – will suffice to satisfy this requirement, though in practice issues relating to breaches of covenant are unlikely to have a great deal of impact in short leases.

There must be a legal assignment

For the benefit and burden to run with the land there must be a legal assignment – that is, the assignment must be made by deed. If the assignment is not made by deed then it is only an equitable assignment – i.e. a contract to assign. In such a situation, the normal rule of contract applies so that only the benefit, not the burden, will be transmitted to the assignee.

It is vitally important to note that, even if the lease is a legal one between the landlord (L) and tenant (T), by virtue of the Law of Property Act 1925 s.54(2) exception the assignment, whether to R or A, *must* nevertheless be contained within the deed.

The legal assignment must be for the whole term

The legal assignment must be for the whole term of the lease for the benefit and burden to run. Essentially, this means that if T has a lease for 25 years he or she will be assigning the remainder of the unspent part of the lease. If the assignment is for even one day shorter than the head lease, then a sub-lease will be created rather than an assignment. For example, if L gives T a lease for 25 years, T then assigns the lease to A and then A assigns the lease to ST for the residue of the 25 years less one day, A's assignment operates as a sub-lease to ST, not an assignment (see Figure 13.8).

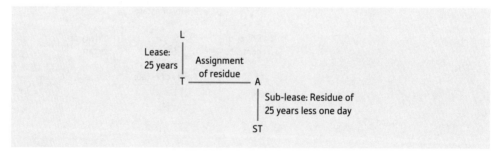

Figure 13.8

This is important because, if ST is in breach of covenant, L will not be able to take direct action against ST since there is neither a relationship of privity of contract nor a relationship of estate between them. In fact, the terms of the sub-lease are normally at least as stringent as the terms in the head lease and often the covenants will be replicated. The effect is that L can take action against T, who is, remember, liable throughout the term of the lease. T in turn will seek an indemnity from A, who in turn will take action against ST. ST, as a sub-tenant, cannot be held liable directly to the head lessor, L.

The covenants must 'touch and concern' the land

The expression 'touch and concern' means that the covenant must be one which affects the landlord in his or her capacity as landlord and the tenant in his or her capacity as tenant. Thus covenants which are personal cannot run with the land on the assignment of the lease. In other words, only covenants that are proprietary in nature are capable of transmission. The reasoning is that such covenants have an enduring impact on the land, whilst personal covenants are just that and only intended to affect a particular individual at a particular moment in time. In practice, arriving at a satisfactory test to distinguish between proprietary and personal covenants has caused some considerable difficulty; however, in *P & A Swift Investments* v *Combined English Stores Group plc* [1989] AC 632 Lord Oliver provided some guidance for a 'satisfactory working test'. It must be emphasised, though, that this test is only a guideline, so each case must be treated on its own merits. Lord Oliver's test consisted of four components:

(a) The covenant must benefit the dominant owner for the time being so that if the owner gives up his estate the covenant ceases to be advantageous to him. If the covenant remains advantageous once the dominant owner gives up his estate then the covenant will be of a personal nature only and will not touch and concern the land;

(b) The covenant must affect the nature, quality, mode of use or value of the land of the dominant owner;

(c) The covenant must not be expressed to be personal;

(d) The fact that the covenant is to pay a sum of money will not prevent it from touching and concerning the land so long as the three forgoing conditions are satisfied and the covenant is connected with something to be done on, or in relation to the land.

Typical examples of covenants that have been held to 'touch and concern' tenants' covenants are: to pay rent; to pay water rates; to repair premises or to cultivate land in a proper husbandry manner; to use the premises for non-business uses only and, importantly, not to assign or sub-let without the landlord's consent.

Typical examples of covenants that have been held to 'touch and concern' landlords' covenants are: to give the tenant quiet possession of the premises; to repair the premises; not to build on the adjoining property. If a landlord's covenant amounts to an estate contract then the enforceability of such an estate contract rests on whether it has been properly protected, not on whether it touches and concerns the land, whether or not the covenant is one entered into by the lessor or lessee – for instance, a covenant giving the lessee the right to renew his or her lease (*Phillips* v *Mobil Oil Ltd* [1989] 1 WLR 888) or a covenant requiring the lessee to offer to surrender his or her lease before assigning or underletting (*Greene* v *Church Commissioners for England* [1974] Ch 467). In unregistered land, such covenants should be protected by registration of a Class C(iv) land charge under the Land Charges Act 1972 and, in registered land, protection should be by way of a notice against the burdened title under the Land Registration Act 2002 s.32(1). It should also be noted that, in registered land, if no notice is registered then the estate contract covenant may take effect as an interest coupled with actual occupation for the purposes of an interest that is overriding within the provision of the Land Registration Act 2002 Schedule 3 para 2.

Before leaving the matter of the liability of the tenant's assignees under privity of estate, one should note that the assignee is only liable for his or her own breaches of covenant. The assignee is not liable for breaches that have occurred prior to him or her obtaining the lease: ***Gresca v Green*** (1700) 1 Salk 199, nor can a landlord levy distress against an assignee with respect to rent arrears accrued by the tenant or a previous assignee: ***Hawkins v Sherman*** (1828) 3 C & P 459. Similarly, an assignee is not liable for breaches of covenant that arise after he or she has assigned the lease: ***City of London Corporation v Fell*** [1994] 1 AC 458. The liability of an assignee is thus restricted to the period in which he or she holds the lease. This is, of course, in sharp contrast to the original tenant, who is liable throughout the term of the lease.

Where the landlord has assigned his or her reversion

The original position where a landlord assigned his or her freehold reversion to an assignee (R) was that neither the benefit nor the burden of the covenants passed to him or her. Thus R could neither sue nor be sued for breaches of covenant. This position changed under the Grantees of Reversion Act 1540 so that the benefit and burden of covenants would pass, provided the covenants 'touch and concern' the land. These provisions are now contained in the Law of Property Act 1925 s.141 and s.142. In these sections, the expression 'touch and concern' is replaced by the expression 'having reference to the subject matter of the lease'.

Before looking at the effects of s.141 and s.142 there are a number of other points that need noting. Firstly, we saw earlier that the lease must be in due form – that is, the lease must be made by deed. A lease created under the doctrine in **Walsh v Lonsdale** will also suffice and, indeed, a lease created orally will also be effective. The reason for this is that the Law of Property Act 1925 s.154 provides that s.141 and s.142 'appl[y] to leases created before or after the commencement of this Act, and "lease" includes an under-lease or *other tenancy*'.

Secondly, whilst, as we have already noted, the landlord remains liable during the whole of the term of the lease even after he or she has assigned his or her reversion, the assignee of the reversion, R, is alone entitled to sue the tenant or his or her assignee for breach of covenant. This entitlement extends to breaches committed prior to the assignment to R as well as breaches occurring whilst the reversion is vested in or her.

Thirdly, whilst we have talked of privity of estate extending between R and T and T's assignee, A, this is not, strictly speaking, correct. Remember that the rights and liabilities of R arise under statute and not under any common law notions of privity of estate which were discussed earlier.

Section 141 – Passing the benefit of the landlord's covenants

Section 141(1) gives R and his or her successors in title the benefit of the landlord's covenants and allows him or her to sue T or A for breaches of covenant that have 'reference to the subject matter of the lease' (see Figure 13.9). This is defined in the same way as 'touching and concerning': ***P & A Swift Investments v Combined English Stores Group plc*** [1989] AC 632.

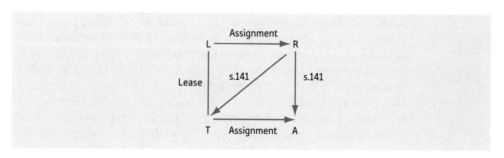

Figure 13.9

Whilst s.141 clearly provides that R has the benefit of L's covenants, we must not ignore the second question that was posed earlier: not only is it necessary to demonstrate that the claimant, R, has the benefit, we must also establish that T or A has the burden of the covenants.

Section 142 – Passing the burden of the landlord's covenants

Section 142(1) gives R and his or her successors in title the burden of the landlord's covenants so that he or she is liable to T or A for breaches of covenant that have 'reference to the subject matter of the lease' (see Figure 13.10). As with s.141(1), the claimant, T or A, has to prove that he or she has the benefit of the covenants. The burden of the covenants passes automatically to R; however, it should be noted that estate contracts, such as covenants to renew the lease, will not bind R unless the registration requirements, as set out above, are complied with.

It should be noted that R will have the benefit of any right of re-entry reserved by L to terminate a tenant's breach of covenant by virtue of s.141(1). A right of re-entry in these circumstances is peculiar since it may be actioned against an assignee of the tenant despite the fact that that assignee has not been in breach of a covenant, though a predecessor has been in breach previously. The reason for this is that a right of re-entry is a proprietary interest that attaches to the land itself so that, where such a right is contained in the head lease or assignment to R, it passes not merely as a benefit under s.141(1) but as a proprietary right that binds the land, whoever is in possession: ***Shiloh Spinners Ltd v Harding*** [1973] AC 691. Even if the assignee of the tenant is not subject to the covenant that is alleged to have been breached, this is immaterial since the right of re-entry attaches to the land.

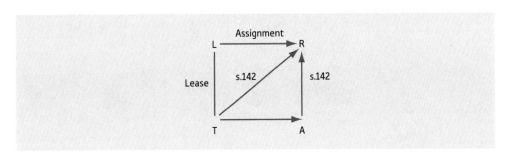

Figure 13.10

The position of sub-tenants ('ST')

We saw earlier that the original tenant or his or her assignee is able to grant a sub-lease that must be shorter than the original lease. If it is not shorter then it operates as an assignment, not as a sub-lease. In a sub-lease, T or A becomes the landlord of ST; however, ST has no relationship at all with L. The relationship can be configured in a variety of ways – see, for instance, Figure 13.11.

Since there is no relationship between L and ST in that there is neither privity of contract nor privity of estate, it stands to reason that the covenants in the head lease cannot be enforced directly against ST, or vice versa. Of course, if the sub-tenant is in breach of

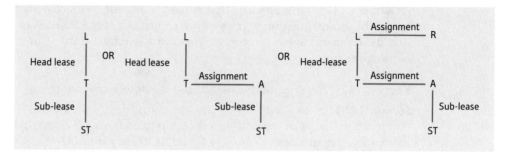

Figure 13.11

a covenant in the head lease then the landlord or his or her assignee may take action against the tenant or his or her assignee, who in turn could take action against ST as the sub-tenant – provided that the covenants in the sub-lease are the same as those in the head lease. T or A will invariably ensure that the terms of the sub-lease are at least as stringent as those in the head lease. Failure to do so will not only render them liable to L or R but, depending on the type of breach, could expose them to having their tenancy forfeited and this in turn would automatically forfeit the sub-lease: *Pennell v Payne* [1995] 2 All ER 592.

It is, of course, possible for ST to assign his or her sub-lease and so a position like that in Figure 13.12 might arise.

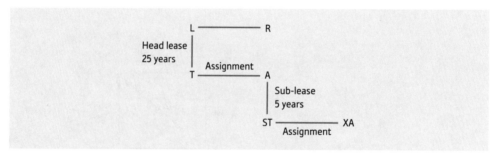

Figure 13.12

Example

In this situation, L has granted a legal lease to T for 25 years who has then assigned his or her lease to A. L has then assigned his or her reversion to R. A then grants a legal sub-lease to ST who has in turn assigned it to XA. XA is not in breach of covenant.

Clearly R cannot take direct action against XA; however, he or she has two options. Under s.141(1) he or she can claim either against T or A, provided the covenant has reference to the subject matter of the lease. If he or she claims against T then T would invariably seek an indemnity from A. A in turn could take action against ST on the basis of privity of contract – as the original sub-tenant, ST, remains liable throughout the term of the sub-lease. ST could then seek an indemnity from XA. Alternatively, assuming the covenant touches and concerns the land, A could take action against XA on the basis of Spencer's Case. Diagrammatically the position therefore is as shown in Figure 13.13.

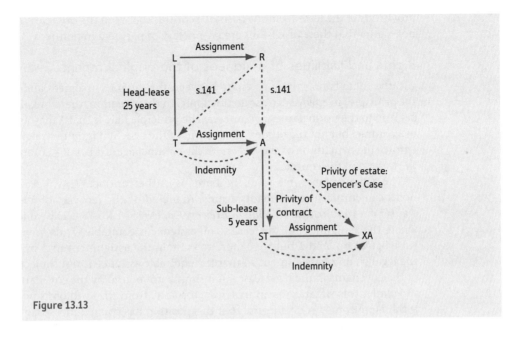

Figure 13.13

There is, however, one exception here. The landlord of the head lease, either L or R as appropriate, can take direct action against ST, or his or her assignee (XA) as appropriate, where the breach is a breach of a restrictive covenant. Since the case of ***Tulk v Moxhay*** (1848) 2 Ph 774 restrictive covenants effectively became a proprietary interest that is enforceable for all persons, except a purchaser of the legal estate for value without notice. In registered land, restrictive covenants, by virtue of the Land Registration Act 2002 s.29(2)b, are automatically binding on any transferee or underlessee. It should be noted that restrictive covenants are not capable of being protected by way of a notice in the register by the Land Registration Act 2002 s.33(c). In unregistered land, restrictive covenants in leasehold premises remain governed by the doctrine of notice since, it will be recalled, Class D(ii) land charges specifically exclude restrictive covenants in leasehold premises.

The principles in the doctrine in ***Tulk v Moxhay*** will be discussed more fully in the next chapter, on freehold covenants.

Equitable leases

So far, in considering the running of covenants in leases we have seen that the principles in relation to ***Spencer's Case*** only apply to leases made in a deed or, following ***Boyer v Warbey***, to leases falling within the three year or less exception contained in the Law of Property Act 1925 s.54(2). Where a lease is an equitable lease then there can be no privity of estate with regard to either an equitable lease or an equitable assignment of a legal lease. As before, we will look at the effect of this between the original parties, L and T, and their assignees.

The original landlord and tenant

Equitable leases generally arise under the doctrine in ***Walsh v Lonsdale*** in which the equitable lease forms the basis of a specifically enforceable contract. It follows therefore that the provisions of the lease form the basis of a contract between the original parties and it does not matter that these provisions are proprietary or personal in nature.

Rights and liabilities of assignees of the original tenant

Clearly, there is no privity of estate between the tenant's assignees and the landlord as the principles in *Spencer's Case* do not apply. In this situation, therefore, the law is thrown back on to the normal rules of contract. The principle here is that T may assign the benefit of a contract but not the burden. So in terms of the benefit it is quite straightforward: A can enforce the benefits he or she has under the contract against L or R – i.e. anyone who takes the burden of the contract.

The assignee takes free from the burdens of the contract. This means that neither L nor R can enforce the covenants against A, including the recovery of rent. This position was set out in *Purchase* v *Lichfield Brewery Co.* [1915] 1 KB 184. The same position arises where the assignment of the lease to an assignee is equitable. Thus there may be a legal lease between L and T but the failure to contain the assignment to A by deed interrupts the legal chain of assignment so that the equitable assignee is not subject to the burdens of the covenants in the legal lease – A is simply not bound by the covenants.

Plainly, this situation is an unsatisfactory one from the landlord's point of view and it therefore comes as no surprise that this position has come under assault in a variety of ways, which we will now examine.

Restrictive covenants

As we saw earlier, restrictive covenants may be enforced by virtue of the doctrine in *Tulk* v *Moxhay* (1848) 2 Ph 744. This doctrine allows a restrictive covenant, because it is a proprietary interest, to be enforced against all persons who may be in possession of the land to which the restrictive covenant applies. It does not matter if the person in possession has a legal estate or an equitable interest – or indeed is a mere squatter or licensee. There are, however, certain conditions that are required to be fulfilled. Firstly, the restrictive covenant must 'touch and concern' the land and it must have become attached to the land. This latter condition normally arises by way of the Law of Property Act 1925 s.79, which provides:

(1) A covenant relating to any land of a covenantor or capable of being bound by him, shall, unless a contrary intention is expressed, be deemed to be made by the covenantor on behalf of himself his successors in title and the persons deriving the title under him or them, and, subject as aforesaid, shall have effect as if such successors and other persons were expressed.

This subsection extends to a covenant to do some act relating to the land, notwithstanding that the subject-matter may not be in existence when the covenant is made.

(2) For the purpose of this section in connexion with covenants restrictive of the user of land 'successors in title' shall be deemed to include the owners and occupiers for the time being of such land.

Secondly, if the claimant is an assignee of the original landlord then that person must have the benefit of the restrictive covenant. This normally arises by the operation of the Law of Property Act 1925 s.141, as previously discussed.

It will be recalled that, in unregistered land, restrictive covenants in leases are subject to the doctrine of notice and do not fall within a Class D(ii) land charge: *Dartstone* v *Cleveland Petroleum Ltd* [1969] 1 WLR 1807. In registered land, restrictive covenants are automatically protected by virtue of the Land Registration Act 2002 s.29(1).

Rights of re-entry

As with restrictive covenants, rights of re-entry are equitable proprietary interests and are enforceable by means of a forfeiture clause, if contained in the original lease (they usually are). Rights of re-entry represent quite a powerful means for a landlord to enforce compliance with a covenant since they allow a landlord to re-enter the premises and terminate the lease even if the covenant itself is not binding on the tenant's assignee: *Shiloh Spinners Ltd v Harding* [1973] AC 691. Rights of re-entry operate in a similar way to restrictive covenants in that the leasehold covenant must 'touch and concern' the land and that if the claimant is an assignee of the landlord he must have the benefit of the right of re-entry – i.e. as per the Law of Property Act 1925 s.141. Finally, the equitable assignee of the tenant must be bound by the right of re-entry. As per restrictive covenants, rights of re-entry are not capable of being registered as a land charge in unregistered land and therefore the doctrine of notice applies. In registered land, rights of re-entry are automatically binding by virtue of the Land Registration Act 2002 s.29(2)b.

Implied periodic tenancy

In Chapter 6 we saw that, where there was an informal lease – that is, a lease outside the requirements of the Law of Property Act 1925 s.52(1) and s.54(2) – the common law and equity took a different stance. In equity, we saw how the doctrine of *Walsh v Lonsdale* applied to create a specifically enforceable contract. At common law, however, where the tenant was allowed into possession and paid rent, a legal periodic tenancy was created. It has been argued that liability under a covenant can be impressed on to an assignee of an equitable lease by way of implied legal periodic tenancy. Such an argument is highly questionable since the whole basis of *Walsh v Lonsdale* is founded on the maxim that equity prevails over the law where there is a conflict. It has been suggested that *Walsh v Lonsdale* is confined to contracts between the original lessor and the original lessee and that there is no reason why it should not apply where an equitable assignee goes into possession and pays rent. The fact, however, that for the principle to apply the assignee must pay rent would tend to eliminate a principal reason for the right of re-entry to be applied – though the right certainly operates in a wider range of breaches of covenant than this. This all assumes, of course, that the covenants in the implied legal periodic tenancy are the same as those in the original lease. It is suggested that they would be to the extent that they are not inconsistent with the implied tenancy.

Boyer v Warbey [1953] 1 QB 234

It was noted earlier that the requirement for a legal lease was extended in the case of *Boyer v Warbey* to include leases within the three-year exception contained in the Law of Property Act 1925 s.54(2) exception. However, in that case Lord Denning went a great deal further and mounted a fundamental assault on the difference between legal and equitable leases. He stated at 246 that there is:

> . . . no valid reason nowadays why the doctrine of covenants running with the land – or with the reversion – should not apply equally to agreements under land as to covenants under seal.

Denning's view was that law and equity had become fused by the Judicature Act 1873. This approach flies in the face of the traditional doctrine that law and equity were only fused administratively in the Judicature Act 1873 and that they still exist as separate distinct bodies of law. Denning's view has not been accepted, but it is clear to see that, if it was, the burden of covenants in an equitable lease would also be transmitted to the assignee, assuming the covenants 'touch and concern' the land as per *Spencer's Case*.

Novation

Novation is a contract entered into between a promisee, a promisor and a third party whereby the benefits of the contract would henceforth be owed by the promisor to the third party. Essentially, this is not an assignment since the enforcement of the contract by the third party is based on the existence of a new contract between him/herself and the promisor. Since there is a new contract, there is now privity of contract between the third party and the promisor, so that all benefits and burdens are enforceable. In the context of transmission of leasehold covenants it may be argued that, if the assignee of the original tenant – the equitable lessee – pays rent (i.e. consideration) and goes into possession and is accepted by the landlord then a new contract arises between the landlord and the assignee which is therefore enforceable. In *Purchase* v *Lichfield Brewery Co.* it was considered this might be a way forward; however, it has been questioned in other cases if novation can arise in the way described above.

Leases created after 1 January 1996

The need for reform

Having considered the rules relating to the transmission of covenants in leases prior to the coming into force of LT(C)A 1995, it is not difficult to see why the need for reform arose. The rules are complex, confusing and intrinsically unfair to the original tenants who were liable for breaches of covenants throughout the term of the lease, despite the fact that it may have been many years since they held the tenancy. The demands made upon original tenants were often completely unexpected; furthermore, the original tenant often had little or no chance of recovering money paid by him or her from the assignee who was in fact in breach of the covenant and over whom the tenant had no control. It should be remembered in this context that leases of 99 years or even 999 years are not uncommon and thus an original tenant could be liable for breaches of covenant after four – or even more – assignments had taken place in the future.

In its report *Landlord and Tenant: Privity of Contract and Estate* (Law Com No. 174, 1988), the Law Commission identified many of the ills afflicting the system of the enforceability of covenants in leases. The Law Commission identified two central pillars that it considered should underlie any reform of the law:

> First a landlord or tenant of property should not continue to enjoy rights nor be under any obligation arising from a lease once he has parted with all interest in the property. Secondly, all the terms of the lease should be regarded as a single bargain for letting the property. When the interest of one of the parties changes hands, the successor should fully take his predecessor's place as landlord and tenant, without distinguishing between different categories of covenant.

These two principles fundamentally changed the position of the various parties; in particular, they meant that the original tenant and landlord would no longer be liable once their interests had been assigned. The principle that a leasehold covenant had to 'touch and concern' the land to be enforceable as a matter of privity of estate would be abolished.

Originally, the Law Commission proposed that the reforms would apply retrospectively; however, this recommendation was not followed through in the LT(C)A 1995 that followed – hence the need to know how the two regimes operate, providing, of course, additional complications.

The LT(C)A 1995 came into force on 1 January 1996 and regulates the transmission of the benefit and burden of leasehold covenants in all new leases, whether legal or equitable, after this date – though, as we have seen, some provisions apply to leases arising before this date. A new tenancy is defined in s.1(3) as a tenancy 'granted on or after the date on which this Act comes into force'. It should be noted, however, that if a lease existing before this date is varied and the variation amounts to a surrender and re-grant of the lease, then the new lease will be regulated by the LT(C)A. The fact that the Act applies to both legal and equitable leases is found within s.28(1), in which a 'tenancy' is to include 'an agreement for a tenancy'.

The LT(C)A provides that covenants are categorised as either 'landlord covenants' or 'tenant covenants'. Thus s.28(1) defines a 'landlord covenant' as one 'falling to be complied with by the landlord of the premises described by the tenancy', whilst a 'tenant covenant' is one which falls 'to be complied with by the tenant of the premises described by the tenancy'.

The liability of the original landlord and the original tenant

The original tenant ('T')

Section 5 provides that when T assigns his or her lease of the premises he or she is thereafter released from his or her 'tenant's covenants' contained in the lease and ceases to have any further benefit of the 'landlord covenants'. The provision relates to any tenant who assigns and thus it also encompasses any assignee of the tenant, who, in any event, even under the old rules, was free from future liability. Effectively, therefore, the enduring liability of T now ceases, though he or she would remain liable for any breaches that have occurred before his or her assignment of the lease: LT(C)A s.24(1). Similarly, T is still able to take action for any breach of a landlord covenant that occurs before he or she assigns his or her lease to an assignee, A: s.24(4).

Since T is now released of his or her enduring liability, the LT(C)A s.30(2) and s.30(3) provides that the statutory implications of indemnity covenants are repealed. It is still possible for the lease to contain an express indemnity clause and indeed, since there are circumstances where T continues to have enduring liability, this is advisable.

The LT(C)A reinforces the fact that T is now released from his or her enduring liability by providing that any attempt to 'exclude, modify or frustrate' the operation of the Act is void: LT(C)A s.25(1). Similarly, if the lease attempts to provide for the lease to be terminated or surrendered, or imposes 'any penalty, disability or liability' in the event of the operation of the Act, such provisions are also void: s.25(1)b(i) and (ii). In conjunction with these provisions s.30(4)a provides that the Law of Property Act 1925 s.79 also no longer applies to new tenancies, so that a tenant as a covenantor is no longer deemed to be covenanting on behalf of him/herself and his or her successors in title, as discussed earlier. There are, however, two circumstances in which the mandatory release provisions in s.5 do not apply.

Excluded assignments

Where an assignment by T to his or her assignee is an excluded assignment, then T retains liability. 'Excluded assignments' are contained in s.11(1) and are described as 'assignments in breach of a covenant' or 'assignments by operation'. In relation to the first category, if T assigns his or her lease in breach of a covenant not to assign or underlet the premises then he or she retains liability for this breach. In particular, if T does assign in breach of such a covenant then he or she would be liable for any unpaid rent of his or her assignee. In relation to the second category, T remains liable for breach of covenant where the assignment arises by operation of law – for instance, on the death of T where the lease passes to his or her personal representative, or, if T becomes bankrupt, to his or her trustee in bankruptcy. T's liability is relieved on the next assignment, which is not an excluded one: s.11(2)b.

Authorised guarantee agreements

It is possible for s.5 to be postponed if T and L enter into an authorised guarantee agreement where T guarantees that his or her assignee will perform the tenant covenants: s.16. The effect of this is that T will retain liability for the duration of his or her assignee's tenure of the lease, but no further than this: s.16(2). L may require T to enter into such an agreement where he or she is required to give consent to the assignment under the lease and where he or she requires T to enter into such an agreement as a condition of giving his or her consent: s.16(3). Clearly, this is a significant concession to landlords but it nonetheless means that T's liability is a significant reduction of his or her previous liability, which was for the full term of the lease.

The original landlord ('L')

The release of a tenant from his or her enduring liability under the LT(C)A is not extended to landlords so that L's assignment of his or her reversion to his or her assignee, R, does not provide L with an automatic release from his or her landlord covenants: s.6. Instead, the LT(C)A provides L with the opportunity to apply to T for such a release when he or she proposes or actually assigns his or her reversion. The application to T by L must be made in writing, either before or within four weeks of the assignment: s.8(1). The written notice must inform T of the assignment and request that L be released from his or her covenants. It should be noted that L cannot use this procedure to be released from his or her personal covenants: **BHP Petroleum Ltd v Chesterfield Ltd** [2002] Ch 194. The landlord is released from his or her landlord covenants:

(a) if T fails to serve a notice in writing of his or her objection to L's request within four weeks of the day on which L made his request to the tenant: s.8(2)a, or

(b) if the court declares, on an application by L, that it is reasonable for L to be released from his or her covenants: s.8(2)b, or

(c) if T serves a written notice on L consenting to the release and if T has previously served a notice objecting to the release stating that his or her objection notice is withdrawn: s.8(2)c.

As with the tenant, a landlord remains liable for any breaches of covenant that arise before his or her assignment of the reversion: LT(C)A s.24(1), but otherwise any release is effective from the date of the assignment to R: LT(C)A s.8(3).

Whilst it appears that, in order to secure release from his or her landlord covenant, a landlord must comply with the above procedures, it seems, following **London Diocesan Fund v Avonbridge Property Co. Ltd (Part 2 Defendant)** [2005] 1 WLR 3956 that an express covenant in a lease relieving a landlord from his or her liability on the assignment of his or her reversion is permissible. The majority of the House of Lords considered this was not an attempt to frustrate the operation of the LT(C)A within s.25(1) and effectively defined the liability of the landlord within the terms of the Act.

The rights and liabilities between assignees

It was seen earlier that, prior to the LT(C)A, the enforceability of covenants between assignees of the landlord and tenant was based on privity of estate, which rested on the principle of touching and concerning contained in **Spencer's Case** and had reference to the subject matter of the lease contained in the Law of Property Act 1925 s.141 and s.142. The rules relating to privity of estate are now governed by LT(C)A s.3(1). This provides:

> The benefit and burden of all landlord and tenant covenants of a tenancy –
>
> (a) shall be annexed and incident to the whole, and to each and every part, of the premises described by the tenancy and of the reversion in them, and
> (b) shall in accordance with this section pass on an assignment of the whole or any part of those premises or of the reversion in them.

The effect of this is that the benefit and burden of the covenants are annexed to the land so that they pass on the assignment of the lease or the reversion. The transmission of the covenants does not apply 'in the case of a covenant which (in whatever terms) is expressed to be personal to any person': s.3(6)a. This effectively eliminates issues of construction as to whether a covenant is one that touches and concerns the land or is of a personal nature, since the Act places the onus on the person drafting the lease to expressly specify covenants which are not intended to run with the land. The courts are thus relieved of having to deduce the nature of the covenant – i.e. whether personal or not – from the characteristics of the covenant.

The result of the above provision therefore does away with the semantics and difficulties associated with the 'touch and concern' principle. Furthermore, as we saw earlier, no distinction is made between legal and equitable leases: LT(C)A s.28(1).

As we noted under our examination of the pre LT(C)A rules, in order for covenants to be enforced, we need to examine if the burden and benefits have passed. We will now look at these matters as regards assignees of the tenant and landlord.

Where the tenant has assigned his or her lease

The first and fundamental principle is that, on assigning his or her lease, the tenant by s.5(2)b ceases to be entitled to the benefit of the landlord covenants and these pass to his or her assignee, though it should be noted that this assignee has no right to take action in respect of breaches of landlord covenants committed prior to the assignment: s.23(1). The assignee therefore has the benefit of all landlord covenants with the exception of personal covenants, as already noted. Such benefits also pass to any subsequent assignees.

Consistent with the principle that the benefit passes to the assignee, so too the burden of the tenant covenants passes to the assignee – again, provided the covenants are not of a personal nature. Just as the assignee does not have the right to take action for breaches committed prior to the assignment, neither does the assignee have the burden and therefore liability with regards to breaches that occurred prior to the assignment: s.23(1). Once the assignee has him/herself assigned the lease, he or she incurs no further liability on the tenant covenants if his or her assignee is in breach of them: s.5(2)a and s.5(2)b – unless he or she has entered into an authorised guarantee agreement, as examined earlier.

In examining the pre LT(C)A principles, we noted the difficulties that can stem from an assignee becoming insolvent or bankrupt. In that situation, we saw that T having enduring liability could be liable to L or his assignee, R. However, under the LT(C)A the position is that T is no longer liable for breaches committed by his or her assignee, such as non-payment of rent arising from the insolvency or bankruptcy of the assignee. The one exception to this is if T has entered into an authorised guarantee agreement with regards to his or her assignee's (or successor in title's) performance of the covenants.

One final word on the assignment of the lease by T is that formerly the assignment had to be a legal assignment. This is no longer the case since s.28(1) provides that 'assignment' includes any equitable assignment.

Where the landlord has assigned his or her lease

When L assigns his or her reversion to R, then R by virtue of LT(C)A s.3(3)b 'becomes entitled to the benefit of the tenant covenants' in the premises, though not any personal covenants: LT(C)A s.3(6)a. Consistent with what we have seen in relation to the liability of assignees of the tenant, R cannot take action to enforce any tenant covenants relating to the period prior to the assignees of the tenant taking the lease: LT(C)A s.23(1), although if L or an earlier assignee of the reversion has expressly assigned such right of action then the current assignee may sue on the basis of that assignment: LT(C)A s.23(2).

We saw earlier that R has the benefit of any right of re-entry reserved by L to terminate a tenant's breach of covenant by virtue of the Law of Property Act 1925 s.141(1). The LT(C)A confirms this position in s.4 so the benefit of L's right of re-entry is annexed to the whole, and to each and every part, of the reversion and this right of re-entry passes on the assignment of the whole or any part of the reversion. Furthermore, the LT(C)A s.23(3) provides that the right of re-entry by R can be exercised in relation to any breach of covenant arising before or after the date of the assignment, unless the right of re-entry was waived so that it was not exercisable immediately prior to the assignment.

As far as the burden of landlord covenants is concerned, R is bound by all these as from the date of the assignment under LT(C)A s.3(3)a with the exception, again, of any personal covenants: LT(C)A s.3(6)a. In parity with the provisions relating to tenants, R is not bound in relation to any liability arising before the assignment to him or her: LT(C)A s.23(1).

When we previously examined the meaning of 'touch and concern' we saw that a landlord covenant in relation to an estate contract (such as a covenant giving the tenant an option or right to renew his or her lease) was one that 'touched and concerned' the land. To this extent, the covenant was enforceable, but only if the option was protected either as a Class C(iv) land charge under the Land Charges Act 1972 in unregistered land and, in registered land, by way of a notice against the burdened title under the Land Registration Act 2002 s.32(1) or as an interest that is overriding under the Land Registration Act 2002 Schedule 3 para 2. The LT(C)A s.3(6)b provides that such estate contracts, options or other obligations that require protection by either the Land Registration Act 2002 or the Land Charges Act 1972 do not bind R unless those obligations are correctly protected under those provisions.

The position of sub-tenants

We have seen that previously there was neither privity of contract nor privity of estate between a sub-tenant of T or a sub-tenant of T's assignee, A, and L or the assignee of the reversion, R. The effect was that neither L nor R could take direct action against ST. We noted that invariably the terms of the sub-lease were at least as stringent as those in the head lease, with the effect that a breach by ST could lead to L or R forfeiting the head lease of T or A – whoever might be vested with the lease at that time. The effect of the re-entry and forfeiture of the head lease would also mean that the sub-lease would be automatically forfeited as well: *Pennell* v *Payne* [1995] 2 All ER 592. The LT(C)A does nothing to change this position. Having said this, it may be possible to deal with this situation by way of other provisions. Thus if the lease was created on or after 11 May 2000 then the Contracts (Rights of Third Parties) Act 1999 might operate to allow a person who is not a party to a contract to enforce the contract if the provisions of the Act have not been excluded – which they probably will be – and the contract either expressly or impliedly purports to confer a benefit on him or her. In this way, a sub-tenant may be able to enforce the terms of the head lease against a head lease landlord. Presumably, it could also operate in the opposite way as well, though it is difficult to envisage a head lease landlord having the benefit of a sub-lease conferred on him or her, either expressly or impliedly.

Technically, it may also be possible for a sub-tenant to bring an action against a head lease landlord by way of the Law of Property Act 1925 s.78(1). This provision provides that a successor in title of a covenantee in relation to a freehold estate could enforce a covenant. Section 78(1) provides:

> A covenant relating to any land of the covenantee shall be deemed to be made with the covenantee and his successors in title and the persons deriving the title under him or them, and shall have effect as if such successors and other parties were expressed.

In order for a successor in title to have the benefit of such a covenant it was believed that he or she had to succeed to the same estate as that held by the original covenantee – i.e. a freehold estate. In *Smith and Snipes Hall Farm Ltd* v *River Douglas Catchment Board* [1949] 2 KB 500 the Court of Appeal held that the benefit of a covenant could also be enforced by a tenant who derived title from the freeholder. It should be noted however that under the LT(C)A s.30(4) the Law of Property Act 1925 s.78(1) no longer applies to new tenancies and thus s.78 only applies to leases created prior to 1 January 1996.

Whilst direct action against a sub-tenant even under the LT(C)A is still not possible, it is, however, possible for direct action to be taken against a sub-tenant if he or she is in breach of a restrictive covenant as per the principle in *Tulk* v *Moxhay* (1848) 2 Ph 774. This has already been discussed earlier and the ability of action here is preserved by the LT(C)A s.3(5), which provides:

> Any landlord or tenant covenant of a tenancy which is restrictive of the user of land shall, as well as being capable of enforcement against an assignee, be capable of being enforced against any other person who is the owner or occupier of any described premises to which the covenant relates even though there is no express provision in the tenancy to that effect.

Summary

There are two sets of rules applicable to leasehold covenants:

(a) Leases created prior to the Landlord and Tenant (Covenants) Act 1995.

(b) Leases created post the Landlord and Tenant (Covenants) Act 1995.

Leases created prior to the Landlord and Tenant (Covenants) Act 1995

The original parties

- All covenants are enforceable between L and T.
- Liability is based on privity of contract.

The original tenant

- T has enduring liability on the covenants throughout the term of the lease, notwithstanding that T might have assigned his or her lease.
- T has a right of indemnity – either expressly, impliedly or whether the rule in *Moule* v *Garrett* (1872) LR7 EX 101.

The original landlord

- L has enduring liability on the covenants throughout the term of the lease, notwithstanding that L might have assigned his or her reversion.
- L is liable to T and T's assignees.
- L loses his or her right to sue once he or she has assigned his or her reversion – Law of Property Act 1925 s.141(1).

The rights and liabilities between assignees

- There is no privity of contract with regards to assignees but there is privity of estate.
- The benefit and burden of covenants under privity of estate is based on *Spencer's Case* (1583) 5 Co Rep 16a.
- For *Spencer's Case* to apply, the lease must be legal and the covenants must 'touch and concern' the land.
- The running of the benefit and burden to L's assignees is based on the Law of Property Act 1925 s.141 and s.142 where the covenant must have 'reference to the subject matter of the lease'.

The position of sub-tenants

- Here there is privity neither of contract nor of estate between a sub-tenant and L or R, neither of whom can take direct action against the sub-tenant, unless the sub-tenant is in breach of a restrictive covenant – *Tulk v Moxhay* (1848) 2 PL 744.

Equitable leases

- In an equitable lease there is no privity of estate with regard to either an equitable lease or an equitable assignment of a legal lease.
- *Spencer's Case* does not apply and therefore the normal rules of contract apply: one can assign the benefit of a contract but not the burden.
- Despite the above, there are a number of possibilities that might allow L to take action:
  - Restrictive covenants
  - Rights of re-entry
  - Implied periodic tenancy
  - *Boyer v Warbey* [1953] 1 QB 234
  - Novation

Leases created post the Landlord and Tenant (Covenants) Act 1995

The original parties

The original tenant

- T is released from his or her tenant covenants once he or she has assigned his or her lease: LT(C)A s.5 but remains liable for any breaches during his or her tenancy: LT(C)A s.24(1).
- No statutory implied indemnity clauses are available to T.
- There are two exceptions to the mandatory release provisions in LT(C)A s.5:
  - Excluded assignments: LT(C)A s.11(1).
  - Authorised guarantee agreements: LT(C)A s.16.

The original landlord

- L is not automatically released from his or her landlord covenants on the assignment of the reversion: LT(C)A s.6; however, L may apply to T for release from his or her covenants: LT(C)A s.8.
- L remains liable for breaches of covenant that arise before his or her assignment of the reversion: LT(C)A s.24(1).

The rights and liabilities between assignees

- ***Spencer's Case*** and the Law of Property Act s.141 and s.142 no longer apply, therefore there is no need to prove that the covenants 'touch and concern' the land: LT(C)A s.3.
- There is no distinction between legal and equitable leases: LT(C)A s.28(1).

The position of sub-tenants

- The position here is the same as for leases prior to the LT(C)A 1995 but note:
  - Contracts (Right of Third Parties) Act 1999
  - Law of Property Act 1999
  - The enforceability of restrictive covenants: LT(C)A s.3(5).

Further reading

Bridge, 'Former Tenants, Future Liabilities and the Privity of Contract Principle: The Landlord and Tenant (Covenants) Act 1995' [1996] 55 *Cambridge Law Journal* 313

Davey, 'Privity of Contract and Leases: Reform at Last' (1996) 59 *Modern Law Review* 78

Fancourt, 'Licences to Assign: Another Turn of the Screw' [2006] 70 *The Conveyancer and Property Lawyer* 37

Law Commission Report, *Landlord and Tenant Law: Privity of Contract and Estate*, Law Com No. 174 (1988)

Walter, 'The Landlord and Tenant (Covenants) Act 1995: A Legislative Folly' [1996] 60 *The Conveyancer and Property Lawyer* 432

14

Freehold covenants

Aims and objectives

After reading this chapter you should:

- Understand the nature of positive and negative covenants.
- Know how covenants are enforced between the original parties.
- Know how the benefit of covenants is transmitted in law and equity.
- Know how the burden of covenants is transmitted in law and equity.
- Understand how restrictive covenants are protected.
- Know the means by which restricted covenants may be modified or discharged.
- Be conversant with the proposals for the reform of covenants.

Introduction

The basis of freehold covenants

In Chapter 13 on leasehold covenants we saw that covenants are enforceable between a landlord and tenant, irrespective of whether the covenants 'touch and concern' the land, at least as far as post 1 January 1996 covenants are concerned. The covenants in leases are enforceable whether or not they are positive or restrictive covenants. Covenants are, of course, very common in leases and control the conduct of both landlord and the tenant, though principally the latter. In leases the relationship between the landlord and tenant is usually an ongoing one, though this is more tentative in long leases of, say, 999 years. Covenants also arise in relation to freehold land and again such covenants are quite common and arise where a freeholder sells the whole or part of the freehold but wishes to impose controls over how the land is going to be used or developed. As we shall see, the issues that arise in relation to freehold land rarely cause a problem between the original parties to the sale; however, if the original parties sell their respective freeholds on to third parties, the question arises as to the extent to which the covenants in the original transaction are enforceable by and between the third parties.

Example

V is the owner of an estate, Blackacre. Blackacre is a sizeable piece of land with expansive gardens which require significant maintenance. Whilst V was at one time a very keen gardener, in his twilight years he has found the work hard and demanding. V therefore decides to sell part of his garden to P. V decides to sell the freehold rather than take a lease; however, he is concerned how P will develop that portion of the land. V does not want P to develop it into commercial premises, nor does he want P to build a small housing estate on the land. V therefore places some covenants on P's land restricting her use. Furthermore, V requires P to maintain the dry stone walls on the boundary of the two pieces of land and thus he places an additional covenant requiring P to maintain these walls. P goes on to the land and builds a house there. Later, V sells Blackacre to W and P sells her land, now named Greenacre, to Q. The question now emerges as to the extent to which W can enforce the covenants against Q. The position can be seen diagrammatically in Figure 14.1.

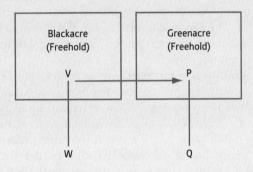

Figure 14.1

The question as to whether the covenants are enforceable depends on two questions:

(i)   Does W have the benefit of the covenants entered into by V? and,

(ii) Does Q have the burden of the covenants entered into by P?

Only if these two questions can be answered in the affirmative can the covenants be enforced by W and Q.

In this example, the question has been raised in absolute terms, but of course the position could be one of V suing Q or P suing W. Since V and P are both the original parties then the questions above have been answered in respect of each – i.e. V has the benefit of the covenants and P has the burden of the covenants – and thus it is only necessary to demonstrate that the covenants have run to the assignees. The original parties, by entering into the contract, will always have either the benefit or burden, depending on whether they are the covenantee (V) or the covenantor (P).

In the example above, we have seen that V has imposed covenants on P, but one should be aware that it is also possible for the reverse to occur within the same contract. Thus P may also wish to ensure that V does not develop Blackacre – for instance, to turn Blackacre into commercial premises. To that extent, P may insist that V enters into similar covenants to her own.

The person making a promise on behalf of his or her own land is known as the 'covenantor' (i.e. P). He or she is the party having the burden of the covenants. The person who takes the benefit of the covenants is known as the 'covenantee' (i.e. V). In the example above, it can be seen that both V and P have entered into covenants, so both V and P are both covenantors and covenantees, depending on which covenants are being referred to. The land owned by the covenantee, V, is known as the 'dominant tenement'; whilst the land owned by the covenantor, P, is known as the 'servient tenement'.

In the example above, it can be seen that the covenants in relation to non-commercial use and the limitations on building are both negative in nature – that is, they are restrictive covenants. The covenant in relation to maintaining the wall appears to be a positive covenant – that is, it requires positive action on the part of P (or Q). The subject of freehold covenants tends to revolve around restrictive covenants since, as we shall see, the enforcement of positive covenants, other than between the original parties, can be difficult.

So far, we have approached the issue of freehold covenants from the point of view of the various parties; however, the macro effect of such covenants on the landscape is not to be underestimated. The law, particularly with regards to restrictive covenants, emerged in the nineteenth century and much of the structure of our towns and cities is due to the imposition of restrictive covenants. But restrictive covenants arise as a matter of private law, while, of course, public law in the form of planning law has also had a significant impact on the modern landscape. However, planning law in relation to restrictive covenants is a more recent phenomenon.

The story of our industrial towns and cities really begins during the industrial revolution, when wealthy landowners took the opportunity to move away from agriculture into the more lucrative economies of the emerging industries. Such entrepreneurs would build factories – usually close to canals and, later, the railway networks. To provide for workers moving off the land and into the towns, such entrepreneurs built rows of terraced, often back-to-back, houses en masse, which are a familiar feature of the industrial landscape. Further away from the factories, the owners built larger houses for more senior workers, foremen, etc. These were still terraced houses, but they often had small gardens. Further out again, still larger houses were built; these were often semi-detached properties. Many, if not all, of these houses were let out on leases; however, as one moves into the leafier suburbs where senior managers, directors and some factory owners lived, parcels of land comprising freeholds were sold. Here the landowners placed conditions on the development of these parcels of land. For instance, they might have required each parcel of land to be at least one quarter of an acre, forbidden the erection of terraced or semi-detached housing and required properties to stand at least 100 feet from the highway. In this way, the landowner intended to preserve the 'leafy' environment of the area. The intention was that these covenants would not only bind the initial purchasers but all their successors in title and, indeed, many of these covenants are still in operation and control the land use today.

If one could transport a Victorian landowner in time to the present day they would certainly be amazed at the materials used and the way buildings are constructed. However, this landowner would no doubt be satisfied that, despite all these changes to construction, the original covenants still hold good and continue to influence the development of the modern landscape. To this extent, freehold covenants demonstrate the dynamic nature of land law – possibly more than any area of the law. Look at your own landscape to see how the influences described above have sculpted it.

The difference between positive and restrictive covenants

So far, covenants have been expressed as positive and restrictive in nature; however, it is important to be able to distinguish between the two since there are limitations on the enforcement of positive covenants. It has to be noted that whether a covenant is positive or restrictive (negative) does not depend on how the covenant is expressed but on whether the covenant is positive or restrictive *in nature*. It is useful to look at some examples of various covenants to illustrate the difference:

(i)   not to use the premises for commercial purposes;

(ii) not to build more than one house on the land;

(iii) not to build any building within 25 metres of Blackacre;

(iv) to maintain the shared drains;

(v)   to maintain the common driveway;

(vi) not to allow the dry stone boundary wall to fall into disrepair.

Looking at these covenants, the first three, (i), (ii) and (iii), are clearly negative in nature and are therefore restrictive covenants. Covenants (iv) and (v) are positive in nature in that they require the covenantor to take some positive action to maintain compliance with the covenant. Covenant (vi) is expressed in negative or restrictive terms but in fact, despite the wording, it is positive in nature, since it requires the covenantor to ensure the wall does not fall into disrepair. In substance, this is a positive covenant. One test that is helpful in identifying a positive covenant is whether the covenant requires the expenditure of money. If it does, then often it will be a positive covenant, not a restrictive one.

Common law and equity

The question of whether the benefit or burden passes to successors in title is approached differently at common law and in equity, though as regards the original covenantor and original covenantee there was no divergence since here there existed a contractual relationship. Since the covenants were included in a deed, there was no requirement for consideration to pass for the covenants to be enforced between those original parties. Where, however, one is seeking to make the covenants 'run' to the assignees of these original parties, there was a significant divergence since at common law it was only permissible to assign the benefit of a contract, not the burden – though, as we will see, some devices were employed to avoid the harshness of this principle. For the benefit to run at common law it had to be shown that the covenant touched and concerned the land and that the covenant was annexed – i.e. 'attached' to the land. In this way, the benefit of both positive and negative covenants would run with the land. The approach of equity was no different since, as regards the running of the benefit, 'equity followed the law'.

With respect to the running of the burden of the covenants, equity again initially followed the law and would not allow the burden to run. However, in the nineteenth century, equity diverged from this position by the doctrine that emerged in the case of *Tulk* **v** *Moxhay* (1848) 2 Ph 774. In this doctrine, equity allowed the burden to run with the land, but only in respect of restrictive covenants. The law on restrictive covenants is therefore very much an equitable doctrine for which there is no counterpart within the common law – hence restrictive covenants are another of the great innovations forged by equity.

The reason why equity would not allow the benefit to run with the land is, at least partly, wrapped up in the remedies available in equity. Where a person is in breach of a restrictive covenant, equity would award an injunction to restrain the breach. In the case of a positive covenant, the proper remedy in equity is an award of specific performance; however, equity will not provide a remedy which requires the constant supervision of the court. In the case of a positive covenant, a court of equity would need to continually supervise that a covenantor complied with the covenant. In this way, equity would not seek to allow positive covenants to run with the land.

The role of equity also changed the characteristics of restrictive covenants so that they emerged out of the law of contract, whereby only the covenantor was bound, to a position that whoever held the land became subject to the burden. In this way, restrictive covenants ceased to be of a personal nature but emerged as a proprietary interest. The modern evidence of this emergence is that, for a restrictive covenant to bind a purchaser it must, in registered land, be entered as a notice against the burdened land under the Land Registration Act 2002 and in unregistered land it must be entered as a Class D(ii) land charge by virtue of the Land Charges Act 1972.

In order to examine the principles governing freehold covenants, we will refer back to the duality issue referred to earlier – that is, firstly, has the benefit passed and, secondly, has the burden passed? We will approach both from the point of view of law and equity and examine the position of the original parties and their assignees.

Enforcement of covenants between the original parties

The original covenantee can always enforce any covenant against the original covenantor and, indeed, unless there is an express statement to the contrary, may take action even if he or she, the covenantee, has parted with the land. Similarly, the covenantor remains liable on the covenants even after he or she has parted with the land. Enforcement and liability here are a simple matter of suing on the contract.

At common law there was a strict rule that no one could sue on a deed who was not a party to the deed; however, this principle was relaxed in the Law of Property Act 1925 s.56(1):

> A person may take an immediate or other interest in land or other property, on the benefit of any condition, right of entry, covenant or agreement over or respecting land or other property, although he may not be named as a party to the conveyance or other instrument.

The effect of this is that a person may take the benefit of a covenant even if he or she was not a party to the deed. Thus, as between V and P, they are clearly parties to the deed, with V having the benefit; however, the deed might also include adjoining property owners. These property owners can sue as original covenantees, even though they were not parties to the deed creating the covenant. In order to fall within the deed, the adjoining property owners must be identifiable and in existence at the time the covenant was made. Thus, X, an adjoining property owner, could take action since he or she would be identifiable and in existence. The concession would not, however, extend to a *future* owner of X's adjoining property since that person would not be identifiable and might not even be in existence: *Re Ecclesiastical Commissioners for England's Conveyance* [1936] Ch 430. It should be noted that X could take action even if he or she was unaware of the covenant having been made. Having said this, it is not sufficient to demonstrate that the covenant merely confers the benefit of the covenant. In *Amsprop Trading Ltd* v *Harris Distribution Ltd* [1997] 1 WLR 1025, the ambit of s.56 was interpreted more strictly in that the third parties, like X, must fall 'within the ambit of the expressly identified covenantee', so that it is not enough merely for P to make a promise to V that the adjoining landowners will benefit from the covenant; P must make a promise to those persons.

The impact of the Contracts (Right of Third Parties) Act 1999 should not be overlooked here. As we have seen previously, this Act enables a person other than a promisee to sue on the contract if the contract either expressly or impliedly confers a benefit on him or her. This position needs some qualification, however, since the third party is not treated as an original covenantee here, but simply given the right to sue under the contract. Thus here V and P would be contracting for the benefit of X, whilst under s.56 X is suing as if party to the deed itself and thus may claim equitable remedies to enforce the contract.

It should be noted that the covenantor would not fall within either the Law of Property Act 1925 s.56 nor the Contracts (Right of Third Parties) Act 1999, since both these refer to persons taking the benefit of the covenants.

In equity, different issues as regards enforcement arise since, rather than claiming damages at common law, the remedies sought will be either specific performance for positive covenants or an injunction for a restrictive covenant. The availability of such remedies will be governed by the normal principles of equity and in any event, such remedies are ineffective against a covenantor who has parted with the land and are unlikely to be awarded anyway since 'equity does not act in vain'. This is not to say that a covenantee would not have any right of action against the covenantor in such circumstances. The original covenantor would always be liable in damages, even if he or she has relinquished ownership of the land, simply on the basis of the contract – though, of course, the liability for damages would be purely of a nominal nature.

Transmission of the benefit of the covenants to successors in title

At common law

In this situation, we are examining whether the benefit of V's covenants with P will pass to W. It should be noted from the start here that if the covenants do run to W it does not matter whether they are positive or restrictive. In order for the benefit to run to W, four conditions must be satisfied, in the absence of an express assignment, so that the covenants are annexed to the land. It should also be noted that these principles have been supplemented by statutory provisions which are not as stringent as the common law rules. The principles for the running of the benefit of covenants were elucidated in the case of *P & A Swift Investments* v *Combined English Stores Group plc* [1989] AC 632.

The covenant must 'touch and concern' the land

This principle is essentially the same as that examined in *Spencer's Case* (1583) 5 Co Rep 16a in the last chapter on leasehold covenants. Thus the covenant must not be one which is personal in nature. It will be recalled that in *P & A Swift Investments* v *Combined English Stores Group plc* [1989] AC 632 Lord Oliver provided guidance for a 'satisfactory working test' as to what constitutes the requirement of 'touching and concerning':

(a) The covenant must benefit the dominant owner for the time being so that, if the owner gives up his or her estate, the covenant ceases to be advantageous to him or her. If the covenant remains advantageous once the dominant owner gives up his or her estate, then the covenant will be of a personal nature only and will not 'touch and concern' the land.

(b) The covenant must affect the nature, quality, mode of use or value of the land of the dominant owner.

(c) The covenant must not be expressed to be personal.

(d) The fact that the covenant is to pay a sum of money will not prevent it from 'touching and concerning' the land so long as the three conditions above are satisfied and the covenant is connected with something to be done on, or in relation to the land.

The basis of the guidelines is that the covenant must be intrinsically attached to the land and must 'either affect the land as regards mode of occupation, or it must be such as per se, and not merely from collateral circumstances, affects the value of the land' per Tucker LJ in **Smith and Snipes Hall Farm Ltd v River Douglas Catchment Board** [1949] 2 KB 600. Essentially, it is a question of fact as to whether the land is benefited by the covenant.

The benefit of the covenant must be annexed to a legal estate

The benefit of the covenant may be annexed either expressly or by implication – however, this is normally apparent from the words incorporated in the original conveyance. Essentially, it must be shown that the covenant has become annexed to the legal estate of the covenantee and must not be for his or her personal advantage. The express words must make it clear either that the covenantee's land is to benefit from the covenant or that successive owners will benefit from the covenant.

Importantly, annexation of the benefit of the land may be accomplished by the operation of the Law of Property Act 1925 s.78(1) which provides:

> A covenant relating to any land of the covenantee shall be deemed to be made with the covenantee and his successors in title and the persons deriving title under him or them, and shall have effect as if such successors and other persons were expressed.
>
> For the purposes of this subsection in connexion with covenants restrictive of the user of land 'successors in title' shall be deemed to include the owners and occupiers for the time being of the land of the covenantee intended to be benefited.

In **Federated Homes Ltd v Mill Lodge Properties Ltd** [1980] 1 WLR 594 it was held that where a covenant, either positive or negative, related to, or touched and concerned the covenantee's land s.78(1) annexed the benefit of the covenant to the covenantee's land so that it was enforceable by the covenantee and his or her successors in title, persons deriving title under him/her or them and the owner and occupier of the benefited land. The effect of this decision was that, if the covenant touched and concerned the land of the covenantee, the benefit of the covenant was automatically annexed to the land when the covenant was made. This was a significant move away from the position prior to the case, where, in order for the benefit to be annexed to the land, it was necessary to show by an indication in the document creating the covenant, or in the circumstances surrounding its creation, that the covenant was imposed for the benefit of the covenantee's land.

The case of **Federated Homes** was not totally accepted since it appeared to create such an automatic annexation of the covenant that express or implied annexation was rendered redundant. In **Roake v Chadha** [1983] 3 All ER 503 the automatic nature of s.78(1) was limited in respect of an express provision to the contrary. The judge considered that whilst s.78(1) was not made subject to express contrary intention, he had to consider the covenant as a whole, including an express exclusion of annexation. Similarly, in **J Sainsbury Ltd v Enfield Borough Council** [1989] 1 WLR 590 it was also held that the court had to construe the conveyance in the light of all the circumstances to find out whether it was intended that the benefit of the covenant was to be annexed.

One of the requirements for the running of the benefit of a covenant set out in **Federated Homes** was that it was necessary for the land to be benefited to be identified or described in the instrument creating the covenant. The issue of description and identification created some difficulties; is it sufficient to merely identify the land even though it was not described in the deed, or was it necessary for the covenant itself to describe the land so that it was capable of being identified? In *Crest Nicholson Residential (South) Ltd v McAllister* [2004] 1 WLR 2409 the court followed its earlier decision in *Marquess of Zetland v Driver* [1939] Ch 1, where the test was that the benefit of a covenant is annexed only to such land as the instrument creating it identifies by express words or by necessary implication as intended to be benefited and only insofar as the instrument does not manifest a contrary intention. The land intended to be benefited will be sufficiently identified if the instrument describes it in terms which enable it to be easily ascertained from other evidence. It is insufficient in the view of the Court of Appeal for the benefited land to be identified from the surrounding circumstances; thus Chadwick LJ stated at para 33:

> In its later decision in the Federated Homes case [1980] 1 WLR 594 this court held that the provisions of s.78 of the 1925 Act made it unnecessary to state, in the conveyance, that the covenant was to be enforceable by persons deriving title under the covenantee or under his successors in title and the owner or occupier of the land intended to be benefited, or that the covenant was to run with the land intended to be benefited; but there is nothing in that case which suggests that it is no longer necessary that the land which is intended to be benefited should be so defined that it is easily ascertainable. In my view, that requirement identified in Marquess of Zetland v Driver [1939] Ch 1, remains a necessary condition for annexation.

Chadwick LJ continued at para 34:

> It is obviously desirable that a purchaser of land burdened with a restrictive covenant should be able not only to ascertain, by inspection of the entries on the relevant register, that the land is so burdened, but also to ascertain the land for which the benefit of the covenant was taken – so that he can identify who can enforce the covenant. That latter object is achieved if the land which is intended to be benefited is defined in the instrument so as to be easily ascertainable. To require a purchaser of land burdened with a restrictive covenant, but where the land for the benefit of which the covenant was taken is not described in the instrument, to make enquiries as to what (if any) land the original covenantee retained at the time of the conveyance and what (if any) of that retained land the covenant did, or might have, 'touched and concerned' would be oppressive. It must be kept in mind . . . the time at which enforceability of the covenant becomes an issue may be long after the date of the instrument by which it is imposed.

The position is therefore that, providing the land that is subject to the restrictive covenant is identifiable, then Federated Homes and Crest Nicholson interprets s.78 as removing the need to demonstrate that the covenant was intended to be capable of enforcement by the successors in title of the covenantee. Thus in *Mohammadzadeh v Joseph* [2008] P & CR 6 Etherton J stated at para 46:

> In short, in the case of a post-1925 conveyance, once it is established that a restrictive covenant relates to, that is to say, 'touches and concerns', the vendor's retained land, section 78(1) obviates the need to show separately and additionally by reference to express terms of, or a necessary implication that the covenant shall benefit the land so as to be enforceable by successors in title of the covenantee rather than enforceable only as a matter of contract by the covenantee and those to whom the covenantee expressly assigns the benefit of the covenant.

The effect therefore is that, providing the covenant 'touches and concerns' the land, s.78 has the effect of automatically annexing the covenants unless the original parties have intended that the covenant was to be a personal covenant for the covenantee only if an express assignment is required to transmit the benefit of the covenant: *Robin v Berkeley Homes (Kent) Ltd* [1996] EGCS 75.

The same is not true of pre-1996 restrictive covenants since here annexation will only occur if there is an intention that the covenant will benefit the land of the covenantee and that intention can be 'expressly or impliedly' deduced from the words of the instrument creating it, as required by the Conveyancing Act 1881 s.58.

One further point before leaving the effect of s.78 is that it casts its net wider than the assignees of the covenantee since it talks also of including 'occupiers for the time being of the land of the covenantee'. Thus the effect of s.78 extends also to licensees and those entitled to occupy by way of adverse possession.

The covenantee must have a legal estate in the land to be benefited

Not surprisingly, since we are examining the running of the benefit of covenants at law, the common law rules insist that the assignees of the covenantee may only take the benefit of a covenant if the original covenantee has a legal estate in land and the covenant will not run if the original covenantee merely has an equitable interest in the land.

The assignee of the covenantee must have the same legal estate as the original covenantee

At common law, the benefit of a covenant could not pass if the assignee had an estate that was less than that of the original covenantee, such as a lease. Thus, if the covenantee had a legal fee simple, the benefit could only pass if the assignee took the same legal estate as the original covenantee: *Westhoughton UDC v Wigan Coal and Iron Co. Ltd* [1919] 1 Ch 159. This is no longer the case since in *Smith and Snipes Hall Farm Ltd v River Douglas Catchment Board* [1949] 2 KB 500 the Court of Appeal held that the Law of Property Act 1925 s.78(1) abrogated this requirement. Section 78(1) talks in terms of the benefit of a covenant running with 'any *land* of the covenantee', not any *estate*.

Smith and Snipes Hall Farm Ltd v *River Douglas Catchment Board* [1949] 2 KB 500

In this case, the defendants entered into a covenant with owners of land that was subject to flooding, under which the defendants were to be responsible for the repair and maintenance of the banks of a river. Mrs Smith was an assignee of one of the original covenantees and she granted a lease of the land to Snipes Hall Farm Ltd, which was the second defendant. The land was flooded on several occasions but eventually a major flood prompted both defendants to take action on the covenant. Since neither was the original covenantee, they had to demonstrate that the benefit of the covenant had passed to them.

It was clear that the covenant touched and concerned Miss Smith's land and that it had been intended that the covenant would run with the land.

The court held that s.78(1) had the effect of rendering the covenant enforceable not only by the original covenantee but by all successors in title – including persons who derived their title from such successors in title. It was held to be sufficient that the defendants had a legal estate but it was unnecessary for them to have the *same* legal estate as the original covenantee.

In equity

As with the position at common law, both positive and restrictive covenants may also run in equity to assignees of the covenantee. The running of the benefit of a covenant in equity is, however, wider than that allowed by the common law. It has been seen that, at common law, the covenantee had to have a legal estate for the benefit to run. This is not necessary in equity, which would allow the covenant to run even if the covenantee had an equitable interest. Similarly, with regards to assignees it was not necessary for the assignee to have the same legal estate as the covenantee; an equitable interest would do. In any event, the operation of s.78 abrogated this requirement since the benefit of the covenant was held to run with the 'land' and not the 'estate' of the covenantee so that the legal or equitable nature of the covenantee became irrelevant: **Smith and Snipes Hall Farm Ltd v River Douglas Catchment Board** [1949] 2 KB 500. As with the running of the benefit at common law, there are a number of conditions that must be satisfied.

(i)   The covenant must 'touch and concern' the land.
      The principle here is the same as at common law – 'equity follows the law'.

(ii) The assignee must establish that the benefit of the covenant has passed to them.
      The assignee may establish this in one of three ways.

Annexation

As we have already noted, annexation is the means by which the benefit is 'fastened' or attached to a clearly defined piece of land in such a way that the benefit will pass automatically with the land on any subsequent transfer of the covenantee's interest in that land to his or her successor in title, tenant or occupier. It should be noted that the benefit of the covenant passes to successors in title, tenants or occupiers of the covenantee even if they are unaware of the existence of the covenant. Thus in **Rogers v Hosegood** [1900] 2 Ch 388 Collins LJ stated at p. 407 that annexation allows the benefit to run 'not because the conscience of either party is affected but because the purchaser has bought something which was inherent in or was annexed to the land bought'.

Annexation may be effected either expressly, impliedly or by statute under the Law of Property Act 1925 s.78(1). We will now consider each of these in turn.

Express annexation

As at common law, it is possible for the benefit of a covenant to be assigned expressly in equity. The instrument annexing the covenant would normally annex the benefit of the covenant in both law and equity at the same time, but in the absence of a legal estate the annexation clearly only takes effect in equity. The express words must sufficiently indicate the land to be benefited and must state either that the covenant is made to benefit certain land or clearly indicate that it is intended that the benefit of the covenant is for the covenantee and his or her successors. It should be noted that it is not necessary for the land to be fully described, provided it is readily capable of identification: **Re Gadd's Transfer** [1996] Ch 56 and must be so at the time of the execution of the instrument creating it. Thus in **Renals v Cowlishaw** (1878) 9 Ch D 125 it was held that the expression 'heirs, executors and administrators, and assigns' was not sufficient to constitute an annexation of the benefit since there was no reference to the land. The same was not true of where the passing of the benefit was expressed to be intended 'that the covenant may enure to the benefit of the [vendors], their successors and assigns and others claiming under them to all or any of their lands adjoining', as held by the Court of Appeal in **Rogers v Hosegood** [1900] 2 Ch 388. The point is that the covenant must not be a personal covenant and the requirement that it is made 'for the benefit of land' or the benefit of a covenantee in his or her capacity as owner of land that is identified or capable of being identified demonstrates that the covenant is not a personal one.

Implied annexation

If on the construction of the instrument creating the covenant it can be established that the covenant is not to benefit the covenantees personally but that it is intended that the covenant is to benefit certain land then the benefit of the covenant will be so annexed that it will run with the land. Note again the two requirements: the intention to benefit and the need to identify the land. It is important that these two elements are construed and implied from the instrument, not the surrounding circumstances: *Sainsbury plc v Enfield London Borough Council* [1989] 1 WLR 590.

Statutory annexation

Statutory annexation is effected by the Law of Property Act 1925 s.78 which has already been examined in the running of the benefit of covenants at law. As we have seen in *Federated Homes Ltd v Mill Lodge Properties Ltd* [1980] 1 WLR 594 the effect of s.78, subject to express provision to the contrary, is to automatically annex the benefit of a covenant to the land of the covenantee. It will be recalled that the effect of s.78 is to do away with the need to find an express intention to annex the covenant to the land – s.78 does this itself, though the land again must be readily identifiable as held in *Crest Nicholson Residential (South) Ltd v McAllister* [2004] 1 WLR 2409. Again, as was stated earlier, the far-reaching impact of s.78 and the decision in *Federated Homes* is to render express or implied annexation virtually defunct, though in practice the instrument creating the covenant will almost invariably still contain an express provision.

Assignment

Should annexation not operate to attach the benefit of a covenant to the land to be benefited, this may be accomplished if the assignee can show that the benefit has nevertheless been assigned to him or her. Essentially, the assignment arises where the covenantee assigns the benefit of the covenant when he or she transfers the land to the assignee. Similar conditions apply as to annexation in that the land must be identifiable and the land must be capable of benefiting from the covenant contained in the assignment. An assignment differs from annexation in two different ways. Firstly, an assignment is an assignment of the contract, not of the land, and thus confers the benefit of the covenant on the assignee personally: *Marten v Flight Refuelling Ltd* (No. 1) [1962] Ch 115. Secondly, an assignment arises at the time of the transfer of the land from the covenantee to his or her immediate successor in title, whilst annexation takes place at the time of the instrument creating the covenant.

With regards to the first difference, because the assignment is effectively to the assignee personally, it does not attach to the land, so if the assignee then sells the land on again there must be a second assignment, and so on at each transfer. In other words, the assignment does not *annex* the covenant to the land. The effect of this process of assignment is that, if a later assignee seeks to enforce the covenant, he or she must be able to demonstrate an unbroken chain of covenants: *Re Pinewood Estate* [1958] Ch 280.

Essentially, to effect an assignment there must be a distinct agreement between the owner of the land and his or her assignee that the benefit of the covenant is to pass. It should be noted that, to effect an assignment at law, this will take effect as an assignment of a chose in action and by the Law of Property Act 1925 s.136 it must be made in writing with written notice to the covenantor.

Finally, it should be stated that it is rarely the case that an assignee of the covenantee has to rely on an assignment as a means of enforcing a covenant since invariably, following

Federated Homes, the covenant will be annexed to the land. If, however, statutory assignment fails because the land has not been identified or rendered capable of identification, assignment may have to be relied upon by the assignee in order to establish that the benefit of the covenant has passed to him or her.

Scheme of development

'Schemes of development' or 'building schemes' commonly arise where a property developer has developed a large parcel of land – as a housing estate, for instance. In such a situation, the developer may wish to impose on each purchaser of a house on the estate a set of covenants aimed at preserving the environment on the estate as an amenity for all the house owners on the estate to enjoy and mutually enforce. One typical example of a covenant under such a scheme is a restrictive covenant preventing householders from delineating their front gardens by way of a hedge, fence or wall. The intention here is to preserve the open-plan nature of the entire estate.

The problem that arises in such a situation is that the developer has the dominant tenement and imposes the covenants on each and every individual plot as that plot is sold. The effect therefore is that, as each plot is sold, the developer's dominant tenement decreases in size until all the plots within the scheme are sold and the developer no longer holds a parcel of land forming the dominant tenement. Clearly, the dominant tenement cannot comprise plots that have already been sold since these are servient tenements in relation to the developer's own (diminishing) dominant tenement. At the point where the developer sells his or her last remaining dominant tenement plot, he or she is unable to annex or assign the benefit of the covenants. The problem that therefore arises is how each owner of a plot can take action to enforce the covenant against owners in breach of the covenants which are otherwise separate or unrelated.

In order to address the problem above, equity developed a set of rules of governance for schemes of development whereby restrictive covenants that are appurtenant to each and every plot within the scheme are mutually enforceable on a reciprocal basis throughout the scheme. The effect of this is to create a community of interest that applies irrespective of the date of purchase by each owner and the timing of entry into the original covenants. In essence, such a scheme is the epitome of equitable intervention in that it effectively enforces reciprocal obligations on a basis of social conscience.

Example

Bird and Drake, property developers, have purchased a plot of land from Giles. Bird and Drake intend to build 16 houses on the estate. They decide to impose a restrictive covenant that no owners of the plots or their successors in title may plant a hedge, erect a fence or build a wall that is more than 18 inches high. When Bird and Drake sell the first plot to A, they impose the restrictive covenant on that plot, the servient tenement. As holders of the dominant tenement, Bird and Drake can enforce the covenant against A. Bird and Drake then sell the second plot to B, who is also under the burden of covenant imposed by the developers. At the time of the transfer of the plot to B they also give him the benefit of their covenant so B is also able to take action against any breach by A. A, however, cannot get the benefit of the covenant against B since B only entered into the covenant after A acquired his or her plot and indeed B's plot would not have existed at that time anyway as a separate parcel of land, since it formed part of Bird and Drake's dominant tenement.

The way around this problem is by way of a scheme of development which ignores the timing issue so that each and every purchase of a plot within the scheme obtains the benefit – and, of course, is subject to the burden – of the covenant. The running of the benefit of the covenant also arises when Bird and Drake sell their last plot, so the scheme looks as shown in Figure 14.2.

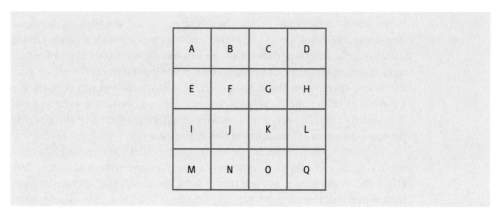

Figure 14.2

All the owners within the scheme can take action against each other, regardless of the time at which they purchased the property, so A could take action against Q, the last purchaser, and indeed vice versa.

The conditions required for the establishment of a scheme of development were originally set out in the case of **Elliston v Reacher** [1908] 2 Ch 374 in which Parker J identified them as being:

(i)   that both the claimant and the defendant derive their title from a common vendor;

(ii) that the common vendor laid the land in identifiable plots;

(iii) that the restrictions imposed by the common vendor were to be for the benefit of all the plots within the scheme;

(iv) that the claimant and defendant purchased their plots on the understanding that the restrictions were to be mutually enforceable;

(v) further, following **Reid v Bickerstaff** [1909] 2 Ch 305, the area covered by the scheme had to be clearly defined.

For many years, the requirements set out in **Elliston v Reacher** placed a significant restriction on the development of schemes of development. However, from 1965 the approach of the courts was to revert to a wider perspective on this creature of equity and, as a consequence, a less prescriptive approach evolved. Thus in **Re Dolphin's Conveyance** [1970] Ch 654, despite the fact that there was no common vendor and the estate had not been laid out in identifiable plots, there was nevertheless held to be a scheme of development in existence. It was stated that it was clearly intended to 'lay down . . . a local law for the estate for the common benefit of all the several purchasers of it'. The decision was based not on the guiding principles set out in **Elliston v Reacher** but on a broader equitable principle founded on 'common interest and the common intention actually expressed in the conveyances themselves'.

Similarly, it was held in **Brunner v Greenslade** [1971] Ch 993 that, where a person has only part of the original plot transferred to him or her, he or she will still be subject to the benefit and burden of the covenants within the scheme of development. Thus by plots being sub-divided it is not possible for purchasers of such plots to avoid the covenants and, equally, they may take action to enforce the covenants against other plot holders. The reasoning behind this again lies in the notion of a 'local law' being established – otherwise 'islands of immunity' would arise within the scheme of development by way of purchasers of sub-plots being outside of the scheme. Just as sub-division of plots within the scheme will not prevent the covenants from being enforceable, nor will amalgamation and then sub-division, as held in **Texaco Antilles Ltd v Kernochan** [1973] AC 609. The effect of this is that, whilst the amalgamation of plots will clearly eliminate the enforcement of the covenants, because the land will be in common ownership the subsequent division of the land will cause the covenants to revive.

Whilst the criteria set out in **Elliston v Reacher** are now looked on in very broad terms, there are certain matters which must exist for the establishment of a scheme of development. Firstly, the area to which the scheme is to apply must be sufficiently defined with reasonable certainty. The whole basis of a scheme is that each purchaser subject to the benefits and burdens must know the extent of the area to which those benefits and burdens apply. This knowledge may not be imparted simply on a transfer of a plot to a purchaser, unless the transfer demonstrates the boundaries of the scheme over which the reciprocal obligations are to operate. Thus in **Whitgift Homes Ltd v Stocks** [2001] EWCA Civ 1732, whilst it was originally contemplated that a scheme would apply, the Court of Appeal held that because there was uncertainty as to which plots fell within the scheme, the scheme could not operate at all, even for those properties within the scheme, since none of the owners could be certain of the extent of their obligations.

Secondly, there must be a perception of a mutual common intention of purchasers within the scheme that they are entering into a relationship of mutual benefits and burdens. Usually, this mutuality will be discovered from the nature of the transfer to the different purchasers, but in the absence of this, a court can have regard to extrinsic evidence – for instance, advertisements relating to the development and site plans available to prospective purchasers in a marketing suite set up by the developer on the site. Often such site plans will have some reference to the scheme and this provides prospective purchasers with at least some knowledge of the reciprocal obligations affecting the plots within the scheme: **Jamaica Mutual Life Assurance Society v Hillsborough Ltd** [1989] 1 WLR 1101.

Transmission of the burden of the covenants to successors in title

At common law

The burden of a freehold covenant cannot run at common law, even by express assignment. The effect of this is that, at law, the burden can only be enforced so long as the original covenantor retains the land. Thus in **Austerberry v Corporation of Oldham** (1885) 29 Ch D 750, it was held that, at common law, an obligation to make up a road and keep it in good repair could not pass to the successor in title of the original covenantor. The principle was upheld in **Rhone v Stephens** [1994] 2 AC 310. This principle of law is clearly consistent with the general principle in the law of contract that, whilst one may assign the benefit of a contract, it is not possible to assign the burden. It was to escape this principle that, in the nineteenth century, equity stepped in to allow the burden of a restrictive covenant to run in equity. It remains the case therefore that the burden of a positive covenant cannot run with the land, either at law or in equity. This should be immediately contrasted with the position with leasehold covenants where the burden of both positive and restrictive covenants will run in relation to assignees of lessors and lessees. This is why occupiers of flats will never have the freehold transferred to them since it would be impossible to enforce compliance with a positive covenant. It is this problem which gave rise to commonhold, as enacted in the Commonhold and Leasehold Reform Act 2002, though this attempt at avoiding the principle in relation to flats is overborne by technicality and complexity in the development of modern land law.

The principle has been subject to significant criticism and in **Rhone v Stephens** Nourse LJ considered it was hard to justify today and saw no reason why the burden of positive covenants should not run on the same basis as restrictive covenants. However, the House of Lords at the end of the day was not prepared to overturn such a pillar of the common law, despite the criticisms levelled at it. In order to escape the principle, various devices have been employed to circumvent or counteract the rule.

The doctrine of mutual benefit and burden

The doctrine of mutual benefit and burden operates on the basis that a person who takes the benefits in a deed must also be subject to the burdens that are also imposed in the deed.

Halsall v Brizzell [1957] Ch 169

There was a conveyance that gave the purchasers of a house on an estate the right to make use of a private road. As part of this, the covenantor also covenanted to contribute to the upkeep of the road. It was held that assignees of the covenantor could not take the benefit without also being subject to the burden, even though the burden does not normally run at law.

Clearly, such a doctrine has the potential to completely circumvent the principle in *Austerberry* and the application of the doctrine has been more constrained recently. Thus in **Rhone v Stephens** Lord Templeman stated at 332:

It does not follow that any condition can be rendered enforceable by attaching it to a right nor does it follow that every burden imposed by a conveyance may be enforced by depriving the covenantor's successor in title of every benefit he enjoyed thereunder. The condition must be relevant to the exercise of the right. In **Halsall v Brizzell** there were reciprocal benefits and burdens enjoyed by the user of the roads and sewers.

Rhone v Stephens [1994] 2 AC 310

In 1960, the freehold owner of Walford House, Somerset, sold off part of the property, which became known as Walford Cottage, the owner covenanting to keep the roof in repair. The roof fell into disrepair and the owner of the cottage sought to enforce the covenant. The ownership of the house and the cottage had changed hands several times. The question therefore was whether the burden of the covenant ran with the land so as to bind the successors in title to the covenantor.

The House of Lords decided that, whilst it was possible to attach conditions to the exercise of a right, this was only possible where the condition was 'relevant to the exercise of the right' – that is, there must be some correlation between the benefit and the burden which a successor has chosen to take. The argument in **Rhone v Stephens** was that, since the covenantor and their successors in title had the benefit of the support of Walford Cottage, they were obliged to accept the burden of keeping the roof in repair. This is an application of what Lord Templeman described as the 'pure principle'. In this case, however, the obligation to repair the roof was an independent provision and thus was not 'relevant to the exercise of the right' of support. Lord Templeman stated that the party must 'at least in theory' be able to elect between enjoying the benefit and performing the burden or renouncing the right and relieving him/herself of the burden. The owner of Walford House could not be deprived of their right of support if they failed to repair the roof. The owner had no choice in the matter. The case is therefore not the same as in **Halsall v Brizzell** where there were reciprocal rights and burdens so that the defendant, at least in theory, could choose between enjoying his right to use the road and other amenities, paying his proportion of the costs or, alternatively giving up the right and saving on the expense of maintaining the road and amenities.

The effect is that, to be able to make use of the doctrine of mutual benefit and burden in order to enforce a positive covenant against a successor in title of the covenantor, the burden must be 'relevant to the exercise of the rights which enable the benefit to be obtained' and the covenantor's successors in title must have the opportunity to elect to take the benefit or renounce it so as to escape the burden of the covenant. In this way, the doctrine of mutual benefit and burden is now very narrowly construed so as to circumvent the common law principle regarding the running of the burden and will not be applied as a 'pure principle'.

Chain of covenants

If V sells land to P and P covenants, say, to erect and maintain a fence, P will remain liable to V on the covenant by virtue of privity of contract, even if P sells the land to Q. In such a situation, P will normally protect him/herself by procuring from Q a covenant of indemnity against future breaches of the covenant to maintain the fence. Thus, if Q fails to maintain the fence, V, who cannot, of course, sue Q, can sue P, who can then sue Q on his indemnity.

The process is unwieldy and its effectiveness questionable, at least in the long term. The reason for this is that, as the chain gets longer, there is more chance of it breaking down if a successor in title to the covenantor becomes insolvent or simply disappears. In any event, the process is flawed in that the covenantee's remedy lies in damages while what he or she really requires is to have the fence repaired.

One way of avoiding the disadvantages of the chain of covenants approach is for V to require P to enter into a direct covenant with V and their successors in title on the same terms as the positive covenant and to require Q to impose the same obligation on their own successor and so on. The effect of this is that the contractual link between the covenantee and their successors in title is directly linked to any successors in title of covenantor P and Q. This process allows the covenant to be directly enforced.

By enlargement of long leases

As already noted, it is possible for the burden of covenants to run with leasehold land, whether the covenant is positive or restrictive; thus it is relatively easy to avoid the consequences of the rules regarding freehold covenants by simply granting a long lease. By the

Law of Property Act 1925 s.153, however, where a lease is granted for more than 300 years without any rent (or a peppercorn rent or other rent having no money value) and having more than 200 years unexpired, the lease may be enlarged into a freehold. The freehold created is then subject 'to all the same covenants . . . as the tenant would have been subject to if it had not been so enlarged'. In this way, the freehold generated is subject to the same principles that apply to leasehold covenants so that the burden of both positive and restrictive covenants will run with the land. A similar effect also arises under the Leasehold Reform Act 1967, which provides for the enfranchisement of long leases into freeholds. The same effect arises under the Housing Act 1985 where a council house tenant exercises his or her 'right to buy' concession.

Positive easements

An easement is a right over another person's land – for example, a right of way or a right of light. We will look at these in more detail in the next chapter but for the moment just think of them in those terms. Whilst an easement provides a right over another's land, it is just that and the holder of an easement is not usually required to incur expenses in maintaining that easement. Thus if one has a right to make use of a driveway across another's land to get to one's house then there is no obligation, on the face of things, to incur the costs of maintaining that driveway. There is, however, an anomaly in this situation in that a landowner may be under a duty to maintain their fence on the boundary with their neighbour. The unusual nature of this type of easement has meant that it is often referred to as a 'spurious easement'.

It cannot be emphasised enough that this easement is confined to the maintenance of fencing and, indeed, all the modern incidents of this easement have been confined to disputes relating to cattle trespass where a landowner alleges that their neighbour had a duty to maintain the fence to prevent the cattle from escaping: *Jones* v *Price* [1965] 2 QB 818; *Crow* v *Wood* [1971] 1 QB 77; *Egerton* v *Harding* [1975] QB 62. It appears that such an easement can only arise by way of prescription – i.e. long use. The effect of this (rare) process is to act as a means by which a positive obligation is imposed as a proprietary right in a context outside of the realm of covenants.

Right of entry annexed to an estate rentcharge

It is possible that a right of re-entry is reserved with regards to freehold land so that a covenantee may exercise the right of non-payment of money or non-performance of some other positive covenants. Such rights of re-entry are usually attached to a rentcharge. As a rule, no new rentcharges can be created after the passing of the Rentcharges Act 1977; however, estate rentcharges were specifically preserved by s.2(4). An estate rentcharge is one where the owner of the servient land is liable to pay money, or make a contribution towards the 'provision of services, the carrying out of maintenance or repairs, the effecting of insurance or the making of any payment by him for the benefit of the land affected by the rentcharge'. Such rentcharges are therefore used to secure positive covenants to repair or provide services.

Rentcharges are enforceable against the owner of the servient land 'for the time being'. Usually, the right of re-entry is annexed to such a rentcharge, so that the dominant owner can re-enter the property to carry out any necessary repairs and then charge the cost to the owner in possession. If the covenantor fails to perform the covenants, however, it is possible that they could ultimately forfeit their freehold estate, though no doubt the covenantor could obtain relief against such an action.

It should be noted that, at common law, it is quite immaterial as to whether the covenantor has any land or whether the covenant is restrictive or positive in nature. In the latter, the remedy normally lies in damages, but note that forfeiture may be possible in an appropriate case.

In equity

We have seen already that covenants are closely aligned with the law of contract and the doctrine of privity that exists within a contract. Contracts are, of course, bilateral and to that extent covenants are enforceable as a matter of contract between the original parties. The problem with covenants is that they are often intended to govern and control the use of the land beyond the original parties but this intention is frustrated once the estates of the original covenantor and covenantee are transferred to third parties. This was the position prior to the nineteenth century in both law and equity, with equity 'following the law'. In the nineteenth century, the limitations of the common law in enforcing covenants drew the attention of equity, which recognised that measures in covenants designed to protect the environment and commercial value of land should move beyond the realms of contract. In this way, what started off as mere contractual rights began to evolve into proprietary interests in land that bound not only the original parties but those deriving title under them.

The process described above did not evolve as a sudden shift in policy but out of the established principles of equity based on conscience and unjust enrichment. Such a sudden shift was never going to occur in the late eighteenth and early nineteenth centuries. The men who developed 'modern' industrial Britain claimed the right to manage their businesses and affairs in their own way. Laissez-faire was the order of the day, so industry and the commercial world were given a free hand. The state abandoned its former claims to regulate trade, business and commerce. Covenants were seen as a mechanism that restricted this bulwark of the industrial revolution – not just for the immediate parties but far into the future. In 1847 Joseph Fletcher, a school inspector, was highly critical of the industrialisation of Britain and its effect on the environment, writing of 'its smoke, its dirt, its bustle, its deformation of the face of nature, and the independent rudeness of its millions'. He claimed that the towns were 'purely places in which to work and make money, not to be at rest and enjoy it'.

For those who had made their fortunes in the industrial revolution, it became important to set themselves apart from the degradation of the environment and to preserve for themselves islands of grandeur where they could demonstrate their success and keep themselves apart from the bustle of the industrial towns they had helped to create. It became important, therefore, to preserve the environment in their immediate vicinity. But things were changing for the ordinary people as well. The early nineteenth century saw the growth of the public parks, created to provide recreational areas for the masses in a clean environment with fresh air. These were often philanthropic gifts to the local community by wealthy industrialists and landowners. Such persons often employed the best landscape designers of the day such as Joseph Paxton, who created Birkenhead Park, and John Claudius Loudon, who created the Derby Arboretum.

Previously, in *Keppell v Bailey* (1834) 2 My & K 517, there had been a rejection of attempts to create covenants that restricted the use and development of land and bound successors in title to the covenantor in perpetuity. Only a few years later, however, times had changed and the need to enforce restrictive covenants was pre-eminent in the light of changing social and political developments. What amounted to private planning law still has a profound effect on the nature of our towns and cities and will continue to do so far into the future, as evidenced by the case of *Tulk v Moxhay* (1848) 2 Ph 774 itself, where the restrictive covenant was upheld in relation to the gardens in Leicester Square, which are still there.

Tulk v Moxhay (1848) 2 Ph 774

In 1808 the plaintiff (claimant) was the owner of a vacant piece of land in the middle of Leicester Square, as well as several houses forming the square. He then sold the square to Mr Elms ('E') who covenanted for himself, his heirs, and assigns that he would 'keep and maintain . . . the ground and square garden . . . in an open state, uncovered by any buildings, in neat and ornamental order' for the inhabitants of Leicester Square and tenants of the plaintiff. The land passed through several owners into the hands of the defendant. The conveyance to the defendant did not contain the covenant, although he acknowledged that he did have notice of the covenant in the deed of 1808. The defendant then indicated his intention to alter the character of the square and build on it. The plaintiff still remained the owner of several houses in the square and sought an injunction restraining the defendant from breaching the covenant.

The court upheld the grant of the injunction with Lord Cottenham LC stating:

> . . . the question is, not whether the covenant runs with the land, but whether a party shall be permitted to use the land in a manner inconsistent with the contract entered into by his vendor, and with notice of which he purchased. Of course, the price would be affected by the covenant, and nothing could be more inequitable than that the original purchaser should be able to sell the property the next day for a greater price, in consideration of the assignee being allowed to escape from the liability which he had himself undertaken.

The case therefore forms the basis of the modern law of restrictive covenants. The decision is not founded on the basis of the covenant being a proprietary interest in land but on the interrelated grounds of conscience and unjust enrichment. In terms of conscience, here is a situation where the defendant, having notice of the covenant, attempts to avoid it by virtue of the covenant being omitted from their conveyance while knowing full well that the owner intended to attach the covenant to the property so that 'no one purchasing with notice that equity can stand in a different situation from whom he purchased'. In other words, E was not only aware of the covenant not to build or change the character of the square but also aware that the original vendor intended that all future purchasers would be bound by the covenant. This clearly became a matter of conscience which a court of equity would not allow E to avoid simply because the covenant was not contained in the conveyance. This is a classic situation in which equity intervenes and in which it will not be constrained by the omission in the deed where issues of conscience arise.

The second aspect which emerges from this case is that of undue enrichment. Obviously, the land is more valuable without the covenant being attached to it and the vendor would have been aware of this but was prepared to accept the lower price in order to preserve the character of the square. All subsequent purchasers would have been aware of the diminution in value because of the restriction in their ability to develop the land. E would have been aware of the fact that the absence of the covenant meant that the parcel of land had a far greater value. Thus a court of equity would intervene to prevent E gaining an unjust (because of his knowledge of the covenant) enrichment.

There is, though, a more subtle interpretation of *Tulk v Moxhay* which is vital in one's understanding of restrictive covenants. In this case, the plaintiff clearly intended that the covenant was to bind all successive owners of the land in that they would be prevented from exercising 'some of the rights inherent in [their] ownership of unrestricted land' – per Lord Templeman in *Rhone* v *Stephens* [1994] 2 AC 310 at 317. Since the ability of a purchaser to develop the land did not and could not form part of their proprietary rights that normally would have enabled them to develop the land, the covenant itself becomes an equitable proprietary right of the covenantee, the plaintiff.

Originally, the decision in *Tulk* v *Moxhay* was capable of applying to both positive and restrictive covenants, albeit the covenant in the case itself was a restrictive covenant. The broad basis of the decision, however, began to be cut down by the courts, which considered that what could become an unruly animal needed to be constrained within strict boundaries. Thus following *London & South Western Railway* v *Gomm* (1882) 20 Ch D 562 it became accepted that a restrictive covenant could not exist '*in gross*' – that is, for the restrictive covenant to be enforceable by equity against a purchaser it had to be made for the protection of other land. In this way restrictive covenants came to resemble easements as being a right over a plot of land (the servient tenement) existing for the benefit of another plot of land (the dominant tenement). In short, the adoption of such a principle took restrictive covenants out of the sphere of contract into the sphere of property law.

The tensions between the need for land to be recognised as a commercial entity and the need to recognise the necessity of restraints in the development of land remain. The law has evolved, however, in order to provide some balance to the juxtaposition of the contrasting positions above. Equity has developed a number of conditions that must be established to render an assignee of a covenantor bound by a restrictive covenant.

The covenant must be negative in nature

In *Haywood* v *Brunswick Permanent Benefit Building Society* (1881) 8 QBD 403 it was held by the Court of Appeal that the equitable principle in *Tulk* v *Moxhay* could only apply to restrictive covenants so as to restrain an assignee of the covenantor from breaching the covenant. The remedy for breach of a restrictive covenant therefore lies in an award of an injunction. Remember the acid test: if the covenant requires the expenditure of money then the covenant is a positive one, regardless of how it is expressed.

At the date of the covenant, the covenantee must own land that will benefit from the covenant

This encompasses two principles. Firstly, there must be a dominant and a servient tenement at the date of the making of the covenant. A restrictive covenant cannot exist 'in gross', so any attempt to annexe the covenant to land that is not owned by the covenantee will render the covenant ineffective. Clearly, this principle is similar to the law of easements which we saw in *London & South Western Railway* v *Gomm* (1882) 20 Ch D 562 as the means by which restrictive covenants were elevated to proprietary interests. There are practical reasons for this principle since the assignees of the covenantor should be able to discover who the assignees of the covenantee are so they are aware of who they are accountable for, and, in particular, who they should negotiate with to either modify the covenant or negotiate a release from the covenant. Further, without this requirement it would be difficult to assess whether any claimant, an assignee of the covenantee, actually has locus standi to bring the action.

In any event, the requirement for a dominant tenement was re-affirmed in *London County Council* v *Allen* [1914] 3 KB 642 and is consistent with the principle that a covenantee, once they have parted with the land, is unable to enforce the covenant against any assignees of the covenant. As a matter of contract, they are always able to take action against the covenantor, though here their claim is limited to damages only. There is an exception to this principle, however, in that under the Town and Country Planning Act 1990 s.106(3) a planning authority may impose a restrictive covenant on a developer in order to ensure compliance with planning conditions designed to enhance local amenities. Clearly, the planning authority does not own any dominant land in such a situation. A further exception is that a landlord's reversion on a lease is sufficient interest to entitle him or her to enforce a covenant against a sub-tenant, as held in *Hall v Ewin* (1887) 37 Ch D 74. Equally, the interest of a mortgagee in the property is also a sufficient interest to ensure that the mortgagor complies with a restrictive covenant since otherwise its equity in the property might well be affected: *Regent Oil Co. Ltd v J A Gregory Ltd* [1966] Ch 402.

Secondly, not only must there be a dominant tenement but it must be shown that the restrictive covenant accommodates or benefits and protects the dominant tenement: *Formby v Barker* [1903] 2 Ch 539. The effect is that the restrictive covenant must benefit the land and not simply confer a personal advantage. Thus the benefit must be 'something affecting either the value of the land or the method of its occupation or enjoyment': *Re Gadd's Land Transfer* [1966] Ch 56. Part and parcel of this requirement is that the dominant and servient tenements must be in proximity to each other, though they do not have to be contiguous. Thus it would be difficult to prove that a piece of land in Liverpool would benefit from a restrictive covenant over a piece of land in Bristol, for instance: *Kelly v Barrett* [1924] 2 Ch 379.

The burden of the covenant must have been intended to run with the covenantor's land

A covenant may be limited, either expressly or impliedly, to binding the covenantor alone and here the assignees will not be bound. There is, however, a statutory presumption contained in the Law of Property Act 1925 s.79(1) which provides:

> A covenant relating to any land of a covenantor or capable of being bound by him, shall, unless a contrary intention is expressed, be deemed to be made by the covenantor on behalf of himself, his successors in title and the persons deriving title under him or them, and, subject as aforesaid, shall have effect as if such successors and other persons were expressed.
>
> This subsection extends to a covenant to do some act relating to the land, notwithstanding that the subject-matter may not be in existence when the covenant is made.

The effect of s.79(1) is to annex the burden of restrictive covenants to the land so that it passes to the covenantor's successors in. We saw earlier that in s.78(1), which relates to the running of the benefit of a covenant, this provision allows the benefit of both positive and restrictive covenants to be automatically annexed to the land. The wording of s.79(1) seems to suggest that it is not limited to restrictive covenants since it states that it 'extends to a covenant to do some act relating to the land' and thus it appears that there is no reason why positive covenants should not be equally annexed. The House of Lords in *Rhone v Stephens* [1994] 2 AC 310 stated that this was not the case and confined its operation to restrictive covenants. Their Lordships considered that s.79 had 'always been regarded as intended to remove conveyancing difficulties' and was only a word-saving device that facilitated the passing of the burden of restrictive covenants.

It should be noted also that by s.79(2) the expression 'successors in title' is deemed to include owners and occupiers for the time being of the land to which the covenant relates and thus the expression extends to licensees and those entitled to occupy by adverse possession.

The protection of restrictive covenants

Restrictive covenants suffer from the same infirmity as all equitable interests, namely they cannot be enforced against a purchaser for value of a legal estate without notice of the covenant, or someone claiming through such a person and the doctrine of notice. This principle still applies as regards leases; however, this common law principle is now largely overturned by statutory intervention and must comply with the rules regarding registration in both unregistered and registered conveyancing.

In relation to unregistered freehold land, a restrictive covenant created after 1 January 1926 must be protected as a Class D(ii) land charge under the Land Charges Act 1972 s.2(5) to be enforceable. Failure to register will render the restrictive covenant void against a subsequent purchaser for money or money's worth of a legal estate in land: s.4(6). Pre-1926 restricted covenants are still dealt with under the doctrine of notice above.

It should be noted that the purchaser described above who purchased an unregistered title will be required to apply for first registration at the Land Registry. If the restrictive covenant is registered as a Class D(ii) land charge, it will be transferred to the newly registered proprietor as a notice against the title. If the restrictive covenant is not registered as a land charge at the time of the first registration then of course it will be void against the purchaser in any event and therefore it is not capable of then being registered as a notice: Land Registration Act 2002 s.11.

In registered freehold land, restrictive covenants must be protected as a notice in the charges register of the title of the burdened or servient land: Land Registration Act 2002 s.32 as either an agreed or unilateral notice: Land Registration Act 2002 s.34. Where the purchaser is the original covenantor then the notice will usually be an 'agreed notice', though if the purchaser does not agree a 'unilateral notice' will be entered. Failure to register will render the covenant void against a purchaser of the burdened or servient land and it will have its priority postponed. It should be noted, however, that an unprotected restrictive covenant will still be enforceable if the new registered proprietor has not purchased the burdened land for valuable consideration as required by s.29(1) by virtue of s.28. Thus if the new registered proprietor receives the title by way of a gift, either inter vivos or under a will, or acquires the title by adverse possession the restrictive covenant will still be binding.

The discharge of restrictive covenants

A restrictive covenant may be discharged or modified in a number of ways.

Express and implied discharge

A covenant is discharged where the person entitled to the benefit expressly releases it. Usually this will be done on the payment of a premium. Thus it is possible for a development company to 'buy out' the covenant if it is going to restrain the development of the land. Similarly, a restrictive covenant will be discharged impliedly if the person entitled to the benefit waives his or her right to enforce it – for instance, by acquiescing in the breach.

Shaw v *Applegate* [1977] 1 WLR 970

In 1967 the purchaser of the property, Applegate ('A'), covenanted not to use it as an amusement arcade. In 1970 he started to install amusement machines and, indeed, added more in subsequent years. Shaw ('S'), the assignee of the benefit of the covenant, did not give notice to A until 1973 prior to taking action for an injunction to restrain the breach.

At first instance, it was held that there had been a continuing breach but the court dismissed the application on the ground that S had acquiesced in the breach. Furthermore, the court refused to grant damages as it considered that these were incapable of assessment.

The Court of Appeal held that the owner of a legal right is only to be deprived of that right on the ground of acquiescence when it can be shown that he or she is acting unconscionably. The court did not consider that Shaw was acting dishonestly or unconscionably in seeking to enforce his contractual rights. However, in the particular circumstances, and especially given the failure of Shaw to protest earlier, his failure to apply for interlocutory relief and the heavy investment made by Applegate, an injunction would not be granted, though an order was made for an inquiry as to damages in lieu of an injunction. Thus unless a claimant is acting unjustly or unconscionably, it is unlikely that acquiescence will cause a discharge of the covenant per se. The effect of delay in applying for relief will, though, have a profound effect on the ability of the claimant to enforce the covenant by injunctive relief and to this extent the ability to enforce becomes sterile outside of an award of damages, which may be nominal.

Unity of seisin

The benefit of a covenant is discharged when the dominant tenement and the servient tenement come into the hands of the same owner. Discharge does not, of course, operate in a scheme of development, as already discussed earlier: ***Texaco Antilles Ltd*** v ***Kernochan*** [1973] AC 609.

Discharge under the Law of Property Act 1925 s.84

It should have been apparent in the analysis of restrictive covenants that they place a long-term restriction on the use of land and that such a restraint may, in some situations, be undesirable. This is particularly the case where the restraint will frustrate development that may be beneficial to a wide community so as to deprive them of the communal utility of the land. In other situations, development of the land or the nature of the restrictive covenant itself might mean that the covenant has become obsolete.

In order to deal with the issues raised above, under the Law of Property Act 1925 s.84 (as amended by the Law of Property Act 1969 s.28), the Lands Chamber of the Upper Tribunal 'Lands Tribunal' has a discretionary power to modify or discharge restrictive covenants, either with or without compensation. The jurisdiction of the Lands Tribunal is confined to restrictive covenants, irrespective of their date of creation, and extends to original covenantees, original covenantors and their assignees. The jurisdiction also extends to schemes of development – though here there is a presumption that the restrictive covenants will be upheld and thus there is a greater burden of proof placed on an applicant: ***Re Lee's Application*** (1996) 72 P & CR 439.

Whilst the Lands Tribunal has extensive powers to discharge or modify restrictive covenants, it is recognised that such powers essentially interfere with the private rights of individuals (often with the result of an applicant making a gain), and thus the powers are exercised with caution. Public interest is also concomitant in considering an application so that the tribunal can take into account the development plan of the local planning authority.

In order for the Lands Tribunal to discharge or modify a restrictive covenant, the applicant must bring their application within one of four grounds.

Obsolesence

By s.84(1)a a restrictive covenant may be discharged or modified 'by reason of changes in the character of the property concerned or the neighbourhood'. This is unlikely to arise if the restriction is of real value or the value of the property is affected: *Re Edwards' Application* (1984) 47 P & CR 458. The Lands Tribunal is unlikely to discharge or modify a restraint if it continues to preserve the environment for public utility. Equally, the fact that a development would be entirely reasonable were it not for the restraint is not per se grounds for the tribunal to strike out the restrictive covenant. In some situations, however, the environment changes so that the restraint is no longer appropriate. For instance, over a period of time, towns expanded into the suburbs and therefore a restrictive covenant requiring residential property to have at least a half-acre of garden may no longer be appropriate in order to meet the housing needs of a growing urban population. Similarly, a covenant not to use the land for business purposes will no longer be appropriate if the land in question is now surrounded by industrial and commercial premises.

It should be noted that, if a restrictive covenant has been created pursuant to an agreement under the Town and Country Planning Act 1990 s.106, it cannot be discharged under s.84. It is also worth bearing in mind that the granting of planning permission does not mean that a restrictive covenant can be ignored. The granting of planning permission is merely a factor that the Lands Tribunal can take into account in deciding whether or not to discharge or modify the covenant.

Consent

The Lands Tribunal may exercise its jurisdiction if the owner of the benefited land impliedly or expressly consents to the covenant being discharged or modified, provided the person entitled to the benefit is of full age and capacity: s.84(1)b.

The proposed modification will not injure the persons entitled to the benefit of the restrictive covenant

By s.84(1) the Lands Tribunal may allow a discharge or modification of a restrictive covenant if this does 'not injure the persons entitled to the benefit of the restriction'. Essentially, this prevents dominant owners from using the 'not in my backyard' or the 'thin end of the wedge' argument. Nevertheless, the tribunal is sensitive to the wider context issues that may result in a discharge or modification of a covenant so that a change made by one application may result in a domino effect across the vicinity, thereby causing a significant change in the wider community.

Impeding the reasonable use of land

This was a new ground introduced in the Law of Property Act 1969 s.28(2) that inserts into s.84 a new subsection – s.84(1)aa and subsection s.84(1)A. This allows the Lands Tribunal to discharge or modify a restrictive covenant if its continued existence 'would impede some reasonable user of the land for public or private purposes'. This jurisdiction may be exercised if the Lands Tribunal is satisfied that the restrictive covenant 'does not secure to persons entitled to the benefit of it [the restrictive covenant] any practical benefits of substantial value or advantage to them' or the restriction 'is contrary to the public interest' and that 'money will be an adequate compensation for the loss or disadvantage (if any)' which the dominant owner would suffer from the discharge or modification.

Reform

It is apparent from this journey through freehold covenants, particularly restrictive covenants, that the law is complex, with areas of great uncertainty. It should come as no great surprise that this area of land law has attracted the attention of the Law Commission – though with no great progress. The Law Commission published reports in 1967 (Law Com No. 11) (*Report on Restrictive Covenants*) and in 1984 (Law Com No. 127) (*Report on the Law of Positive and Restrictive Covenants*). In the intervening years, the Wilberforce Committee also published a report, *Report on Positive Covenants Affecting Land* (Cmnd 2719, 1968). All these reports raised matters of concern; however, no reform emanated from any of them.

The development of the Land Registration Act 2002 prompted a further review of covenants, alongside easements and profits à prendre, and to this end in 2008 the Law Commission published a consultative paper: *Easements, Covenants and Profits à Prendre* (Law Com No. 186, 2008). This culminated in a Law Commission Report: *Making Land Work: Easements, Covenants and Profits à Prendre* (Law Com No. 327, 2011).

In its lengthy 2011 report, the Law Commission identified the difficulties associated with the law of freehold covenants and prepared a draft bill in response to its recommendations for reform. The identified difficulties were:

(a) It is difficult to identify who has the benefit of a restrictive covenant for two reasons:
   (i) There is no requirement that the instrument creating the covenant should describe the benefited land clearly enough without extrinsic evidence; and
   (ii) The *benefit* of a restrictive covenant, being an equitable interest, cannot be registered as an appurtenant interest on the register of title of the dominant land.

(b) There are differing and complicated rules for the benefit and burden of restrictive covenants.

(c) The contractual liabilities of the original parties continue despite the changes in ownership of the land. The original covenantor remains liable when the land is sold.

(d) Whilst the benefit of a positive covenant can run at law, the burden of a positive covenant cannot run so as to bind successors in title.

The response of the Law Commission to these issues was to recommend the creation of a new type of interest, an 'obligation'. Past reports had used the expression 'land obligation' and the report acknowledges that this expression is probably more convenient. Land obligations as proposed in earlier reports were surrounded by complex technicalities. In this report, the Law Commission was proposing land obligations without those complexities.

With regard to land obligations, the Law Commission considered that an estate owner will be able to create positive and negative obligations that will take effect as *legal* interests that are appurtenant to another estate in land. Such legal interests will be registrable interests under the Land Registration Act 2002, provided that:

1 The benefit of the obligation touches and concerns the benefited land;

2 The land obligation is either:

    (a) an obligation not to do something on the burdened land;

    (b) an obligation to do something on the burdened land or on the boundary (or any structure or feature that is treated as marking or lying on the boundary of the burdened and benefited land); or

    (c) an obligation to make a payment in return for the performance of an obligation of the land mentioned in (b) above; and

3 The land obligation is not one made between a lessor and lessee relating to described premises, the effect being that leasehold covenants fall outside the Law Commission's proposals.

The Law Commission recommended that covenants made by the owner of an estate in land that satisfy the above conditions will not take effect as promises/covenants but as legal interests in the burdened land that are appurtenant or attached to the benefited estate in land. Such land obligations will therefore be outside of the law relating to restrictive covenants. The report indicated that there would be no need for any special drafting requirements and that conveyancers could continue to draft such obligations in the same form, providing the above conditions are met.

The decision to make land obligations a legal interest is an interesting one. The effect of this is that there is no longer a contract and thus the issues surrounding privity of contract disappear. Such a change also means that the rules in **Elliston v Reacher** and **Tulk v Moxhay** will no longer be relevant since the new interests will not be covenants. It is important not to speak of the new land obligations as 'covenants'. This expression would now be misleading as land obligations are set very firmly outside this regime. It should be noted that it will no longer be possible to create freehold covenants enforceable under **Tulk v Moxhay**; equally, however, the Law Commission did not propose that existing covenants under **Tulk v Moxhay** will cease to exist. The result is that the new land obligation will exist alongside the old, which are likely to continue 'perhaps forever'.

Since a land obligation will be a legal interest, it will fall within the Law of Property Act 1925 s.1(2)a. The Law Commission considered that the existing language used there was wide enough to encompass the new land obligations. Similarly, land obligations will be registrable interests and thus fall within the Land Registration Act 2002 s.2(a)(v). This refers to 'any other interest or charge which subsists for the benefit of an interest the title to which is registered' and thus the Law Commission also considered this was wide enough to encompass the new interest.

It will be noticed that the new land obligations are still required to meet the 'touch and concern' requirement. Whilst this has been removed in other common law jurisdictions, the Law Commission considered that the expression is so well established in English law that no new fresh test was required. Thus an obligation that does not 'touch and concern' the land in that it does not benefit the estate to which it is appurtenant will remain a personal obligation to be enforced by way of the law of contract and, as such, will not run with the land.

As legal interests, the new obligations will have to be granted by deed, as per the Law of Property Act 1925 s.52, and if the title is registered the transfer will have to be completed by registration, as per the Land Registration Act 2002 s.27. The Law Commission considered that the new obligations should be created expressly and that they should not be capable of being created by implication or by presumption. Equally, the Law Commission considered that the Law of Property Act 1925 s.62 should not be allowed to operate to create a land obligation or to convert one from a leasehold interest to a freehold interest. It should be noted that there are no provisions for equitable land obligations because none are needed – they can only exist as legal interests, remember. In particular, if an equitable land obligation was to arise for want of the correct formality in order to bind a purchaser, it would have to be contained in the transfer and therefore would become legal anyway on registration.

In relation to unregistered land, the Law Commission noted that a restrictive covenant currently has to be registered as a Class D(ii) land charge under the Land Charges Act 1972 against the name of the owner of the burdened land. If it is unregistered, it is void against a purchaser for money or money's worth of a legal estate in the land charged with it: Land Charges Act 1972 s.4(b). Whilst a land obligation as a legal interest will bind the world at common law, the Law Commission considered that this position is unacceptable in the context of land obligations since a purchaser 'should not be taken by surprise by an obligation attached to his or her property'. The Law Commission proposed that land obligations, whether positive or negative, legal or equitable, should be capable of being registered as land charges within the Land Charges Act 1972 so that unregistered charges would be void against a purchaser of the burdened land. To that extent, the Law Commission recommended the creation of a new Class G land charge within the Land Charges Act 1972.

In the case of registered land, since land obligations will now fall within the Law of Property Act 1925 s.1(2)a, the creation of an obligation will amount to a registrable disposition for the purposes of the Land Registration Act 2002 s.27(2)(d). Thus the land obligation cannot take effect at law until the burden is registered on the title to the burdened land. The burden of the land obligations is, of course, noted in the charges register of the burdened land. Equally, if the benefited land is registered, the benefit is registered on the title to the benefited land. Both of these positions take effect by reason of the Land Registration Act 2002 s.27. The Law Commission recommended that the new obligations should not be capable of being overriding interests and thus, pursuant to the Land Registration Act 2002 s.29, they will not bind a purchaser of land unless their priority is protected on the register.

The Law Commission also recommended that the powers of the Lands Tribunal should be extended and enhanced so that they encompass the new land obligations. In particular, it recommended that the Lands Tribunal should also extend to positive covenants if the performance of the obligation 'ceases to be reasonably practicable' or it 'has become unreasonably expensive when compared with the benefit that it confers' because of changes in circumstances.

Whether or not the proposals set out by the Law Commission in its proposed bill actually get to the statute book is still a matter of speculation. The history of intervention by the Law Commission in this area is not encouraging and one will just have to wait and see if a new chapter will open in the saga of land law.

Summary

Enforcement of covenants between the original parties

Rule 1

The original covenantee can always enforce any covenant against the original covenantor and may take action even if the covenantee has parted with possession. Similarly, the covenantor is also liable after they have parted with ownership of the land. The relationship between the covenantee and the covenantor is based on contract.

Exceptions

Law of Property Act 1925 s.56(1)

Whilst at common law there was a strict rule that no one could sue on a deed who was not a party to the deed, this rule was relaxed by the Law of Property Act 1925 s.56(1). The effect of this is that a person may take the benefit of a covenant even if they were not a party to the deed. Such a person must be identifiable and in existence. The concession does not extend to future third parties (***Armsprop Trading Ltd v Harris Distribution Ltd*** [1997] 1 WLR 1025).

Contracts (Rights of Third Parties) Act 1999

Note that the third party, unlike s.56(1) above, is not treated as an original covenantee. Otherwise, a person other than the promisee may sue on the contract if the contract either expressly or impliedly confers a benefit on them.

Rule 2

In order to enforce a covenant the covenantee (or their assignees) – see below – must be able to show:

(i)   that they (or their assignees) have the benefit of the covenant, AND

(ii) that the covenantor (or their assignees) has the burden of the covenant.

Transmission of covenants to the successors in title of the covenantee and covenantor

COMMON LAW	
BENEFIT	*BURDEN*
The benefit of both positive or restrictive covenants may run	The burden of a freehold covenant *cannot* run at common law:
Subject to conditions: –	***Austerberry v Corporation of Oldham*** (1885) 29 ChD 750. Upheld in **Rhone v**
a. The covenants must 'touch and concern' the land.	***Stephens*** [1994] 2 AC 310.
Same test as in ***Spencer's Case*** but note the 'satisfactory working test' in **P & A Swift Investments v Combined English Stores Group plc** [1989] AC 632 and **Smith and Snipes Hall Farm Ltd v River Douglas Catchment Board** [1949] 2 KB 600.	Means of circumventing the rule: a. Doctrine of mutual benefit and burden: **Halsall v Brizzell** [1957] Ch 169.
b. The benefit must be annexed to a legal estate. This may be done expressly or impliedly but note also the Law of Property Act 1925 s.78(1) and **Federated Homes Ltd v Mill Lodge Properties Ltd** [1980] 1 WLR 594: automatic annexation. Also **Crest Nicholson Residential (South) Ltd v McAllister** [2004] 1 WLR 2409.	b. Chain of covenants c. Enlargement of long leases: Law of Property Act 1925 s.153.
c. The covenantee must have a legal estate in the benefited land.	d. Positive easements: **Jones v Price** [1965] 2 QB 818; **Crow v Wood** [1971] 1 QB 77;
d. Assignee of the covenantee must have the same legal estate as the original covenantee. Since **Smith and Snipes Hall Farm Ltd** this is no longer required: s.78(1) states the covenant runs with 'any land of the covenantee' not any estate.	**Egerton v Harding** [1975] QB 62. e. Right of entry annexed to a rentcharge.

EQUITY	
BENEFIT	*BURDEN*

The benefit of both positive and negative covenants may run subject to conditions:
 	
a. The covenants must 'touch and concern' the land. The principle here is the same as at common law: 'equity follows the law'.
 	
b. The assignee must establish that the benefit of the covenant has passed to him or her. This can be shown in three ways:
 	
● Annexation: This is the means by which the benefit is 'fastened' to the land and may be accomplished by
  – Express annexation
  – Implied annexation
  – Statutory annexation: Law of Property Act 1925 s.78; *Federated Homes Ltd v Mill Lodge Properties Ltd* [1980] 1 WLR 594.
 	
● Assignment: Similar conditions apply as with annexation: the land must be identifiable and the land must be capable of benefiting from the covenant.
 	
● Schemes of Development: See the conditions set out in *Elliston v Reacher* [1908] 2 Ch 374
 	
  – *Re Dolphin's Conveyance* [1970] Ch 654
  – *Whitgift Homes Ltd v Stocks* [2001] EWCA Civ 1732
  – Mutuality: *Jamaica Mutual Life Assurance Society v Hillsborough Ltd* [1989] 1 WLR 1101
	The burden of a restrictive covenant may run in equity:
	Tulk v Moxhay (1848) 2 Ph 774
	
	For the burden to run in equity the following conditions are required:
	
	a. The covenant must be negative in nature – i.e. must be a restrictive covenant:
	Hayward v Brunswick Permanent Benefit Building Society (1881) 8 QRD 403
	
	b. At the date of the covenant, the covenantee must own land that will benefit from the covenant. Thus:
	
	● There must be a dominant tenement.
	● The restrictive covenant must accommodate the dominant tenement.
	
	c. The burden of the covenant must have been intended to run with the land. This may be accomplished by express words but the effect of the Law of Property Act 1925 s.79 is to imply an intention that the burden of a restrictive covenant will run with the land.

Protection of restrictive covenants

Unregistered land

● Covenants created prior to 1926 are governed by the doctrine of notice.

● Covenants created after 1 January 1926 must be protected as Class D(ii) land charges under the Land Charges Act 1972 s.2(5). An unregistered restrictive covenant is void against a purchaser for money or money's worth of the legal estate.

Registered land

● Restrictive covenants must be entered as a notice in the charges register of the title of the burdened land: Land Registration Act 2002 s.32. The notice may be either an agreed or unilateral notice, depending on the circumstances: Land Registration Act 2002 s.34.

Discharge of a restrictive covenant

● An express or implied discharge.
  Shaw v Applegate [1977] 1 WLR 970
  ● Unity of seisin.
  ● Discharge under the Law of Property Act 1925 s.84 by the 'Lands Tribunal'.

Further reading

Bullock, 'Federated Homes Revisited' (2005) 155 *New Law Journal* 238

Dixon, 'Is There Any Value in Restrictive Covenants? Enforceability and Remedies' [2007] 71 *The Conveyancer and Property Lawyer* 70

Gouldry, 'Privity of Estate and the Enforcement of Real Covenants' (2007) 36 *Common Law World Review* 3

Gravells, 'Enforcement of Positive Covenants Affecting Freehold Land' (1994) 110 *Law Quarterly Review* 346

Law Commission, *Report on Restrictive Covenants* (1967, Law Com No. 11)

Law Commission, *Report on the Law of Positive and Restrictive Covenants* (1984, Law Com No. 127)

Law Commission, *Easements, Covenants and Profits à Prendre* (2008, Law Com No. 186)

Law Commission, *Making Land Work: Easements, Covenants and Profits à Prendre* (2011, Law Com No. 327)

Martin, 'Remedies for Breach of Restrictive Covenants' [1996] 60 *The Conveyancer and Property Lawyer* 329

Snape, 'The Burden of Positive Covenants' [1994] 58 *The Conveyancer and Property Lawyer* 477

Todd, 'Annexation After Federated Homes' [1985] 49 *The Conveyancer and Property Lawyer* 177

Wilberforce Committee, *Report on Positive Covenants Affecting Land* (1968, Cmnd 2719)

15

Easements and profits à prendre

Aims and objectives

After reading this chapter you should be able to:

● Know the nature of easements and profits and the criteria needed under *Re Ellenborough Park*.

● Understand the legal and equitable nature of easements and profits.

● Know and understand the means of acquiring easements and profits.

● Know and understand how easements and profits are protected.

● Recognise how easements and profits may be extinguished.

● Understand the need for the reform of the law on easements and profits.

Introduction

What is an easement?

Easements are rights exercised by one person over land belonging to another and are incorporeal hereditaments. They are very common – for instance, many houses have shared drains running through the land and thus neighbours have a right of drainage across their land. Some properties may share a driveway so that they have a right of way, an easement, running across their neighbour's land, depending on who is claiming the easement. Equally, properties may have a right to light, though it should be noted that there is no general right to light, thus one has a right to such light as enables one to make reasonable use of a room.

There is no exact definition but a useful one is found in *Halsbury's Laws of England*, 4th edition, vol. 64, para 1:

> An easement is a right annexed to land to utilise other land of different ownership in a particular manner (not involving the taking of any part of the natural produce of the land or of any part of its soil) or to prevent the owner of the other land from utilising his land in a particular manner.

Thus easements can be positive or negative, but there is no limit to the types of right that can exist as an easement. One simply has to apply certain criteria, which we will examine later, in order to discover if the right is in the nature of an easement. It is important that it is recognised that an easement is a proprietary right that is annexed to the land and will therefore bind not only the current owners but also their successors in title. The existence of an easement is therefore important from a conveyancing perspective in both registered and unregistered land.

It can be seen already that an easement will exist as a benefit for one piece of land, the owner of which will have a right over the land burdened with the easement. Where land has been *granted*, the benefit of the covenant is known as the *dominant* tenement, whilst the land that has the burden of the covenant is known as the *servient* tenement. Thus if B, the owner of Whiteacre, sells a piece of her land, Blackacre, to A, she may grant the right to cross over Whiteacre to reach the main road. Blackacre has the dominant tenement and Whiteacre has the servient tenement (see Figure 15.1).

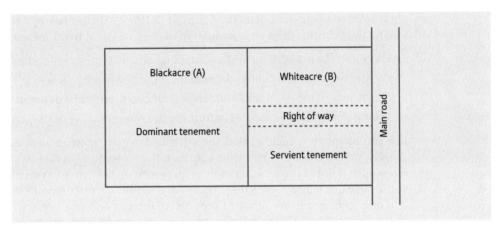

Figure 15.1

Such a situation may have arisen where B has sold Blackacre to A and granted him the right to cross over her, B's, land.

When B sold Blackacre to A she may have *reserved* her right to make use of a drain crossing from Whiteacre over Blackacre. In such a situation B has the benefit of the easement and thus Whiteacre is now the dominant tenement whilst Blackacre carries the burden and is the servient tenement (see Figure 15.2).

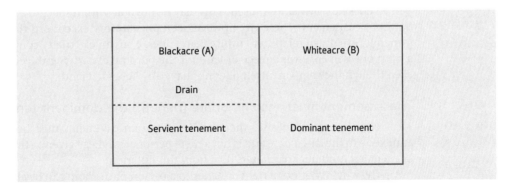

Figure 15.2

From the above it can be seen that, in assessing which piece of land has the dominant tenement, one has to consider which has the benefit and this may depend on whether the easement has been created by *grant* or by *reservation*. It is vital to remember that an easement is not a personal right but a proprietary interest.

The essential characteristics of an easement

Clearly, easements are important in order to safeguard the utility of the dominant land. Without easements of drains or rights of way, for example, the use of the land would be incapable of being utilised as a useful amenity. Having said this, the law has to maintain limits on the burdens that can be attached to a piece of land since both the value and amenity of the land may be so burdened that its value and its alienability would be placed in jeopardy. The usual criteria that are applied in assessing whether a right is an easement or not are found in the case of **Re Ellenborough Park** [1955] 3 All ER 667. In this case the court referred to criteria originally set out in *Cheshire's Modern Law of Real Property*. These criteria were gleaned from an examination of the case law at that time and are as follows:

1 There must be a dominant and a servient tenement.
2 The easement must accommodate (benefit) the dominant tenement.
3 The owners of the dominant and servient tenements must be different.
4 The easement must be capable of forming the subject matter of the grant.

It is important to remember that the criteria above are mere guidelines. At the end of the day, even if the first three criteria are met, the recognition of an easement may still be refused if it is not in the general nature of an easement. Reference to precedent is obviously useful here but it also means that courts have significant discretion in deciding whether a right is sufficient to amount to a proprietary interest and an easement. If a court is not so satisfied, the 'right' becomes merely a personal licence, only affecting individuals and providing only personal rights.

We will now consider each of the criteria above in turn.

There must be a dominant and a servient tenement

We have already examined what amounts to a dominant and a servient tenement above, but it is worth re-stating that an easement must exist for the benefit of one piece of land over another burdened piece of land. The effect of this is that an easement cannot exist 'in gross' – that is, it is not possible for a person to enjoy a right over burdened land when that person does not own land himself. This may be possible with respect to a profit à prendre but not an easement. There are, however, certain statutory exceptions that apply to this principle, usually in relation to utility companies. Thus an electricity company may have a right of easement over a piece of land for the purpose of carrying the electricity cables, even though the company itself does not have any benefited land.

The easement must accommodate (benefit) the dominant tenement

This requirement emphasises that the benefit of an easement must be attached – i.e. annexed – to the land per se and is not a mere personal privilege given to the current owner or occupier. A number of matters flow from this criterion.

Firstly, whether or not a right attaches to a person or the land can be elusive, but if the right benefits the use of the land, or affects its value or the mode of occupation then it will attach to the land. The test is therefore very similar to the 'touch and concern' criterion in **Spencer's Case** (1583) 5 Co Rep 16a. The problem here is that often the right is being claimed by a person and one has to extrapolate from the claim a right that benefits the land.

Hill v *Tupper* (1883) 2 H & C 121

In this case, the claimant claimed the right to put pleasure boats on a canal which bordered the claimant's land.

It was held that 'right' was a mere personal privilege since there was no evidence that the right benefited the claimant's land. Clearly, there was no connection between the easement and the dominant tenement and, indeed, the right claimed could have existed even if the claimant owned no land.

The fact that the easement provides a commercial advantage to the dominant tenement is not fatal to a claim, provided it attaches to the land and not the person or business owning or occupying the land.

Moody v *Steggles* (1879) 12 Ch D 261

In this case, it was held that the right to hang a pub sign on neighbouring land was capable of being an easement in that it benefited the business taking place on the land. The possible reason for this is that pubs tend to remain in operation for many years so that the business and the land are so intertwined that they cannot be separated.

On the other hand, a contrast can be seen in the case of **Re Webb's Lease** [1951] Ch 808 where an advertisement for matches was held to be of no benefit to a butcher's shop and was therefore not held to be an easement.

Secondly, there can be no easement for purely recreational purposes or personal amusement. Thus in **Mounsey v Ismay** (1865) 3 H & C 486 Mounsey B stated that the right 'must be a right of utility and benefit, but not one of mere recreation and amusement'. The case of **Re Ellenborough Park** [1955] 3 All ER 667 itself provides an interesting insight here, however.

Re Ellenborough Park [1955] 3 All ER 667

The owners of the park also owned the land surrounding the park and, over a period of time, sold off individual plots for development purposes. Each transfer gave the new plot owner the right to use the park, subject to a maintenance fee. The owners of the park then sold it to the plaintiffs, who intended to develop and build on the park. The surrounding owners sought to prevent the development and claimed the right to use the park.

The Court of Appeal upheld the claim. Evershed MR stated that the use of the garden undoubtedly enhanced and was connected with the normal enjoyment of the house to which it belongs. The 'garden' in question was a communal one, the use of which the Court of Appeal felt was 'for the purposes, not only of exercise and rest but also for such domestic purposes as . . . taking out small children in perambulations or otherwise' and this was 'not fairly to be described as one of mere recreation or amusement', and was clearly beneficial to the premises to which it was attached.

In **Mulvaney v Gough** [2002] EWCA Civ 1078 the Court of Appeal again upheld as an easement 'a commercial garden for recreational purposes' since, as Latham LJ explained, this would not exclude the owners of the servient tenement from any use which they might wish to make of the land. 'It restricted that use only to the extent necessary to ensure that the servient land as a whole could still be enjoyed by the dominant owners as a communal garden for recreational and amenity purposes.' The case demonstrated two points. Firstly, an easement is a right over someone else's land but not a right to the land itself. Secondly, the deciding factor is whether the dominant land per se is benefited by the right. Thus a recreational right to ride a horse over someone's land would not be an easement, but a mere licence, whilst a right of way on horseback is capable of being an easement in that it benefits the dominant tenement by providing a right of access or egress. The issue therefore is that the alleged easement must be connected with the dominant tenement so that the owner has the benefit of the easement because he or she is the owner of that land. Thus the commercial nature, or not, of the benefit is largely irrelevant. Recreational use, however, is often ill-defined and insufficiently precise to be an easement. In **Re Ellenborough Park** the actual use was, in fact, defined and annexed specifically to the houses surrounding the park – hence the finding that it was an easement. The right therefore was very different from an indefinite and unregulated privilege – a 'jus spatiandi' (i.e. a privilege of wandering at will over every part of another's field, park or other land).

Secondly, to demonstrate that the easement benefits the land, it is unnecessary to prove that the dominant tenement cannot be enjoyed without the benefit of the easement. It simply has to be shown that the easement provides a utility to the dominant tenement. Clearly, a right of way, for instance, would provide such utility but if the owner of the land has some alternative means of access this does not prevent the easement being claimed from being something less than an easement. The position was established in **Polo Woods Foundation v Shelton-Agar** [2009] EWHC 1361 (Ch). Whilst this decision relates to profits à prendre, the position is the same for easements.

Thirdly, there must be a connection between the dominant and servient tenements. This does not mean to say that the two tenements must be contiguous, though the further apart the two tenements are, the less likely it is that the easement is capable of benefiting the dominant tenement. Thus in **Bailey v Stephens** (1862) 12 CBNS 91 Willes J stated 'there cannot be a right of way over land in Kent appurtenant to an estate in Northumberland'. In **Re Ellenborough Park** some of the houses claiming the easement were not immediately fronting the park. In relation to these few houses it was stated, '. . . the extension of the right of enjoyment to these few houses does not negative the presence of the necessary "nexus" between the subject matter enjoyed and the premises to which the enjoyment is expressed to belong . . .' (per Evershed MR).

The owners of the dominant and servient tenements must be different

A person cannot have an easement over their own land. For instance, in the earlier example of Blackacre and Whiteacre, if both pieces of land were in the common ownership of A, when A makes use of the right of way he is simply making use of his own land. There is no need for them to be given a 'right' to use the land as it is theirs already!

It should be noted, however, that it is not just a question of the two pieces of land being in common ownership; there must also be common occupation. Thus if A has the common fee simple ownership of Blackacre and Whiteacre but in fact leases each property to X and W respectively then X could enjoy the easement over Whiteacre. Here the two tenements are in separate ownership and occupation and an easement can exist.

If, however, the fees simple of both Blackacre and Whiteacre are owned by different persons but both are leased to the same tenant this will not destroy the easement as regards the fee simple ownership. Here the easement is merely suspended during the currency of the lease and will revive at the end of the lease: **Thomas v Thomas** (1835) 2 Cr M & R 34.

It should be noted that, in some situations, where a person makes use of a right – for instance, a right of way over part of their land – if that part subsequently becomes owned by another then that right may become elevated to become an easement. These types of easement are referred to as 'quasi-easements' until such time as the land in question becomes partitioned.

The easement must be capable of forming the subject matter of the grant

The right claimed must be capable of being sufficiently certain to be contained within a deed. This gives the court discretion in determining whether any right is capable of being an easement. In addressing this matter, courts need to be assured that the right claimed is precisely defined so that the owner of the servient tenement understands the extent of the right that imposes the obligation on him or her. Precedent is a useful guide here – thus, for instance, a right of privacy has been held to be insufficiently definite: *Browne* v *Flower* [1911] 1 Ch 219. Similarly, there is no right to 'a good view': *Re Aldred* [1610] 9 Co Rep 576; nor a general right to air since neither of these is capable of sufficient definition. (In the case of the latter example, though, one can have an easement of air through a defined duct or channel: *Wong* v *Beaumont Property Trust Ltd* [1965] 1 QB 173.)

An easement cannot exist unless there is a capable grantor – that is, the person granting the easement must have legal capability to grant the easement. So, for example, if the grantor is a public authority with no power to grant an easement then no easement will be created. Equally, there must be a capable grantee – i.e. someone in whose favour an easement may be legally granted. So, for example, if the person or persons claiming the easement is a fluctuating body of people, such as all the inhabitants of a particular village, an easement could not be established. It must be borne in mind that proprietary interests in land easements have an enduring quality and therefore must be able to be sustained over an extensive period of time.

The right claimed must be within the general nature of rights that are recognised as easements. Whilst it is possible for novel easements to be recognised, they must be analogous to existing rights, though these may, of course, change over a period of time. Having said this, the courts are reluctant in any event to allow easements to place onerous obligations on the servient tenement, by restricting the use of the servient tenement, or by giving the claimant tenement control over the servient tenement.

Positive easements are easements which require the owner of the servient tenement to spend money; the courts are most reluctant to allow these. For instance, *in Regis Property Co. Ltd* v *Redman* [1956] 2 QB 612 it was held that there could be no easement to maintain a supply of hot water since this would require the servient owner not only to supply water but also to heat it. Similarly, with regards to drains, no duty lies on the servient tenement to keep the drains in repair, even if the drains also serve the servient tenement. More recently in *Old (William) International Ltd* v *Arya* [2009] EWHC 599 (Ch), following *Jones* v *Pritchard* [1908] 1 Ch 630, it was held that the servient owner has no obligation to repair a right of way and the judge stated that easements can generally not impose positive obligations on the servient owner. That said, there is one notable exception which was alluded to in the previous chapter and that is easements of fencing. Thus in *Crow* v *Wood* [1971] 1 QB 77 it was held that a right to have a fence maintained and repaired by the servient owner was 'a right which was capable of being granted at law . . . because it is in the nature of an easement'. Lord Denning went on to say, 'it is not an easement strictly so-called because it involves the servient owner in the expenditure of money. It was described by Gale [*Easements*, 11th edition, p.422] as a "spurious kind of easement" . . . there seems to be little doubt that fencing is an easement.'

In terms of easements restricting the ability of the servient owner to make use of land it must be remembered that easements should not act as restrictive covenants so as to prevent a servient owner from doing something on their own land. An example of an attempt to impose such an easement can be seen in the case of *Phipps v Pears* [1965] 1 QB 76 where an owner of one half of a semi-detached house demolished it. The result of this was that the wall of his neighbour's house was left unprotected from the weather. The neighbour claimed that he was entitled to an easement of protection from the elements. The Court of Appeal did not agree and considered that there was no known category of easements of protection and refused to allow it.

An easement cannot entitle the owner of the dominant tenement to possession or control of the servient land. An easement is a right over the land for a defined purpose and not a right in the land such as a freeholder or leaseholder has by way of an estate in the land. Thus if the easement prevents the servient owner from using their land then the easement will be regarded as too extensive in terms of the ambit of its operation and will fail to be recognised.

Copeland v Greenhalf [1952] Ch 488

In this case, the defendant was a wheelwright and he, and his father before him, had used a strip of the plaintiff's land for storing and repairing vehicles. Notwithstanding that use of the land, they had always allowed the plaintiff access to his orchard. Upjohn J stated at p. 498 that there could be no easement because:

> The right claimed goes wholly outside any normal idea of an easement, that is, the right of the owner or occupier of a dominant tenement and a servient tenement. This claim . . . really amounts to a claim to a joint user of the land by the defendant. Practically, the defendant is claiming the whole beneficial user of the strip of land on the south-east side of the track there; he can leave as many or as few lorries there as he likes for as long as he likes; he may enter on it by himself, his servants and agents to do repair work thereon. In my judgment, that is not a claim which can be established as an easement. It is virtually a claim to possession of the servient tenement, if necessary to the exclusion of the owner; or, at any rate, to a joint user.

Grigsby v Melville [1973] 1 All ER 385

In this case, it was held that a right of unlimited storage within a defined, confined space amounted to the whole beneficial use of the servient tenement and could not therefore be an easement. The space in question was a cellar beneath one of two adjoining cottages. Melville claimed the right of storage for the benefit of his cottage. Brightman J commented, 'A purchaser (Grigsby had bought his adjoining cottage from Melville) does not expect to find the vendor continuing to live mole-like beneath his drawing room floor'!

The question as regards having an easement over a defined part of the servient tenement is always one of degree, both in terms of area and in terms of impact. Is the servient owner still able to make reasonable use of their own land? In *Reilly v Booth* (1890) 44 Ch D 12 it was stated by Lopes LJ at 26 that 'there is no easement known to law which gives exclusive and unrestricted use of a piece of land'. This principle is sometimes referred to as the 'ouster' principle.

One particular aspect of the ouster principle is the question of car parking spaces. Various permutations exist here. Thus in an apartment block, for instance, an owner of an apartment may be allocated a defined space. In some circumstances this may form part of their lease of the apartment, in which case there is no problem. In other cases this might not be so. In some developments, an apartment owner does not have a defined space but has the right to park their car anywhere they can find a space within the car parking area.

Such a situation may, of course, give rise to a contractual licence but where there is a claim to an easement the position is less clear. In **London and Blenheim Estates v Ladbrooke Retail Parks Ltd** [1992] 1 WLR 1278 it was held that the question was one of degree, thus in relation to a claim to an easement of parking it was stated that if the easement amounted to occupation of the land it could not be an easement. On the other hand, if there was sufficient space for the servient owner to carry on their normal activities on the land and for the dominant owner to park their car then such an easement could exist.

Similarly, in **Batchelor v Marlow** (2001) P & CR 36 it was held that the right to park six cars on a strip of land throughout the day was, by analogy with **Copeland**, too extensive to be an easement since it would deprive the servient owner of a significant part of his user of the land. On the other hand, a right to park one car on a piece of land that was, in fact, large enough to accommodate several cars, was held to be an easement in **Hair v Gilman** (2000) 80 P & CR 108.

The issue of car parking was considered by the House of Lords in **Moncrieff v Jamieson** [2007] UKHL 42.

Moncrieff v Jamieson [2007] UKHL 42

Here there was a piece of land that was divided into two parts. The Moncrieffs owned a plot of land at the bottom of a cliff and the only means of access was down a steep flight of steps, the Moncrieffs having parked their cars at the top of the cliff on land belonging to the Jamiesons. The Jamiesons proceeded to build a wall around their property which effectively would have cut off the parking area used by the Moncrieffs. The case was a Scottish case and under Scottish law it was undecided whether one could have a 'servitude' – i.e. an easement of a right to park a car as an ancillary right to a right of access. The case then came to the House of Lords for consideration.

The House of Lords unanimously held in favour of the Moncrieffs. Their lordships considered not only the matter of a right to park as ancillary to a right of access but also whether a freestanding right to park could exist at all. On this latter point, the House of Lords by a majority considered that such an easement could so exist; though clearly one could not consider the issue raised without considering the latter situation. In the case the House of Lords considered the ouster principle and the 'degree of control' approach considered in **London and Blenheim Estates v Ladbroke Retail Parks Ltd** [1992] 1 WLR 1278 and **Batchelor v Marlow** (2001) P & CR 36 and questioned whether this was correct. Lord Scott considered that **Batchelor v Marlow** was wrongly decided and that the test which would cause a claim for an easement to be rejected 'if its exercise would leave the servient owner with no "reasonable use" to which he could put the servient land' needs to be qualified. He considered that, just because the servient owner had granted an easement over their land, that did not necessarily deprive them of user of the land. Lord Scott did not see any reason why a landowner should not grant easements over their land to any degree they wished and to this extent the grant could be any way of an express grant or by presumption. The point he made was that the servient owner remained the owner of the land and in possession and control over it. He noted that if an area of land can hold nine cars why should not the servient owner be able to grant an easement to park that many cars? Why should the servient owner be limited to grant the dominant owner to park five, six or seven cars for instance, as the ouster/reasonable use test constrains them to do? Lord Scott considered that that test should be rejected in favour of a test which 'asks whether the servient owner retains possession and, subject to the reasonable exercise of the right in question, control over the servient land'.

The judgments in *Moncrieff* are merely obiter dicta, so the decision in *Batchelor* v *Marlow* (2001) P & CR 36 has not been overruled, but the effect of such a test being adopted would be profound on cases like *Batchelor* v *Marlow* since there would no doubt be a finding for an easement. The proposed test does make a lot of sense since to distinguish between cases where a plot of land is capable of being an easement because it is large enough to hold multiple cars against a finding for no easement because a car takes up the entire servient tenement is clearly inconsistent. The test propounded by Lord Scott places more emphasis on the nature of the right rather than the ouster principle and indeed the Law Commission in its consultative paper *Easements, Covenants and Profits à Prendre* (2008, Law Com No. 186) has also advocated a more relaxed approach to this question.

Another area, not too dissimilar to the right to park, is the right of storage. This has generated some academic debate since, although it might give rise to a sole user situation, such rights have been held to be capable of existing as an easement. Much of the controversy on this matter surrounds the decision in *Wright* v *Macadam* [1949] 2 KB 744.

Wright v Macadam [1949] 2 KB 744

Wright had a weekly tenancy of two rooms on the top floor of a house owned by Macadam. Wright needed more storage space and asked Macadam if she could make use of a coal shed at the bottom of the garden for this purpose, to which Macadam agreed. Later, Wright took a new tenancy over the two rooms, plus one more. The new tenancy agreement made no reference to the use of the coal shed as a store for Wright, though she in fact continued to make use of it. Macadam then asked Wright for a payment for the privilege of using the coal shed. Wright refused to pay, stating that she had an easement of storage by virtue of the operation of the Law of Property Act 1925 s.62.

The matter of the application of the Law of Property Act 1925 s.62 will be considered later; here we will discuss the matter of the easement of storage. In the case, it was decided that such a right could indeed exist as an easement, though it appears that the claimant had sole use of the coal shed. This appears to contradict the ouster principle contained in *Reilly* v *Booth* (1890) Ch 12. On the facts, there appears to be no difference between this and the decision in *Copeland* v *Greenhalf*, where the claim to an easement was rejected on the basis that the defendant was claiming the whole beneficial use of the strip of land.

If one applies the standard test, the ouster test, the question as to whether the servient owner is still able to make reasonable use of their own land must be answered in the negative as regards the easement to store in the coal shed. The case of *Wright* v *Macadam* tended to focus on the means by which the easement was created, rather than on the nature of the easement. Lord Scott in *Moncrieff*, however, considered that sole use does not prevent the servient owner from using the shed for their own purposes that do not interfere with the dominant owner's reasonable use of the shed for storage. Sole use, therefore, is very different from exclusive possession. Scott LJ considered that sole use for a limited purpose was neither inconsistent with the servient owner's retention of possession and control, nor inconsistent with the nature of an easement. This would not have been the case if the dominant owner, Wright, was able to prevent Macadam from entering the shed or using it at all. A similar point is made in *Re Ellenborough Park* itself where Evershed MR stated:

> . . . the right conferred no more amounts to a joint occupation of the park with its owners, no more excludes the proprietorship or possession of the latter, than a right of way granted through a passage . . .

In *Copeland* v *Greenhalf* [1952] Ch 488 no reference was made to the decision in *Wright* v *Macadam* but, as we have seen, the opposite view was taken, since the claim was 'virtually a claim to possession of the servient tenement, if necessary to the exclusion of the owner'. Lord Scott approved of that decision in *Moncrieff*.

It appears that the difference between *Wright* v *Macadam* and *Copeland* v *Greenhalf* is one of degree. This was certainly how the difference was reconciled in both *Grigsby* v *Melville* and *London and Blenheim Ltd* v *Ladbroke Parks Ltd*, with Judge Paul Baker QC stating at 1286 in the latter case, 'A small coal shed is one thing. The exclusive use of a large part of the servient tenement is another.' The 'reasonable use test' in *Batchelor* v *Marlow* undoubtedly provides a flexible approach to the finding of an easement and allows a court to judge the degree to which the servient owner is prevented from using their land. The approach propounded in *Moncrieff* in which the question is one of whether the servient owner retains control and possession casts the net wider so that more extensive easements are capable of being recognised.

What is a profit à prendre?

Essentially, a profit à prendre ('profit') is a right to take something from the land of another. The matter being removed could be wild animals found naturally on the land, such as fish, grouse, rabbits, deer or pheasants, things growing on the land, such as grass for grazing, or matter that is part of the land, such as gravel or peat. It should be noted that the taking of water is not a profit as this amounts to an easement.

Many of the profits are ancient in origin and this is often reflected in the language used to describe them, thus:

- A right of piscary = a right to take fish.
- A right of estover = a right to cut or take wood for fuel or domestic use.
- A right of turbary = a right to cut peat for fuel.

We saw earlier that an easement cannot exist in gross: it must be for the benefit of a dominant tenement that is appurtenant to the servient tenement. A profit, however, is capable of existing in gross – that is, there is no need for the owner to own land. A profit may exist for the personal benefit of the owner of the profit and, whilst it can exist to the exclusion of the owner of the servient tenement, it can also exist in common with that owner or indeed jointly with others.

The legal and equitable nature of easements and profits

An easement or a profit can exist as a legal or equitable interest in land. In order to exist as a legal interest the easement must comply with two conditions:

(i) It must be held for an interest equivalent to a fee simple absolute in possession or a terms of years absolute: Law of Property Act 1925 s.1(2)a; and

(ii) It must be created either by statute, deed or prescription.

With regard to the first requirement it can be seen that the interest must be created by way of a fee simple absolute in possession – i.e. an indefinite period – or for a fixed term under a lease: for example, 20 years. The requirement set out in the Law of Property Act 1925 s.1(2)a clearly precludes an easement or profit for life which must therefore exist as an equitable interest.

The second requirement means that usually to create a legal easement or profit a deed is required, as under the Law of Property Act 1925 s.52(1). Failure to use a deed renders the easement or profit only existing in equity. It should be noted, however, that if a deed is not used but there is a valid contract to grant an easement or profit within the ambit of the Law of Property (Miscellaneous Provisions) Act 1989 s.2 equity may treat the contract as specifically enforceable to grant the interest.

There are two principal exceptions to the requirement for a deed – firstly, if the easement or profit is created by statute; and, secondly, if the easement or profit is created by prescription. Both of these will be looked at more closely later on but, with regards to prescription, this is a means by which an easement or profit can be acquired by long use. In the case of prescription this can arise by a variety of means – however, all rely on a fiction that a deed has been used in the proper form. Technically, therefore, a deed is used in this instance to create a legal easement or profit.

The means of acquiring easements and profits

Easements and profits may arise either expressly, by implication or by presumption and we shall look at the modes of creation within these three contexts. Before doing so, it must also be borne in mind that easements may be created by statute. This usually applies to utility companies which may require an easement with regards to electricity, gas, water pipes, etc. Thus, if a gas pipe requires repair, the utility company will normally have a statutory right to enter the land to conduct the repair. Similar statutory easements may also be given to local authorities.

By express grant or reservation

Often easements or profits arise where a landowner sells off part of their land and retains a portion of it. We saw an example of this at the start of this chapter where B, the owner of Whiteacre, sold Blackacre to A.

In relation to the right of way enjoyed by A: this would usually have been included in the deed of conveyance or transfer to A. A thus enjoys this right of way by reason of an express *grant*.

On the other hand, the seller, when they sell part of their land, may wish to retain rights across the land they have sold. Again, referring back to the earlier example, B, when she sold Blackacre, reserved the right to use the drains across Blackacre. B thus enjoys her right to use the drains by reason of an express *reservation*.

We have looked at these positions by way of easements but, equally, B could have given A the right to pick fruit on Whiteacre or reserved a right for herself, B, to cut timber from Blackacre. Here A enjoys an express grant to pick fruit and B enjoys an express reservation to cut timber. Both these rights are, of course, profits à prendre.

It is important that, if there is any ambiguity as regards the extent or nature of a reservation, it is always construed against the person reserving the right – i.e. B, the grantor/vendor: *Cordell* v *Second Clanfield Properties Ltd* [1969] 2 Ch 9; *St Edmundsbury and Ipswich Diocesan Board of Finance* v *Clark (No. 2)* [1975] 1 WLR 468.

An express reservation is usually contained in the transfer of the land to the new servient owner, A. This is provided for in the Law of Property Act 1925 s.65(1), which states:

A reservation of a legal estate shall operate at law without any execution of the conveyance by the grantee of the legal estate out of which the reservation is made, or any re-grant by him, so as to create the legal estate reserved, and so as to vest the same in possession in the person (whether being the grantor or not) for whose benefit the reservation is made.

Essentially this is a 'word-saving device'. Without it when B sells Blackacre to A, in order to reserve her right to use the drains, A would have to make a re-grant to B. Section 65(1) does away with the need for the regrant by A so that the reservation can be included within the original transfer from B to A.

By express grant under the Law of Property Act 1925 s.62

The principles of Section 62

An easement or profit may be created by express grant, even though the easement or profit is not included in the deed of conveyance or transfer. The vehicle for achieving this is the Law of Property Act 1925 s.62(1) which provides:

A conveyance of land shall be deemed to include and shall by virtue of this Act operate to convey, with the land, all buildings, erections, fixtures, commons, hedges, ditches, fences, ways, waters, water-courses, liberties, privileges, easements, rights, and advantages whatsoever, appertaining or reputed to appertain to the land, or any part thereof, or, at the time of conveyance, demised, occupied, or enjoyed with, or reputed or known as part or parcel or appurtenant to the land or any part thereof.

On the face of things, this appears to be nothing more than another 'word-saving' provision so that a conveyance of an estate to another is deemed to include any buildings, fences, ditches, etc. which exist for the benefit of the estate. Prior to this provision, deeds of conveyance had to expressly set all these out, with the result that conveyances could be astonishingly complex documents. The effect of s.62 is to do away with this necessity, so any existing easements or profits that benefit the land are deemed to be included in the conveyance without any need for them to be expressly set out.

Section 62(1) clearly makes a good deal of sense; however, the interpretation of s.62 transforms it into an extremely powerful vehicle for converting precarious 'rights' such as permissions or licences into legal easements in their own right. The interpretation will also include quasi-easements.

Before looking at some cases where s.62 has been considered, some basic points should be noted. Firstly, s.62 only applies where there has been a sale or a lease (including a renewal of a lease) made in a conveyance so that a legal estate is transferred or granted – i.e. a deed has been used. From this it can be gathered that s.62 operates to grant a legal easement since it will be implied into the deed of conveyance or transfer. Secondly, by s.62(4) the provision in s.62(1) applies only if a contrary intention is not expressed in the transfer. In modern transfers s.62 is invariably excluded from operation since the consequences of failing to do so may be to create a legal easement which is neither intended nor, indeed, envisaged. Thirdly, s.62 cannot elevate 'rights', permissions, etc. which the grantor has no power to create by express grant: *Quicke v Chapman* [1902] 1 Ch 659; or where the 'rights' themselves are not in the nature of an easement of profit. Thus in *Phipps v Pears* [1965] 1 QB 76, which was examined earlier, an easement of protection from the elements could not be elevated into an easement by way of s.62 because it was not a category of easement known to law. Fourthly, s.62 only applies to 'grants', not 'reservations'.

The powerful nature of s.62 can be discerned from the following cases:

Wright v *Macadam* [1949] 2 KB 744

We have looked at the facts of this case earlier but, to recall: Wright had the tenancy of two rooms in Macadam's house. Macadam gave Wright permission to use the coal bunker in the garden for storage. Later Macadam gave a new tenancy to Wright for one year. This grant was not contained in a deed but it was in writing and fell within the Law of Property Act 1925 s.54(2) 'three years exception'. Macadam then tried to charge Wright for the use of the coal shed and Wright alleged that she had easement of storage.

The Court of Appeal held that, by giving Wright a new tenancy, there was essentially 'a conveyance' within the terms of s.62, with the effect that Wright acquired an easement of storage. Thus what started off as a mere permission or licence by Macadam to help Wright ended with him giving her a legal easement over his land.

International Tea Stores v *Hobbs* [1903] 2 Ch 165

A tenant was given permission to use a path over his landlord's property. Later, the landlord transferred the freehold to the tenant and then attempted to stop his former tenant from making use of the path.

It was held that the conveyance had the effect of converting the permission he gave to the tenant into a legal easement.

Whilst the operation of s.62, if it is allowed at all, can arise unexpectedly, certain conditions are required before this will occur.

Other conditions required for s.62 to operate

Diversity of occupation

Section 62 will only operate where, at the time of the grant, the two tenements are in separate occupation, but *not* ownership.

Long v *Gowlett* [1923] 2 Ch 177

Here a miller claimed the right to go on to his neighbour's river bank to cut weeds, as they were impeding the flow of water running through the mill. Previously, the two pieces of land had been held by a common owner who had also cleared the weeds and maintained the river banks. The miller claimed that, when the mill was conveyed to him, the Conveyancing Act 1881 s.6(2) (the predecessor to the Law of Property Act 1925 s.62) also conveyed to him an easement for the benefit of the mill and binding the remaining land.

The court rejected the miller's claim and found that no such right had been conveyed to him. The court stated that, since the same person had held the quasi-dominant and quasi-servient tenements, there was no privilege, easement or advantage being exercised at the date of the conveyance to the miller. Clearly, what the original owner did on his own land he did as owner – not by virtue of some 'right' over one part of his land for the benefit of another part. This decision was also re-affirmed in the case of **Sovmots Investments Ltd v Secretary of State for the Environment** [1979] AC 144 and in **Payne v Inwood** (1996) 74 P & CR 42. On the other hand, in **Broomfield v Williams** [1987] 1 Ch 602 there was no diversity of occupation. In that case, two pieces of land were held by one owner, who sold part of it to the plaintiff, who then claimed a right to light from adjoining land retained by the owner. It was held that the purchaser had acquired a right to light by virtue of the Conveyancing Act 1881 s.6(2) (i.e. s.62). Apparently a right to light is an exception to the principle of diversity of occupation, such a right having its own characteristics.

Continuous and apparent quasi-easements

Whilst we have already seen that a person cannot have an easement over their own land, it would appear that the point has not been universally accepted and that quasi-easements that are both continuous and apparent are an exception to this principle. 'Continuous and apparent' means the claimed easement must be evidenced by some visible sign on the servient tenement that is detectable on 'a careful inspection by a person ordinarily conversant with the subject': *Pyer v Carter* (1857) 1 H & N 916. Thus a worn pathway which clearly benefits the quasi-dominant tenement would fall within this category: *Millman v Ellis* (1996) 71 P & CR 158. The same would also be true of an underground drain that disperses surface water from the gutters of a house: *Pyer v Carter* (1857) 1 H & N 916. It should be noted that 'continuous' use does not necessarily mean that it must be used regularly but refers to the need for the use to be a permanent one that has been exercised over a significant period of time. The principle is based on the wider and deeper principle that a 'grantor may not derogate from his grant': that is, a grantor cannot transfer land to another on such terms that the utility of the land is rendered unusable.

It appears that diversity of ownership is not always required, however; thus in *P & S Platt v Crouch* [2004] 1 P & CR 18 Gibson LJ stated:

> ... the rights in question did appertain to and were reputed to appertain to and were enjoyed with [the land in question] ... The rights were continuous and apparent, and so it matters not that prior to the sale of the hotel there was no prior diversity of occupation of the dominant and servient tenements ... Accordingly s.62 operated to convert the rights into full easements ...

Undoubtedly this appears to be a stark interpretation of s.62 itself which says that a 'conveyance of land shall be deemed to include ... rights ... appertaining or reputed to appertain to the land'. The provision itself, therefore, does not per se require diversity of ownership. Thus diversity of ownership is merely a means of inferring the existence of some 'right' over the quasi-servient tenement. By the same token, in the absence of diversity of ownership, establishing a 'right' by way of it being exercised continuously and apparently over the quasi-servient tenement is an evidential principle for establishing 'right ... appertaining or reputed to appertain to the land'. Certainly, if this is the case, the decision in *P & S Platt v Crouch* [2004] 1 P & CR 18 would appear to widen the scope of s.62 considerably.

It should be noted that the operation of the Law of Property Act 1925 s.62 has been treated here as the express grant, whilst, of course, s.62 implies an easement or profit into a deed. Some textbooks treat s.62 as a category of implied easements, though technically, because the easement or profit is implied into the deed, it is an express easement or profit. The actual means of classification is not significant, though the Law Commission Report (2011, Law Com No. 327) also considers that easements created under s.62 should be treated as express grants.

By implied grant of reservation

The vast majority of easements are created by deed and therefore are legal. They are generally created either by way of grant to a grantee or lessee or by reservation of a right by the grantor. It may happen, however, that an easement may have to be implied into a transfer of the land because of failure by the grantor to include the easement in the grant or reservation. Often this arises by oversight but if an easement is implied it may be implied into the deed or disposition and in this way the implied easement takes on a legal mantle. Equally, of course, the easement may be implied into a specifically enforceable contract, in which case it takes on an equitable form.

Easements, whether by grant or reservation, may be implied by way of necessity or by common intention. In addition, easements by grant may also be implied by way of the rule in *Wheeldon v Burrows* (1879) 12 Ch D 31. We will now look at each of these in turn.

Easements by way of necessity

The reasoning behind easements of necessity arises because without the easement the land would be rendered unusable. Necessity may be used to imply an easement, whether by grant or by reservation.

Grant

The classic example of an implied grant is what is sometimes referred to as the 'landlocked close'. This may arise where a vendor sells land to a purchaser but provides no means of access for the purchaser (P) to reach his or her land ('close'), as shown in Figure 15.3.

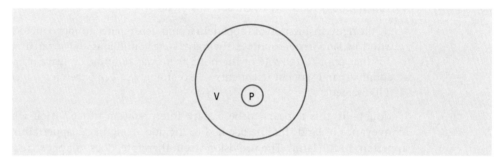

Figure 15.3

In such a situation, an implied right of way would be implied into the conveyance so as to give P access to his or her land. The position would also be the same if P's land was also partially bordered by that of a third party (X) as well, as considered obiter in *Adealon International Proprietary Ltd v Merton* LBC [2007] 1 WLR 1604 (see Figure 15.4).

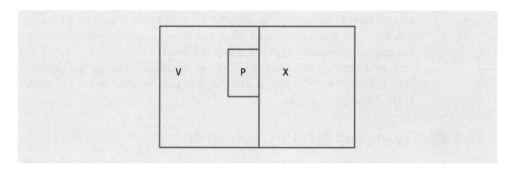

Figure 15.4

In such a case an implied easement of necessity would also be required to enable P to make use of his or her land.

The underlying reason behind the rule has been thought to rely on public policy in that, as land is a finite resource, it is not in the public interest to allow it to be rendered unusable by what is often clumsy conveyancing. In *Nickerson v Barraclough* [1981] Ch 426 this public policy idea was rejected in that there was no reason why such a situation could not be upheld if it is clear that the vendor had clearly stated that no access would be given. It is hard to imagine, though, why a person would purchase such a plot of land and, in any event, the value of the land would be much diminished in such a case. In *Nickerson v Barraclough* Buckley LJ stated at 447 that an easement arises from the fact that an 'implication arises that the parties must have intended that some way giving access to the land should have been granted'. The two positions lead to very different outcomes. If the approach taken in *Nickerson v Barraclough* is used, a claim for an easement of necessity may be refused where there is evidence that there was no intention that such an easement would arise. If, on the other hand, the principle is based on public policy grounds, such an implied easement could never be refused.

It should always be borne in mind that the easement required must be one of necessity and in terms of access this would amount to bare necessity. Thus access would normally mean access by foot, not by car, however inconvenient this may be: *Re MRA Engineering* [1988] P & CR 1. The easement is therefore not implied to allow reasonable enjoyment of the property.

Another example of an easement of necessity is *Wong v Beaumont Property Trust Ltd* [1965] 1 QB 173.

Wong v Beaumont Property Trust Ltd [1965] 1 QB 173

In this case the basement of the premises was let for the purpose that it was to be used as a restaurant. Later, the assignee of the original tenant was required to improve the ventilation in order for the premises to be allowed to continue as a restaurant because of health regulations. The lease also contained a covenant not to create a nuisance by the generation of smells and odours from the kitchen. The assignee claimed an easement permitting the installation of a ventilation duct over the landlord's premises. However, the landlord refused to allow this.

It was held that because the very purpose of the lease was for the basement to be used as a restaurant, an easement permitting the installation and use of a ventilation shaft would be implied. A refusal by the landlord would amount to a derogation of his grant.

Reservation

Implied easements of necessity with respect to a reservation arise in much the same way as seen above under a grant except the positions are reversed so that the vendor (V) sells land to the purchaser (P) but fails to ensure that he or she has a right of access to the land he or she has retained; thus the 'landlocked close' principle applies again, as in Figure 15.5.

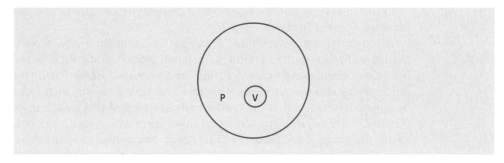

Figure 15.5

It should be stated that such a situation would be quite rare since clearly the vendor must know the implications of the sale and the fact that he or she could be left with a piece of land that is completely unusable or saleable. It should be borne in mind that there must be no possible means of access to the land. If access is available but difficult, no implied reservation will be awarded: *Titchmarsh* v *Royston Water Co.* (1900) 81 LT 673. Similarly, the inconvenience of the route will be no grounds for an implied reservation if some other route is available: *Re Dodd* [1843] 6 Man & G 672.

It should be remembered that easements by reservation are always interpreted contra proferentem to the person claiming the right. The law takes the view that, as grantor or lessor, he or she should be fully aware of the need to create an express reservation and thus he or she is under a heavy burden of proof to establish his or her reservation by implication.

Easements by way of common intention

Such easements are implied, whether by grant or by reservation, to give effect to the common intentions of the parties with respect to the use of the land at the date of the transfer. In *Pwllbach Colliery Co. Ltd* v *Woodman* [1915] AC 634, Lord Parker provided one test for the establishment of common intention. The test has two arms. Firstly, there must be a common intention that the right is 'necessary for the enjoyment of some other right expressly granted [or reserved]'. For example, a right to take fish from a river must require a right of access to the river. Secondly, the easement must be implied from the circumstances or purposes for which the grant or reservation was made. He stated at 646:

> The law will readily imply the grant . . . of such easements as may be necessary to give effect to the common intention of the parties to a grant of real property, with reference to the manner or purposes in and for which the land was granted.

Lord Parker also found that common intention will only produce an implied easement if the subject matter is intended by the parties to be used 'in some definite and particular manner'.

Stafford v *Lee* (1993) 65 P & CR 172

Here there was a gift of a wood access to which was via a private road which bordered the wood and which was the only means of access. Later the owners of the wood wanted to build a house and claimed a right of way by foot or vehicles for the purpose of accessing a residential property. The owners of the servient land claimed that the right of access was limited to purposes necessary for the reasonable enjoyment of the land as woodland.

The court held that the deed of gift of the wood indicated that the parties intended that the land was to be used for the construction of a building. The parties were thus held to have a common intention to use the land for that particular purpose and a right of way had been impliedly granted.

It should be noted that the use of common intention for implying an easement is wider than that of necessity. There the easement is implied because of necessity, whilst with common intention the easement is not implied because it is necessary for the use of the land, but because both the parties intend that the land is granted for a particular purpose and the easement is required to give effect to that intention.

In claims involving implication of a reservation by common intention the issue of contra proferentem must always be borne in mind. *Peckham* v *Ellison* (2000) 79 P & CR 276 provides an illustration of such a case.

Peckham v *Ellison* (2000) 79 P & CR 276

A council sold off a block of four council houses under the 'right to buy' scheme. When the council sold the end house, the council failed to reserve a right of way across the back of the house and along the side of it so that other owners could remove rubbish from their back gardens. The pathway was clearly marked and had been previously used by the former tenants of the four terraced houses.

The Court of Appeal held that there was a clear common intention to reserve a right of way and, whilst acknowledging the difficulty in establishing a reservation, considered the burden of proof had been discharged in this case. The case has been criticised on the grounds that the implied reservation seemed to have been given too readily. In *Webb's Lease* [1951] Ch 808, the heavy onus of proof required to prove an implied easement of reservation was emphasised. Certainly, in order to reserve a right, the nature and extent of the right need to be precise. It is not enough that a transferee of land knows that the transferor, who has retained adjoining land, would like to carry on using the right just as he or she did before. The right claimed will only be upheld if the facts are 'not reasonably consistent with any explanation other than that of an implied reservation' (per Cazalet J in *Peckham* v *Elliston* (2000) 79 P & CR 276 at 291).

Easements by way of the rule in *Wheeldon v Burrows* (1879) 12 Ch D 31

Before examining this means of implying an easement, it must be emphasised that the rule only applies in relation to grants, *not* reservations.

In order to fully understand the rule, the principles regarding quasi-easements should be remembered. If a person owns a piece of land and makes use of a track connecting one part of their property over another part of their property they do not have an easement. The fact that they own both parts means they do not need a 'right' since they own the land in any event. Such a situation is usually described as a 'quasi-easement'.

The rule in *Wheeldon* v *Burrows* provides that, in a situation of the type described above, if the owner transfers part of their land to another, the transfer impliedly includes the grant of all rights in the nature of an easement – i.e. quasi-easements – that the owner enjoyed and used prior to the transfer. The conditions required for the rule to apply were set out by Thesiger J at 49 as follows:

> . . . on the grant by the owner of a tenement of part of that tenement as it is then used and enjoyed, there will pass to the grantee all those continuous and apparent easements (by which, of course, I mean quasi-easements), or, in other words, all those easements which are necessary to the reasonable enjoyment of the property granted, and which have been and are at the time of the grant used by the owners of the entirety for the benefit of the part granted.

The rule can therefore be distilled into three conditions that must be present for the rule to operate; thus the quasi-easement must be:

(i)   continuous and apparent;

(ii) necessary for the reasonable enjoyment of the land transferred; and

(iii) used by the owners at the time of the grant.

'Continuous and apparent'

The principles relating to the quasi-easement being 'continuous and apparent' are the same as we have previously examined under the Law of Property Act 1925 s.62. The quasi-easement must therefore be evidenced by some visible sign of the easement on the servient land by way of an inspection of the land. Clearly, in the case of a track or a drain this is fairly straightforward but it is less so in the case of a right to light, though here the apparent nature of the easement will be discerned from a window.

Borman v *Griffith* [1930] 1 Ch 493

The claimant held a house on an equitable lease for seven years, during which time he used a driveway that crossed his landlord's property. The landlord then tried to prevent the claimant from using the driveway. It was held that, since the contract had not excluded the ability of the tenant from using the driveway, which was clearly visible, the use of the driveway was implied as an easement.

Again, as we saw earlier, the need for the easement to be continuous refers to the need for its use to be permanent and not necessarily regularly used, though it should have been exercised over a significant period of time so that there is a sense of permanence.

'Necessary for the reasonable enjoyment of the land transferred'

The emphasis here is on 'necessary for reasonable enjoyment', not on necessity, although there appears to be some uncertainty as to the degree of necessity required. It may be that the test is merely one that requires the easement to accommodate the dominant land and, to that extent, the focus is on reasonable enjoyment rather than necessity. Certainly, in *Millman* v *Ellis* (1996) 71 P & CR 158 it was stated that a lay-by used as part of an easement of access could be implied. It made access safer, thereby aiding the reasonable enjoyment of the land, despite the fact that the lay-by per se was not actually necessary to access the land. There are, however, conflicting authorities here – for instance, in *Wheeler* v *JJ Saunders Ltd* [1996] Ch 19.

Wheeler v JJ *Saunders Ltd* [1996] Ch 19

Wheeler was a veterinary surgeon who owned, with his wife, Kingsdown Farm House. The farm itself was owned by Kingsdown Farm Ltd which was 85% owned by JJ Saunders Ltd and 15% by Wheeler. They fell out in 1988. In 1990 JJ Saunders Ltd constructed some pigsties near Kingsdown Farm House. Wheeler brought an action claiming he was entitled to one of two ways of access as an easement by virtue of the rule in **Wheeldon v Burrows**.

It was held that it was not possible to establish the second access as an easement as it was not necessary for the reasonable enjoyment of the property. This decision appears to elevate necessity in this context to one closer to easements of necessity and this is unfortunate since the principle under *Wheeldon* v *Burrows* is broader than that. Both Staughton LJ and

Gibson LJ accepted that point. Staughton LJ relied on the statement by Lord Wilberforce in *Sovmots Investment Ltd* v *The Secretary of State for the Environment* [1979] AC 144 at 168 in which he referred to:

> Easements . . . necessary to the reasonable enjoyment of the property granted and which have been and are at the time of the grant used by the owners of the entirety for the benefit of the part granted.

Thus Staughton LJ concluded that the second entrance was not necessary for the reasonable enjoyment of the farm since the second access was usually gated, not the main entrance and only used on very rare occasions. Gibson LJ took the view expressed in *Cheshire and Burns Modern Law of Real Property*, 15th edition, that 'necessary' means 'conduces to the reasonable enjoyment of the property'.

This distinction between the two tests may be seen in the sense that 'necessity' in easements of necessity is something which is indispensable for the functioning of the land that has been granted. Without it the ability to use the land would be moribund and as such amounts to a derogation of the grant since the land is 'absolutely inaccessible or useless': *Union Lighterage Co.* v *London Graving Dock Co.* [1902] 2 Ch 577. An easement of necessity is therefore not implied as a matter of conveyance. On the other hand, 'necessary' within the meaning of *Wheeldon* v *Burrows* is a right without which the land is incapable of functioning usefully so as to allow a reasonable enjoyment of the land. In the later case of *Hillman* v *Rogers* (Unreported, Court of Appeal, 19 December 1997), however, it was made clear that necessity should not be equated with 'necessary for reasonable enjoyment'.

A further issue with the requirement for the easement to be necessary for the reasonable enjoyment of the land transferred is its relationship with the 'continuous and apparent' requirement. Thesiger J in *Wheeldon* v *Burrows* speaks of 'all those continuous and apparent easements . . . OR . . . those easements which are necessary to the reasonable enjoyment of the property granted'. There are a number of cases, *Borman* v *Griffiths* [1930] 1 Ch 493 and *Millman* v *Ellis* (1996) 71 P & CR 158 included, that indicate that both requirements are cumulative and must be met. On the other hand, in *Wheeler* v *JJ Saunders Ltd* [1996] Ch 19 at 31 Gibson LJ stated it was 'tolerably clear from Thesiger LJ's introduction of the test of necessity by the words "or in other words" that he was treating the first requirement as synonymous with the second'. The position remains unclear and it will no doubt have to be decided by the Supreme Court in due course.

'Used by the owners at the time of the grant'

The rule in *Wheeldon* v *Burrows* only applies if the *owner* of the entire land uses the quasi-easement before the sale or lease of the dominant tenement. Presumably, this would also extend to the agent of the owner or persons acting with the owner's permission.

Clearly, there are grant similarities between *Wheeldon* v *Burrows* and the operation of the Law of Property Act 1925 s.62 which was examined earlier. However, there are some significant differences that need to be noted:

(i) The Law of Property Act 1925 s.62 requires diversity of ownership for an easement to be implied, whilst *Wheeldon* v *Burrows* requires the two pieces of land to be in the same ownership immediately before the sale or lease of the dominant land.

(ii) The Law of Property Act 1925 s.62 applies to both easement and profits, whilst *Wheeldon* v *Burrows* is confined to easements only.

(iii) The Law of Property Act 1925 s.62 is limited to conveyances and gives rise to a legal easement. *Wheeldon* v *Burrows* only applies in the case of a sale of the dominant part by means of a deed (i.e. a registered disposition that is registered) thereby giving rise to a legal easement; however, it also operates where the sale or lease is contained in a specifically enforceable contract and thus gives rise to an equitable easement.

(iv) The Law of Property Act 1925 s.62 requires that the quasi-easement be 'continuous and apparent', whilst *Wheeldon* v *Burrows* requires the 'continuous and apparent', 'reasonable enjoyment of the land' and 'use by the owner at the time of the grant' criteria for an easement to be established.

By presumed grant: prescription

The basis of prescriptive acquisition

Easements and profits may be presumed to exist by way of long use so that the enjoyment of the right claimed must at some point have had an origin that was lawful – i.e. there must have been an earlier grant but the evidence of the grant is no longer available. The establishment of an easement or profit by prescription is brought about by presuming a grant.

There are three methods by which a right can be established by prescription:

- common law prescription;
- lost modern grant;
- prescription Act 1832.

Prescription acquisition is often considered to be based on long use but this is not strictly the case since it arises by way of acquiescence by the servient owner in long use by the dominant owner, resulting in a presumption of a grant that allows the dominant owner to *acquire* the easement. This distinction is important since long use of itself may give rise to rights by adverse possession so that the rights of an owner over their land are *extinguished*. Prescriptive acquisition is not adverse to an owner in the sense that the right was always present but the grant 'lost'. Thus in *Dalton* v *Angus* (1881) 6 App Cas 740 Fry J stated:

> . . . the whole law of prescription and the whole law which governs the presumption or inference of a grant or covenant rests upon acquiescence . . .

More recently, in *R* v *Oxfordshire County Council Ex parte Sunningwell Parish Council* [2000] 1 AC 335 Lord Hoffman stated at 349:

> [English law] has never had a consistent history of prescription. It did not treat long enjoyment as being a method of acquiring title. Instead, it approached the question from the other end by treating lapse of time as either barring the remedy of the former owner or giving rise to a presumption that he had done some act which conferred a lawful title upon the person in de facto possession or enjoyment.

Whichever of the three methods of prescriptive acquisition are used, the methods are not mutually exclusive, so a person may claim under any or all three and thus may fail at common law but succeed under the Prescription Act 1832 or vice versa, or indeed, succeed (or fail) under all three. The different methods have a common lineage and thus share three basic principles.

The use must be as of right

The claimant must be able to prove that he or she has enjoyed the right claimed 'as of right' and that the exercise of the right over the servient land cannot be explained by any other reason. In other words, the use of the right is only explicable by the fact that the dominant claimant had been granted that right sometime in the past and is relying on the grant in order to make use of the right that is being claimed. This process is often explained as the claimant having exercised his or her right 'nec vi, nec clam, nec precario': that is, 'without force, without secrecy, without permission' respectively.

Nec vi – without force

Clearly, if one has to exercise one's right by way of force then a grant cannot be presumed. Actions such as breaking down a gate or continuing to exercise the right in the face of protests by the (alleged) servient owner, as in *Eaton* v *Swansea Waterworks Co.* (1851) 17 QB 267, would constitute force. The unlawfulness of a right does not necessarily prevent an easement from arising – for instance, it might be the case that what would otherwise be an unlawful act could become lawful if the right was expressly given. On the other hand, if the unlawful could never become lawful, this might well prevent a right being acquired by prescription: *Hanning* v *Top Deck Travel Group Ltd* (1993) 68 P & CR 14; *Bakewell Management Ltd* v *Brandwood* [2004] 2 AC 519.

Hanning v Top Deck Travel Group Ltd (1993) 68 P & CR 14

Here the defendant drove buses along a track across a common for some 27 years to reach a farm. The Law of Property Act 1925 s.193(4) made it an offence to drive a vehicle on any common land without lawful authority or in breach of any conditions or limitations imposed in respect of such land. The effect of this was to preclude the defendant from acquiring a prescriptive easement to use the track for his buses.

Nec clam – without secrecy

The right must be exercised openly and without stealth. The servient owner has to be aware of the exercise of the right so that they can protest at the exercise of the right. This strikes at the basic premise of acquiescence being the source of prescriptive acquisition since, in order to acquiesce, one must be aware of the action taking place. Thus, in *Union Lighterage Co.* v *London Graving Dock* [1902] 2 Ch 557, a company could not claim a right of support provided by steel reinforcing bars that were driven under the land of the servient owner as the servient owner was not aware of the presence of the reinforcing bars. Similarly, in *Liverpool Corporation* v *H Coghill and Son Ltd* [1918] 1 Ch 307, no easement could be claimed because the servient owner was not aware that the dominant owner had been secretly discharging waste into a sewer at night for 20 years or more.

Nec precario – without permission

Whilst the servient owner must acquiesce in the exercise of the right, consent to the exercise of the right will prevent prescriptive acquisition from arising. The giving of consent or the giving of a licence to exercise the right will defeat a claim, whether or not the consent or licence is acquired expressly or impliedly: *R (Beresford)* v *Sunderland City Council* [2004] 1 AC 889. Unsolicited consent, as a rule, will not prevent a claim from arising since otherwise the servient owner would be able to defeat the claim by a simple unilateral act: *London Tara Hotel Ltd* v *Kensington Close Hotel Ltd* [2011] EWCA Civ 1356. In *Odey* v *Barber* [2008] 2 WLR 618, however, such unsolicited consent was held to be sufficient as the claimant had accepted that permission.

In *Dalton* v *Angus* (1881) 6 App Cas 740 it was stated that in many cases acquiescence, as opposed to consent, can be found by:

> . . . first, the doing of some act by one man upon the land of another; secondly, the absence of right to do that act in the person doing it; thirdly, the knowledge of the person affected by it that the act is done; fourthly, the power of the person affected by the act to prevent such act either by action on his part or by action in the courts; and lastly, the abstinence by him from any such interference for such a length of time as renders it reasonable for the courts to say that he shall not afterward interfere to stop the act being done.

Broadly speaking, therefore, if the servient owner has knowledge of the acts done by a claimant and the power to stop the claimant or to sue the claimant to restrain the acts and the servient owner has abstained from the exercise of such power, then the servient owner will be deemed to have acquiesced in the exercise of the acts, allowing a prescriptive claim to arise.

The use must be continuous

This does not mean that the use must never have ceased, but that the frequency of use must be such as to allow a claimant to assert continuous use. The more infrequent the use, the more difficult it will be to establish the claim. Thus in *Diment* v *NH Foot Ltd* [1974] 1 WLR 1427 it was held that use six to ten times a year over 35 years was sufficient. On the other hand, in *Hollins* v *Verney* (1884) 13 QBD 304, use on three occasions, each occasion being separated by a period of 12 years, was held to be insufficient.

Prescription lies in fee simple only

Prescriptive acquisition can only be claimed by a fee simple user against another fee simple user. Clearly, since the claim is based on a grant sometime in the past, it is not appropriate for a claim to be made by or against a tenant. The effect of this is that it is not possible for a tenant to claim a prescriptive right against his or her own landlord: *Gayford* v *Moffat* (1868) LR 4 Ch App 133. Furthermore, a tenant cannot claim such a right against another tenant of the same landlord: *Kilgour* v *Gaddes* [1904] 1 KB 457.

Similarly, it is not possible to claim a prescriptive right against a tenant since the fee simple owner may not be aware of the prescriptive use that has arisen and which in any event the fee simple owner would not be able to prevent: *Pugh* v *Savage* [1970] 2 QB 373. Again, this comes down to a principle of acquiescence since a landlord in such circumstances would be 'blind' to the use and could not acquiesce in it.

The above principles require some refinement where the alleged prescriptive use covers both freehold and leasehold land – for example, where a right of way crosses freehold land of the servient owner together with land leased by that owner. The Court of Appeal in *Williams* v *Sandy Lane (Chester) Ltd* [2007] 1 EGLR 10 considered such a circumstance and rejected a claim that prescriptive acquisition could not arise because the servient owner was unable to acquiesce in use over the leased property. The court held that the servient owner could disrupt the right of way by preventing its use over the freehold land that the servient owner also held. The court reviewed the issue of prescriptive acquisition over leasehold land. Chadwick LJ observed that if the use commenced before the grant of the lease and the servient owner knew of the use then he or she would be deemed to have acquiesced in it, allowing the prescription period to commence running at that time. Further, he stated that if the use commenced during the period of a tenancy then the prescription period would begin when the fee simple owner re-entered at the end of the lease. He did, however, qualify the last point in that, if the fee simple owner knew about the use and was in a position to prevent it, then the prescription period might begin to run at the time of the use if no steps were taken to prevent it. It must be emphasised that Chadwick LJ's observations are obiter dicta only.

The grounds for prescriptive acquisition

Common law prescription

In order to establish a claim to an easement or profit by prescriptive acquisition it is necessary to establish that the right has been enjoyed 'from the time whereof the memory of man runneth not to the contrary' or 'time immemorial'. Clearly, there are significant obstacles involving proof over such a period of time and the phrases provide no real guidance here. Thankfully, the difficulties were recognised fairly early on in the history of the common law and so 'legal memory' was defined as dating from 1189 by the Statute of Westminster 1275. In the modern context this is also well-nigh impossible to prove and for many years use was usually established by records (where they existed) but also by asking the oldest inhabitants about the length of time the use had continued. Claims that a profit or easement had been exercised since 'time immemorial' were only a presumption, though, and could be defeated if it could be shown that it must have commenced later than 1189. In the vast majority of such cases this is quite easy to do. For example, a claim of a right to light can easily be defeated if the building itself is only 100 years old, since the right clearly could not go back to 1189. In the nineteenth century, however, it became accepted practice that 20 years' use gave rise to an easement or profit by prescription: *Dalton v Angus & Co.* (1881) 6 App Cas 740.

Lost modern grant

The difficulty with the common law rule as regards the establishment of prescriptive rights gave rise to this second method. The rule is based on a fiction that at least 20 years' use of a right is conclusive evidence of the right being granted by the servient owner. Often the evidence may be provided by local inhabitants, Ordnance Survey maps, etc. However the evidence is presented, if the court is satisfied, then it presumes the right has been exercised as a result of a modern (that is, since 1189) grant but that grant has been lost at some point: *Dalton v Angus & Co.* (1881) 6 App Cas 740.

The presumption of a lost modern grant cannot be defeated by the servient owner producing evidence that no grant has been made. It is possible to defeat the claim if it can be shown that, at the date the alleged grant is supposed to have been given, there was no person capable of making the grant – for instance, the person was a minor, suffered from mental incapacity or was an incorporated body which lacked the capacity to grant an easement or profit: *Rochdale Canal Co. v Radcliff* (1852) 18 QB 287. It is also possible to defeat the claim if it can be shown that the dominant and servient tenements were in common ownership: *Neaverson v Peterborough Rural District Council* [1902] 1 Ch 557. It should be added that it is quite difficult to establish a profit à prendre by this method since such rights by their very nature exist in gross and thus evidence may be very thin on the ground: *Bettison v Langton* [2000] Ch 54.

Prescription Act 1832

The difficulties associated with common law prescription and lost modern grant gave rise to the Prescription Act 1832. It must be emphasised that it is not a replacement for the first two methods of prescriptive acquisition. The idea was to make the issues of proof easier. Unfortunately, the Act has the ignominious distinction of being regarded as the worst-drafted Act on the statute book and has been described as an 'eyesore'. That may be the case, and it is well overdue for reform; however, at the moment the law is stuck with it!

The Act divides easements into two classes: profits and easements other than light and easements of light themselves. It also introduces two periods of prescription.

Easements and profits other than light

Section 2 of the Act provides that a period of 20 years is sufficient to establish an easement (30 years for a profit à prendre), provided the right was exercised without interruption. The Act provides that no prescriptive right at common law can be defeated if the appropriate period was first enjoyed prior to the 20-year period. The effect of this, since the claim is being made at common law, is that no evidence that the right has only commenced after 1189 will cause the claim to fail. The 20-year period must be the period immediately prior to the 'suit or action' in which the claim is challenged. Thus it does not matter how long the right has been enjoyed, 100 or 200 years or more, no absolute or indefeasible right can be established until the claim to the right is challenged by action in the courts. Further, under s.4 a servient owner can only defeat a claim if the alleged dominant owner tolerated an interruption/obstruction by the servient owner for one year or more within the 20-year period. The effect therefore of these provisions is that, no matter how long the right has been enjoyed, it stands to be defeated if the conditions required at common law are not complied with within the 20-year period before the action. In any event, the claim will fail if the dominant owner has notice of an interruption (and the person making it) for a period of one year within that 20-year period of grace to bring his or her action before the courts.

Section 2 also provides that if the easement is enjoyed for 40 years (60 years for a profit à prendre) as of right and without interruption the right is 'absolute and indefeasible, unless it shall appear that the same was enjoyed by some consent or agreement expressly given or made for the purpose of by deed or writing'. The effect is that, if the servient owner provides consent to the easement at the commencement of the 400-year period, then this will only defeat the right if that consent was made by deed or writing.

It should, however, be noted that even oral permission given within the prescribed period will negate any user as of right or any claim to user as of right: ***Jones v Price and Morgan*** (1992) 64 P & CR 404. Similarly, any user based on a common understanding that the use is, and continues to be, permissive will also defeat a claim; thus Parker LJ stated:

> If both parties have such a common understanding it cannot be, in my judgment, that there is an assertion to a claim as of right.

The 40 years' use must also be immediately prior to a 'suit or action' as for the 20-year period. Similarly, the one-year rules applicable to interruption/obstruction also apply to the 40-year period.

Rules governing the prescriptive acquisition of a right to light

By section 3, slightly different rules apply to the prescriptive acquisition of a right to light. The provision states that actual enjoyment of access to light for a period of 20 years without interruption renders the right 'absolute and indefeasible'. The matter of actual enjoyment means just that, so in ***Tamares (Vincent Square) Ltd v Fairpoint Properties (Vincent Square) Ltd*** [2007] 1 WLR 2148 it was held that no easement of light was established where the windows were blocked off by internal panelling throughout the 20-year period as there was no light 'actually enjoyed'.

Again, if the right was enjoyed by reason of written consent or agreement, that will defeat a claim. It appears that the consent or agreement will defeat the claim whether given or made before or after the 20-year period has commenced: ***Hyman v Van den Burgh***

[1907] 1 WLR 516. From the decision in **RHJ Ltd v F T Patten (Holdings) Ltd** [2008] EWCA Civ 151, the consent or agreement does not have to make reference to a claim to light per se to fall within s.3 if it does so by implication.

At one time, it was not unusual for servient owners to erect structures to block light in order to prevent an easement of light arising. Since the Right to Light Act 1959 such action is now unnecessary since a servient owner is able to register a notice as a local land charge that acts as an interruption of the right in order to prevent s.3 from operating.

The protection of easements and profits

Easements and profits are proprietary interests – and thus the benefit of an easement or a profit – *may* run with the dominant tenement so that the owner of an estate may enforce a right. Similarly, the burden of the easement *may* run with the servient tenement so that the owner is liable to have the easement or profit enforced against him or her. The question of enforcement and liability (as with other interests in land we have examined) depends on the nature of the easement or profit – that is, whether it is legal or equitable and whether the relevant registration and other mechanisms within unregistered or registered land have been complied with.

Unregistered land

A legal easement or profit granted over unregistered land is binding for all purchasers on the basis that legal interests 'bind the whole world' and thus an owner of the dominant tenement will always be able to enforce it against the owner of the servient tenement.

An equitable easement or profit over unregistered land must be registered as a Class D(iii) land charge under the Land Charges Act 1972 s.2(5). Failure to register will render the easement or profit void against a purchaser for money or money's worth of a legal estate in land charged with it: Land Charges Act 1972 s.4(6). These registration requirements are only necessary for easements or profits created after 1 January 1926; any easement or profits created before this date are governed by the doctrine of notice. It should be noted that any easements or profits created by estoppel are also governed by the doctrine of notice, whenever created, as these do not fall within a Class D(iii) land charge: **E R Ives Investments Ltd v High** [1967] 2 QB 379.

It should be borne in mind that the above principles are only applicable prior to compulsory first registration of title by a purchaser; following this, the issue of priority is governed by the Land Registration Act 2002 below.

Registered land

Prior to the Land Registration Act 2002, a legal easement or profit was an overriding interest under the Land Registration Act 1925 s.70(1)a and therefore bound a purchaser automatically. On the other hand, where an easement was equitable, it generally had to be protected as a minor interest by entry on the servient tenement's register. As indicated in Chapter 5, the case of **Celsteel Ltd v Alton House Holdings Ltd** [1986] 1 WLR 512, however, provided that an *equitable* easement could fall within s.70(1)a, provided the right was 'openly exercised and enjoyed' at the time the servient land was transferred. This decision was subsequently upheld by the Court of Appeal in **Thatcher v Douglas** [1996] 146 NLJ 242. Given the fact that there is still a significant, though declining, amount of land that has not been subject to the new Land Registration Act 2002 regime, it is worth bearing in mind that the above principles will continue to apply.

As we know from Chapter 5, the aim of the Land Registration Act 2002 is to bring as many interests as possible on to the register so that there is transparency about the title to the land. In relation to easements, however, this transparency has to extend to the dominant and servient titles, so that a purchaser can discover the respective benefits and burdens that fall on to each title. The result is that the registration requirements have to be effected across each title so that each title mirrors the other one – that is, if there is a benefit then there must be a burden. Prior to the Land Registration Act 2002, easements were either protected on the servient land or not at all if they were overriding interests, so the position is now a great deal clearer – but more complicated. The rules on registration of easements can thus be difficult to follow since there are a number of factors that have to be taken into account. Firstly, there are two pieces of land involved: the dominant and servient tenements. Secondly, each piece of land may be registered or unregistered or subject to the rules of first registration. Thirdly, easements can be legal or equitable and therefore different rules will apply to each type. Fourthly, the land may be freehold or leasehold. These factors are important since, of course, easements and profits are proprietary interests and whilst the benefit and burden of easements are capable of running with the dominant and servient tenements respectively, in order to do so they must comply with the rules set out in the Land Registration Act 2002. Generally speaking, easements are the concern of the purchaser of the servient tenement; however, it should be borne in mind that the existence (or not) of an easement may have a profound effect on the value of the land with regards to both the dominant and servient tenements.

Before embarking on an examination of the Land Registration Act 2002 in respect of first registration of title and subsequent dealings, it must be emphasised that the Land Charges Act 1972 (unregistered land) and the Land Registration Act 1925 continue to apply until the land falls within the Land Registration Act 2002 regime.

First registration

Legal easements

First registration of the dominant land

With regard to legal easements in first registration of the dominant land ,the legal estate is vested in the first registered proprietor and this will include 'all interests subsisting for the *benefit* of the estate' – that is, the dominant tenement: Land Registration Act 2002 s.11(2),(3) (freehold estates) and s.12(2),(3) (leasehold estates). Thus if the transfer of the dominant land is a 'trigger' disposition, the easements that benefited the land before it was registered will continue to benefit it after registration.

Following the need to 'mirror' the interests that are protected, the dominant land adjustments need to be made on the servient land. If the servient land comprises unregistered land then the dominant owner may lodge a caution against first registration on the servient land: Land Registration Act 2002 s.15, following which the Land Registry will notify the servient owner of their right to object to the caution: Land Registration Act 2002 s.16. If the servient land is a registered title but the easement is not currently noted against that title then the Land Registry will note the burden of the easement on the servient land.

First registration of the servient land

Where there is first registration of the servient land, the land that has the *burden* of an easement or profit, then the registered title will be automatically bound by any legal easements or profits by virtue of Schedule 1 para 3. Furthermore, the servient title will be subject to any notices or cautions against first registration (see above) by s.11(4) (freehold land) and s.12(4) (leasehold land).

Equitable easements

First registration of the dominant land

With regards to equitable easements: on first registration of the dominant land, the registration of the legal estate will (just as with legal easements) also include 'all interests subsisting for the benefit' of the dominant land: Land Registration Act 2002 s.11(2),(3) (freehold land) and s.12,(3) (leasehold land).

Again, it must be remembered that the servient land must reflect the position on the dominant land and thus the owner of the dominant land must protect his or her equitable easement or profit on the land. If the servient land comprises unregistered land then the dominant owner will do this by registering a Class D(iii) land charge under the Land Charges Act 1972 on the servient land. This is already likely to have been done. However, in any event, the dominant owner should register a caution against the first registration of the servient land: Land Registration Act 2002 s.15, following which the Land Registry will notify the servient owner of his or her right to object to the caution: Land Registration Act 2002 s.16.

If the servient land has a registered title, on the first registration of the dominant land, the dominant owner should apply to enter an agreed or unilateral notice on the title of the servient land: Land Registration Act 2002 s.32(1), s.34(1),(2). These processes ensure that the presence of equitable easements and profits is 'mirrored' on the dominant and servient titles, thus embodying the principles and objectives of the Land Registration Act 2002.

First registration of the servient land

As indicated above, the presence of an equitable easement or profit would normally have been registered as a Class D(iii) land charge and therefore bind subsequent purchasers – that is, a person or persons applying for first registration of the servient land. If, however, no such Class D(iii) land charge has been registered then it will 'be void against a purchaser for money or money's worth of a legal estate in the land charged with it': Land Charges Act 1972 s.4(6). It is worth remembering that this position is the same even if the purchaser of the servient land has actual notice of the existence of the equitable easement or profit: Law of Property Act 1925 s.199. Additionally, if the person acquiring the servient land does not fall within the ambit of the Land Charges Act 1972 s.4(6) – if, for instance, they received the servient land as a gift so that they are not a purchaser – then the doctrine of notice applies.

Assuming there is a Class D(iii) land charge when the purchaser applies for first registration of the servient land, they will, of course, usually accompany their application with a copy of the land charges search certificate that contains the Class D(iii) land charge. The Land Registry will note the existence of the Class D(iii) land charge on the title. The effect therefore is that the protection afforded to the dominant title by the Class D(iii) land charge is now effectively transferred on to the newly registered title of the servient land.

One further point that should be noted is that, following *Celsteel Ltd* v *Alton House Holdings Ltd* [1986] 1 WLR 512, certain equitable easements are capable of existing as overriding interests under the Land Registration Act 1925 s.70(1)a. This anomaly continues to be recognised under the Land Registration Act 2002 so that such equitable easements will continue to override by virtue of Schedule 12 para 9.

Subsequent dealings

In this section, we are dealing with legal and equitable easements in transactions taking place after 13 October 2003 and which therefore fall squarely within the Land Registration Act 2002.

Legal easements

Subsequent dealings with the dominant land

Here a purchaser of a registered estate of the dominant land must register their disposition, which includes the easements or profits, for the disposition to take effect in law: s.27(1) and s.27(2)d. If the legal easement is a new one that is *expressly* created then, again, this is a disposition that must be completed by registration: s.27(1) and s.27(2)d. In either case, failure to complete the disposition by registration will result in the disposition taking effect in equity only: s.27(1). Once the disposition has been registered, the legal easements and profits are automatically protected by entry of a notice on the servient tenement's register of title, thus completing the mirror process described above.

Where, however, the legal easement arises other than by express creation – i.e. by implied grant or reservation, by prescription or by virtue of the Law of Property Act 1925 s.62 – it cannot be registered. The result is that, by s.29, s.30 and Schedule 3 para 3, the easement or profit will take effect as an interest that is overriding, provided one of the following conditions applies:

(a) The legal easement or profit is within the knowledge of the purchaser; or

(b) The purchaser did not know about the easement or profit but it is obvious on a reasonably careful inspection of the land over which the easement or profit is exercisable; or

(c) The person entitled to the legal easement or profit has proved it has been exercised in the period of one year ending with the date of the dispositioning; or

(d) The legal easement or profit is registered under the Commons Act 2006, as noted in Chapter 5, referring to certain specialist easements or profits that apply in relation to common land.

Despite a legal easement falling within the above conditions becoming an overriding interest, it would of course be advisable for the dominant purchaser to protect their easement or profit by entering a notice against the servient title, and, by s.29(3) the easement or profit then ceases to be an overriding interest.

Subsequent dealings with the servient land

In the case of legal easements or profits *expressly* created, we have seen above that, on the disposition being completed by registration by the dominant owner: s.27(1) and s.27(2)(d), the legal easements and profits are automatically protected by entry of notice on the servient tenement's register of title, thus binding the purchaser of the servient tenement.

If the legal easement has arisen other than by express creation, we saw above that the easement or profit will take effect as an overriding interest, provided one of the four conditions are met. In such a situation, the purchaser will be bound by s.29 as the legal easement or profit will be overriding under Schedule 3 para 3. If the conditions are not met, there will be no overriding interest and the purchaser will not be bound unless the dominant owner was protected by the legal easement or profit by way of a notice.

Equitable easements

An equitable easement may arise because it is not for a period of a fee simple absolute in possession or a term of years – for example, an easement for life. Equally, it could arise because the dominant owner has not completed his or her transaction by registration: s.27(1). An equitable easement cannot qualify as an overriding interest under Schedule 3 para 3 as this only pertains to legal easements or profits. Furthermore, such easements cannot fall within Schedule 3 para 2 (the interests of persons in actual occupation) since it was held in *Chaudhary* v *Yavuz* [2011] EWCA Civ 1314 that a dominant owner is not in actual occupation of the servient land but simply uses it.

In order to protect an equitable easement, it must be registered as either an agreed or unilateral notice on the title of the servient land. Failure to register such notices will render the equitable easement unenforceable against a purchaser of the servient land: s.29. It follows from this that if the person acquiring the land is not a purchaser in that he or she has not provided valuable consideration but received the land as a gift inter vivos or under a will he or she will be bound by any equitable easement: s.28.

Leasehold land

Where a legal lease was granted before 13 October 2003 then, if the lease did not have to be registered, such leases, including any legal easements, were binding 'against the world'. If the easement was merely equitable then it had to be protected as a Class D(iii) land charge.

After 13 October 2003 the disposition of an unregistered lease with more than seven years unexpired became compulsorily registrable: s.4(1)c, with the result that any easements contained in such a lease will be noted on the title by the Land Registry.

Legal easements in leases granted after 13 October 2003 *must* be noted on the title even if the lease is incapable of substantive registration: s.27(2)b and Schedule 2. If they are not registered then they may only take effect in equity: s.27(1). Equitable easements in leaseholds of the servient land should be noted on the register: s.32(1).

The extinguishment of easements

Whilst easements and profits can exist over many years, there are ways in which they can be brought to an end – extinguished.

Unity of seisin

As we have already seen, a person cannot have an easement or profit over his or her own land and therefore if the dominant and servient tenements come into common ownership *and* possession then the easements and profits will be extinguished. This will occur if the dominant owner, being the fee simple owner, acquires the fee simple of the servient tenement, but not if the claimant owner takes a lease of the servient tenement. In such a case, the operation of the easements and profits is merely suspended for the period of the lease and will revive when the lease expires: *Simper* v *Foley* (1862) 2 John & H 555. If the dominant fee simple owner takes the fee simple of the servient tenement then the easements and profits will be completely extinguished and cannot be revived if the two plots of land are again separated in the future.

Mergers of leases with reversions

As we have already examined in Chapter 6, when a leasehold estate merges with its reversion then the leasehold estate comes to an end. Until recently, it was generally considered that, as far as the benefit of an easement in a lease granted by a third party is concerned, if the lease is extinguished by merger, surrender or disclaimer – indeed, if the lease determines by expiration or any other means – then any easements over third party land come to an end also. This is because easements are regarded as being appurtenant to the leasehold estate and therefore end when the lease is brought to an end: *MRA Engineering Ltd v Trimster Co. Ltd* (1988) 56 P & CR 1. In *Wall v Collins* [2007] EWCA Civ 444 the Court of Appeal took a different view of this commonly regarded position.

Wall v Collins [2007] EWCA Civ 444

A developer had been granted a lease over some development land in 1910. In 1911, the developer sold one house (No. 231) and assigned the lease to the purchaser, retaining another house (No. 233) for himself. The assignment of No. 231 contained an express right of way down an entry situated on No. 233. Subsequently, the successors in title to the leases of No. 231 and No. 233 acquired the freeholds in their properties. Originally, when the freehold to No. 231 was acquired it was subject to the lease assigned in 1911 and an entry was made in the charges register of the freehold title, noting the lease. The Land Registry maintained separate registers for the freehold and leasehold titles for both properties but, when the litigation commenced, the leasehold registers had both been closed and the entry on the charges register removed from the freehold title. At that moment, the freehold and leasehold estates had become merged so that the leasehold estates ceased to exist. Wall, who was the owner of No. 231, claimed he was entitled to the right of way over No. 233, owned by Collins.

At first instance, the judge held that the right of way was attached to the lease, so that when the lease was extinguished by the merger of the freeholder titles the right of way was lost.

In the Court of Appeal, this argument was rejected on the basis that, whilst the easement could last no longer than the 1910 lease, the easement had become attached to the land that benefited from it, i.e. No. 231, irrespective of whether the easement had arisen by way a conveyance, a lease or a separate grant. The effect therefore was that the merger of the lease with the freehold did not extinguish the right of way. The Court of Appeal considered that, whilst s.1(2)a provided that a legal easement could be created for a term of years, it does not necessarily mean that it is attached to a lease of the same length. The effect therefore was that the easement could continue on the freehold estate – albeit only for the rest of the term of years originally granted. Carnworth LJ stated:

> As a matter of common sense, it is difficult to see why a lessee should be worse off, so far as concerns an easement annexed to the land, merely because he has acquired a large interest in the [benefited land].

The reactions to *Wall v Collins* [2007] EWCA Civ 444 appeared mixed. Certainly, if an easement is regarded as being appurtenant to a lease, then the decision is incorrect, but it is correct if the easement is regarded as attached to the land. In theory, the former is correct but practically the second position makes a great deal of sense since otherwise there is potential for the right to be lost inadvertently where a merger takes place and the wider effect is not considered.

These difficulties attracted the attention of the Law Commission in its 2011 report (2011, Law Com. 327). The Law Commission considered that the effects of the decision in *Wall v*

Collins seemed to be confined to cases of merger. The Law Commission was less sure whether the principle could apply to surrender, since the legal position is not known here, and considered it would be unfair if, on a surrender by a tenant to his or her landlord, the landlord could not take the benefit of a right granted by a third party to his or her tenant. If *Wall* v *Collins* extends to surrender then the landlord would take the benefit, which may be a positive effect from the decision.

The Law Commission also considered the situation would be of benefit where a landlord and tenant agree an extension or reduction of the term of a lease. This situation operates as a surrender and a re-grant and the orthodox approach here is that the tenant loses the rights that were formerly enjoyed under the lease. The decision in *Wall* v *Collins*, if extended to easements, would avoid such a consequence.

The position is not the same with forfeiture or disclaimer. The Law Commission considered that those were non-consensual situations. In particular, it considered that to extend the decision in *Wall* v *Collins* to forfeiture could give landlords, in some situations, an incentive to forfeit in order to gain the advantage of any rights that might attach to the lease. The Law Commission considered that disclaimer (see Chapter 6) was closely aligned to forfeiture and the same reasoning might apply also.

At the end of its deliberations, the Law Commission considered that the decision in *Wall* v *Collins* should be statutorily reversed in order to bring about consistency with forfeiture and disclaimer and, at the same time, clarify the position with surrender. The Law Commission did consider, though, that a simple saving mechanism should be introduced, whereby interests appurtenant to leases on merger and surrender could be preserved.

Release

An easement or profit can be relinquished, 'released', by the dominant owner at any time. Such release would be granted by deed. A release may, however, be effected informally, either by way of estoppel or under the rule in *Walsh* v *Lonsdale*. The effect of the release is to return the easement or profit to the servient owner so that it merges into his or her estate, thus extinguishing the easement or profit.

Abandonment

In rare cases, release from the burden of an easement may be implied where the dominant owner is deemed to have abandoned his or her right; however, mere non-use will not amount to abandonment: *Seaman* v *Vawdrey* (1810) 16 Ves Jr 390. Every case turns on its own facts and in *Tehidy Minerals Ltd* v *Norman* [1971] 2 QB 528 Buckley LJ stated at 553 that only 'where the person entitled to it has demonstrated a fixed intention never at any time thereafter to assert the right himself or attempt to transmit it to anyone else' would the easement or profit be extinguished. Similarly, in *Swan* v *Sinclair* [1924] 1 Ch 254 at 266 Pollock MR stated:

> Non-user is not by itself conclusive evidence that a private right of easement is abandoned. The non-user must be considered with, and may be explained by the surrounding circumstances. If those circumstances clearly indicate an intention of not resuming the user then a presumption of a release of the easements will, in general, be implied and the easement will be lost.

Often the physical fact of abandonment is clearly evident to substantiate abandonment – for instance, if the owner of a building claimed a right to light through its windows but later demolished the building and replaced it with another building with no windows, they would not, after 14 years, be able to claim the right to light when their neighbour sought to construct a building next to theirs. It was clearly evident here that the dominant owner had abandoned their right: *Moore v Rawson* (1824) 3 B & C 332. Non-use, however, is rarely sufficient evidence of abandonment, since it is one thing for a person 'not to assert an intention to use a right, but quite another thing to assert an intention to abandon it': *James v Stevenson* [1893] AC 162. Thus in *Benn v Hardinge* (1992) 66 P & CR 246 the Court of Appeal held that non-use of a right of way for 175 years was not abandonment.

There is no process for judicial intervention in the case of easements or profits becoming obsolete in English law. No doubt there are instances where such a power might be useful – for instance, in the case of a mill having an easement for the flow of water in a river when the river, years after a mill had ceased operating, had been diverted along another course. The issue did, however, arise in *Huckvale v Aegean Hotels Ltd* (1989) 58 P & CR 163 where the Court of Appeal considered the question as to whether obsolescence should be a ground for extinguishing an easement that ceases to accommodate the dominant tenement. Slade LJ stated that it should be possible to countenance extinguishment where the circumstances:

> . . . have changed so drastically since the date of the original grant of an easement (for example by supervening illegality) that it would offend common sense and reality for the court to hold that an easement still subsisted.

Slade LJ considered that if there was 'no practical possibility' of the dominant tenement regaining the accommodation of an easement in the form envisaged in the original grant then the court should have the power to extinguish the easement by operation of law or by extinguishment by frustration.

Reform

The Law Commission in 2011 published its final report *Making Land Work: Easements, Covenants and Profits à Prendre* (2011, Law Com No. 327). The report followed on from the Law Commission Consultative Paper published in 2008 (2008, Law Com No. 186). We have already considered this report in relation to restrictive covenants; however, the report also covers issues relating to easements and profits. The Law Commission considered that the law of easements and profits à prendre was in need of reform in that currently it is unduly complex, founded in antiquity and unnecessarily costly. The Law Commission identified five areas that required reform:

(i) The various means by which easements and profits can be created have become numerous and too complex.

(ii) The acquisition of an easement or profit by presumption is complex, and not helped by the fact there are three ways in which prescriptive rights can arise.

(iii) The difficulties arising where there is a purported grant of a right to make extensive use of land: for example, the right to park.

(iv) Issues arising out of the extinguishment of easements and profits by abandonment.

(v) Powers of the court to modify or discharge an easement or profit in the same way as restrictive covenants.

The Law Commission report made a range of recommendations intended to make the law more transparent with regard to the above matters.

The creation of easements and profits

The creation of profits

The Law Commission considered that the creation of profits by implication and by prescription was particularly oppressive to servient owners because it involved something being taken from the land. The Commission judged that such an arrangement was more in the nature of a commercial arrangement and found it difficult to imagine how the grant or reservation of a profit was essential to make the land more useable. The Law Commission therefore recommended that, in future, profits should only be capable of being created by an express grant or reservation or by statute.

Creation by implication

In examining the different ways in which easements may arise by implication, the Law Commission rejected a proposal that all such means should be brought together into a codifying statute. The Law Commission did, however, propose that when an easement is implied, it should not be material whether the easement takes effect by way of grant or reservation.

The Law Commission recognised the complexity of the rules on the creation of easements by implication – not least the fact that, whilst they operate differently, they nevertheless overlap, so that litigation is often conducted across several heads. The Commission took the view that a single statutory test was required. It examined a range of alternatives in establishing such a test that came out of the consultation paper. It was clear that reform was appropriate but there was a significant divergence of opinion as to how such a test was to be achieved. The Commission certainly considered that it would be wrong to introduce a test based on contractual principles such as the business efficacy or officious bystander tests, and in any event such a test would be inappropriate in the context of proprietary rights. The Commission also rejected an intention-based test, not least because, where an easement arises by implication, there is no such intention present and thus this runs into evidential difficulties. The fact that a 'right is reasonable or necessary does not mean that someone intended to grant it'. Such a test therefore was considered unrealistic and would eventually descend 'into inference and thence into fiction'.

The Law Commission considered that the best way forward was to formulate a test based on what is necessary for the reasonable use of the land, to be accompanied by a non-exclusive list of factors that a court should bear in mind in assessing what is necessary for the reasonable use of land. The Law Commission therefore recommended that an easement should be implied as a term of disposition where it is necessary for the reasonable use of the land at that date, bearing in mind:

(i) the use of the land at the time of the grant;
(ii) the presence on the servient land of any relevant physical features;
(iii) any intention for the future use of the land, known to both the parties at the time of the grant;
(iv) so far as relevant, the available routes for the easement sought; and
(v) the potential interference with the servient land or inconvenience to the servient owner.

The Law Commission also considered that it should remain possible for the parties to be able to prevent easements from arising by implication by express agreement since it could envisage a situation where without this a transaction may not proceed.

The Law of Property Act 1925 s.62

The Law Commission also examined the impact of the Law of Property Act 1925 s.62 and considered it should be seen as a form of express creation (as in this chapter) rather than implication. Clearly, s.62 talks in terms of rights being implied into a 'conveyance' and thus they take on the form of an express easement. Dissatisfaction was expressed at the way s.62 converts what are precarious rights (i.e. those enjoyed by permission) into full-blown legal easements. The Law Commission judged that s.62 should no longer be able to operate in this way and considered the unexpected results of s.62 were unwelcome, quoting from the Chancery Bar Association, which submitted:

> [The creative effect] of section 62 is capricious and has led to pernicious results where the creation of a legal easement was clearly not intended, but was not properly excluded.

Prescription

In its consultation, the Law Commission found that most consultees were against the abolition of prescription, though it considered the rules complex, being based in three different methods of establishing a prescriptive right which were often used interchangeably by claimants. Despite the fact that prescription almost legitimises a trespass, the Commission's investigation revealed the feeling that it was invaluable since it legitimised long use and brought the legal position into line with 'practical reality'. The Law Commission therefore did not recommend an outright abolition of prescription but it proposed that a new statutory scheme for prescriptive acquisition should be introduced.

In formulating a new statutory scheme, the Law Commission had the following objectives in mind:

(i) simplicity;

(ii) the avoidance of litigation;

(iii) compatibility with land registration principles, and

(iv) ensuring that the scope for prescription is not extended.

Furthermore, it recommended that:

(i) an easement will arise by prescription on completion of 20 years' continuous qualifying use;

(ii) qualifying use shall be use without force, without stealth and without permission; and

(iii) qualifying use shall not be use which is contrary to the criminal law, unless such use can be rendered lawful by the dispensation of the servient owner.

Clearly the nec vi, nec clam, nec precario reference is well established and, to that extent, there is no change. The Law Commission used the word 'permission' specifically since it considered that the word 'consent' is too easily confused with acquiescence. It should be noted that continuous use need not be by one and the same person.

The 'qualifying use' must be carried out by, and against the freehold owner. The Law Commission was, however, concerned that freeholders who do not have capacity to grant an easement should not be the subject of a prescriptive claim. That is the position now and the Law Commission considered that this immunity should continue. Equally, it was concerned at the possibility of 'qualifying use' being established at a time when the freehold owner of the servient land does not have the power to prevent such use arising during the currency of a lease or where the freeholder does not know about the use or could not reasonably have discovered it. The Law Commission therefore proposed one exception, so that a servient freeholder may become subject to prescriptive acquisition if the qualifying 'use began before the lease was created; and at the time when the lease was granted the landlord knew about the use or could reasonably have discovered it'.

It will be noted that the new statutory scheme does not contain any special rules as regards rights to light as seen under the Prescription Act 1832. The Law Commission's view was that these distractions should be abolished in favour of a common scheme for presumption, whatever the type.

Purported grants of extensive use of land

The problem here is where the easement (usually) confers a right to park or otherwise provides the grantee an extensive right in relation to the servient land. As we saw earlier in this chapter, matters such as parking have created significant problems in some cases. We have seen that an easement must not amount to exclusive possession of the land – it is a right over the land, not in the land. Furthermore, the 'ouster principle' means that the servient owner must not be left without reasonable use of his or her land. Such principles can be seen in the cases of **London and Blenheim Estates v Ladbroke Retail Parks Ltd** [1992] 1 WLR 1278 and **Batchelor v Marlow** (2001) P & CR 36 above.

The Law Commission considered that, whilst an easement must continue not to give exclusive possession of the land, the ouster principle should be abolished. This would reverse the decision in **Batchelor v Marlow** (2001) P & CR 36 and follow the line suggested in **Moncrieff v Jamieson** [2007] UKHL 42 by Lord Scott.

Extinguishment of easements – abandonment

In examining this area, the Law Commission was cognisant of the fact that a balance had to be maintained in preserving property rights and avoiding deprivation of those rights, whilst attempting to ensure that land is not burdened by rights that have become obsolete. The Law Commission expressed concern at the difficulty in establishing abandonment as a ground, referring to **Benn v Hardinge** [1992] 66 P & CR 246 (above) where an easement not used for 175 years was held not to be abandoned because 'it might have significant use in the future'. One of the contradictions here is that, whilst an easement cannot be extinguished in such a case, it is quite easy to establish an easement by presumption after only 20 years!

The Law Commission proposed two ways of dealing with this problem. Firstly, it recommended that the jurisdiction of the Lands Tribunal (the Lands Chamber of the Upper Tribunal) be extended so that it is able to discharge obsolete easements or profits. Secondly, the Law Commission had recommended in its consultation paper that, where the title to land is registered and an easement or profit has been entered on the register of the servient title, it should not be capable of being extinguished by abandonment. Where the land is not registered or title is registered but the easement or profit has not been entered on the register of the servient title, it should be capable of being extinguished by abandonment, and where it has not been exercised for a specified continuous period a presumption of abandonment should arise.

The Law Commission considered that it should not proceed with its first proposal as to registered titles since it would cause insuperable difficulties if abandonment rested on the registered or unregistered nature of the title because some properties would be subject to abandonment whilst others, in similar circumstances, would not be. Thus it decided that abandonment could give rise to extinguishment whether or not the title was registered.

The Law Commission therefore recommended that, if there had been 20 years of continuous non-use, a presumption of abandonment should arise. This period was consistent with the law prior to **Benn v Hardinge** [1992] 66 P & CR 246 and provides a parallel period of time with prescription.

Powers of the court to modify or discharge easements and profits

As alluded to above, the Law Commission recommended changes to the jurisdiction of the Lands Tribunal so that it has the power to modify or discharge easements and profits. The grounds for modification should fall within the Law of Property Act 1925 s.84, which was considered in the previous chapter. Where, however, more than one person can enforce a benefit, an order can be on differing grounds under s.84 in relation to each of them, thus withdrawing the need for any applicant to have to show the same ground or grounds as the other applicants.

The Law Commission recommended that the Lands Tribunal should only be able to modify or discharge an easement or profit if it is satisfied that the modified interest will not be materially less convenient to the benefited owner and will be no more burdensome to the land affected. The power to modify should also include a power to provide for the interest to have effect as a different kind of easement or profit – that is, for the owner to change the nature of the easement, if such a change appears to be reasonable and the applicant does not object. Equally, the Lands Tribunal may refuse to modify an easement or profit unless such a change is accepted by the applicant.

Summary

Essential characteristics of an easement

The traditional criteria for the establishment of an easement are set out in **Re Ellenborough Park** [1955] 3 All ER 667:

1 There must be a dominant and servient tenement.
2 The easement must accommodate (benefit) the dominant tenement.
3 The owners of the dominant and servient tenements must be different.
4 The easement must be capable of forming the subject matter of the grant.

If the court is not satisfied that a 'right' has arisen under the criteria above then only a mere licence is created.

The legal and equitable nature of easements and profits

Legal easements and profits

In order for an easement or profit to exist as a legal interest it must:

(a) be held for an interest equivalent to a fee simple absolute in possession or a term of years absolute: Law of Property Act 1925 s.1(2)a; and
(b) be created either by statute, deed or prescription.

Equitable easements and profits

An equitable easement arises if it is for less than a freehold or leasehold – for example, an easement for life. Further, even if created within s.1(2)a, the easement or profit will be equitable if it is not created properly – i.e. within a deed. It should be noted that, should that be the case, the easement must be contained within a written document under the Law of Property (Miscellaneous Provisions) Act 1989 s.2.

The test set out in this case is:

- There must be a common intention that the right is necessary for the enjoyment of some other right expressly granted, and
- The easement must be implied from the circumstances or purposes for which the grant or reservation was made.

Stafford v *Lee* (1993) 65 P & CR 172

Peckham v *Ellison* (2000) P & CR 276

The rule in *Wheeldon* v *Burrows* (1879) 12 Ch D 3: quasi-easements

'On a grant of part of a tenement there will pass to the grantee as easements all quasi-easements which are continuous and apparent or are necessary for the reasonable enjoyment of its land granted and were used by the grantor for the benefit of the part granted' (per Thesiger J).

The following conditions/limitations apply:

- Only applies in relation to grants, NOT reservations.
- The quasi-easement must be 'continuous and apparent': *Borman* v *Griffiths* [1930] 1 Ch 493.
- The easement must be necessary for the reasonable enjoyment of the property: *Wheeler* v *JJ Saunders Ltd* [1996] Ch 19.
- The quasi-easement must be used by the owner immediately before the grant.

Presumed grant – prescription

Easements and profits may be presumed to exist by way of long use so that a presumption of the enjoyment of the right claimed must at some point have had an origin that was lawful.

The means of acquiring easements and profits

Easements and profits may be acquired in the following ways:

Express grant or reservation: deed

Express grant under the Law of Property Act 1925 s.62

This provision contains 'general words' which, unless expressly excluded, will imply into a conveyance of a legal estate a number of rights (including easements) which are then enjoyed by the grantee of that estate. There are certain limitations on the operation of s.62:

- There must be a deed.
- S.62 only applies in absence of express contrary intention.
- S.62 cannot elevate rights which the grantor has no power to create by express grant.

Other conditions required for the operation of s.62:

- There must be diversity of occupation: *Long* v *Gowlett* [1923] 2 Ch 177.
- The quasi-easements must be 'continuous and apparent': *P & S Platt* v *Crouch* [2004] 1 P & CR 18.

Implied grant or reservation

Easements of necessity

- *Nickerson* v *Barraclough* [1981] Ch 426
- *Wong* v *Beaumont Property Trust Ltd* [1965] 1 QB 173

Easements by common intention

Such easements are implied intentions of the parties with respect to use of land at the date of the transfer: *Pwllbach Colliery Co. Ltd* v *Woodman* [1915] AC 634.

The requirements for common law prescription are:

- The use must be exercised as of right: nec vi, nec clam, nec precario.
- The use must be continuous.
- It lies in fee simple only.
- It must lie in grant.

Prescription can arise in three ways: common law prescription, lost modern grant, lost modern grant.

Common law prescription

A grant will be presumed if continuous use as of right has continued from 'time immemorial' (i.e. 1189) but can be rebutted by showing the right must have arisen since 1189.

Lost modern grant

The rule is based on a legal fiction. The court *may* presume, if it can be established, that there has been use for a sufficient period of time (usually 20 years), i.e. there was an actual grant subsequent to 1189 but the grant has been lost.

> *Dalton* v *Angus & Co.* (1881) 6 App Cas 740

Prescription Act 1832

Short period

- 20 years' use prior to the 'suit or action'
- Exercised without interruption that has been acquiesced in for one year
- Used as of right

Long period

- 40 years' use prior to the 'suit or action'
- Long use as of right
- Without interruption
- = Absolute and indefeasible

Easement of light

- 20 years' use without interruption
- Must be 'actual enjoyment'
- = Absolute and indefeasible

The extinguishment of easements

Easements may be extinguished by:

Unity of seisin

Thus arises where a fee simple owner acquires the fee simple in both the dominant and servient tenements.

Merger of lease with reversions

The general rule used to be the case that if a leasehold estate merges with the freehold estate then any easements that benefit the lease granted by the lessor are extinguished. But now consider the Court of Appeal decision in *Wall* v *Collins* [2007] EWCA Civ 444.

Release

An easement can be released expressly by the dominant owner at any time by way of a deed. Release may however arise informally by way of estoppels or the rule in *Walsh* v *Lonsdale*.

Abandonment

A release may be implied where the dominant owner is deemed to have abandoned his or her right. Non-use will not amount to abandonment. To establish this, an intention to abandon must be properly inferred from all the circumstances of the case: *Benn* v *Hardinge* (1992) 66 P & CR 246.

Further reading

Barnsley, 'Equitable Easements – Sixty Years On' (1999) 115 *Law Quarterly Review* 89

Battersby, 'More Thoughts on Easements under the Land Registration Act 2002', [2005] 69 *The Conveyancer and Property Lawyer* 195

Bunns, 'Prescriptive Easements in England and Legal "Climate Change"' [2007] 71 *The Conveyancer and Property Lawyer* 133

Goymour, 'Easements, Servitudes and the Right to Park' [2008] *Cambridge Law Journal* 20

Haley, 'Easement, Exclusionary Use and Elusive Principles – The Right to Park' [2008] 72 *The Conveyancer and Property Lawyer* 244

Land Registry, Practice Guide 62 – Easements, February 2011

Law Commission, *Easements, Covenants and Profits à Prendre* (2008, Law Com No. 186)

Law Commission, *Making Land Work: Easements, Covenants, and Profits à Prendre'* (2011, Law Com No. 327)

Spark, 'Easements of Parking and Storage: More Easements Non-Possessory Interests in Land' [2012] 76 *The Conveyancer and Property Lawyer* 6

Tee, 'Metamorphoses and s.62 of the Law of Property Act 1925' [1998] 62 *The Conveyancer and Property Lawyer* 115

West, 'Wheeldon v Burrows Revisited' [1995] 59 *The Conveyancer and Property Lawyer* 346

Xu, 'Easement of Car Parking: The Ouster Principle is Out but Problems may Aggravate' [2012] 76 *The Conveyancer and Property Lawyer* 291

16

Mortgages

Aims and objectives

After reading this chapter you should be able to:

- Know and understand how legal and equitable mortgages are created.
- Understand the registration requirements under the Land Registration Act 2002.
- Evaluate the rights of the mortgagor.
- Understand the rights and remedies of the mortgagee.
- Understand the rights of the deserted spouse and cohabitant in mortgage transactions.
- Know and understand how the priority of mortgages is determined.
- Understand the role of undue influence in mortgage transactions.

Introduction

Mortgages are a vital part of land law and enable a person to purchase a piece of land. They are also possibly the most familiar part of land law from the point of view of laypeople as they are the primary means by which a person funds home ownership. Mortgages, of course, are not confined to home ownership and provide an extremely valuable means by which capital investment is raised for commercial, business and industrial development.

Essentially, a mortgage or 'charge' is a device by which money is lent by a 'mortgagee' (the lender) to a 'mortgagor' (the borrower) which is secured against an estate or interest in the mortgagor's land. The security provided by a mortgage to a mortgagee is ultimately the means by which the mortgagee can recover the capital debt that they have provided. Normally, the debt, plus interest, is repaid by instalments over a period of time. In the event of the mortgagor being unable to pay the instalments or debt, the mortgagee may enforce their 'security' by compelling the sale of the land so as to recoup money lent plus interests and costs. Mortgagees also enjoy certain privileges which are not accorded to ordinary creditors in that mortgagees are preferential creditors, having priority over the ordinary creditors with respect to the assets of the debtor.

The mortgage has an almost reverential quality in the life of the nation as a property-owning democracy. To the layman it is a matter of status – not just in the type and size of the home he or she enjoys but as a means of moving away from the stigma often associated with renting property, particularly council-owned property. In the 1980s, under the Housing Act 1980 and 1985, the Conservative government provided council tenants with the 'right to buy' their rented council properties as a means of 'liberating' them from the regulation of councils and, debatably, giving the private individual control over his or her own destiny. The transformation of the country from the point before the Second World War when renting was by far the most common means of having a place to live into a property-owning democracy that is pre-eminent amongst European countries has been remarkable. It is not therefore hard to see why property ownership and the availability of mortgages is one of the primary indices of the nation's wealth.

Before embarking on an examination of the law of mortgages, it is important to bear in mind some of the terminology associated with mortgages. As already stated, the lender is the 'mortgagee' and the borrower is the 'mortgagor'. This may seem obvious, but the student of land law often reverses this terminology. So far, we have talked of 'mortgages' and 'charges' and today the terms are often used interchangeably. Essentially, a mortgage is a loan raised on security of an estate or interest in land which gives the mortgagee an interest in the land. A 'charge', on the other hand, whilst being raised over an asset, which may or may not comprise land, provides the lender no such interest in the asset charged but merely confers certain rights and powers in relation to the asset, including the power to take possession and sell the asset as security for the loan. The interchangeability of the terminology can also be seen in the Law of Property Act 1925 s.205(1)(xvi) where a mortgage is described as including 'any change or lien on any property for securing money or money's worth; "legal mortgage" means a mortgage. . . or a charge by way of a legal mortgage'.

As with other interests in land, mortgages can arise in either a legal or equitable form and therefore, just as in other estates and interests we have examined so far, there is an element of both contractual and proprietary rights in the institution of the mortgage.

Creation of legal mortgages

Pre-1926

Whilst it seems something of an anachronism to be dealing with the creation of pre-1926 mortgages, it is a useful exercise since it will provide some of the concepts that underlie modern mortgages, particularly that other great contribution of equity outside of the trust, the equity of redemption.

Prior to 1926, a legal mortgage of freehold land was created by transferring the whole of the mortgagor's fee simple to the mortgagee subject to a covenant by the mortgagee that they would re-convey the fee simple back to the mortgagor once the mortgage (plus interest, etc.) had been repaid to the mortgagee. Essentially, therefore, the mortgagee owned the property but the mortgagor could recover it on repayment of the loan. The mortgage contract required the mortgagor to repay the mortgage on a particular date, neither before nor after. If the mortgagor failed to repay the mortgage on the contractual date, known as 'the legal date for redemption', then they lost all entitlement to their land *and* they had to repay the mortgage.

If the mortgagor appealed to the common law courts they would not help them, as these courts looked to the terms of the contract and nothing else. On the other hand, if the mortgagor appealed to the courts of equity they would be able to obtain some relief. It should be remembered that, at law, even if the mortgagor was one day late they lost their property, but equity regarded this as unfair. Equity recognised that a mortgage was simply security for a loan and that security was not lost simply by one day's lateness, for instance. In other words, equity applied a policy of 'once a mortgage, always a mortgage'. Equity allowed the mortgagor to repay the mortgage and recover their land even though the legal date for redemption had passed. Equity therefore applied an 'equitable right of redemption'. At first this could only applied in certain circumstances – for instance, if the mortgagor could prove some special hardship, or illness had prevented them from repaying the mortgage on the correct date, or where the mortgagor was personally owed money. The underlying basis, then, was to prevent the mortgagee taking the property when the mortgagor was otherwise able to pay. Eventually, equity allowed the mortgagor to redeem the mortgage whatever the circumstances, provided the debt was paid.

Today, the equitable right to redeem goes beyond the right to redeem the mortgage and forms a bundle of rights which is in itself a proprietary right in the property and indeed has a value that can be sold or transferred to others. In addition, since the equitable right to redeem is a proprietary right, it can be enforced against third party purchasers. The equitable right to redeem is usually referred to as the 'equity of redemption'.

In the face of the intervention by equity in mortgages the legal date for redemption became far less important, to the extent that it became a nominal date only, usually set six months after the date the mortgage was entered into. Technically, of course, the mortgagee could call in the loan immediately after this date or claim possession of the property (though, in the very early days of the history of the mortgage, the mortgagee could take this anyway). Mortgagees, however, were fully aware that there was little point in doing this since a court of equity would protect the mortgagor. The effect of all this was that mortgages were simply recognised as being securities for a loan – indeed the equity of redemption itself could be a valuable asset and was capable of being mortgaged in its own right.

The equity of redemption remains an important right of the mortgagor and, as we shall see later, attempts to restrict the right are subject to strict control.

Post-1926

Mortgages of the fee simple

By the Law of Property Act 1925 s.85, legal mortgages are created by granting a long lease to the mortgagee with a provision that the lease comes to an end when the mortgage is redeemed – i.e. repaid. This method avoids the need for the mortgagor to transfer their legal fee simple to the mortgagee as we saw earlier and, indeed, if one attempts to create a mortgage by this method it is automatically converted to a long lease anyway. The lease given to the mortgagee is by s.85(2)a a lease for 3000 years on the first mortgage, a second mortgage is granted for a term of 3000 years plus one day and any subsequent mortgages are increased proportionately by a day each time, so a third mortgage would be for 3000 years plus two days, and so on. This method of creating a mortgage has advantages over the old method since the transfer of a fee simple can only be done once (there is only ever one fee simple over a piece of land). Technically, each subsequent mortgagee has a leasehold reversion so, as each mortgage is redeemed, the next mortgagee moves up the chain of priority. It should be stated that the granting of longer and longer leases as subsequent mortgages are created is more or less a convention and there would be little difference if all the mortgages were created for the same period, though perhaps this could lead to confusion in terms of priority.

Mortgages of leases

By the Law of Property Act 1925 s.87 mortgages of leases are created by way of a sub-lease (or 'sub-demise'). This avoids the necessity of the mortgagor having to assign their lease to the mortgagee. Section 87 provides that any attempt to create a mortgage by assignment is now automatically converted to a sub-demise. Again, this method now allows more than one mortgage to be created, which would otherwise not be possible. The sub-demise given to the mortgagee on a first mortgage is by s.87(2) for a term of the original lease less 10 days, whilst each subsequent mortgage is for a term of years that is one day longer than the mortgage sub-demise before it. Once again, when a mortgage is redeemed the sub-lease ceases.

Charges by way of a legal mortgage

This method of creating a mortgage is provided for by the Law of Property Act 1925 s.87 and is the most common method of creating a mortgage today. Indeed, by the Land Registration Act 2002 s.23(1)a it is now the only way that a mortgage over registered land can be effected. In this form of mortgage there is no conveyance of any estate – i.e. a lease or sub-lease – to the mortgagee. Here the mortgagor executes a deed which declares that they are charging their property with the capital of the mortgage plus interest, etc. In this way, the mortgagee has the benefit of the charge that provides them with the same rights over the property, such as the right to take proceedings to obtain possession on the event of non-payment of the mortgage, as if the mortgagee had actually been granted a lease or sub-lease as per s.85 and s.86, though no estate is actually granted to the mortgagee.

Mortgages created by way of a charge have certain advantages over the other methods. Such a method can be used for both freehold and leasehold land. A further advantage is that, with regard to leasehold land, the lease generally contains a covenant preventing a tenant from assigning their lease or creating a sub-lease. Clearly, therefore, the creation of a mortgage by way of s.86 is a breach of such a covenant. A charge by way of a legal mortgage ensures that no such breach is likely to arise by this method.

On the face of things, charges by way of a legal mortgage should be simpler and shorter. This is not necessarily the case since the mortgagee generally places all sorts of restrictions on the way the land may be used, as well as the normal terms governing the mortgage, such as the repayment mechanism and the term of the mortgage (often 20 or 25 years in a residential mortgage). For instance, there is usually a covenant preventing the mortgagor from granting a lease or a sub-lease over the property since this may affect the ability of the mortgagee to exercise their rights over the property, e.g. their right to take possession and re-sell it if the mortgagor fails to maintain their repayments. Where the mortgagor is buying the property with the intention of letting it out – i.e. a 'buy to let' purchase – then specific authorisation would be required of the mortgagee in such a circumstance. The result of all this is that even mortgages by way of a charge can be lengthy and technical.

Post-2002

Generally

As we have indicated earlier, the Land Registration Act 2002 s.23(1)a provides that a registered proprietor has the 'power to make a disposition of any kind permitted by the general law . . . other than a mortgage by demise or sub-demise'. Thus the only way that mortgages of registered land can be created is by way of a registered charge – i.e. a charge by way of a legal mortgage. It should be remembered that the general provisions of the

Land Registration Act 2002 apply here also, so the execution of the deed does not per se create the legal mortgage. It will be recalled that s.4 requires that certain events are required to be registered and the creation of a legal mortgage is one of those events. S.27 provides that a registered charge that is not completed by registration does not operate at law, with the result that only an equitable mortgage is created.

As we have seen, a charge by way of a legal mortgage must be executed by way of a deed and thus the requirements of the Law of Property Act 1925 s.52(1) must be complied with. Apart from the requirement that a deed must be used, the Land Registration Act 2002 s.25 provides that a charge 'only has effect if it complies with such requirements as to form and contents'. There are no strict requirements as to form, provided the deed makes it clear that the property is to be charged with the loan: *Cityland and Property (Holdings) Ltd* v *Dabrah* [1968] Ch 166.

Registration requirements of legal mortgages under the Land Registration Act 2002

The creation of a legal mortgage or charge in unregistered land is a 'trigger' event that requires both the estate charged and the charge or mortgage to be registered by virtue of s.4(1)g. It should be noted that, by s.6(2), where the requirement of registration applies because of s.4(1)g then it is the registrable estate that must be registered and not only the mortgage/charge. By this process, the unregistered land will become registered land. Following on from this, once the land becomes registered land then, by s.27(2)f, the grant of the legal mortgage must be completed by registration.

One effect of non-registration of a legal mortgage is that it takes effect in equity only s.27(1). Registration is crucial for the mortgagee to maintain their priority over prior rights – except registered interests and overriding interests by virtue of s.29(2): *Barclays Bank plc* v *Zaroovabli* [1997] 2 All ER 19. It is also vital in electronic conveyancing in order to avoid the 'registration gap' discussed in Chapter 5.

The effect of s.51 should also be noted in that, if one attempts to create a mortgage under either s.85 or s.86 of the Law of Property Act 1925, on completion of the relevant registration requirements the mortgage takes effect as a 'charge by deed of a legal mortgage'.

Creation of equitable mortgages

Whilst mortgages are usually created at law, it is nevertheless possible for a mortgage or a charge to be created in equity. This can arise in a number of ways.

Mortgage of an equitable interest in land

Where a person only has an equitable interest in land then only an equitable mortgage can be created, since one cannot carve a legal interest out of an equitable interest, such as a beneficial interest under a trust of land. A mortgage of such an interest is effected by the whole equitable interest being assigned to the mortgagee as security for the loan, with a proviso that the equitable interest will be re-assigned to the mortgagor when the loan is repaid. It can be seen therefore that neither the Law of Property Act 1925 nor the Land Registration Act 2002 has made any changes to this mode of creation for equitable mortgages. In order to effect an equitable mortgage of an interest in land by the Law of Property Act 1925 s.53(1)c, the assignment must be made in writing and signed by the mortgagor. A deed is therefore not required; however, failure to comply with s.53(1)c will render the assignment void.

Informal and incomplete mortgages of a legal estate

Equitable mortgages may arise either because a deed is not used or because the registration requirements have not been followed, so that the mortgage only takes effect in equity: Land Registration Act 2002 s.27(1).

The former situation will arise where there is a contract to create a legal mortgage. In such a situation, the principle follows the doctrine in *Walsh v Lonsdale*: 'equity regard that as done that ought to be done' so that equity recognises the informal mortgage. The contract must comply with the Law of Property (Miscellaneous Provisions) Act 1989 s.2 and must be in writing. Technically, the ability of equity to recognise such a mortgage is reliant on the willingness to enforce the contract by way of specific performance. It should be noted, however, that equity will not make such an award to compel a mortgagee to make the advance of the loan on the basis that damages would be an adequate remedy here. The effect therefore is that an informal mortgage will only be recognised once the advance has been made.

The effect of failure to comply with the Law of Property (Miscellaneous Provisions) Act s.2 is to render the contract void. This can produce two effects. Firstly, if the contract is void then the mortgage itself becomes ineffective so that the security in the mortgage fails, with the result that the mortgage becomes immediately repayable. Rarely is it possible to sidestep this effect by the use of proprietary estoppels. In *Taylor Fashions Ltd v Liverpool Victoria Trustees* [1982] QB 133n it was held that, where a person promises to dispose of an interest in land to another and that other relies on that promise to their detriment, then equity will enforce the promise. Thus if there is an oral agreement to mortgage a legal estate and the mortgagee advances the money on reliance of a promise given by the mortgagor so that a detriment is incurred by the mortgagee, then equity may enforce the mortgage. This process is, however, controversial since, essentially, the mechanism is sidestepping the statutory requirements of s.2. In *Kinane v Mackie-Conteh* [2005] EWCA Civ 45 the Court of Appeal considered that the failure of contract to comply with the statutory formalities nevertheless formed the basis of an assurance that gave rise to the necessary unconscionability to form the basis of an estoppel. The result is that the estoppel is not founded on the unenforceable agreement but on the conscience of the defendant by way of their conduct.

Secondly, if the mortgage is void for non-compliance of s.2 it is not possible for a later deed to make good the defect by acknowledging the existence of the contract because there is no contract: *United Bank of Kuwait plc v Sahib* [1997] Ch 107.

Where an equitable mortgage arises because the registration requirements for a legal mortgage have not been complied with in accordance with s.27(1) then the purported mortgage takes effect as an equitable charge which should be protected by the entry of a notice in the mortgagor's register of title: Land Registration Act 2002 ss.32–34. In this way, the mortgagee's interest is protected against further interests coming on to the mortgagor's title.

Mortgages by deposit of title deeds

Prior to the passing of the Law of Property (Miscellaneous Provisions) Act 1989 it was possible to create a mortgage by simply handing the title deeds to the mortgagee in return for the loan. No written contract was required to create this type of mortgage since the deposit and receipt of the deeds by the mortgagee and the making of the loan to the mortgagor were regarded as a sufficient act of part performance for equity to recognise the contract. Furthermore, such an act of part performance was recognised by virtue of the Law of Property Act 1925 s.40(2). This was a convenient and cheap way of creating a mortgage for short-term loans; however, since the Law of Property (Miscellaneous Provisions) Act 1989, mortgages cannot be created by this method. Whilst it was originally considered that the Law of Property (Miscellaneous Provisions) Act 1989 had not done away with this type of mortgage – a topic over which there was much debate – the Court of Appeal in **United Bank of Kuwait plc v Sahib** [1997] Ch 107 put this matter 'to bed' and stated that non-compliance with s.2 rendered the mortgage void. Mortgages created by this method prior to 27 September 1989 still have validity; however, given that this method was normally used for short-term loans, it would be rare to come across them today.

Protection of equitable mortgages

We have seen that equitable interests are vulnerable to loss of priority against legal interests and the same applies, of course, to equitable mortgages. Equitable mortgagees must therefore take appropriate steps to protect their interest.

In unregistered land the equitable mortgage should be protected as a Class C(iii) land charge under the Land Charges Act 1972 s.2(4)(iv) – a general equitable charge. As we saw in Chapter 3, this is registered against the name of the estate owner (the mortgagor) who granted the mortgage and, as such, will bind all subsequent purchasers of the land. Failure to register will render the mortgage void against a purchaser for valuable consideration whether of a legal or an equitable interest in the land.

As indicated earlier, an equitable mortgage is registered land that should be entered as a notice in the mortgagor's register of title by way of the Land Registration Act 2002 ss.32–34. Usually this will be in the form of an 'agreed notice'. Registration is clearly vital in order to protect the mortgagee against any subsequent dealings with the registered title, including the granting of any subsequent legal easements: Land Registration Act 2002 s.29 and s.30. If the equitable mortgagee does not register the mortgage then its priority will be lost to a subsequent registered proprietor of the land or to a later legal mortgage. Section s.29(2) provides that such priority is maintained if an interest falls within interests that are over-riding under Schedule 3. Whilst technically it might be possible for the equitable mortgagee to bring themselves within Schedule 3 para 2 – interests of persons in actual occupation – such a situation, it is suggested, would be rare indeed.

Rights of the mortgagor

Borrowers of money are, almost by definition, necessitous and thereby are vulnerable to unscrupulous moneylenders. Even the earliest civilisations have therefore controlled the lending of money – if not outlawing it entirely. Usury, the practice of making unethical or immoral monetary loans, has been condemned from the earliest days of the common law and the violators have been subject to sweeping, extreme punishment and invective – for example, Shylock in Shakespeare's *The Merchant of Venice*. Given the historical backdrop to moneylending, it is not surprising that the law has evolved to protect mortgagors from the unconscionable actions of the mortgagees.

The right to redeem

The 'equity of redemption' – the right to redeem – is the primary right of the mortgagor that evolved out of the court of conscience that is equity. The mortgage contract requires the mortgagor to redeem their mortgage on a specific date and also sets out the terms for repayment. The legal date for redemption did not allow for redemption earlier, thus saving on interest, or later, when the property might be forfeited to the mortgagee. Furthermore, if the legal date for redemption was passed, the mortgagor, having lost their property, also had to repay the loan plus interest.

As we noted earlier, equity stepped into this unhappy situation and recognised that a mortgage was simply a security for a loan and enabled the mortgagor to redeem their mortgage either before or after the legal date for redemption set out in the contract, provided the mortgagor was able to pay the mortgage debt. In this way, equity protected the mortgagor against losing their property if some unforeseen event occurred that caused them to miss the legal date of redemption for redeeming their mortgage, though later equity allowed the mortgagor to redeem the mortgage whatever the circumstances. Equity therefore recognised a bundle of rights which all fell within the equitable notion of the right to redeem. It is this bundle of rights that separates the right to redeem from the mortgagor's equity of redemption – the two are not the same. The latter simply involves paying off the loan and does not represent the bundle of wider rights possessed by the mortgagor that prevents the mortgagee using the mortgage as a means of acquiring property rather than as security for a loan. The courts of equity intervene to protect the mortgagor's rights and thus a body of rules has developed to protect those rights.

'Clogs or fetters' and the rule against irredeemability

The essence of the mortgage, as equity saw it, was that, once the mortgage was paid, the mortgagor received back that which they owned, their security, free from any burdens that a mortgagee might attempt to impose on the property after the date the mortgage was redeemed. 'Once a mortgage always a mortgage' was the avowed principle of equity so that it was assiduous in protecting the mortgagor from transactions which, while purporting to be a mortgage, in fact prevented the mortgagor from redeeming their security or imposed harsh and onerous terms on the mortgagor. The principle was summed up by Lord Lindley in *Samuel v Jarrah Timber and Wood Paving Co. Ltd* [1904] AC 323 at 329 in the following terms:

> The doctrine . . . means no contract between a mortgagor and a mortgagee made at the time of the mortgage and as part of the mortgage transaction, or, in other words, as one of the terms of the loan, can be valid if it prevents the mortgagor from getting back his property on paying off what is due on his security. Any bargain which has that effect is invalid, and is inconsistent with the transaction being a mortgage.

This principle is grounded in the fact that borrowers are in a vulnerable position and their need for money may drive them into oppressive and unconscionable transactions. Thus in *Vernon v Bethall* (1762) 2 Eden 110 Lord Henley stated:

> . . . there is great reason and justice in this rule, for necessitous men are not, truly speaking, free men, but to answer a present exigency will submit to any terms that the crafty may impose upon them.

The first principle that equity adopts in protecting the mortgagor is that it will take no cognisance of the label that is attached to the transaction entered into. The question is one of substance, not form, so that if the transaction is essentially a mortgage then it will be treated as such, thus providing the mortgagor with the protection of equity: *Lavin v Johnson* [2002] EWCA Civ 1138.

The second principle is that equity will strike down any provision which renders the mortgagor's equity of redemption irredeemable or which places any undue limitation on the mortgagor's right to redeem: *Toomes v Conset* (1745) 3 Atk 261.

Samuel v Jarrah Timber and Wood Paving Co. Ltd [1904] AC 323

Here the mortgagor granted a mortgage on some debentures (i.e. loan stock) for £5000. The mortgage provided that the mortgagee had an option to purchase the stock at any time within the next year at a given rate.

The House of Lords held that the option was illegal and void since it prevented the mortgagor from recovering their security on the repayment of the mortgage, thereby excluding the mortgagor's equity of redemption. The House of Lords considered that an option granted contemporaneously with a mortgage carried with it a risk that the mortgagee could proceed to exercise their option and deprive the mortgagor of their legal estate despite the mortgagor having paid off the mortgage.

It has to be stated that the House of Lords reached its conclusion with some reluctance and considered that a doctrinaire approach to the inclusion of options in the mortgage transaction might well cause an otherwise fair bargain to fail. Their Lordships considered that, whilst the existence of an option might raise a presumption of the existence of an unfair bargain, there was a danger that this was applied too forcefully. The result of these deliberations later led the courts to avoid the 'clogs and fetters' rule if an option was entered into in a separate, independent transaction, even if the result would be to wholly or partially destroy the mortgagor's equity of redemption. Thus in **Reeves v Lisle** [1902] AC 461, an option was entered into eleven days after the mortgage was upheld since it was regarded as a separate and independent transaction. The principle therefore is that, once a mortgagor has obtained and entered into their mortgage, they are free from the possibility of being compelled to enter into an unfair bargain and are thus more likely to enter into the option consensually and by exercising their free will. It should be noted, however, that the above arguments do not apply to a right of pre-emption being given to the mortgagee since here the discretion to sell or not rests with the mortgagor – unlike in an option – so the mortgagor cannot be compelled to sell.

The matter as regards a time gap between entering into the mortgage and the inclusion of an option was also considered in **Jones v Morgan** [2002] 1 EGLR 125.

Jones v Morgan [2002] 1 EGLR 125

The parties entered into an agreement in 1994 by which J advanced £105,000 secured by way of a legal charge over M's property in order to fund the development of the property. The development did not take place and so, in order to raise funds for another development, M entered into an agreement to sell 40 acres of the charged land to a third party. J's consent was required for the sale and therefore an agreement was entered into by which J agreed to the sale in return for a 50% share in the remaining land. The land was then sold and the proceeds were used to partially pay off the outstanding charge. J then commenced proceedings for specific performance of the agreement to give him a 50% share in the remaining property.

The Court of Appeal held that the agreement to give J a 50% share was not unconscionable since J had not acted in a morally reprehensible manner. The Court of Appeal nevertheless held that the agreement was void as a clog on the equity of redemption. The court considered that, had the later agreement been part of the 1994 agreement, it would have been integral to that agreement and not a collateral contract. The court considered that the 1997 agreement essentially converted a single indivisible mortgage into two separate mortgages which were not independent of each other. It was clear that, but for the later agreement, M would have been able to redeem his mortgage free from any encumbrance created at the time of the mortgage and thus the imposition of the conditions in the later agreement must amount to a clog on the equity of redemption.

So far, we have considered the principles where the terms of the mortgage render it irredeemable; however, in some situations, the mortgage terms provide that the equity of redemption is postponed for a longer period then the customary six-month period for the legal date of redemption – for instance, 40 years. Essentially, there is nothing wrong with this, providing that the provision does not render the equity of redemption illusory or so unconscionable and oppressive that a court of equity would not enforce it. Thus in *Fairclough* v *Swan Brewery Co. Ltd* [1912] it was held that a mortgage of a lease for 20 years was struck down because a term prevented the mortgage from being redeemed six months before the end of the lease. Here the equitable right to redeem was held to be illusory and therefore void. Generally, however, the court will not interfere in the mortgage transaction unless it is found to be oppressive or unconscionable. It should be borne in mind that, in examining the agreement between the parties as a whole, the mortgagee may be taking considerable risks in making their loan and thus postponement of the right of redemption may be perfectly reasonable. Issues of equal bargaining power and mutuality are also valid considerations in assessing the arrangement – for instance, if the mortgagee can demand earlier repayment then it is equally reasonable for the mortgagor to exercise their right to redeem earlier.

Knightsbridge Estates Trust Ltd v *Byrne* [1939] Ch 441

Knightsbridge took a loan of £310,000 from Byrne on a 40-year term at an interest rate of 6.5% per annum. Later, the interest rates fell and Knightsbridge, wanting to avail itself of the lower rates, attempted to pay off the mortgage earlier, even though the agreement stated that the mortgage should not be repaid before the expiry of the 40-year term.

In the Court of Appeal it was held that the postponement of the date of redemption could not be challenged on the ground of its excessive length. The court held that the agreement was a commercial agreement between two parties acting 'at arm's length', who had entered into an agreement on terms that were advantageous at the time of the agreement. Sir Wilfred Greene MR stated at 457:

> . . . equity does not reform mortgage transactions because they are unreasonable. It is concerned to see . . . that oppressive or unconscionable terms are not enforced. Subject to this it does not . . . interfere.

The effect – certainly in business transactions – is that the courts will not interfere in the absence of oppressive or unconscionable mortgage terms since to do otherwise would be to interfere with the 'liberty of contract of competent parties who are at arm's length'.

Unfair collateral advantages

Whilst the essence of a mortgage is a loan in return for security, there are occasions when terms are added into the agreement which provide for the mortgagee to have some additional advantages – i.e. a collateral advantage. In equity there developed a wide discretionary power to strike down collateral advantages within a mortgage transaction if they were deemed to be unfair and unconscionable. Typical examples arising in relation to collateral advantages are breweries requiring landlords to purchase all their drinks from the brewery in return for a loan, or oil companies requiring petrol station owners to purchase all their petroleum from the oil company, again, in return for a loan.

Originally, such collateral advantages were struck down automatically as being an undue clog or fetter on the equity or redemption, as in **Bradley v Carritt** [1903] AC 253, where the collateral advantage extends beyond the date of redemption. In that case, a holder of shares ('B') in a tea company mortgaged his shares to secure a loan and also agreed to 'use his best endeavours' to ensure that the mortgagee tea broker would be able to purchase all the company's tea. If the company's tea was sold elsewhere, the mortgagor was to pay the mortgagee the amount of commission he would have earned if the tea had been sold through him. The mortgage was paid off and the company then changed its broker. The House of Lords held that the agreement was not binding on the basis that, once the mortgage had been paid off, B would have been unable to sell or dispose of his shares in order to ensure that C would continue to be the company's broker. Their Lordships referred to the judgment of Rigby LJ in **Noakes v Rice** [1900] 2 Ch 445, in which he stated at 457 that:

> the property, which comes back to the mortgagor must not be worse than it was when it was mortgaged, and the mortgagee must not, either expressly or by implication, reserve to himself any hold upon the property after the time for redemption has arrived and the right of redemption has been put in force.

In **Biggs v Hoddinott** [1898] 2 Ch 307 it had been held that, if the collateral ends on the date of redemption and is not unduly oppressive or unconscionable, then it may be upheld. This position is not invariable, however, since a sea change began to arise with **G & C Kreglinger v New Patagonia Meat and Cold Storage Ltd** [1914] AC 25.

G & C Kreglinger v New Patagonia Meat and Cold Storage Ltd [1914] AC 25

The mortgagees were a firm of wool brokers who lent the mortgagees £10,000 on the basis that, for a period of five years, the mortgagees should have the right of first refusal over all sheepskins sold by the mortgagors as a by-product of their meat processing business. The mortgagors paid off the loan after two and a half years; however, the mortgagees claimed they were entitled to continue to exercise that right of first refusal for the remaining part of the five-year agreement. The mortgagors considered that this was unfair as it extended beyond the redemption date of the mortgage.

The House of Lords held that the right of first refusal formed no part of the mortgage transaction, that it was a collateral advantage entered into as a condition of the company obtaining the loan and that the mortgagee was entitled to enforce it. The House of Lords considered that this was an agreement entered into at arm's length and, as such, it was simply a commercial transaction between two commercial parties. The court did not consider the agreement to be unfair or unconscionable. Lord Haldane stated at 38 and 39:

> What was the true character of the transaction? Did the appellants make a bargain such that the right to redeem was cut down, or did they simply stipulate for a collateral undertaking, outside and clear of the mortgage, which would give them an exclusive option of purchase of the sheepskins of the respondents? The question is in my opinion not whether the two contracts were made at the same moment and evidenced by the same instrument, but whether they were in substance a single undivided contract or two distinct contracts.

The effect therefore in **Kreglinger** is that, whilst the first refusal was made at the same time as the loan agreement and evidenced by the same document, it was a separate and independent transaction and so valid. One therefore has to examine the substance of the agreement, not the form, particularly in the case of a legitimate commercial agreement.

The difference between **Kreglinger** and **Bradley v Carritt** can be seen by the fact that in **Bradley** there continued to be a restriction in that, even once the mortgage had been redeemed, the shares could not be sold in order to ensure that the mortgagor had sufficient control to ensure that the mortgagee continued to act as broker. In *Kreglinger*, though, the property that was mortgaged was returned unfettered. *Kreglinger* represents a sea change in that it enabled the courts to break away from a doctrinaire approach and look behind the transaction, as summed up by Lord Mersey who stated that the clogs and fetters doctrine is 'an unruly dog, which, if not securely chained to its own kennel, is prone to wander into places where it ought not be' – that is, legitimate business transactions.

The change seen in *Kreglinger* is, however, tempered by the doctrine of restraint of trade, which will invalidate any contract that places unreasonable restrictions on an individual pursuing their trade, profession or commercial ability. Such contracts are void as being contrary to public policy. Public policy arises here in two ways. First, the common law seeks to protect an individual from negotiating away their livelihood to another, possibly contractually stronger, party, particularly where the restraint is a general one. Second, the law understands that it is not in the public interest for the state to be deprived of a valuable benefit in allowing a person to be restricted in carrying out his lawful trade or business.

Contracts in restraint of trade may be upheld, provided that the restraint can be shown to be reasonable, not only as regards the parties themselves, but also as regards the interests of the public, having regard to the extent, area and duration of the restraint. In the context of mortgages and collateral advantages, the problem commonly arises where a manufacturer or wholesaler attempts to restrict a retailer in a method of distribution or pricing policy or seeks to tie the retailer to a chain of supply so that they are prevented from selling similar goods by competing manufacturers or wholesalers in return for a loan. Such agreements are commonly referred to as 'solus agreements' or 'vertical agreements'.

Esso Petroleum Co. Ltd v *Harper's Garage (Stourport) Ltd* [1967] 1 All ER 699

The respondent owners of two garages entered into a solus agreement with the appellants whereby they contracted to purchase all their petrol from the appellants. The agreement was to last four years and five months in respect of one garage, during which the owners would receive a discount in the price of petrol purchased from the appellants. In respect of the other garage the 'tie' was to last 21 years in return for a mortgage of £7000. The covenants in the second agreement stated that the owner had also to comply with the covenants contained in the first agreement. Further, the respondent owners were not entitled to redeem the 21-year mortgage before the end of the term of the mortgage. When the respondents started to sell another brand of petrol, they were sued by the appellants. The respondents argued that they were not bound by the contracts since they were an unreasonable restraint of trade.

The House of Lords held that both transactions fell within the doctrine of restraint of trade and were thus prima facie void. Their Lordships decided that there was nothing unlawful per se in a solus agreement, since very often both parties benefited from the transaction. One party benefited from acquiring a chain of distribution which made the supply of its products efficient and economical. On the other hand, the other party, the respondents in this case, gained by acquiring extra capital finance and a preferential wholesale price. On this basis there were clearly interests that merited protection. Nevertheless, the restrictions could only be enforced if they could be reasonable, not only between the parties, but also as regards the public interest. With regard to the first agreement, the House of Lords found that it was reasonable since it protected a legitimate interest of the parties and at the same time it was not contrary to the public interest. The court, however, decided that such agreements would become unreasonable if they operated for an excessive period and in this regard considered the second agreement to be unreasonable and void.

The stance taken by the House of Lords with regard to the second mortgage is also consistent with the general principles seen in the law of mortgages. As we have seen, equity will not allow a clog or fetter on the equity of redemption so as to either postpone the right of redemption or render it illusory. The court, however, stated that the doctrine of restraint of trade still applied, albeit there was a crossover into the field of land law. Their Lordships then adopted an unusual stance and stated that the doctrine did not apply where the restriction was applied to covenants contained in leases or conveyances of land. Thus if one purchases a garage or takes a lease of a garage and the oil company imposes covenants akin to those found in *Harper's Garage*, then such restrictions will be prima facie valid. This presumption as to validity will only be rebutted if it can be shown that the restrictions are contrary to the public interest, as stated in *Cleveland Petroleum Co. Ltd* v *Dartstone* [1969] 1 All ER 201, where the Court of Appeal considered that to find otherwise would be to allow the doctrine of restraint of *trade* to be sidestepped by the adoption of a conveyancing device.

An attempt to make use of the above distinction between a person who is already in possession of their business premises entering into a solus agreement, thereby surrendering rights, and a person who enters into restrictions as they acquire their business premises can be seen in the case of *Alec Lobb (Garages) Ltd* v *Total Oil Great Britain Ltd* [1983] 1 WLR 87, where the plaintiff company was a petrol filling station. In 1969 it found itself in financial difficulties and turned to the defendants for help. This help took the form of the defendants taking a 51-year lease of the garage forecourt for £35,000 plus a nominal rent. There was an immediate lease-back arrangement whereby the directors of the plaintiff company acquired a 21-year sub-lease at a rent of £2,500 per annum, together with a solus clause whereby the plaintiffs agreed to buy all their petrol from the defendants. The reason the sub-lease was granted to the two directors of the plaintiff company was to avoid the solus clause being challenged, since if the clause was contained in what might be considered a separate transaction, namely the sub-lease, it would not be subject to the doctrine of restraint of trade.

The plaintiff company relied on an earlier decision of the Privy Council in *Amoco Australia Pty Ltd* v *Rocca Bros Motor Engineering Co. Pty Ltd* [1975] AC 561 that a lease and a lease-back were held to be a single transaction, and that, since the result of the solus clause was to render the sub-lease unenforceable, the effect was to render both transactions – that is, the lease and the sub-lease – unenforceable. This decision was followed in the *Alec Lobb* case, although the effect of the solus clause was not quite so fundamental as to render both transactions unenforceable. The Court of Appeal decided that the solus clause was severable from the sub-lease, with the result that both the lease and the sub-lease were upheld as valid but without the benefit of the solus clause.

Unconscionable terms

The principle here is all-embracing and applies to all terms in the mortgage transaction. Equity will provide relief against terms in a mortgage transaction if they are regarded as oppressive and unconscionable. As we saw earlier in *Knightsbridge Estates*, the ability of equity to interfere is based not on unreasonableness but on unconscionability, particularly in commercial transactions. One particular area that has attracted attention here is high interest rates. The modern mortgage offered by institutional lenders is quite remarkable in that banks and building societies provide an open-ended mortgage whereby they are free to increase their rates. The point is made in Gray and Gray, *Elements of Land Law*, (2009):

The modern mortgage is a quite remarkable form of transaction. In most cases in this jurisdiction the rate of interest payable by the mortgagor is not fixed throughout the loan period or for any defined period thereof, but fluctuates in accordance with the rate stipulated from time to time by the mortgagee. The open-ended nature of this contract is little short of astonishing. The borrower generally agrees to pay any rate of interest demanded by the lender.

This power to increase interest rates is not completely unfettered, though, since in *Paragon Finance plc* v *Nash* [2002] 1 WLR 685 it was stated that the discretion to increase interest rates cannot be exercised 'dishonestly, for an improper purpose, capriciously or arbitrarily'. If, however, the discretion is exercised in response to market forces, such as the Bank of England raising its base rate, then the rise cannot be challenged. Furthermore, the courts will act to declare void any transaction which they regard as 'unfair or unconscionable'.

Cityland and Property (Holdings) Ltd v *Dabrah* [1968] Ch 166

Here the mortgagor was a tenant of limited means buying the freehold land from his landlord with the help of a loan from the landlord. Not only was there unequal bargaining strength between the parties but the tenant had been threatened with eviction at the end of his lease. The landlord lent the tenant £2900 which, on the terms of the agreement, required the tenant to pay £4553 for redemption. The difference of £1653 was described as a 'premium' in lieu of interest but in fact this amounted to a capitalised interest rate of 57%. It was held that, in the circumstances, this was unfair and unconscionable and that the lender was only entitled to a reasonable rate of interest of 7% per annum.

Leaving aside the privileges afforded to the large institutional lenders, the courts are willing to intervene where there is inequality of bargaining power and unconscionable conduct between lender and borrower and to re-write the mortgage contract between the parties. This is more likely to arise between private individuals, and in the case of loans from money lenders and from the less mainstream financial institutions, where the borrower is more likely to be necessitous. In commercial transactions, the position may be very different since here the parties enter into the transaction at arm's length with their 'eyes open'. In addition, there is an element of public policy which recognises the need for lenders to maintain the value of their capital assets, particularly at times of high inflation, by way of index-linked loans. Without such a facility, the amount of venture capital required to ensure industrial and commercial development would be drained. This can be seen in the case of *Multiservice Bookbinding Ltd* v *Marden* [1979] Ch 84.

Multiservice Bookbinding Ltd v *Marden* [1979] Ch 84

In 1966 a company mortgaged its business premises for a loan of £36,000 in terms which provided that the loan could not be called in by the mortgagee, nor redeemed by the mortgagor within 10 years of the grant of the mortgage. The interest rate was to be 2% above the Minimum Lending Rate on the whole loan throughout the duration of the loan. The agreement also provided that the repayment of interest or capital would increase or decrease according to the exchange rate of the Swiss franc against the pound sterling. Ten years after the commencement of the loan, the mortgagor sought to redeem the mortgages, at which point the interest due amounted to £45,380. The mortgagor claimed that the mortgage was void and unenforceable as being contrary to public policy.

The terms of the mortgage were clearly aimed at preserving the capital value of the money lent by the mortgagee against domestic inflation and any fall of the pound sterling on the international money markets.

It was held that the index-linked money obligation was not contrary to public policy. Browne-Wilkinson J considered that the index linking was clearly aimed at preserving the real value of the money lent since otherwise the availability of loan capital would be diminished, which would not be in the public interest. The terms of the mortgage would only be objectionable if they were unfair and unconscionable. He considered that a mortgage would only be regarded as unfair and unconscionable if it was 'imposed in a morally reprehensible manner . . . in a way which affects [the mortgagee's] conscience'. Browne-Wilkinson J considered that the parties were of equal bargaining power and, whilst the terms may have been unreasonable, they were not unfair, oppressive or morally reprehensible and thus the court would not intervene to strike down the terms of the mortgage.

Whilst the interest rate cases illustrate the rule against oppressive or unconscionable mortgage agreements, it should be borne in mind that a court may set aside 'any oppressive bargain, or any advantage exacted from a man under grievous necessity': per Stuart VC in **Barrett v Hartley** (1866) LR 2 Eq 789. In **Harwood v Millars Timber Trading Co. Ltd** [1917] 1 KB 305 the court struck down a mortgage arrangement where the mortgagor had been reduced to a condition 'savouring of slavery'.

Statutory regulation of credit bargains

It should be noted before embarking on the means by which statute has interfered to control mortgage and credit agreements that such agreements are outside of the scope of the Unfair Contract Terms Act 1977.

Consumer Credit Act 1974

This Act has been amended by the Consumer Credit Act 2006, which repeals and replaces ss.137–140 of the 1974 Act by which a court could intervene and protect a borrower, if necessary by varying or re-writing the terms of an 'extortionate credit bargain'. The 2006 Act relates to second mortgages and other consumer credit agreements. First mortgages are regulated by the Financial Services and Markets Act 2000.

The 2006 Act applies to loans taken out by individuals on or after 6 April 2007 and from April 2008 applies retrospectively to existing loan agreements where there is an 'unfair credit relationship'. Section 19 of the Act inserts a new s.140A into the 1974 Act, thus it provides:

(1) The court may make an order under section 140B in connection with a credit agreement if it determines that the relationship between the creditor and the debtor arising out of the agreement (or the agreement taken with any related agreement) is unfair to the debtor because of one or more of the following –
   (a) any of the terms of the agreement or of any related agreement;
   (b) the way in which the creditor has exercised or enforced any of his rights under the agreement or any related agreement;
   (c) any other thing done (or not done) by, or on behalf of, the creditor (either before or after the making of the agreement or any related agreement).

This provision gives a court wide discretion in considering whether an agreement amounts to an unfair credit relationship and, indeed, it may look outside of the agreement in that it can take into account how the terms have been operated and applied by the creditor. Further by s.140A(4) a court has jurisdiction to make a determination even if the relationship may have ended. Section 140B gives the court a wide range of powers in relation to unfair relationships, thus it provides:

(1) An order under this section in connection with a credit agreement may do one or more of the following –
  (a) require the creditor, or any associate or former associate of his, to repay (in whole or in part) any sum paid by the debtor or by virtue of the agreement or any related agreement (whether paid to the creditor, the associate or the former associate or to any other person);
  (b) require the creditor, or any associate or former associate of his, to do or not to do (or to cease doing) anything specified in the order in connection with the agreement or any related agreement;
  (c) reduce or discharge any sum payable by the debtor or by a surety by virtue of the agreement or any related agreement;
  (d) direct the return to a surety of any property provided by him for the purposes of a security;
  (e) otherwise set aside (in whole or in part) any duty imposed on the debtor or on a surety by virtue of the agreement or any related agreement;
  (f) alter the terms of the agreement or of any related agreement;
  (g) direct accounts to be taken, or (in Scotland) an accounting to be made, between any persons.

Of particular significance is s.140B(9) which provides that if a debtor (or surety) alleges that the relationship between the creditor and debtor is unfair to the debtor, it is for the creditor to prove to the contrary, thereby providing the debtor with a significant procedural advantage. It must be emphasised, though, that the provisions contained in s.140A and s.140B do not apply to first legal mortgages of residential property.

Financial Services and Markets Act 2000

The vast majority of residential mortgages that are first mortgages are regulated by the Financial Services and Markets Act 2002 ('FSMA 2000'). The scope of the Act extends far beyond mortgages, however, and it regulates many areas of the financial services industry. In relation to mortgages the Act provides that, in relation to 'regulated mortgage contracts', anyone engaged in mortgage lending and administration must 'pay due regard to the interests of its customers and treat them fairly'.

Conformity with good practices in relation to mortgages is provided by way of the Financial Services Authority handbook, *Mortgages: Conduct of Business*, issued under the auspices of the FSMA in 2000. This provides that, in relation to regulated mortgage contracts entered into on or after 31 October 2004, firms dealing with such contracts must adhere to its formula in calculating the annual percentage rate on a mortgage and that the 'total charge for credit' must be included, including any premiums for insurance. The handbook also provides detailed guidelines for ensuring that customers are dealt with fairly in cases of arrears and repossession. Thus a firm must 'make reasonable efforts to reach an agreement with a customer over the method of repaying any payment shortfall' where a customer is in difficulty in making repayments. When such an agreement is not possible, the lender must allow the customer to remain in possession for a reasonable period so as to effect a sale, and must not repossess the property unless all reasonable attempts to resolve the position have failed.

The rights and remedies of the mortgagee of a legal mortgage

Much has been said in the popular press about the big, bad banks – however, the property-owning aspirations of the vast majority of the population have meant that obtaining and paying for a mortgage is an everyday reality, despite the emotive reactions towards lenders. As we have seen, there is nothing new here, as demonstrated by the usury laws of the past and, in the opinion of some, the present. The fact remains, though, that, whilst mortgagors require protection, so do mortgagees whose capital may be at risk. A balance therefore has to be struck between the need to protect both parties to the mortgage contract. In this section we will focus on the rights and remedies of the mortgagee when things go wrong. These rights and remedies are not just important to the mortgagee but they are vital when advising a mortgagor, since he or she needs to know how the mortgagee will deal with them and how to meet that challenge to produce the best outcome for them.

The rights and remedies of the mortgagee are heavily dependent on the circumstances of a particular case. At one end of the scale is a simple action to recover money owed, and at the other is forfeiture that results in the mortgagee not only taking possession of the property but seeking repayment of the mortgage itself.

Action on the mortgagor's personal covenant to repay

The essence of a mortgage is that it is a contract between the parties under which the mortgagor agrees to repay the sum borrowed plus interest in return for a loan. Once this term is breached by the mortgagor, the mortgagee has a right to sue the mortgagor at common law.

In the mortgage contract, the mortgagor agrees to pay the capital and interest by a certain date – the legal date for redemption – and at any time after this date has passed the mortgagee can sue. As we saw earlier, the legal date for redemption is a notional one, normally set within six months of the date of the commencement of the mortgage. Once this date has passed, the mortgagee has a right to sue on the mortgagor's covenant to repay, though the mortgagee normally defers this right whilst the mortgagor continues to repay their mortgage instalments.

Usually, suing on the covenant to repay is a mortgagee's secondary remedy and tends to arise where the mortgagee has sought possession and sale of the mortgaged property but the ultimate sale has failed to pay off the capital sum and any interest owed, in the case of a 'negative equity' type of situation. In such a situation, the mortgagee sues the mortgagor for the recovery of the balance and may obtain satisfaction against any of the mortgagor's other personal property since the action is a personal remedy of the mortgagee. This position also exposes the common misconception that a person who is living in a property with negative equity and who cannot make the mortgage repayments simply 'hands the keys over' to the bank or building society. Even if the lender takes over the property, the mortgagor is still liable on the covenant to repay since the debt is not satisfied by handing the property over. Ultimately, of course, if the mortgagor has no money or assets at all there is little the lender can do other than making the borrower bankrupt. However, it should be borne in mind that the liability of the mortgagor continues for 12 years from the date that the right to receive the money accrued by virtue of the Limitation Act 1980 s.20(1). The extended limitation period from the normal period of 6 years for contract lies in the fact that the mortgage contract taking under a deed is a speciality contract. Should the mortgagee fail to bring the action within the 12-year period then his action is statute-barred and the debt then becomes irrecoverable: *Wilkinson* v *West Bromwich Building Society* [2004] EWCA Civ 1063. Some care needs to be exercised here since any acknowledgement of the debt by the mortgagor will result in the limitation period re-starting from the date of the acknowledgement and thus can trap the unwary: s.29(5). Legal privilege does not operate here and therefore if, as in *Bradford and Bingley plc* v *Rashid* [2006] UKHL 37, a letter is sent on behalf of the mortgagor from a legal advice centre, this will amount to an acknowledgement causing the period to re-start. It should be noted that the 12-year limitation period only applies in relation to the capital owed: s.20(1). In relation to any interest owed the limitation period is six years: s.20(5).

Whilst the action is being taken for breach of a covenant within a contract, this is not an action for damages but an action for debt and, as such, the mortgagee is under no obligation to mitigate its loss.

The power of sale

Generally

The power is often expressly conferred in the mortgage contract but, whether it is or not, such a power is implied and regulated in the Law of Property Act 1925 ss.101–107. By s.101, in the absence of express contrary intention in the mortgage (s.101(4)), a mortgagee has a power of sale, provided the mortgage is made by deed and the mortgage money is due – that is, the legal date for redemption has passed: s.101(1)(i).

Once the above conditions are satisfied, then it is said that the power of sale *arises*; however, the power is only *exercisable* when one of the conditions in s.103 has been met:

(i) Notice requiring payment has been served on the mortgagor or one of two mortgagors, and default has been made in payment of the mortgage money, or part thereof, for three months after such service; or

(ii) Some interest under the mortgage is in arrear and unpaid for two months after becoming due; or

(iii) There has been some breach of some provision in the mortgage deed or in this Act . . .

Once the power of sale has arisen and become exercisable by the occurrence of one of the three events above, the mortgagee may proceed directly to sale of the whole or part of the mortgaged land. There is no requirement for the mortgagee to obtain the leave of the court and by s.104(1) the mortgagee has the full power to transfer the mortgagor's estate free from all estates, interests and rights to which the mortgage has priority, but subject to all estates, interests and rights which have priority to the mortgage.

If the mortgagee proceeds to sale without the power arising or becoming exercisable, the mortgagee, nevertheless, subject to contrary intention in the mortgage deed, has all 'the powers of disposition conferred by law on the owner of the legal mortgage'. The effect therefore is that a purchaser (or 'disposee') acquires the title and this cannot be questioned on the basis that the sale is improper. Of course, the mortgagee has acted improperly so that the mortgagor, whilst being unable to challenge the title of the purchaser, may sue the mortgagee for damages. The mortgagor's equity of redemption is thereby extinguished and, in the absence of some fraud, mistake or irregularity in the conduct of sale, they are unable to re-open the sale. Whilst this is possible in the mortgagee's right of foreclosure (see later) it is not possible in relation to sale.

The effect of a transfer of the legal estate to the purchaser operates to give the purchaser the same legal estate as that enjoyed by the mortgagor, subject to any interests that take priority to the mortgagee's mortgage. There is no obligation on the purchaser to investigate whether the mortgagee has the power to sell within the terms of s.101 and s.103 – i.e. whether it was exercised improperly or irregularly, by virtue of s.104(2)d.

Duties of the mortgagee as regards the proceeds of sale

Once the mortgagee has sold the property, they become the trustee of the proceeds of sale, so that the proceeds have to be applied according to the order laid down in s.105.

The mortgagee has to apply the proceeds of sale initially to pay off any prior mortgages and then:

(i)   in the payment of all costs, charges and expenses properly incurred by the mortgagee in effecting the sale – for example, estate agents' fees;

(ii) in the discharge of mortgage money, interests and costs, and any other money, if any, due under the mortgage;

(iii) the residue of the money received to be paid to any person entitled to the mortgaged property. That is, the mortgagee must pay the residue to any subsequent mortgagees of whom they have notice and, if there are none, to the mortgagor himself.

Duties of the mortgagee on selling the property

Whilst the mortgagee is a trustee of the proceeds of sale, he is *not* a trustee of the exercise of the power of sale itself: ***Cuckmere Brick Co. Ltd* v *Mutual Finance Ltd*** [1971] Ch 949. It should be borne in mind that the mortgagee is only intent on recovering the amount owed under the mortgage – i.e. capital and interest, plus costs. The mortgagee is not necessarily interested in obtaining the best price for the property or becoming involved in protracted negotiations with estate agents, etc. Indeed, in order to speed up the sale, they may auction the property off rather than attempting to effect a sale by private treaty. That said, the law does attempt to balance the interests of both parties and, to that extent, duties of good faith and reasonable care are imposed on the mortgagee, though as seen in ***Palk* v *Mortgage Services Funding plc*** [1993] AC 330 the mortgagee is entitled to give consideration to their own interests first, but not exclusively so.

In carrying out the sale, the mortgagee must act in good faith. Subjectively, the mortgagee's motive in selling the property is not relevant, provided the need to satisfy the mortgage debt is at least partly the reason for the sale: ***Meretz Investments NV* v *ACP Ltd*** [2007] Ch 197. Traditionally, however, a wider duty of good faith required that the mortgagee should not deal wilfully and recklessly with the property so that the interests of the mortgagor are not prejudiced: ***Kennedy* v *De Trafford*** [1897] AC 180, or calculate to cheat him, as indicated in ***Cuckmere Brick Co. Ltd***. Thus a mortgagee would be found to be in breach of this duty if they colluded with a particular purchaser so as to execute a sale at a low price, with or without providing that purchaser with a preference over other potential purchasers: ***Stockl* v *Rigura Pty Ltd*** (2004) 12 BPR 23151. In more recent years there has been a move towards a more objective view of the duty of the mortgagee so that they must take reasonable care and take due diligence in obtaining a proper price and in this respect act in good faith: ***Forsyth* v *Blundell*** (1973) 129 CLR 477.

Duty with regards to the sale price

Mortgagees have a duty of due diligence with respect to the price at which the property is sold. The general duty was set out in ***Cuckmere Brick Co. Ltd* v *Mutual Finance Ltd*** [1971] Ch 949 where Salmon LJ stated at 968 that mortgagees have a responsibility to:

> . . . take reasonable precautions to obtain the true market value of the mortgaged property at the date on which he decides to sell it.

Equally in ***Michael* v *Miller*** [2004] EWCA Civ 282 it was stated by the Court of Appeal that:

> . . . a mortgagee will not breach his duty to the mortgagor if in the exercise of his power to sell the mortgaged property he exercises his judgment reasonably; and to the extent that that judgment involves assessing the mortgage value of the mortgaged property the mortgagee will have acted reasonably if his assessment falls within an acceptable margin of error.

The mortgagee therefore is not obliged to obtain the *best* price but, on the other hand, they cannot accept *any* price. The mortgagee equally cannot adopt just any type of arrangement for selling the property and need not attempt to sell by private treaty. Inevitably, many mortgagees wanting to dispose of the property efficiently will offer the property for sale by auction and here the price may be said to reflect the market value. At the end of the day, whether reasonable steps have been taken to obtain the best price depends on the circumstances of a particular case and is a question of fact. Against this background, the mortgagee must be seen to have made an informed judgment as to the state of the property market and even sales by auction may not reflect those conditions. The mortgagee must also take into account the characteristics of the property, so that if a property has outline planning permission as regards part of the property this may well make the property inherently more valuable.

Cuckmere Brick Co. Ltd v *Mutual Finance Ltd* [1971] Ch 949

Here the mortgagee was aware that the property had planning permission attached to it for two alternative schemes – one to build houses and the other for the building of flats. The mortgagee sold the property by auction; however, the particulars of sale failed to make adequate reference to the planning permissions existing on the property. The property was sold for £44,000 but the mortgagor obtained an independent valuation that placed a price of £75,000 on the property, taking into account the planning permissions.

In the Court of Appeal it was held that whilst the mortgagee in exercising his power of sale not only had to act in good faith but also had to take reasonable care to obtain the true market value. As a consequence the Court of Appeal found that the mortgagee was in breach of his duty and was liable to the mortgagor for damages for the difference.

There is a degree of debate about the basis of liability in such a case. In *Standard Chartered Bank Ltd* v *Walker* [1982] 1 WLR 1410 Lord Denning suggested liability arose out of the law of negligence, as set out in *Donoghue* v *Stevenson* [1932] AC 562. Salmon LJ in *Cuckmere Brick Co. Ltd* also appeared to have alluded to this as the underlying basis for liability. Equally, it was stated by Slade LJ in *Bishop* v *Bonham* [1988] 1 WLR 742 that liability arises out of the contractual relationship between the parties in that it is an implied term that the mortgagor will use their best efforts to secure the best price for the mortgaged premises. The better view, however, is that liability derives from the intervention of equity that imposes a requirement of due diligence rather than a tortious duty of care. The duty here is similar to that set out in *Speight* v *Gaunt* (1883) 9 App Cas 1 where Sir George Jessel stated:

> It seems to me that on general principles a trustee ought to conduct the business of the trust in the same manner that an ordinary prudent man of business would conduct his own . . .

Translated into the duty of a mortgagee it seems that the mortgagee has to act in a prudent, business-like manner to obtain the best price that may fairly and reasonably be realised by acting with due diligence: *Matthie* v *Edwards* (1846) 2 Coll 465. The effect therefore is that the remedy, for a mortgagor who can demonstrate such a breach of duty, lies in a duty to account for the difference between the price realised and the true market value rather than in damages.

The right to possession

This is probably the most important right of the mortgagee, though the right is tempered by the fact that, if there is an existing lease on the property which the mortgagee has taken subject to or has agreed with the mortgagor, then possession is limited to the mortgagee simply being placed in the same shoes as the mortgagor in terms of being in receipt of the rents and profits due under the lease and payable to the mortgagor.

The right to possession arises because, in the case of a legal mortgage, a legal estate is conferred on the mortgagee: Law of Property Act 1925 s.87. The effect is that the mortgagee's right to possession arises as soon as the mortgage is entered into and is not dependent on any default by the mortgagor. Thus in *Four Maids Ltd* v *Dudley Marshall (Properties) Ltd* [1957] Ch 317 Harman J stated at 320 that the mortgagee 'may go into possession before the ink is dry on the mortgage unless there is something in the contract, express or by implication, whereby he has contracted himself out of that right'. It is remarkable that the right of the mortgagee to go into possession arises irrespective of whether there is any default by the mortgagor by, for example, failing to make the repayments on the mortgage. Clark LJ in *Ropaigealach* v *Barclays Bank plc* [1999] 4 All ER 235 stated at 253:

> . . . in the absence of a provision to the contrary in the mortgage, a mortgagee has a right of immediate possession (as the ink dries on the document). Although I suspect that many mortgagors would be astonished to discover that a bank which had lent them money to buy a property for them to live in could take possession of it the next day.

It would, however, be unusual for a mortgagee to take such action since its business is lending money and profiting from the interest, so it makes little sense for a mortgagee to exercise its right in this way. Possession is generally a remedy that is a precursor to the remedy of sale and indeed mortgagees generally have no interest in going to possession except to effect a sale. In any event, there are often significant disadvantages in taking possession.

Statutory limitations on the right of possession

In *Esso Petroleum Co. Ltd* v *Alstonbridge Properties* [1975] 1 WLR 1474 Walton J considered that if a mortgagor was not in default in their instalment payments, in the absence of an express term, a court would be particularly ready to find an implied term entitling the mortgagor to remain in possession, though there must be 'something upon which to hang such a conclusion in the mortgage other than the mere fact that it is an instalment mortgage'. It follows that a mortgagee can take possession without first obtaining a court order, though it would be unusual to do so. In *Quennell* v *Maltby* [1979] 1 WLR 318 Lord Denning stated at 322:

> . . . a mortgagee will be restrained from getting possession except when it is sought bona fide and reasonably for the purpose of enforcing the security and then only subject to such conditions as the court thinks fit to impose.

The discretion suggested by Lord Denning has not been without challenge and, more recently, there has been a re-affirmation of the orthodox position that a mortgagee has an absolute right to possession that derives from the fact that the mortgagee has a deemed legal estate in land, as provided in the Law of Property Act 1925 s.87, subject, of course, to the mortgage contract and the statutory protection provided by the Administration of Justice Act 1970 (AJA 1970) s.36(1).

Where the mortgaged property consists of or includes a dwelling house, the court has wide powers to provide relief to the mortgagor by way of AJA 1970 s.36, as amended by AJA 1973 s.8, which provides:

(1) Where the mortgagee under a mortgage of land which consists of or includes a dwelling-house brings an action in which he claims possession of the mortgaged property, not being an action for foreclosure in which a claim for possession of the mortgaged property

is also made, the court may exercise any of the powers conferred on it by subsection (2) below if it appears to the court that in the event of its exercising the power the mortgagor is likely to be able within a reasonable period to pay any sums due under the mortgage or to remedy a default consisting of a breach of any other obligation arising under or by virtue of the mortgage.

(2) The court –

    (a) may adjourn the proceedings; or

    (b) on giving judgment, or making an order, for delivery of possession of the mortgaged property, or at any time before the execution of such judgment or order, may –

        (i) stay or suspend execution of the judgment or order, or

        (ii) postpone the date for delivery of possession.

for such period or periods as the court thinks reasonable.

In *Royal Bank of Scotland* v *Miller* [2002] QB 255 it was held that the relevant date for determining whether there was a dwelling house was the date on which the mortgagee claims possession, not the date of the execution of the mortgage. The fact that only a small part of the building is used as a dwelling does not alter the ambit of the provision since s.39 provides that 'dwelling-house' includes 'any building or part thereof which is used as a building'. The fact that part of the premises is used as a shop, office or for trade, business or professional purposes does not prevent the premises from being a dwelling house.

As originally drafted, s.36(1) presented a problem since the court's discretion could only be exercised where it appeared to the court that the mortgagor was likely to be able within a reasonable period to pay 'any sums due under the mortgage'. In itself, the provision seems innocuous until it is realised that this expression does not refer to the actual arrears but, on the usual terms of a mortgage, once the mortgage becomes 'due' then the *whole* of the unpaid capital and interest becomes payable. An example of the application of the unamended s.36(1) can be seen in the case of *Halifax Building Society* v *Clark* [1973] Ch 307 where the mortgagee had deserted his wife and was £100 in arrears on the mortgage of the matrimonial home. The wife could have taken advantage of the right to make the mortgage repayments under the Matrimonial Homes Act 1967 s.1(5) (now the Family Law Act 1996 s.30(3)); however, the AJA 1970 s.36(1) required her to pay not just the £100 but the whole of the capital and interest 'due' under the mortgage. Since this was not possible, the building society was granted possession. Clearly, the interpretation of s.36(1) as it originally stood rendered the original intention behind s.36(1) otiose since very few people indeed could find these sums of money and, if they could, they would not be in arrears anyway! Section 8(1) of the AJA 1973 now provides that 'any sums due' is confined to the actual payments which are in arrears, so that any requirement in the mortgage agreement requiring the whole debt to be paid in the event of a default can be ignored by the court under s.36(1) as amended.

The question as to what is a 'reasonable period' for the mortgagor to be able to pay any sums under the mortgage is determined by the facts of each case. Prior to 1996, it became the practice, perpetuated by The Supreme Court Practice guidance to the judiciary, that the normal period to enable the mortgagor to repay the sums due should be at least two years. Despite the fact that s.36(1) provides no time limits, it seemed a two-year period became the norm. In *Cheltenham and Gloucester Building Society* v *Norgan* [1996] 1 All ER 449 Waite LJ considered that 'the starting point for determining the reasonable period for repayment of the outstanding arrears is the outstanding term of the mortgage'. He further stated that the court should 'pose at the outset the question: would it be possible for the mortgagor to maintain payment of the arrears by instalments over that period?'

Evans LJ concurred with the view of Waite LJ that it was appropriate to take into account the whole of the remaining part of the original term when assessing a reasonable period for payment of arrears. Evans LJ went further and suggested several relevant considerations for a court when applying its discretion under s.36:

(a) How much can the borrower reasonably afford to pay, both now and in the future?

(b) If the borrower has a temporary difficulty in meeting their obligations, how long is the difficulty likely to last?

(c) What was the reason for the arrears which have accumulated?

(d) How much remains of the original term?

(e) What are relevant contractual terms, and what type of mortgage is it, i.e. when is the principal due to be repaid?

(f) Is it a case where the court should exercise its power to disregard accelerated payment provisions (s.8 of the 1973 Act)?

(g) Is it reasonable to expect the lender, in the circumstances of the particular case, to recoup the arrears of interest (1) over the whole of the original term, or (2) within a shorter period, or even (3) within a longer period – i.e. by extending the repayment period?

(h) Are there any reasons affecting the security which should influence the length of the period for payment?

In the light of the above answers, a court can begin to formulate how to exercise its discretion on the facts of a particular case, taking into account any further matters as appropriate. That said, the court must actually define the period over which the action for possession is to be stayed and it has no jurisdiction to postpone the proceedings for an indefinite period of time: *Royal Trust Co. of Canada v Markham* [1975] 1 WLR 1416. A court may, however, adjourn proceedings in order to assess whether there is any prospect of the mortgagor paying off the arrears within a reasonable period of time. For instance, in *Skandia Financial Service Ltd v Greenfield* [1997] CLY 4248, in the case of a student studying for qualifications, the court decided to wait and see if the student at the end of her studies could secure employment which would enable her to pay off the arrears.

A further consideration in determining the reasonable period is whether the mortgaged property was intended to be sold by the mortgagor. In *Cheltenham and Gloucester Building Society plc v Krausz* [1997] 1 WLR 1558 it was held that the court had discretion to suspend an application for possession for a reasonable period in such circumstances, provided the sale would realise a sufficient sum to pay off the entire mortgage debt. Furthermore, there has to be evidence that a sale is likely to take place within the foreseeable future: *Mortgage Service Funding plc v Steele* (1996) 72 P & CR D40, and a mere intention to sell by the mortgagor is insufficient: *National and Provincial Building Society v Lloyd* [1996] 1 All ER 630.

One interesting issue with the power of the court to suspend possession proceedings under s.36 is the interaction between this and the Law of Property Act 1925 s.91(2). In re-possessing a mortgaged property, a mortgagee may well find that property values have become so depressed that, if the property was sold, the price yielded would be too low to enable the mortgagee to recover their security, the mortgage debt. This presents two problems for the mortgagor: firstly, they will continue to be liable personally for the mortgage; and, secondly, if the property values continue to deflate the balance of the mortgage debt will increase. Section 91(2) provides that, in circumstances such as these, the mortgagor himself can apply to the court for an order of sale and the court is then able to order a sale 'on such terms as it thinks fit'. The effect of this is that, in a negative equity situation, a court may suspend the mortgagee's application for possession in order for a sale to take place following a s.91(2) application by the mortgagor.

Palk v Mortgage Services Funding plc [1993] Ch 330

At the time of this case, the property market had become depressed and mortgage rates were very high. Mr and Mrs Palk ('P') had a £300,000 mortgage on their matrimonial home. They had decided to sell the house but a prospective purchaser was only willing to pay £283,000. The mortgage debt had then increased to £358,587 and so the mortgagee ('M') refused to allow the sale to go through as their security would be in jeopardy. M made an application for possession but had no intention of selling the property into the depressed market. M intended, on obtaining the property, to rent it out so as to obtain some return and eventually sell the property once the property market had picked up. Clearly, this would have an adverse effect on P since, apart from losing their home and even offsetting the rental income against their mortgage repayments, the debt would increase by £30,000 for every year the property was not sold. At the time the case came to court, the debt had increased to £409,000. Mr P was then bankrupt and Mrs P then applied for an order of sale under s.91(2), which the mortgagee resisted. Essentially, M was, at no risk to itself, speculating on the property market. The level of indebtedness against Mr and Mrs P was increasing so that, even if the market did not recover before a sale, they would be liable on their personal covenant anyway. M was in a 'win-win' situation.

The Court of Appeal decided that its discretion to order a sale under s.91(2) was not limited by the fact that there was a negative equity in the property. Further, the court's discretion was not limited by the mortgagee being deprived of its contractual rights with regard to its security and its statutory rights under AJA s.36. The Court of Appeal considered that the actions of the mortgagee were 'likely to be highly prejudicial to [Mr and Mrs P's] financial position as a borrower' and that mortgagees had a duty to be fair to the mortgagor. Nicholls VC referred to the judgment of Lord Templeman in *China and South Sea Bank Ltd v Tan Soon Gin* [1990] 1 AC 536 in which he stated at 545:

> If the creditor chose to exercise his power of sale over the mortgaged security he must sell for the current market value but the creditor must decide in his own interest if and when he should sell . . . The creditor is not obliged to do anything.

Nicholls VC continued at 337:

> But if he does take steps to exercise his rights over his security, common law and equity alike have set bounds to the extent to which he can look after himself and ignore the mortgagor's interests. In the exercise of his rights over his security the mortgagee must act fairly towards the mortgagor . . . he is not entitled to conduct himself in a way which unfairly prejudices the mortgagor.

Nicholls VC thus considered that a mortgagee 'must act fairly towards the mortgagor' despite the fact that their own interests have priority to the mortgagor. He considered that it was unfair for Mrs P to be compelled 'to underwrite the risk' the mortgagee wished to take in relation to house prices and that 'in common fairness . . . it should not be able to saddle Mrs Palk with that risk and a rising debt against her wishes'. The Court of Appeal considered that it had a wide and unfettered discretion under s.91(2) in the particular circumstances and against a background that a mortgagee owes at least some duties in law to a mortgagor. The Court of Appeal therefore directed that it should order an immediate sale to protect Mrs P from the rising mortgage debt.

Clearly, therefore, *Palk* provides the mortgagor with an important safety net by way of its discretion under s.91(2). In *Cheltenham and Gloucester Building Society plc v*

Krausz [1997] 1 WLR 1558 it was held that the court's discretion to suspend an application for possession under the AJA 1970 s.36(1) was dependent on any subsequent sale realising a sufficient sum to pay off the entire mortgage debt.

The Court of Appeal in *Krausz* doubted the decision in *Palk*. In *Krausz* Phillips LJ provided the leading judgment and considered that previously s.36(1) and s.91(2) were complementary to each other in that an application under s.91(2) would only be contemplated where the proceeds of sale exceeded the debt and that it was in these circumstances that s.36 provided the court the power to suspend possession in order for application for sale under s.91(2) to be made. He considered at 1566 that s.36 'does not empower the court to suspend possession in order to permit the mortgagor to sell the mortgaged premises where the proceeds of sale will not suffice to discharge the mortgage debt' unless the mortgagor has funds to make up the shortfall. On the face of things, *Palk* appears to be an exceptional case decided on its own extreme facts. The better position seems to be that expressed in *Krausz*, though the matter has not been completely settled and indeed *Palk* was followed in *Polonski* v *Lloyds Bank Mortgages Ltd* [1998] 1 FLR 896 where the court again reiterated its unfettered discretion to order a sale under s.91(2) and did so not on financial grounds but taking into account social considerations.

It was held in *Bank of Scotland* v *Grimes* [1985] 2 All ER 254 that s.36 applies equally to endowment mortgages as to repayment mortgages; however, it does not apply to a mortgage to secure an overdraft since here no money is due until the bank has demanded repayment of the loan: *Habib Bank Ltd* v *Tailor* [1982] 1 WLR 1218.

Before leaving the examination of s.36, one further point of limitation on its exercise needs to be considered in that the court's discretion does not operate where a mortgagee has acquired possession without a court order, as we saw earlier it is entitled to do. It is rare for mortgagees to proceed in this way since they can potentially face the sanctions of the criminal law. Thus, under the Criminal Law Act 1977 s.6(1) any person who, without lawful authority, uses or threatens violence in order to secure entry into any premises, commits an offence if there is someone present on the premises at the time who is opposed to the entry. Since it is highly likely that a mortgagor is likely to resist such an entry, mortgagees rarely take the risk of seeking possession in this way. If, however, a mortgagee does exercise their right to possession – for instance, if the premises are unoccupied – then the mortgagor cannot avail themselves of the protection of s.36 and a court is unable to exercise its discretionary powers under s.36 to stay the possession. Such was the decision in *Ropaigealach* v *Barclays Bank plc* [2000] QB 263 where the Court of Appeal held that s.36 impliedly requires a court order. The Court of Appeal considered that the common law entitlement of a mortgagee to take possession on a self-help basis emanates from the fact that the mortgagee has a legal estate in land and is entitled to possession on that basis. The effect therefore is that a mortgagee intent on taking possession can circumvent the protection provided to mortgagors by way of s.36. It should be noted also that in *Ropaigealach* the Court of Appeal considered that a mortgagee could proceed to selling the property without actually taking possession, relying on the sale to extinguish the mortgagor's equity of redemption. It is suggested that it would be rare for a mortgagee to proceed in this way since invariably the value of the property would be affected by the mortgagee not having possession, particularly if the mortgagor was in possession of the property.

The court's inherent power to grant relief

A court has an inherent equitable jurisdiction to stay possession proceedings. This discretion is based on the principle that a court will not allow a mortgagee to enforce its rights where the mortgagor is in a position to redeem their mortgage. Thus if a mortgagor is having short-term difficulties in making their repayments or where there has been some error in the banking process so that their payments have not been processed, a court will grant relief to provide them with time to sort their financial affairs out. Whilst in the past this inherent jurisdiction has been granted quite liberally, in **Birmingham Citizens Permanent Building Society v Caunt** [1962] Ch 883 it was stated that the inherent power can only operate to adjourn proceedings for a relatively short time and that this would be unlikely to be for more than 28 days.

Pre-Action Protocol for Possession Claims

The Pre-Action Protocol for Possession Claims based on Mortgage or Home Purchase Plan Arrears in Respect of Residential Property was issued by the Ministry of Justice and became applicable from 6 April 2011. The protocol, which only relates to residential property, describes the behaviour that a court expects from the parties *prior* to the start of a possession claim. The aim of the protocol is to ensure that a standard process is adopted and to encourage more pre-action contact between the lender and borrower in an effort to seek agreement between the parties and, where this cannot be reached, to enable efficient uses of the court's time and resources.

The intention is to encourage communication between the parties in a clear and fair way so as not to be misleading, particularly if the lender is aware that the borrower has difficulty in reading the information. The lender must provide the borrower with the information concerning the amount of the arrears, the total outstanding on the mortgage and whether interest or charges will be added. Guidance is provided in terms of requiring the lender to inform the borrower to consult various professionals and agencies for independent legal advice. The protocol sets various means by which the matter may be resolved in terms of instalments and the process by which the lender can proceed, together with time limits. In particular para 6.2 provides:

> If a borrower can demonstrate that reasonable steps have been or will be taken to market the property at an appropriate price in accordance with reasonable professional advice, the lender must consider postponing starting a possession claim. The borrower must continue to take all reasonable steps actively to market the property where the lender has agreed to postpone starting a possession claim.

The protocol therefore provides the borrower with a lifeline to be able to secure a sale and obtain a better price without the ensuing costs that can result from a possession claim. Indeed para 7 provides that a possession claim by a mortgagee should normally be the last resort and that such a claim should not be commenced unless all reasonable attempts to resolve the position have failed. In particular, the parties should consider whether, given the individual circumstances of the borrower and the form of the agreement, it is reasonable and appropriate to do one or more of the following: extend the term of the mortgage; change the type of mortgage; defer payment of interest due under the mortgage; capitalise the arrears; or, make use of any government forbearance initiatives in which the lender chooses to participate.

Whilst mortgagees are free to pursue possession claims, the parties must be able to explain at any hearings what actions they have taken to comply with the protocol. In fairness most reputable lenders will usually have such processes in place already; however, the penalty for non-compliance with the protocol will lie in the mortgagee being penalised in terms of costs orders by the court.

The right of foreclosure

Foreclosure is rarely used today but its effects may be drastic and draconian. It is extremely potent since the effect is to vest the mortgagor's estate in the mortgagee free from any rights of the mortgagor and, in particular, it extinguishes the mortgagor's right of redemption: Law of Property Act 1925 s.88. The right to foreclose arises after the legal date of redemption has passed. Foreclosure must be commenced by a court order whereby the mortgagee makes a request for foreclosure unless the mortgage debt is not paid by a certain date. If the debt is not paid by that date, the mortgagee obtains a foreclosure nisi, following which the mortgagor has a further period in which to pay the debt. Failure to pay by that date generates a foreclosure absolute, after which the mortgagee becomes the registered proprietor of the property, whether it is freehold or leasehold, and the totality of the mortgagor's interest is extinguished.

The draconian nature of foreclosure can be seen from the fact that a mortgage may be considerably less than the value of the property and therefore the vesting of the mortgagor's estate in the mortgagee may deprive the mortgagor of their equity in the property. It is for this reason that foreclosure is subject to statutory controls aimed at protecting the mortgagor. Thus, under the Law of Property Act 1925 s.91(2), a court may substitute a sale rather than order foreclosure. Further, the Law of Property Act 1925 s.105 provides that, should a sale occur, then any surplus is distributed to the mortgagor, just as we saw earlier under the right of the mortgagee to sell the property.

Even if a foreclosure absolute has been given, that is not the end of the matter for the mortgagor. It is possible for the action to be re-opened on an application of the mortgagor – for instance, if they obtain the financial resources to pay off the mortgage. This would not generally be possible if the mortgagee had sold the property to a third party, though even here a court technically could do so.

The fact that courts normally order a sale and the possibility of the action being re-opened have conspired to make foreclosure a right of action that is rarely pursued by mortgagees.

The effects of foreclosure on other mortgagees raise clear issues of consequence for them. If there is a mortgage created *prior* to the mortgage under which the mortgagee is applying for foreclosure, then the foreclosure will take place subject to that mortgage as it has priority. If any mortgage has been entered into *after* the mortgage under which the mortgagee is applying for foreclosure, then the foreclosure will destroy that mortgage or any subsequent mortgage. The foreclosing mortgagee will usually give notice to the subsequent mortgagees of their application for foreclosure. This will give the subsequent mortgagees the opportunity to redeem the mortgage of the foreclosing mortgagee and so protect their interest in the property. This process is sometimes referred to as 'redeeming up, foreclosing down'.

The right to appoint a receiver

A further right of the mortgagee is the right to appoint a receiver under the Law of Property Act 1925 s.101(1)(iii). The right may also be expressly granted by the mortgage document itself. A receiver is appointed to take over the management of the mortgaged property – for instance, to collect rent and income, and pay any expenses, including the mortgage debt itself. Receivers are normally appointed in relation to commercial premises and only rarely used in relation to domestic property.

The power to appoint a receiver arises and becomes exercisable in the same way as the power of sale: s.109(1) and the appointment must be made in writing. By s.109(2) the receiver is an agent of the mortgagor, *not* of the mortgagee, so that if the receiver acts negligently in the management of the mortgaged property, the mortgagee cannot be held liable for the acts of the receiver. Clearly this is a great advantage to the mortgagees.

By s.109(8) a receiver who receives income must apply the income in a particular order:

(a) the payment of all rents, taxes, rates and outgoings affecting the mortgaged property;

(b) in keeping down all annual sums or other payments, and the interest on all principal sums having priority to the mortgage;

(c) in payment of his commission and premiums for fire, life or other insurances, if any, properly payable under the mortgage;

(d) in payment of the interest accruing under the mortgage;

(e) in payment towards the principal money owed under the mortgage if so directed in writing by the mortgagee.

The rights and remedies of the mortgagee of an equitable mortgage

Essentially, the rights and remedies of a mortgagee of an equitable mortgage are the same as those for a legal mortgage, though there are some differences that need noting.

Action on the mortgagor's personal covenant to repay

The mortgagee has the right to sue the mortgagor in the same way as for legal mortgages since the liability is founded in contracts in just the same way.

The power of sale

Generally speaking, even equitable mortgages are created by deed and, if this is the case, then the power of sale exists in just the same way as for legal mortgages. If this is not the case, however, the mortgagee can apply to the court to exercise its discretion under the Law of Property Act 1925 s.91(2).

The right to possession

The right to possession may be expressly granted under the mortgage contract; however, if the mortgage has been created by way of a lease or sub-lease, then the mortgagee will have a right to possession as an equitable tenant. On the other hand, if the equitable mortgage is granted by way of a charge, since the mortgagee has no estate in land, they have no right to possession unless, again, this right is conferred by way of the mortgage contract.

The right of foreclosure

This right is applicable to an equitable mortgagee as to a legal mortgagee. It does not apply, however, where the equitable mortgage is created by way of a charge since the charge has no estate in land for the right of foreclosure to attach to.

The right to appoint a receiver

The position here is the same as for the power of sale above.

The rights of spouses and cohabitants

One particular problem that can arise in relation to mortgages is where a partner is unaware that the mortgagor is in financial difficulties and has defaulted on the mortgage repayments, so putting at risk the family home. In such cases, the law has intervened to provide them with the discretionary powers of the court in possession proceedings under the AJA 1970 s.36. It is important to understand that the situation here is not one where both spouses are co-owners of the family home, since here both parties will automatically be joined together in the possession proceedings.

The starting point for the spouse is that, at common law, a mortgagee is under no obligation to inform the spouse that his or her partner is in default on the mortgage payments. This was so held in *Hastings and Thanet Building Society* v *Goddard* [1970] 3 All ER 954, where the Court of Appeal stated that it was clearly impracticable to expect a mortgagee to keep track of the marital status of the mortgagors and their spouses, cohabitants or civil partners. Spouses and civil partners fall within the same legislation, as do cohabitees, though the rules are slightly different here. The Court of Appeal also stated that, where a mortgagor's spouse is not a joint tenant of the property, his or her statutory rights of occupation of the matrimonial home were not binding on the mortgage. The practical effect of this decision is that, if a spouse only discovers that his or her partner is in substantial arrears of the mortgage repayments very late in the action for possession taken by the mortgagee, then he or she may well be precluded from invoking the court's discretionary powers under the AJA 1970 s.36.

The common law principles set out in *Goddard* have been mitigated by subsequent statutory provisions. Thus under the Family Law Act 1996 ('FLA 1996'), as amended by the Civil Partnership Act 2004, certain 'connected persons' may apply for relief under the AJA 1970 s.36. By the FLA 1996 s.54(5), a connected person is the mortgagor's spouse, civil partner or cohabitant. Such connected persons are, by s.55(1) and s.55(2), entitled to apply to the court to be made a party to any possession proceedings brought by the mortgagee, provided the circumstances set out in s.55(3) are satisfied. These are:

(a) the connected person is enabled by s.30(3) or s.30(b) or by section 30(3) or (6) as applied by section 35(13) or section 36(13), to meet the mortgagor's liability under the mortgage;

(b) he has applied to the court before the action is finally disposed of in that court; and

(c) the court sees no special reason against his being made a party to the action and is satisfied –
   (i) that he may be expected to make such payments or do such things in or towards satisfaction of the mortgagor's liabilities or obligations as might affect the outcome of the proceedings; or
   (ii) that the expectation of it should be considered under section 36 of the Administration of Justice Act 1970.

The FLA 1996 s.30(1) confers on a spouse rights where that spouse is entitled to occupy the home by virtue of any beneficial estate or interest or by virtue of some other piece of legislation, and that the other spouse is not so entitled to occupy the home by virtue of such beneficial interests, etc. The rights conferred on the spouse are set out in s.30(2) and form the so-called 'matrimonial home rights' of the spouse, stereotypically the wife. These are:

(a) a right not to be evicted or excluded if she is already in occupation; and

(b) a right with the leave of the court, to enter and occupy if not already in occupation.

The rights above do not apply to any other dwellings, only the dwelling that is or is intended to be the matrimonial home: s.30(7). The matrimonial home rights are brought to an end by the death of a spouse or the termination of the marriage (or civil partnership).

By the FLA 1996 s.30(3) a spouse who falls within the above criteria is entitled to make payments towards the mortgage repayments, and by s.55 that spouse is then entitled to be joined into the possession proceedings. By this process, a spouse is able to step into the proceedings and stave off any possession proceedings initiated by the mortgagee.

These processes are all well and good, but they do not, of themselves, solve the problem where a spouse is completely unaware of what has been taking place between the other spouse and the mortgagee bank or building society. This is important since, by s.55(3)b, if the matter has already been disposed of by the court before that spouse can intervene, then he or she will be deprived of any discretionary relief under the AJA 1970 s.36. In order to overcome this situation, any mortgagee seeking to enforce its security over the home must first serve notice on a spouse who has protected their matrimonial home rights by way of a notice (in registered land) or a Class F land charge (in unregistered land): s.56. By this process, the spouse is able at least to be joined into the proceedings for possession and have an opportunity to protect his or her rights so as not to lose their home.

The above procedures apply to both married persons and those in a civil partnership; however, in relation to cohabitees, the statutory rights of occupation are more limited. The FLA1996 s.62 describes cohabitants as two persons living together as 'husband and wife or as if they were civil partners'. As before, a court can make an order providing the applicant partner is not entitled to occupy the home by virtue of a beneficial estate or interest, contract or by any other piece of legislation. Co-owners, therefore, are excluded since they are automatically joined into the possession proceedings anyway. An order under s.36(5) provides the court with the power to give a cohabitant a right not to be evicted or excluded from the property and a right to enter and occupy the home. Also by s.36(5), a court may make an order excluding the owning cohabitant from the property. These orders are, of course, made against the owning cohabitant; however, where the owning cohabitant is the subject of possession proceedings then the other cohabitant may also be brought within those proceedings by virtue of s.30(13) and s.55(3)a.

Clearly, cohabitation is a very fluid relationship and, in determining whether to make an order under s.36(5), a court can test the permanency of the relationship by reference to a set of circumstances set out in s.36(6). These include the nature and duration of the relationship; the housing needs and resources of the parties; whether there are any children and the health, safety and wellbeing of any child; the conduct of the parties and, if they have ceased to cohabit, the length of time that has elapsed since the parties ceased living together. In particular, the Domestic Violence, Crime and Victims Act 2004 s.2(2) provides that, in considering the circumstances in s.36(6), a court should have regard to the level of commitment involved in the relationship.

In terms of making an order giving a cohabitant a right to occupy the home, etc., the rights here are far less than they are for married partners, where the occupation orders may last forever. In the case of cohabitants, however, an order of the court may only last for six months, subject to a single extension of another period of six months; thus the maximum period is for one year only: s.36(10). Furthermore, no order can be made after the death of either of them: s.36(a).

The difficulty for cohabitees in mortgage possession proceedings is that, whilst they can avail themselves of the discretionary power of the AJA 1970 s.36 via the FLA s.55(3), they are not able to protect their occupation rights by way of either a Class F land charge or a notice in the register of title. There is thus no incumbent duty on the mortgagee to serve notice of the impending possession proceedings, with the result that a non-owning cohabitee is vulnerable to such proceedings.

Undue influence

Equity has always been more flexible in the way it grants or refuses relief. While the common law required concepts to be strictly defined, this was never the case in equity which, partly because it was discretionary and partly because it acted according to the principles of good conscience, developed concepts that fell short of the requirements of the common law. Undue influence was defined in *Allcard* v *Skinner* (1887) 36 ChD 145 as some unfair and improper conduct, some coercion from outside, some overreaching, some form of cheating and generally, though not always, some personal advantage obtained by the guilty party where equity would grant relief from a contract that had been entered into because improper pressure had been placed on one of the parties.

With undue influence, the courts will intervene where a relationship between the two parties has been exploited by one party in order to gain an unfair advantage. It follows that the exploitation can arise where there is an abuse of a particular confidence placed in a party or where that party is in a position of dominance over the victim. It should be stressed, however, that with regard to the latter category, it was held in *Goldsworthy* v *Brickell* [1987] 1 All ER 853 that domination is not a prerequisite of undue influence and that this was merely an example of conduct that might amount to undue influence. In the case of *Bank of Credit and Commerce International SA* v *Aboody* [1990] 1 QB 923 it was held that, whatever category of undue influence is alleged, it is a requirement that the transaction entered into must have been to the manifest disadvantage of the victim, though this must now be read in the light of the House of Lords' decision in *Barclays Bank plc* v *O'Brien and Another* [1993] 4 All ER 417, *CIBC Mortgages plc* v *Pitt* [1993] 4 All ER 433 and the case of *Royal Bank of Scotland* v *Etridge (No. 2)* [2001] 4 All ER 449 ('*Etridge No. 2*').

Undue influence has arisen on many occasions where a mortgagor has claimed that the mortgage against him or her is voidable because of the operation of this equitable concept. The undue influence might arise directly from the mortgagee or by way of a third party. In the latter case, it may arise where a wife has been unduly influenced by her husband to sign a charge over the matrimonial home that is jointly owned or where she acts surety or guarantor.

In examining whether a mortgage can be set aside for undue influence it should be noted that undue influence may be either actual or presumed. In *BCCI* v *Aboody* [1990] 1 QB 923 the Court of Appeal adopted the following classification:

(a) Class 1: actual undue influence;

(b) Class 2: presumed undue influence, which had two sub-classifications.

In *O'Brien* the Class 2 presumed undue influence was further recognised as being sub-divided into types 2A and 2B. This classification was also broadly recognised in *Etridge No. 2* where Lord Nicholls stated:

Equity identified broadly two forms of unacceptable conduct. The first comprises overt acts of improper pressure or coercion such as unlawful threats . . . The second form arises out of a relationship between two persons where one has acquired over another a measure of influence, or ascendancy, of which the ascendant person then takes unfair advantage . . . In cases of this latter nature the influence one person has over another provides scope for misuse without any acts of persuasion. The relationship between the two individuals may be such that, without more, one of them is disposed to agree a course of action proposed by the other. Typically this occurs when one person places trust in another to look after his affairs and interests, and the latter betrays this trust by preferring his own interests. He abuses the influence he has acquired.

On this basis, one can begin to examine the nature of undue influence by dividing the subject into two areas: actual and presumed undue influence. It should be noted, however, that Lord Nicholls did not approve of this way of classifying undue influence on the grounds that he considered it tended to confuse the issues of definition and the requirements of evidence or proof. Moreover, he disapproved of dividing presumed undue influence into two further subdivisions, stating that this tended to 'add mystery rather than illumination'. The reasoning behind this re-evaluation is that the expression 'presumed' relates to an evidential requirement and does not point to a conclusion that there was 'undue' influence. Whether or not influence is undue has to be evidentially ascertained from the facts. Bearing in mind this reservation, it is nevertheless a convenient tool in understanding the concept of undue influence to divide the concept into two: actual and presumed undue influence.

Actual undue influence

In this classification it is necessary for the claimant to prove affirmatively that the wrongdoer exerted undue influence on the complainant to enter into a particular transaction which is thus impugned. This type of undue influence arises where there is no special relationship between the parties so that there is no abuse of a particular confidence.

The leading case on this area is that of **Williams v Bayley** (1866) LR 1 HL 200, where a father, to save his son from being prosecuted and possibly transported for giving his bank promissory notes on which he had forged his father's signature, was forced to give security for the debts of the son. It was held that the father's agreement had been extracted by virtue of undue influence being exerted on the father. The agreements were held to be invalid.

Other examples of such undue influence include taking advantage of persons acting under religious delusions, as in **Norton v Reilly** (1764) 2 Eden 286; or a young man's mentor influencing him to incur liabilities, as in **Smith v Kay** (1859) 7 HLC 750.

In **National Westminster Bank plc v Morgan** [1985] 1 All ER 821 it was held that in presumed undue influence (i.e. formerly Class 2 undue influence) a claim to set a transaction aside for undue influence could not succeed unless the claimant could prove that the transaction was manifestly disadvantageous. This requirement was taken up and applied to cases of actual undue influence (i.e. formerly Class 1 undue influence) by the Court of Appeal in **BCCI v Aboody**. In **CIBC v Pitt**, Lord Browne-Wilkinson did not agree with **Aboody** and considered the requirement that the undue influence had to be manifestly disadvantageous, as laid down in **Morgan**, had no application to cases of actual undue influence. He stated:

> Actual undue influence is a species of fraud. Like any other victim of fraud, a person who has been induced by undue influence to carry out a transaction which he did not freely and knowingly enter into is entitled to have that transaction set aside as of right . . . A man guilty of fraud is no more entitled to argue that the transaction was beneficial to the person defrauded than a man who has procured a transaction by misrepresentation. The effect of the wrongdoer's conduct is to prevent the wronged party from bringing a free will and properly informed mind to bear on the proposed transaction, which accordingly must be set aside in equity as a matter of justice.

Thus, where there is no special relationship and the claimant proves actual undue influence, they are not under a further burden of proving that the transaction induced by this undue influence was manifestly disadvantageous to them and they may have it set aside as of right. *Etridge No. 2* makes it clear that the undue influence, whilst not being manifestly disadvantageous, must not be innocuous. The onus of proof is, however, on the claimant to prove the presence of undue influence. This position was affirmed by the House of Lords in *Etridge No. 2*, where it was stated that the question as to whether a transaction has been brought about by the exercise of undue influence is one of fact. The evidence to discharge this burden of proof depends on various factors, such as the nature of the alleged undue influence, the personalities of the parties, their relationship to one another, the 'extent to which the transaction cannot readily be accounted for by the ordinary motives of ordinary persons in that relationship, and all the circumstances of the case'. This is the general rule regarding the burden of proving the existence of undue influence.

Thus it is not sufficient simply to show 'influence'. The claimant must prove that the influence has been 'undue' as well. In *Dunbar Bank plc* v *Nadeem and Another* [1998] 3 All ER 876, it was stated *obiter* that it is not enough simply to show that one party dominated another, but that there had to be an actual unfair advantage exacted over the victim. In this case the Court of Appeal decided that there was no actual undue influence since there was a 'clear finding that Mr Nadeem did not take unfair advantage of his position. Seen through his eyes, the transaction was obviously beneficial to his wife and was intended to be for her benefit.' This approach, however, had the great danger of being too subjective as regards the intentions of the dominant party. Simply because the dominating party considers the transaction to be of benefit to the victim, should this necessarily be so? There is a certain arrogance in assuming that the dominating party knows what is beneficial or advantageous for the victim. The test set out in *Etridge No. 2* provides a more objective assessment of what is 'undue'.

This type of undue influence is becoming much rarer today since there is a continuing blurring of this area with duress. For example, in *Flower* v *Sadler* (1882) 10 QBD 572 a promise to pay a sum of money extracted by the threat of criminal prosecution was held to be invalid for undue influence. Today such conduct would no doubt fall within the ambit of duress. Similarly, the case of *Williams* v *Bayley* would probably be considered to be a case of duress today.

Presumed undue influence

As stated earlier, the Court of Appeal in *BCCI* v *Aboody*, approved by the House of Lords in *O'Brien* and *Etridge No. 2*, established that a confidential relationship could arise in two ways, thus creating two sub-classes.

Class 2A Presumed undue influence

Certain types of relationship automatically presume the existence of undue influence: for instance, the relationship between trustee and beneficiary (*Benningfield* v *Baxter* (1886) 12 App Cas 167); solicitor and client (*Wright* v *Carter* [1903] 1 Ch 27); parent and child (*Powell* v *Powell* [1900] 1 Ch 243); religious leader or adviser and disciple or parishioner (*Allcard* v *Skinner* (1887) 36 ChD 145). Not surprisingly, therefore, Class 2A presumed undue influence is unusual in mortgage transactions, but not unknown.

The use of the expression 'presumption' here is one which describes the shift in the evidential burden of proof on the question of fact. The claimant has to show, first, that there is a relationship of trust or confidence between him/herself and the wrongdoer and, second, the existence of a transaction which calls for an explanation.

On proof of these two matters there is an inference that the transaction has arisen from undue influence and the evidential burden of proof shifts to the defendant to provide evidence that counters the presumption. Not every type of fiduciary relationship gives rise to such a presumption since it has to be shown that the confidence placed in the wrongdoer gives that person some authority over the victim or that it creates an obligation on the wrongdoer to offer or recommend the victim to seek independent advice. The person in whom the confidence is reposed is in such a position that that person has an obvious opportunity of enhancing their position, to the extent that they must prove that they have not exercised their position of influence in that manner.

There is thus no need for the victim to prove that undue influence has actually taken place, since all they have to do is to prove that a confidential relationship has arisen and that the transaction itself calls for an explanation. Once the victim has done that, a rebuttable evidential presumption of undue influence automatically arises at law. The burden of proof then shifts to the wrongdoer to prove that the victim entered into the transaction of their own volition – for instance, by showing that the victim had received independent advice. The court, in turn, then has to draw 'the appropriate inferences of fact upon a balanced consideration of the whole of the evidence at the end of the trial in which the burden of proof rested upon the plaintiff' (*per* Lord Nicholls in *Etridge No. 2*). The second requirement therefore is an evidential presumption which can be rebutted by the so-called wrongdoer.

In *Etridge No. 2* it was considered that it is only in Class 2A undue influence that a true presumption of influence arises. It was stated that 'the law has adopted a sternly protective attitude' towards the types of relationship described above, where one party acquires influence over another vulnerable person. It is sufficient for the claimant to prove the existence of such a relationship and that the the the transaction 'calls for an explanation'. 'Alternatively the claimant must demonstrate that the transaction is not one that is readily explicable by the relationship of the parties.' The second presumption found in Class 2A undue influence is a necessary constraint on the width of this type of undue influence. Thus Lord Nicholls stated in *Etridge No. 2*:

> The second pre-requisite . . . is good sense. It is a necessary limitation upon the width of the first requisite. It would be absurd for the law to presume that every gift by a child to a parent, or every transaction between a client and his solicitor or between a patient and his doctor, was brought about by undue influence unless the contrary is affirmatively proved . . . The last would be rightly opened to ridicule, for transactions such as these are unexceptionable. They do not suggest that something may be amiss. So something more is needed before the law reverses the burden of proof, something which calls for an explanation.

Despite the definitive statements by Lord Nicholls, individual cases continue to throw up anomalies, such as that of *Leeder* v *Stevens* [2005] EWCA Civ 50. The facts of the case are that Denis Stevens, a married man, for many years had an affair with Maureen Leeder. Maureen owned a house worth £70,000 subject to a mortgage of £5,000. The couple discussed marriage and, as part of these discussions, Denis offered to pay off the mortgage, in return for which the house would be transferred into joint names. Subsequently, Maureen agreed to the transaction and the house was transferred into joint names as tenants in common in equal shares. At the time of the transfer a Deed of Trust was drawn up under which either party could force a sale of the property, subject to a right of pre-emption (a right of first refusal). Soon after the transfer, Denis forced a sale and Maureen argued that the Deed of Trust should be set aside on the grounds of undue influence. Her action failed at first instance and she appealed to the Court of Appeal.

It was held that this was a case of presumed undue influence and that there was no evidential reason to rebut it. The decision is remarkable in that in *Etridge No. 2* it was clearly stated that the presumption of undue influence can only arise in two situations: first, where the relationship is one in which the law presumes the existence of undue influence; second, where the wrongdoer has acquired an influence over a vulnerable party so that the existence of the relationship 'calls for an explanation'. The Court of Appeal considered that the relationship which exists between an engaged couple falls within the type of relationship that presumes undue influence. The court considered that the relationship between Denis and Maureen was analogous to that position. This decision appears to be at odds with *Etridge No. 2* itself since it was held in the House of Lords that a presumption of undue influence does not apply to a husband and wife relationship. If that is the case, then it is clearly anomalous that such a presumption should exist in the case of an engaged couple. This would mean that their relationship, in terms of presumed undue influence, would change, possibly for the worse, simply because they became married. Furthermore, the relationship of an engaged couple did not fall within Lord Nicholls's examples of relationships that give rise to presumed undue influence in *Etridge No. 2*. The decision also appears to contradict the earlier Court of Appeal decision in *Zamet v Hyman* [1961] 3 All ER 933 where the court considered that the presumption of undue influence would not arise in the case of engaged couples unless the transaction was clearly unfavourable to the party attempting to avoid the transaction or, in modern parlance, the transaction 'calls for an explanation'.

Class 2B Presumed undue influence

Where there is no special relationship that falls within Class 2A giving rise to an automatic presumption of undue influence, it may nevertheless be the case that the victim can prove as a fact the existence of a relationship in which they have placed a trust and confidence in the wrongdoer. The victim will therefore be able to have the transaction set aside merely by proving that they have placed a trust and confidence in the wrongdoer, without the need to prove that an actual undue influence arose.

The husband and wife relationship is a good example of a category of relationship within Class 2B that does not exist per se but which has to be proved as a fact. This was established in *Howes v Bishop* [1909] 2 KB 390 and *Bank of Montreal v Stuart* [1911] AC 120, and again confirmed in *Midland Bank plc v Shephard* [1988] 3 All ER 17. In *Kingsnorth Trust Ltd v Bell* [1986] 1 All ER 423 the wife was able to prove undue influence as a fact where the husband was regarded as an agent of the bank in procuring the agreement of the wife to a particular transaction. Similarly, in *BCCI v Aboody* a wife was able to avoid liability to the bank in respect of a surety transaction, which she was induced to enter by her husband, on the basis that the bank had notice, actual or constructive, of the husband's actions in either exercising undue influence over his wife or misrepresenting the extent of his indebtedness to the bank.

But why doesn't the relationship fall into Class 2A? In *Yerkey v Jones* (1939) 63 CLR 649 Dixon J explained that the courts were not blind to the opportunities that a husband may have in unfairly influencing the decisions of his wife. The actions of a wife, however, could also arise from motives of affection or some other such reason and there was nothing strange or unusual in that. Thus whilst there is no presumption of undue influence in such a relationship, the court will note, as a matter of fact, the opportunities a husband may have in abusing his wife's confidence in him. This is taken into account alongside all the other evidence put forward in the case.

While the cases which cause most concern arise out of the husband and wife relationship, Class 2B undue influence may arise in any transaction where the victim can prove as a fact that when he or she entered into a transaction there was a relationship of trust and confidence between the victim and the wrongdoer. This being done, a court will presume that the victim has been subject to undue influence.

Lloyds Bank Ltd v *Bundy* [1975] QB 326

The defendant was an elderly farmer whose only asset comprised a farmhouse that was also his home. The defendant shared the same bank as his son and his son's company. The company ran into financial difficulties and so the defendant gave a guarantee in respect of the company to the bank, the guarantee being secured by a charge over the farmhouse. In fact, the fortunes of the company failed to improve and the defendant was then approached by his son and the manager of the bank, who informed him that the bank was unwilling to continue to support the company without additional security. In response to this approach, and without seeking independent advice, the defendant extended the guarantee and with it the charge over his property. Eventually, a receiver was appointed in respect to the company and, as a result, the bank sought to enforce its security against the farmhouse. The defendant pleaded undue influence, based on the fact that there was a long-standing relationship between himself and the bank, and as such he had placed confidence in it in that he looked to the bank for financial advice. Clearly, the bank, since it had a financial interest in the company, could not present itself as being able to give independent financial advice. It was incumbent upon the bank to advise the defendant to seek such advice, which it failed to do, and therefore it could not rebut the presumption of undue influence.

It has to be stated that the ***Bundy*** case is a somewhat exceptional one and turns on its own facts, since the presumption of undue influence does not normally arise between banks and their customers.

National Westminster Bank plc v *Morgan* [1985] 1 All ER 821

A husband and wife were the joint owners of the family home, which was mortgaged to a building society. The husband became unable to meet the mortgage repayments because his business began to fail. When the building society began to take proceedings for possession of the property in order to enforce the mortgage, the husband decided to seek new finance from the bank, which had agreed to help. The bank manager then called at the family home to have the relevant documents executed by the wife, who did not receive any independent legal advice before signing the new mortgage. Although the husband was initially present, the wife insisted that she wished to discuss the mortgage with the bank manager privately. During her discussions with the manager, she stated that she had little confidence in her husband's business ventures and that she did not want the legal charge to cover her husband's business liabilities. The manager assured her, incorrectly, that the legal charge would cover only the refinancing of the mortgage and that it did not extend to the business liabilities. The financial difficulties of the husband and wife continued and they again fell into arrears with the mortgage repayments, although the husband's business was not in debt to the bank. The bank sought to enforce their security on the charge by seeking possession of the property. Soon afterwards the husband died. The wife then appealed against the order for possession on the grounds that the mortgage had been obtained by virtue of undue influence and therefore the legal charge should be set aside. The Court of Appeal allowed her appeal but she failed in the House of Lords.

The House of Lords rejected the contention that undue influence arose simply out of the relationship of the parties and that the presence of such undue influence allowed the transaction to be set on one side. Lord Scarman (who delivered the only judgment) referred to the judgment of Sir Eric Sachs in ***Lloyds Bank Ltd*** v ***Bundy***, where he considered that undue influence does not simply arise because of the relationship of banker and client, as in a simple case of the bank going about its normal duties where it is, for instance, obtaining a guarantee and in the course of that explains the legal effect of the guarantee and the sums involved. For the presumption of undue influence to arise, the bank must normally 'cross the line' into the area of confidentiality. Lord Scarman did not approve of the latter expression, preferring to find whether or not a dominating influence was present by a 'meticulous examination of the facts', an expression used by Sir Eric Sachs in determining whether or not an area of confidentiality had been crossed into. He considered that, on the facts, the bank had not exercised a dominant influence over the wife.

Lord Scarman decided that on a 'meticulous examination of the facts' the bank in the *Morgan* case had not crossed the line to where a presumption of undue influence existed. In any event, he considered that the presence of this presumption was not, of itself, sufficient. He stated that one also had to show that the transaction was, of itself, wrongful in that it constituted a manifest disadvantage to the person influenced. He found that the transaction had not been unfair to the wife; indeed, quite the contrary, since it had allowed Mr and Mrs Morgan to stay in their house on terms that were not substantially different from those of the building society. The transaction, if anything, was to their advantage and thus the bank had no duty to ensure that Mrs Morgan received independent advice.

But what of the effect of *Etridge No. 2* on this analysis of presumed undue influence? *Etridge No. 2* provides authority that presumed undue influence merely shifts the evidential burden of proof from the claimant to the wrongdoer. It is *not* a presumption that undue influence exists per se, but rather that the burden of explaining why the transaction was not caused by undue influence is shifted to the wrongdoer. The wrongdoer may therefore dispel any notion of undue influence by producing evidence that the transaction was properly entered into. Thus the 'presumption' of undue influence, by way of either a 'relationship' (as in Class 2A cases) or demonstrating a relationship of trust and confidence (as in Class 2B cases), arises in circumstances that require 'explanation', for instance because the transaction is manifestly disadvantageous. This then shifts the burden of proof on to the wrongdoer to provide an explanation for the transaction. If the wrongdoer is unable to discharge this burden of proof by providing an explanation then undue influence will be found to exist.

From this it may be seen that the difference between the 'old' Class 2A and 2B categories is that, in the former, the relationship of trust and confidence cannot be disputed. In the latter, the wrongdoer is entitled to provide evidence that no such relationship existed, which in turn means it is unnecessary to provide an explanation for the transaction.

The requirement of 'manifest disadvantage' and transactions 'calling for an explanation'

To what extent is 'manifest disadvantage' a necessary prerequisite to establishing presumed undue influence? As already stated, there are two prerequisites that bring about a shift in the evidential burden of proof. To reiterate, the first is that the complainant must have placed trust and confidence in the other party, or that the other party had influence over the complainant. The second prerequisite is that the transaction is not one which is explicable by the relationship of the parties to each other. In the past this second prerequisite was proved by the complainant proving the transaction was to his or her manifest disadvantage. This, as seen in *Morgan*, was therefore a significant factor in limiting the application of undue influence. The courts would nevertheless enforce a transaction where the potential benefits outweighed the disadvantages.

The requirement to prove manifest disadvantage is a contentious one and has been much criticised. It appears to derive from the case of ***Allcard v Skinner*** (1887) 36 ChD 145, where Lindley LJ indicated that the mere existence of influence was not enough – it had to be undue.

The intention behind this prerequisite is to limit the first prerequisite so that undue influence does not arise from innocuous transactions that take place within the trust and confidence relationship. Not to do so would mean that every transaction between persons in such a relationship, such as children and parents, patient and doctor, client and solicitor and so on, stood to be overturned on grounds of undue influence. Something more is required before a court will reverse the burden of proof. There must be a transaction that requires an 'explanation' as to why the weaker party entered into the transaction. As Nicholls LJ in ***Etridge No. 2*** indicates:

> . . . the greater the disadvantage to the vulnerable person, the more cogent must be the explanation before the presumption will be regarded as rebutted.

Lord Nicholls considered that the label 'manifest disadvantage', as used by Lord Scarman in explaining the second prerequisite, was too limited and gave rise to misunderstandings; indeed, he considered that it was not being used in a manner intended by Lord Scarman. In the context of a wife guaranteeing her husband's debts, one had to consider whether such a transaction by which she not only guaranteed the debts but charged her share of the matrimonial home was to her manifest disadvantage. He stated that, in the narrow sense, such a transaction is clearly or 'manifestly' disadvantageous to the wife. She undertakes a 'serious financial obligation' for which 'she personally receives practically nothing'. However, in the wider sense, there are advantages to the wife in embarking on such a transaction. If the husband's business is the provider of the main income, the wife has an interest in supporting her husband.

Lord Nicholls considered neither the narrow nor the wider interpretations to be correct in deciding whether or not the transaction is disadvantageous to the wife. He considered that the label 'manifest disadvantage' should be abandoned in favour of the test set out by Lindley LJ in ***Allcard* v *Skinner***, above, and adopted by Lord Scarman in ***Morgan***.

In relation to husband and wife cases, Lord Nicholls considered that, in the ordinary course of things, a guarantee by the wife should not be regarded as a transaction that is explicable only on the basis that it has been procured by undue influence on the part of the husband, unless there is proof to the contrary. The fact that wives enter into such transactions with a pessimistic view of the outcome does not provide prima facie evidence of undue influence. His conclusion is salutary:

> Wives frequently enter into such transactions. There are good and sufficient reasons why they are willing to do so, despite the risks involved for them and their families. They may be enthusiastic. They may not. They may be less optimistic than their husbands about the prospects of the husbands' businesses. They may be anxious, perhaps exceedingly so. But this is a far cry from saying that such transactions are to be regarded as prima facie evidence of the exercise of undue influence by their husbands.

Lord Nicholls states this situation as applying 'in the ordinary course of things' and he acknowledges that there are cases where a husband deliberately misleads his wife as to the proposed transaction, so that he prefers his own interests to those of his wife. Here the husband abuses his position and the influence he has over his wife and 'fails to discharge the obligation of candour and fairness he owes a wife who is looking to him to make the major financial decisions'.

Rebutting the presumption – what is the effect of independent advice?

While it has been seen that the presumption of undue influence may be rebutted by the person having the dominating influence showing that the other party had had access to independent advice or at least been in a position to exercise free judgment, such advice is not always successful in saving the situation. It must be competent advice and made in the knowledge of all the facts of the case: *Inche Noriah v Shaik Allie Bin Omar* [1929] AC 127.

The weight the court must place on the advice depends on the circumstances. Ordinarily, advice from a solicitor or a financial adviser might normally be expected to make the complainant aware of the nature of the transaction about to be entered into. This does not necessarily preclude undue influence since a person who is aware of the nature of the transaction may still be acting under the influence of another. Whether or not independent advice precludes the effects of undue influence is a question of fact to be decided by reference to the evidence of the facts of the case.

The effect of undue influence on third parties

So far, the examination of undue influence has been looked at in the context of where the victim is attempting to avoid a transaction entered into with the wrongdoer. However, as alluded to above, it sometimes arises, particularly in the context of a husband and wife relationship, that the victim is persuaded to enter into a guarantee or surety contract with a bank or some other mortgagee on the basis of some undue influence, misrepresentation or other legal wrong, not by the bank or creditor, but by some third party – for instance, a husband. The question arises, therefore, to what extent that undue influence will affect the transaction between the victim and the bank/creditor. If one adopts the usual rule of privity of contract, the actions of the wrongdoer should have no effect on the transaction; however, in certain instances, the courts have allowed the victim to have the transaction set aside.

The law whereby mortgagees have been affected by the actions of the wrongdoer and thus been unable to enforce the surety contract/guarantee has evolved in three phases that encompass different approaches – agency, special equity and the doctrine of notice. The first two have now been laid to rest and rejected in *Barclays Bank plc v O'Brien* where Lord Browne-Wilkinson considered the correct approach in protecting the interests of wives was by way of a more wide-ranging doctrine of notice.

Barclays Bank plc v O'Brien [1993] 4 All ER 417

Mr O'Brien wanted to increase the overdraft facility of a company in which he was a shareholder. The bank agreed a loan of £120,000 that was to be guaranteed by Mr O'Brien, his liability in turn being secured by a second charge over the matrimonial home, which was jointly owned by Mr O'Brien and his wife. The bank manager gave instructions for the relevant documents to be prepared, including a legal charge to be signed by both Mr O'Brien and his wife, together with a guarantee to be signed by the husband alone. Instructions were also given that both Mr O'Brien and his wife should be advised as to the nature of the transactions and that, if they had any doubts, they should obtain independent advice. These instructions were not complied with and subsequently both husband and wife signed the documents without reading them. The company's indebtedness then increased beyond the agreed limit and the bank took proceedings to enforce its security against the husband and wife. In her defence, the wife contended that her husband had put undue pressure on her to sign the surety agreement and, second, that her husband had misrepresented the effect of the legal charge in that she believed it was limited to a sum of £60,000 over three weeks.

> The judge at first instance, and the Court of Appeal and House of Lords, dismissed the wife's contention that she had been subject to undue influence by her husband. The case therefore turned on the misrepresentation of the husband as to the extent and the duration of the liability and whether the bank's ability to enforce the surety contract against the wife was prejudiced by the actions of her husband.
>
> On the facts, the bank was aware that the parties were husband and wife and thus was put on notice as to the circumstances in which the wife would have been asked to stand as surety. The bank failed to warn the wife of the risks she ran in entering into the surety contract or as to her potential liability in respect of her husband's debts. Furthermore, the bank had not advised her to seek independent legal advice. On this basis, the bank was fixed with constructive notice of the misrepresentation made by the husband to induce his wife into the surety contract and therefore the wife was entitled to have the legal charge on the matrimonial home securing her husband's liability to the bank set aside.

Lord Browne-Wilkinson thus considered that the key to whether a mortgagee is bound by the wrongdoings of the mortgagor ('principal debtor'), and thereby unable to enforce security against a guarantor or surety, lay in whether the mortgagee had actual or constructive notice of the equitable right of the surety to have the transaction set aside on the basis of the mortgagor's wrongdoings. He stated that 'the doctrine of notice lies at the heart of equity' and 'provides the key to finding a principled basis for the law'. He went on to state that where there are two innocent parties, both of whom enjoy rights, the earlier right prevails against the later one if the holder of that later right has actual notice of the earlier one or has constructive notice of it and would have discovered it by making proper inquiries. Translating this to the husband and wife scenario, where the wife has agreed to stand as surety for the debts of her husband by virtue of some undue influence or misrepresentation, then the mortgagee will be deemed to have constructive notice of the equitable right of the wife to have the surety agreement set aside, provided the circumstances are such as to put the mortgagee on inquiry. Lord Browne-Wilkinson thus applied the equitable maxim – since undue influence is an equitable doctrine – that 'where the equities are equal the first in time prevails'. Thus, since the first equity is the wife's and the second equity belongs to the bank, the wife's interest should prevail. In **Barclays Bank plc v Boulter** [1997] 2 All ER 1002, however, it was held that the burden of proof lay on the bank to prove that it did not have constructive notice of the undue influence or misrepresentation. It was not incumbent on the surety to prove that the bank had constructive notice.

Lord Browne-Wilkinson considered that it was at this point that the special position of wives became important since, even today, many wives place a confidence and trust in their husbands in relation to their financial affairs. Thus the relationship between a husband and wife in these circumstances gave rise to an 'invalidating tendency' which meant that a wife was in a better position to be able to establish Class 2B presumed undue influence by her husband. The informality of the dealings between a husband and his wife meant that there was a higher likelihood of the husband misrepresenting the liability of the undertaking to the wife in order to secure her assent to the surety contract. His Lordship considered that the informality of the business dealings between a husband and his wife would be sufficient to put a mortgagee/bank on notice if two factors are satisfied:

(a) the transaction is on its face not to the financial advantage of the wife; and

(b) there is a substantial risk in transactions of that kind that, in procuring the wife to act as surety, the husband has committed a legal or equitable wrong that entitles the wife to set aside the transaction.

Thus where a mortgagee is put on inquiry it is incumbent on them to ensure that the wife's consent to act as surety has been properly obtained, since otherwise they will be deemed to have constructive notice of the wife's right to have the surety agreement set aside, on the basis of either undue influence or misrepresentation. This position has now been affirmed by the House of Lords in *Etridge No. 2* where it was stated that 'a bank should take steps to ensure that it is not affected by any claim the wife may have that her signature . . . was procured by the undue influence or other wrong of her husband'.

But what of the situation outside the husband and wife relationship?

Lord Browne-Wilkinson stated that the special position of wives does not arise out of the status of the husband and wife relationship but out of the emotional ties that arise within that relationship. These emotional ties also arise in the case of cohabitees, whether of a heterosexual or homosexual nature. Where the mortgagee knows that a surety or guarantor is cohabiting with the principal debtor, the nature of the surety contract and the relationship of the parties means that the possibility of undue influence or misrepresentation can be inferred, with the consequence that the mortgagee will have constructive notice of the equitable right of the surety to have the transaction set aside, just as in the husband and wife situation.

Of course, these principles are not confined to cohabitees but will arise in any situation where a mortgagee is aware that the surety places a confidence and trust in the principal debtor. Lord Browne-Wilkinson gave an example of this type of relationship in the following case.

Avon Finance Co. Ltd v *Bridges* [1985] 2 All ER 281

In this case a son persuaded his parents to act as surety for his debts by means of a misrepresentation. It was held that the surety contract was unenforceable by the finance company, *inter alia*, because the finance company had knowledge of the trust the parents reposed in their son with regard to their financial dealings. One may discern a difference of approach here since there would appear to be a requirement to prove actual knowledge by the creditor of the confidence and trust reposed in the debtor by the surety, while in the cohabitee scenario undue influence or misrepresentation may be inferred.

The problem now remained as to how mortgagees could avoid the consequences set out above. Lord Browne-Wilkinson considered that the answer to this question lies in good banking practice by the various financial institutions. He stated:

Where one cohabitee has entered into an obligation to stand as surety for the debts of the other cohabitee and the creditor is aware that they are cohabitees: (1) the surety obligation will be valid and enforceable by the creditor unless the suretyship was procured by the undue influence, misrepresentation or other legal wrong of the principal debtor; (2) if there has been undue influence, misrepresentation or other legal wrong by the principal debtor, unless the creditor has taken reasonable steps to satisfy himself that the surety entered into the obligation freely and in knowledge of the true facts, the creditor will be unable to enforce the surety obligation because he will be fixed with constructive notice of the surety's right to set aside the transaction; (3) unless there are special exceptional circumstances, a creditor will have taken such reasonable steps to avoid being fixed with constructive notice if the creditor warns the surety (at a meeting not attended by the principal debtor) of the amount of her potential liability and of the risks involved and advises the surety to take independent legal advice.

By 'reasonable steps' he considered that financial institutions could lend in confidence on the basis of a surety contract, provided the surety is warned, independently of the principal debtor, of the extent of his or her liability and the risks involved. Furthermore, the surety should be advised to seek independent advice. His Lordship also considered that notices in the documentation did not provide an adequate warning, no matter what prominence such warnings are given, since very often such written warnings were not read by potential sureties or they were intercepted by the principal debtor. There is thus a legal requirement on financial institutions to explain the matters indicated above to the potential surety in a personal interview from which the principal debtor is excluded.

Lord Browne-Wilkinson also referred to 'exceptional circumstances' that would still cause the transaction to fail, even if a creditor took the above precautions. What sort of 'exceptional circumstances' did he envisage? His Lordship did not give explicit examples but it would appear that such circumstances might arise if the mortgagee had knowledge of facts that made the presence of undue influence highly likely rather than a mere possibility. In such a situation the transaction would be set aside unless the mortgagee ensured that the innocent party was *actually* independently advised.

Avoiding constructive notice

The case of *O'Brien* contained within it procedures that are required to be taken by creditors when entering surety transactions in order to avoid being fixed with constructive notice of the principal debtor's misrepresentations, undue influence or other wrongdoing. Lord Browne-Wilkinson considered these procedures to be good banking practice. To reiterate:

1 There is a legal requirement that the innocent party is called in for a personal interview. It is important that the principal debtor is excluded from this interview. Written advice is not regarded as being adequate.

2 The extent of the proposed liability of the innocent party (the potential surety) should be explained at the interview.

3 The risks of entering into the transaction should be explained.

4 The innocent party should be encouraged to seek independent legal advice.

Clearly, the procedures are designed to ensure that the innocent party is given a maximum degree of protection; however, the question arises as to whether the procedures are to be regarded as best practice guidelines rather than hard-and-fast rules.

In *Massey* v *Midland Bank plc* [1995] 1 All ER 929 Steyn LJ made two observations: first, the guidance given does not need to be exhaustive to satisfy the *O'Brien* requirements; second, the guidance requirements in *O'Brien* should not be applied mechanically. This position accords with that set out in the earlier decision of *Bank of Baroda* v *Shah* [1988] 3 All ER 24, where it was stated that the bank can assume that the solicitor is honest and competent and that any conflict between the solicitor and the wife is not for the concern of the bank. This position was also affirmed in the Court of Appeal decision in *Banco Exterior Internacional* v *Mann* [1995] 1 All ER 936.

The principles applied in these were followed and extended in the subsequent cases of the *Bank of Baroda* v *Rayarel* [1995] 2 FLR 376 (CA) and *Halifax Mortgage Services Ltd* v *Stepsky* [1996] 2 All ER 277. In the former it was held that where a surety was advised by a solicitor acting for the alleged wrongdoer, the bank was entitled to assume that the surety had been properly advised as to the nature and extent of the transaction. It was also stated that it was a matter for the solicitor to decide if there was a conflict of interest. In *Stepsky* the solicitor was acting for the wife, the husband and the building society. The Court of

Appeal decided that the knowledge gained from the husband relating to the true purpose of the loan could not be imputed to the building society since the knowledge had been gained prior to the appointment of the solicitor by the building society.

The issue of whether a bank has taken 'reasonable steps' to avoid constructive notice by ensuring that the surety has obtained independent legal advice continued to be blurred by subsequent cases.

Barclays Bank plc v Thomson [1997] 4 All ER 816

A bank instructed a solicitor to act on its behalf for the purpose of ensuring that the wife received independent legal advice as to her liabilities under a charge in the bank's favour; the bank was entitled to rely on the solicitor's assurance that he had discharged his duty and given her professional independent advice. This was so even where the solicitor was also acting for both the bank and the husband. It was stated that deficiency in the advice given by the solicitor could not be imputed to the bank. On the other hand, in *Royal Bank of Scotland v Etridge* [1997] 3 All ER 628 it was held that the bank was not discharged of its duty to take reasonable steps to ensure that the wife received independent advice simply by the fact that the solicitor had signed a certificate stating that the nature and effect of the transaction had been explained to her. This was because the wife had signed the charge in the presence of the husband; she regarded the solicitor as employed by her husband; and, lastly, the solicitor had been appointed by the bank and was therefore regarded as being an agent of the bank. The case thus distinguished the cases of *Massey* and *Mann*.

Undoubtedly, the contradictory decisions in these two cases are unsatisfactory and produced further uncertainty and confusion in this increasingly complex area of the law. The case of **Royal Bank of Scotland v Etridge** was followed by the case of **Crédit Lyonnaise Bank Nederland NV v Burch** [1997] 1 All ER 144 (CA), which applied a principle first set out by Lord Browne-Wilkinson in **O'Brien**. He stated that, in an exceptional case, a creditor may be so aware of the fact of undue influence by the third party wrongdoer that it would be inadequate for the mortgagee simply to advise the wife/surety to obtain independent advice; the mortgagee must insist upon it so that independent advice is actually received. The case is also authority for the proposition that if the transaction is one for an unlimited guarantee then it must be regarded as onerous. In such circumstances, the solicitor is bound to inquire as to the nature of any onerous clauses. If the solicitor does discover such clauses, they should advise their client not to enter into the transaction. If the client persists in carrying on with the transaction, the solicitor should then refuse to act any further for the client, unless satisfied that the transaction is one which, given the overall circumstances, the client should sensibly enter into free from improper pressure.

In both the **Massey** and **Mann** cases, the Court of Appeal considered that the **O'Brien** principles set out by Lord Browne-Wilkinson were not exhaustive ones that had to be applied in all cases. Both Steyn LJ (in the **Massey** case) and Morritt LJ (in the **Mann** case), considered the principles in **O'Brien** to be simply an indication of 'best practice'. Thus Steyn LJ stated:

The guidance ought not to be mechanically applied . . . It is the substance that matters.

Morritt LJ stated:

I do not understand Lord Browne-Wilkinson to be laying down for the future the only steps to be taken which will avoid a bank being fixed with constructive notice of the rights of the wife, rather he is pointing out . . . best practice.

On this basis, the absence of a private meeting will not necessarily be fatal to the agreement, provided the overall objective of the guidelines is met in ensuring that the innocent party is made sufficiently aware of the consequences of entering into the proposed transaction so that the undue influence, misrepresentation or other wrong committed by the principal debtor is counteracted.

It cannot be doubted that the decisions in the *Massey* and *Mann* cases considerably weakened the ability of sureties to have transactions set aside following *Barclays Bank plc v O'Brien*. Conflicting decisions in subsequent cases such as *Etridge* and *Thomson* exacerbated the situation. The result was a growing uncertainty that made it almost impossible at times for either the banks or sureties to predict the outcome of their respective positions. The problem appeared to be that the banks and other financial institutions involved in lending money adopted a variety of different practices, believing that these met the *O'Brien* principles. The other problem was that, at times, the courts also seemed to produce equally varied responses. If the *O'Brien* guidelines were to be viewed as 'best practice' then the confusion being created by subsequent decisions was making the law so confused and unpredictable that it could only be labelled as 'worst practice'.

Into this picture came the case of *Royal Bank of Scotland* v *Etridge (No. 2)* [2001] 4 All ER 449 (HL). As indicated earlier, the leading judgment in the House of Lords was delivered by Lord Nicholls. He first of all directed his attention to the criticisms that had been made of the decision in *O'Brien*. He reiterated the process in which the doctrine of constructive notice had been applied by Lord Browne-Wilkinson in *O'Brien*. Usually, a bank that takes a guarantee from the wife of a customer will be completely ignorant of any undue influence that might be brought to bear in order to compel her concurrence with the loan arrangements. As we have seen, Lord Browne-Wilkinson used constructive notice as a means of putting the mortgagee on notice of the wife's rights unless the mortgagee has taken reasonable steps to satisfy themselves that the wife's agreement has been properly obtained.

As Lord Nicholls pointed out, this is an unusual use of constructive notice in that the law does not impose an obligation on one party to check whether the other's agreement was obtained by undue influence. Usually in a situation such as a surety transaction where there are three persons involved, the wife only avoids liability if it can be shown that the bank has been a party to the conduct that caused the wife to enter into the transaction. What *O'Brien* essentially does is to introduce a concept that the bank will lose the benefit of a contract if it 'ought' to have known that the other's concurrence has been procured by the misconduct of the third party.

Another unusual feature of constructive notice as applied in *O'Brien* was considered by Lord Nicholls. Under conventional principles, a person is deemed to have constructive notice of a prior right when they do not actually know of the prior right but would have learned of it had they made those inquiries that a reasonably prudent purchaser would have made. In *O'Brien*, however, the bank is not required to make such inquiries. The decision merely sets out the steps to be taken by the bank to reduce or eliminate the risks incurred by the wife entering into a transaction by way of some misrepresentation or undue influence by her husband. The steps here are to *minimise* the risk, not *discover* if the husband has exerted influence over his wife by misrepresentation or undue influence. Thus, in establishing guidelines as to when a bank is put on inquiry, the use of the expression 'constructive notice' is not technically correct since a bank is not required to make such inquiries but to ensure that the risk of undue influence being exerted upon the wife has been reduced.

Lord Nicholls then set out some principles and guidelines regarding the position of lenders and the duties of solicitors in advising wives in transactions where a wife proposed to charge her share of the matrimonial home as security for a loan to her husband or a company within which the husband operates his business.

When is the bank put on inquiry?

A bank is put on inquiry when a wife offers to stand as surety for her husband's debts. This arises from the fact that the transaction is not, on the face of things, to the wife's financial advantage. Further, in such transactions there is a substantial risk that the husband has committed a wrong that would entitle the wife to set the transaction aside. These two factors provide the underlying rationale for the bank to be put on inquiry. Both do not, however, have to be proved before the bank is put on inquiry.

The above principles apply not just in the case of married couples, but also in the case of unmarried couples, whether homosexual or heterosexual, where the bank is aware of the relationship. Couples do not have to be cohabiting, thus affirming the decision in *Massey*, above, nor indeed does there have to be a sexual relationship. Lord Nicholls in *Etridge No. 2* considered that banks will always be put on inquiry in all cases where there is a non-commercial relationship between the surety and the mortgagor, referring to this as the 'wider principle'. Thus he stated:

> . . . the only practical way forward is to regard banks as 'put on inquiry' in every case where the relationship between the surety and the debtor is non-commercial. The creditor must always take reasonable steps to bring home to the individual guarantor the risks he is running by standing surety. As a measure of protection, this is valuable. But, in all conscience, it is a modest burden for banks and other lenders. It is no more than is reasonably to be expected of a creditor who is taking a guarantee from an individual. If the bank or other creditor does not take these steps, it is deemed to have notice of any claim the guarantor may have that the transaction was procured by undue influence or misrepresentation on the part of the debtor.

Lord Nicholls therefore suggests that, in any non-commercial situation, a bank/lender must assume that it is put on inquiry and must take appropriate action to avoid being fixed with constructive notice.

In *First National Bank plc* v *Achampong* [2003] EWCA Civ 487 a wife attempted to establish that a bank was put on inquiry because the loan had been made to benefit her husband's business and that she had received no benefit from the loan. The Court of Appeal considered it was unnecessary to inquire into the latter two matters and considered that undue influence arose on the basis of the 'wider principle' as set out above.

The bank is also put on inquiry if the wife acts as surety for the debts of a company whose shares are held by the wife and her husband, even where the wife is a director or company secretary. Lord Nicholls did not consider this type of situation to be a joint loan since shareholders' interests and the identity of directors provide an accurate guide as to who has de facto control of the company's business. The case of *Bank of Cyprus (London) Ltd* v *Markou* [1999] 2 All ER 707 provides an example of such circumstances.

What steps should the bank take when put on inquiry?

When a bank has been put on inquiry it need only take such reasonable steps as are necessary to satisfy itself that the practical implications of the proposed transaction have been brought home to the wife in a meaningful way. Lord Nicholls states:

> The furthest a bank can be expected to go is to take reasonable steps to satisfy itself that the wife has had brought home to her, in a meaningful way, the practical implications of the proposed transaction. This does not wholly eliminate the risk of undue influence or misrepresentation. But it does mean that a wife enters into a transaction with her eyes open so far as the basic elements of the transaction are concerned.

There is no requirement on a bank to discharge its responsibility by having a personal meeting with the wife – provided a suitable alternative means of communicating the necessary information to her is used. Lord Nicholls considered that the risk of litigation ensuing by having a personal meeting with the wife was high and that it was not unreasonable for the bank to insist that she receive advice from an independent financial adviser. Ordinarily it is reasonable for a bank to rely upon confirmation from a solicitor that they have given the wife appropriate advice. It would not, however, be reasonable if the bank knows that the solicitor has not duly advised the wife or, from the facts, the bank knows that the wife has not received appropriate advice. Normally, the deficiencies in the advice provided by the solicitor are a matter between the wife and the solicitor. The solicitor is regarded as acting solely for the wife and is not an agent of the bank. Thus the quality of the advice given is a matter between the wife and the solicitor.

In assessing what steps the bank should take when put on inquiry, Lord Nicholls considered that many of the cases already discussed featured the wife becoming involved at a very late stage of the transaction between the bank and the husband. She often had little opportunity to express a view on the identity of the solicitor who advised her. She was often unaware that the purpose of the interview was for the solicitor to confirm to the bank the fact that she had received advice. It was not unusual for the solicitor to act for both the wife and her husband.

Lord Nicholls considered that, in future transactions, banks should take the following steps when looking for the protection of legal advice given to the wife by the solicitor. He considered that the bank should check directly with the wife the name of the solicitor she wishes to act for her. The bank should also communicate directly with the wife, informing her that, for its own protection, it will require confirmation by the solicitor acting for her that they have fully explained to her the nature of the documents and the practical implications the transaction may have for her. She should be informed that the purpose of this requirement is that she should not be able to dispute that she is legally bound by the documents once she has signed them. She should be asked to nominate a solicitor whom she is willing to instruct to advise her, separately from her husband, and act for her in giving the necessary confirmation to the bank. She should be informed that, if she wishes, the solicitor may be the same solicitor as is acting for her husband in the transaction. If the solicitor is already acting for both herself and her husband, she should also be asked whether she would prefer that a different solicitor should act for her regarding the bank's requirement for confirmation from a solicitor. The bank should not proceed with the transaction unless it has received an appropriate response from the wife directly.

Since the bank's representatives are likely to have a better idea of the husband's financial affairs than the solicitor, the bank must provide the solicitor with the financial information necessary to provide an explanation to the wife, unless the bank is willing to take on the role itself. In practice, it has become usual for banks to supply the solicitor with the necessary financial information. The information required will largely depend on the facts of the case. Ordinarily, this will include information on the purpose for which the loan is required, the husband's current level of indebtedness, the amount of his current overdraft facility, and the amount and terms of any new facility. If the bank's requirement for security arises from a written application by the husband for a facility, a copy of the application should be sent to the solicitor. Of course, the bank would need to obtain the consent of the husband for this confidential information to be circulated, but if this consent is not forthcoming the transaction would not be able to proceed.

If the bank suspects that the wife has been misled by her husband or is not acting of her own free will, the bank must inform the wife's solicitor of the facts giving rise to that belief or suspicion.

The bank should in every case obtain from the wife's solicitor a written confirmation to the above effect. It should be noted that the steps set out will apply only to future transactions. In respect to past transactions, the bank will usually be regarded as having discharged its obligations if the solicitor acting for the wife has given the bank confirmation that they have brought home to the wife the risks she is running in acting as surety in the transaction.

Banks regulate their affairs on the basis that they are put on inquiry in every case where the relationship between the surety and the mortgagor is not a commercial one. A bank must always take care therefore to ensure that reasonable steps are taken to inform the individual guarantor as to the risks he or she is taking by acting as surety. If the bank or other creditor does not take such steps, it will be deemed to have any notice of any claim the guarantor may have that the transaction was procured by undue influence or misrepresentation on the part of the mortgagor.

What are the responsibilities of the solicitor in advising the wife?

It must always be remembered that the solicitor is acting solely for the wife and is not an agent of the bank. The solicitor will need to explain to the wife the purpose for which they have become involved. They should also advise the wife that their involvement may be used by the bank to counter any suggestion that she has been compelled to enter the transaction by the husband or that she has not properly understood the implications of the proposed transaction. The solicitor will need to obtain confirmation from the wife that she wishes them to act for her in the matter and to advise her on the legal and practical implications of the proposed transaction. Once the instruction has been obtained from the wife, the content of the advice provided by the solicitor will be dictated by the facts of the case.

As a minimum the solicitor would typically be expected to cover the following matters:

1 The solicitor will need to explain the nature of the documents and the practical consequences these will have for the wife if she signs them. The solicitor should draw her attention to the fact that she could lose her home if her husband's business fails to prosper.

2 The solicitor should advise her that her home may be her only substantial asset, as well as the family home, and that she could be made bankrupt.

3 The solicitor will need to point out the seriousness of the risks involved.

4 The wife should be told the purpose of the new lending facility – its amount and principal terms. She should be informed that the bank may increase the loan facility, change its terms, or grant a new facility without further reference to her. She should be told the extent of her liability under the guarantee.

5 The solicitor should discuss the wife's financial means, including her understanding of the property to be charged, and whether the wife or her husband has any other assets out of which payment can be made if the husband's business fails.

6 The solicitor should explain clearly to the wife that she has a choice whether or not to enter the arrangement and the decision is hers alone. In explaining this choice, the solicitor should discuss the current financial position, including the amount of the husband's present indebtedness and the amount of his current overdraft facility.

7 The solicitor should check whether the wife wishes to proceed. They should ask if she is content for the solicitor to write to the bank, confirming that they have explained the nature of the documents and the practical implications they may have for her.

They should also ask if she would prefer the solicitor to negotiate with the bank on the terms of the transaction – for instance, the sequence in which various securities are called in or the level of her liability. The solicitor should not give any confirmation to the bank without the wife's authority.

The solicitor's meeting with the wife should take place face-to-face, without the husband being present. The solicitor's explanations should be in non-technical language in order to ensure that the wife has a clear understanding of her position. The interview should not be regarded as a formality since the solicitor has an important task to perform in such transactions.

The solicitor must ensure that they obtain from the bank any information necessary. If the bank fails to provide this information, then the solicitor must decline to provide the confirmation required by the bank. It is not, however, the solicitor's role to veto the transaction by declining to provide the confirmation. The solicitor's role is to explain the documents to the wife and the risks involved. If the solicitor considers that the transaction is not in the best interests of the wife, she should be told so. Ultimately, the decision whether or not to enter into the transaction is the wife's, not the solicitor's, since the wife may have her own reasons for entering into a transaction that might be regarded as unwise. If it is clearly apparent that the wife is being seriously wronged, then the proper action for the solicitor is to decline to act for her.

Can the solicitor act for the husband or the bank and the wife at the same time?

As seen earlier, this has been a vexed question that has arisen over the years. Lord Nicholls considered that a clear and simple rule was required to provide an answer to this question. He considered it was confusing to use a rule based on whether the bank deals directly with the husband and the wife, or whether the bank deals with the solicitors acting for the husband and the wife, as seen in *Bank of Baroda* v *Rayarel* [1995] 2 FLR 376. He considered that some balance was required here depending on the circumstances. Thus, some factors clearly pointed to the need for the solicitor to act for the wife alone. For example, a wife may be inhibited in discussing the transaction with a solicitor who is also acting for her husband, as in *Banco Exterior Internacional* v *Mann* [1995] 1 All ER 936, above. A solicitor may not be able to give the same single-minded attention to the wife's interests as they would if they were acting solely for her. Lord Nicholls considered that, as a matter of general understanding, 'independent advice' would suggest that the solicitor should not be acting within the same transaction for the person who is the source of any undue influence.

Lord Nicholls thought that there was nothing inherently wrong in the solicitor also acting for the bank or the husband and the wife, provided it is in the wife's best interests and no conflicts of duty or interest arise. For instance, the costs of the transaction may be lower than if the solicitor acts for her solely; the wife may be happier being advised by the family solicitor; sometimes the solicitor who knows the husband and wife and their histories may be better placed to give advice than a solicitor who is a complete stranger.

Lord Nicholls considered that the advantages attached to the solicitor acting for both parties outweighed independent advice being applied prescriptively to each party. Once the solicitor receives instructions from the wife, the solicitor assumes legal and professional responsibilities directed towards her alone and is concerned only with her interests. In every case, the solicitor must consider whether there is any conflict of interest or duty and decide whether it is in the wife's best interests for them to accept instructions from her. The House of Lords, however, did recognise that there could be some circumstances where a solicitor should decline to act for the wife and refuse to supply the bank with confirmation that the wife had been advised appropriately. The court stated that such circumstances arose in 'exceptional cases where it is obvious that the wife is being grievously wronged'. The case of *Credit Lyonnaise Bank Nederland NV v Burch* [1997] 1 All ER 144 (CA) is often cited as an example here.

The facts were that Mrs Burch was only a modestly paid employee who, despite having no financial interest in a company, was persuaded to act as surety for the company's debts by way of a second charge on her small flat. The flat was valued at £100,000 and was already subject to a charge of £30,000. The second charge exposed her to unlimited liability for an unlimited period of time. At the time she entered into the second charge, she was not aware that the current level of indebtedness of the company would have meant that she would have lost her home and incurred a personal debt of £200,000. Clearly, this was a transaction which not only was manifestly to her disadvantage but was one which shocked 'the conscience of the court'.

The House of Lords' decision in *Etridge No. 2* now provides for a coherent process for dealing with surety arrangements. It should be noted that the principles apply to any lender embarking on such a transaction – they are not confined to banks. Effectively, both lenders and solicitors are now put on notice that married couples must no longer be considered as a single unit, but as two separate individuals who may have conflicting interests. It is to be hoped that this decision will also put to bed the catalogue of confusion that has arisen since the decision in *O'Brien*.

The effects of undue influence

The effect of undue influence on a contract is to render it voidable, rather than void. It follows that the victim must take steps to void the contract by rescinding it. As in other instances where rescission is the remedy, it may be lost where restitutio in integrum is impossible, or where the contract has been affirmed or where a bona fide third party has acquired the title to any property sold.

It should be noted that restitution does not have to be precise but merely substantial, as in *O'Sullivan v Management and Music Ltd* [1985] QB 428. In *TSB Bank plc v Camfield* [1995] 1 All ER 951, however, it was stated that where rescission is ordered the whole transaction is to be set aside (restitutio in integrum). In that case, the wife was persuaded by her husband to charge her beneficial interest as security for a loan facility for the husband's business. The husband, on the basis of an innocent misrepresentation, falsely told his wife that the maximum liability on the loan would be £15,000, being his share of a £30,000 loan to himself and his partner. In fact the charge was an unlimited one. It was held that the charge should be set aside in its entirety and that the wife was not required to make restitution of even the £15,000 she thought the charge amounted to. The basis of the decision was that the wife would not have agreed to the transaction at all had she known that the charge was to secure unlimited liability. In *Newbigging v Adam* (1887) 34 ChD 582, Bowen LJ described the principle in the following terms:

> There ought, as it appears to me, to be a giving back and a taking back on both sides, including the giving back and taking back of the obligations which the contract has created, as well as the giving back and taking back of the advantages.

This principle is important since it is designed to prevent unjust enrichment arising. In *Camfield*, however, the wife obtained no benefit whatsoever and therefore the principle had no application as regards the wife since she had nothing to give back. By the same token, it would be wrong to impose terms on any relief that she sought.

But what of the situation where a benefit is obtained? At what level should the restitution be assessed? At first instance in *Dunbar Bank plc* v *Nadeem and Another* [1997] 2 All ER 253, whilst finding that undue influence was present, the judge refused to set the transaction aside unconditionally, as occurred in *Camfield*. He found that case to be quite different because there the wife received no benefit from the transaction. Relying on *Erlanger* v *New Sombrero Phosphate Co.* (1878) 3 App Cas 1218, he concluded that there could be no setting aside of the transaction unless Mrs Nadeem accounted to the bank for the benefit she received from the money advanced. Since she had received a half-share in the home, the question arose as to whether she should refund either the full amount of the loan or half that plus interest. The judge concluded that the latter should be repaid since otherwise the wife would be funding her husband's share of the loan and interest in the home. In the Court of Appeal it was stated that the judge at first instance was wrong in principle to impose the condition he did. Millett LJ considered that there were two agreements. The first was made between Mr Nadeem and his wife, that he would give her a half-interest in the home on the basis that she would join him in charging the property with the moneys advanced by the bank to effect the purchase. Thus Mrs Nadeem would get a beneficial interest or share in the property. The second transaction was between Mr and Mrs Nadeem and the bank on the terms set out in a letter describing the loan facility.

On the basis of the two agreements, Mrs Nadeem obtained, first, an interest in the property and, second, a loan advance of £260,000 on the basis that £210,000 would be used to purchase the property, which she and her husband would charge to the bank to secure the repayment of the loan moneys. In relation to the second agreement there was no question of Mrs Nadeem getting a free-standing loan to do with what she wanted. The loan had to be applied for the purpose of acquiring the property.

In assessing the level of restitution it is necessary to consider the level of Mrs Nadeem's enrichment since it is this which restitution seeks to redress. Millett LJ and Morritt LJ held that this should not be based on the money advanced but on the interest she obtained in the property by way of the loan because this was the extent of her enrichment. They thus concluded that, in having the legal charge discharged as against her, she should restore the beneficial interest to her husband. It should be noted that her obligation to restore the beneficial interest was not an obligation to restore it to the bank since it was not derived from the bank. The consequence of the beneficial interest being restored to the husband would mean that the whole beneficial interest would come within his charge to the bank. A further consequence, however, would be that the wife would have no defence to claims for possession of the property brought by the bank in order to recoup the loan.

Problems can arise where restitution is ordered but the value of the property in question has changed. Such a situation arose in the case of *Cheese* v *Thomas*.

Cheese v Thomas [1994] 1 WLR 129

In this case the plaintiff (Cheese) bought a house with his great-nephew (Thomas) for £83,000. The money for the purchase was raised by the plaintiff contributing £43,000 and the defendant £40,000 by way of a mortgage on the property for that amount. The house was purchased in the defendant's name, though it was agreed that the plaintiff would have sole use of the house for the rest of his life. It was further agreed that, on the plaintiff's death, the house would belong to the defendant exclusively. Eventually, the plaintiff became worried that the defendant was not paying the mortgage repayments, conduct which inevitably would have placed his interest in the property at risk. The plaintiff thus sought to have the arrangement set aside on the basis of undue influence.

The judge at first instance ruled that the agreement could be set aside for undue influence. Normally, where restitution is ordered, the plaintiff should have been able to recover his full £43,000 contribution since the principle behind this remedy is that the parties should be restored to their original positions. In this case, however, the house was sold for £55,400 – i.e. a £27,600 loss. Should the plaintiff receive his £43,000 in full or only a proportion of it to reflect the loss sustained on the sale of the property? The Court of Appeal held that it was appropriate that the loss should be shared since each party had contributed to the purchase of a house in which each would have an interest. Further, the defendant's personal conduct was not found to be open to criticism – he had acted as an 'innocent fiduciary' rather than in some unconscionable manner. Presumably, the result of this decision is that, if the parties can show that they have an interest in the property, then, if the property had been sold at a profit, the parties would have likewise been entitled to a share of the profit.

Priority of mortgages

Clearly, it is possible to have one or more mortgages over the same piece of land. The number of mortgages that can be taken is ultimately one of commercial judgment for lenders. The limiting factor is whether there is sufficient equity in the property to secure an individual lender's requirements for the loan since there is little point in providing a mortgage if, on default by the mortgagor, one is not going to recover the capital monies plus interest. It is at this point that the issue of priority of mortgages arises.

Issues of priority that arise are decided by two factors: firstly, whether a particular mortgage has been protected appropriately as an estate registered at the Land Registry or as a land charge under the Land Charges Act 1972 and secondly, whether the mortgage is created out of a legal or equitable interest in the land. If created out of an equitable interest, the mortgage must necessarily be an equitable mortgage. On the other hand, a mortgage created out of a legal estate may be legal or equitable.

Registered land

Legal mortgages of a registered estate

The grant of a legal mortgage over a registered legal estate is a disposition of the registered estate by virtue of the Land Registration Act 2002 s.27(2)f. To be effective, the legal charge must be registered: s.27(1), s.59 and Schedule 2 para 8 and failure to do so renders the charge effective in equity only: s.27(1). The legal charge is registered in the charges register of the mortgagor's registered title, the chargee being entered on the register as the proprietor of the charge: Schedule 2 para 8.

The Land Registration Act 2002 s.28(1) provides that the priority of interests in registered land is determined by the order in which they are created, so therefore, as the provision states, a disposition of a registered estate will not affect the priority of an existing interest. As against competing charges, however, s.29 is excepted from s.28 so that priority is determined not by the chronological order in which charges are created but by the order in which they are registered.

Section 29(2) provides additional means by which interests are capable of being protected. Section 29(2) states:

For the purposes of subsection (1), the priority of an interest is protected –

(a) in any case if the interest
(i) is a registered charge or notice in the register,
(ii) falls within any of the paragraphs of Schedule 3, or
(iii) appears from the register to be excepted from the effect of registration, and
(b) in the case of a disposition of a leasehold estate, if the burden of the interest is incident to the estate.

Thus if the legal charge has not been registered, so that it takes effect in equity only, that charge must be entered as a notice on the register in order to maintain its priority.

Summing up, therefore, if M1 is entered on the register of title as the registered proprietor of a charge, their charge will take priority over M2's legal charge which is subsequently registered: s.29(1). It is the time of registration that is crucial, not the time a charge was created, so that, even if M2's charge was created before M1's charge, they will lose their priority to M1 if they have not registered their charge. Similarly, M1 will take priority over any equitable interest created *before* their own charge unless the equitable mortgage was entered as a notice: s.29(2)(a)(i). In the same way, M1's registered charge will take priority over any equitable charge created after M1 has registered their charge.

Equitable mortgages of a registered estate

An equitable mortgage can arise either because a mortgagee has failed to register their charge: s.27(1), where the charge is expressed to be an equitable one, or where there is a contract to create a charge over the mortgagor's land. In all cases of equitable charges, they should be protected by entry of a notice in the charges register of the mortgagor's title: s.32. If an equitable charge is protected in this manner then it will take priority over any subsequent charges, subject to the existing entries in the register by virtue of s.29(1), s.29(2)(a)(i). If the equitable charge is not protected by notice, it will lose its priority to any legal charge that is then registered on the title.

Priority amongst equitable charges is governed by the basic rule as set out in s.28(1) so that competing interests rank in priority to each other by way of the order in which they are created.

Unregistered land

Legal mortgages of a legal estate

Prior to April 1998, the mortgagee taking the first legal mortgage ('M1') would take the title deeds relating to the property. This deposit of title deeds provided M1 with an unimpeachable position as against any subsequent mortgagees since, if the mortgagor attempted to take out another mortgage with M2, M3, etc., the subsequent mortgagees would inevitably ask to see the title deeds. The absence of the title deeds would alert the subsequent mortgagees to the existence of a first legal mortgage but not to any others. Thus if a third mortgage was taken out, with M3, then M3 would be alerted to the existence of the mortgage with M1 but not M2.

If a mortgage is not protected by deposit of title deeds relating to the legal estate then the mortgage has to be registered as a Class C(i) puisne mortgage under the Land Charges Act 1972 s.2(4). The Land Charges Act 1972 s.4(5) and s.17(1) provides that an unregistered Class C(i) land charge created after January 1926 shall be void against a purchaser for valuable consideration of an estate in the land or of any interest in the land. It should be remembered that the expression 'purchaser' includes a mortgagee. Thus, if M1 fails to take the title deeds, they must protect their legal mortgage as a C(i) land charge and register this against the name of the estate owner taking the mortgage. If M1 does this then they will have priority over M2 and subsequent mortgages, irrespective of whether they are taking a legal or an equitable mortgage and whether they have actual notice of the prior mortgage.

If M1 fails to register their land charge, it will be void for want of registration and therefore M2 will take priority. If the mortgagor creates three mortgages to M1, M2 and M3 and none is registered then effectively the order of priority is reversed to M3, M2 and M1 since M1 is void against M2 and the mortgage to M3 and so on. If, on the other hand, all the mortgages are registered, the Law of Property Act 1925 s.97 provides that the mortgages will rank according to their date of registration.

A potential conflict between s.4(5) and s.97 can arise if the first mortgage is registered after the second mortgage is created, thus:

June 1st	A grants a mortgage to M1
July 2nd	A grants a mortgage to M2
August 3rd	M1 registers their mortgage
September 4th	M2 registers their mortgage

According to s.4(5) the order of priority is M2 and then M1 since M1's mortgage is void as against M2's mortgage. However, according to s.97, the mortgages rank according to the date of the registration – i.e. the order of priority is M1, M2. This problem is still to be resolved and indeed, because of the impact of the Land Registration Act 2002, probably never will be. Nevertheless, it is generally assumed that the registration requirements of s.4(5) take precedence over s.97 since the effect of s.97 would be to reactivate a charge that would otherwise be void.

It should be borne in mind that, following the Land Registration Act 2002, the creation of a protected first legal mortgage to M1 is a 'trigger' requiring an unregistered estate to be the subject of mandatory first registration at the Land Registry: Land Registration Act 2002 s.4(1)g and S.6(2)a and gives rise to the mortgage being entered as a registered charge: s.27(1) and s.27(2)f. A later mortgage to M2 now becomes a disposition of the registered estate over which M1's mortgage has priority by virtue of s.29(1) and s.29(2)(a)(i).

If the creation of the mortgage to M1 fails to bring about the registration of the mortgagor's estate at the Land Registry: s.6(4) then M1's charge will take effect in equity only and becomes void as a legal charge: s.7(1). The mortgagor will continue to hold a legal estate in unregistered land. In such a case, the creation of the mortgage will have to be protected as an estate contract (by virtue of LRA s.7(2)b) and be registered as a Class C(iv) land charge under the Land Charges Act 1972 s.2(6). Failure to register will render it void as against a subsequent purchaser (or mortgagee) of the mortgagor's legal estate for money or money's worth. If a subsequent mortgage is an equitable mortgage, M1's equitable mortgage, even though unregistered, will still take priority since the rule is that 'where the equities are equal, the first in time prevails'.

Equitable mortgages of a legal estate

If M1 takes an equitable mortgage secured by deposit of title deeds, priority will be determined by whether a subsequent mortgagee has a legal or equitable mortgage. In the case of a legal mortgage, priority is determined by the doctrine of notice under the Law of Property Act 1925 s.199(1) so that if M2 takes their mortgage without actual or constructive notice of M1's earlier mortgage they will take priority to it. It should be borne in mind that, since the title deeds are in the hands of M1 and the mortgagor will be unable to produce them to M2, this will inevitably place M2 on notice of M1's prior to the mortgage.

If M2's mortgage is also an equitable mortgage then priority is again determined by the rule 'where the equities are equal, the first in time prevails' so M1 will take priority. This may be lost if M1 has acted with gross negligence in relation to the title deeds and left them in the hands of the mortgagor so that the mortgagor can present them to M2 as if they were to be the first mortgagee. Similarly, M1 will lose their priority if there has been some fraud or misrepresentation on their part as to the title deeds.

Where M1 has not secured their equitable mortgage by deposit of title deeds then they should have secured their priority by registering it as a Class C(iii) general equitable charge under the Land Charges Act 1972 s.2(4). Failure to do so will render the land charge void against a purchase for valuable consideration of the land charged with it or of any interest in such land: Land Charges Act 1972 s.4(5).

Mortgages of an equitable interest

As we have seen, it is not possible to carve a legal interest out of an equitable interest and therefore it stands to reason that all mortgages of an equitable interest must necessarily be equitable themselves. The rule for determining the priority of equitable interest is set out in the maxim 'where the equities are equal, the first in time prevails'.

The above rule is modified where there is a mortgage of a beneficial interest under a trust and, of course, the nature of a beneficial interest in land normally pre-supposes the existence of a trust of land. The problem here is that, where a beneficiary under a trust defaults on a mortgage of his or her interest, the mortgagees will look to the trustees in order to recoup their security since the property will be sold and the capital monies paid to the trustees. If there is more than one mortgage, the trustees need to know in what order they should pay out the capital monies in respect of each mortgagee.

The rules of priority here are determined by the rule in *Dearle* v *Hall* (1823) 3 Russ 1, as amended by the Law of Property Act 1925 s.137. Under the rule, the priority between competing mortgagees (assignees, since mortgages of the beneficial interests essentially amount to an assignment of the beneficial interest to the mortgagees) is determined by the order in which notice of the assignments is received by the trustees. However, the normal rules of equity as regards notice and good faith also apply. Thus, in the following example we have:

(i)   mortgage given to M1;

(ii) mortgage given to M2;

(iii) M2 gives notice to the trustees;

(iv) M1 gives notice to the trustees.

On the basis of notice being given to the trustees, M2 should gain priority. On the normal basis of good faith and conscience, though, equity would not allow M2 to gain priority if he or she knew of the existence of M1's mortgage at the time the mortgage to M2 was created. By s.137 notice must be given in writing and served on the trustees; however, it is not the time at which the notice is served but the time at which the notice is *received* by the trustees that determines the order of priority. It is important that notice is served on the trustees holding the legal estate and thus particular care is required in the case of settled land within the Settled Land Act 1925. In such an instance, the notice must be served not on the tenant for life who holds the legal estate but on the trustees of the settlement. Furthermore, notice must be served on *all* the trustees, irrespective of the type of trust involved. Provided notice is served to all trustees it remains effective, even if a trustee dies or retires from office without communicating the notice to those trustees taking his or her place: *Re Wasdale* [1899] 1 Ch 163. If there are several trustees and notice is given to only one trustee, the notice will become ineffective if that trustee dies or retires unless they have communicated the notice to at least one other surviving trustee: *Timson* v *Ramsbottom* (1836) 2 Keen 35; *Ward* v *Duncombe* [1893] AC 369.

Summary

Nature of a mortgage

A mortgage or charge is a device by which money is lent by a mortgagee (the lender) to a mortgagor (the borrower) which is secured against an estate or interest in the mortgagor's land.

Creation of mortgages

Legal mortgages

Pre-1926

Freehold: Created by a transfer of the whole fee simple subject to a covenant by the mortgagee that the fee simple would be re-conveyed to the mortgagor once the mortgage had been repaid.

Leasehold: Created by an assignment of the lease to the mortgagee subject to a covenant that the lease would be re-assigned to the mortgagor once the mortgage had been repaid.

Post-1926

Freehold: Created by granting a lease to the mortgagee with a provision that the lease comes to an end when the mortgage is redeemed: Law of Property Act 1925 s.85.

Leasehold: Created by way of a sub-lease to the mortgagee. Once the mortgage is redeemed, the sub-lease comes to an end: Law of Property Act 1925 s.86.

Freehold/leasehold: Charge by deed and expressed by way of legal mortgage: Law of Property Act 1925 s.87.

Post-2002

Freehold/leasehold: By virtue of the Land Registration Act 2002 s.35(1) the only permissible way to create a legal mortgage is by way of a registered charge. To take effect in law the 'registrable charge' must be registered against the title, otherwise it only takes effect in equity: Land Registration Act 2002 s.27.

Equitable mortgages

Equitable mortgages arise by way of an informal mortgage, a mortgage of an equitable interest in land or lack of registration under the Land Registration Act 2002 s.27(1).

Rights of the mortgagor

The primary right of the mortgagor is the equity of redemption. Until the legal date for redemption has passed, the mortgagor has a contractual right to redeem. After this date has passed, equity would allow the mortgagor to redeem their mortgage. The mortgagor has certain other rights within their right to redeem – there must be no 'clogs and fetters' on the right to redeem; the rule against irredeemability; no unfair collateral advantages; no unconscionable terms.

Mortgages also have statutory protections under the Consumer Credit Act 1974 and 2006 and the Financial Services and Markets Act 2006.

Rights and remedies of the mortgagee of a legal mortgage

Mortgagee may sue on the mortgagor's covenant to repay the mortgage

The power of sale

If not expressed or conferred in the mortgage, such a power is implied and regulated by the Law of Property Act 1925 ss.101–105. If the mortgage is in a deed and the mortgage money is due – i.e. the legal date for redemption has passed – the power of sale is said to '*arise*'. The power of sale only becomes '*exercisable*' under s.103.

The right to possession

This is probably the most important right of the mortgagee and arises because, in the case of a legal mortgage, a legal estate is conferred on the mortgagee. The mortgagee is thus able to enter into possession 'before the ink is dry on the mortgage': *Four Maids Ltd* v *Dudley Marshall Properties Ltd* [1957] Ch 317.

There are certain limitations on the right to possession, not least the fact that by the AJA 1970 s.36 if the house is a dwelling house the court has wide powers to grant relief to the mortgagor. In addition, the court has an inherent power to grant relief. Note also that mortgagees embarking on possession proceedings should have regard to the Pre-Action Protocol for Possession Claims.

The right of foreclosure

It is rarely used today, but the effect of foreclosure is to extinguish the mortgagor's right of redemption: Law of Property Act 1925 s.88. The draconian nature of this remedy is that a court, by s.91(2), may substantiate a sale rather than order foreclosure. Further, s.105 provides that any surplus must be distributed to the mortgagor on sale.

The right to appoint a receiver

This right is normally expressly provided for in the mortgage, but in the absence of this such a right is implied by s.101(1)(iii). The receiver is an agent of the mortgagor, not the mortgagee, so the mortgagee is not liable if the receiver acts negligently. By s.109(8) a receiver must apply any income according to a strict order.

Rights and remedies of a mortgagee of an equitable mortgage

Essentially, these rights are the same as for a mortgagee of a legal mortgage. The mortgagee has the right to sue on the personal covenant to repay by the mortgagor if the equitable mortgage is created by deed. If the equitable mortgage is not contained in a deed then the mortgagee may ask the court to exercise its discretion under s.91(2). A mortgagee has the right to possession if this is expressly conferred on them by the mortgage contract, otherwise they have no right to possession as they have no legal estate in land. An equitable mortgagee has the same rights of foreclosure as for a legal mortgage. The right to appoint is the same as for the power of sale.

Undue influence

- The transaction entered must be of manifest disadvantage to the victim – *Bank of Credit and Commerce International SA* v *Aboody* [1990].
- *Royal Bank of Scotland* v *Etridge (No. 2)* [2001] (HL) confirmed the two types of undue influence:
  - (a) Class 1: actual undue influence.
  - (b) Class 2: presumed undue influence, which had two sub-classifications:
    - – Class 2A. Overt acts of improper pressure or coercion such as unlawful threats.
    - – Class 2B. Interparty relationships where one has acquired a measure of influenc or ascendancy over another and then takes unfair advantage.

Class 1: Actual undue influence

- Occurs where there is no special relationship between the parties so that there is no abuse of a particular confidence.
- The claimant must prove that the transaction was manifestly disadvantageous.
- *National Westminster Bank plc* v *Morgan*.
- The exercise of undue influence is one of fact.

Class 2: Presumed undue influence

2A Presumed undue influence

- Examples of automatic presumed undue influence:
  - – trustee and beneficiary: *Benningfield* v *Baxter*;
  - – solicitor and client: *Wright* v *Carter*;
  - – parent and child: *Powell* v *Powell*;
  - – religious leader/adviser and disciple/parishioner: *Allcard* v *Skinner*.
- The claimant must show:
  1 a relationship of trust or confidence exists between him/herself and the wrongdoer, and
  2 the existence of a transaction which calls for an explanation.
- NB: The victim need not prove that the undue influence has actually taken place; all he or she has to prove is that a confidential relationship has arisen and that the transaction itself calls for an explanation.
- In *Etridge No. 2* it was considered that it was only in Class 2A undue influence that there was a true presumption of influence.

2B Presumed undue influence

- Example: Husband and wife relationships: *Midland Bank plc* v *Shephard*.
- The burden of proof: The victim will be able to set aside a transaction by proving as of fact that they have placed trust and confidence in the wrongdoer, without the need to prove that actual undue influence arose.
- *Etridge No. 2* provides authority that presumed undue influence merely shifts the evidential burden of proof from the claimant to the wrongdoer.
- It is *not* a presumption that undue influence exists *per se*, but rather that the burden of explaining why the transaction was not caused by undue influence is shifted to the wrongdoer.

Avoiding constructive notice

- A bank must take reasonable steps to avoid constructive notice by ensuring that the innocent party has obtained independent legal advice (***Royal Bank of Scotland* v *Etridge (No. 2)*** [2001]).
  - (a) When is the bank put on inquiry?
  - (b) What steps should the bank take when put on inquiry?
  - (c) What are the responsibilities of the solicitor in advising the wife? The House of Lords decision in ***Etridge No. 2*** now provides for a coherent process for dealing with surety arrangements.
- The effects of undue influence.
- The effect of undue influence on a contract is to render it voidable rather than void.
- The victim must take steps to avoid the contract by rescinding it.
- Rescission may be lost where restitutio in integrum is impossible, or where the contract has been affirmed or where a bona fide third party has acquired the title to any property sold to him or her.
- Restitution does not have to be precise but merely substantial (***O'Sullivan* v *Management and Music Ltd*** [1985]).

Rights of spouses and cohabitants

At common law there is no obligation on the mortgagee to inform a spouse who does not hold a beneficial interest in the land that the other spouse is in default and that possession proceedings are being taken: ***Hastings and Thanet Building Society* v *Goddard*** [1970] 3 All ER 954.

By the FLA 1996 s.55(3) 'connected persons' may be made party to the possession proceedings and may apply for the court to exercise its discretion under the AJA 1970 s.36. A connected person is a person who enjoys matrimonial home rights under the FLA 1996 s.30. Where such a person has protected his or her rights by way of a notice in the land register as a Class F land charge, the mortgagee must serve notice on the spouse about the possession proceedings. Similar but more limited rules apply for cohabitants, though here any rights of occupation are limited to a maximum period of one year. It should be noted, however, that cohabitants have no right to enter a notice on the land register or a Class F land charge to protect their rights of occupation.

Priority of mortgages

Registered land

Legal mortgages

By the Land Registration Act 2002 s.27(1) and s.27(2)f legal mortgages must be completed by registration, otherwise they only take effect in equity. The entry is made in the charges register of the mortgagor's title, the charge being entered on the register as the proprietor of the charge: Schedule 2 para 8. The priority of competing interests is determined by the order in which they are registered: Land Registration Act 2002 s.28(1).

Section 29, however, provides that if any person has an interest before a registered disposition that interest is postponed when disposition is registered, unless the priority of the first interest is protected by registration. The effect therefore is that s.28(1) is displaced in favour of a priority based on registration.

Equitable mortgages

Equitable mortgages should be protected by entry of a notice in the charges register of the mortgagor's title: s.32. If an equitable charge is not protected in this way it will lose its priority to any charge that is then registered on the title: s.29.

Unregistered land

Legal mortgages

- If there is a legal mortgage protected by title deeds the legal mortgage will be good as against the whole world.

- Where a legal mortgagee does *not* have possession of the title deeds they must protect their mortgage as a Class C(i) land charge – a puisne mortgage.

- If there is an equitable mortgage and the mortgagee has possession of the title deeds then (1) this will bind a later acquirer of a legal estate or interest by reason of the doctrine of notice: Law of Property Act s.199(1); and (2) if there is a later equitable interest then the principle is 'where the equities are equal, the first in time prevails', so the first equitable mortgage will take priority.

- If there is an equitable mortgage and the mortgagee does *not* have possession of the title deeds they should protect their interest as a Class C(iii) land charge – a general equitable charge.

Further reading

Bently, 'Mortgagee's Duties on Sale – No Place for Tort' [1990] 54 *The Conveyancer and Property Lawyer* 431

Bigwood, 'Undue Influence in the House of Lords: Principles and Proof' (2002) 65 *Modern Law Review* 435

Chen-Wishart, 'Loss Sharing, Undue Influence and Manifest Disadvantage' (1993) 110 *Law Quarterly Review* 173

Clements, 'Residential Mortgages and the Administration of Justice Act 1970 and 1973: A Case for Reform' (1999) 3 Web *Journal of Current Legal Issues*

Conaglen, 'Mortgagee Powers Rhetoric' (2006) 69 *Modern Law Review* 583

Copper, 'Undue Influence and Unconscionability' (1998) 114 *Law Quarterly Review* 479

Dixon, 'Combating the Mortgagee's Right to Possession: New Hope for the Mortgagor in Chains?' (1998) 18 *Legal Studies* 279

Dixon, 'Mortgage Duties and Commercial Property Transactions' [2006] 70 *The Conveyancer and Property Lawyer* 278

Dixon and Harpum, 'Fraud, Undue Influence and Mortgages of Registered Land' (1994) 58 *The Conveyancer and Property Lawyer* 421

Doyle, 'Borrowing Under the Influence' (1994) 15 *Business Law Review* 6

Greer, 'Watching the Clock' (2008) 158 *New Law Journal* 7317

Griffiths, 'Mortgages, Repossession and Limitation Periods' [2005] 69 *The Conveyancer and Property Lawyer* 469

Haley, 'Mortgage Default: Possession, Relief and Judicial Discretion' (1997) 16 *Legal Studies* 483

Hanbury, 'Limiting the Shortfall' (2006) 156 *New Law Journal* 7215

Henry, 'No Postponement of the Evil Day' [1998] 62 *The Conveyancer and Property Lawyer* 223

Korotana, 'Undue Influence in the Context of the Residential Mortgage Transaction' (2000) 21 *Business Law Review* 226

Levy, 'Under Duress' (2006) 156 *New Law Journal* 936

Nash, 'A Killer Contract' (2006) 156 *New Law Journal* 280

O'Neill, 'The Mortgage Repossessions (Protection of Tenants etc.) Act 2010 – Sufficient Protection for Tenants?' [2011] 75 *The Conveyancer and Property Lawyer* 380

Pawlowski and Greer, 'Constructive Notice and Independent Legal Advice: A Study of Lending Institution Practice' [2001] 65 *The Conveyancer and Property Lawyer* 229

Pawlowski and Greer, 'Undue Influence: Back Door Tactics?' (2001) 31 *Family Law* 275

Phang and Tijo, 'The Uncertain Boundaries of Undue Influence' [2002] *Lloyd's Maritime and Commercial Law Quarterly* 231

Whitehouse, 'The Mortgage Arrears Pre-action Protocol: An Opportunity Lost' (2009) 72 *Modern Law Review* 793

Wong, 'Revisiting *Barclays Bank* v *O'Brien* and Independent Legal Advice for Vulnerable Sureties' [2002] *Journal of Business Law* 439

Glossary

As we have seen throughout this book, land law has a language very much of its own, based on Latin, Norman-French, Anglo-Saxon and English. This terminology frequently creates difficulty for students since many of the expressions have a technical meaning and even apparently familiar words are given a different meaning. To understand the subject of land law you need to be familiar with the language and the best way to do this is to read the material as often as you can.

This glossary aims to explain the meanings of words and phrases which commonly arise in the subject. The glossary does not provide an exhaustive list, though the most frequently used expressions are explained here. If you do come across a term you do not understand immediately, take steps to ascertain its meaning in the context in which it is used, and add it to the glossary.

abatement The removal of an obstruction to the exercise of an easement by the dominant tenement owner.

absolute (of an interest) neither conditional nor determinable by some specified event.

abstract of title A summary of all matters which affect the title offered by the vendor, including the various dispositions; it is the narrative summary of title, consisting of documents or events affecting the title, that must be supplied by a landowner to a purchaser under a contract of sale. See LPA 1925 s.10. See also **epitome of title**.

acquiescence Failure to take steps to prevent some act, such as the exercise of a right which has not been granted, or an obstruction to the exercise of a right which is in the course of being acquired.

administrators Persons appointed by the court to administer the estate of a person who died intestate, i.e. without leaving a will.

adverse possession A means by which an adverse possessor can acquire the title to land, thus dispossessing the previous 'paper-title' owner.

adverse possessor A person who enters land as a trespasser or 'squatter' but who subsequently acquires title to the land by way of long occupation without challenge by the 'paper owner'.

alienation The transfer of interests in property from one owner to another. This can be by way of sale, gift or some other transaction.

animus possidendi The intention to (adversely) possess the land of another.

annexation The attaching of the benefit of a restrictive covenant to the dominant tenement so that it will run with the land.

ante-nuptial Prior to marriage.

appurtenant
1 A right which is attached to the land by agreement between the parties.
2 A profit à prendre which benefits a piece of land, and not merely the owner of it.

assent The means by which personal representatives vest the deceased's property in those entitled under his or her will or intestacy. An assent need not be by deed.

assignment The transfer of property, usually a lease.

barring the entail The means by which an entailed interest can be disentailed and converted into a fee simple.

beneficial owner A person having an equitable interest who is entitled to an interest for their own benefit and not, for example, as trustee.

beneficiaries Those entitled under a trust having an equitable interest in the property.

bequest Gift of personalty made by will.

bona vacantia Property which reverts to the Crown for lack of any other owner.

caution Formerly, any person interested in registered land could lodge a caution with the registrar against any proposed registered dealing with that land. Entry of dealing with such land could not then be made on the register unless the cautioner had received notice: LRA 1925 s.53 and s.54. Now repealed under the LRA 2002. Cautions are protected as **unilateral notices** under the LRA 2002 s.35.

cesser on redemption The automatic ending of a mortgage upon the mortgagor complying with all their obligations to the mortgagee, e.g. paying off the monies lent and interest thereon as agreed.

cestui que trust The original terminology describing a beneficiary under a trust.

charge An incumbrance upon the land – either legal or equitable – by which a debt or other obligation is secured, e.g. a mortgage.

chattel Any property other than freehold land.

chattels real Leasehold land.

choses in action Intangible rights in property other than land, e.g. copyrights, debts.

choses in possession Tangible property other than land, e.g. cars, jewellery.

clog Some restriction placed by the mortgagee upon the mortgagor's right to redeem.

commonhold A method by which flats can be held as freeholds and under which obligations – either positive or negative – can be enforced.

conditional interest An interest which is subject to some conditioning event – either a condition precedent or subsequent. Until a condition precedent is satisfied, the holder of it has merely a hope of attaining the interest. Upon the happening of a stipulated subsequent event, the grantor has a right of re-entry.

consolidation The means by which a mortgagee can require a mortgagor to redeem more than one mortgage at the same time.

constructive notice A person has constructive notice of any interest that they would have had actual notice of if they had made those inquiries or inspections that a prudent purchaser would reasonably have made.

constructive trust A trust imposed by equity in order to give effect to some common intention between the parties. See also **notice.**

conversion An equitable doctrine under which the interests of beneficiaries behind a trust for sale are treated as interests in the proceeds of sale, not in the land.

co-ownership Ownership which is shared by two or more persons at the same time, holding as joint tenants (legal estate and/or equitable interests) or tenants in common (equitable interests only).

corporeal Capable of being physically possessed, e.g. soil, bricks.

covenant A promise made by deed.

covenantee The person who has the benefit of a covenant.

covenantor The person who has the burden of a covenant.

deed
1 Prior to the passing of the Law of Property (Miscellaneous Provisions) Act 1989 – a document which has been signed, sealed and delivered.
2 Following the passing of the Law of Property (Miscellaneous Provisions) Act 1989 – a document which has been executed and signed as a deed in the presence of witnesses, and then delivered.

deed of discharge A document which brings a strict settlement to an end.

demise The grant of a lease.

determinable interest An interest which will determine automatically upon the happening of some specified event.

determine Come to an end.

devise Gift of realty made by will.

distrain, distress The legal right to seize chattels, without a court order, in order to satisfy some debt or claim. Usually exercised by a landlord against his or her tenant by way of compensation for unpaid rent.

dominant tenement Land which enjoys the benefit of some right, e.g. an easement or restrictive covenant.

donee The recipient of funds or other benefits.

donor The person who makes a gift of property.

easement A right enjoyed over the servient tenement for the benefit of the dominant tenement, e.g. a right of way.

encumbrance A liability attached to a piece of land, e.g. the burden of a restrictive covenant.

entail An interest in land which lasts only as long as there is issue of the relevant gender of the original grantor.

epitome of title This is a schedule of documents going back to the good root of title supplied by a landowner to a purchaser under a contract of sale. See also **abstract of title.**

equitable interests Interests, the recognition and protection of which were originally within the province of the courts of equity. See, e.g., LPA 1925, s.1(1)–(3), in which they are defined by exclusion; s.4(1).

equitable lease A lease which does not satisfy the necessary requirements for a legal lease but is, nevertheless, valid in equity. There must be a valid contract to create a lease and the contract must be specifically enforceable. See *Walsh* v *Lonsdale* (1882) 21 Ch D 9; Law of Property (Miscellaneous Provisions) Act 1989 s.2.

equitable mortgage A mortgage which transfers an equitable interest only, either because the mortgagor's interest is equitable, or because the conveyance or other mode of transfer is equitable. See LPA 1925, s.53(1)(c). It may be created, e.g., by agreement to create a legal mortgage; or by creation of an equitable charge (i.e., where property is charged with payment of the debt, but there is no transfer of possession or ownership of the property). Deposit of title deeds alone no longer suffices to create an equitable mortgage, by virtue of the Law of Property (Miscellaneous Provisions) Act 1989. The equitable mortgagee's remedies include foreclosure, appointment of a receiver and power of sale.

equity of redemption The sum total of the mortgagor's rights in equity, i.e., their rights of ownership of the property subject to the mortgage. The right of redemption is inviolable and may not be restricted unduly. See *Kreglinger* v *New Patagonia Meat Co. Ltd* [1914] AC 25; *Knightsbridge Estates Trust Ltd* v *Byrne* [1939] Ch 441 (postponement of right to redeem); *Pye* v *Ambrose* [1994] NPC 53. In *Jones* v *Morgan* (2001) *The Times*, 24 July, the Master of the Rolls stated that the doctrine of a clog on the equity of redemption (in relation to mortgages) no longer serves a useful purpose and would be better excised.

equity's darling A bona fide purchaser for value of the legal estate without notice.

estate
1 An interest in land for a prescribed period.
2 The whole of the property left by a deceased person.

estate contract A contract to create or convey an estate or interest in land.

estate rentcharge A means by which a positive covenant can be made to run with freehold land.

estoppel Equitable doctrine under which any person who makes a promise or representation to another and allows the other person to act to their detriment in reliance thereon, will be precluded from denying that promise or representation.

execute To complete a conveyance or other transaction.

executors Persons appointed by will to administer the deceased's estate.

executory Remaining to be done.

fee simple absolute in possession A legal estate in land which lasts indefinitely whilst there are persons entitled under the prior owner's will or intestacy. One of two legal estates in land provided for by LPA 1925 s.1(1).

fee tail An entailed interest. Such interests were abolished by the Trusts of Land and Appointment of Trustees Act.

fine Payment of a capital sum. Also called a 'premium'.

fittings Personal property which has not become a fixture and which can, therefore, be removed by a vendor (subject to any contrary agreement in the contract).

fixed-term tenancy A tenancy of a specified length of time, which is not a **periodic tenancy**.

fixtures Items which have become attached to the land and are, therefore, realty. Fixtures can only be removed by a vendor if the contract specifically so provides.

flying freehold A freehold property above ground level.

foreclosure Method by which a mortgagee acquires the whole of the mortgagor's equity of redemption in order to satisfy the mortgage debt or other obligation.

freehold The fee simple absolute in possession.

gazumping Where a would-be purchaser of land is defeated by another who offers a higher price after the vendor has agreed to sell at the lower price, but before contracts have been exchanged.

gazundering Where a vendor of land is forced to accept an unreasonably low offer from a purchaser who reduces their previous higher offer at the last minute. The opposite of **gazumping**.

grant Formal transfer of property under a written instrument such as a deed.

hereditaments Inheritable rights in land. Hereditaments may be

(a) corporeal, i.e. tangible, physical, such as the soil, or any physical structure attached thereto; or

(b) incorporeal, i.e. intangible rights over land, such as easements, profits and rentcharges.

inchoate Commenced, or in an early stage but not yet complete.

incipient Only partly in existence; imperfectly formed.

indenture A term for a deed – now largely outmoded.

infant Under the Family Law Reform Act 1969 anyone under 18 years of age. Also called a 'minor'.

in gross Existing without a dominant tenement. Easements cannot exist in gross, though profits à prendre can.

inhibition A method of protecting minor interests in registered land.

in possession Method of holding an interest in land, whereby the holder has immediate enjoyment of it.

instrument Any legal document.

intestacy State of dying without leaving a valid will, so that the deceased's estate is subject to intestacy rules. Even where a person has left a will, any property for which he or she does not provide therein will be subject to intestacy.

inter vivos During one's lifetime.

issue Offspring. A person's issue comprises their children, grandchildren and other lineal descendants.

joint tenancy A form of co-ownership under which all the joint tenants own the whole property without individually owning any separate share in it. (Hence the expression, 'joint tenants own everything and yet own nothing'.) As between the joint tenants, the right of survivorship, or **jus accrescendi**, applies. Contrast joint tenancy with **tenancy in common**.

jus accrescendi The right of survivorship whereby, upon the death of a joint tenant, the whole of his or her interest devolves upon the surviving joint tenants.

laches The equitable doctrine of delay; negligence or unreasonable delay in the assertion of a right will defeat equities.

land obligation Proposed new interest in land to replace restrictive covenants.

lapse The failure of a gift, e.g. where a beneficiary dies before the testator.

lease Also known as a 'term of years absolute' and a 'tenancy'. Can only exist where one party (the lessee or tenant) is granted exclusive possession of land for a fixed term, usually (though not necessarily – see LPA 1925 s.205(xxvii)) at a rent, by the other party (the lessor or landlord). The second legal estate in land provided for by LPA 1925 s.1(1). Also the document which creates the same . . .

Lease of the reversion Also known as a concurrent lease. Arises where a fee simple owner (lessor or landlord) grants a second lease on property which is already subject to a subsisting lease. Not to be confused with a **reversionary lease** (see below).

lessee A tenant.

lessor A landlord.

letters of administration Granted to personal representatives in order that they may administer the estate of a deceased person.

licence Permission, e.g. to do on another's land something which would otherwise amount to a trespass.

lien A form of security over land or property for money that remains unpaid.

limitation of actions The barring of a right of action after a specified period, currently governed by the Limitation Act 1980. See **adverse possession**.

limited owner One who holds an estate less than a fee simple absolute in possession.

matrimonial home The domicile of a husband and wife who live, or have lived together.

matrimonial home right Right of occupation of a non-owning spouse as against the other spouse. Where one spouse is not a co-owner of the home, certain matrimonial home rights, e.g., the right, if in occupation, not to be evicted or excluded from the home by the other spouse, except by leave of the court, and, if not in occupation, the right, by leave of the court, to enter and occupy the home: see FLA. 1996, Part IV. A right of this type is registrable as a Class F land charge in the register of land charges. See *Bull v Bull* [1995] 1 QB 234; *Baroden v Dhillon* [1998] 1 FLR 524.

merger Where two or more estates or interests are fused together. To be distinguished from **surrender**.

mesne Intermediate, as in 'mesne lord'.

mesne profits, claim for Claim in trespass brought against an occupier of premises who remains in possession after the termination of their interest in those premises, to recover damages suffered by the plaintiff as the result of their having been out of possession. Damages are generally assessed on the basis of a rent representing fair value of premises during the relevant period of occupation.

minor An infant.

minor interest Term formerly used in land registration under the LRA 1925 where minor interests were defined as 'the interests not capable of being disposed of or created by registered dispositions and capable of being overridden (whether or not a purchaser has notice thereof) by the proprietors unless protected as provided by this Act, and all rights and interests which are not registered or protected on the register and are not overriding interests': LRA 1925, s.3(*xv*). Originally they were protected by **notice**, **inhibition**, **restriction** or **caution**. See *Peffer* v *Rigg* [1977] 1 WLR 285; *Lyus* v *Prowsa Developments Ltd* [1982] 1 WLR 1044. Under the LRA 2002 the term has supposedly been abandoned, though it continues to be used colloquially. The LRA 2002 has reduced the categories whereby such interests can be protected to two: cautions and notices.

mortgage Grant of an interest in property as security for a loan or other obligation.

mortgagee The person who lends the money and to whom the mortgage is granted.

mortgagor The person who borrows the money and the one who grants the mortgage.

nec vi, nec clam, nec precario 'Without force, without secrecy, without permission' – the way in which a person must act if he or she is to be able to claim an easement or profit by prescription.

notice
1 Notices in registered land were originally classified as minor interests and protected by notice of an interest entered on the Charges Register (see LRR 1925, rr 2, 7); they were then protected by making them binding on any third party who acquired interests thereafter in the land. See LRA 1925, ss.48(1), 52(1). Notices have now been subject to reform under the LRA 2002, s.32(1) where they are defined as 'an entry in the register in respect of the burden of an interest affecting a registered estate or charge'. The fact that a notice is registered does not necessarily mean that it is valid, though if it is valid it is protected against a purchaser of the registered estate for valuable consideration. Notices now exist in two forms: 'agreed notices' (LRA 2002, s.32) and 'unilateral notices' (LRA 2002, s.35), the latter protecting what were formerly cautions.
2 Knowledge which a person has or which is attributed to them under the doctrine of notice, i.e.
   (a) actual notice – actual knowledge;
   (b) constructive notice – knowledge which a person would have had, had they made all necessary enquiries;
   (c) imputed notice – the actual and constructive notice of a person's agent, e.g. their solicitor.

3 Notice attributed to a person by virtue of the registration of a land charge in accordance with the Land Charges Act 1972.

All three forms of notice need to be distinguished.

notice to quit Method by which a landlord or tenant may terminate a periodic tenancy.

option to purchase A right whereby the holder can require an estate owner to convey that estate to the option holder. A form of estate contract.

overreaching Method by which interests in land are shifted from the land into the proceeds of sale, thereby enabling a purchaser to take the legal estate free of any equitable interests existing behind a trust of land or strict settlement, provided they pay the capital (purchase) monies to at least two trustees or a trust corporation.

overriding interest Those encumbrances, interests, rights and powers that were originally stated in LRA 1925, s.70(1) as not entered on the register but subject to which registered dispositions of land take effect. Hence, a registered proprietor is bound by such rights, irrespective of registration and notice. Such interests were always regarded as a defect in the system of land registration because they bound a purchaser but did not appear on the register, e.g. legal easements, profits, local land charges, rights of persons in occupation. See LRA 1925, s.70. Overriding interests are now dealt with by the Land Registration Act 2002 which has reduced the number of potential overriding interests and has attempted to limit their effect so that the registers reflect the original concept behind the land registration system in that all incumbrances should be capable of being detected from the registers. There are now two lists of overriding interests to be found in Sch. 1 and 3 of the LRA 2002.

parcel A piece of land.

parol By word of mouth, oral.

partition Method by which a piece of land is physically divided so that what was previously a single plot held by several co-owners becomes several plots, each held by a sole owner.

periodic tenancy Form of tenancy whereby the tenant is in possession of the land and paying rent calculated on a periodic basis, e.g. weekly, monthly, quarterly, annually, to the landlord.

perpetually renewable lease A lease which contains a covenant by the landlord that they will from time to time renew the lease (i.e. grant a new one to the tenant) at the termination of the current lease. Such leases are automatically converted into a term of 2000 years – see LPA 1922 s.145.

personal property Property other than freehold land.

personal representatives Persons authorised to administer the estate of a dead person:

(a) executors – appointed by will;
(b) administrators – appointed by the court where the deceased died intestate (or where an executor is unwilling or unable to act).

personal rights Rights which attach only to the person, and not to the land, e.g. licences (other than estoppel licences).

personalty Personal property (as opposed to **realty**).

possession The immediate right to occupation of land or receipt of rents and profits therefrom.

post-nuptial After marriage.

pre-emption, right of A right whereby the holder is entitled to first refusal of property should the owner decide to sell. A form of estate contract.

prescription Method of acquiring an easement or profit à prendre by long user.

privity of contract The relationship between contracting parties, especially between the original landlord and tenant.

privity of estate The relationship existing between landlord and tenant, or current lessor and lessee.

probate The granting by the court of approval of a will.

profit à prendre The right to take something from the land of another, e.g. grass by grazing cattle. Can be:

(a) in gross – benefiting the holder of the profit only, there being no dominant tenement; or
(b) appurtenant – benefiting a piece of land, a dominant tenement.

proprietary rights Rights which attach to the land and are thus capable of binding third parties.

puisne mortgage A legal mortgage which is not protected by a deposit of the title deeds.

pur autre vie For the life of another.

purchaser A person who acquires an estate or interest by act of the parties, though not necessarily a 'buyer', e.g. a person who takes under a deed of gift (a 'donee'). However, see the definition section in each statute for particular meaning, e.g. LPA 1925, s.205(l)(xxi).

quasi-easement A right enjoyed by the owner of land which has the potential to be an easement, if enjoyed by someone else.

realty, real property Freehold land.

registered proprietor In registered land, the person registered as legal estate owner.

remainder An interest which is subject to a prior interest, e.g. 'to Kamala for life, remainder to Rajiv absolutely'. Interests in remainder can only exist in equity (although they can become legal when they fall into possession) – LPA 1925 s.1(3).

rentcharge The right of the holder to receive a periodic sum of money from the current owner of the land charged with it. To be distinguished from rent, i.e. payments made by a tenant to his or her landlord under a lease.

reservation Method whereby a grantor of land retains for him/herself an easement or a profit.

residual interests Those interests in unregistered land which, being neither registrable as land charges nor overreachable, remain subject to the doctrine of notice.

residue That which remains of an estate after payment of debts, funeral expenses, testamentary expenses, legacies, annuities, costs of administration, etc.

restriction Under the LRA 1925 s.58(1) a restriction was a method of protecting minor interests in registered land, especially beneficial interests behind a trust, that were entered on the Proprietorship Register at the Land Registry. This has now been replaced by the LRA 2002 s.41(1) which defines a restriction as 'an entry in the register regulating the circumstances in which a disposition of a registered estate, may be the subject of an entry in the register', i.e. a restriction on dealings with the registered estate. The restriction may impose a complete ban on any dealings or could impose conditions that must be met before any dealing will be registered.

restrictive covenant A covenant which restricts the use of land in a specified way.

resulting trust A trust which arises in circumstances where the beneficial interest comes back ('results') to the person (or their representative) who transferred the property to the trustee. See LPA 1925 s.60.

reversion The right remaining in a grantor who has not parted with the whole of their interest. Usually used with reference to the remaining estate of a landlord and their right, during the continuance of the lease, to receive rents and profits and to regain possession of the land at the end of the term granted. Also applies to settlements under which the fee simple owner grants an interest less than they have – for example, a life interest – at the end of which the land will revert to the fee simple owner.

reversionary lease A lease the term of which is to begin in the future. See LPA 1925, s.149.

rights in personam Rights enforceable against the person only.

rights in rem Rights enforceable against the land.

root of title The earliest document upon which clear title can be proved. The root must be traced back at least 15 years to form a 'good root of title' – LPA 1969, s.23 – unless a contrary intention appears in the contract.

seisin Possession of land by a freeholder.

servient tenement Land which carries the burden of some right, e.g. an easement or restrictive covenant.

settlement Method of creating a series of successive interests. See SLA 1925.

settlor One who makes a settlement of their property. See **settlement**.

severance
1 A method of converting a joint tenancy, or the interest of a joint tenant, into a tenancy in common. Operates upon the equitable interests only – see LPA 1925, s.1(6).
2 See **words of severance**.

socage The last surviving tenure, known today as 'freehold'.

squatter A trespasser, a person wrongfully occupying land.

strict settlement Defined under the Settled Land Act 1925 s.1 (as amended). It arises from an instrument such as a deed or will that provides for:

(a) successive equitable interests limited in trust, or

(b) where an interest in land was conferred on a grantee in possession subject to some contingency or disability that qualified his r her entitlement or capacity to hold the interest and this conferment was limited in trust.

sub-lease A lease granted by a tenant to a sub-tenant (the tenant becoming the sub-tenant's landlord). May also be known as an 'underlease'.

sui juris Not subject to any legal disability, e.g. not a minor or a person who is insane.

surrender The transfer of an interest to the person next entitled, e.g. surrender of the remainder of a term by a tenant to their landlord. To be distinguished from **merger.**

survivorship See **jus accrescendi.**

tacking Method by which a mortgagee can extend their security by adding a later loan (a further advance) to an earlier one secured by mortgage. In this way, the mortgagee can defeat later mortgagees by increasing their priority to cover the later loan.

tenancy A **lease**.

tenancy at sufferance Where a tenant remains in possession following the termination of his or her lease.

tenancy at will Where a tenant enjoys possession of the land with the landlord's consent, it being agreed that the tenancy can be terminated by either party giving notice to the other.

tenancy by estoppel Where a landlord has, in fact, no legal title, the parties will be estopped from denying their obligations under the lease. When the landlord's title is perfected, the estoppel is 'fed' and the lease becomes a full legal lease.

tenancy in common A form of co-ownership under which each tenant in common has an identifiable (an undivided) share. The right of survivorship does not operate upon tenancies in common, therefore each tenant's share will pass, on their death, by their will or intestacy. Tenancy in common can only exist in regard to the equitable interests – LPA 1925, s.1(6). To be contrasted with a joint tenancy.

tenant for life The person who, in a strict settlement, holds the legal estate and enjoys all the powers of management and disposition over the settled land provided for by SLA 1925.

tenure The conditions upon which a tenant held land from his lord in the feudal system. Today only the tenure of **socage** remains.

term of years absolute A **lease**.

time immemorial Beyond legal memory. Fixed arbitrarily as the first year of the reign of Richard I (1189).

transfer In registered land, the deed used to pass the legal estate from one owner to another.

trust In essence, an equitable obligation which imposes on a person described as a trustee certain duties of dealing with property held and controlled by him or her for the benefit of the persons described as the beneficiaries, or, if there are not such persons, for some purpose recognised and enforceable at law. See Trustee Act 1925, 2000.

Example: A, the owner of Blackacre, conveys it to B in fee simple, directing B to hold it in trust for C: A is the settlor; B is the trustee; C is the beneficiary.

trustee One who holds property on trust for another, known as the 'beneficiary'. Capacity to be a trustee exists where there is capacity to take or hold property. Trustees may be appointed by the settlor, under express power conferred by a trust instrument, or by court, under Trustee Act 1925, s.36. See Trusts of Land and Appointment of Trustees Act 1996, s.20; Trustee Delegation Act 1999.

trust for sale Method of holding concurrent interests, prior to 1 January 1997, by which a duty to sell was imposed.

trust instrument Document setting out a settlor's wishes – the terms of the trust/settlement.

trust of land Method of holding successive and concurrent interests in land subject to any trust of property which consists of or includes land, by which a power to sell is vested in the trustees (who have all the powers of an absolute owner). Established under the Trusts of Land and Appointment of Trustees Act 1996.

undivided shares in land The interests of tenants in common. Also a tenancy in common. Can only exist in equity – LPA 1925 s.1(6).

unilateral notice See **notice**.

unity of seisin Where the same person owns both the dominant and servient tenement.

valuable consideration

1 At common law – money, money's worth, or a valid deed.
2 In equity – money, money's worth, or marriage consideration.
3 For the purposes of the Land Registration Act 2002, s.132(1) provides that 'valuable consideration' no longer includes marriage consideration or a nominal consideration in money.

vested Owned unconditionally, not contingent:

(a) in possession – with immediate right to possession, e.g. 'to Fatimah for life . . .';
(b) in interest – with future right to possession, e.g. '. . . and then to Ali absolutely'.

voluntary conveyance Conveyance not granted for consideration that is money or money's worth (cf. 'good consideration' which is founded on generosity or natural affection). A settlement that is founded on 'good consideration' is regarded as 'voluntary'. Thus because equity will not assist a volunteer, should A promise B that she will create a trust and should she fail to do so, B cannot compel performance of A's promise unless he, B, has provided valuable consideration. See *Midland Bank Trust Co.* v *Green* [1981] AC 513.

waiver Abandonment of a legal right.

waste An act or omission committed by a limited owner, e.g. a tenant for life, which alters the land for better or for worse:

(a) voluntary waste – a positive act of injury to the land;
(b) ameliorating waste – a positive act which enhances the land;
(c) permissive waste – an act of omission which results in injury to the land;
(d) equitable waste – acts or omissions which a reasonable person would not commit in the management of their own property.

words of limitation Words which delimit the estate granted – see LPA 1925 s.60.

words of severance Express words which show an intention to create a tenancy in common, and not a joint tenancy, of the equitable interests.

Index

Note: page references in bold refer to entries in the Glossary